Νικολεοντω Κόπερνικον

Hector Berlioz.

Cornwallis

Oliver Cromwell

Henrik Ibsen

Mozart   C. G. Jung.

G. Bernard Shaw

Zion-Benton Twp. High School
Instructional Materials Center

Friedrich Fröbel

James

Serge Prokofieff

G. Garibaldi

James

I olgay Calving.

Louis

Claude Monet

Ludwig van Beethoven   Freud.

A. Einstein
1946.

Vincent   Carl Johan.

EUROPEAN
HISTORICAL BIOGRAPHY

Research Guide to
EUROPEAN
HISTORICAL BIOGRAPHY
1450 ——————————————————————————— PRESENT

R
920
RES
v5

Volume V
A-Ed
(2139-2850)

950287

Zion-Benton Twp. High School
Instructional Materials Center

BEACHAM PUBLISHING, INC.
WASHINGTON, D.C.

RESEARCH GUIDE TO EUROPEAN HISTORICAL BIOGRAPHY

Editor
James A. Moncure

Staff Editors
Walton Beacham
Laura A. Bergheim
Don Raymond Marr
Katharine D. McLucas
Charles J. Moseley

Editorial Assistant
Stephanie A. Fox

Book and Cover Design
Amanda Mott

Production
Deborah M. Beacham
Dolores M. May

Library of Congress
Cataloging-in-Publication Data

Research Guide to European Historical Biography/ edited
by James A. Moncure.
Washington, D.C.: Beacham Publishing, Inc.

Includes bibliographical references and index

1. Celebrities—Europe—Biography. 2. Celebrities—Europe—Biography—Bibliography. 3. Europe— History-Bio-bibliography
I. Moncure, James A., 1926-.
Z5304.C44R47 1993(CT759) 016.92004—dc20 92-8935

Description and evaluation of the most important secondary and primary sources for 450 European historical figures in 2 sets of 4 volumes each.

© 1993, by Walton Beacham

All rights to this book are reserved. No part of this work may be used or reproduced in any manner whatsoever or transmitted in any form or by any means, electronic or mechanical, including photocopy, recording, or in any information storage and retrieval system, without written permission from the copyright owner, except in the case of brief quotations embodied in critical articles and reviews. For information, write the publisher: Beacham Publishing, Inc., 2100 ''S'' Street, NW, Washington, D.C. 20008

Library of Congress Card Number: 92-8935
ISBN: 0-933833-30-X
Printed on acid-free paper in the United States of America
First printing, November 1993

Preface

The lives of four-hundred fifty prominent men and women who shaped European civilization since 1450 are brought together in this eight-volume set. The subjects have generally been grouped into two categories. The first four volumes cover explorers, monarchs, heads of state, diplomats, political and military leaders, and social reformers. These second four volumes cover scientists, philosophers, political theorists, theologians, popes, artists, writers, and musicians.

As with its companion set, the *Research Guide to American Historical Biography,* edited by Professor Robert Muccigrosso, each article contains a biographical chronology with an incisive synopsis of the individual's life. The following section, Activities of Historical Significance, explains the issues and areas in which the subject made an impact. Written by professional historians and teachers, this important section alerts readers to directions for further reading and research.

Of special value to researchers are two other sections. The Overview of Biographical Sources examines the changing interpretations of the subject's life and work, enabling the reader to gain perspective about the response different ages have had to his/her importance. The Evaluation of Principal Biographical Sources section annotates the most important works on the life of the subject. These annotations are particularly useful to teachers developing course materials or who are assisting students with research. Librarians will find this section useful in helping students take command of their own research, as well as for collection development. The section, where applicable, Evaluation of Biographies for Young People, will help librarians identify historical reading for their younger patrons and alert researchers to works that interpret history from a different perspective. The works cited in several sections carry A, G, or Y designations, which suggest the academic, general, or young audience orientation of the resources, based on subject matter, readability, and availability.

Students will find the guide invaluable as they explore possible topics for research papers. The biographical data quickly sets students on their way with information roughly equivalent to a road map. By referring to the *Research Guide* before embarking on a topic, students can learn what body of primary and secondary sources is available, quickly compare related subjects, and develop an approach to forming a research topic and identifying materials.

The Overview and Evaluation of Primary Sources section provides readers with autobiographical materials, memoirs of family members and acquaintances, official documents, and manuscripts and correspondence. In many instances the location of these materials is given. When the subject has been treated in films, plays, novels, and other creative media, the Fiction and Adaptations section evaluates the quality and historical accuracy of the adaptation. One function of this section is to alert researchers to the popular image of the subject, which often differs from the historical portrait. The section Museums, Historical Landmarks, Societies indicates special places relevant to the life of the subject, enabling readers to contact institutions for specialized information, or to visit these places. A final section, Other Sources, expands bibliographical data to include monographs and works that place the subject within a broader historical context.

As is usual with a publishing project of this scope, deciding who to include, and who for various reasons to exclude, is the editor's dilemma. The first criteria for inclusion was that sources about the subject are available in English and generally available in American libraries. We have relied where possible upon English-language biographies, citing foreign-language works when English editions were not available or when such works were compelling in their own right. In some cases, important Europeans were not included because there is a paucity of sources in English. In other cases, as with the arts and sciences, we could only include representatives of a period or movement because of the great number of accomplished people in the field. Some writers are included when their work has influenced the political development of Europe or is representative of a movement. Because most British writers are included in Beacham's *Research Guide to Biography and Criticism,* they have not been included in this series to avoid duplication in library collections. As this series evolves, we expect to include many more subjects and we welcome recommendations from our readers.

The subjects are arranged A-Z by the name by which they are most commonly known. The index lists all the alternative names and titles. Readers studying Bolshevik Revolution Russians should note that each article designates whether the dates are in old or new style. If the first date given in the article is indicated as new style, then all subsequent dates are also given in new style. For clarity, however, we consistently refer to the February and October Revolutions by those names without regard to old and new style dates.

Two appendices are included in volumes 5-8 to provide students with a starting point for comparative analysis of subjects. Appendix A groups subjects by the historical period in which they achieved their most significant accomplishments. Appendix B groups subjects by their principal position or area of historical activity. Neither of the appendices is intended to reflect academic opinions about the activities or importance of the subjects, only to provide a starting point for student research.

The *Research Guide* owes its existence to many contributors who labored diligently to fulfill the purposes of this research tool, and I wish to express my sincere appreciation to our talented writers who have made this guide possible. During the three years of preparation, the scope of both events and materials continued to expand, and the contributors and editors worked hard to meet the challenge of this ambitious project.

As always, we are interested in producing research materials that are most useful to students, teachers, and librarians. To make suggestions, or for further information, write to Beacham Publishing, Inc., 2100 "S" Street, NW, Washington, DC 20008.

James A. Moncure
Elon College

Figures Appearing on the Cover

(Rear cover, left corner) Ptolemaic universe; Martin Luther (above the universe); 16th c. Italian Carvel ships; Amerigo Vespucci (below the ships); Columbus; 15th c. astrolabe and Galileo; Ivan the Terrible; 16th c. musical score; Queen Elizabeth I; Philip II imposed over a manuscript of *In Praise of Folly*. (Front cover, left corner) 18th c. French cotton press; DaVinci's Vetruvian man; Michelangelo's elevation of St. Peter's; Cardinal Richelieu; Mozart; Napoleon; steam locomotive; Einstein; construction of a letter; Marie Curie; DNA molecular structure; "Solidarity" symbol.

Autographs Appearing on the Endpages

Line 1: Henry VIII, Bernadotte Croce, Robespierre, Copernicus, Margaret Thatcher

Line 2: Catherine the Great, Michelangelo, William Pitt the Younger, Lenin, Charles I,
Hector Berlioz

Line 3: Lord Nelson, Mikhail Gorbachev, Alexander I, Oliver Cromwell, General Cornwallis

Line 4: Konrad Adenauer, Leonardo da Vinci, Anne Boleyn, Mozart, Carl Jung, Henrik Ibsen

Line 5: Albert Schweitzer, James Watt, Captain James Cook

Line 6: Benjamin Disraeli, Joseph Goebbels, George Bernard Shaw, Charles De Gaulle

Line 7: Voltaire, Henry Cavendish, Dr. F. W. Froebbel

Line 8: Richard Wagner, Elizabeth I, Serge Prokofiev, James I, Eugene Delacroix

Line 9: Paul Gaugin, Benjamin Britten, Catherine of Aragon, Giuseppe Garibaldi

Line 10: Machiavelli, Erasmus, James II, Napoleon Bonaparte

Line 11: Johann Sebastian Bach, Leonid Brezhnev, Columbus, Heinrich Himmler, John Calvin,
Louis XIII

Line 12: Cardinal Richelieu, Marie Antoinette, Francisco Franco, Claude Monet

Line 13: Helmut Schmidt, Edward Degas, Winston Churchill, Beethoven, Sigmund Freud

Line 14: George III, Galileo, Queen Victoria, Albert Einstein, Vincent Van Gogh,
Charles XIV of Sweden

Contents

Contents
Subjects in Volumes 5-8

Contributors to Volumes 5-8

Mathé Allain
Southwestern Louisiana University

Stanley Archer
Texas A&M University

Karl Avery

Joachim T. Baer
University of North Carolina,
Greensboro

Margaret Barnett
University of Southern Mississippi

Rosalie Murphy Baum
University of South Florida

Peter W. Becker
University of South Carolina

Jonathan Beecher
University of California, Santa
Cruz

Kirk H. Beetz

Laura A. Bergheim

Dianne C. Betts
Southern Methodist University

Franz G. Blaha
University of Nebraska-Lincoln

William E. Blake, Jr.
Virginia Commonwealth University

George P. Blum
University of the Pacific

Mark Blum
University of Louisville

Monica Brown
Pembroke State University

Robert W. Brown
Pembroke State University

Donald D. Hook
Trinity College

Karen M. Bryan
Georgia State University

Hallman Bell Bryant
Clemson University

Arden Bucholz
State University of New York,
Brockport

June K. Burton
University of Akron

Kenneth L. Campbell
Monmouth College

Marie Carani
Université Laval, Quebec

Robert B. Carlisle
St. Lawrence University

David E. Cartwright
University of Wisconsin-
Whitewater

Alva V. Cellini
St. Bonaventure University

Gale E. Christianson
Indiana State University

Henry C. Clark
Canisius College

Lorraine Coons
Chesnut Hill College

Frank J. Coppa
St. John's University, New York

Frederic M. Crawford
Middle Tennessee State University

Daniel Crews
Central Michigan State University

Kathryn Moore Crowe
University of North Carolina at
Greensboro

Loralee Davenport
Mississippi State University

Frank Day
Clemson University

Robert K. DeKosky
University of Kansas

Phyllis T. Dircks
Long Island University
C. W. Post Campus

Richard J. Dircks
St. John's University, New York

Justus D. Doenecke
New College, University of South
Florida

Conrad L. Donakowski
Michigan State University

Richard Drake
University of Montana

Seymour Drescher
University of Pittsburgh

Sina Dubovoj

Kathleen E. Dunlop
East Carolina University

Evelyn Edson
Piedmont Virginia Community
College

Joann Eisberg
Harvard University

Ann W. Engar
University of Utah

Kurt F. Flexner
Memphis State University

Elizabeth Lane Furdell
University of North Florida

Jerry L. Gaw
David Lipscomb University

C. Herbert Gilliland
U. S. Naval Academy

Nancy M. Gordon

Gerald L. Gutek
Loyola University, Chicago

John Haag
University of Georgia

James G. Harper
University of Pennsylvania

C. James Haug
Mississippi State University

Leo Hecht
George Mason University

Kathleen Rout
Michigan State University

Arthur Herman

James Hitchcock
St. Louis University

James C. Holland
Shepherd College

Niles Holt
Illinois State University

Elizabeth Alexander Holtze
Metropolitan State College
of Denver

Barbara J. Horwitz
C. W. Post Campus of Long Island
University

William V. Hudon
Bloomsburg University

E. D. Huntley
Appalachian State University

McKellar Israel
Sandhills Community College

Charles M. Joseph
Skidmore College

Richard Keenan
University of Idaho

Ruthmarie Kelley
Bowling Green State University

Peter C. Kent
University of New Brunswick

Heather Kiernan
Edinburgh, Scotland

W. Laird Kleine-Ahlbrandt
Purdue University

Isabel F. Knight
Pennsylvania State University

Benjamin G. Kohl
Vassar College

Gary Land
Andrews University

Oscar E. Lansen
Elon College

Carole Levin
SUNY/College at New Paltz

Leon Lewis
Appalachian State University

Brad Loudenback
University of Southwestern
Louisiana

Paul Lucas
Clark University

Robert B. Luehrs
Fort Hays State University

Lois N. Magner
Purdue University

Martin J. Manning
United States Information Agency

Howard Marblestone
Lafayette College

Katherine Kearney Maynard
Rider College

Len McCall
Clemson University

Amy Thompson McCandless
College of Charleston

Timothy L. McDonald
Rockhurst College

William Melin
Lafayette College

Henry P. Meyer
George Mason University

Eugene W. Miller, Jr.
Pennsylvania State University,
Hazleton

Suzanne M. Munich

Pellegrino Nazzaro
Rochester Institute of Technology

Martin Needels
Southeast Missouri State University

Gregory L. Nehler

Henry Paolucci
St. John's University

Anthony Papalas
East Carolina University

Robert J. Paradowski
Rochester Institute of Technology

Marvin Perry
Baruch College
City University of New York

John R. Pfeiffer
Central Michigan University

Larry Portis
American University of Paris

Dorothy Potter
Lynchburg College

Rado Pribic
Lafayette College

Mary Ellen Priestley
Elon College

S. E. Gerard Priestley
Elon College

Eugene L. Rasor
Emory & Henry College

Alan J. Reinerman
Boston College

Samuel J. Rogal
Illinois Valley Community College

Sven Hakon Rossel
University of Washington

Leonid Rudnytzky
La Salle University

Rose-Mary Sargent
University of Minnesota

Rose-Mary Sargent
University of Minnesota

Mark Schumacher
University of North Carolina at
Greensboro

Lucy M. Schwartz
Pennsylvania State University
Wilkes-Barre Campus

Joseph N. Scionti
University of Massachusetts,
Dartmouth

Daniel E. Shannon
DePauw University

George Shepperson
Edinburgh University

Jack Shreve
Allegany Community College

Arthur J. Slavin
University of Louisville

David C. Smith
University of Maine

Clyde Curry Smith
University of Wisconsin,
River Falls

F. B. Smith
Australian National University

Richard Francis Spall, Jr.
Ohio Wesleyan University

S. J. Stearns
College of Staten Island
City University of New York

Suzanne Stratton

Roland N. Stromberg
University of Wisconsin,
Milwaukee

Claude C. Sturgill
University of Florida

Alexander Sydorenko
Arkansas State University

Carol G. Thomas
University of Washington

Constantin Toloudis
University of Rhode Island

Alexander Varias
Villanova University

Gordon De La Vars
Keuka College

Lauren Pringle De La Vars
St. Bonaventure University

Jane Karoline Vieth
Michigan State University

William Weisberger
Butler Community College

Barbara Whitehead
DePauw University

Leland Edward Wilshire
Biola University

Jonathan W. Zophy
University of Houston-Clear Lake

John Emerich Edward Dalberg Acton
1834-1902

Chronology

Born John Emerich Edward Dalberg Acton on January 10, 1834, at the Villa Acton on the Riviera di Chiaja, Naples, Kingdom of the Two Sicilies, where his grandfather Sir John Acton, a general and admiral, had been prime minister; son of Sir Ferdinand Richard Acton, and Marie Louise Pelline de Dalberg, daughter and heiress of Emerich, duc de Dalberg, representative of Louis XVIII at the Congress of Vienna; his father's only brother, Charles Edward Januarius, as Cardinal Acton, becomes advisor to Pope Gregory XVI on English affairs; his father's only sister, Elizabeth, marries Sir Robert Throckmorton, a leader of the Cisalpine Catholics; *1837* succeeds as Sir John Emerich Edward Dalberg Acton, eighth baronet and master of Aldenham (Shropshire), upon the premature death of his father in Paris; *1840* Lady Dalberg-Acton marries Granville George Leveson-Gower, gaining for her son, though Catholic, future access to the inner circle of the Protestant Whig establishment; Lord Leveson succeeds his father in 1846 as second Earl Granville; *1842* begins formal education at Saint Nicholas du Chardonnet, near Paris (Gentilly) where he begins a life-long familiarity with the inner workings of the clerical world; *1843-1848* attends St. Mary's College, Oscott, a center for converts from the Oxford Movement, including John Henry Newman; begins collecting his vast personal library, eventually numbering sixty thousand volumes; *1848-1850* tutored in the Edinburgh home of Henry F. C. Logan; *1850-1857* denied admission to Cambridge and Oxford because of his religion; moves to Munich to study with Johann Joseph Ignaz von Döllinger; attends lectures at the university; travels with Döllinger to archives, libraries, and homes of intellectuals; *1853* visits the United States with his relation Lord Ellesmere; *1856* accompanies Lord Granville as personal secretary to the coronation of Alexander II; *1855-1857* travels through Europe to attend lectures and do research; *1857* visits Rome with Döllinger and is shocked by the low state of historical studies, a turning-point in his intellectual outlook; returns to England, purchases half interest in the *Rambler*, a journal run by Oxford Movement converts; *1858-1864* serves as chief contributor and literary partner of Richard Simpson in the *Rambler* and its successor; makes it the voice of English Liberal Catholicism until its demise in 1862; founds the *Home and Foreign Review* with Simpson, serving in the same capacity until its demise in 1864; *1859-1865* serves as member of Parliament for Carlow, Ireland; *1860* Lady Granville dies; inherits her ancestral home at Worms, Herrnsheim Castle; *1864-1868* works extensively in archival collections at Bologna, Brussels, Florence, London, Mantua, Modena, Paris, Rome, Simancas, Venice, Verona, and Vienna; *1865* marries his maternal cousin Marie Anna Ludomilla Euphrosyne Arco-Valley, daughter of Count Johann Maximilian Arco-Valley, a Bavarian diplomat whose Munich home and country villa at Tegernsee become social and intellectual centers for the remainder of Acton's life; six children are borne to this union; *1867-1868* writes for the *Chronicle*; *1869* created Baron Acton of Aldenham on the recommendation of Prime Minister William E. Gladstone, with whom a close friendship had developed; *1869-1870* advises and encourages the bishops at Vatican Council I who opposed promulgation of the dogma of papal infallibility; writes for the *North British Review*; *1871* delivers lecture at Kidderminster on the Roman Question; *1874-1875* writes four letters to the *Times* in response to Gladstone's *Vatican Decrees,* prompting Cardinal Henry Edward Manning's failed attempt to have Acton excommunicated; *1877* delivers lectures before the Bridgnorth Institute on the history of freedom in antiquity and Christianity; *1887* reviews Bishop Mandell Creighton's *History of the Papacy* in the *English Historical Review,* a journal he helped found the year before; *1890* made Honorary Fellow of All Souls, Oxford; *1892-1895* Lord-in-Waiting to Queen Victoria; *1895-1902* Regius Professor of Modern History at Cambridge; *1895* delivers Inaugural Lecture, "The Study of History"; *1895-1899* delivers lectures on the French Revolution; *1896-1902* plans and begins to edit the *Cambridge Modern History*; *1896* founds the Trinity Historical Society; *1897* delivers the Eranus Club lecture, "Notes on Archival Researches 1864-1868"; *1899-1901* delivers lectures on modern history; *1902* dies of heart disease on June 19, and is buried at Tegernsee, Bavaria.

Activities of Historical Significance

Lord Acton's pursuit of historical studies and his concern with the history of freedom occurred at a most opportune time historically, and in a most favorable circumstance personally. From start to finish his intellectual energies focused on what he described to Mary Gladstone (Drew) as the "wavy line" between religion and politics, along which he discerned the advance of human freedom. His perspective was the product of his lineage and education. A Catholic of ancient descent who was comfortable in the Whig establishment, an Englishman who was more Continental than English, and an intellectual who gained the confidence of Prime Minister William E. Gladstone, the most durable politician of the century, Acton was an enigma in his time and has been an evasive, confounding figure to posterity. He became an intellectual tour de force unparalleled in the English-speaking world: his was an extraordinary intellect committed to historical inquiry and its canons, unfettered by the restraints of authority or convention, with an all-absorbing faith in the capacity of scientific, historical inquiry to uncover error and right the wrongs of the ages.

The deepest stamp on his mind was his German education under Johann Joseph Ignaz von Döllinger's careful direction. The German Catholic scholars who were Acton's teachers argued that only through disciplined searches in archives and libraries can the truth of the past (and present) be unfolded, the crimes of commission and omission divulged, and time-honored falsehoods dissolved. Only through uninhibited examination of the evidence can the divine nature of the Catholic Church be distinguished from the cumulative knavery of its human custodians. In this milieu free intellectual inquiry becomes the requisite condition for the emancipation of history and the sole path along which could be found the ultimate vindication of God's institution on Earth. History, properly understood and pursued, would come down on the side of the Catholic Church, but it neither could nor should be a painless victory. Such was the new world of understanding and hope that Acton entered in his sixteenth year.

At the time Acton departed England to study in Munich, Catholicism in Britain was dramatically changing. What the English Catholicism of that day lacked in intellectual depth it asserted in its tripartite tensions among old Catholics, Oxford Movement converts, and Irish immigrants. Emancipation came in 1829, the defections of prominent Anglicans commenced in the 1840s, while the influx of Irish poor—already underway since the eighteenth century—grew to a flood during the famine. In 1850—the year Acton went to Munich—Pius IX restored the hierarchy in England, marking the onset of a triumphal Romanization policy that would drastically alter the nature and practice of Catholicism in England.

For nearly three centuries Catholicism in England had been under the protection and patronage of the small Catholic gentry and aristocracy, a leadership firmly rooted in Lockean principles of governance, and whose liturgical taste reflected its own indigenous Anglo-Saxon cultural sensitivities, which were decidedly not Latinate. With Romanization came progressive subordination of the laity to clerical authority, plus a radical turn liturgically towards Latin piety. The restored hierarchy and its advocates were motivated by a desire for uniformity of Catholic behavior and practice in England, shaped by the communicated objectives and understanding of their superiors in Rome.

When Acton returned to a changing England in 1857, he was filled to the brim with enthusiasm for the ideas of his Continental tutors. He turned to journalism to convey the new learning to the tired ways of his countrymen, and to that end he acquired half interest in the *Rambler*. Acton and his literary partner, Richard Simpson, an England-wise convert from the Anglican priesthood, soon made the journal the voice of English Liberal Catholicism, best defined as a movement fostering unfettered freedom of intellectual inquiry, toward the end of vindicating the claims of their religion. By bringing the high standards of German historical scholarship to his English co-religionists, Acton hoped to raise the intellectual level of that community, long comfortable with cultivating a submissive, inconspicuous presence in exchange for toleration. Complaining of Catholic indolence and mental lethargy in his essay ''The Catholic Press'' (February 1859), he saw an even darker side: ''One of the fruits of this system is mendacity. Ignorance can only be defended by falsehood; every artifice is deemed lawful; a little fraud becomes a necessary ingredient in controversy. Hence means which only the most worthless of her adversaries have the baseness still to use are sometimes pressed into the service of the Church by those who have not the candor or the courage to adopt that method of defence by which alone success is ultimately infallible.''

As a result of timely articles over three years on highly sensitive issues—education, history, philosophy, politics, the press, and theology—the *Rambler* aroused the severe criticism of a hierarchy and its underlings pursuing different objectives. Far from wanting to air the Catholic Church's own dirty linen, Wiseman and others labored prodigiously to expand the authority of an increasingly Romanized clergy, to tend to the immediate desparate needs of the ever-growing numbers of Irish poor, and to instill a disciplined compliance into the laity regarding clerical leadership on the controversial questions of the day. The clergy viewed the *Rambler* as transgressing upon their prerogatives, sowing confusion and scandal among the faithful, and giving comfort to the enemy. This was set against a backdrop of an intractably reactionary papacy caught up in the death throes of its temporal power. When a formal censure appeared imminent in 1862, either from the bishops or from Rome itself, Acton transformed the journal into a quarterly (the *Rambler* had been a monthly), calling it the *Home and Foreign Review.*

Though in a new format, the old hostilities continued at an even more intense level as the unification of the Italian kingdom progressed. From July 1862 until April 1864 the *Home and Foreign Review* published a wide range of critical writing by various authors whose interests and thought ran counter to the current in Rome. In July 1863 Acton and Simpson published "Ultramontanism," a compelling assault on those who sought to make the papal monarchy absolute in its authority. By the following April, Acton concluded that the existence of the journal had become untenable in the face of imminent condemnation—Pius IX's Syllabus of Errors was to appear that December—and he terminated its publication. In "Conflicts with Rome" he gave his reasons, ending on a characteristically hopeful note: "If the spirit of the *Home and Foreign Review* really animates those whose sympathy it enjoyed, neither their principles, nor their confidence, nor their hopes will be shaken by its extinction. It was but a partial and temporary embodiment of an imperishable idea—the faint reflection of a light which still lives and burns in the hearts of the silent thinkers of the Church."

The *Home and Foreign Review* was the greatest achievement of the short-lived English Liberal Catholic movement. The depth and profundity of its writings attracted the praise of the foremost critic of Victorian civilization, Matthew Arnold, who noted that "in no organ of criticism in this country was there so much knowledge, so much play of mind . . ."

Acton now embarked upon his remarkable archival tour, a four-year interval during which he gathered vast materials on broad topics pertaining to what he would call "the wavy line" between religion and politics," which he believed shaped the history of freedom.Commencing at Vienna in the summer of 1864, he went on to Bologna, Brussels, Florence, London, Mantua, Modena, Paris, Rome, Simancas, Venice, and Verona, employing copyists, cultivating archivists and their staffs, and shipping the treasure back to Aldenham for later scrutiny. Home in January 1866, he presented his deeply felt pro-Southern views at Bridgnorth in the lecture "The Civil War in America: Its Place in History." During the winter of 1866-1867 he settled in Rome, befriended Augustin Theiner, prefect of the Vatican Archives, and proceeded to gain access to priceless documents relating to highly sensitive subjects from the sixteenth and seventeenth centuries. Theiner's cooperation in allowing Acton into the holdings of the Secret Archives eventually brought down censure (1870) and restrictive access to the collections over which he ostensibly presided.

By the convening of Vatican Council I in December 1869, Acton was again settled in Rome, where he aimed to do all in his power to prevent the promulgation of papal infallibility, a task at which he and Döllinger labored tirelessly. In October Acton had written "The Pope and the Council" for the *North British Review*—an essay review of *Der Papst und das Council*, by Janus, Döllinger's pseudonym—a compelling historical argument against the proposed doctrine. During the Council itself Acton took a prominent part in organizing the opposition bishops, furnishing them with historical evidence for their position, as well as using his friendship with Gladstone in an unsuccessful effort to have the governments intervene on the opposition side. He left Rome a month before the approaching Ultramontane victory in July, exhausted and demoralized by the steady defection of the minority bishops in the face of Vatican pressure. Following the promulgation of the dogma he wrote the pamphlet, *Sendschreiben en einen Deutschen Bischof*, an eleventh-hour effort to reinforce the German bishops of the minority in continuing their resistance to the doctrine. Finally, in the October issue of *North British Review* appeared "The Vatican Council," Acton's account of events and their meaning, and a final utterance of residual hope. His experience at the Council would remain the low point of his life.

Four years later, in 1874, Gladstone published *The Vatican Decrees in Their Bearing on Civil Allegiance*, in which he employed in part some of Acton's arguments from earlier years. Between November and December Acton wrote four letters to the *Times* refuting Gladstone's assertions while at the same time expressing biting criticisms of the Catholic Church. Manning, soon to be archbishop of Westminster and a leading Ultramontane, suspected heresy and moved to press Acton on the Vatican decrees, hoping for his excommunication. Though fully expecting to be excommunicated, Acton was in the end saved from Manning's designs by his own bishop, James Brown of Shrewsbury. Still, the acrimony further distanced Acton from the episcopacy and the institutional church. He had minimal expectations of clergy and church thereafter; in his mind the Liberal Catholic experiment had ended.

It was Mandell Creighton's *History of the Papacy During the Reformation* (4 vols. 1882-1887) that occasioned Acton's most quoted aphorism. The first two volumes were reviewed by Acton in the *Academy* of December 1882, which gave rise to a lengthy correspondence between the two men. Acton's chief criticism was Creighton's reluctance to impose rigid moral standards in history, especially in the history of the Church. The final two volumes received a more substantial review in the 1887 *English Historical Review*. Acton's remarks were even harsher this time around. Responding to Creighton's specific request for his philosophy of history, Acton wrote on April 5, 1887, his celebrated letter, which includes his familiar judgment: "Power tends to corrupt and absolute power corrupts absolutely." This hardening commitment to stern moral judgment in history had ruptured Acton's intellectual harmony with Döllinger, who called his most brilliant student a hanging judge.

Acton's most ambitious undertaking was a history of freedom—what Mary Gladstone (Drew) teasingly called his "Madonna of the Future," a play on the short story by Henry James so titled. Although he assembled massive amounts of materials, and completed prodigious reading, he never wrote the monumental work. An exacting perfectionist, he held that history should not be written before the materials were mastered and concluded in middle life that his materials could never be mastered. Yet his two lectures before the Bridgnorth Institute in 1877—"The History of Freedom in Antiquity" and "The History of Freedom in Christianity"—present a glimpse into his brilliant command of the subject.

Acton's inaugural lecture as Regius Professor at Cambridge reaffirmed his now unshakable conviction that the historian must serve as moral magistrate, for "if we lower our standard in history, we cannot uphold it in Church and State." In his remarks made before the tiny Eranus Club in May 1897, he summed up the meaning of his intellectual odyssey: "To renounce the pains and penalties of exhaustive research is to remain a victim to ill informed and designing writers, and to authorities that have worked for ages to build up the vast tradition of conventional mendacity. By going on from book to manuscript and from library to archive, we exchange doubt for certainty, and become our own masters. We explore a new heaven and a new earth, and at each step forward, the world moves with us."

Overview of Biographical Sources

By the year of his death Acton's reputation seemed secure as an extraordinarily erudite, if somewhat remote, Cambridge don with deep Continental connections, who had launched a great work, the *Cambridge Modern History*. Painful memories of struggles with the Church had faded, as he himself had long since avoided the topic with family and associates, maintaining a great silence on his religious views and the intellectual impasse posed by them. The earliest reliable biographical writing came from those who had known him in various capacities in earlier days. The most telling was from the hand of Lady Charlotte Blennerhassett, with whom Acton had shared many of his deepest thoughts over a long span of years: "Acton-," *Biographisches Jahrbuch deutscher Nekrolog* (Vol 7. 1902: 16-22); "The Late Lord Acton," *Edinburgh Review* (Vol. 197. 1903: 501-534); and "Lord Acton," *Deutsche Rundschau* (Vol. 122. 1905: 64-92). John Neville Figgis, a Cambridge colleague and co-editor with Reginald V. Laurence of Acton's lectures and correspondence, wrote an entry for the *Dictionary of National Biography* (1912).

Another contemporary, Herbert Paul, an author and politician, edited some of Acton's letters to Mary Gladstone (1904; see below). The strong language of the letters, plus Paul's sharp comments in a lengthy introduction, raised anew questions as to the orthodoxy of Acton's Catholicism, opening again old charges from Manning's arguments.

The first full-length biography did not appear until the three volumes of Ulrich Noack, *Geschichtswissenschaft und Wahrheit* (Frankfurt: G. Schulte-Bulmke, 1935); *Katholizität und Geistesfreiheit* (Frankfurt: G. Schulte-Bulmke, 1936); and *Politik als Sicherung der Freiheit* (Frankfurt: G. Schulte-Bulmke, 1947), works riddled with serious defects in methodology. Less analytical are Frank E. Lally's *As Lord Acton Says* (Newport, RI: Remington Ward, 1942)—largely an anthology of Acton's writings laced together with narrative—and David Matthew's treatment of Acton's early years, *Acton: The Formative Years* (London: Eyre & Spottiswoode, 1946), which is quite rich on the social aspect of the family, both in England and on the Continent. None of these works comes to grips with the controversial questions in Acton biography, namely how he came to his understanding of moral judgment in history, why he failed to produce his history of freedom, and the precise nature of his Catholicism.

In 1948 there appeared two publications which stimulated two decades of intense analysis of Acton's thought and life: "Lord Acton," by Herbert Butterfield, a pamphlet for the English Historical Association, and *Essays on Freedom and Power,* edited by Gertrude Himmelfarb, a collection of Acton's essays and lectures (see below). Thoughts on the history of freedom and its enemies took on special meaning to a fresh generation of intellectuals struggling to comprehend World War II. Acton was now relevant, a prophetic figure, a voice from the past speaking to the experience of the present. Interest in his intellectual life, his political philosophy, his thought on history and much more prompted scholarly inquiry into his pre-Cambridge years.

Momentous developments within the Roman Catholic Church—the pontificate of John XXIII and the Second Vatican Council—intensified the search for the lost Acton: the Liberal Catholic Movement in its many manifestations became the focal point of doctoral dissertations on both sides of the Atlantic; moral judgment in history was cast in a new light by a generation reeling from the stark horrors of the modern age. Flawed scholarship was reworked in the 1970s as Cambridge published the full correspondence between Acton and Simpson.

A rather more critical opinion of Acton began to appear with Owen Chadwick's lecture, "Acton and Gladstone" (London: Athlone Press, 1976). Far more stinging was the writing of Hugh Tulloch, who published his more negative judgments in *Acton* (1988), notwithstanding that he had not studied the major primary sources. Despite the appearance of the new biographical studies and a massive three-volume anthology of his writings, a definitive life has yet to be written, though a promising work by Roland Hill is in production.

Evaluation of Principal Biographical Sources

Gunn, Peter. *The Actons.* London: Hamish Hamilton, 1978. (**A, G**) Highly readable survey of the remarkable family. Though it contains only a brief chapter on Lord Acton, the book offers a splendid overview. Lacks documentation but contains a general bibliography.

Himmelfarb, Gertrude. *Lord Acton: A Study in Conscience and Politics.* London: Routledge and Kegan Paul, 1952. (**A, G**) An excellent treatise on Acton's intellectual biography. Thoroughly documented with a full bibliography for its date. It's weakness is that the author did not have access to the largest manuscript collection of Acton papers, now at Cambridge, but her judgments remain, for the most part, sound.

Mathew, David. *Lord Acton and His Times*. London: Eyre and Spottiswoode, 1968. This work is a rewrite and expansion of Mathew's *Acton: The Formative Years*. London: Eyre and Spottiswoode, 1946, (**A, G**) Though the author did not research the most important manuscript collections—his knowledge of the social and ecclesiastical orders of Acton's time is helpful. Limited documentation and bibliography.

Schuettinger, Robert L. *Lord Acton: Historian of Liberty*. LaSalle, IL: Open Court, 1976. (**A, G**) Though flawed in scholarship and didactic, this work does present a useful survey of Acton's life. As with the other works cited here, the principal manuscript collections were not consulted. Documentation shows that this book is largely a rewrite from published sources. Good bibliography.

Tulloch, Hugh. *Acton* London: Weidenfeld and Nicolson, 1988. (**A, G**) More an extended essay than a monograph, this is the latest work to appear. It is one of a series by the publisher on English historians. Tulloch praises Acton's intellect but faults him as a flawed man and historian. Provocative thought with documentation but no bibliography. The major manuscript collections were not used.

Overview and Evaluation of Primary Sources

The flagship collection of Acton manuscript material is housed in the University Library, Cambridge University. In addition to numerous collections of correspondence, there exists over two hundred boxes (the "black boxes") in which Acton kept his extensive notes and extracts from a lifetime of reading and research. Since it is often impossible to distinguish whether a given writing is in fact Acton's or merely copied from an unidentified source, extreme caution is necessary in using these materials. In another wing of the library are housed the sixty thousand volumes of Acton's personal library, many volumes of which contain marginalia in Acton's hand, as well as thousands of slips of paper marking passages of significance to his thinking.

The Shropshire County Council Archives in Shrewsbury constitutes the only other major repository of Acton manuscripts. In addition to miscellaneous correspondence of Acton and other members of the family—complementing the Cambridge holdings—there is extensive documentary material pertaining to the history of the family and its Aldenham Hall estate, dating from the sixteenth century.

Published primary sources are somewhat extensive but varied in quality. Herbert Paul's edition of selections form the *Letters of Lord Acton to Mary Gladstone* (London: George Allen, 1904. Rev. ed. London: Macmillan, 1913) marked the first publication of Acton's letters, causing alarm in some quarters owing to his unconventional views of the Church. This prompted Abbot Gasquet's scandalously edited selection from Acton's letters to Richard Simpson, *Lord Acton and His Circle* (London: George Allen and Burnes & Oates, 1906). In an ill-judged effort to reclaim Acton as a loyal, dutiful son of the Church, Abbot Gasquet edited Acton's words to give the appearance of orthodoxy. He radically altered crucial sentences, reversing their meaning, and his introductory essay portrays a highly inaccurate interpretation of Acton's views. When Figgis and Laurence brought forth the first of several projected *Selections from the Correspondence of the First Lord Acton* (London: Longmans, Green, 1917), the old doubts and anxieties surfaced again, leading the family to terminate the project. It was not until 1963 that the world began to receive the fullness of Acton's thought in the magisterial *Ignaz v. Döllinger Briefwechsel mit Lord Acton 1850-1890* (3 vols. Munich: C. H. Beck, 1963-1971), edited by Victor Conzemius. Acton letters containing great substance appeared in *Lord Acton: The Decisive Decade 1864-1874* (Louvain: Bibliothèque de l'Université, 1970), edited by Damian McElrath, James C. Holland, Ward White, and Sue Katzman. Gasquet's mischief was finally set right with the publication of *The Correspondence of Lord Acton and Richard Simpson* (3 vols. Cambridge: Cambridge University Press, 1971-1975), edited by Josef L. Altholz, Damian McElrath, and James C. Holland. James C. Holland and Mary G. Holland are currently (1993) compiling an edition of the full correspondence of Acton and Gladstone.

There have been numerous editions of Acton's lectures and anthologies of his writings. Figgis and Laurence led the way with four volumes: *Lectures on Modern History* (London: Macmillan, 1906); *The History of Freedom and Other Essays* (London: Macmillan, 1907); *Historical Essays and Studies* (London: Macmillan,

1907); and *Lectures on the French Revolution* (London: Macmillan, 1910). Additional collections of Acton's writings include the following: *Essays on Freedom and Power* (Boston: Beacon Press, 1948), edited by Gertrude Himmelfarb; *Essays on Church and State* (London: Hollis and Carter, 1952), edited by Douglas Woodruff; *Lord Acton: Essays in the Liberal Interpretation of History* (Chicago: University of Chicago Press, 1967), edited by William H. McNeill; *Lord Acton on Papal Power* (London: Sheed and Ward, 1973), edited by H. A. MacDougall; and the most useful *Selected Writings of Lord Acton* (3 vols. Indianapolis, IN: Liberty Classics, 1984-1988), edited by J. Rufus Fears.

Museums, Historical Landmarks, Societies

Cambridge University Library (Cambridge). There is a striking photograph of Lord Acton taken in his study at his desk, piled high with books. The framed photograph hangs in the Acton Library Special Collection.

National Portrait Gallery (London). The collection includes the oil portrait of Acton by Franz von Lenbach.

James C. Holland
Shepherd College

Hans Christian Andersen
1805-1875

Chronology

Born Hans Christian Andersen on April 2, 1805, in Odense, Denmark, son of Hans Andersen, an impoverished shoemaker, and Anne Marie Andersdatter; grows up in Odense with very little schooling; hears from his grandmother tales of Danish folk culture; spends most of his time daydreaming and playing with his puppet theater; *1816* father dies; spends as much time as possible with the local theater; *1819* moves to Copenhagen in order to fulfill his dreams of becoming an actor at the Royal Theater; *1819-1822* attempts unsuccessfully to establish a career as an actor, singer, and ballet dancer; manages to find generous benefactors among artists and government officials; his first plays, submitted to the theater, are rejected; *1822-1827* receives public support for a basic education at Slagelse School; *1827* publishes his first poem, "The Dying Child"; *1828-1831* writes several works that gain him an enthusiastic readership but are harshly treated by the critics; *1831* leaves for Germany on the first of thirty foreign journeys and publishes his first travelogue based on the trip, *Shadow Pictures*; *1831-1833* financial needs force him to translate, write, and rework libretti for operas; *1833-1834* travels to France, Switzerland, and Italy, which has a decisive impact on his artistic development; *1835* publishes *The Improvisatore,* a veiled autobiography in novel form and his first international success; publishes *Tales, Told for Children,* the first of twenty-four collections of tales and stories; *1835-1840* consolidates his national and international reputation with additional novels, *O.T.* (1836) and *Only a Fiddler* (1837) as well as several volumes of tales and stories; *1840* falls in love with Jenny Lind, a young Swedish soprano who does not reciprocate his affections; his first major stage play, *The Mulatto,* is successfully performed at the Royal Theater; *1840-1841* undertakes his most ambitious journey, to Italy, Greece, and Turkey; *1842* becomes acquainted in Paris with the great writers of French Romanticism, Balzac, Dumas, Hugo, Lamartine, Vigny, and the renowned actress Rachel; *1844* invited to stay with the royal family; knighted with the Order of Dannebrog; *1847* travels to Holland, England, and Scotland and becomes acquaint-

Zion-Benton Twp. High School
Instructional Materials Center

ed with his admirer Charles Dickens; his collected works begin to appear in Germany; *1848* publishes *The Two Baronesses*; *1851* appointed titular professor, a royal appointment not affiliated with any institution; *1853* publishes his collected works; *1863* publishes his last significant travelogue, *In Spain,* based on an extensive journey the previous year; *1867* made an honorary citizen of his native town of Odense; *1870-1875* with his health deteriorating, spends his last years in the homes of wealthy and attentive friends in Copenhagen and at manor houses in the Danish countryside; *1875* becomes Commander of the Order of Dannebrog; dies on August 4, at the home of friends, and is buried in Copenhagen.

Activities of Historical Significance

Hans Christian Andersen was the first prominent Danish writer of proletarian origin. Although later in life he moved in upper-class and aristocratic circles, he never disguised his background and always considered himself an outsider. This position explains both his social insecurity and vanity, and his ability to observe the most minute detail of his environment, especially the shortcomings in society, particularly among the upper classes. However, he never attacked royalty, whom he placed above any criticism. Andersen, in his adherence to idealistic philosophy and fierce rejection of materialism, was a child of romanticism. He nevertheless pointed ahead to the succeeding period of realism—through his keen awareness of external reality, including its negative aspects and social flaws.

In particular his use of plain, everyday language in his tales and stories, and the oral quality which he himself continuously emphasized, make Andersen a forerunner of later literary trends. Indeed, it is the colloquial tone of his tales and stories which have made them so appealing to an audience of all ages and nations. Nevertheless, this stylistic quality should not conceal that these texts are also highly sophisticated, psychological and philosophical statements.

Andersen was productive in a variety of literary genres. Some of his poetry, with its simple style and musicality, has maintained its Danish readership, probably assisted by that touch of sentimentality which mars so much of Andersen's writings.

With his first novel, *The Improvisatore* (1835), Andersen wrote the first European novel that successfully incorporated colorful Italian nature and picturesque folklore in a narrative frame. With *Only a Fiddler* (1837), he wrote a European bestseller and predicted through the novel's tragic ending what he saw as a possible outcome of his own career. It is this extreme fascination with himself as an individual and his interrelationship with the external world that makes Andersen a forerunner of modern European psychological writers.

This self-analysis also permeates Andersen's travelogues, which successfully combine an introverted preoccupation with a unique sensory awareness surrounding the traveler's experience abroad. Andersen's constant craving for new impressions took him to places which in the mid-nineteenth century were off limits to most: Greece, Turkey, Bulgaria, North Africa, and Portugal.

However, it is his tales and stories, 156 in all, for which Andersen is best remembered. He began, as a typical Romanticist, by rewriting folktales he had heard as a child, such as *The Tinderbox* and *The Traveling Companion*; but he soon developed his talents to compose texts based exclusively on personal experiences. His social background is commented on in *She Was No Good,* a stirring tribute to his alcoholic, impoverished mother, and expressed more generally through his compassion for the poor and lonely in *The Little Matchgirl*; frequently his social awareness takes on a stinging satirical direction as in *The Ice Maiden* or *The Gardener and the Lord and Lady*. His affairs of the heart can be followed in a series of tales, of which *The Nightingale* stands out both as a heartfelt glorification of the Swedish singer Jenny Lind and of true, natural art in general. The demands and dilemmas of being an artist are dealt with in the dissatisfied and ambitious title character of *The Fir Tree*, as well as in Andersen's last tale, the complex and ambiguous *Auntie Toothache,* in which he—with abysmal pessimism —discusses the artist's choice between sacrificing himself completely for his art and rejecting inspiration in favor of a safe and pleasant bourgeois life.

The modernity of Andersen comes forth in his ambiguous attitude towards accepting absolute existential statements. In *The Shadow* he holds forth the crushing defeat of idealistic philosophy, to which he otherwise basically adheres. The story is the description of triumphant nihilism and a capital text in the history of nineteenth-century ideas. The absurdity of all human efforts in making the right choice is demonstrated with merciless consequence in *The Story of a Mother*. And the existence, if not predominance, of absolute evil both in a metaphysical and social sense permeates both *The Snow Queen* and *A Drop of Water* respectively. Optimism and pessimism, good and evil, continuously alternate in Andersen's tales and stories and gives them a modern relativistic view of values. Nevertheless, he desperately wished to adhere to a belief in the divine symbolized by the mysterious sound which is heard, but ignored by most, in *The Bell,* and in immortality as so stirringly demonstrated in *The Little Mermaid. The Ugly Duckling* is permeated with his firm belief that, in spite of any handicaps, it is possible for any individual to achieve his or her goals and find happiness and success.

Andersen dared to replace the academic, often stilted language of his fellow Romanticists with a fresh approach to everyday language, which so violently upset his critics. Indeed, the innovation, variety, and universality of Andersen's artistic achievements are amazing seen against the backdrop of his social origin, the literary conventions of his time, and the narrow-mindedness and provincialism of his critics—all obstacles which he successfully overcame.

Overview of Biographical Sources

The earliest discussions of Andersen were published by the Danish scholars Georg Brandes, ''H. C. Andersen som Eventyrdigter'' (H. C. Andersen as a Fairy-Tale Writer) in *Kritiker og Portraiter* (Critiques and Portraits) (Copenhagen: Glydendal, 1870) and Hans Brix, *H. C. Andersen og hans Eventyr* (H. C. Andersen and his Fairy-Tales) (Copenhagen: Glydendal, 1907). In particular Brandes's essay contains brilliant aesthetic observations and judgments, whereas the strength of Brix's work lies in its biographical detail, though Brix has a tendency to draw too many far-fetched parallels between the author and his works.

The first English-language biography is Robert Nisbet Bain's *Hans Christian Andersen: A Biography* (1895). Several decades passed before the biographical study of Andersen gathered momentum, based on research by Hans Brix and foremost by Helge Topsøe-Jensen. An impressive number of these works were translated from Danish to English.

Introducing this renewed interest in Andersen was the actor and writer Elith Reumert, whose biography, *Andersen the Man* (1925), focuses on biographical detail rather than on Andersen's artistic achievement. Reumert toured England and the U.S. giving exceptionally fine readings of Andersen's tales and stories which revived interest in his life and work.

In the strict biographical tradition of Reumert are Signe Toksvig's *The Life of*

Hans Christian Andersen (1933), Svend Larsen's *Hans Christian Andersen* (1949), and Rumer Godden's, *Hans Christian Andersen* (1955), whereas Monica Stirling's *The Wild Swan: The Life and Times of Hans Christian Andersen* (New York: Harcourt, Brace and World, 1965) renders a free, almost fictitious account based on Andersen's life. A more successful balance between biography and literary criticism is found in the monograph by the Swedish scholar Fredrik Böök, *Hans Christian Andersen: A Biography* (1938). More popular and with a clearer informational aim are Erling Nielsen's *Hans Christian Andersen: 1805-1875* (1963), Reginald Spink's picture book *Hans Christian Andersen and His World* (London: Thames and Hudson, 1972), and Elias Bredsdorff's *Hans Christian Andersen: An Introduction to his Life and Works* (Copenhagen: Hans Reitzel, 1987). In the much more comprehensive volume *Hans Christian Andersen: The Story of His Life and Works 1805-1875* (1975), Bredsdorff attempts to combine biography with some critical analysis, whereas Bo Grønbech's *Hans Christian Andersen* (1980) mainly focuses on interpretation.

More specialized studies of Andersen have been published exclusively in Scandinavia. Eigil Nyborg's *Den indre linie i H.C. Andersens eventyr* (The Underlying Thread in H. C. Andersen's Tales) (Copenhagen: Glydendal, 1962) is heavily indebted to Jungian psychology; Norwegian critic Arne Duve, in *H. C. Andersens hemmelighet* (The Secret of H. C. Andersen) (Oslo: Psychopress, 1969), adheres to a dogmatic psychoanalytical approach; and the Dane Peer E. Sørensen presents with *H. C. Andersen og herskabet* (H. C. Andersen and the Lord and Lady) (Grenå: GMT, 1973) a thought-provoking Marxist analysis. Klaus P. Mortensen's study, *Svanen og skyggen* (The Swan and the Shadow) (Copenhagen: Gad, 1989) is more of a traditional biography. However, most contemporary Danish studies focus on Andersen's writings rather than on his biography, frequently analyzing their language and style, relationship to other prose genres, mythic content, and narrative technique.

Evaluation of Principal Biographical Sources

Bain, Robert Nisbet. *Hans Christian Andersen: A Biography*. London: Lawrence and Bullen, 1895. (G) The first American biography, displaying a thorough familiarity with Andersen's published letters, autobiographies, other relevant secondary literature, and contemporary criticism. In spite of its occasional unreliability and penchant for anecdotes, this 461-page study is a pioneering work in the biographical study of Andersen. Bain meticulously lists most of Andersen's writings in all his genres, and usefully summarizes the novels and major plays. The volume concludes with an index.

Böök, Fredrik. *Hans Christian Andersen: A Biography.* 1938. Translated by George Schoolfield. Norman: University of Oklahoma Press, 1962. (**A, G**) A stimulating and accurate, mainly biographical account. Andersen's other works are only briefly mentioned. However, in two separate chapters, Böök discusses the genesis of the tales and stories, the uniqueness of their style, and their philosophical content. The biography offers new insights into Andersen's complex personality: the discussion of his religious views is brilliant, and the interpretations are innovative and stimulating.

Bredsdorff, Elias. *Hans Christian Andersen: The Story of His Life and Work 1805-1875.* London: Phaidon, 1975. (**A, G**) The best, most thorough and reliable biography. Though critical analysis is sketchy, Bredsdorff, by extensively quoting from Andersen's letters and other primary sources, adds numerous significant details. Strong emphasis on Andersen's relationship with England and English personalities. The volume has an excellent bibliography.

Godden, Rumer. *Hans Christian Andersen.* London: Hutchinson, 1955. (**G**) Godden is heavily indebted to Andersen's autobiography, *The Fairy Tale of My Life,* and accepts the information he provides at face value. Most attention is given to Andersen's early years, whereas his last fifteen years are covered in only seven pages and the tales and stories not introduced until two-thirds into the volume. There is a glaring lack of dates, only a few, often incorrect, titles are mentioned in passing, and there is no attempt at interpretation. Scholarship after 1900 is only rarely considered. Reads well as a somewhat disorganized biographical novel but has only little scholarly merit.

Grønbech, Bo. *Hans Christian Andersen.* Boston: Twayne, 1980. (**A, G**) The biographical sections of this volume uncritically utilizes Andersen's own autobiography, *The Fairy Tale of My Life,* but ignores some important data on Andersen's life. Grønbech's discussion of the tales and stories is extremely valuable. His study also offers the only available overview in English of Andersen-criticism and research in Denmark and abroad. Less satisfactory is the discussion of the other genres in which Andersen wrote. Some major works are given several pages of analysis, others only a few lines.

Larsen, Svend. *Hans Christian Andersen*. 1953. Translated by Mabel Dyrup. Odense: Flensted, 1961. (**G**) Traditional, popular, and somewhat wordy biography focusing on Andersen's childhood in Odense, early experiences in Copenhagen, and his many travels and connections with celebrities in Denmark and abroad. Not up-to-date on newer Andersen research and contains no original observations or evaluations. Andersen's works are only introduced in a biographical context without any additional interpretation.

Nielsen, Erling. *Hans Christian Andersen, 1805-1875*. 1963. Translated by Reginald Spink. Copenhagen: Royal Danish Ministry of Foreign Affairs, 1983. (**A, G**) In this acute and penetrating study, Nielsen, a recognized Andersen scholar, outlines the main features of Andersen's life and works, placing special emphasis on his greatest achievement, the tales and stories. Beautifully illustrated. Probably the most handy introduction to Andersen and the romantic epoch in Danish culture. Highly recommended.

Reumert, Elith. *Hans Andersen the Man*. 1925. Translated by Jessie Bröchner. London: Methuen, 1927. (**G**) This enthusiastically written, but rather uncritical glorification of Andersen, provides an abundance of biographical information about the numerous personalities that surrounded and interacted with Andersen. The broad cultural-historical sections of the book provide information that is not available in English elsewhere. In addition to the chronological treatment, sections include "Andersen and Religion," "Imagination and Fantasy," and "Andersen and his Fellow-Men."

Spink, Reginald. *Hans Christian Andersen and His World*. London: Thames and Hudson, 1972. (**G**) A brief, reliable biography enhanced by numerous illustrations. Particular attention is given to Andersen's Danish contemporaries. The volume, which reads like a novel, closes with a bibliography and an index.

Toksvig, Signe. *The Life of Hans Christian Andersen*. New York: Harcourt, Brace, 1934. (**A, G**) Like most of the other biographies, this one focuses on Andersen's early years. Toksvig embellishes and fictionalizes the material she has taken from Andersen's autobiography, *The Fairy Tale of My Life*. Her intent (as stated in the preface of the second Danish edition, 1970) is "to further a better understanding of Andersen's so-called vanity."

Overview and Evaluation of Primary Sources

It is possible to find autobiographical features in almost everything Andersen wrote. He was fascinated by his own life and career, wrote four autobiographies, made daily notes in his almanac, and kept a diary. All this material, together with his extensive correspondence, comprises a unique wealth of sources.

Andersen wrote four autobiographies, of which the first (1832) and the third (1855) have never been translated into English. His second attempt (1847) was translated from German by Mary Howitt, *The True Story of My Life* (London: Longman, 1847). The final version, covering the years up to 1868, was translated by Horace E. Scudder, *The Story of My Life* (New York: Hurd and Houghton, 1871) and W. Glyn Jones, *The Fairy Tale of My Life* (New York: British Book Centre, 1954). Apart from the first version, Andersen's biographies are written in retrospect, with posterity in mind, and provide an idealized and often manipulated account of his life and career. Whereas the early chapters prove most successful with their flamboyance, candor, and honest judgments, the latter occasionally approach a mere catalogue of the flattery, honors, and decorations that were bestowed upon Andersen. Nevertheless these volumes are written by a great artist and constitute fascinating readings for a general audience. Only very little of Andersen's large correspondence has been translated: *Hans Christian Andersen's Correspondence with the Late Grand-Duke of Saxe-Weimar, Charles Dickens, Etc., Etc.* (London: Dean and Son, 1891); *Hans Christian Andersen's Visits to Charles Dickens, As Described in His Letters, Published with Six of Dickens' Letters in Facsimile* (Copenhagen: Levin and Munksgaard, 1937); and *The Andersen-Scudder Letters: Hans Christian Andersen's Correspondence with Horace Elisha Scudder* (Berkeley: University of California Press, 1949). Andersen was an avid letter writer—regarding letter writing as an art form—and he became increasingly dependent on receiving letters on a daily basis, in particular when traveling abroad. He corresponded not only with his close friends in Odense and Copenhagen but also with fellow artists and writers as well as dignitaries from various European countries. Of particular interest to English-speaking readers is correspondence with friends in England, such as Charles Dickens, and the young American publisher Horace E. Scudder. It is his quite candid correspondence, as well as his diaries, that provide the most lifelike and correct information about his life.

Andersen's diaries have been published in twelve volumes as *H. C. Andersen's dagbøger 1825-1875* (Copenhagen: Gad, 1971-1976). Selections in English have been translated by Patricia L. Conroy and Sven H. Rossel, *The Diaries of Hans Christian Andersen* (Seattle: University of Washington Press, 1990). This edition is illustrated with Andersen's own drawings and paper cuts and contains an introduction, annotations, and a detailed index. The diaries provide fascinating insights into the complexity of Andersen's psyche, his perceptions of the people, landscape, and art of the countries he visited, and concrete details which comprise the raw materials of his tales and stories.

In 1990 Andersen's almanacs were published, *Almanakker 1833-1873* (Copenhagen: Gad, 1990). They are made up by brief, daily notes, often in an almost shorthand form. They contain a multitude of information about his everyday tasks, his visitors, and his working habits. Whereas Andersen's diaries focus on his travel experiences, his almanacs focus on his daily life in Denmark.

Fiction and Adaptations

The Danish playwright Kjeld Abell wrote on the occasion of Andersen's 150th anniversary in 1955 a play for the Royal Theater in Copenhagen entitled *Andersen eller hans livs eventyr* (Andersen or the Fairy Tale of His Life). By boldly employing the theater's technical equipment he was able to create a magic fairy tale world in which characters from Andersen's life and from his writings appear. The play requires considerable knowledge of Andersen's biography and the characters of his tales and stories. Danny Kaye starred in the movie *Hans Christian Andersen* (1952), which provided considerable misinformation and greatly distorted Andersen's life. This film is an extremely free adaptation completely ignoring the tragic outcome of the love story and the metaphysical aspect of the tale. Numerous films have been adapted from Andersen's stories, the most popular of which is Disney's *The Little Mermaid* (1989).

Museums, Historical Landmarks, Societies

Bust (Sydney, Australia). By Wendy Solling, 1955.

Central Park (New York). Contains a statue by George Loeber, 1956.

H. C. Andersen Samfundet i København (The H. C. Andersen Society in Copenhagen, Denmark).

H. C. Andersen-Samfundet (The H. C. Andersen Society, Odense, Denmark). Published the journal *Anderseniana*, 1933-1954.

Hans Christian Andersen House and Museum (Odense, Denmark). Houses Andersen's personal belongings, drawings, paper cuts, and an extensive library with a collection of all of Andersen's works in translation. Also displays a painting by C. A. Jensen, 1836, and a bust by Joseph Durham, 1847. Has published the journal *Anderseniana* since 1955.

Lincoln Park (Chicago). Contains a statue by J. Gelert, 1896.

National Historical Museum (Frederiksborg, Denmark). Holds a painting of Andersen by Albert Küchler, 1833.

The King's Garden (Copenhagen). Houses a statue by August Saabye, 1880.

Hans Christian Andersen House and Museum (Odense, Denmark). Houses a drawing by H. Olrik, 1859.

Town Hall Square (Copenhagen). Contains a statue by Henry Luckow-Nielsen, 1961. In the harbor is a statue of the Little Mermaid by Edvard Eriksen, 1913.

Other Sources

Anderseniana, journal and major forum for national and international Andersen research. Published by *The H.C. Andersen Society* 1933-1954; by *The Hans Christian Andersen House and Museum* 1955-. Also publishes articles in English, French, and German and provides summaries in the same languages.

Bredsdorff, Elias. *Hans Andersen and Charles Dickens: A Friendship and Its Dissolution. Anglistica,* Vol. 7. Copenhagen: Rosenkilde and Bagger, 1956. A fascinating account of a friendship between two writers, which was not without its frictions.

Dal, Erik. "Hans Christian Andersen's Tales and America." *Scandinavian Studies* 40 (1968): 1-25. Discusses the relationship of Andersen and his tales and stories in the United States. Special attention is given to Horace E. Scudder, Andersen's American editor and publisher.

Heltoft, Kjeld. *Hans Christian Andersen as an Artist.* Translated by Reginald Spink. Copenhagen: Royal Danish Ministry of Foreign Affairs, 1977. A splendidly illustrated book about Andersen's extraordinary artistry with pen and pencil drawings, collages, and paper cuts.

Marker, Frederick J. *Hans Christian Andersen and the Romantic Theatre.* Toronto: University of Toronto Press, 1971. A study and evaluation of Andersen as a playwright in the romantic tradition.

Sven Hakon Rossel
University of Washington

Giacomo Antonelli
1806-1876

Chronology

Born Giacomo Antonelli on April 2, 1806, in Sonnino in the Southern tier of the Papal States, the third son of Domenico Antonelli, and Loreta Mancini; his father amasses a considerable fortune serving lay and clerical patrons and places his sons in important positions; *1816-1823* attends the Collegium; Romanum; completes the seven-year course in grammar and rhetoric; *1823* enters the University of the Sapienza, where he receives his degree in canon and civil law; studies under Nicola Manari of the Apostolic Chamber; *1830* enters the *Prelatura*—the higher civil and diplomatic service of state; *1832* named an associate judge of the Civil Congregation of the Apostolic Chamber; *1834* secures admission in the Criminal Tribunal in Rome and the following year appointed apostolic delegate to the Province of Orvieto, charged with supervising civil and ecclesiastical affairs; *1836* sent by Pope Gregory XVI to Viterbo; *1839* sent to Macerata, the largest of the apostolic delegations in size and population; two years later the conservative Gregory brings Antonelli back to Rome as under-secretary of state for internal affairs; *1841* agrees to receive sacred orders up to the deaconate, resisting parental pressure to become a priest; *1844* following three and a half successful years in the Ministry of the Interior, Gregory makes him deputy treasurer; *1845* made minister of finance; *1846* among the chosen few to attend Pope Gregory XVI on his deathbed; Gregory's successor, the more liberal Giovanni Maria Mastai-Ferretti, who assumes the name Pius IX, proves equally solicitous toward Antonelli who shows himself prone to moderate opinions and friends, seconding the course of the new Pontiff; *1847* rewarded by being raised to the dignity of cardinal deacon; appointed president of the *Consulta,* the consultative chamber that Pius creates; *1848* when the call for broader reforms threatens the quiet of the Papal State, helps draft the Constitution of Papal Rome and is subsequently appointed secretary of state and effective head of the first Constitutional Ministry in Rome; when nationalists in Rome demand that the pope join the crusade for national liberation against Austria, and the pope's conscience prevents his declaration of war, the Antonelli ministry resigns, but Antonelli remains Pius's trusted advisor; arranges the pope's flight from Rome; *1849* while at Gaeta, in the Kingdom of Naples, named acting secretary of state; following the intervention of the Catholic powers (Austria, France, Spain, and the Kingdom of the Two Sicilies) arranged by Antonelli, and the fall of the Roman Republic, he returns to Rome with the pope; serves as papal secretary of state and effective head of the papal government until the total collapse of the temporal power provoked by the Italian seizure of Rome in 1870; *1870-1876* remains by the side of Pius IX, sharing his "imprisonment" in the Vatican and serving as papal secretary of state until his death; *1876* dies on November 6; buried in the chapel of the Church of Santa Agata alla Suburra, beside his mother.

Activities of Historical Significance

The last of the "lay Cardinals," Giacomo Antonelli, the chief minister and advisor of Pope Pius IX, played a remarkable role in nineteenth-century Italian and European affairs. Associated initially with the reforms of the "liberal" Pius IX, and head of the first Constitutional Ministry of Papal Rome, he had to confront the revolutionary whirlwind of 1848, and was deemed responsible for the Restoration which ensued. Although some mistakenly place the entire responsibility for papal intransigence during these decades upon his shoulders, he did play an important role in executing the policy of *non-possumus*, and was unquestionably the most talented figure of the counter-*Risorgimento*. Directing Vatican diplomacy in the decades when nationalism disrupted the Restoration of 1815, the Americas were troubled by the Civil War and the Maximilian affair, Italy and Germany were unified, and the Roman question and the *Kulturkampf* burdened the papacy, Antonelli crossed swords with the leading practitioners of *Realpolitik* of the century. Supervising the religious interests of the Catholic church as well as protecting its political affairs, his influence was far reaching. Thus he was called upon to explain the meaning of the "Syllabus of Errors" as well as papal infallibility to the powers. His achievements during the course of the long pontificate of Pius IX (1846-1878) may be divided into phases.

In the first, 1846-1848, Antonelli provided technical and political support for Pius IX's reforms, serving as head of his Consultative Assembly. He also presided over the first Constitutional Ministry and confronted a host of technical and economic issues.

A second phase ensued following the revolution in Rome in November 1848, when Antonelli arranged for the pope's flight from the capital, his transport to Gaeta in the Kingdom of Naples, and the intervention of the four Catholic powers that overturned Mazzini's Roman Republic and restored the pope. In this stage, when Pius emphatically abandoned his earlier liberal and reformist sentiments, Antonelli drafted the *motu proprio* of September 12, 1849, which reflected the pope's new political philosophy. Antonelli's structure mirrored the change, providing for juridical and administrative concessions for the people of the Papal States, but retaining political power in the hands of the pope and his ministers.

In the years from 1849 to 1870, which constitute a third phase, Antonelli remained indispensable to Pius, assuming many of the burdens of state, while the pope increasingly focused on religious issues and questions troubling the universal church. While Antonelli fought against the Piedmontese consolidation of the peninsula, Pius IX issued his "Syllabus of Errors" and convoked the Vatican Council, among other things. Unable to prevent Cavour from absorbing the greater part of the Papal States in 1860, and the proclamation of the Italian Kingdom in 1861, Antonelli did manage to constrain Napoleon to retain his troops in Rome, preserving it for the papacy until the Franco-Prussian War and the withdrawal of the French contingent. Had Antonelli not bound Napoleon to protect Rome, the French emperor would have been able to conclude the triple alliance among France, Italy, and Austria against Prussia, and the outcome of the Franco-Prussian War and subsequent European history might have taken a different turn.

There were those who predicted that Antonelli's long career was over following the fall of the temporal power, but the pundits miscalculated. Pope Pius IX refused to dismiss the man who provided the diplomatic justification for his intransigent stance on the Roman question. In this fourth phase the pope depended not only on Antonelli's diplomatic savvy, but his financial expertise as well. Antonelli, with the assistance of his elder brother Filippo, revised the collection and investment of Peter's Pence, converting it into the primary source of papal income, allowing Pius to scorn the offer of Italian financial assistance that would have bound the pope to accept the loss of his territory.

Overview of Biographical Sources

Until recently no scholarly biography of the "villain" of the *Risorgimento* (movement for Italian unification) was available in English or any other language. To make matters worse, a popular but polemical literature appeared which presented Antonelli not only as the opponent of unification, but as a corrupt brute with fang-like teeth and a sexual appetite as insatiable as Casanova and as perverted as the marquis de Sade. The campaign against Antonelli, who was denounced as Machiavelli, Richelieu, and Mazarin rolled into one, commenced early. In 1861 there appeared a study by A. Bianchi-Giovini entitled *Quadro dei costumi della corte di Roma* (3d ed. Florence: Libreria speciale della novità, 1861) accusing Antonelli and his family of the most lurid crimes. Edmund About's *The Roman Question* (1859), translated from the French, proved equally libelous and indifferent to the truth, presenting Antonelli as a virtual savage and holding him responsible for the problems and abuses in papal Rome. Likewise Hippolyte Castille in his short, pseudobiography, *Le Cardinal Antonelli* (Paris: E. Dentu, 1859), harped upon the unfortunate influence Antonelli allegedly had upon Pius IX and the papal regime. Veturio Vetere's *I ventidue anni di governo di Cardinale Antonelli* (Rome: Stabilumento Civelli, 1871) presents a negative assessment of the person and policies of Antonelli. To be sure there were contemporary apologetic works which defended the regime of Pius IX, but often in their ardor to defend the pope, they were less than fair or objective regarding Antonelli, who was often burdened with much of the responsibility. Two notable exceptions were a review that appeared in the *Dublin Review* 28 (January, 1877: 74-78) after Antonelli's death, and David Silvagni's article "Il Cardinale Antonelli," which was included in *La corte e la società romana nei secoli XVIII e XIX* (1882. Reprint. Naples: Berisio Editore, 1967). Both articles sought to present Antonelli in an objective light, providing considerable information about the minister who was already enveloped in controversy. Only in the twentieth century were these works supplemented by serious scholarly articles, including those of Armando Ladolini in *Studi Romani* Anno I (July-August, 1953: 410-424; and September-October, 1953: 510-520); Pietro Pirri in *Rivista della Storia della Chiesa in Italia* XII (1958: 81-120); Roger Aubert in Volume 3 of the *Dizionario Biogafico degli Italiani* (Rome: Instituto della Encyclopedia Italiana, 1961, vol. III: 484-493); and Frank J. Coppa in *Journal of Church and State* (1974) and in *Biography* (1979). In 1983 Carlo Falconi's *Il*

Cardinale Antonelli. Vita e carriera del Richelieu italiano nella Chiesa di Pio IX was published, and in 1990 Coppa's *Cardinal Giacomo Antonelli and Papal Politics in European Affairs* appeared.

Evaluation of Principal Biographical Sources

About, Edmund. *The Roman Question.* Translated by H. C. Coape. New York: Appleton, 1859. (**G**) This slim volume on the personalities and policies of papal Rome is ultracritical of Cardinal Antonelli who is held responsible for most of the abuses in the Papal States following the Restoration of 1849. A good example of the polemical literature on Antonelli that contributed to his legend as a manipulator and corrupter. The work seeks to undermine the person as well as the political course pursued by Antonelli.

"Cardinal Antonelli." In *Dublin Review* 28 (January, 1877): 74-84. (**A, G**) This unsigned article published following Antonelli's death is one of the few early works favorable to him. While somewhat apologetic in tone, it is generally accurate, providing useful information about the early life and later career of the secretary of state of the longest reigning pope.

Coppa, Frank J. "Cardinal Antonelli, the Papal States and the Counter Risorgimento." In *Journal of Church and State* 16 (Autumn, 1974): 453-471. (**A, G**) Examines the political relationship of Pius IX and his secretary of state, and the alleged and real role played by Antonelli in the transformation of Pius from the patriotic leader of 1846-1848 to the leader of the reaction and opponent of unification. It assesses the part played by each in the counter-*Riorgimento* and the final days of the temporal power. In the process, Coppa dispels a number of the myths.

————. "Cardinal Giacomo Antonelli: An Accommodating Personality in the Politics of Confrontation." *Biography* 2 (Fall 1979): 288-302. (**A, G**) This article focuses on the character and career of Antonelli as well as his role and responsibility in setting and executing papal policy on the thorny Roman question. Shows Antonelli to be far more accommodating on political issues than his sovereign, whose position he executed if he did not always reflect.

————. *Cardinal Giacomo Antonelli and Papal Politics in European Affairs.* Albany: State University of New York Press, 1990. (**A, G**) This is the first scholarly biography on the life and times of Antonelli in English. Based on the documents of the Secret Vatican Archive and the neglected papers of the family in the State Archive in Rome, it provides an important reevaluation of this key figure who opposed Italian unification and directed papal diplomacy for three crucial decades. The early chapters delve into his formation and career while the later ones emphasize his relationship to Pius IX, his part in the counter-*Risorgimento* and papal reaction, and his activity during such crucial events as the Vatican Council and the *Kulturkampf*. Almost one third of the volume is devoted to notes and bibliography, and the annotated bibliography, which lists Italian and English works, will prove useful to those wishing to study the life and times of Antonelli.

De Cesare R. *The Last Days of Papal Rome, 1850-1870.* Translated by Helen Zimmern. New York: Houghton Mifflin, 1909. (**A, G**) This work, republished in Italian in 1970, remains a classic. Its reputation rests not only upon its own obvious merits but also on the dearth of objective studies of Pius IX, Cardinal Antonelli, and papal Rome. The author utilizes a series of anecdotes and a host of oral reports in this study, which is far more social than political.

Falconi, Carlo. *Il Cardinale Antonelli. Vita e carriera del Richelieu italiano nella chiesa di Pio IX.* Milan: Mondadori, 1983. (**A**) This is the first full-length, serious study of Antonelli in Italian, providing a historical rather than a polemical or apologetic approach. The first fourteen chapters, which dwell upon his family background and economic activities, as well as his youth and early career, supply information not readily available elsewhere. The remaining twenty-two chapters, which trace his activities from the revolutionary upheaval of 1848 to his death in the Vatican in 1876, recount more widely known developments, but are useful for the depth of their coverage and their insights. Contains an exhaustive forty-page bibliographical essay, but does not include Falconi's notes.

Martina, Giacomo. *Pio IX (1846-1850); Pio IX (1851-1866); Pio IX (1867-1878).* Rome: Università Gregoriana Editrice, 1974, 1986, 1990. (**A, G**) This three-volume Italian biography of Pius IX, which focuses on his Pontificate, devotes considerable attention to Cardinal Antonelli who served as his chief minister and adviser for most of these years. In the first volume Martina presents a more critical view of the cardinal than he does in the two subsequent volumes in which he has moderated his earlier critical assessment. Among other things Martina now refutes the charge that Antonelli and his family encouraged "brigandage" in the newly formed Kingdom of Italy. The author's reevaluation of Antonelli apparently has played a part in his overall assessment of the papal regime, which is far more balanced than that of the liberal historiography on the one hand and the work of the clerical apologists on the other.

Overview and Evaluation of Primary Sources

Most of the primary sources on the personal life and diplomatic and political policies of Antonelli are in Italian, Latin, or French, although some material is available in English. In the early 1960s Mariano Gabriele edited the correspondence found in the *Archivio di Stato di Roma* between Antonelli and Carlo Sacconi, the nuncio at Paris, in the volume *Il Carteggio Antonelli-Sacconi 1850-1860* (Rome: Istituto per la Storia del Risorgimento, 1962; **A**). Only following the opening of the Vatican Archives for the Pontificate of Pius IX was Carla Meneguzzi Rostagni able to edit the correspondence between Antonelli and the apostolic nuncio at Madrid, published as *Il Carteggio Antonelli-Barili, 1859-1861* (Rome: Istituto per al Storia del Risorgimento, 1973; **A**). More recently Lajos Lukacs has edited part of the correspondence between Antonelli and the various nuncios in Vienna in *The Vatican and Hungary 1846-1878: Reports and Correspondence of the Apostolic Nuncios in Vienna* (Translated by Zsofia Karmos. Budapest: Akademiai Kiado, 1981; **A, G**). While the documents included herein have not been translated from the original Italian, the editor's precis of each is in English, providing a good synthesis of what is included in the documents for the English-speaking reader. The introduction and the first five chapters of historical analysis, some two hundred pages of the volume, are likewise in English, and they shed considerable light on the personalities and events covered in the correspondence. Also useful for those who rely primarily on English sources is Noel Blakiston, ed., *The Roman Question: Extracts from the Dispatches of Odo Russell from Rome, 1858-1870* (London: Chapman and Hall, 1962; **A, G**). This volume includes the most important dispatches of Russell, who served as the unofficial representative to Rome and came into frequent contact with Antonelli. They provide an eyewitness account of Antonelli's effort to salvage the Papal States and preserve the temporal power. Written by a Protestant who was not friendly to the temporal power, the dispatches provide interesting if sometimes biased reports on the activities and motivation of Pius IX and Antonelli. As early as 1797 the United States commissioned a consul to represent them in the Papal States, and in the year of revolutionary upheaval, 1848, opened formal relations with the Papal States. The Americans retained a representative at the Roman court until 1867. The reports of the American ministers are found in Leo Francis Stock, ed., *United States Ministers to the Papal States: Instructions and Dispatches, 1848-1868* (Washington, DC: American Catholic Historical Association, 1933; **A, G**). Although long neglected, these dispatches provide invaluable accounts of the personalities and developments in papal Rome during the Antonelli years. Removed from the bitter diplomatic struggle, the reports of the American ministers provide some of the earliest objective accounts of Antonelli and his role in the counter-*Risorgimento.* The comments of Dudley Mann sent to the court of Pius IX, include comments on Secretary of State Antonelli. They can be found in *The Messages and Papers of Jefferson Davis and the Confederacy including Diplomatic Correspondence, 1861-1865* (New York: Chelsea House, 1966; **A, G**).

The most important papers on the person and policies of Cardinal Giacomo Antonelli are found in two archives in Rome: the *Archivio di Stato di Roma* and the *Archivio Segreto del Vaticano.* The State Archive in Rome contains the private papers of the Antonelli family, including those of Giacomo, which are found in the *Fondo Famiglia Antonelli.* Among the important documents found therein are Antonelli's will and that of his mother. The *Carte Miscellanea Politiche O Riservate,* those of the *Consiglio di Stato,* and those of the *Consulta di Stato,* provide valuable information on Antonelli's policies in the first half of the nineteenth century. The *Archivio Segreto del Vaticano* the *Archivio della Segreteria di Stato,* and the *Archivii delle Nunziature,* are particularly important for understanding and assessing Antonelli's diplomacy. The Central Museum of the Risorgimento in Rome has important material on the person and policies of Antonelli.

Frank J. Coppa
St. John's University

Johann Sebastian Bach
1685-1750

Chronology

Born Johann Sebastian Bach on March 21, 1685, in Eisenach, Germany, the son of Johann Ambrosius Bach, a court musician, who performed on the violin and viola, and Elisabeth Lämmerhirt Bach; *1693* attends the Latin school in Eisenach; *1694* his mother dies on May 3; his father remarries in November; *1695-1699* his father dies on February 24, 1695; moves to Ohrdruf to live with his oldest brother Johann Christoph and to study at the Latin school; *1700-1703* moves to Lüneburg for further education and to sing in the *Mettenchor,* a prestigious choir associated with St. Michael's Church; *1703-1707* serves as organist at the New Church in Arnstadt; *1705* obtains a leave of absence and travels to Lübeck to hear the music of the famous organist and composer Dietrich Buxtehude; *1707* begins working as an organist at St. Blasius's Church in Mühlhausen; marries his second cousin Maria Barbara Bach, with whom he has seven children, three of whom die; their eldest son, Wilhelm Friedemann (1710-1784), composes keyboard works and cantatas during the period of transition between Baroque and Rococo styles; their second surviving son, Karl Philipp Emanuel Bach (1714-1788), becomes a leading composer of the pre-Classical period, appointed harpsichordist to Frederick II of Prussia in 1740; *1708* his first published work, the cantata *Gott ist mein König* (God is my King), is performed on February 4 at the installation of the Mühlhausen Town Council; on June 25 resigns his position in Mühlhausen and accepts a prestigious offer as court organist to Duke Wilhelm Ernst of Weimar; *1714* elevated to the position of concertmaster of the Weimar court; *1717* accepts the position of director of music and chapelmaster to Prince Leopold of Anhalt in Cöthen after the duke of Weimar bypasses Bach for that position at his court; the duke of Weimar refuses to release him as concertmaster, and he is jailed from November 6 to December 2 for "too obstinately requesting his dismissal"; released from prison and his service, possibly to avoid a dispute with the court at Cöthen; *1720* his wife dies; *1721* marries Anna Magdelena Wilcken, daughter of the town trumpeter, with whom he has thirteen children, six of whom die; their youngest son, Johann Christian Bach (1735-1782) writes symphonies, concertos, sonatas, and operas, and serves for many years as music master to England's Queen Charlotte; their longest surviving son, Johann Christoph Friedrich Bach (1732-1795), becomes concertmaster to Count Wilhelm at Bückeburg, writes symphonies, motets, oratorios, piano sonatas, and chamber sontatas; six *Brandenburg Concertos* dedicated to the Margrave Christian Ludwig of Brandenburg; *1722* composes *The Well-Tempered Clavier, Book I*; *1722-1725* composes *The English Suites* and *The French Suites,* to further the keyboard education of his wife; *1723* installed as cantor of St. Thomas's Church in Leipzig, a post that was offered first to Georg Philipp Telemann of Hamburg and Christoph Graupner of Darmstadt; *1723-1744* writes the bulk of 250 cantatas in Leipzig; *1729* organizes the Collegium Musicum, a group that includes students from the University of Leipzig as well as professional musicians; the group performs weekly concerts on a regular basis and is under his direction until 1737; *1738-1742* composes *The Well-Tempered Clavier, Book II*; *1739-1741* continues his association with the Collegium Musicum; *1741-1742* composes for harpsichord *The Goldberg Variations*, thirty variations on a sixteen-measure sarabande theme; *1745-1750* composes but does not complete *Die Kunst der Fuge* (The Art of the Fugue); *1747* joins the Societät der musikalischen Wissenschaften (Society of Musical Sciences), an honorary society founded by former member of the Collegium Musicum Lorenz Mizler; composes *The Musical Offering*; *1747-1749* assembles *Mass in B Minor* from previously composed Sanctus, Kyrie and Gloria and newly composed Credo, Agnus Dei works; *1750* health deterioates as a result of two unsuccessful eye operations; after an unidentified prolonged illness, dies on July 28, and is buried in the churchyard of St. John in Leipzig with no gravemarker; *1894* during excavations to the foundation of the church, his coffin is found, and is reburied in a sarcophagus underneath the church.

Activities of Historical Significance

Johann Sebastian Bach was unquestionably one of the most brilliant composers in the history of music. He was born to a family of musicians; seven generations of Bachs were professional musicians. At one time, early in the eighteenth century, thirty Bachs held organ posts in Germany. Johann Sebastian Bach was primarily known as a performer by his contemporaries, and in particular as an organist. His mastery of the organ was so renowned that several times during his career he was asked to supervise the construction of organs at churches other than his own.

The enormous amount of music that remains as Bach's legacy attests to his compositional skill, despite the fact that many of his works have been lost. Indeed, only nine or ten of his compositions were printed during his lifetime and nothing else for half a century after his death. Bach came at the end of an epoch in musical history in which compositions were constructed polyphonically, emphasizing the use of several melodies simultaneously, each equally important. The age of homophony, which stressed the single melody and its accompaniment, came after Bach. Because Bach's music was essentially the product of an earlier era, many of his contemporaries regarded him as old-fashioned. However, a turning point came in the appreciation of Bach's legacy when, in 1829, a Berlin revival of the *Passion According to St. Matthew* under Felix Mendelssohn, awakened the world to this master's long-neglected music. By 1850 awareness of Bach's greatness encouraged the formation of the Bach Gesellschaft to gather and publish all of his works, a process which took fifty years to complete.

Bach's compositions display an absolute command of the technical aspects of music, an expressiveness rare among his contemporaries, and a fascination with the symbolic power of numbers, gesture, and words. Bach's music exhibits remarkable originality and resourcefulness regarding melodic, harmonic, and textural techniques. In addition, he demonstrates an awareness of the primary national styles employed at the time: French, Italian, and German. Rather than exploiting a single style at one time, Bach often combined them.

Bach's organ works came in the Weimar period of his life, his first great creative phase (1708-1717). He drew from organ forms from his predecessors, Frescobaldi and Buxtehude, which included the passacaglia and chaconne, both old dance forms characterized by a series of variations on a recurring theme in the bass; the toccata, characterized by grand passages in which the organist could exhibit virtuosity; the fantasia, an improvisational style; chorale-prelude, which combined traits of both the toccata and the fantasia; and the fugue, a network of contrapuntal voices on a single theme, one voice following another at measured intervals. Bach produced forty-six such compositions in his *Orgelbüchlein* (Little Organ Book). In whatever organ form he wrote, Bach became a channel through which he transmitted great art. Unlike his predecessors for which these forms had been mere technical exercises, he brought a blending of technique with emotion in a way no one before him had produced.

Bach's works are often encyclopedic in scope, as demonstrated by *Die Kunst der Fuge* (The Art of the Fugue), begun in 1745, in which he took a single melodic idea in D minor and subjected it to virtually every technical device used in fugal writing. The result was a monumental work comprising sixteen fugues, two canons, two fugues for two claviers, and a final fugue which his death kept him from completing. With the exception of the two fugues for two claviers, Bach did not specify the instrument for which he wrote this fugal exercise. However, it has been performed most often on piano or harpsichord.

Bach was one of the first composers to demonstrate a historical awareness with respect to musical style and creativity. He consciously composed portions of compositions, specifically sacred vocal works in a style resembling that of Giovanni Pierluigi da Palestrina and his contemporaries. In addition, the fact that he assembled the *Mass in B Minor* late in his life is likely an acknowledgement of the importance of the Mass in the history of music.

Several of Bach's appointments were important ones, especially those at Weimar, Cöthen, and Leipzig. The directorship of music at St. Thomas's in Leipzig was the leading position for a Lutheran composer in northern Germany. An element of his compositional style that is often overlooked is the practical nature of his output. The bulk of his organ works, for example, were written during the Weimar period when he was employed as an organist, while most of his orchestral and chamber works stem from the Cöthen years, when he served as director of music to Prince Leopold and had an orchestra at his disposal. During the Leipzig period his large scale works for soloists, chorus, and orchestra were written.

In addition to contributing an enormous body of music himself, four of Bach's sons, who trained with their father, became established in their time, as well. The oldest son of Bach and Maria Barbara was a distinguished composer of chamber and piano music, Wilhelm Friedemann (1710-1784), whose style led to the development of expressiveness, which led music away from Baroque objectivity and began endowing it with dramatic and emotional interest. Karl Philipp Emanual (1714-1788), the second surviving son of Bach and Maria Barbara, developed the sonata form, still in its infancy when he began composing. He became a significant transitionary figure between the age of counterpoint, which his father had brought to a magnificent culmination and the age of homophony and the sonata. Both Haydn and Mozart knew the piano sonatas of Karl Philipp Emanuel and expressed their indebtedness to him. John Christian (1735-1782), youngest son of Bach and Anna Magdalena, also wrote symphonies, concertos, and sonatas, as well as operas. Because of his long residence in England, where for many years he served as music master to Queen Charlotte, he is known as the "English Bach." Johann Christoph Friedrich (1732-1795), longest surviving son of Bach and Anna Magdalena, had a steady career and composed motets, oratorios, piano sonatas, chamber cantatas, and symphonies.

Overview of Biographical Sources

Any biographical study of Bach should begin with the invaluable collection of English translations of all extant documents concerning Bach's life, *The Bach Reader* (1966), edited by Hans T. David and Arthur Mendel.

The most reliable biography of Bach appears in the standard English-language reference work on music: *The New Grove Dictionary of Music and Musicians* (1980). The article has been revised and published as *The New Grove Bach Family* (1983).

Nineteenth-century biographies resulted from the growing German discipline of musicology, and Philipp Spitta's two-volume *Johann Sebastian Bach* (1889) is quite remarkable for its time, although now of limited use due to later discoveries.

Twentieth-century biographies written before the mid-1950s need to be used with care, due to research conducted by two German scholars, Alfred Dürr in "Zur Chronologie der Leipziger Vokalwerke J. S. Bachs," in *Bach Jahrbuch* 44 (1957): 5-162, and Georg von Dadelson's *Bemerkungen zur Handschrift J. S. Bachs, seiner Familie und seines Kreises* (Trossingen, 1957); *Beitrage zur Chronologie der Werke J. S. Bachs* (Habilitationsschrift, University of Tubingen, 1958, Trossingen, 1958).

A study of the handwriting of Bach and his copyists as well as watermark analyses led to a radically different chronology of Bach's cantatas, and this in turn resulted in a different interpretation of some biographical data. According to the earlier biographies of Bach, he wrote his choral cantatas throughout much of the Leipzig period (1723-1750), along with his compositions written for the *Collegium*

Musicum. Instead, watermark and handwriting analysis showed that the vast majority of the cantatas were composed for church services at St. Thomas's in the first three years of his employment in Leipzig, and that he used the same works and those of other composers throughout his career. This corresponds to the disillusionment with his position that is apparent from many letters of the Leipzig period. It also suggests that, apart from an occasional cantata, his later career was to a great extent taken up with the composition of instrumental works for the Collegium and the challenge of technical mastery of musical techniques such as the fugue that were explored in works like *Die Kunst der Fuge* late in life.

Curiously, there is currently no definitive biography that does justice to Bach's life and works that incorporates the most recent research. Part of the reason for this is the massive output of the composer. Spitta's monograph from the latter part of the nineteenth century, for example, is over 1,800 pages in length and could not begin to deal with the wealth of information that has come to light in the century since the work first appeared. Much of the recent research is summarized in *The New Grove Dictionary of Music and Musicians* (see Emery, Wolff, and Temperly, below). In addition, the bibliography supplied is the most complete in any English language source. In general, the best single-volume discussion of Bach's life and works remains Karl Geiringer's *Johann Sebastian Bach: The Culmination of an Era* (1966).

Evaluation of Principal Biographical Sources

Boughton, Rutland. *Bach, the Master.* New York: Harper and Brothers, 1930. **(G)** This popular biography of the composer is an unreliable approach to Bach's life and should be avoided by anyone pursuing a serious study.

Boyd, Malcolm. *Bach.* London: J. M. Dent, 1983. **(A, G)** This third volume on Bach in Dent's Master Musician Series is readable and generally reliable. In addition to biographical materials, it includes a stylistic discussion of Bach's music.

David, Hans T., and Arthur Mendel, eds. *The Bach Reader.* Rev. ed. New York: W. W. Norton, 1966. **(A, G)** In addition to translations of all existing documents regarding Bach, this work includes references to Bach by his contemporaries, an obituary begun in March 1751 (but not published until 1754) by Bach's son Karl Philipp Emanuel Bach and pupil J. F. Agricola, and a translation of the 1802 biography of Bach by Johann Nikolaus Forkel.

Emery, Walter, Christoph Wolff, and Nicholas Temperley. "Johann Sebastian Bach." In *The New Grove Bach Family*. New York: W. W. Norton, 1983. (**A, G**) This revision from an article from *The New Grove Dictionary of Music and Musicians* provides an excellent concise study of the life and works of Bach, with a valuable bibliography and works list.

Felix, Werner. *Johann Sebastian Bach*. New York: W. W. Norton, 1985. (**A, G**) A useful popular study of the life and music of Bach. This volume is replete with photographs, accessible to a general reader, up-to-date in terms of factual information, and it contains a lucid discussion of Bach's music.

Field, Laurence N. *Johann Sebastian Bach*. Minneapolis, MN: Augsburg, 1943. (**G**) This popular biography is factually unreliable, and it paints an overly romanticized picture of the composer.

Geiringer, Karl. *The Bach Family: Seven Generations of Creative Genius*. New York: Oxford University Press, 1954. (**A**) Contains chapters on Bach and other family members. Written by an important musicologist, this work is valuable, but superseded by Geiringer's later monograph.

―――. *Johann Sebastian Bach: The Culmination of an Era*. New York: Oxford University Press, 1966. (**A**) A more thorough treatment of Bach's life and music than *The Bach Family*, this well-written and readable volume incorporates recent findings of Dürr and von Dadelsen.

Grew, Eva Mary, and Sydney Grew. *Bach*. London: J. M. Dent, 1947. (**A, G**) The second of three studies of Bach's life and works to be issued in the popular Master Musician Series. Although once helpful, it has been superseded by the third version by Boyd.

Herz, Gerhard. *Essays on J. S. Bach.* Ann Arbor: University of Michigan Research Press, 1985. (**A**) Many of the articles in this volume. by a major Bach scholar deal with musical style and technique, and some articles handle his biography. In particular, "Johann Sebastian Bach in the Age of Rationalism and Early Romanticism," a translation of Herz's 1935 dissertation, traces the Bach revival of the nineteenth century. "Toward a New Image of Bach" is an important essay interpreting the implications of the research of Dürr and von Dadelsen.

Hindemith, Paul. *Johann Sebastian Bach: Heritage and Obligation.* New Haven, CT: Yale University Press, 1952. (**A**) This brief work is the transcript of an address given in Hamburg to commemorate the two-hundredth anniversary of Bach's death in 1950. Although somewhat interesting in terms of the opinions of Hindemith, an important composer, this work is not particularly helpful.

Loon, Hendrick Willem van. *The Life and Times of Johann Sebastian Bach.* New York: Simon and Schuster, 1940. (**G**) This is the worst of the popular biographies. Full of errors, it was apparently written by a person unfamiliar with music.

Meynell, Esther. *Bach.* New York: A. A. Wyn, 1949. (**G**) Like so many other popular biographies, this one presents a romanticized and misleading picture of the composer. It should be avoided for any serious biographical study.

Neuman, Werner. *Bach: A Pictorial Biography.* Translated by Stephan de Hann. London: Thames and Hudson, 1961. (**A, G**) Pleasant and accessible, this book is full of photographs of the places where Bach lived and worked. Recommended for the general reader not particularly interested in technical aspects of Bach's music.

Parry, C. Hubert H. *Johann Sebastian Bach.* New York: G. P. Putnam's Sons, 1909. (**A**) This work, once a standard, is now quite outdated.

Pirro, André. *J. S. Bach.* Translated by Marvyn Savill. 1911. Reprint. New York: Bonanza Books, 1957. (**A**) Like Parry's book, this former standard biography has been superseded by later works.

Schweitzer, Albert. *J. S. Bach.* 2 vols. Translated by Ernest Newman. 1911.

Reprint. New York: Dover, 1966. (**A, G**) One of the classic English-language biographies of Bach. Originally published in French in 1905, it was translated into German and expanded in 1908, and Newman's translation is of this later edition. Schweitzer, the noted humanitarian and organist, intimately knew the works of Bach. Because Schweitzer was a performer, he argues a somewhat biased view that Bach's organ music served as the core of his total repertory, a view not shared by most later scholars. Nevertheless, this is a remarkable work, encyclopedic in nature. Since it is dated, it should be used with caution, and factual material, especially dates, should be checked against more recent works. One of the most interesting aspects of Schweitzer's work is his attempt to relate musical ideas to poetic ones. Although his discussion is often highly subjective and disputable, the relation of music and rhetoric has become an important area of study in recent years.

Schwendowius, Barbara, and Wolfgang Domling, eds. *Johann Sebastian Bach: Life, Times and Influence*. New Haven, CT: Yale University Press, 1984. (**A, G**) Contains articles originally written in 1974 and 1975 to accompany recordings made for Archiv Productions. Although not originally intended to be published together, these articles were written by important Bach scholars from the German musicological community: Georg von Dadelsen, Alfred Dürr, Ludwig Finscher, Christoph Wolff, Walter Blankenburg, and others. It is eminently readable, and yet contains an immense amount of important material. Highly recommended for any research work and also for general readers who may want to increase their knowledge of the composer and his music.

Smend, Friedrich. *Bach in Köthen*. Translated by John Page and edited by Stephen Daw. St. Louis: Concordia, 1985. (**A**) This work by a major Bach scholar originally appeared in German in 1951. The subsequent translated edition contains editorial revisions and a chapter by Daw that discusses the court at Cöthen.

Spitta, Philipp. *Johann Sebastian Bach*. 2 vols. Translated by Clara Bell and J. A. Fuller Maitland. London: Novello, 1889. Reprint. New York: Dover, 1951. (**A, G**) Spitta's monumental and encyclopedic study of the life and music of Bach remains in some ways unsurpassed to this day. Includes several chapters that provide a historical background about Bach's ancestors, predecessors, and contemporaries to show how his life and musical style were affected by them. The exhaustive biographical portions of the book contain all information known to the date of publication. Only a relatively small portion of compositions had appeared in print, and in numerous cases Spitta dealt with primary sources. Although this is one of the most remarkable monographs in musicological history, much factual material, as was the case in Schweitzer's book, has been proven incorrect. Several cantatas attributed to Bach, for example, have subsequently been shown to belong to other composers.

Taylor, Sedley. *The Life of Johann Sebastian Bach in Relation to His Work as a Church Musician and Composer.* Cambridge: Macmillan and Bowes, 1897. (**A, G**) A poorly written and unreliable biography, this book presents a highly romanticized picture of the composer and should be avoided.

Terry, Charles Stanford. *Bach: A Biography.* 2d ed., rev. New York: Oxford University Press, 1933. (**A**) Well written and factually reliable for the most part. However, despite the fact that it is a classic in the Bach biographical literature, it suffers from being dated.

The Universal Bach. Philadelphia, PA: American Philosophical Society, 1986. (**A**) The result of a series of lectures by important scholars Christoph Wolff, Robert Marshall, Laurence Dreyfuss, and others on various aspects of Bach's life, works, and biblical interpretation. A valuable book, although more specialized in approach than some of the standard biographical works.

Williams, C. F. Abdy. *Bach.* Rev. ed. New York: E. P. Dutton, 1934. (**A, G**) The first of three biographies of Bach in the Master Musicians Series. The fact that the publisher felt it necessary to have entirely new volumes written about Bach (see Boyd and Grew, above) suggests that they realized the outdated quality of the book.

Overview and Evaluation of Primary Sources

After Bach's death in 1750, his manuscripts were divided among his widow,

Anna Magdelena, and his eldest sons, Wilhelm Friedemann, Johann Christian, and Karl Phillip Emanuel. Unfortunately, few of the manuscripts distributed to Wilhelm Friedemann and Johann Christian can now be traced. However, Anna Magdelena and Karl Philipp Emanuel proved to be better stewards of the music. K. P. E. Bach's manuscripts are now divided between the Staatsbibliothek and the Deutsche Staatsbibliothek in Berlin. Anna Magdelena's holdings were transferred to St. Thomas's School in Leipzig.

A helpful guide to Bach manuscripts in the United States is Gerhard Herz's *Bach Sources in America* (New York: Bärenreiter, 1984; **A**). Written in German and English, the book describes every known manuscript in the U.S. In addition, photographs are included at the end of the book.

There are two collected editions of the music of Bach. The first, *Werke Johann Sebastian Bach* (1851-1899. Reprint. 1926. 46 vols. Leipzig: Bach-Gesellschaft), was reprinted unchanged in 1947. A new edition, *Neue Ausgabe samtlicher Werke* (Kassel: Barenreiter, 1954-) was begun in 1954 and remains incomplete to date. It is sponsored by the Bach Archive of Leipzig and the Johann Sebastian Bach Institute of Göttingen.

A catalogue that lists every work of Bach, along with its principal melodic themes and location of the works in both Bach editions, is Wolfgang Schmieder, *Thematisch-systematisches Verzeichnis der musikalische Werke von Johann Sebastian Bach, Bach-Werke-Verzeichnis* (7th ed. Leipzig: Breitkopf und Härtel, 1990; **A**) The end of this lengthy title, "Back-Werke-Verzeichnis" is the source of the abbreviation BMV often found before a work of Bach. For example, the Mass in B Minor, BMV 232, is the 232nd composition of Bach listed in Schmieder's catalogue. A companion is Ray Reeder, *The Bach English-Title Index* (Berkeley, CA: Fallen Leaf Press, 1993; **A, G**) that provides an English index for the BMV.

Principal Works

Organ works: fantasias, fugues, preludes, toccatas, chorale preludes, and passacaglias; *Little Organ Book*; *Passacaglia and Fugue in C minor*.

Orchestral works: six Brandenburg Concertos, four orchestral suites, concertos for one and two violins; and concertos for one through four harpsichords.

Chamber works: six sonatas for flute and clavier; three sonatas for unaccompanied violin; three partitas for unaccompanied violin;, viola da gamba, six cello suites, *The Musical Offering,* six sonatas for violin and harpsichord, and six sonatas for unaccompanied violin; four trio sonatas.

Keyboard works: fifteen inventions, fifteen sinfonias, two volumes of *The Well-Tempered Clavier,* six French Suites, six English Suites, partitas, fugues, *The Italian Concerto, Chromatic Fantasy and Fugue, The Goldberg Variations,* and *The Art of the Fugue.*

Sacred vocal works: over two hundred church cantatas, *Magnificat, St. Matthew Passion, St. John Passion, Mass in B Minor, Christmas Oratoria,* and six motets.

Museums, Historical Landmarks, Societies

Historisches Museum der Stadt (Leipzig, Germany). Houses one of two versions of the only authentic portrait of Bach. Painted by Elias Gottlob Haussman in 1746.

Library of William H. Scheide (Princeton, NJ). Contains the second version of Haussman's official portrait of Bach. Painted in 1748, and originally obtained from the estate of Bach's son Karl Philip Emanuel Bach, the portrait was originally painted as a condition for admission into Mizler's musical society, although it is unlikely that it ever made its way there.

Other Sources

Bukofzer, Manfred. *Music in the Baroque Era.* New York: W. W. Norton, 1947. A classic, though dated, work on seventeenth- and early eighteenth-century music.

Chiapusso, Jan. *Bach's World.* Bloomington: Indiana University Press, 1968. Examines the ideological, theological, and philosophical aspects of Bach's music.

Cox, Howard H., ed. *The Calov Bible of J. S. Bach.* Ann Arbor: University of Michigan Research Press, 1985. This volume of Bach's Bible is particularly interesting and well presented. Of particular value are the passages Bach underlined and some of the marginalia.

Grout, Donald Jay, and Claude Palisca. *A History of Western Music.* 4th ed. New York: W. W. Norton, 1988. The best one-volume music history text.

Leaver, Robin, ed. *J. S. Bach and Scripture: Glosses from the Calov Bible Commentary.* St. Louis, MO: Concordia, 1985. Attempts to provide the same service as Cox, but the quantity and quality of Leaver's material is of less value.

Mellers, Wilfrid. *Bach and the Dance of God.* London: Faber and Faber. 1980. Critically analyzes Bach's style with the aim of deriving philosophical and theological intent from his music.

Palisca, Claude. *Baroque Music.* 3d ed. Englewood Cliffs, NJ: Prentice-Hall, 1991. Contains a brief but useful discussion of Bach.

Pelikan, Jaroslav. *Bach among the Theologians.* Philadelphia, PA: Fortress, 1986. **(A)** Pelikan, a historian of the development of Christian doctrine rather than a music scholar, studies Bach's choice of texts in his Passion settings and discusses their theological implications.

Stiller, Günther. *Johann Sebastian Bach and Liturgical Life in Leipzig.* Edited by Robin Leaver. St. Louis, MO: Concordia, 1984. **(A)** Originally published in German in 1970, this work supplies readers with a wealth of information regarding liturgical practices in Leipzig in the first half of the eighteenth century and Bach's relationship to them. This book is important for anyone studying Bach's work as cantor at St. Thomas's Church, or his sacred music and organ works in general.

Timothy L. McDonald
Rockhurst College

Francis Bacon
1561-1626

Chronology

Born Francis Bacon on January 22, 1561, at York House, London, England, son
of Sir Nicholas Bacon and his second wife; grows up at York House; *1573-1575*
attends Trinity College, Cambridge; *1576* admitted as an "ancient" (senior governor) of Gray's Inn, one of the Inns of Court which serves as an institution of legal
schooling; *1576-1579* lives in France as a member of the English ambassador's
suite; *1579* takes up residence at Gray's Inn; *1582* becomes a barrister, moving
successively to the positions of reader (lecturer at the Inn), bencher (senior member), and queen's counsel extraordinary; writes "Temporis Partus Maximus" (The
Greatest Part of Time); *1584* sits as a member of Parliament; *1589* writes a
"Letter of Advice" to Queen Elizabeth I and *An Advertisement Touching the
Controversies of the Church of England*; *1593* takes a stand against the revenue
raising policies of the government during the war with Spain, which results in
Elizabeth's displeasure and his disgrace at court for several years; *1593-1600* gains
the patronage of Robert Devereux, the earl of Essex, with whom he had become
acquainted in 1591; Essex, one of the queen's favorites, repeatedly but unsuccessfully attempts to have him named to various high offices, including attorney
general; *1600* as queen's learned counsel is forced to take part in the trial of his
patron, Essex, who returns from an expedition to Ireland against orders; *1601-1603*
after an abortive attempt by Essex to force the queen to dismiss his rivals, Essex
is executed; draws up the official report of the incident, depicting Essex as a
traitor; *1603* using his ability to write, secures himself a place in the court of
James I, becoming one of the three hundred new knights dubbed in the first year
of James I's reign; *1604* confirmed as learned counsel and sits in Parliament;
during this time finishes writing *Apologie in Certaine Imputations Concerning the
Late Earle of Essex,* which defends his action in that affair; *1605* publishes *Advancement of Learning*; *1606* marries Alice Barnham, the daughter of a London
alderman; *1608* begins the first of several drafts of *Novum Organum*; *1609* publishes *De Sapientia Veterum* (The Wisdom of the Ancients), which expounds the

practicality of the hidden meanings in ancient myths; *1613* appointed attorney general; *1614* writes *The New Atlantis* (not published until 1626); *1617* appointed lord keeper of the great seal; *1618* appointed lord chancellor and Baron Verulam; makes an enemy of George Villiers when he interferes in the marriage of Villiers's younger brother and the daughter of the former chief justice, Coke; *1620-1621* publishes *Novum Organum* and created Viscount St. Albans; *1621* convicted on charges, in which Villiers plays a role, of bribery and fined forty thousand pounds, imprisoned in the Tower of London, and prohibited from holding any state, court, or parliamentary office; *1622-1625* writes his collection of *Essayes*; *1626* dies April 9 of bronchitis at the earl of Arundel's house.

Activities of Historical Significance

Although politically active most of his adult life, Francis Bacon was a relatively minor governmental figure. He had little influence until 1613 when he persuaded James I to replace Edward Coke with himself as attorney general. In subsequent years he advocated the royal prerogative in opposition to Coke's support of common law. He appears to have been aware of the constitutional problems that would ultimately lead to civil war. Unfortunately, political enemies and his carelessness in handling finances, which made him vulnerable to charges of bribery, ended his political career in 1621.

Bacon's significance lies primarily in his writings. In *The Advancement of Learning* (1605) and *De Augmentis Scientiarum* (1623), he attempted a systematic classification of all branches of knowledge, and became a model for later systematizers such as the eighteenth-century Encyclopedists and the nineteenth-century Comteans. He distinguished between divine knowledge, with which reason has no relation, and secular knowledge, which is acquired through the application of reason. He assigned history, literature, and philosophy respectively to the faculties of memory, imagination, and reason. Philosophy in turn he divided into "first philosophy," which is concerned with general principles, and "natural philosophy," which investigates the physical world. He also distinguished between science and technology. Bacon furthermore criticized scholasticism, humanism, and occultism—the prevailing methodologies of the day.

Novum Organum (1620) argues that human errors resulted from four causes, or "idols" as he called them. These included limitations common to all humans, individual idiosyncrasies, the nature of language, and erroneous systems of thought. To overcome these predilections to error, Bacon advocated the inductive method, whereby generalities would be built up by "gradual ascent" from particulars. This empirical approach particularly contrasted with the deductive method of René Descartes. In his advocacy of induction, however, Bacon gave little attention to the role of mathematics. Hence, while popularizing scientific research, Bacon did not fully appreciate the actual methodology of science that was developing in the seventeenth-century. His attention to the limitations of language, however, did influence later critical analysis, leading ultimately to logical positivism in the twentieth century.

Bacon's utopian fable, *New Atlantis* (1627), tells the story of a voyage to the imaginary Pacific island of "Bensalem," describing the government and social conditions of the people. The description of "Solomon's House," the island's institution for scientific study, helped inspire the founding of the Royal Society.

Overview of Biographical Sources

The earliest biographies of Bacon, written in the wake of political scandal, defended his reputation. Pierre Ambrose began this defense with his *Discourse on the Life of M. Francis Bacon, Chancellor of England* (1631), praising him both as a man and as a government official. Bacon's chaplain and personal secretary, William Rawley, perpetuated the defense in *Life of Bacon* (1658). A more tempered view appeared in Thomas Fuller's *The History of the Worthies of England* (1662). The first balanced biography was David Mallett's *The Life of Francis Bacon, Lord Chancellor of England* (1740), which admired Bacon as a scholar but criticized his political ambition and methods.

The nineteenth century saw the emergence of two schools of thought regarding Bacon. Thomas Macaulay helped shape a negative viewpoint with his essay "Lord Bacon," published in the *Edinburgh Review* in 1837. He described Bacon as cold of heart and mean of spirit. John Lord Campbell, *The Lives of the Lord Chancellors and Keepers of the Great Seal of England* (1851), attacked Bacon's handling of chancery. Influenced by Macaulay, Edwin Abbott's *Francis Bacon: An Account of His Life and Works* (1885) argued that Bacon's scientific interests made him too rational and that he had no moral sense. R. W. Church, *Bacon* (1901), saw him as a lackey of James I. Such criticism provoked defenses of Bacon. The most significant effort was James Spedding's edition of *The Works of Francis Bacon (1861-1864)* which, in addition to collecting the primary sources, defended Bacon's character, seeing him as victimized by Parliament. Other favorable accounts of Bacon included Thomas Martin's *The Character of Lord Bacon* (1835), which examined Bacon's legal ideas; Basil Montagu's *Life of Bacon*, included in *The Works of Francis Bacon, Lord Chancellor of England* (1842); William Hepworth Dixon's *Personal History of Lord Bacon* (1861), which presents a rhetorical defense; and Thomas Fowler, *Bacon* (1881), which attack on Macaulay's characterization. John Nichol's *Francis Bacon: His Life and Philosophy* (1907) admired Bacon's political ideas while suggesting that his defects arose from a lack of passions.

A curious sideline of scholarship that emerged in the nineteenth century was the argument that Bacon was actually the author of Shakespeare's plays. This allegation seems to have begun with an unsigned article, written by Adelia Bacon, which appeared in *Putnam's Magazine* in 1856, and mushroomed into popularity.

The twentieth century has seen several superficial biographies, including Mary Sturt's *Francis Bacon* (1932), Charles Williams's *Bacon* (1933. Reprint. Norwood, PA: Norwood, 1978), and Bryan Bevan's *The Real Francis Bacon* (London: Centaur, 1960). But more scholarly and analytical books have also appeared, revealing Bacon to be more complex than previously described and attempting to understand the relationship between his political and philosophical careers.

Evaluation of Principal Biographical Sources

Anderson, Fulton H. *Francis Bacon: His Career and Thought.* 1962. Reprint. Westport, CT: Greenwood Press, 1978. (**A**) Anderson argues that previous biographers and historians have been philosophically naive and therefore have not recognized Bacon's originality. The author states that Bacon was a distinctive and original thinker who divided knowledge into three areas—theological, political, and natural. The latter was to be explored through the inductive method. Although primarily interested in Bacon's philosophy, Anderson also examines his political activities. This work is the most scholarly recent study of Bacon's life and thought.

Bowen, Catherine Drinker. *Francis Bacon: The Temper of a Man*. Boston, MA: Little, Brown, 1963. (**G**) The author organizes Bacon's life into five parts: childhood and youth, the effort to win Queen Elizabeth's favor, work as attorney general and lord chancellor, impeachment and conviction, and banishment from London. She sees Bacon as a sensitive personality who held conflicting ambitions: the desire for power and wealth and the wish to pursue a life of study. Bowen appears to believe that Bacon's embezzlement arose out of his naivite. This work is the most readable and balanced recent biography, but gives little attention to Bacon's ideas.

Crowther, J. G. *Francis Bacon: The First Statesman of Science*. London: Cresset Press, 1960. (**A, G**) This volume is divided into two parts: part one examines Bacon's understanding of scientific activity, which he regarded as essential for the advancement of humanity; part two presents a more conventional biography. This organization reflects the author's belief that Bacon entered politics for scientific purposes but that his personal ambition sometimes conflicted with his desire to serve mankind. Does not fully develop the political side of Bacon's personality.

Dodd, Alfred. *Francis Bacon's Personal Life-Story*. 2 vols. Vol. 1, 1910. Reprint. London: Rider, 1986. (**A, G**) The author writes a spirited defense of Bacon, stating that he was "the greatest man in the world." He argues that Bacon laid the basis for modern science, ethics, literature, and philosophy and that he led in the creation of the English Renaissance. Dodd further asserts that Bacon wrote Shakespeare's plays as well as plays ascribed to other writers. The biography is useful primarily when seen as part of a long-standing debate over Bacon's character. The second volume apparently was not published until the appearance of this edition.

Epstein, Joel J. *Francis Bacon: A Political Biography*. Athens: Ohio University Press, 1977. (**A**) Believing that Bacon's political career must be examined separately from his thought, Epstein presents a chronologically organized account. He emphasizes Bacon's role in attempting to reconcile the king and Parliament and argues that Bacon's impeachment came about because Parliament saw him as a symbol of royal power. Although the volume does not contain much new information of Bacon as a politician, it has an excellent bibliographical essay.

Farrington, Benjamin. *Francis Bacon: Philosopher of Industrial Science*. New York: Schuman, 1949. (**A**) Although presenting some biographical information, Farrington primarily studies Bacon's understanding of technology. He argues that Bacon devoted his life to the idea that scientific knowledge should have practical application. Therefore, Bacon believed, men must organize themselves for human improvement. Places Bacon's views within the context of the history of science. The appendix reprints the description of "Solomon's House" from *New Atlantis*.

—————. *Francis Bacon: Pioneer of Planned Science*. New York: Praeger, 1969. (**Y**) Concentrating on the relationship of his thought and political activity, this volume is illustrated with photographs.

Green, A. Wigfall. *Sir Francis Bacon: His Life and Works*. Denver, CO: Alan Swallow, 1952. (**A, G**) Green regards Bacon as a leading figure of the Renaissance who nonetheless was closely connected with medieval thought. In addition to having wide intellectual interests, Bacon also became an effective government official who kept the state financially solvent and promoted religious toleration. This readable biography emphasizes Bacon's education and preparation for government service, and his attraction to both science and justice.

—————. *Sir Francis Bacon*. New York: Twayne, 1966. (**G**) This is a commonly available introduction and is useful for students despite its superficiality. It contains a chronology of major events in Bacon's life and, in Part One, a five-chapter biographical sketch. Part Two, titled "The Mind," summarizes Bacon's intellectual activity by category, such as essayist or biographer, or provides brief analyses of individual works. The bibliography annotates manuscript collections and secondary works.

Luxembourg, Lilo K. *Francis Bacon and Denis Diderot: Philosophers of Science*. New York: Humanities Press, 1967. (**A**) Luxembourg attempts to determine Diderot's response to Bacon's ideas. He argues that despite a number of differences, the two men held similar purposes, particularly in their effort to classify all the scientific knowledge of their day and to improve human welfare. This work is useful for placing Bacon in historical perspective. It contains an extensive bibliography, including French sources on Bacon.

Rossi, Paolo. *Francis Bacon: From Magic to Science.* Translated by Sacha Rabinovitch. Chicago: University of Chicago Press, 1968. (**A**) The author examines Bacon's relationship to his time. After discussing elements of Bacon's intellectual heritage, including the occult and classical traditions, Rossi then analyzes Bacon's own thought, method, and language. He argues that Bacon sought to change the nature of philosophy because, in Bacon's view, it had failed. His advocacy of induction sought to provide a basis for the domination of nature. Rossi states that Bacon was most surely modern in his rejection of preestablished limits to scientific investigation. This work is an excellent study of Bacon's role in the development of modern science.

Steel, Byron. *Sir Francis Bacon: The First Modern Mind.* Garden City, NY: Doubleday, Doran, 1930. (**G**) This is a readable but superficial biography which, despite its title, gives little attention to Bacon's thought. The text reproduces a number of Bacon's letters. The appendix contains an extensive bibliography through 1930 of "Baconia," the literature arguing that Bacon wrote Shakespeare's plays.

Stephens, James. *Francis Bacon and the Style of Science.* Chicago: University of Chicago Press, 1975. (**A**) Stephens has written a fine literary study that shows the relationship between Bacon's "plan" for science and his stylistic accomplishment as a writer. He argues that Aristotle significantly influenced Bacon's break with rhetorical tradition. Bacon developed literary principles that led him to the use of aphorism and acroamatic, the latter referring to such intellectual games as secret alphabets and hieroglyphs. Stephens concludes that Bacon combined both the rational and the imaginative.

Sturt, Mary. *Francis Bacon.* London: Kegan Paul, Trench, Truber, 1932. (**G**) In this popularly written biography, Sturt emphasizes Bacon's role as a civil servant. She regards Bacon as one who was born out of his time, one whose vision moved too far ahead of his fellows. The author argues that Bacon's ambition lay behind his flaws but that his intellectual judgment was usually correct. She also notes that Bacon's political fall was typical of what happened to many government officials of his time. Recent scholarship disagrees about the value of this biography; Rossi calls it the best available while Epstein refers to it as superficial.

Whitney, Charles. *Francis Bacon and Modernity*. New Haven, CT: Yale University Press, 1986. (**A**) In contrast to Anderson's view that Bacon was a systematic thinker, Whitney argues that his writings reveal an "unresolved modernity," a conflict between tradition and innovation. The author also maintains that Bacon was prophetic in that he regarded humanity as both producing and controlling change. The book concludes that Bacon's modernity lies in the very discontinuity between old and new that characterizes his writings. Whitney's study is considerably influenced by Paul de Man's deconstructionist theory.

Overview and Evaluation of Primary Sources

Manuscript collections relating to Bacon may be found in the Bodleian Library of Oxford University and the British Museum. An exhaustive listing of Bacon's works can be found in R. W. Gibson, *Francis Bacon: A Bibliography of His Works and of Baconia to the Year 1750* (Oxford: Scrivener Press, 1950; **A**). There are many published editions of Bacon's works; the standard collections are: James Spedding, ed., *The Letters and the Life of Francis Bacon Including all His Occasional Works* (7 vols. London: Longmans, Green, 1861-1864; **A, G**), and James Spedding, Robert Leslie Ellis, and Douglas Denon Heath, eds., *The Works of Francis Bacon* (7 vols. London: Longmans, 1879-1890; **A, G**). David W. Davies and Elizabeth S. Wrigley have prepared *A Concordance to the Essays of Francis Bacon* (Detroit: Gale, 1973; **A**), which uses the Spedding edition. Although several editions of Bacon's essays have appeared, the first critical edition since the nineteenth century is Michael Kiernan, ed., *The Essayes or Counsels, Civill and Morall* (Cambridge, MA: Harvard University Press, 1985; **A**). Kiernan regards Bacon as one of the chief exponents of the seventeenth-century essay and in his introduction carefully analyzes the evolution of these writings. Benjamin Farrington presents some essential philosophical works in *The Philosophy of Francis Bacon: An Essay of Its Development from 1603 to 1609 with New Translations of Fundamental Texts* (Liverpool, England: Liverpool University Press, 1964; **A**). James Edward Creighton's introduction to *Advancement of Learning and Novum Organum* (1890. Reprint. New York: Willey Book Co., 1944; **A, G**) argues that Bacon is important because he aroused mankind to the practical significance of extending the knowledge of nature. Similarly, Thomas Fowler's *Bacon's Novum Organum* (Oxford:

Clarendon, 1899; **A, G**) comments that Bacon's contribution lies in showing what might be achieved through scientific inquiry. Alfred B. Gough's edition of *New Atlantis* (Oxford: Clarendon, 1924; **A, G**) anticipates more recent interpretations of Bacon in stating that this utopian work showed the unity of his political and scientific thought. The themes of these editors have persevered in more recent editions of Bacon's works, including Sidney Warhaft, ed., *Francis Bacon: A Selection of His Works* (New York: St. Martin's, 1965; **G**); Fulton Anderson, ed., *The New Organon and Related Writings* (Indianapolis: Bobbs-Merrill, 1960; **G**); and Arthur Johnston, ed., *The Advancement of Learning and New Atlantis* (Oxford: Clarendon, 1974; **A, G**). These editions have useful introductions and critical notes. *Essays, Civil and Moral* and *New Atlantis* appear in Charles W. Eliot, ed., *The Harvard Classics*, vol. 3 (New York: P. F. Collier and Son, 1909; **G**) and *The Advancement of Learning, Novum Organum*, and *New Atlantis* may be found in Robert Maynard Hutchins, ed., *Great Books of the Western World*, vol. 30 (Chicago: Encyclopedia Brittanica, 1952; **G**). These two collections have the advantage of being widely available in libraries but they carry no critical apparatus apart from brief biographical sketches.

Museums, Historical Landmarks, Societies

Francis Bacon Foundation (Claremont, CA). Organized in 1938. Promotes the study of science, literature, history and philosophy with special reference to the works of Bacon. Maintains a rare book library on the campus of the Claremont Colleges.

Francis Bacon Research Trust (Northampton, England). Organized in 1980. Promotes public education in the works of Bacon and provides funding for centers of research.

Francis Bacon Society (London). Organized in 1886. Promotes the study of the works of Bacon and examines evidence that Bacon may have written Shakespeare's plays and other Elizabethan works.

Gorhambury House (Hertrfordshire, England). Residence of Bacon. Houses busts of Bacon as a child and adult.

National Portrait Gallery (London). Contains Paul von Sumer's portrait, "Francis Bacon, Lord Chancellor."

Other Sources

Kocher, P. H. "Bacon on the Science of Jurisprudence." *Journal of the History of Ideas* 18 (January 1957): 3-26. Argues that Bacon applied the inductive method to law as well as science. Concludes that he was a great jurist as well as a great philosopher of science.

Prior, E. Moody. "Bacon's Man of Science." *Journal of the History of Ideas* 15 (July 1954): 348-370. Suggests that Bacon created the first clearly realized image of the scientist which in turn put forward a new ideal of man.

Rossi, Paolo. "Baconianism." *Dictionary of the History of Ideas: Studies of Selected Pivotal Ideas*, edited by Philip P. Wiener, vol. 1. New York: Scribner's, 1973. A succinct summary of Bacon's ideas and their impact on subsequent thought. Contains a brief but useful bibliographical essay.

Stephen, Leslie, and Sidney Lee, eds. "Bacon, Francis." In *The Dictionary of National Biography*. Vol. 1. London: Oxford University Press, 1917. This dated but useful entry sees Bacon as a man greater than his age.

Vickers, Brian, ed. *Essential Articles for the Study of Francis Bacon*. Hamden, CT: Archon Books, 1968. Includes articles from scholarly journals dealing with Bacon as a scientist, writer, historian, and political and legal thinker.

Gary Land
Andrews University

Honoré de Balzac
1799-1850

Chronology

Born Honoré Balzac in Tours, France, on May 20, 1799, oldest of four children of Bernard-François Balzac, the deputy mayor and a descendent from Gascon peasants, and Anne-Laure Sallambier, of the Parisian bourgeoisie; *1799-1807* grows up in Tours, but spends little time with his parents; *1807-1813* attends the Collège de Vendôme, in Vendôme; his family visits him only once or twice; *1814-1816* attends the lyceé in Tours for one year; moves with his family to the Marais district of Paris and attends two schools; receives degree; *1816-1819* studies law at the University of Paris while clerking for Guyonnet-Merville; *1819-1821* spends two years in a garret in Paris, trying to write, while being supported by his family; *1821* meets Laure de Berny, a woman twenty-two years his senior, with whom he has a liaison until 1830, and who remains his friend and supporter until her death in 1836; *1821-1829* publishes gothic novels under several pseudonyms, including Lord R'hoone and Horace de Saint Aubin; works as a printer and publisher, incurring heavy debts; meets Zulma Carraud, who becomes his life-long friend; becomes involved with the Duchess of Abrantès; *1829* father dies; publishes *Les Chouans*, his first important novel, under the name Balzac; *1830-1831* publishes dozens of short stories and articles; begins using the name "de Balzac," with the publication of *La Peau de Chagrin*; *1833* publishes *Eugénie Grandet,* a huge success; meets Countess Eveline Hanska, whom he will marry months before his death; *1834* publishes *La Recherche de l'Absolu* and *Père Goriot*; outlines to Mme. Hanska his plans for *La Comédie Humaine*: a three-part organization, including "Studies of Manners," "Philosophical Studies," and "Analytical Studies"; *1836-1838* starts a legitimist magazine, *Chronique de Paris*, which soon goes bankrupt; continues to struggle with personal and family debts; starts a silver mining operation in Sardinia which fails; *1840* writes several plays, including *Vautrin*, which is a failure on stage; founds the *Revue Parisienne; 1841* falls seriously ill but organizes the publication of his novels as *La Comédie Humaine* (to contrast with Dante's *Divine Comedy*); *1842-1848* continues to write voluminously, even as his health deteriorates; visits Mme. Hanska in Dresden and travels with her throughout Europe and in Russia; *1848* publishes *La Cousine Bette* and *Le Cousin Pons*, his last two masterpieces; *1849* travels to the Ukraine; *1850* returns to Paris; becomes very ill in the summer and dies late in the evening of August 18, with his mother at his bedside; buried in Père-Lachaise cemetery, as Victor Hugo delivers the eulogy.

Activities of Historical Significance

Honoré de Balzac, along with Gustave Flaubert and Emile Zola, was one of the most productive and influential nineteenth-century French novelists. Along with Victor Hugo, Balzac dominated the literary scene of the first half of the century. A prolific and successful writer, he lived extravagantly and passionately, and worked tirelessly, completing, for instance, the first section of *Les Illusions Perdues* in a mere eight days. It was in part the exhausting pace of literary production that he set for himself which led to his death at the relatively young age of 50. Yet in that time he wrote over one hundred novels.

Balzac's major achievement was the creation of *La Comédie Humaine*, a group of ninety-five novels (he at one time had envisaged 144 titles) depicting the rich variety of life in France between 1789 and the 1840s. Whether describing life in the French countryside and towns, as in *Les Illusions Perdues* (1837-1843), or portraying the crowded urban scenes of Paris, as in *Père Goriot* (1834), Balzac captured not only the motivations, desires, fears, and ambitions of his individual characters, but also painted in often devastating detail the social contexts in which his figures moved and acted.

Balzac began his writing at a time when the Romantic movement was in full flower in France. Poets, such as Lamartine and Vigny, and novelists, such as Hugo and Chateaubriand, were the major figures of the literary world of the 1820s. Sir Walter Scott's historical novels served as early models for the young novelist; Anne Radcliffe, Rabelais, Rousseau, Goethe, and Byron were also influences on Balzac in the late 1820s. Furthermore, in his personal life and in his passion and energy for writing, Balzac embodied much of the romantic personality. His flamboyant dress and his turquoise-encrusted walking stick were fabled Parisian sights. (He would normally write from midnight to eight, drinking endless cups of coffee, and sending off his night's work to the printer before breakfast.) The poet Charles Baudelaire called him a passionate visionary. Yet his novels contain the seeds of the realism which dominated French fiction well into the twentieth century. Writers such as Flaubert and the Goncourts, and later Zola and the Naturalists would extend the principles and techniques of observation and documentation which give Balzac's opus its depth and breadth. In fact his depictions of French society have been considered more revealing and insightful than those of the social scientists of the time. Sainte-Beuve, a leading critic, and a frequent adversary of Balzac, wrote, shortly after his death, "Who has painted better than he the old men and the beautiful women of the Empire? . . . Who has better grasped and depicted in all its amplitude the bourgeois society triumphant under the dynasty of the weak?''

Overview of Biographical Sources

As befits an author of his importance, who was also extremely popular during his lifetime, the biographical and critical literature on Balzac is enormous. William Royce's comprehensive 1929 bibliography lists over four thousand items, and this before the great increase in academic scholarship on nineteenth-century French literature. The MLA bibliography details another 1,787 books and articles on Balzac published between 1965 and 1989.

One of the earliest biographies of Balzac was written by his friend and fellow writer Théophile Gautier and was published in 1858 in a single volume with a brief critical analysis of *La Comédie Humaine* by Hippolyte Taine, one of the most important nineteenth-century literary critics in France. (Taine's essay was finally translated into English in 1973.) In the same year, Balzac's sister, Laure Surville, published a memoir entitled *Balzac, sa vie et ses oeuvres*. In 1875 Spoelberch de Lovenjoul published the first major critical study of Balzac's work, *Histoire des Oeuvres d'Honoré de Balzac*, which was revised twice in the 1880s but never translated into English. In 1976 David Bellos published a study on French Balzac criticism which outlines the growth of his reputation in the nineteenth century.

Early discussions of his literary achievement, including comments by Flaubert and Guy de Maupassant, derided his rough and sloppy style. Academic critics of the early twentieth century such as Brunetière and Lanson, who preferred the classical literature of the sixteenth century, held similar views and influenced much of the study of Balzac's life and work into the 1930s.

Because of the nature of Balzac's lifestyle, his life has not been one that is easily chronicled. Many of the French biographies and some of the English ones, such as those by Frederick Lawton, *Balzac* (New York: Wessels, 1910) and Francis Gribble, *Balzac, the Man and the Lover* (New York: E. P. Dutton, 1930), tend to stress "the sentimental, the sensational and the anecdotal."

With the centennial of Balzac's death in 1950, and in the years following, scores of books, both biographical and critical, have appeared in English, including Herbert W. Hunt's *Honoré de Balzac: A Biography* (1957), V. S. Pritchett's *Balzac* (1973), and the translation of André Maurois's standard work, *Prometheus: The Life of Balzac* (1965). Literary studies by Leo Bersani, *From Balzac to Beckett* (1970); Anthony Pugh, *Balzac's Recurring Characters* (Toronto: University of Toronto Press, 1974); William Stowe, *Balzac, James, and the Realistic Novel* (1983. Reprint. Princeton, NJ: Princeton University Press, 1986), and many others have explored the many facets of the powerful novelistic achievement represented by *La Comédie Humaine*. The ongoing interest in Balzac's work assures him an everlasting place in the pantheon of French fiction.

Evaluation of Principal Biographical Sources

Bardèche, Maurice. *Balzac*. Paris: Julliard, 1980. (**A**) As yet untranslated, this 700-page volume is a highly detailed life. Full of wit, this entertaining intellectual biography examines Balzac the philosopher as well as Balzac the writer. Bardèche argues that Balzac built the entire system of the *Comédie Humaine* around several basic ideas about the relationship of the individual to the society in which he lives. The forces of tradition (society) and innovation (individual) may collide, deforming and often destroying the individual.

Gerson, Noel. *The Prodigal Genius: The Life and Times of Honoré de Balzac*. New York: Doubleday, 1972. (**G, Y**) A lively life by a prolific popular biographer, but it generally lacks depth. More anecdotal than analytical, it only sketches the social context of Balzac's world. Gerson captures well Balzac's flamboyant energy, his womanizing and his amazing work schedule, but does not help us fully grasp his creative literary genius.

Hunt, Herbert J. *Honoré de Balzac: a Biography*. London: Athlone, 1957. (**A**) A concise distillation of the vast information on Balzac, clear and straightforward. Hunt captures the flavor of the period, and concludes with an excellent chapter summarizing the preceding material. Hunt does not claim to bring "new facts or new documents to light," but rather recapitulate what was known at the time. This work, which focuses on Balzac's life, including his passionate eccentricities, may be read in conjunction with Hunt's detailed study of the novelist's work, Balzac's *Comédie Humaine* (London: Athlone Press, 1959).

Maurois, André. *Prometheus: The Life of Balzac*. New York: Harper and Row, 1965. (**A**) A vast and rich biography, extensively documented. Maurois states in the forward that his work is not a critical study, and lists many other critics and literary historians who have analyzed diverse aspects of Balzac's work. He nevertheless offers numerous judgments on the qualities of Balzac's writing. He argues that although Balzac's works cannot be accounted for by his life, the events of that life nourished the *Comédie Humaine*. The standard source.

Pritchett, V. S. *Balzac*. New York: Alfred A. Knopf, 1973. (**G, Y**) A heavily illustrated work, placing Balzac within the context of French cultural life of the nineteenth century. It is anecdotal and quite readable; by providing numerous contemporary illustrations of nineteenth-century Paris, of people Balzac knew and places he frequented, the work gives the reader an excellent sense of Balzac's world. Frequent quotations from Balzac's writings—letters and novels—also give a flavor of his literary style.

Zweig, Stefan. *Balzac*. New York: Viking, 1946. (**A**) Translated from the German text left unfinished by Zweig at his death in 1942 and completed by Richard Friedenthal, this work is more impressionistic and subjective than the Maurois biography. Zweig held Balzac in high regard, calling him the greatest writer of his age. His biography reflects the warm affection he had for the novelist.

Overview and Evaluation of Primary Sources

Very few Balzacian primary materials such as manuscripts are held in U.S.

libraries. The largest specialized collections are to found in the Hobart-Royce Collection at Syracuse University and in the Croue Collection at the University of Chicago. However, numerous libraries do hold copies of the first edition of Balzac's complete works, including *La Comédie Humaine*, published in Paris between 1842 and 1855.

Balzac's correspondence, particularly that with Madame Hanska and Zulma Carraud, has been published; many of these letters have been translated into English. (Most of the letters between Balzac and Laure de Berny were later burned by her son.) The standard French edition of the letters is the five-volume collection edited by Roger Pierrot in the 1960s; the three-volume *Lettres a Mme Hanska* was also published during this period. English translations date from earlier French editions; his letters to Mme. Carraud, edited by Walter Scott Hastings, *Letters to his Family in 1934* (Princeton, NJ: Princeton University Press, 1937), and his correspondence with Eve Hanska in several different editions between 1900 and 1920, (e.g., Volume 34 of *The Works of Balzac,* Centenary Edition, Little Brown, 1900).

Fiction and Adaptations

Because of the inherent visual richness of the world which Balzac presents in his fiction, several of his numerous works have been adapted to film, both in the United States and France. One of the most important is the 1921 silent film *The Conquering Power*, adapted from *Eugénie Grandet*, in which Rudolph Valentino appeared in his first starring role. A 1915 five-reel production of *La Peau de Chagrin* was directed by Richard Ridgely, while a 1923 version of the same work, *Slave of Desire*, took considerable liberties with Balzac's original. *La Duchesse de Langeais* became *The Eternal Flame* in 1922 and *Père Goriot* was filmed as *Paris at Midnight* in 1926. In France, Jean Epstein directed *L'Auberge Rouge* in 1923, based on a novella of the same name. The playwright Jean Giraudoux wrote the screenplay for a 1942 film verion of *La Duchesse de Langeais*. Gabriel Axel filmed *Le Cure de Tours* as a teleplay in 1980 starring Michel Bouquet and Micheline Boudet. In 1978, Guy Jorre directed *Pierrette* also for French television.

In 1980, Fritz Geissler wrote an opera in seven scenes based on *La Peau de Chagrin*. Charles Levade had created a lyric comedy from the same work in 1929.

Other works which have served as a basis for musical works, usually operas or *drames lyriques*, include *La Grande Bretèche*, *Les petites misères de la vie conjugale*, *La belle Imperia mariée*, and *Le shérif*.

Museums, Historical Landmarks, Societies

Maison de Balzac (Paris). Balzac's former residence in the rue Raynouard is open to the public as a museum, with manuscripts and other memorabilia.

Musee Carnavalet (Paris). This museum of Parisian history contains many materials on the nineteenth-century world depicted in *La Comédie Humaine*, as well as items once belonging to Balzac.

Statues (Paris and New York). Copies of Rodin's famous sculpture can be found in Pari son the Boulevard Raspail and in the Rodin Museum. Copies are also on display at the Museum of Modern Art in New York and at the Hirshhorn Museum in Washington, DC.

Other Sources

Affron, Charles. "Honoré de Balzac." In *European Writers*, Vol. 5 (The Romantic Century), edited by Jacques Barzun. New York: Scribner's, 1985. A twenty-page presentation of Balzac's life and, more importantly, his writings. Provides insightful analysis into the themes, organization, and character development in *La Comedie Humaine* through discussion of selected works. Contains a useful bibliography.

"Balzac, Honoré de." In *Dictionary of Modern French Literature*. New York: Greenwood, 1986. A chronological presentation of the life and writings of Balzac, with a brief analysis of his place in nineteenth-century literature, and a useful bibliography of recent critical articles.

Festa-McCormick, Diana. *Honoré de Balzac*. Boston: Twayne, 1979. A short introduction in the Twayne World Author Series to the works of Balzac, focusing on several major novels, but also incorporating biographical information.

Nelles, Charles. "Honoré de Balzac." In *Great Lives from History*. Englewood Cliffs, NJ: Salem, 1989. Concise outline of Balzac's life and work, with a brief annotated bibliography.

Mark Schumacher
Jackson Library
University of North Carolina at Greensboro

Béla Bartók
1881-1945

Chronology

Born Béla Bartók on March 25, 1881, in Nagyszentmiklós, Hungary (now Sinnicolau Mare, Romania), son of Béla Bartók, the headmaster of the Nagyszentmiklós Agricultural School, and Paula Voit, a schoolteacher and amateur musician; *1881-1887* suffers from poor health; begins piano lessons with his mother; *1887-1899* upon his father's death, accompanies his mother from town to town in search of a livelihood; studies piano with László Erkel, then harmony and piano with Anton Hyrtl; *1899-1903* attends the Academy of Music in Budapest, where he studies piano with István Thomán and composition with Hans Koessler; *1903* transcribes for the piano Richard Strauss's *Ein Heldenleben* and composes his symphonic poem *Kossuth*; *1904* discovers authentic Hungarian folksong in the village of Gerlicepuszta and composes the *Scherzo* for piano and orchestra; *1905* enters the Rubenstein Competition in Paris as both a composer and a pianist; begins his collaboration with Zoltán Kodály on research into Hungarian folk music; *1906* tours Spain and Portugal with the violin prodigy Ferenc Vécsey; *Twenty Hungarian Folksongs,* a collection that he and Kodály arranged for voice and piano, is published; *1907* succeeds István Thomán as professor of piano at the Academy of Music in Budapest; spends the summer in Transylvania collecting ancient folk music and finishing *Suite No. 2* for small orchestra; *1908* composes *Violin Concerto* and writes his first mature piano pieces including the *Fourteen Bagatelles*; *1909-1910* marries his pupil, Márta Ziegler, with whom he has a son; composes *String Quartet No. 1*; *1911-1912* completes the opera *Duke Bluebeard's Castle* with libretto by Béla Balázs; helps found the New Hungarian Music Society; *1913* tours North Africa in search of folk music; publishes his first collection of ethnomusicological essays; *1914* excused from military service as war in Europe begins; *1915* spends time in Slovakia collecting folksongs; *1916* composes the *Suite* for piano and a song cycle after five poems of Endre Ady; *1917 The Wooden Prince,* a one-act ballet, successfully premieres; completes *String Quartet No. 2*; *1918-1920* makes several public appearances; attacked in the press for a "lack of patriotism'' and contemplates emigration; *1921* finishes his seminal monograph *Hungarian Peasant Music* and composes *Sonata No. 1 for Violin and Piano*; *1922* performs all over Europe where his reputation as a pianist as well as a composer grows; *1923* finishes *Dance Suite*, which premieres at a festival concert also featuring the works of Kodály and Ernst von Dohnányi; divorces Márta Ziegler and marries his pupil Ditta Pásztory, with whom he has another son; *1925 Dance Suite* premieres in Europe and America; *1926* his ballet, *The Miraculous Mandarin,* which had been under a censor's ban in Hungary since its completion in 1919, premieres in Cologne; composes the *Sonata for Piano, Out of Doors,* and the *Piano Concerto No.1*; *1927-1928* writes *String Quartets No. 3 and 4*; gives recital tours in America and in Russia; *1929-1930* composes the Cantata Profana; *1931* attends the League of Nations Congress for International Cooperation at Geneva; completes the *Piano Concerto No. 2*; *1932* attends a folk music conference in Cairo; *1933* performs the premiere of *Piano Concerto No. 2* in Frankfurt; *1934* retires from teaching to devote himself to music research; composes *String Quartet No. 5*; *1935 The Wooden Prince* revived in Budapest; *1936* travels to Turkey to collect folksongs; composes *Music for Strings and Percussion and Celesta*; *1937* completes *Sonata for Two Pianos and Percussion*; effects a ban on broadcasts of his concerts to Italy and Germany; *1938* finishes *Violin Concerto No. 2* and composes *Contrasts* for violin, clarinet, and piano; transfers from the Austrian to the London branch of the Performing Rights Society; leaves his Viennese publisher for one in London; *1939* composes his *Divertimento,* for string orchestra and the *String Quartet no. 6*; 1940 tours the United States and, after an unofficial farewell concert in Budapest, settles in New York; *1941* receives a research fellowship at Columbia University; *1942* learns his appointment will not be renewed and, suffering from ill health including arthritis and leukemia, becomes inactive; *1943* gives his last concert appearance, performing with his wife the American premiere of *Concerto for Two Pianos*; composes the *Concerto for Orchestra,* a work commissioned by Serge Koussevitzky; *1944* composes the *Sonata for Solo Violin,* commissioned by Yehudi Menuhin; *1945* writes *Piano Concerto No. 3* and, while at work on *Viola Concerto* dies in West Side Hospital in New York on September 26.

Activities of Historical Significance

It is now generally agreed that Béla Bartók belongs among the elite composers of the twentieth century. He explored ways of transcending the major-minor system of Western music, a system of tonality based on the uneven division of the octave. But he never entirely abandoned tonality, which is present in even his least accessible works. Rather he refined and developed it into a non-hierarchic system of pitches which, cohering around an axis, bear a symmetrical relationship to one another. This system seems to have evolved organically as Bartók worked out methods to adapt Eastern European folk music to the Western art music tradition.

Hungary, like nineteenth-century Europe in general, was entrenched in the German-Austrian musical tradition. But the winds of change were blowing from both the East and West, as composers began to turn to native folk sources in their endeavors to fashion music peculiarly suited to their own nationality. It is revealing that early in 1902, beginning his mature years, Bartók wrote four songs after the "folk-national" poems of Lajos Pósa, in the popular song idiom (népies műdal) reminiscent of the gypsy style he was soon to deprecate as being not truly Hungarian. Around this time, moreover, he was frequently attired in national costume, and on occasion was even heard reprimanding his mother for her lapses into German. In other words, his early devotion to the by then somewhat outmoded anti-Habsburg, pro-Hungarian cause was expressed both in his everyday behavior and in his music. Yet, as it turned out, Bartók's passing fancy with the popular song style reflected a deeper desire to discover more genuine expressions of folk attitudes and sentiment. It was not long after making his first notation of a Hungarian folksong, in 1904 in the district of Gömör, that he recognized that peasant styles, differing though they do to some extent along ethnic lines, betray enough mutual influences to suggest a cultural unity possibly transcending ethnic differences. Therefore, unlike his friend Zoltán Kodály, Bartók extended his investigations into the folk music of neighboring nationalities. Eventually, his interest in folk music, and particularly his *ideé fixe* regarding common origins, led him far beyond the borders of Hungary, to Turkey and even Algeria.

He maintained that peasant music was a practically inexhaustible resource with which Western music could renew itself. He warned against stylization or imitation and instead urged a thorough assimilation of peasant music, in order that it might act upon the composer as a genuine influence.

Nevertheless, Bartók always sought corroborating examples of what he found in peasant music in the music of the West. If he had not found them—as he did, for example, in the pentatonic phrases of Debussy or the Russian folk motifs of

Stravinsky—it is by no means certain that he would have persevered in his devotion to folk music.

Early in Bartók's career as a composer, however, he seemed destined to work in the German Romantic tradition. His compositions from the late 1890s to the early 1900s—written mainly for the piano—were influenced by Mosonyi, Erkel, Liszt, Beethoven and, most of all, of Brahms. Such works include the *Sonata in A Major for Violin* (1897, unfinished) and the *Piano Quartet in C Minor* (1898). Around the turn of the century he discovered Wagner, and certain distinctly Wagnerian effects and even quotations—from the *Ring Cycle*, *Tristan und Isolde* and *Die Meistersinger*—can all be detected in the music of his early and early—middle periods. Then, after a brief fallow period while still at the academy, he found the inspiration he was looking for in Richard Strauss's *Also sprach Zarathustra*. Bartók's symphonic poem *Kossuth* (1903), which was modelled on Strauss's work but retained many of the old influences, was intended to be his first major venture towards a specifically Hungarian style.

During the next few years Bartók devoted much of his time to collecting and studying authentic Hungarian folksong. Particularly significant in terms of his own development was his discovery, in Transylvanian folk music, of ancient modes such as the Dorian and Phrygian. The *Fourteen Bagatelles for Piano*, op. 6 (1908) was one of Bartók's first pieces to exploit these new discoveries. Later, he found in Debussy's music a kindred tendency towards a tonal-modal musical language characterized by unordered pitch collections linked by a common axis of symmetry. Meanwhile his experiments with post-Wagnerian chromatic melody, dating from around the same time, suggest the influence of Max Reger, whose scores Bartók is known to have studied.

During the first period of his mature style (1908-1926)—often referred to as his expressionist period—Bartók produced a series of works characterized mainly by their technical experimentation and intellectual abstraction. In his *Allegro Barbaro for Piano* (1911), which exhibits some characteristic features of Romanian folk music, Bartók employed dissonant effects such as tone clusters, and in so doing stressed the percussive nature of the instrument. The one-act opera *Duke Bluebeard's Castle* (1911) was created in the spirit of Symbolism, and contains reverberations of Debussy's *Pellas et Melisande*, whereas in its orchestration it even recalls the older influence of Richard Strauss. *The Miraculous Mandarin* (1919) employs free twelve-tone groups as do the *Studies for Piano* (1918) and the two

Sonatas for violin and piano (1921, 1922).

By the mid-1920s Bartók was in transition towards his neo-classical style, so called for its relatively less dissonant and complicated character, and for the balance it achieves between the emotional and the intellectual. Such a designation naturally recalls Stravinsky. There are Stravinskian features in much of Bartók's music of this period, though most of them are attributed to parallel development, not influence. The orchestration of *Village Scenes* (1926), however—originally composed for voice and piano—is attributable to the direct influence of Stravinsky, who had just been in Budapest for a performance of his *Concerto for Piano and Wind*. It was also around this time that Bartók began studying the early keyboard composers, particularly Bach, whose influence can be heard in the contrapuntal inflections of the *Nine Little Piano Pieces*. Both Bartók's *Sonata* (1926) and *Concerto No. 1* (1926), on the threshold of his classical period, make use all the same of such dissonant devices as tone clusters—by now a Bartókian trademark. In the *String Quartet No. 4* (1928) the standard quartet form is expanded from four to five movements, the third movement of which links the outer pairs of movements which are thematically related. In the *String Quartet No. 5* (1934), the palindromic principle governing the structure of the whole also finds an application in the sonata structure of the opening movement. If not every work is shaped by the palindromic principle, still the concern for structure which it evinces is evident in practically all of Bartók's music from this time on. The *Cantata Profana* (1930), originally intended as the first installment of a trilogy, makes use of a text drawn from a Romanian colinda, translated into Hungarian, but is curiously devoid of Romanian folk music influences. Bartók is said to have been studying Palestrina's choral style around this time, hence the work's Baroque flavor and polyphonic richness.

From the mid-1930s on, Bartók wrote much of the music for which he would be remembered. Although he continued to emulate classical forms and genres, there appears in his music a gradual shift from a classical to a romantic sensibility. It is during this period that Bartók composed *Music for Strings, Percussion, and Celesta* (1936), the *Sonata for Two Pianos and Percussion* (1937) and the *Divertimento* (1939), a series of pieces reflecting a variety of folk music influences including Hungarian, Romanian, and Bulgarian, and which exhibit the composer's rhythmic and metrical inventiveness. *Contrasts* (1938) for violin, clarinet and piano, commissioned by the American jazz artist Benny Goodman, included a novel and unexpected use of *verbunkos* rhythms. The *String Quartet No. 6* (1939), written at a singularly gloomy time of Bartók's life, is suffused with a pessimism that maintains itself through the *mesto* conclusion. After a period of depression, impecuniosity, and relative inactivity, Bartók wrote what would become perhaps his most popular work, the *Concerto for Orchestra* (1943), which so enthralled Koussevitzky that he called it the best orchestral work of the last twenty-five years. The *Sonata for Solo Violin*, written for the violinist Yehudi Menuhin, owes much in its basic conception to Baroque music and to Bach in particular. The *Piano Concerto No. 3* (1945), complete but for the orchestration of the last few measures, filled in subsequently by Tibor Serly with the aid of Bartók's notes, includes in the second movement a quotation from the Heiliger Dankgesang of Beethoven's op. 132.

Bartók's international reputation rests primarily on his work as a composer but he was a multifaceted talent who made significant contributions in many other fields. He was an ethnomusicologist of the first rank, whose indefatigable and systematic work in collecting, sorting, and classifying folk music from numerous ethnicities, including Hungarian, Romanian, Slovak, Serbo-Croatian, Bulgarian, Ruthenian, Turkish, and Arab—he even annotated a few West Virginian folk ballads—has proven an invaluable tool for later ethnomusicologists. Bartók also distinguished himself as a pedagogue. His *Microcosmos* (1926-1939), consisting of 153 piano pieces ranging from the elementary to the most technically demanding, runs the full gamut of his ouevre and was originally conceived as a teaching aid for his son Péter. Over the years Bartók prepared a number of annotated editions of piano works, including, in the period from 1908 to 1912, editions of Haydn, Mozart, Beethoven, and Bach which would become the standard pedagogical texts of Hungary. Finally, Bartók was also a renowned concert performer and an impeccable studio artist. Were it not for his enormous reputation as a composer, which tends to overshadow his other musical pursuits, Bartók would doubtlessly occupy a more secure place in the pantheon of twentieth-century pianists.

Overview of Biographical Sources

Literature on Bartók originally appeared in Hungarian, German, and French; English works, including biographies, hardly existed until the early 1950s. One of the first biographies in English was a translation of Serge Moreaux's likeable but now extremely dated French-language opus, *Béla Bartók* (1953). Halsey Stevens's *The Life and Music of Béla Bartók* (1953) was much acclaimed at its release and regarded for years thereafter as the definitive biography in English. Interested primarily in the composer and musician, Stevens refrained from sentimentalizing Bartók's utopianism. Moreover, Stevens had the advantage of knowing Hungarian and was able to consult the important Hungarian sources. Nothing offers a starker contrast to Stevens's scholarship than *The Naked Face of Genius: Béla Bartók's Last Years* (1958), written by Agata Illés under the pseudonym of Agatha Fassett. Although a personal acquaintance of her subject—she hosted the Bartóks at her seaside home in Vermont in the summer of 1941—she provides a highly romanticized, to some extent even fictionalized, account of Bartók's American years.

The 1960s marked a curious hiatus, if not in Bartók scholarship, then in Bartók biographies. Except for the reissuing of Stevens's work in 1964, nothing of note appeared. By the early 1970s, however, a spate of biographies became available, most of which were translations from Hungarian and German. One exception to this was Everett Helm's *Bartók* (1971), which, though still identifying Eastern European folk music as the singularly most important element in Bartók's music, did much to redirect attention to the composer's Western heritage. Lajos Lesznai's *Bartók* (1973), translated from German, presents a more conventional picture of Bartók, emphasizing his folk-music influences and humanitarianism.

Even the most basic biographical accounts, which put relatively little stress on musical analysis, have traditionally devoted considerable attention to Bartók's relationship with folk music. This was largely in keeping with the notion of Bartók as a "primitive," a label not chosen to stigmatize, but which necessarily called up associations that tended to distort the public view of Bartók, whose music is anything but the analogue of primitive or naive pictorial art. More recently, however, there has been a shift in emphasis from Bartók's Eastern European folk influences to his Western music heritage. Among the works in this vein are Paul Griffith's valuable monograph *Bartók* (1984) and Elliott Antokoletz's *The Music of Béla Bartók* (Berkeley: University of California Press, 1984).

Evaluation of Principal Biographical Sources

Bónis, Ferenc. *Béla Bartók: His Life in Pictures and Documents.* Budapest:

Corvina, 1981. (**A, G, Y**) A special edition for the Bartók centenary, this book may be said to supersede in its richness and accuracy the earlier version entitled *Béla Bartók: His Life in Pictures* (London: Boosey and Hawkes, 1964). An iconography containing photographs of Bartók, his family, friends, colleagues, and places where he resided or visited, as well as maps (providing guides to Bartók's travels as an ethnomusicologist and performing artist) and facsimiles of letters, program notes, and scores. The text accompanying the illustrations is on the mark and helpful.

Fassett, Agatha. *The Naked Face of Genius—Béla Bartók's Last Years.* London: Gollancz, 1958. (**G**) Written by a personal acquaintance of Bartók during his last years in America. Conversational in tone, rich in anecdotes, and, here and there, so full of sympathetic imagination as to border on the fictional. It can be recommended to the reader with a passing interest in Bartók and who wants merely to be entertained.

Gillies, Malcolm. *Bartók in Britain: A Guided Tour.* Oxford: Clarendon, 1989. (**A**) This book is an extremely well written and documented account of Bartók's twenty concert tours in Britain from 1904 to 1938. The circumstances and particulars of Bartók's concert appearances are examined together with the reaction of the British press and public. Gillies takes a fresh look at Bartók the man in light of the latest findings about his music. Includes a helpful bibliography.

―――. *Bartók Remembered.* New York: W. W. Norton, 1991. First American edition. (**A, G, Y**) Gillies brings together in one volume nearly one hundred recollections of Bartók, illuminating aspects of both the private and public man. Although there are reminiscences for every period of Bartók's life, the volume concentrates on the composer's most fruitful years, 1920 to 1940. Gillies's selection will guide the reader to the not unreasonable view that Bartók's public life—comprised of performance, teaching, musicology, and composition—was more varied than is generally thought. The volume includes an introduction, select bibliography, and an index.

Griffiths, Paul. *Bartók.* London: J. M. Dent, 1984. (**A**) This work is intended for the cultivated music listener if not the musicologist. Nevertheless, there is a highly readable biographical account, skillfully interwoven with a musical analysis that does not seem to avail itself of the most up-to-date Bartók scholarship. Among its helpful appendices is a select bibliography, a list of Bartók's compositions, and a glossary of names.

Helm, Everett. *Bartók.* London: Faber and Faber, 1971. (**A, G**) Basic and reliable, striking just the right a balance between biography and musicology. Illustrated.

Juhász, Vilmos. *Bartók's Years in America.* Washington, D.C.: Occidental Press, 1981. (**G**) Preface by Yehudi Menuhin. Introduction by Sándor Veress. Written by an acquaintance, this account is full of personal reminiscences and anecdotes. However, the author has an axe to grind and aims to characterize Bartók as an anti-Communist as well as an anti-Fascist, thus making it clear that his target audience consists of like-minded Hungarian émigrés.

Lesznai, Lajos. *Bartók.* London: J. M. Dent, 1973. (**A**) Translated by Percy M. Young. The original German version, *Bela Bartók, seine Leben, seine Werke* (Leipzig: Deutscher Verlag für Musik, 1961), was apparently translated for the Master Musicians series only to be replaced a decade or so later by Paul Griffith's much superior work. Both books contain illustrations and musical examples, and follow roughly the same format, but all comparisons end there.

Milne, Hamish. *Bartók: His Life and Times.* New York: Hippocrene, 1982. (**G**) A readable popular biography, this book spares the reader any but the most general kind of musical analysis. The text is accompanied by illustrations, a bibliography, and a list of the composer's works (except juvenilia).

Moreaux, Serge. *Béla Bartók.* London: Harvill, 1953. (**A, G**) Translated from French by G. S. Fraser and Erik de Maury. Preface by Arthur Honegger. Moreaux's is a lively and informative work, but it is dated in several important respects. The effusive musical analyses are no longer of any but historical interest. The English translations of the Ady poems (those set to music by Bartók), as well as those of Béla Balázs's libretti, are excruciatingly bad. For scholars.

Stevens, Halsey. *The Life and Music of Béla Bartók.* New York: Oxford University Press, 1953. (**A**) Though its reputation may have tarnished somewhat—this work was once considered the definitive work on Bartók in English—it is still an exemplary piece of scholarship. Although much more space is devoted to the explication of Bartók's works than to the recounting of his life, there is enough to qualify it as a biography. It contains not only illustrations, a bibliography, and a list of works, but also a discography (not updated in later versions) and a helpful guide to Hungarian pronunciation.

Újfalussy, J. *Béla Bartók.* Budapest: Corvina, 1971. (**A, G**) Translated by Ruth Pataki. Revised by Elisabeth West. Informative but exasperating reading. It is full of pre-Glasnost prejudices and terminology, a fact that makes the labored explication of Bartók's philosophy particularly painful reading.

Overview and Evaluation of Primary Sources

A good place to begin studying Bartók's music is his ethnomusicological essays. Interesting in their own right, they also offer important insights into Bartók's attitude towards music and, specifically, his philosophy as a composer. His landmark *Hungarian Folk Music* (London: Oxford University Press, 1931; **A**) translated by M. D. Calvocoressi, a personal acquaintance, appeared only five years after its publication in Hungary. The treatise covers both "new" and "old" styles of Hungarian peasant music, as well as miscellaneous or hybrid melodies. In Calvocoressi's version, the illustrative song texts appear both in English and in the original Hungarian.

The distinguished English folklorist Albert B. Lord is cited as the co-author of Bartók's posthumously published *Serbo-Croation Folk Songs* (New York: Columbia University Press, 1951; **A**). In all likelihood, the finished text is by Lord, but it is based on the notes compiled by Bartók during his research appointment at Columbia University. *Rumanian Folk Music* (5 vols. The Hague: Mortinus Nijhoff, 1967-1975; **A**), edited by Benjamin Suchoff, presents the written record of Bartók's research in the former Hungarian provinces of Transylvania, the Banat, Bihor (Bihar), and Maramures between 1908 and 1917. Consisting mainly of Bartók's transcriptions of his wax-cylinder recordings, the volumes cover instrumental melodies, vocal melodies, texts, carols, and songs from Maramures. A project of the New York Bartók Archive, it includes an informative foreword by Victor Bator.

The single volume *Letters* (Budapest: Corvina, 1971; **A, G**) edited by János Demény, was prefaced by Sir Michael Tippett. Though filling a gap by making available in English a representative sampling of Bartók's correspondence, it lacks the unity of style which a single translator could have provided. The work as it stands was translated by Péter Balabán and István Farkas, and revised by Elisabeth West and Colin Mason.

Bartók also wrote essays, which appeared over the years in a variety of periodicals. It is from these writings that the volume *Essays* (New York: St. Martin's, 1976; **A, G**) selected and edited by Benjam Suchoff, is compiled. The essays deal with various aspects of the national characteristics of Eastern European folk music. Similar in scope and size to the multi-volume set on Romanian folk music is *Yugoslav Folk Music* (Albany: State University of New York, 1978; **A**), edited by Benjamin Suchoff. Among its four volumes is the material first published in *Serbo-Croation Folk Songs*. This edition, unlike its predecessor, reflects not only the labors of Bartók's Columbia University appointment, but also those of his seminal field work in those parts of Yugoslavia still under Hungarian rule. Besides the transcription of 3,349 melodies and detailed ananlysis, the volumes also contains valuable commentary by the editor.

Principal Works

Stage Works

Duke Bluebeard's Castle (1911), a one-act opera.
The Wooden Prince (1917), a one-act ballet.
The Miraculous Mandarin (1919), a one-act pantomime.

Orchestral Works

Three Piano concertos (1926, 1931, 1945)
Two Violin concertos (1908, 1938)

Two Rhapsodies for Violin and Orchestra (1928)
Divertimento for string orchestra (1939)
Concerto for orchestra (1943)
Viola Concerto (1945)

Chamber Music

Six String quartets (1909, 1917, 1927, 1928, 1934, 1939)
Sonata for Violin and Piano (1903)
Piano Quintet (1904)
Two Sonatas for Violin and Piano (1921, 1922)
44 Duos for Two Violins (1931)
Sonatat for two Pianos and percussion (1937)
Sonata for solo Violin (1940)

Piano Music

Three Hungarian Folk Songs (1907)
14 Bagatelles (1908)
For Children (43 pieces in 4 volumes) 1908-1909
Four Dirges (1910)
Allegro Barbaro (1911)
Sonatina (1915)
Six Romanian Folk Dances (1915)
15 Hungarian Peasant Songs (1914-1918)
Out of Doors (1926)
Mikrokosmos (153 pieces in 6 volumes) 1926-1939

Vocal Music

20 Hungarian Folk Songs (in collaboration with Kodály) (1906)
Village Scenes (1924)
20 Hungarian Folk Songs (in 4 volumes) (1929)
Ukrainian Folk Song (1945)

Choral Music

Four Old Hungarian Folk Songs (1910)
Two Romanian Folk Songs (1915)
Five Slovak Folk Songs (1917)
Four Hungarian Folk Songs (1930)
Cantata Profana (1930)
25 Choruses for two- and three-part children's choir (19350
From Olden Times (1935)

Museums, Historical Landmarks, Societies

Béla Bartók Archive (Budapest). Part of the Hungarian Academy of Sciences, where it was established in 1981, the centenary of Bartók's birth.

Béla Bartók Archive (New York). Long in the planning stages, finally established in the early 1960s.

Bartók Béla Memorial Museum (Budapest). Located in the house on Csalán Street where Bartók and family lived from 1932 to 1940.

Bust (Budapest). This 1970 work of Erzsébet Schnár is in the Ministry of Art and Culture.

Monument (Budapest). András Beck completed this impressive bronze monument in 1955.

Portraits. Bartók has been frequently portrayed by painters, graphic artists, and sculptors. The following is a representative list of such artists and their works: Róbert Berény, "Portrait of Béla Bartók" (1913), painting at the Hungarian National Gallery in Budapest; Imre Pérely, "Portrait of Béla Bartók" (1926), drawing at the Bartók Archive in Budapest; Béni Ferenczy, "Portrait of Béla Bartók" (1936), drawing at the Hungarian National Gallery; and Tibor Borbás, "Portrait of Béla Bartók," bronze bust at the Bartók Archive in Budapest.

Other Sources

Antokoletz, Elliott. *The Music of Béla Bartók: a Study of Tonality and Progression in Twentieth-Century Music.* Berkeley: University of California Press, 1984. The most exhaustive, systematic, and definitive analysis of Bartók's musical language as exemplified in a few representative works. Describes how Bartók used both Eastern folk and Western music to develop a unique system in which tonal priority is retained outside the standard major-minor paradigm.

Bator, Victor. *The Béla Bartók Archives—History and Catalogue.* New York: Bartók Archives Publication, 1963. Brief description of the founding of the Archives, followed by summary inventories of the contents including tapes, discs, and photographs, concert programs, clippings, and manuscript facsimiles. Not available are the original documents, which are stored in a bank vault in New York City.

Kroó, György. *A Guide to Bartók.* Translated by Ruth Pataki and Mária Steiner. Budapest: Corvina, 1974. A handy and informative reference work.

Lampert, Vera, and László Somfai. "Béla Bartók." In *The New Grove Modern Masters.* New York: W. W. Norton, 1984: 1-101. An exhaustive, chronological study of Bartók's music together with a fairly detailed biographical account. Though incorporating much of the latest Bartók scholarship, it is not entirely up to date. Concludes on a dubious note, suggesting that Bartók was a *creative synthesizeró* rather than a true innovator. Contains illustrations, musical examples, list of works, and a bibliography.

Lendvai, Ernő. *Béla Bartók: An Analysis of His Music.* London: Kahn and Averill, 1971. Introduction by Alan Bush. A serious probe into the underlying logic and structure of Bartók's music. Argues that Bartók devised a method of integrating all the elements of music; also that the principle of Greek and Roman architecture known as the Golden Section informs both small and large-scale structure in several of Bartók's mature works.

Greg Nehler

Simone de Beauvoir
1908-1986

Chronology

Born Simone Lucie Ernestine Marie Bertrand de Beauvoir on January 9, 1908, in Paris, France, daughter of Georges de Beauvoir, bourgeois lawyer, and Francoise Brasseur; *1910* learns to read; sister Hélène ("'Poupette'") born; *1913-1925* attends Cours Adeline Désir, an exclusive private girls' school, where she meets her friend Elisabeth ("'Zaza Mabille'") Le Coin; *1919* moves from Boulevard du Montparnasse to less affluent Rue de Rennes upon her father's declaring bankruptcy; *1922* rebels against her conservative bourgeois Catholic upbringing; reads controversial works of literature; questions, and finally breaks with all aspects of Roman Catholicism; *1924* completes first program of studies at Cours Adeline Désir; *1925* completes program of study in philosophy and mathematics from Cours Désir; attends classes at two Paris secondary schools; *1925-1927* studies philosophy at the Sorbonne and receives her *licence-ès-lettres* and her degree in philosophy; *1928-1929* studies at the École Normale Supérieure for teaching certification; meets Paul Nizan and Jean-Paul Sartre; begins her lifelong liaison with Sartre; *1931-1936* teaches philosophy at a girls' schools in Marseille and Rouen; *1936-1943* teaches philosophy at various girls' schools in Paris; *1937-1943* writes five short stories (published in 1979 under the title *When Things of the Spirit Come First*); writes novels *She Came to Stay* and *The Blood of Others*; begins *All Men are Mortal*; *1941* father dies; *1943* publishes *She Came to Stay*, the story of her student Olga Kosakiewicz's sexual and emotional intrusion into her relationship with Sartre; dismissed from her teaching position after a student accuses her of condoning immoral behavior; works as a researcher for German-controlled Radio Paris; *1944* assists Sartre and friends at *Combat*, a magazine of the French Resistance against the Germans; with Sartre, founds *Les Temps Modernes*, a radical monthly journal; *1945* travels to Spain and Portugal; publishes *The Blood of Others*; *1946* publishes *All Men Are Mortal* and articles on Existentialism in *Les Temps Modernes*; lectures on Existentialism and contemporary French literature in Tunisia and Algeria; *1947* visits the United States twice, lecturing at universities and initiating a romance with Chicago novelist Nelson Algren; publishes *The Ethics of Ambiguity*, her analysis of Existentialism; *1947-1951* continues her affair with Algren through frequent letters and yearly meetings in the United States, Central America, France, Italy, and North Africa; *1949* publishes *The Second Sex*, a historical, sociological, and philosophical analysis of women that elicits both critical acclaim and hostility; *1950* travels through North and sub-Saharan Africa; *1951* completes a draft of *The Mandarins*; ends affair with Algren despite his proposal of marriage; *1952* undergoes surgery for a breast tumor; begins a seven-year relationship with Claude Lanzmann, a young member of *Les Temps Modernes*' advisory board; *1954* publishes *The Mandarins*, a novel about postwar French intellectuals that receives the prestigious Prix Goncourt; *1955* visits China for two months; *1956* publishes her experiences in China in *The Long March*; *1958-1960* publishes *Memoirs of a Dutiful Daughter* and *The Prime of Life*, the first and second volumes of her autobiography; speaks out against France's policies in Algeria; meets Sylvie Le Bon, a young student, whom she later legally adopts; *1960-1968* with Algren, travels to Greece and Turkey; with Sartre, travels to Brazil, Cuba, the Soviet Union, Japan, Egypt, Israel, Denmark, Sweden, and Yugoslavia; *1963* publishes *Force of Circumstance*, the third volume of her autobiography; *1964* publishes *A Very Easy Death*, based on her mother's death in 1963; *1966* publishes novel *Les Belles Images*; *1968* publishes a short-story collection, *The Woman Destroyed*; supports the Parisian student uprising in May; *1972* publishes *All Said and Done*, the fourth volume of her autobiography; *1975* receives the Jerusalem Prize in honor of her advocacy of human rights; *1980* collapses after Sartre's death in April and recovers slowly; *1981* publishes *Adieux: A Farewell to Sartre*; learns of Algren's death; *1982* refuses French Legion of Honor; *1983* receives the Sonning Prize for European Culture in honor of her lifetime achievements; visits the United States; edits a collection of Sartre's World War II letters; *1985* visits Hungary and Austria; *1986* dies in Paris of pulmonary edema on April 14; buried next to Sartre in Montparnasse Cemetery in Paris.

Activities of Historical Significance

Simone de Beauvoir was the most prominent of women intellectuals and authors in twentieth-century France. Her writings embody philosophies of Existentialism and feminism that span a period of some five decades, but writing was by no means her sole method of commitment to what she defined as a "life of action." She was also a teacher of philosophy and an active sociologist, studying and lecturing on the "human condition," as she called it, especially those aspects concerning the roles of women as dictated by a male-dominated society. Throughout her life she, she was often at the forefront of the social issues of the day: She was politically active as a reporter for the Resistance magazine *Combat*; participated in the anti-fascist movement; vocally favored Algerian independence from French control; sympathized with the May, 1968 student uprising in Paris; and continued to advocate human rights and feminist causes until the time of her death.

Long before Beauvoir made the conscious decision to follow in the footsteps of Existentialists such as Georg Wilhelm Hegel, Søren Kierkegaard, Gabriel Marcel, and Sartre, she had been acutely aware of the disparity that existed among social classes, of the often hypocritical teachings of the Catholic Church, and of her own propensity toward a life of intellectual rather than maternal and domestic activities. In an effort to deal with these concepts, quite in conflict with the strict teachings of her somewhat overzealous mother, Beauvoir chose to reject all parental authority. She read controversial works of literature and she questioned and later broke off with the Catholic Church. Instead of marrying, she successfully completed university degrees, taught philosophy, and maintained a committed but unmarried relationship with Jean-Paul Sartre. She also became an esteemed author and leader of the feminist movement in France. In the details of her life, we see Beauvoir's personal application of the philosophy of Existentialism, whereby she herself took control of and responsibility for her own life.

In the 1930s, during the early years of her association with Sartre, she was thought of merely as his "companion," and Sartre's followers believed that she had no true convictions of her own. It was this misconception of her role in society, especially in politics, that resulted in her undergoing an intense process of questioning the validity of her opinions and of reevaluating her place in society. To accomplish this, she immersed herself in the "act of living," separating herself philosophically and psychologically from Sartre. She recognized herself as an individual, free to realize her acts and decisions, forge her own destiny, and accept responsibility for her own life. This personal existentialist struggle for independence and autonomy in a world quick to stereotype people is the struggle Beauvoir chronicles in virtually all of her published works, from her earliest fiction of the 1930s to her political and philosophical treatises up until the 1970s.

Beauvoir recognized as early as the 1930s the importance of individual political action to the securing of an environment in which individuals could freely pursue their personal quests for meaning. However, it was not until after the Second World War that Beauvoir truly associated literary and political activity. For her, the goal of literature was not primarily aesthetic in nature but rather a means by which one could demonstrate commitment to a political cause and bring about widespread change. But the individual alone could not promulgate such radical change—this could only be accomplished through the solidarity of all humanity, striving toward a common cause. In novels such as *The Blood of Others* (1945) and *The Mandarins* (1954), Beauvoir expounds not only the need for political "engagement" but also the need for people to join forces in combatting their common enemy.

It is these vital issues that underlie Beauvoir's masterpiece, *The Second Sex* (1949), the work for which she is best known today. Having comprehended what a life committed to action entailed, she felt the need to examine the overall condition of women in society to determine the degree to which they did or did not participate actively in the creation of their own destiny. Topics covered in *The Second Sex* include the historical "enslavement" of women by men and the influence of society on roles available to women, primarily those centered on motherhood and care-taking. Beauvoir's famous statement, "One is not born, but rather becomes a woman," implies that indeed all women are directly responsible for the direction that their lives take. Feminists of the 1950s and 1960s took *The Second Sex* as their authority on feminism, but more contemporary feminist critics have quarreled with some of Beauvoir's reductive and classist statements. Although many of the questions raised by Beauvoir in *The Second Sex* may seem outdated a half-century later, her underlying belief in the ideal of the self-created, self-determining, independent woman is as vital today as it was in 1949.

Beauvoir's dual role in twentieth-century Western culture—as the doyenne of Existentialism and the mother of modern feminism—demonstrates her intellectual versatility and assures her an enduring place in history. She should also be remembered as a tireless advocate for human rights, fighting against the forces of sexism, ageism, and other "isms" that in her view limited the individual's freedom to assert himself or herself as "subject" rather than "object" or "other."

Overview of Biographical Sources

Beauvoir's biographers have been blessed with the wealth of information and self-interpretation she provides in her autobiographies, and burdened with the essential unreliability of a highly subjective text. Beauvoir's anomalous position—as a prominent intellectual who happened to be a woman—has so far been the key issue for her biographers. No book-length studies were published in English until the 1980s, after the academic feminist movement was well established, and this academic feminism is amply represented in the biographies.

Two general tendencies are apparent in the contemporary biographies. The first is to take an adulatory and intensely personal view of her life. Some feminist biographers have identified strongly with Beauvoir's commitment to personal freedom and her repudiation of stereotypical feminine roles. They have thus written defenses of her radical lifestyle and philosophy while at the same time authenticating their own experiences as women intellectuals. These biographers tend to either accept Beauvoir's autobiographical self-portrait relatively uncritically or revise her image in positive and sympathetic ways. Works by Carol Ascher (1981), Claude Francis and Fernande Gontier (1985), Judith Okely (1986), and Lisa Appignanesi (1988) fit into this category.

The second general tendency in recent Beauvoir biography is likewise personal, but it is not uncritical. Analyses of a recently deceased subject are frequently less forgiving than those written during the subject's lifetime. Some feminist scholars have felt betrayed by the inconsistencies between Beauvoir's public repudiation of stereotypical feminine roles and what now appears to have been, based upon new evidence from letters and from interviews with her surviving circle, her private ambivalence in her relationships with men, Jean-Paul Sartre and Nelson Algren in particular. Deirdre Bair's *Simone de Beauvoir: A Biography* (1990) carries traces of this tendency, and several reviewers of Bair's book echoed this feeling. Renee Winegarten's *Simone de Beauvoir: A Critical View* (Oxford: Berg, 1988) extends this disillusionment beyond biography into literary criticism as well.

Evaluation of Principal Biographical Sources

Appignanesi, Lisa. *Simone de Beauvoir.* London: Penguin, 1988. (**G, Y**) Brief, admiring study of Beauvoir's life and work, tracing her life chronologically and thematically, stressing Beauvoir's significance as an exemplary woman who freed herself form conventional social restraints. Readers new to Beauvoir studies may wish to start with this book.

Ascher, Carol. *Simone de Beauvoir: A Life of Freedom*. Boston: Beacon, 1981. (**G**) Quirky "part biography, part literary criticism, part political and personal commentary" stressing Beauvoir's implication in the central issues of twentieth-century life.

Bair, Deirdre. *Simone de Beauvoir: A Biography*. New York: Summit Books, 1990. (**A, G**) The definitive biography, undertaken with Beauvoir's general cooperation. Thoroughly researched, exhaustively documented, monumental in size, readable, and interesting. Draws on extensive interviews with Beauvoir and her circle as well as unpublished archival material. Includes illustrations, notes, and index.

Francis, Claude, and Fernande Gontier. *Simone de Beauvoir: A Life, A Love Story*. 1985. Translated by Lisa Nesselson. New York: St. Martin's, 1987. (**G**) Sometimes sensationalized biography stressing Beauvoir's romantic relationships. Draws on newly accessible Beauvoir letters to Nelson Algren. Some factual error; criticized by Beauvoir in *Le Matin* 16 (December, 1985).

Okely, Judith. *Simone de Beauvoir*. New York: Pantheon, 1986. Virago/Pantheon Pioneers Series. (**A, G**) Thoughtful feminist analysis, with extensive application of ideas from *The Second Sex* to Beauvoir's own life and other writings. Okely's analysis is conducted on several levels, citing her personal response to *The Second Sex* in the 1960s and the 1980s as well as Beauvoir's revisionary comments in the decades since its publication.

Overview of Primary Sources

The most obvious primary sources are Beauvoir's autobiographical works. The first volume, *Memoirs of a Dutiful Daughter*, translated by James Kirkup (1958.

Reprint. Harmondsworth: Penguin, 1984; **A, G, Y**), covers her childhood from 1908 to 1929. The second, *The Prime of Life*, translated by Peter Green (1960. Reprint. New York: Paragon House, 1992; **A, G, Y**), deals with her young womanhood and the war years, 1929 to 1944. The third, *Force of Circumstance*, translated by Richard Howard (1963. Reprint. New York: Harper and Row, 1977; **A, G, Y**), discusses her years of growing fame, 1944 to 1962. The fourth, *All Said and Done*, translated by Patrick O'Brian (1972. Reprint. New York: Paragon House, 1993; **A, G, Y**), covers her life of political and social action, 1962 to 1972. The fifth, *Adieux: A Farewell to Sartre*, translated by Patrick O'Brian (1981. Reprint. New York: Pantheon, 1984; **A, G, Y**), discusses Sartre's decline and death, and her own old age from 1972 to 1981.

Throughout the works, Beauvoir presents herself as a rational, sensible, intellectual who made her life choices freely and deliberately and who was consistently self-possessed and self-reflective. This personal account of her life and the evolution of her philosophy is an invaluable resource. Nevertheless, because of her wish to exhibit a particular, coherent, and consistent portrait of herself and her suppression of some information to protect friends' privacy, her autobiography is selective, skewed, and faulty in dates and details. This unreliability is, of course, one of the autobiography's primary attractions, as it has provoked and will continue to provoke extensive commentary and revision by scholars.

After abandoning her teaching career in her mid-thirties, Beauvoir became a full-time writer, and she produced an impressive body of material that varied in both genre and subject matter. She is best known as a novelist, an autobiographer, and a sociologist, but she also wrote a play, three philosophical monographs, and documentary studies on such diverse topics as her American and Chinese travels, old age, and her mother's death. She also spent forty years editing, writing, and reviewing books for the radical journal *Les Temps Modernes*, which she, Sartre, and their circle founded in 1945. Taken as a whole, her writings span the central issues of mid-century thought and life—Existentialism, political engagement, roles for women and men, and the condition of the individual in society from childhood to old age. Few twentieth-century writers can demonstrate such a broad sweep and great impact.

There is, to date, no standard English-language collection of Beauvoir's works. All of her books, though not all of her essays, have been translated into English and are generally easily available; most are still in print. Because there are several editions and reprints of her works by various French, British, and American publishers, bibliographic information in this section is limited to the date of first French publication and the most recent English-language edition.

Beauvoir is best known for her pioneering socio-historical treatise on the condition of women in Western society, *The Second Sex*, translated by H. M. Parshley (1949. Reprint. London: David Campbell, 1993; **A, G**). In it, Beauvoir attempts to explain why women have been relegated to the margins of Western culture. Her basic premise is that, for various reasons, men have historically viewed women as "other," and that this "otherness" came to be seen as inferiority. The result: Women essentially have been deleted from the historical record kept by men. Beauvoir asserts that this presumed inferiority stems not from physiological difference but from cultural conditioning. According to the existentialist concept that all individuals possess the freedom to choose their actions and thus may remake themselves and the world, women and men need not persist in this unequal relationship; society can learn to accept equality of the sexes, despite their differences.

Beauvoir's five long works of fiction are all thesis novels; each illuminates an aspect of her Existentialist and feminist concerns. The first, *She Came to Stay*, translated by Yvonne Moyse and Roger Senhouse (1943. Reprint. New York: Norton, 1990; **A, G, Y**), is a semi-autobiographical story of a couple dedicated to existential freedom whose invitation to a younger woman to join their relationship has disastrous effects as shifting alliances within the trio consistently alienate one or another member. *The Blood of Others*, translated by Yvonne Moyse and Roger Senhouse (1945. Reprint. New York: Pantheon, 1983; **A, G, Y**) is a novel of commitment, presenting characters who forswear their political detachment and class allegiances in order to dedicate themselves to the Resistance against the German occupation of France. *All Men Are Mortal*, translated by Leonard Friedman (1946. Reprint. New York: Norton, 1992; **A, G, Y**), according to Beauvoir scholar Catherine Savage Brosman, examines the "dominant existentialist themes" of "action, happiness, freedom" in a story about an immortal man and a mortal woman, the futility of their choices, and their ultimate powerlessness against the course of history.

Beauvoir's great critical and popular success came in 1954 when she received the Prix Goncourt, France's premier literary prize, for *The Mandarins*, translated by Leonard Friedman (1956. Reprint. New York: Norton, 1991; **A, G, Y**). The

"Mandarins" of the title are a group of postwar French intellectuals, much like Beauvoir's own circle, who are deeply committed to politics and writing and profoundly perplexed by the challenges of maintaining love and friendship in the face of the alienation of the human condition and the degradations of women. Beauvoir's last novel, *Les Belles Images* (title same in French and English), translated by Patrick O'Brian (1966. Reprint. New York: Putnam, 1968; **A, G, Y**), continues her analysis of the peculiar problems women face in a society that limits their freedom by bombarding them with images of how they should look, act, and ultimately be.

Beauvoir also published two collections of short stories with feminist and existentialist themes: *The Woman Destroyed*, translated by Patrick O'Brian (1967. Reprint. New York: Pantheon, 1987; **A, G, Y**), and *When Things of the Spirit Come First*, translated by Patrick O'Brian (1979. Reprint. New York: Pantheon, 1984; **A, G, Y**). Her play, *Who Shall Die?*, translated by Claude Francis and Fernande Gontier (1945. Reprint. Florissant, MO: River, 1983; **A, G**), is a kind of dramatized philosophical essay posing ethical questions about the value of the individual life. Beauvoir's important monograph, *The Ethics of Ambiguity*, translated by Bernand Frechtman (1947. Reprint. Secaucus, NJ: Citadel, 1980; **A**), explores the problem of the individual creating an ethical system in an ambiguous, absurd, and chaotic world.

Besides *The Second Sex*, Beauvoir's other book-length, nonfiction documentary studies are: *America Day by Day*, translated by Patrick Dudley (1948. Reprint. New York: Grove, 1953; **A, G**), a pseudo-diary of her 1947 American lecture tour; *The Long March*, translated by Austryn Wainhouse (1957. Reprint. Cleveland: World, 1958; **A, G**), a commentary on the Socialist transformation of mainland China based on Beauvoir's official 1955 tour; *A Very Easy Death*, translated by Patrick O'Brian (1964. Reprint. New York: Pantheon, 1985; **A, G, Y**), a chronicle of her mother's illness and death from cancer; and *The Coming of Age*, translated by Patrick O'Brian (1970. Reprint. New York: Putnam, 1974; **A, G**), an analysis of the deplorable condition of elderly people in Western society.

One volume of the journal Beauvoir kept sporadically throughout her lifetime has been published: *Journal de Guerre: Septembre 1939-Janvier 1941,* edited by Silvie Le Bon de Beauvoir (Paris: Gallimard, 1990), not yet translated.

Beauvoir's correspondence is in the process of being published. Her adopted daughter Sylvie Le Bon de Beauvoir issued two volumes of Beauvoir's *Letters to*

Sartre, covering the years 1930 to 1963, translated, edited, and abridged by Quintin Hoare (1990. Reprint. New York: Arcade, 1992; **A**). Summaries of Beauvoir's letters in English to American novelist Nelson Algren comprise Lauren Helen Pringle's *An Annotated and Indexed Calendar and Abstract of the Ohio State University Collection of Simone de Beauvoir's Letters to Nelson Algren, 1947-1964* (Ann Arbor: University Microfilms International, 1985; #86-03042; **A**). Other correspondence of interest to Beauvoir students is the collection of letters Sartre wrote to her during their intermittent separations between 1926 and 1939: *Witness to My Life: The Letters of Jean-Paul Sartre to Simone de Beauvoir, 1926-1939* (New York: Scribner's, 1992; **A, G**), edited by Simone de Beauvoir in 1983 and translated by Lee Fahnestock and Norman MacAfee.

German feminist and critic Alice Schwarzer has published a transcription of six interviews she conducted with Beauvoir from 1972 to 1982. The work, *After the Second Sex: Conversations with Simone de Beauvoir*, translated by Marianne Howarth (1983. Reprint. New York: Pantheon, 1984; **A, G, Y**), chronicles Beauvoir's mature attitudes toward feminism and the female condition in the decades following the publication of *The Second Sex* in 1949.

Students seeking a bibliography of Beauvoir's publications, including translations, should consult Claude Francis and Fernande Gontier's excellent though necessarily, by its date, incomplete *Les Ecrits de Simone de Beauvoir: la vie, l'écriture, avec en appendice textes inédits ou retrouvés* (Paris: Gallimard, 1979; **A**), not yet translated into English. Joan Nordquist's *Simone de Beauvoir: A Bibliography* (Santa Cruz, CA: Reference and Research Services, 1991; **A, G**) lists books, essays, and interviews by Beauvoir as well as books, book reviews, articles, and dissertations about her work. Nordquist's bibliography is limited to works in English and is not annotated. Anne-Marie Lasocki has compiled a listing of contemporary book reviews of Beauvoir's volumes of autobiography: "Simone de Beauvoir" in *A Critical Bibliography of French Literature* (Syracuse, NY: Syracuse University Press, 1980, Vol. 6, Part 3: 1682-1683; **A**), edited by Douglas W. Alden and Richard A. Brooks. The essential bibliography of critical books and articles is by Joy Bennett and Gabriella Hochmann, *Simone de Beauvoir: An Annotated Bibliography* (New York: Garland, 1988; **A, G, Y**), which lists and summarizes books, articles, interviews, theses, and book reviews of books by and about Beauvoir for the years 1940 to 1986. Works in five languages are included—French, English, German, Italian, and Spanish.

Fiction and Adaptations

Three film documentaries have been made of Beauvoir's life and work. The first, *Simone de Beauvoir* (directed by Josée Dayan and Malka Ribowska, 1978; in French), is a series of conversations among Beauvoir, Sartre, Claude Lanzmann, and Alice Schwarzer; the filmscript has been published as *Simone de Beauvoir* (Paris: Gallimard, 1978; not translated). Josée Dayan also directed a four-hour documentary for French television on Beauvoir's role in modern feminism: *The Second Sex* (1985). Most recently, Penny Forster produced and Imogen Sutton directed a one-hour documentary for the British Broadcasting Corporation, *Daughters of de Beauvoir* (New York: Filmmakers Library, 1989), a series of interviews with women from many countries (including Kate Millett, Marge Piercy, Eva Figes, and Sylvie le Bon de Beauvoir) who are continuing Beauvoir's feminist and humanitarian work. The filmscript for this documentary has been expanded and published as *Daughters of de Beauvoir,* edited by Penny Forster and Imogen Sutton (London: Women's Press, 1989).

Museums, Societies, and Historical Landmarks

Centre Audiovisuel Simone de Beauvoir (Paris). Cinematographic archives on women, founded in 1982 by Carole Roussopoulos, Delphine Seyrig and Ioana Wieder, open to the public.

Plaque (Hôtel Mistral, Paris). December 10, 1991: inauguration of a plaque dedicated to Simone de Beauvoir and Jean-Paul Sartre, commemorating their residence at the Hôtel (24 rue Cels, Paris 14e) before and during the Second World War. The plaque is attached to the hotel's facade for public viewing.

Simone de Beauvoir Institute (Montreal). Located at Concordia University, the Institute, founded in 1978, houses an extensive library of books and periodicals relating to Beauvoir and to women's studies in general.

Simone de Beauvoir Society (Hayward, California). The Society has an international membership of students and scholars, publishes a quarterly newsletter and an annual journal of scholarship on Beauvoir, and sponsors a biennial conference.

Other Sources

Bennett, Joy, and Gabriella Hochmann. *Simone de Beauvoir: An Annotated Bibliography*. New York: Garland, 1988.

Bieber, Konrad. *Simone de Beauvoir.* Boston: Twayne, 1979. Good summary of Beauvoir's autobiographies. Elementary discussion of the literary and philosophical works.

Brosman, Catharine Savage. *Simone de Beauvoir Revisited*. Boston: Twayne, 1991. Clear and cogent exposition of ''Beauvoir's literary, philosophical, and other works . . . against the background of her life and career.'' (Introduction). Recommended for readers wishing an introduction to or a review of Beauvoir's work. Excellent annotated bibliography.

Cottrell, Robert D. *Simone de Beauvoir*. New York: Frederick Ungar, 1975. Modern Literature Monographs. Concise analysis of Beauvoir's use of existentialist ideas in her fiction.

Evans, Mary. *Simone de Beauvoir: A Feminist Mandarin*. London: Tavistock, 1985. Excellent philosophically oriented study focusing on Beauvoir's evolving Existentialism and feminism.

Fallaize, Elizabeth. *The Novels of Simone de Beauvoir.* London: Routledge, 1988. Discusses issues of historicity, political commitment, and gender roles in Beauvoir's five novels and two short-story collections. Asserts that women's narrative authority decreases markedly in Beauvoir's fiction, from the powerful female monologues in the 1930s to the muffled intermittent narration by the female protagonist in the 1966 *Les Belles Images.*

Heath, Jane. *Simone de Beauvoir.* New York: Harvester Wheatsheaf, 1989. Key Women Writers Series. Feminist analysis of the autobiographies, *She Came to*

Stay, The Mandarins, and *Les Belles Images.* Heath's premise is that Beauvoir's writing stance was neither feminist nor consciously feminine and that she consistently identified with masculine values.

Keefe, Terry. *French Existentialist Fiction: Changing Moral Perspectives.* London: Croom Helm, 1986. A consideration of popular notions of Existentialism as communicated through the fiction, not the theoretical writings, of Beauvoir, Albert Camus, and Jean-Paul Sartre. Keefe demonstrates that Beauvoir's and Camus' works are remarkably similar in their ambivalence about the individual's situation in society.

―――――――. *Simone de Beauvoir: A Study of Her Writings.* London: Harrap, 1983. Emphasizes Beauvoir's seriousness as a writer and her engagement with moral questions in every work, regardless of genre. Balances analysis of the novels with analyses of her sociopolitical and philosophical essays and her autobiographies.

Leighton, Jean. *Simone de Beauvoir on Woman.* Foreword by Henri Peyre. Rutherford, NJ: Fairleigh Dickinson University Press, 1975. Early feminist analysis of "the woman question" as a base for Beauvoir's writings. Leighton argues that Beauvoir is often anti-feminist; for instance, the confident assertion in *The Second Sex*—that women can reject their inferior "other" status and can choose autonomy and freedom—is never manifested in Beauvoir's fictional women characters.

Madsen, Axel. *Hearts and Minds. The Common Journey of Simone de Beauvoir and Jean-Paul Sartre.* New York: William Morrow, 1977. A dual biography that explores the long, intertwined relationship of Beauvoir and Sartre. Includes correspondence, translated by the author. Minimal documentation; dated and contradicted by recent accessible primary materials.

Marks, Elaine. *Simone de Beauvoir: Encounters with Death.* New Brunswick, NJ: Rutgers University Press, 1973. Clear and convincing analysis of Beauvoir's existential fear of emptiness, meaninglessness, and the annihilation of the self in death. Marks notes that Beauvoir is preoccupied with this theme in all her writings and that in every genre Beauvoir depicts mature women in anguish over the prospect of death.

—————. *Critical Essays on Simone de Beauvoir.* Boston: G. K. Hall, 1987. Includes twenty-seven essays by noted scholars and critics utilizing a variety of approaches. Useful as a gauge of critical opinion of Beauvoir at the time of her death.

Moi, Toril. *Feminist Theory and Simone de Beauvoir.* Cambridge, MA: Basil Blackwell, 1990. Bucknell Lectures in Literary Theory Series. Two lectures given by Moi in 1989: "Politics and the Intellectual Woman," an analysis of French and Anglo-American feminists' differing receptions of Beauvoir's work, plus a commentary on Western culture's ambivalence about women as intellectuals; and "Intentions and Effects: Rhetoric and Identification in *The Woman Destroyed.*" Helpful introductory essay by Michael Payne.

Patterson, Yolanda Astarita. *Simone de Beauvoir and the Demystification of Motherhood.* Ann Arbor: UMI Research, 1989. Important contribution to the history of ideas in its depiction of Beauvoir's attitudes toward women's family roles set against the backdrop of shifting Western attitudes about motherhood in the past century. Interviews with Simone de Beauvoir and her sister Hélène are appended. Patterson, a professor at California State University, Hayward, also edits the annual *Simone de Beauvoir Studies* and the quarterly *Simone de Beauvoir Society Newsletter.*

Peters, Hélène. *The Existential Woman.* Foreword by Germaine Brée. New York: Peter Lang, 1991. American University Feminist Studies. A study of Sartre's and Beauvoir's literary representations of women within the existentialist context of freedom, choice, and responsibility. Counters Leighton by asserting that providing role models of successful women was never Beauvoir's intent.

Wenzel, Hélène Vivienne, ed. *Simone de Beauvoir: Witness to a Century.* Special edition of *Yale French Studies* 72 (1986). Collection of ten essays on various aspects of Beauvoir's work, plus a transcription of a 1984 interview.

Whitmarsh, Anne. *Simone de Beauvoir and the Limits of Commitment.* London: Cambridge University Press, 1981. Emphasizes Beauvoir's metamorphosis from apoliticism to political engagement, with extensive reference to Existentialism.

Good summaries of the novels.

Winegarten, Renee. *Simone de Beauvoir: A Critical View*. Oxford: Berg, 1988. A very critical view, highlighting the disparities between Beauvoir's professed ideals and her life as actually lived. Winegarten undercuts the popular heroic images of Beauvoir and presents instead a view of an egocentric and inconsistent rationalist.

Mary Anne Kucserik
Cedar Crest College

Lauren Pringle De La Vars
St. Bonaventure University

Cesare Beccaria
1738-1794

Chronology

Born Marchese di Cesare Beccaria Bonesana on March 15, 1738, in Milan, Italy, the son of Giovanni Saverio Beccaria Bonesana, a modestly endowed Milanese aristocrat, and Maria Visconti da Rho; *1746-1754* studies at the College of the Jesuits in Parma where he excels in mathematics; *1754-1758* studies law at the University of Pavia, earning his doctorate at the age of twenty; *1758-1761* returns to Milan and joins the literary club Accademia dei Trasformati (Academy of the Transformed), where he is befriended by Count Pietro Verri; against his father's wishes marries Teresa Blasco, daughter of an army colonel, and is temporarily disinherited; *1762* joins Verri's newly created literary circle, the Accademia dei Pugni (Academy of Fists); his daughter Giulia is born; on Verri's suggestion writes *Del disordine e de'rimedii delle monete nello stato di Milan nell'anno 1762*, (On the Disorders and the Remedies of the Currency in Milan in the year 1762), an economic treatise on the currency problem in Milan which becomes the basis for the Milanese Currency Reform Acts of 1777; *1763-1764* again on Verri's advice, begins work on a study of criminal law in March 1763; anonymously publishes his findings, *On Crimes and Punishments*, in July 1764, only to be recognized as the author shortly thereafter; *1764-1765* co-founds with Pietro and Alessandro Verri in June 1764 a short-lived newspaper, *Il Caffé*, modeled after the English *Spectator*; writes a total of seven articles for *Il Caffé*: "Il Faraone" (Faro), on statistical probabilities; "Tentativo analitico su i contrabbandi" (Analytical Essay on Smuggling Operations), an attempt to compute a cost-benefit equation balancing the risks of smuggling against its profits; "Risposta alla rinunzia" (In Response to the Renunciation) and "Frammento sullo stile" (Fragment on Style), two studies of linguistic problems; "De'fogli periodici" (The Periodicals), an examination of the function of newspapers in a society; and "I piaceri dell'immaginazione" (Pleasures of the Imagination) and "Frammento sugli odori" (Essays on Odors), two collections of Beccaria's thoughts on human behavior; *1766* the Vatican places *On Crimes and Punishments* on the index of condemned books for its extreme rationalist philosophy; begins a correspondence with the Abbé Morellet, author of the first French translation of Beccaria's masterpiece, and Voltaire, who writes a commentary endorsing the principles of *On Crimes and Punishments*; *Il Caffé* ceases publication in June; leaves Milan with Alessandro Verri for Paris in October, on the invitation of the Abbé Morellet; due to extreme homesickness, returns to Milan four months early; *1767* declines an invitation from Catherine II to come to St. Petersburg and assist in the preparation of a uniform penal code; daughter Maria is born; *1768* accepts the chair of Public Economy and Commerce at the Palatine School; *1769-1771* teaches at the Palatine School; publishes *Ricerche intorno alla natura dello stile* (Research on the Nature of Style) in 1770; *1771-1785* serves on the Supreme Economic Council of Milan; *1771* wife Teresa dies on March 14; marries Anna Barbó, daughter of the wealthy Count Barnaba Barbó, on June 4; *1775* son Giulio is born; *1777* is instrumental in achieving monetary reform in Milan; *1780* presents his report, *Della riduzione delle misure di lunghezza all úniformitá per lo stato di Milano* (On the Reduction of the Measures of Length to Uniformity in the State of Milan), where he proposes a uniform system of weights and measures based on a decimal system; *1785-1794* serves as a member of the Imperial Government Council which replaces the Supreme Economic Council of Milan; *1785-1789* runs the Department of Agriculture, Industry, and Commerce; *1788* daughter Maria dies; *1789* under his guidance the first veterinary school opens in Milan; *1790-1794* serves on the Public Commission for the Reform of Civil and Criminal Jurisprudence in Lombardy; *1794* overweight throughout his life, dies of apoplexy on November 28 in Milan and is buried in the cemetery of San Gregorio.

Activities of Historical Significance

Cesare Beccaria lived in a world where the judicial system was characterized by cruelty and arbitrariness. Death, bodily mutilations, and flogging were common punishments for most crimes; the use of torture to obtain confessions and secret proceedings governed by capricious magistrates were normal practices throughout Europe. Although earlier authors had condemned these abuses, Beccaria's *On Crimes and Punishments* was singularly important in galvanizing reformers in the field of law. For the first time, the call to rationalize the legal systems of Europe was systematically and succinctly stated. Basing his principles of reform on the argument that government policy should seek the greatest good for the greatest number, Beccaria used logic to defend his proposed humane and reasonable system of justice against the current barbaric practices supported solely by tradition. Alone among reformers, Beccaria also wrote in favor of the abolition of the death penalty.

On Crimes and Punishments was an immediate success; within a few years of publication, translations could be found in French, English, German, Polish, Spanish and Dutch. The first French translation ran through seven printings in six months. Beccaria's influence on English reformers was especially profound. William Blackstone's 1765 book on criminal laws in his *Commentaries* often refers to Beccaria. Both Jeremy Bentham and Samuel Romilly acknowledged their great debt to Beccaria, in particular to his idea that public utility should be used as the ultimate test of morality.

Beccaria's later writings show the diversity of his interests and the international influence of his work. Late eighteenth-century French reformers used his 1780 report, *On the Reduction of the Measures of Length to Uniformity in the State of Milan,* in their successful battle to convert France to the metric system. His lecture notes on economics from the Palatine School, posthumously published in Milan in 1804 as *Elementi di economia pubblica* (Elements of Public Economy) and containing such concepts as the division of labor and the relationship between food supply and population, anticipated some of the ideas of Adam Smith and Thomas Malthus.

Overview of Biographical Sources

Despite the tremendous influence of Beccaria's treatise, few biographies have been written on his life. Until Marcello Maestro's scholarly biography, *Cesare Beccaria and the Origins of Penal Reform* (1973), the only English studies on the Italian author were incomplete, focusing narrowly on his life prior to and immediately after publication of *On Crimes and Punishments*. These works routinely summed up the remaining thirty years of his life in two pages or less, often ignoring his later years altogether. Such studies took the form of chapters from books concerned with broader topics such as Coleman Phillipson's *Three Criminal*

Law Reformers, Beccaria, Bentham, Romilly (1923), or prefaces to English editions of his treatise, including James Anson Farrer's lengthy preface to his 1880 translation of *On Crimes and Punishments*, and Henry Paolucci's introduction to his 1963 translation of the work.

The Italian sources are only slightly more numerous and complete. Within twenty years of his death, Beccaria was the subject of Italian biographers. The first scholarly Italian biography, however, did not appear until 1862, when Cesare Cantú's *Beccaria e il diritto penale* was published. Cantú's work remains one of the foremost biographies of Beccaria and is an excellent source. Relatively more recent is C. A. Vianello's documentary history of Beccaria's life, *La Vita e l'opera di Cesare Beccaria, con scritti e documenti inediti* (1938). Combining biography with documentary evidence, Vianello's book is extremely useful.

Evaluation of Principal Biographical Sources

Farrer, James Anson. *On Crimes and Punishments.* 1880. Reprint. Ann Arbor, MI: University Microfilms. (**A, G**) Farrer's simple and incomplete biographical introduction to this translation of *On Crimes and Punishments* is notable only because it is the only English nineteenth-century biography of Beccaria. The early years of Beccaria's life are dealt with up through and including his disastrous trip to Milan. Beccaria's influence on English judicial policy and penologists throughout the mid-nineteenth century is analyzed. Those facets of Beccaria's life which do not relate to *On Crimes and Punishments* are ignored. Farrer's work is out of date and surpassed by more recent biographical studies.

Maestro, Marcello. *Cesare Beccaria and the Origins of Penal Reform.* Philadelphia, PA: Temple University Press, 1973. (**A**) Maestro's book is the first full biography of Beccaria in English, and the only complete recounting of Beccaria's life from his early school years to his death. Unique to every other biography of Beccaria to date, nearly half of Maestro's work is devoted to Beccaria's life after the publication and success of *On Crimes and Punishments*. Although Beccaria's fame rests on this work, Maestro emphasizes the importance and influence of both his later writings and his work in the Economic Council of Milan. In order to make this point effectively, Maestro includes numerous translated quotes from

Beccaria's essays and letters, many in English for the first time.

Paolucci, Henry. *On Crimes and Punishments.* Indianapolis, IN: Bobbs-Merrill, 1963. (**A, G**) Paolucci's biographical preface to his translation of Beccaria's treatise discusses the historical significance of Beccaria's treatise and the events of Beccaria's life connected with the publication of *On Crimes and Punishments.* The international reception of the work along with Beccaria's relationship with the Verri brothers is emphasized. Paolucci ends his brief biography with Beccaria's flight from France during his triumphal European tour following the publication of *On Crimes and Punishments.* The remaining twenty-eight years of Beccaria's life is passed over in a cursory manner.

Phillipson, Coleman. *Three Criminal Law Reformers, Beccaria, Bentham, Romilly.* 1923. Reprint. Montclair, NJ: Patterson Smith, 1970. (**A**) Phillipson divides his book into three parts beginning with a discussion of Beccaria, his life and works. The subsequent sections show the influence of Beccaria's ideas on both Bentham and Romilly. Much attention is paid to conditions in Europe in the seventeenth and eighteenth centuries in order to highlight the later changes brought about by the influence of Beccaria's ideas not only on Bentham and Romilly but on political leaders around the world. As the intent of the book is to trace the development of the ideas of penal reform contained in *On Crimes and Punishments*, the biography of Beccaria is compressed into a single chapter, and only that portion of his life having to do with the publication of his famous treatise is emphasized.

Overview and Evaluation of Primary Sources

The modern English translations of Beccaria's *On Crimes and Punishments* are few in number. There are four widely available today: Farrer's (London: Chatto & Windus, 1880), Paolucci's (Indianapolis, IN: Bobbs-Merrill Educational Publishing, 1963), David Young's (Indianapolis, IN: Hacket Publishing, 1986), and most recently, a reproduction of F. Newberry's 1775 English edition containing Voltaire's commentary on the treatise (Birmingham, AL: Legal Classics Library, 1991). Also available in English is Beccaria's *A Discourse on Public Economy and*

Commerce (New York: Burt Franklin Research and Source Works Series, 1970; **A**). Unfortunately, with the exception of these two examples, the writings of Beccaria are not available in English. In Italian numerous editions of his complete works exist, beginning as early as 1770 with Giovanni Gravier, ed., *Opere diverse*, 3 vols. (Naples: 1770; **A**), through 1958 with the definitive collection of the writings of Beccaria, Sergio Romagnoli, ed., *Opere*, 2 vols. (Florence: Sansoni, 1958; **A**). Beccaria's private letters and documents are untranslated as well, one of the best collections being Franco Venturi, ed., *"Dei delitti e delle pene," con usa raccolta di lettere e documenti relativi alla nascita dell'ópera e alla sua fortuna nell'Europa del Settecento* (Turin: Einaudi, 1965; **A**). The letters of the Verri brothers, also untranslated, are collected by Carlo Casati in *Lettere e Scritti inediti di Pietro e Alessandro Verri*, 4 vols. (Milan: Galli, 1879-1881; **A**). Articles from *Il Caffé* have been edited by Ezio Colombo in *Antologia de Il Caffé (1764-1766)* (Milan: Bompiani, 1945; **A**).

Museums, Historical Landmarks, Societies

Birthplace and residence (Milan, Italy). The family house is located at 6 Via Brera. A plaque near the door reads, "In this house Cesare Beccaria was born in 1738 and died on November 28, 1794."

Gravesite (Milan, Italy). Beccaria was buried in the San Gregorio cemetery under a simple stone with a Latin inscription: "Councillor in the public administration, expert in criminal jurisprudence, writer of clear intellect."

Monuments (Milan, Italy). Several streets in Milan have been named after Beccaria, and two statues of him have been erected in the city.

Other Sources

Maestro, Marcello T. *Voltaire and Beccaria as Reformers of Criminal Law.* New York: Columbia University Press, 1942. Beccaria's treatise is analyzed in light of its influence on Voltaire. Only one of the seven chapters of the book deals with Beccaria, narrowly focusing on the influential nature of *On Crimes and Punishments*.

Schumpeter, Joseph A. *History of Economic Analysis.* New York: Oxford University Press, 1954. A brief evaluation of the contributions of Beccaria's economic writings to western economic thought is included in this survey.

Barbara J. Whitehead
DePauw University

Thomas Beecham
1879-1961

Chronology

Born April 29, 1879, St. Helens, Lancashire, near Liverpool, the son of Sir Joseph Beecham, a pharmaceuticals magnate, and Josephine Burnett Beecham; *1892-1897* studies at Rossall, a school for boys; *1897-1898* studies at Wadham College, Oxford University, where he receives private lessons in music theory from Dr. John Varley Roberts, organist and choir trainer at Magdalen College, Oxford; *1899* serves as substitute for internationally known conductor Hans Richter at a performance of the Hallé Orchestra in St. Helens; *1902* serves as accompanist and conductor of the short-lived Imperial Grand Opera Company; *1903* marries Utica Celestina Welles; *1903-1905* joins, along with Charles Kennedy Scott, the Oriana Madrigal Society; studies orchestration in Paris with composer Moritz Moszkowski; *1905-1908* gives various concerts with an orchestra made up of members of various established orchestras; *1906* officially names this ensemble the New Symphony Orchestra; directs the Birmingham City Choral Society; *1909* organizes a new orchestra, which he names the Beecham Symphony Orchestra; *1915* forms the Beecham Opera Company; *1916* knighted by George V in the New Year's Honours List; upon the death of his father ascends to the Baronetcy of the United Kingdom, a hereditary honor first instituted by King James I in 1611; *1927* begins his quest to stabilize the performance of opera in England by means of the Imperial League of Opera; *1932* forms the London Philharmonic Orchestra; *1933* becomes artistic director of the Royal Opera House at Covent Garden; *1936* becomes managing director of the Royal Opera; *1940-1944* serves as director of the Seattle Symphony Orchestra; conducts often at New York City's Metropolitan Opera; tours the United States, Canada, Mexico, and Australia; 1943 divorces his first wife Utica and marries pianist Betty Humby Thomas; *1944* publishes an autobiography, *A Mingled Chime*; *1946* founds the Royal Philharmonic Orchestra; *1957* invested by Elizabeth II with the insignia of the Companions of Honour, a British honorary order instituted by George V in 1917 for men and women who have rendered conspicuous national service; *1958* publishes his biography of

Frederick Delius; wife dies; *1959* marries Shirley Hudson; *1961* dies in London on March 8 of a cerebral thrombosis.

Activities of Historical Significance

Sir Thomas Beecham is the most prominent English conductor of his generation, and arguably, of all time. He commanded an enormous repertory and often had an intense performance schedule, as in 1910, when he conducted more than 100 operas. A large number of his performances were recorded, some of which have been remastered for release on compact disc. (See *Sir Thomas Beecham Discography* and *17th Edition Artist Issue* in Other Sources, below.) In addition to forming and conducting two of the most important orchestras in the world, he was enormously influential in bringing attention to eighteenth-century music and in promoting contemporary composers.

Beecham's background was unusual for an English musician. Whereas most conductors were trained in a conservatory or a cathedral school, Beecham was self-trained as a conductor. He was born to a wealthy family—his grandfather founded a prosperous family pharmaceutical business, a legacy which granted Thomas financial independence and the ability to hire his own orchestras early in his career. He excelled in drawing the best players available for his ensembles, but his autocratic style of orchestral management led to his dissociation with the New Symphony Orchestra, which he founded in 1906.

Further tension regarding the degree of artistic control and business management desired by Beecham led to the formation of the London Philharmonic Orchestra. First appearing in a Queen's Hall concert on October 7, 1932, the ensemble dominated the London orchestral scene until World War II. Under Beecham's direction, the group performed its own series of concerts as well as a summer opera series at Covent Garden and a highly acclaimed tour of Germany in 1936. During World War II, while Beecham toured with other orchestras, the London Philharmonic became a self-governing organization. Although Beecham was offered reinstatement as Music Director after the war, he would have lost much management control, and he emphatically refused the contract. He subsequently formed the Royal Philharmonic Orchestra in 1946.

The first concert of this new orchestra took place on September 15, 1946, and the players were contracted in the preceding three-week period. The Royal Philharmonic Orchestra became associated with both the Glyndebourne and Edinburgh Festivals as well as its own series of subscription concerts. During Beecham's tenure as music director, he controlled the orchestra's policy and business matters. It was only in 1963 that the ensemble became a self-governing organization.

Beecham's attraction to early- and mid-eighteenth-century composers foreshadowed society's subsequent interest in early music. Although a great deal of research on and performance of Baroque music was taking place in Germany, Beecham was one of the most important musicians performing these works in the English-speaking world. He displayed a special interest in the music of George Frideric Handel, adapting some of his pieces as concert suites and ballets. In addition to Handel, Beecham also performed works of other Baroque composers who were not well-known in the early twentieth century except to musical scholars. Included in his concert programs were many Italian Baroque composers, such as Antonio Vivaldi, Giovanni Battista Pergolesi and Leonardo Leo, as well as Giuseppe Tartini and Pietro Locatelli.

Beecham was well-known for his performances of the music of Wolfgang Amadeus Mozart, Joseph Haydn, Hector Berlioz, Antonin Dvořák, and Richard Strauss, but early in his career he championed the music of contemporary composers, especially English composers. Among the better known are Frederick Delius, Jean Sibelius, Ralph Vaughn Williams, Arnold Bax, and Frank Bridge. The accessibility of these works in live performances and recordings made them better-known to later generations. It is likely that Beecham's predilection toward some of these works saved them from obscurity.

Early in his career Beecham wrote three works for the lyric stage, but none were ever performed, and two of the manuscripts have been lost. Beecham was reputed to have been particularly good at communicating with his orchestras. Although a very eloquent speaker, at times he could not find the words to describe the effect he wanted and would instead sing the line or communicate with expressive hand gestures. He was well known for the beautiful singing quality and shaping of his melodic phrases, as well as a firm rhythm and an economy of musical accent. Humphrey Procter-Gregg, in *Sir Thomas Beecham: Conductor and Impresario* (1972) also discusses his effective climaxes and his long and expressive technique of diminuendo.

Overview of Biographical Sources

There is no definitive or critical biography of Sir Thomas Beecham. Although much has been written about the conductor, most of it is in the form of anecdotal remembrances, popular "chatty" biographies, and general writings by those who are so obviously in awe of this major twentieth-century performer that an unbiased representation is impossible. This is partly because writings about performers generally tend toward the popular rather than the historical.

A starting point for any biographical inquiry, however, are the standard references on music and music biography: *The New Grove Dictionary of Music and Musicians* (1980) and *Baker's Biographical Dictionary of Music* (8th ed. New York: Schirmer, 1992). The entries on Beecham are not very long, but they are well written and offer bibliographic information.

Although certain aspects of Beecham's career were discussed in English-language works in the 1930s and 1940s, biographies did not begin to appear until 1961, the year of his death. In some cases these served more as memorial tributes than biographies. A few biographical works also appeared around the centenary of Beecham's birth in 1979. These are also essentially popular remembrances and tributes.

Evaluation of Principal Biographical Sources

Capell, Richard. "Sir Thomas Beecham." In *The Musical Times* 102 (1961): 283-286. (**A**) Published as an obituary in one of England's most important music periodicals, this is very useful as a summation of the importance of Beecham's work in the English music world. It was written in 1953, and an editorial addition to the end of the article lists some of the performing highlights of the conductor's last years.

Cardus, Neville. *Sir Thomas Beecham: A Memoir.* London: Collins, 1961. (**G**) This brief work by a journalist with the *Manchester Guardian* is largely a collection of anecdotes and is of limited use biographically.

Crichton, Ronald. "Thomas Beecham." In *New Grove Dictionary of Music and*

Musicians, New York: Macmillan, 1980. Vol. 2: 349-351. (**A, G**) The *Dictionary* is the standard English-language reference work on music and should be the starting point for virtually any biographical or bibliographical study in music. The article on Beecham, although brief, is objective and useful.

Geissmar, Berta. *The Baton and the Jackboot.* London: Hamish Hamilton, 1944. (**A, G**) Geissmar, who worked for Beecham, has provided an interesting, if slanted, view of English and German concert life before and during World War II. Most interesting is the discussion of the London Philharmonic Orchestra's tour to Germany in 1936.

Jefferson, Alan. *Sir Thomas Beecham: A Centenary Tribute.* London: Mac-Donald and Jane's, 1979. (**A, G**) Well written and insightful, this biography does not follow a strict chronological style but rather deals with various aspects of the composer's life. Jefferson begins with Beecham's family life and follows with discussions of his orchestras, operatic work, and touring abroad, and he concludes with a discussion of Beecham's repertory. This biography is somewhat more objective than others, but nevertheless, the author seems to be in awe of his subject. The bibliography included at the end of the book is the most complete one available.

Procter-Gregg, Humphrey. *Sir Thomas Beecham, Conductor and Impresario: As Remembered By His Friends and Colleagues.* Westmoreland, United Kingdom: private publication, 1972. (**A, G**) An invaluable collection of materials related to Beecham, Procter-Gregg's book is primarily a collection of reminiscences by prominent English musicians and writers. But it also contains an introductory essay on Beecham's life and work; a list of conductors, singers and professionals who worked with Beecham; the testimonial given when Beecham was granted an honorary Doctor of Music degree from the University of Manchester in 1937, as well as a description of his reply; a collection of Beecham's observations on topics as diverse as modern art and America; the text of Beecham's 1956 lecture on the English playwright John Fletcher; Beecham's 1935 funeral oration for Frederick Delius; memorial articles from the *London Times* by Frank Howes and Sir Malcolm Sargent soon after Beecham's death; a memorial article by Neville Cardus from the *Manchester Guardian*, written ten years after the conductor's death; a selected bibliography and discography. A revised and enlarged version of this book, *Beecham Remembered*, appeared in 1977.

   Reid, Charles. *Thomas Beecham: An Independent Biography*. New York: Dutton, 1962. (**A, G**) Reid's biography is the only lengthy chronological account of Beecham's life and career. Although he attempts to address certain omissions in the composer's autobiography, much more emphasis is placed on the period covered by *A Mingled Chime* than on Beecham's later years. The tone of the book is conversational, and it is based on discussions with family members and musicians who worked under Beecham.

   Smyth, Dame Ethel. *Beecham and Pharaoh*. London: Chapman and Hall, 1935. (**G**) This book by an English composer contains an essay about Beecham. It is "chatty" and generally unreliable, but it does provide some insight into Beecham's stature in the English music community during the early twentieth century.

Overview and Evaluation of Primary Sources

A Mingled Chime (New York: Putnam's, 1943; **A, G**), Beecham's autobiographical account of his early years, is lively and obviously needs to be consulted in any study of his life. The reader can experience some of Beecham's wit and opinionated nature, which have been described in so many other sources. However, the work needs to be compared to other biographical accounts, such Reid's, as there are some omissions. In addition, the work is limited since it only discusses his life up to 1924.
   Harold Atkins and Archie Newman have edited *Beecham Stories: Anecdotes, Sayings and Impressions of Sir Thomas Beecham* (London: Robson Books, n.d.), an entertaining but anecdotal work of questionable biographical value.
   Some of Beecham's writings on Frederick Delius can be found in "Beecham on Delius," in *A Delius Companion*, edited by Christopher Redwood (London: Calder, 1976).

Fiction and Adaptations

Films for the Humanities and Sciences, Princeton, New Jersey, released a videotape, *Sir Thomas Beecham,* (1991) in which Timothy West portrays Beecham in this dramatization made for British television.

Museums, Historical Landmarks, Societies

Beecham Society (London). Located at 46 Wellington Avenue, Westcliff-on-Sea, Essex, England SSO 9XB.

Other Sources

Abromeit, Kathleen A. "Ethel Smyth, *The Wreckers,* and Sir Thomas Beecham," *Musical Quarterly* 73 (1989): 196-212.

Gilmour, J. D. *Sir Thomas Beecham—The Seattle Years.* Aberdeen, WA: World Press, 1978.

————. *Sir Thomas Beecham—50 Years in the New York Times.* London: Thames and Hudson, 1988.

Gray, Michael H. *Beecham: A Centenary Discography.* London: Duckworth, 1979.

Sir Thomas Beecham Society. *Sir Thomas Beecham Discography.* Westport, CT: Greenwood, 1978.

17th Edition Artist Issue. Sante Fe, NM: Stereophile, 1992.

Timothy L. McDonald
Rockhurst College

Ludwig van Beethoven
1770-1827

Chronology

Born Ludwig van Beethoven—exact date uncertain, but baptized December 17, 1770, at Bonn in the German Rhineland, son of Johann van Beethoven, a court musician, and pious Maria Magdalena Keverich, widow of Johann Lym, valet to the Elector of Trier; *1770-1782* grows up in a servant-class environment; talent recognized by his alcoholic father, who has a violent temper and treats him roughly; plays viola and violin in the court orchestra; typical of his time, receives only an elementary school education; plays organ in the local church, where the needs of the Catholic liturgy allow him to develop his improvisational skills; *1782* becomes assistant court organist to his teacher, Christian Gottlob Neefe; *1783* his first composition, *Variations on a Theme by Dressler,* is published at Mannheim; appointed continuo player to the Bonn opera; compared as child prodigy to Wolfgang Amadeus Mozart by Cramer's *Magazin der Musik; 1784* appointed organist by the new elector, Maximilian Francis, brother of the Habsburg emperor Joseph II; *1787* sent by Maximilian Francis to Vienna, to study with Mozart; the visit is cut short by the news of his mother's death; *1789* returns to Bonn where playing viola in the theatre orchestra is added to his court duties; successfully petitions to be considered head of the family, displacing his dissolute father; *1790* composes his most important work of the Bonn years, *Cantata on the Death of Emperor Joseph II,* who embodied the progressive ideas of the Enlightenment; travels throughout Germany as part of the elector's entourage, attracting admiration of other professional musicians and notice of the powerful and talented Count Waldstein, eight years his elder, whose friendship—characteristic of the rebellious composer's ability to cultivate aristocratic patrons—would ease Beethoven's way into the high society of Vienna; befriended by Frau von Breuning, a widow with four children, who remains his lifelong friend and who becomes almost a second mother; cultivates a social life and musical activities unconnected with the court; *1792* moves permanently from Bonn to Vienna, the musical capital of Europe, and enters his so-called "First Period" of composition, producing music resembling that of his two great predecessors in the "First Viennese School," Haydn and Mozart; *1793* earns money by writing and publishing chamber music; *1793-1794* studies with the composer Franz Joseph Haydn, probably only polishing compositions of the later Bonn years; *1794* studies with contrapuntist Johann Georg Albrechtsberger, organist at St. Stephen's Cathedral; studies vocal composition with Antonio Salieri, imperial Kapellmeister; *1795* performs successful private concerts in great houses of Vienna; establishes himself as virtuoso at charity concerts in the Burgtheater; publishes *Three Trios for Piano, Violin and Cello,* Opus 1, meant to appeal to aristocratic musical amateurs; *1796* his brothers join him in Vienna; travels to Dresden—where the king of Prussia, impressed by the sonata, op. 5, for his own instrument, the cello—gives the composer a gold snuff box filled with gold coins, and to Pressburg (now Bratislava, Slovak Republic); *1798* begins to publish chamber music dedicated to the elite musical amateur friends for whom it was composed; meets General Bernadotte, sent from the Directory now ruling France, who suggests writing a heroic symphony dedicated to the young general Napoleon Bonaparte; meets violinist Kreutzer travelling with Bernadotte; impresses Bohemian composer and critic Václav Tomasek; challenged and inspired in Vienna by rival keyboard virtuosi Joseph Wölff from Salzburg and Baptist Cramer from London; further challenged by Haydn's late quartets, symphonies, and masterly oratorio, *The Creation;* attempts to write a symphony and begins to write string quartets; *1798-1799* begins keeping systematic sketchbooks of ideas for new compositions, expanding a practice begun in Bonn; *1799* meets the soon to be unhappily married young Countess Giuletta Guicciardi, who would later become the subject of much conjecture concerning his love life; *1800* performs for profit a public concert including his *First Symphony* and works by Haydn and Mozart; visits Hungarian estates of aristocratic friends; compositions include the ballet *The Creatures of Prometheus; 1801-1802* again studies with Antonio Salieri; publishers now compete for his work; detects impairment in his hearing, which he reveals to trusted friends; letters reveal that melancholy mingles with professional success; moods of exaltation, "I will seize fate by the throat," join confessions of love for a "dear Charming girl,"—probably Giuletta; *1802* on a sojourn in nearby village of Heiligenstadt, writes a despairing note, the *Heiligenstadt Testament,* which illuminates his struggle with suicidal thoughts engendered by incipient deafness, as well as by his inability or unwillingness to conform to societal norms; *1803* recovering from despondency, enters his "Second Period," often called "externalization," for a decade during which his uniquely self-assertive, turbulent style reflects the turbulence of the post-revolutionary era; attracted to the lucrative operatic medium, composes his first vocal-dramatic work, *The Mount of Olives,* an oratorio on the life of Christ; composes his *Third Symphony,* the "Eroica," originally dedicated to Napoleon, employing the largest, most diverse, yet most tightly unified compositional techniques for purely instrumental music yet conceived; "Waldstein" Sonata and the string quartets, dedicated to Count Razumovsky, show the same triumphant spirit; *1805-1806* first version of his only opera, *Fidelio,* the tale of a political prisoner's rescue by his wife, Leonora, disguised as a man; idealization of married love therein seems to match his intense friendship with a widow, Josephine von Brunsvik; accepts suggestions of cuts in the opera; provides a new overture for it, *Leonora No. 3,* to succeed the symphony-sized *Leonora No. 2; 1806-1808* produces a steady stream of masterpieces, including the *Fourth Symphony, Violin Concerto, Fourth Piano Concerto,* and *Coriolan Overture,* resulting in offers from London publishers; receives commissions from Prince Esterhazy to compose the setting of the Mass for his wife's name's day—resulting in unfavorable comparison between this *Mass in C* and those of his former teacher, Haydn; *1807-1808* completes at Heiligenstadt the *Fifth Symphony* as well as the *Sixth,* the "Pastorale," both premiered at a four-hour long concert on December 22, 1808, whereby he hoped to secure additional income; *1809* negotiates lifetime subsidy with three patrons, the princes Kinsky and Lobkowitz and the youngest brother of the emperor, Archduke Rudolf, his only composition pupil and dedicaté for some of his greatest works; *1810* provides on commission the successful incidental music to Goethe's play, *Egmont,* the story of a leader who foresaw the liberation of his homeland, though he would not live to experience it; establishes friendships with Bettina Brentano, a friend of Goethe, and Therese Malfatti, niece of his physician; *1811* travels; *1812* returns to Vienna and completes the *Seventh Symphony; 1812* completes the *Eighth Symphony;* meets Goethe, who finds him "untamed," as Beethoven finds Goethe too much the courtier; seeks to end his brother's illicit liaison, yet writes his famous love letter "to the distant beloved"—apparently a married woman; *1813* relinquishes hope of any successful courtship and marriage; accepts guardianship of Karl, son of brother Caspar Carl; falls into financial difficulties because accidents and the Napoleonic wars have undermined the Hapsburg currency and his patrons' resources; achieves popular following; composes probably his worst piece, the wildly acclaimed

Wellington's Victory, employing a mechanical instrument with orchestra to celebrate the defeat of the French emperor; *1814* revises his opera and adds a new "Overture to *Fidelio*"; meets Anton Schindler, law student and musician who becomes his irritatingly obsequious volunteer factotum and unreliable biographer; composes the bombastic *Der glorreiche Augenblick* (The Glorious Moment), op. 136, for festivities welcoming royalty to the Congress of Vienna; full annuity restored; *1815* brother Caspar Carl dies; begins five-year conflict over custody of his nephew with his sister-in-law, Johanina, whom he vilifies as "the Queen of the Night;" *1816* completes song cycle *An die ferne Geliebte;* no other major works completed during these years of conflict with Johanina, accompanied by his own unfulfilled conjugal desires and deteriorating health; deafness causes him to resort to handwritten conversation books; begins his "Third Period" of composition, usually labelled "internalization" during which he demonstrates his conquest both of personal problems and of new compositional frontiers; *1818* writes *Hammerklavier Sonata,* op. 106, which explores the possibilities of the piano, then still a relatively new musical instrument; works on *Missa Solemnis,* planned for the consecration of Archduke Rudolf as archbishop of Olmutz in 1820 but completed too late; *1821-1822* writes piano sonatas, op. 109; *1822* begins the *Ninth Symphony; 1824* completes *Diabelli Variations,* op. 120, thirty-three seemingly inscrutable variations (instead of the one requested by the publisher for an album anthologizing music from various composers of the Hapsburg Empire); *1824* conducts, though deaf, the premier at the Kärnthnerthor Theatre of the *Ninth Symphony* and of *Missa Solemnis,* which he believed to be his greatest work; *1824-1827* his last works, the "late [string] quartets," bewilder listeners; encounters problems with patrons not paying his annuity and confusion among publishers; attempts to continue managing the life of his nephew, who attempts suicide in 1826; string quartet in F finale deemed too difficult by his publisher, so a new last movement is substituted and the original published separately as the *Grosse Fuge,* op. 133; returning to Vienna from a visit to brother Johann, contracts pneumonia from which he never fully recovers; *1827* after bequeathing his estate to nephew Karl, dies from cirrhosis of the liver on March 26; funeral attended by ten thousand people; the oration, written by Franz Grillparzer, is delivered graveside by actor Heinrich Anschütz; *1888* remains moved to Zentralfiedhof and now lies next to composer Franz Schubert.

Activities of Historical Significance

As a composer, Ludwig van Beethoven culminated the classical style of music of the eighteenth century, helped found the romanticism of the nineteenth century, and foreshadowed the post-tonal music of the twentieth century. His personal, as well as musical autonomy inspired a continuing idealization of the artist as creator, rebel, and hero.

The continuing global fame and influence of Beethoven, whose outward life was relatively uneventful, depends on the manifold appeal of his music. First, Beethoven's music resonates with the condition of modern humanity. His most characteristic pieces communicate a sense of restless drive sustained despite dissonances and abrupt mood changes. Listeners sense an interior psychological struggle that overcomes adversity. This sense of struggle for a noble goal that is not definable in words was already recognized in his lifetime as corresponding to the historic struggles in the wider culture of that era of the American, French, and industrial revolutions with their attendant upheavals accompanied by a basically confident attitude. The compositions of his last decade are often so dense and complex that they seem to forecast the tribulations of the whole modern era, as well as being direct ancestors of the agonies of twentieth century music. Second, Beethoven compositions, though often complex, are characteristically constructed of extraordinarily simple musical ideas. More than any other composer, he is able to balance the clarity of traditional classical canons, which require that art conform to a clear rational design, with the unpredictability and sense of spontaneity typical of later romantic attitudes, which crave art that is unique, nonconformist. Third, Beethoven's artistic independence combined with his ability to reach a wide audience helped to change the way people thought about music. Instead of expecting only a pleasant decoration to life, the shared experience of an inspiring piece of music now seemed a rite that offers fulfillments formerly sought in religion. Beethoven's struggle against deafness seemed to justify his assertion that listening to his music could show listeners how to overcome fate. Thus Beethoven epitomized the idea that music can bring messages from—if not define—a spiritual world.

Skeptical of authority, Beethoven was personally and artistically unconventional. His insistence that aristocratic patrons treat him as an equal (including allowing Germans and Austrians to think that the "van" in his name signified nobility), combined with his sympathy for liberal ideas, fostered the image of the independent artist. His disgust with Napoleon for declaring himself Emperor of the French while posing as son of the Revolution helped to inspire the Romantics' pronouncements that ideals are enshrined better in art than in institutions or ideology. Yet Beethoven's life seems a great irony, for he prided himself upon being a self-made prince of art although he was dependent for sustenance upon aristocratic patronage in the conservative capital of Vienna that was prenational and feudal. A populist roughness seems to pervade much of the music of his middle period that gained so much popularity—as well as criticism—because it seemed to express rebellion against artificial conventions.

Beethoven's more massive compositions, such as the choral finale of the *Ninth Symphony,* owe something to the democratic spirit of civic celebrations during the French Revolution, whose slogan "Liberty, Fraternity, and Equality," spread through the world during Beethoven's time. Music more for a mass audience, including participation by hundreds of performers, became an ideological and economic necessity as the middle class replaced the nobility and churches as principal art patrons and consumers. Such a combination of high art with popular appeal became a norm followed by the great symphonists and choral composers of the nineteenth century, such as Hector Berlioz, Felix Mendelssohn, Johannes Brahms, Antonin Dvorak, Anton Bruckner, and Gustav Mahler. Their sometimes-massive compositions were part of the artistic and commercial movement that spurred the construction of imposing civic temples for the performing arts worldwide, from the Gesellschaft für Musikfreunde in Vienna and Royal Albert Hall in London through the music halls of smaller cities in Europe and the Americas, such as the music halls of Boston, Philadelphia, and Cincinnati, and down to the performing arts centers on university campuses and in westernized cities worldwide. The existence of these monuments to the transcendental mission of music—and its commercial desirability—depends in part on the legacy of Beethoven.

Beethoven's religious impulse was profound though incapable of definition in the traditional formulas of any single theology. His compositions on religious texts, such as those of the *Missa Solemnis,* summarized the whole of the European musical heritage while still providing a vehicle for Beethoven's individual expression. To compose that Mass, he researched ancient sacred music from the medieval Gregorian chant and Renaissance polyphony, Baroque soloistic styles, congregational chorales, and the orchestrally-backed and operatically-dramatic Mass settings by Haydn and Mozart. These precedents he combined with the stirring rhythms and big sounds derived from the national and democratic Mass-oriented music of his age. Beethoven can, therefore, be seen as helping to set a precedent for historical research as source for inspiration, as did others like the monks of Solesmes—who worked on the restoration of Gregorian chant, or Felix Mendelssohn—who fostered a revival of public interest in the music of Johann Sebastian Bach. Such an eclectic, even nostalgic, mixture of styles and devices became a hallmark not only of nineteenth- century European music but of modern civilization in general. At the same time he introduced startling textual interpretations in music that seemed to subordinate ecclesiastical religion to the service of a wider humanistic enterprise. Many modern thinkers found such aspects of Beethoven's music congenial. As a result, his compositions have been used as evidence that music is a higher language that is above sectarian or ethnic division.

Beethoven's stature was such that the subsequent history of European music may be considered a dialogue between two ways of appropriating his legacy. One school of followers emphasized his "classical" side. His tight thematic unification of huge musical compositions that may last hours encouraged their view of music as an art that is autonomous, or "absolute." Beethoven's instrumental works encouraged a tendency to think that music does not need the pretext of words or ceremony in order to make sense. Thus Beethoven's example encouraged the growth of music for its own sake, which is to be consumed in concerts, rather than in an ancillary role at church liturgies, public celebrations, musical theater, or courtly ceremonies. His typical method of composing was to establish a simple musical motive (a brief melodic figure) as the raw material of a vast edifice in which he developed every conceivable permutation of that motive in ways that were undreamed-of previously and still challenge the imagination of listeners, analysts, and composers. Beethoven's shadow fell on a hero of the classical purists, Johannes Brahms, who disdained the entanglement of music with extra-musical ideas, who postponed for forty years the writing of his first symphony, quickly dubbed "Beethoven's Tenth."

Beethoven's admirers espoused a second way of looking at his legacy, which stressed connections between music and extra-musical ideas, such as nationalism and idealistic philosophy. From their point of view, Beethoven's compositional method of "motivic expansion" seemed to offer evidence in support of theories about organic growth from tiny seeds or primitive ideas. Such ideas were being applied by analogy to everything from biological evolution to cultural nationalism in the century that followed his death. His compositional procedure in which simple elements functioned as the seeds of a great organism was adduced in support of the vogue for seeing high culture as the logically evolving ramification of folk roots. Beethoven had sometimes taken inspiration literally from folk songs, as in the string quartets dedicated to the Russian Count Razumovsky. The *Sixth Symphony* had bird calls and other nature sounds; the choral movement of the *Ninth* celebrated union of the arts and grass roots political systems. The Romantic movement, for which Beethoven became the virtual idol, often viewed music as the ideal voice of a people and their pre-literate culture. Romantic music represented the voice of the uncorrupted human heart. The undecorated simplicity of much of Beethoven's raw material, combined with his use of hymn or folk-like melodies encouraged biographers to think of him as a democratic hero who rose from the people, retained his connections with those roots, and returned his art to them as a monument to a common humanity where distinctions were based upon merit. Such sympathy for folk-like expression as the model for art readily blended with the most abstruse theories and grand pattern-making, such as Hegel's theory of historical dialectic, where the simplest beginnings work themselves out in the most complex ramifications.

Whatever the bent of the writer, Beethoven's legacy has usually seemed that of a mythic figure who was the very archetype of the artist. In general, he appealed to the new middle class audience so much that his symphonies, overtures, and more famous sonatas became such staples that their obsessive repetition by symphony orchestras and pianists, reinforced in the twentieth century by electronic media, may actually have hindered the widening of public musical taste in later times, thus functioning contrary to the way in which Beethoven helped to expand musical taste in his own day.

Professional musicians eventually came to rate Beethoven's last compositions as his best. In these he stretches the tonal system and familiar forms beyond recognition, thus becoming a prophet of post-tonal and free-form developments of the twentieth century. Of course the example of the great musician isolated by deafness and whose best work is inaccessible to the uninitiated multitude is not lost upon critics seeking analogies for the plight of a truly unique individual alienated from a society that purports to enshrine liberty but actually punishes deviation from mediocrity. Thus the cult of Beethoven as man and artist is refurbished in every generation.

The fascination with Beethoven's music and personality inspired the Romantic composers who consciously imitated his compositional methods and publicized his music. Franz Schubert's sweet-song and dance-based music shows in his later output the influence of Beethoven's "storm and stress." Hector Berlioz, probably the ultimate Romantic, who made his living largely as a music critic in an age of burgeoning literacy and newspaper reading, tried to gain a public for Beethoven's music in Paris, Europe's most cosmopolitan cultural capital, but found that a fundraising campaign to erect a monument to Beethoven did not even meet advertising expenses. Berlioz's compositional method, the *ideé fixe* employed in his *Symphonie fantastique* (1830), deliberately combines a Beethoven-like unity with an extra-musical program, like that in Beethoven's *Sixth Symphony,* that might make daring new music accessible to the public. Richard Wagner, too, emulated the continuous unfolding of musical ideas in his *Leitmotiv* system of composition. The complex situation of the alienated artist who seeks to sell his output to a mass audience while living off the upper classes provided additional stimulus to Wagner's—and indeed most Romantics'—public image and self esteem.

Some other great late nineteenth-century composers sought to blend both the "absolute" and "program" music sides of Beethoven's legacy. Antonin Dvorak represented a Brahmsian vocation of "absolute" music and a nationalistic interest in furthering the folk music of his submerged Czech nation. The goal in such instances is the combination of democratic impulse with sophisticated product.

At the turn of the twentieth century, the eclectic Viennese symphonist Gustav Mahler seemed to have taken Beethoven's expansion, dissolution, and reconstruction of traditional forms to their logical conclusion. Richard Strauss, primarily known for his programmatic tone poems for orchestra, continued the Wagner line of combining music with other arts.

In the twentieth century, a "Second Viennese School" led by Arnold Schoenberg played a role analogous to that of the First Viennese School of Haydn, Mozart, and Beethoven a century before. Again musical habits were stretched beyond recognition in the name of further development of tradition. The Hungarian composer and ethnomusicologist Béla Bártok developed the compositional strategies inspired by Beethoven's late string quartets in combination with material derived from research into the traditional music springing from the ethnic traditions of central Europe. The search for cultural roots of submerged nationalities became a well-nigh universal cultural and political phenomenon that owes much to the romantic quest for the spontaneous outpouring of the human heart. The continuing irony is that Beethoven's meritocratic stance may be less egalitarian than elitist.

Overview of Biographical Sources

Beethoven's musical reputation became inseparable from his personal image. Together they fascinated the nineteenth-century Romantics and assumed a mythic stature that caused his biographers to hang on his every recorded syllable as much as on his every note. Two nineteenth century-studies of Beethoven's life remain among the bases of modern scholarship—A. W. Thayer, *Thayer's Life of Beethoven* (1866-1889), the first biographer to base his work on primary sources, and Franz Gerhard Wegeler, *Beethoven Remembered: the Biographical notes of Franz Wegeler and Ferdinand Ries* (1860). W. von Lenz, *Beethoven et ses trois styles* (Brussels: Stapleaux, 1852) elaborated the "three periods" interpretation of Beethoven's life and work begun during his lifetime. Subsequent great composers who felt a debt to Beethoven also wrote biographies or critical appreciations, which include Hector Berlioz, *Beethoven: a Critical Appreciation of Beethoven's Nine Symphonies and His Only Opera, "Fidelio," with its Four Overtures* (Boston: Crescendo, 1975; translated by Ralph De Sola). Berlioz includes such statements as "the only answer for the critic who reproaches the composer for having violated the law of unity is: So much the worse for the law." Franz Liszt, wrote in his *Letters* (1894) "The works for which I openly confess my admiration and predilection are for the most part amongst those which . . . are commonly described nowadays as belonging to Beethoven's last style (and which were, not long ago, with lack of reverence, explained by Beethoven's deafness and mental derangement.)" Richard Wagner, *Beethoven* (Leipzig: E. W. Fritsch, 1870) perhaps setting up a fictional ideal for his own autobiography spoke of Beethoven in terms traditionally reserved for the channels of supernatural Revelation, "The more he lost connection with the outer world, the clearer was his inward vision . . . A musician without hearing! could a blind painter be imagined? But we know of a blind Seer, Teiresias, to whom the phenomenal world was closed, but who, with inward vision, saw the basis of all phenomena."

In *Kreutzer Sonata,* Leo Tolstoy, ever suspicious about the dangers of a passion for art and artists wrote "On me, at least, this music had a devastating effect. It seemed to reveal to me entirely new feelings and capabilities of which I had been utterly unaware."

The appropriation of Beethoven by nationals pre-dates the establishment of a German state in 1870. Typical of a French musical skepticism which thereafter found that Germanic music-making and philosophizing takes itself all too seriously, is the satiric vein of the witty Parisian composer, Erik Satie, *Memoirs of an Amnesiac* (1912) "[Beethoven's] form and technique are always portentous. . . . As an artist he can easily stand up to any counterfeit attributed to him." But the German social theorist Theodore W. Adorno's many works pontificate that Beethoven is beyond ideology, "Beethoven does not bring about . . . synthesis. He tears asunder in time, as a power of dissociation, perhaps in order to perpetuate them for eternity." As music has long been thought to mirror interior states of soul, it is no surprise that, beginning in Vienna itself with Sigmund Freud himself—who professed to admire Beethoven even though he did not attend concerts, there have been dozens of psychoanalytic articles discussing the composer as exemplar of diverse psychological virtues and problems, including the law enforcement question of whether intervention in Beethoven's abusive childhood might have deprived us of his artistic profundity.

Early twentieth century treatments still showed the residues of the previous century's hero worship. Some of these include Romain Rolland's *Beethoven the Creator* (1929. Reprint. New York: Dover, 1964; translated by Ernest Newman), which is written in a tone of virtual worship, and R. H. Schauffler, *Beethoven: The Man Who Freed Music* (New York: Doubleday, 1929) which exemplifies the continued early twentieth-century idealization of Beethoven. And yet, the 1920s also saw the publication of Vincent D'Indy's excellent *Beethoven: A Critical Biography* (1926), one of the first objective treatments of both the life and the work.

In contrast, in this century there have still been a few harsh critics, usually polemics, such as Bishop Fan Stylian Noli, whose *Beethoven and the French Revolution* (New York: International, 1947) argue's unpersuasively that Beethoven's Romanticism and music about Napoleon spread Napoleon's immorality.

One of the best examinations of the transformation of Beethoven's reputation from mortal man to musical myth is Alexandra Comini's *The Changing Image of Beethoven: A Study in Mythmaking* (New York: Rizzoli, 1987), which examines the nineteenth and early twentieth century treatments, revealing Beethoven's mythological metamorphoses.

Recent biographies have offered a more scholarly, removed appreciation of Beethoven's life, stepping back from earlier hagiographies and toward a fuller, more realistic appreciation and interpretation of his character and work. Among these are George Marek's *Beethoven: A Biography* (1969), considered, upon its publication, the best since Thayer's; Solomon Maynard's *Beethoven* (1977), an impressive scholarly account; and Denis Mathews's *Beethoven* (London: Dent, 1985), a fine study of Beethoven's work that includes a lengthy biographical overview. Other important recent works include Martin Cooper's *Beethoven's Last Decade, 1817-1827* (1970), a philosophical examination of the end of his life; and Irving Kolodin's *The Interior Beethoven: A Biography of the Music* (1975), which studies how the music developed within Beethoven throughout his life.

Evaluation of Principal Biographical Sources

Bekker, Paul. *Beethoven.* 1925. Reprint. New York: AMS Press, 1972. (**A**) Translated and adapted from German by M. M. Bozman. One of the better early twentieth century works, Bekker's *Beethoven* is divided into two parts, the first a thorough biography, the second a study of the music. Considered the first modern biography.

Cooper, Martin. *Beethoven's Last Decade, 1817-1827.* London: Oxford University Press, 1970. (**A, G**) Takes the high road to connect Beethoven's more demanding compositions with the leading philosophical and theological currents of the era.

D'Indy, Vincent. *Beethoven: A Critical Biography.* 1926. Reprint. New York: Da Capo Press, 1970. (**A, G**) Considered the first modern biography, D'Indy's study broke new ground in scholarly analysis and as a retreat from the typical hagiography that had marked previous works. D'Indy divides Beethoven's life into three periods—his early life until 1801, his middle period, 1801-1815, and his later years, 1815-1827. In each, the music as well as the man are thoroughly examined in a readable, reasonable tone.

Kolodin, Irving. *The Interior Beethoven: A Biography of the Music*. New York: Alfred A. Knopf, 1975. (**A, G**) A fascinating study that examines the genesis of the music, and how the seeds for his great works were sown throughout his life. As an alternative biography, this works quite well, revealing in reverse how the music was shaped by the man. Kolodin's method included a close study of the sketchbooks, making this a worthwhile companion to those primary sources.

Marek, George R. *Beethoven: Biography of a Genius*. New York: Funk and Wagnalls, 1969. One of the best of this century's biographies, Marek's work is organized around universal themes such as love and family relationships. Examines Beethoven's style and substance as well as his temperament and talent.

Schindler, Anton Felix. *Beethoven as I Knew Him*. Edited by D. W. MacArdle. Translated by Constance S. Jolly. 1840. Rev. ed., 1966. Reprint: New York: W. W. Norton, 1972. (**A, G, Y**) Consists of the conversation books used by Beethoven when he became totally deaf. Published in 1840 they were retained selectively and sometimes falsified by the self-appointed aide, Schindler, who wanted to make the most of his relationship to the great man.

Solomon, Maynard. *Beethoven*. New York: Macmillan, 1977. (**A, G**) A full-fledged biography based on primary sources and a close study of contemporary accounts, Solomon's brings Beethoven to life in one of the best works ever written about the composer. Like some previous biographers, Solomon psychoanalyzes his subject, but not to the point of Freudian obsession. The best of recent biographies.

Thayer, A. W. *Ludwig van Beethoven's Leben*, vols. 1-3, edited by H. Dieters (Berlin: 1866-1879): vols. 4-5, edited by H. Riemann (Leipzig: 1907-1908). Published in English as *Thayer's Life of Beethoven*. 1921. Rev ed. 2 vols. Princeton: Princeton University Press, 1964, 1967. (**A, G**) Remains in its many editions the standard biography, by an American determined to base his biography directly upon primary sources. It was never completed, perhaps because the real Beethoven could not match the hagiographic image already so widespread.

Wegeler, Franz Gerhard. *Beethoven Remembered: the Biographical Notes of Franz Wegeler and Ferdinand Ries*. 1860. Reprint. Arlington, VA: Great Ocean

Publishers, 1987. (**A, G**) Ferdinand Ries, piano pupil of Beethoven for four years beginning in 1801 when Ries was seventeen, sets down his recollections in collaboration with Franz Gerhard Wegeler, son-in-law of Mme von Breuning. They report Beethoven's disdain for the normal routines of social relationships, whether in his sometimes violent relationships with his brothers or his single-minded devotion to his metier.

Overview and Evaluation of Primary Sources

Musical materials can present problems for research because they are not always catalogued under a uniform title system. Beethoven, Ludwig van. *Symphony no. 9, in D, op.* 125, may also be catalogued as the *Ninth Symphony, Choral Symphony,* or under other spellings according to the language(s) used by the publisher or cataloguer. Beethoven himself may sometimes be listed under ''Van Beethoven,'' or ''L. van Beethoven.'' Beethoven's music catalog is further complicated by the fact that, upon moving to Vienna, he overlooked his many previous compositions in order to begin numbering ''opus 1'' with the first piece he published there. He published several compositions simultaneously with different publishers in different countries in order to overcome the absence of international copyright agreements. Like most other composers, he mined his existing works for ideas to use in new music. These editorial problems fascinate specialists trying to learn how the great composer worked. There are three authoritative editions of Beethoven's musical compositions: *Werke: Vollständige kritisch durchgesehene überall Ausgabe* (24 - vols. Leipzig: Breitkopf und Härtel, 1861-1865; vol. 25, supplement 1888); *Sämtliche Werke: Supplemente zur Gesamtausgabe* (Wiesbaden: 1959-1971), a further supplement of music discovered and studied during the following century; and *Werke: neue Ausgabe sämtlicher Werke,* edited by Joseph Schmidt-Georg (Munich and Duisberg: Henle, 1961-), a new edition sponsored by the Beethoven-Haus and monument in Bonn.

Beethoven's sketchbooks, in which he kept notes and about his works in progress, are the subject of Douglas Porter Johnson's *The Beethoven Sketchbooks: History, Reconstruction, Inventory* (Berkeley: University of California Press, 1987; **A**), which reconstructs and reproduces a number of the sketchbooks that had been disassembled or destroyed over the years.

After falling deaf, Beethoven began carrying on conversations with acquaintances in a series of books he kept. His longtime friend Anton Felix Schindler reprinted a number of these, in an edited form, in his remembrance *Beethoven as I Knew Him* (1840. Rev. ed., 1966. Reprint: New York: W. W. Norton, 1972). They are not necessarily to be trusted, as Schindler's editing was designed to highlight his close relationship with Beethoven, often at the expense of others who may have also been mentioned in the books. Donald W. MacArdle's *An Index to Beethoven's Conversation Books* (Detroit, MI: Information Coordinators, 1962; **A**) covers the topics discussed in the conversation books.

Beethoven's letters, diaries and conversations also have appeared in a variety of other collections in this century, including such early collections as Friedrich Kerst's *Beethoven: The Man and the Artist, as Revealed in his Own Words* (New York: Huebsch, 1905; **A, G**), a composite autobiography created from diaries, letters and conversation books. *Beethoven's Letters*, edited by A. Eaglefield-Hull and translated by J. S. Shedlock (New York: Dutton, 1926), based on a collection published in 1909, arranged the letters chronologically, with explanatory notes added by A. C. Kalischer. In 1951, Michael Hamburger's short but excellent collection, *Beethoven: Letters, Journals and Conversations* (1951. Reprint. New York: Thames and Hudson, 1993; **A, G**) first appeared, providing a fine overview of the primary source writings, including new translations of the letters and journals. Donald MacArdle and Ludwig Misch's *New Beethoven Letters* (Norman: University of Oklahoma Press, 1955; **A, G, Y**) offered readers of earlier collections a new sampling of previously unpublished letters.

Emily Anderson edited and translated *The Letters of Beethoven* (3 vols. New York: Norton, 1985; **A, G**), the most thorough collection yet of the letters, with accompanying portraits of Beethoven and his correspondents.

Perhaps the best introduction to Beethoven through his primary sources is H. C. Robbins Landon's *Beethoven: A Documentary Study* (New York: Macmillan, 1970; **A, G, Y**), a lavish art-style book published to commemorate the bicentennial of Beethoven's death. It is overflowing with selections from Beethoven's letters and journals, as well as with hundreds of illustrations, including portraits, landscapes, and reproductions of his scores. The work was later adapted and revised as Landon's *Beethoven: His Life, Work and World* (New York: Thames & Hudson, 1992; **A, G, Y**).

Evaluation of Selected Critical Sources

Cooper, Barry, ed. *The Beethoven Compendium: A Guide to Beethoven's Life and Music.* London: Thames and Hudson, 1991. Has virtually all one could ask, including genealogical tables, a "who's who" of Beethoven's time, chronological tables, pictures, maps, and quotable quotes.

MacArdle, Donald W. *Beethoven Abstracts.* Detroit, MI: Information Coordinators, 1973. Abstracts articles about Beethoven from the eighteenth century through 1964 in four sections: primary periodicals, secondary periodicals, newspapers, and catalogs.

Nottebohm, Gustav. *Two Beethoven Sketchbooks* 1929. Reprint. London: Gollancz, 1979. Contains translations of Beethoven's musical sketchbooks, and analyzes the music in the light of the sketch books to show how painstaking work and reworking of basic ideas achieved results that sound spontaneous.

Repertoire international de littérature musi-cal/Repertoirum der Musik-literatur/ International Repertory of Music Literature (RILM Abstracts). New York: RILM, 1967. This contains an ongoing compilation of "Abstracts of all significant literature on music that has appeared since January 1, 1967. RILM is also available online through DIALOG and on CD-ROM. Has a companion thesaurus of terms.

Sadie, Stanley, ed. *The New Grove Dictionary of Music and Musicians.* 20 vols. London: Macmillan, 1980. Authoritative treatment and bibliography concerning Beethoven (and indeed all musical topics) are in this standard comprehensive music encyclopedia in English. The article on Beethoven is published as a separate paperback: *The New Grove Beethoven,* ed. Joseph Kerman. A complete list of Beethoven's musical works follows the biography. Then follows an extensive bibliography of his writings and the literature about him, beginning with a bibliography of bibliographies.

Tovey, Donald F. *Beethoven.* 1944. Reprint. London: Oxford, 1965. Exemplifies the school of musicology closer to music theory, which would study Beethoven's music in and for itself.

Tyson, Alan. *The Authentic English Editions of Beethoven.* London: Faber and Faber, 1963. Applies detailed bibliographical analysis to early nineteenth-century music printing, thereby making important revisions in the chronology of Beethoven's works.

Fiction and Adaptations

The aesthetic controversies over Beethoven's extra-musical image boil down to two: One is the continuing debate over Plato's suspicion of art and artists expressed in the *Republic,* which insists upon keeping the creative imagination subordinate to established norms; the other is question of Beethoven's appropriation by nationalistic partisans of the superiority of German culture. Both are well-exemplified in Robert Schumann's fictionalized essays from his days as a musical journalist, *On Music and Musicians* (New York: Pantheon, 1946), edited by Konrad Wolff, and translated by Paul Rosenfeld. In "The Poet and the Composer," Schumann treats the figure of "Ludwig" as having a musical talent superior to language.

The standard for Beethoven criticism and novelistic idealization of the artist as preternatural hero was set by E. T. A. Hoffmann's stories, such as those found loosely strung together in his fantasies, *E. T. A. Hoffmann's Musical Writings: "Kreisleriana"* (New York: Cambridge University Press, 1989). The fantasies, which became Hoffmann's "tales," to offer an analysis of Beethoven's music while asserting that the [*Fifth*] "Symphony in C minor irresistibly draws the listener in an ever-rising climax into the spirit-realm of the infinite."

Cinematic treatments of Beethoven include Abel Gance, *Un grand amour de Beethoven* (1936), the first film to use a sound-track, wherein the composer loves, loses, and almost regains his ideal woman only to be thwarted by his deafness, which causes him to write a reply that is mistakenly read by another lady.

Problematic aspects of the romantic cult of music in general and Beethoven in particular were faced in Anthony Burgess's novel (and subsequent film), *A Clockwork Orange* (1962), in which hearing the finale from the *Ninth Symphony* induces a sociopathic frenzy. Director Stanley Kubrick's film version of the book is relatively faithful, though sensationalized.

Walt Disney's *Fantasia* (1940. Reissue on home video, 1991) is a visually programmatic treatment of the *Sixth Symphony,* the "Pastorale." Paradoxically, the the music of the rebel Beethoven came to symbolize the high culture against which pop culture purports to rebel.

In the most literal sense, Beethoven's music and reputation as symbol for highbrow music have been adapted to popular culture. Contrast the respectful treatment of "Pathetique" by Jimmie Lunceford (1939) with Chuck Berry's, "Roll Over Beethoven" (Chess Records 1979); the same song was recorded by the Beatles in 1963.

Museums, Historical Landmarks, Societies

Because of the historic division among German-speaking lands, archives containing material concerning someone of Beethoven's stature are found in more than one place. Researchers would find useful guides to the principal Beethoven haunts, archives, and artifacts in these major repositories and exhibitions:

Beethoven-Haus (Bonn, Germany). Beethoven's birthplace, near the town hall, established at the time of German unification in 1870. Houses his pianos, portraits, letters, manuscripts, and the eartrumpet devices he used as hearing aids. Curates the Bodmer Collection, perhaps the world's greatest accumulation of Beethoven documents. There are two catalogs describing the collection: *Eine Schweizer Beethovensammlung,* edited by Max Unger (Zurich: Verlag der Corona, 1939), which lists hundreds of letters, music manuscripts, first editions, facsimile plates, index of names; and *Die Beethovenhandschriften des Beethovenhauses in Bonn,* listing 489 letters and documents in Beethoven's hand. Open to the public.

British Museum (London). The collection of materials is described in *Beethoven and England: An Account of Sources in the British Museum,* by Pamela J. Willetts (London: The Trustees of the British Museum, 1970).

Deutsche Staatsbibliothek (Berlin). *Die Beethoven-Sammlung in der Musikabteilung der Deutschen Staatsbibliothek* (Berlin: Deutsche Staatsbibliothek, 1970) is a well-organized bibliography of all types of material in the Beethoven collections of the then-East German State Library.

Gewandhaus Concert Hall (Leipzig). Holds a nude statue by Max Klinger made for the Seccessionist exhibition at the turn of the century in Vienna where Beethoven sits enthroned as a god. During the course of the nineteenth century, in according with phrenological theories, representations gave Beethoven an ever-increasing cranium.

Österreichische Nationalbibliothek (Vienna). *The Music Collection of the Austrian National Library*, by Franz Grasberger (Vienna: Federal Chancellery, Federal Press and Information Department, 1972) describes the Beethoven collection in Vienna.

Other Sources

Abraham, Gerald, ed. *The Age of Beethoven, The New Oxford History of Music,* Vol. 2. New York: Oxford University Press, 1982. Impressive, authoritative, and presuming readers of some education and wide cultivation.

Beethoven-Zentenarausstellung. *Führer durch die Beethoven Zentenarausstellung der Stadt Wien: "Beethoven und die Wiener Kultur seiner Zeit"*. Vienna: Selbstverlag der Gemeinde Wien, 1927. Exhibition catalog of 1,070 items, including letters documents, pictures, musical instruments, scores, and prints related to Beethoven and his circle in and around Vienna.

Donakowski, Conrad L. *A Muse for the Masses: Ritual and Music in an Age of Democratic Revolution, 1770-1870*. Chicago: University of Chicago Press, 1977. Sets the trends of the era in cultural and spiritual context.

Dorfmüller, Kurt. *Beiträge zur Beethoven Bibliographie. Studien und Materialen zum Werkverzeichnis von Kinsky-Halm*. Munich: G. Henle, 1978. Brings the catalogues up to date with more entries on various Opus and WoO (without an opus number) pieces.

Elvers, Rudolf, and Hans-Günter Klein, eds. *Ludwig van Beethoven 1770-1970. Autographe aus der Musikabteilung der Staatsbibliothek Preussischer Kulturbesitz.*

[Ausstellung 1-30 Dez., 1970 im Mendelssohn-Archiv der Staatsbibliothek]. Berlin-Dahlem: Staatsbibliothek Preussischer Kultur Besitz, 1970. Exhibition catalog of one of the more important collections of Beethoven sources, by the curator of the collection and one of the outstanding Beethoven scholars.

Gyimes, Ferenc, and Veronika Vavrineca, eds. *Ludwig van Beethoven: a magyar konyvtarakban es gyujtemenyekben. Bibliografia I-III.* 3 vols. Budapest: Allami Gorkij Konyvtar, 1970-1972. A union catalog of Beethoven documentation in Hungarian libraries. Hungary, part of the Habsburg Empire, contained the estates of some of Beethoven's aristocratic friends, whom he visited from time to time.

Hess, Willy. *Verzeichnis der nicht in der Gesamtausgabe veröffentlichten Werke Ludwig van Beethovens.* Wiesbaden: Breitkopf und Härtel, 1957. Catalogues the musical compositions not in the collected edition (Gesamtausgabe).

Kinsky, G., and H. Halm. *Das Werk Beethovens.* Munich and Duisberg: Henle, 1955. The standard catalogue of Beethoven's music.

Lang, Paul Henry. *The Creative World of Beethoven.* New York: W. W. Norton, 1971. A masterful combination of the study of music with cultural history.

Raeburn, Michael, and Alan Kendall, eds. *The Heritage of Music,* Vol. II, *The Romantic Era.* New York: Oxford University Press, 1990. Lavishly illustrated essays on topics in and around the music of Beethoven's time. Lacks a bibliography.

Sterba, Edith, and Richard Sterba. *Beethoven and His Nephew: A Psychoanalytic Study of Their Relationship.* 1954. Reprint. New York: Schocken, 1971. Translated from German by Willard R. Trask. The authors find much to criticize in the composer's character and in his difficult relationship with his nephew Karl.

Conrad L. Donakowski
Michigan State University

Jeremy Bentham
1748-1832

Chronology

Born Jeremy Bentham on February 15, 1748, in London, England, the son of an attorney; spends childhood mainly at his two grandmothers' country houses, and gains a reputation for writing verse in Greek and Latin; *1760-1763* studies at Queen's College, Oxford, then enters Lincoln's Inn to study law; *1776* publishes *A Fragment on Government* which criticizes Sir William Blackstone's *Commentaries* for its antipathy to reform; *1781-1785* becomes acquainted with Lord Shelburne; spends much of this period writing what is later published in French as *Theorie des peines et des recompenses* (1811) and in English as *The Rationale of Reward* (1825) and *The Rationale of Punishment* (1830); *1785-1788* visits his brother, Samuel Bentham, in Russia, and while there writes *Defence of Usury* (1787); *1788* returns to England with the hope of a political career; this failing, turns to the study of the principles of legislation; *1789* publishes *An Introduction to the Principles of Morals and Legislation*, a work that has taken him many years to complete; *1792* due to his spreading fame, is made a French citizen; *1809* writes *A Catechism of Parliamentary Reform* (published 1817); *1818* drafts a series of resolutions that are introduced in the House of Commons; *1823* helps found the *Westminster Review* in order to spread the principles of philosophic radicalism; *1830* publishes one volume of his *Constitutional Code*; *1832* dies on June 6 in London, while writing his *Constitutional Code*, which is never finished.

Activities of Historical Significance

Jeremy Bentham began addressing issues of legal, penal, and political reform shortly after the American Revolution (1776-1783) and prior to the French Revolution (1789-1799). This political upheaval created a climate receptive to Bentham's reform ideas, although no country adopted his code of laws.

In his economic thought Bentham followed a largely laissez-faire philosophy.

Defence of Usury (1787) went beyond Adam Smith in arguing that because each individual can best judge his own interest, the public good demands that this principle be extended to the matter of money loaned at interest. His "Manual of Political Economy," published in *Theorie de peines et des recompenses* (1811), presented a lengthy list of prohibitions against state activity in the economic realm.

Ethical theory was a more significant element of Bentham's thought. He fought against the two dominant ethical viewpoints of his time: that all human activity is based on self-interest and that moral rules are binding regardless of their results. He sought instead a basis for moral judgement that was purely objective. He concluded that one could speak of measurable units of pleasure or pain which could then be calculated to determine the relative value of any action. This position became known as utilitarianism, and it provided the basis for his contribution to political reform. Bentham posited that all legislation could be evaluated through a "felicific calculus." This method could, he believed, precisely determine the amount of pleasure and pain produced within society by any particular legislative action. Because human beings are motivated by pleasure and pain, the utility principle, he argued, provided a rational guide to the best social legislation. He spelled out this theory in *An Introduction to the Principles of Morals and Legislation* (1789).

Bentham also gave considerable attention to the codification of law and the reform of prisons. He corresponded with European and American leaders, hoping to receive an appointment to prepare a code of laws for a specific nation. In *Panopticon* (1791) he proposed a model prison system which he thought would improve the morals, health, intellect, and industriousness of prisoners and he later suggested other reforms in the administration of British justice. Although Bentham had little direct effect on legislation during his lifetime, his work with James Mill in founding the *Westminster Review* (1824-1914) provided a means for spreading the ideas of "philosophic radicalism," as his concepts became known. The "Philosophic Radicals," sometimes called Benthamites, in Parliament systematized public relief of the destitute in the Poor Law Amendment Act (1834) and reformed the governments of towns and cities through the Municipal Corporation Act (1835).

Many of Bentham's writings were published only after friends rewrote his memoranda. Etienne Dumont of Geneva compiled his *Theories des Peines et des Recompenses* (1811), which was later translated into English. John Stuart Mill prepared the five-volume *Rationale of Judicial Evidence* (1827) and Peregrine Bingham strengthened *The Book of Fallacies* (1824).

Overview of Biographical Sources

Because Bentham's life was generally uneventful, most studies have concentrated on his thought rather than his biography. Volumes ten and eleven of *The Works of Jeremy Bentham* (1843), edited by Sir John Bowring, contain Bentham's memoirs and correspondence, which provide a starting place for research. John Stuart Mill's essay ''Bentham'' (1832) set the tone for most nineteenth-century opinion. Mill argued that Bentham's originality lay in his introduction of precise, analytical thought into moral and political philosophy. Most subsequent interpretations, however, emphasize Bentham's significance in jurisprudence and politics rather than moral issues.

C. B. R. Kent, *The English Radicals* (1899), called Bentham a law reformer while Leslie Stephen, *The English Utilitarians* (London: Duckworth, 1900), described him as a theorist of legislation who did not need philosophy. Similar viewpoints also appeared in Ernest Albee, *A History of English Utilitarianism* (New York: Macmillan, 1902); A. Seth Pringle-Pattison, *The Philosophical Radicals* (London: Duckworth, 1907); John MacCunn, *Six Radical Thinkers* (London: E. Arnold, 1910); and J. L. Stocks, *Jeremy Bentham* (Manchester, England: Manchester University Press, 1933).

C. K. Ogden in *Jeremy Bentham, 1832-2032* (London: K. Paul, Trench, Trubner, 1932), sought to rescue Bentham's reputation as a philosopher by predicting that his greatest influence was still to come. David Baumgardt's *Bentham and the Ethics of Today* (1952. Reprint. New York: Octagon, 1966) perhaps fulfilled Ogden's prediction by arguing for Bentham's significance as an ethicist. Recent studies, however, have continued to see Bentham primarily in political and legal terms.

Evaluation of Principal Biographical Sources

Atkinson, Charles Milner. *Jeremy Bentham: His Life and Work.* 1905. Reprint.

Westport, CT: Greenwood Press, 1970. (**G**) Chapters 1 through 8 present a biographical sketch of Bentham's life, organized chronologically. Extracts from the "Historical Preface to the Fragment on Government" appear on pages 58-71. Chapter 9 gives an overview of Bentham's ideas. Atkinson argues that Bentham had an exaggerated faith in the principle of utility as a means of resolving moral, political, and legal problems. He concludes that Bentham's primary contribution lay in legal reform.

Crimmins, James E. *Secular Utilitarianism: Social Science & the Critique of Religion in the Thought of Jeremy Bentham.* New York: Oxford University Press, 1990. (**A**) This volume, which examines Bentham's attempt to understand religion scientifically, is divided into three parts. Part One analyzes the utilitarian effort to develop a science of society. Part Two looks at controversies revolving around the Church of England as the established church. Part Three describes Bentham's views of natural and revealed religion. In contrast with Mack and Steintrager, who understand Bentham's religious views in terms of their political function, Crimmins argues that they must be understood as part of Bentham's effort to develop and apply his principle of utility. Appendix B reprints Bentham's account of a "dream," much of which paraphrases biblical language.

Everett, C. W. *Education of Jeremy Bentham.* New York: Columbia University Press, 1931. (**A**) The author examines the first forty years of Bentham's life, concentrating on the events, friendships, and acquaintances that helped shape his thought. The volume is particularly interesting because it prints extracts from Bentham's letters to his brother Samuel. It also discusses Bentham's education from childhood through early manhood, emphasizing particularly his study of the physical sciences. The book's primary value lies in its more broadly human, rather than strictly intellectual, view of Bentham.

Harrison, Ross. *Bentham.* London: Routledge and Kegan Paul, 1983. (**A**) Harrison argues that Bentham's major works in political and moral theory should be understood within the context of his analysis of sense and nonsense. Although providing little biographical information, the book identifies Bentham's key arguments and contains a useful "Note on Texts."

Long, Douglas G. *Bentham on Liberty: Jeremy Bentham's Idea of Liberty in Relation to His Utilitarianism.* Toronto: University of Toronto Press, 1977. (**A**) This study of Bentham's philosophy is divided into three parts. Part One examines the enlightenment background to Bentham's thought. Part Two studies Bentham's terminology and basic concepts. Part Three addresses the development and application of Bentham's philosophy. Long argues that Bentham's passion was the pursuit of happiness and security through order. He produced, therefore, "an illiberal defence of liberty." The author suggests that Bentham was an eighteenth-century prototype of the modern social theorist.

Mack, Mary P. *Jeremy Bentham: An Odyssey of Ideas.* New York: Columbia University Press, 1963. (**A**) Mack presents the most thorough biographical study of Bentham beginning with his birth in 1748 and ending in 1792. Believing Bentham to be both misunderstood and undervalued, the author argues that he created a general method for analyzing all aspects of human life. She states that the French Revolution played the decisive role in making Bentham a full-fledged democrat and parliamentary reformer. The appendices contain excerpts from Bentham's political writings. Due to Mack's untimely death, a projected second volume did not appear.

Manning, D. J. *The Mind of Jeremy Bentham.* New York: Barnes and Noble, 1968. (**A**) The author analyzes Bentham's ideas in both a social-political and intellectual context, organizing his work thematically. Although Manning has little interest in Bentham's theories, he believes that his prescriptive writing remains significant, for it anticipated much of the modern welfare state. Manning argues that Bentham's prescriptions arose from a common-sense understanding of the social changes taking place in his time and that he developed the elements of a post-Hobbesian philosophy of state.

Steintrager, James. *Bentham.* Ithaca, NY: Cornell University Press, 1977. (**A**) Steintrager has written a largely intellectual biography, although organized thematically. He argues that Bentham was unable to define progress within a utilitarian ethic but was tenacious in pursuing such issues as opinion and truth, democracy and science, and the common person and the experts. The author believes that Bentham significantly affected the direction of nineteenth-century British politics.

He states that Bentham's relationship to the Church of England caused him deep distress and produced hostility to religion. He also notes that Bentham's thought and utilitarianism are not identical.

Overview and Evaluation of Primary Sources

Collections of Bentham's manuscripts are located in the British Museum, London; University College, London; and the University of Geneva. A. Taylor Milne prepared his *Catalogue of the Manuscripts of Jeremy Bentham in the Library of University College, London* (1937. Reprint. London: Athlone Press, 1962; **A**). The most commonly available, though often inaccurate, collection is John Bowring, ed., *The Works of Jeremy Bentham* (11 vols. 1838-1843. Reprint. New York: Russell and Russell, 1962; **A, G**). A useful guide to the rather disorganized Bowring edition appears in David Lyons, *In the Interest of the Governed* (Oxford: Oxford University Press, 1973; **A**) and is reprinted in Nancy L. Rosenblum, *Bentham's Theory of the Modern State* (Cambridge: Harvard University Press, 1978; **A**). A new complete and scholarly edition of Bentham's writings under the general editorship of J. H. Burns, *The Collected Works of Jeremy Bentham* (London: Athlone Press, 1968-; **A**), is being published, although Oxford University Press has recently taken over the project. This ongoing effort includes both correspondence and individual works.

A number of critical editions of various Bentham writings have also appeared. C. K. Ogden argues for Bentham's continuing philosophical significance, particularly in language, in his introductions to *The Theory of Legislation* (New York: Harcourt, Brace, 1931; **A**) and *Bentham's Theory of Fictions* (1931. Reprint. Paterson, NJ: Littlefield, Adams, 1959; **A**). Bentham's legal views appear in C. W. Everett, ed., *A Comment on the Commentaries: A Criticism of William Blackstone's Commentaries on the Laws of England* (1938. Reprint. New York: Columbia University Press, 1945; Aalen, Germany: Scientia Verlag, 1976; **A**). Harold A. Larrabee attempts to clarify Bentham's tortured English in his edition of *Bentham's Handbook of Political Fallacies* (Baltimore: Johns Hopkins University Press, 1952; **A**).

Bentham's economic concerns receive attention in W. Stark, ed., *Jeremy Bentham's Economic Writings: Critical Edition Based on His Printed Works and*

Unprinted Manuscripts (3 vols. London: George Allen and Unwin, 1952; **A**). The lengthy introductory essays provide historical background but do not try to analyze the documents. W. H. Harrison provides critical editions of *A Fragment on Government* (Oxford: Basil Blackwell, 1960; **A**) and *The Principles of Morals and Legislation* (Oxford: Basil Blackwell, 1960; **A**). J. H. Burns and H. L. A. Hart argue in their edition of *A Fragment on Government* (Cambridge: Cambridge University Press, 1977; **A**) that Bentham provides an instructive example of an attempt to develop an account of law and government from independent rational principles. Although their introduction is new, the text of *A Fragment on Government* is the same as that appearing in the *Collected Works of Jeremy Bentham*. A student-oriented collection of Bentham's writings appears in Mary Mack, ed., *A Bentham Reader* (New York: Pegasus, 1969; **A, G**).

Museums, Historical Landmarks, Societies

National Portrait Gallery (London). Houses the portrait of Bentham by H. W. Pickersgill and other portraits.

University College (London). Anatomical Museum contains Bentham's skeleton.

Other Sources

Brinton, Crane. *English Political Thought in the 19th Century*. 1933. Reprint. New York: Harper and Row, 1962. Chapter one contains an extended discussion of Bentham, suggesting that he never understood the utilitarianism he had created.

Halévy, Elie. *The Growth of Philosophic Radicalism*. London: Faber and Faber, 1928. A critical analysis of Bentham's thought by an astute French student of English history.

Hart, H. L. A. *Essays on Bentham: Studies in Jurisprudence and Political Theory*. Oxford: Clarendon Press, 1982. Collected essays by one of the foremost Bentham scholars.

Himmelfarb, Gertrude. *Victorian Minds*. New York: Alfred A. Knopf, 1968. The chapter titled ''The Haunted House of Jeremy Bentham'' suggests that, contrary to dominant scholarly opinion, nineteenth-century English political reform was brought about by other men with other ideas than those of Bentham and his followers.

Keeton, George W., and Georg Schwarzeberger. *Jeremy Bentham and the Law: A Symposium*. London: Stevens and Sons, 1947. Contains thirteen essays on Bentham's thought and influence.

Leavis, F. R. *Mill On Bentham and Coleridge*. London: Chatto and Windus, 1950. Includes Mill's influential essay on Bentham. Introduction provides a literary perspective on Mill's analysis.

Monro, D. H. ''Utilitarianism.'' In *Dictionary of the History of Ideas Studies of Selected Pivotal Ideas*, edited by Philip P. Wiener, vol. 4. New York: Charles Scribner's Sons, 1973. Provides a succinct overview of Bentham's ideas and influence.

Parekh, Bhikhu. *Jeremy Bentham: Ten Critical Essays*. London: Frank Cass, 1974. A collection of nineteenth- and twentieth-century essays.

Stephen, Leslie, and Sidney Lee, eds. ''Bentham, Jeremy.'' In *Dictionary of National Biography*. Vol. 2. London: Oxford University Press, 1917. Describes Bentham as a writer on jurisprudence who pursued truth single-mindedly.

Gary Land
Andrews University

Nicholai Berdyaev
1874-1948

Chronology

Born Nicholai Aleksandrovitch Berdyaev on March 6, 1874, in Kiev, Russia, son of Alexander Michailovitch Berdyaev, a member of the military aristocracy, and of Princess Alexandra Sergeevna Kudasheffa, daughter of Prince Serge Kudasheeff, Court Chamberlin; grows up in aristocratic household and learns to read in three languages; *1884-1890* spends six years in the Cadet Corpus in Kiev in preparation for career as an army officer; dislikes school intensely and is a poor student, but studies philosophy on the side; reads Immanuel Kant, Georg Hegel, and the German religious mystics, Jakob Boehme and Meister Eckhart; *1890* leaves the Cadet Corpus, and studies for three years to pass qualifying examination for the University of Kiev; *1894* enters University of Kiev to study natural sciences, but pursues his own philosophical interests; joins the Social Democratic Party shortly after entering; *1898* arrested along with one hundred and fifty other members of the Social Democratic Party after an older member, Peter Struve, publishes a manifesto; taken with the others to the Lukianovski prison near Kiev, but is treated leniently because of family connections in the upper nobility; *1900* sentenced after a two year deliberation to a three-year exile in the northern province of Vologda; publishes his first article, "F. A. Lange and Critical Philosophy, in its Relation to Socialism" (1899) in the interval between arrest and sentencing; corresponds with German socialist leader Karl Kautsky for a time, but is too idealistic in his beliefs for the revisionist Marxist; settles in the city of Vologda during his exile; *1901* writes his first book, *Subjectivism and Individualism in Social Philosophy*, an attempt to integrate Kantian idealism and Marxist theory; *1903* enrolls for a semester in the University of Heidelberg, and takes a class with Wilhelm Windelband, who is reviving an interest in Kant; *1904* present at Schaffhausen in Switzerland when the Union of Liberation is organized with the object of providing Russia with freedom backed by a constitution; renews acquaintance with Serge Bulgakov whom he had known in his student days, and learns that Bulgakov has abandoned Marxism for Christianity, a direction he also is taking;

marries Lydia Trusheff; moves to St. Petersburg where he and Bulgakov take over the editorship of *The New Way*; *1905* begins a new magazine, *Life's Problems*, which is also dedicated to philosophical religious questions after *The New Way* fails; attends meetings held by novelist Dimitri Merezhkovsky and his wife, poet Zinaida Hippias; undergoes a period of crisis, but his spiritual life develops; *1907* after a summer in the country, moves to Moscow; becomes a Christian and joins the Russian Orthodox Church (the date is somewhat uncertain); gives a public lecture on Dostoevsky's "Legend of the Grand Inquisitor," and says that in this story presents the image of Christ he prefers; publishes *Sub-Specie Aeternitatis* explaining the religious foundations of his thinking; *1907-1908* spends winter in Paris and is active as a lecturer/debater in the Religious-Philosophical Society, which is in his words "a spiritual reform effort"; *1910* publishes *The Spiritual Crisis of the Intelligentsia*, in which he defends his religious views against the ideas of his secular and religious contemporaries; *1912* publishes *A. S. Khomyakov*, a study of an earlier poet/philosopher whose views were similar to his; visits Italy; inspired by the beauty of Renaissance art, begins writing what he considers to be his most important book, *The Meaning of the Creative Act*; *1913* writes "Quenchers of the Spirit," an attack on the Holy Synod and is arrested, with all copies of the article confiscated; charged with blasphemy, he is automatically exiled to Siberia for life; *1914* his case is annulled due to the Revolution; *1916* publishes *The Meaning of the Creative Act* which contains all of the ideas of his mature philosophy, but the book is only partially a study of art because he expounds on the idea that men share with God the ability to create an aspect of their spiritual freedom, and is essential to the understanding of historical progress; *1917* takes no active part in the February Revolution, but becomes, for a short time, a member of the Council of the Republic in the newly proclaimed Republic under Kerensky; *1918* establishes the Free Academy of Spiritual Culture in Moscow where he lectures on religious subjects; *1920-1921* arrested for discussing controversial topics in meetings at his home; questioned by Felix Dzerzhinsky, the founder of the Cheka, the first Soviet secret police organization and released; becomes a professor of philosophy at Moscow University; *1922* arrested again by the Cheka, and exiled; received cordially by Germans in Berlin, but he and seventy other exiles are viewed with suspicion by the Russian émigrés; becomes dean of the newly founded Russian Scientific Institute where he teaches ethics and the history of Russian thought; *1923* helps establish the Religious-Philosophical Academy, which is financed by the Y.M.C.A.; publishes *Dostoevsky*, a study of the novelist's Christian philosophy to which he owes much of his own thinking; publishes *The Philosophy of Inequality*, written before his exile, a passionate attack on the Soviet regime, and *The Meaning of History*, also written earlier, expressing his growing interest in the destiny of man; *1924* publishes *The New Middle Ages*, the first of his works to attract world-wide attention: in it he insists that mankind has entered a new and terrible Middle Ages, and challenges men everywhere to fight the powers of darkness; moves to Paris because of economic conditions in Germany; *1925* edits *Put*; *1926* organizes ecumenical meetings, which include Jacques Maritain, Gabriel Marcel and many other notable Frenchmen; *1928* inherits money from a friend, Florence West, and buys a house in Clamart; publishes *Leontieff*, a biography of Constantine Leotieff, another aristocratic writer of religious subjects; *1927-1939* writes more than ten books and sixty articles for *Put*; speaks and debates frequently at conferences, condemning National Socialism as worse than the repressive communism of the Bolsheviks; publishes *The Destiny of Man* (1931), and *The Fate of Man in the Modern World* (1934), in which he argues that the combined will of God and free men will usher in the heavenly kingdom; publishes *Slavery and Freedom* (1939), the clearest explication of his philosophy; *1940* leaves Clamart to seek refuge in Pilat near Arcachon after the fall of France, but Pilat also becomes occupied by the Germans after his arrival and he returns to Clamart; interrogated several times by Gestapo agents, but never charged; *1942* undergoes an operation after becoming ill; writes *The Divine and the Human* during the war years; *1945* wife dies; *1947* finishes his autobiography *Dream and Reality* (published 1949); receives an honorary degree from Cambridge University; *1948* dies March 24, sitting at his writing desk in Clamart; three books are published posthumously, *Self-Knowledge* (1949), *The Realm of Spirit and the Realm of Caesar* (1949), and *Truth and Revelation* (1953).

Activities of Historical Significance

Nicolai Berdyaev realized even as a teenager that the world was radically changing, that the era of his class, the aristocratic landowners in Russia, was ending. Despite the attempts of the czarist government to maintain rigid controls over the country, social changes were already evident. At fourteen Berdyaev had begun reading philosophy and was to become a convinced Kantian. But Kant's idealism like that of Hegel, whose works Berdyaev read later, did not give sufficient scope to the individual human personality. By the time he entered the University of Kiev he was much more advanced than his fellow students in his thinking. He joined the Marxists and became a member of the Social Democratic Party because he believed that Marx's analysis of capitalism was essentially correct, although he did not accept Marx's views on materialism. In the eyes of the authorities, however, he was a radical, and he was eventually arrested and exiled. During his exile in Volgda (1901-1903), he gradually turned from Marxism to a more spiritual position in philosophy. He was not yet ready to commit himself to any Christian church, but the appeal of the Russian Orthodox Church was beginning to influence him. He defended his spiritual ideas in debate with the convinced Marxist, A. V. Lunacharsky, with whom, even after the 1917 revolution, he remained on good terms. A descendent of generations of military aristocrats, Berdyaev, in a sense, carried on the family tradition by being a fierce polemicist whether in debate or in his writings. During the two revolutions of 1905 and 1907 he participated in political meetings, but always with the awareness that the ideology of such movements was wrong. Russia, he felt, had to go through these terrible periods of social upheaval because it had allowed itself to turn away from its true mission as a spiritual leader of the nations. This was God's terrible judgment, but the country would finally turn to its true vocation. Berdyaev had become a religious mystic, and would remain one. His philosophy, too, was formed by the time of the revolution of 1917, and he declared himself a Russian Orthodox Christian.

Berdyaev's philosophy is founded in the belief that intuition is a better judge of reality than logic. God, who represents the real truth about the human personality, freedom and the supreme values, is out of reach of the rational processes used in analytical philosophy, which was the prevailing mode of twentieth century thinking. Immanuel Kant, Berdyaev's philosophical mentor, distinguished between the noumenal, ultimate reality impenetrable by the intellect, and the phenomenal, the more superficial outward manifestations of reality. This provided Berdyaev with a foundation for his metaphysics, although Berdyaev disagreed with Kant's insistence that ultimate truths were unknowable. Berdyaev argued that they could be grasped by intuition; his confidence in the powers of his intuitions was unshakable.

The concept of freedom was for Berdyaev his chief philosophical concern since it was for him the foundation of the individual human being's personality, insisting that freedom in its origins must be absolutely unconditioned. He adapted mystical philosopher Jakob Boehme's (1575-1624) concept of the *Ungrund* to express the primacy of freedom over that of being itself. The *Ungrund* is the dark, primordial source of both God and freedom, and accordingly of the will for good and evil. God did not create freedom, but was himself produced in the *Ungrund*. God, then, could not interfere with the freedom of any human personality. Berdyaev argued that God is not omnipotent, which became the most controversial idea in his metaphysics as far as Christian theologians are concerned. Berdyaev's critics responded by asking how could such a limited God create the world? Berdyaev's reply was that the creation lies beyond rational demonstrations as do all intuitively grasped ideas.

Berdyaev invented the term "objectification" to explain the source of the problem of evil. History began when the human imagination allowed itself to ignore its natural free condition, and started thinking of itself as an object in a world of objects, to treat humans not as ends in themselves but as means to ends. Humans became pawns in military ventures, cogs in industrial machinery, or mere instruments in the employ of all powerful states. Kant, who is the source of this idea, argued that every human being should be treated as an end unto himself, not as a means to an end. In his *Critique of Practical Reason* Kant called this the "categorical imperative." Berdyaev took Kant's idea another step, postulating that history is the record of humankind's struggle to throw off the effects of objectification and resume the free existence which is its natural right. Complete victory can come only after history has ended. For this reason, Berdyaev calls himself a "metahistorian" because he is primarily interested in the origin of history and coming of the Kingdom of God after history has ended. Both of these developments are beyond the usual scope of history.

At no time in history have people been reduced to objects as systematically as in the totalitarian state of the twentieth century, and he insists that no human ideal can ever be fully realized in the historic process. The victors of revolutions try to eliminate the last vestige of freedom in their states. Berdyaev saw history as the gradual working out of the divine plan, a view resulting from his turning to Christianity after his involvement with radical politics. Taking some suggestions from a medieval mystic philosopher, Joachim de Floris (ca. 1130-1201), he divided history into three epochs which correspond to the three Persons of the Trinity: the

Epoch of the Law (God the Father), the Epoch of Redemption (Christ), and the Epoch of Creativity (the Holy Spirit). The coming of Christ is the central event in history because He enabled the human personality to cooperate with God to bring history to an end. The Orthodox Church never accepted the total depravity of man, nor does it believe that divine revelation ended with the scriptures. Berdyaev believed that the Christ presented by Feodor Dostoevsky in his parable "The Legend of the Grand Inquisitor" (*The Brothers Karamazov,* Book V, Chapter V) supplements the Gospel records. This great liberator of the human spirit is the one he accepts most fully. This Christ returns to Earth in the sixteenth century, performs a few miracles, and preaches his message of freedom. He is soon arrested by the Grand Inquisitor who is convinced that men function best as slaves, and do not really want freedom. He will have Jesus burned at the stake on the following day. Berdyaev in his books is battling the followers of the Grand Inquisitor who have made their impact on the twentieth century in such a terrible fashion.

Berdyaev defied the czarist regime, the Holy Synod of the Orthodox Church, and later the officials of Lenin's government in his lectures and writings. He seemed to be almost fearless. When his sister-in-law, Eugenie Rapp, warned him to be careful, he replied, "it would be better to be honest and die before a firing squad, than to be careful and die in your bed." He had accused the Holy Synod of failing completely to meet the spiritual needs of the Russian People. His Free Academy of Spiritual Culture survived for three years under the Bolsheviks and enabled him to bring his religious ideas to the capacity audiences who regularly attended the lectures. As a result, Berdyaev was arrested and banished from Russia, a tragic event for the philosopher who was still convinced that the country would again become Holy Russia before the Epoch of Creation was realized. Russian philosophers and writers had been declaring their faith in "Holy Russia" since the fifteenth century, and Berdyaev, Russian to the core, shared this conviction that the country had a messianic role to play in history.

Exile made of Berdyaev an even more prolific writer. During the two years spent in Germany he published his *Dostoevsky* (1923) based on lectures he had delivered at the Free Academy of Spiritual Culture, which explains his reasons for making Dostoevsky his spiritual mentor. *The Meaning of History* (1923), also written in Russia, is at once a commentary of recent events in Russia, and a fuller explication of his philosophy of history. Under the auspices of the American Y.M.C.A., Berdyaev formed the Religious Philosophical Society, an ecumenical organization which functioned much as his Free Academy in Moscow had done. For Berdyaev the West needed spiritual instruction, too, because capitalism still treated people as machines. The Y.M.C.A. also funded a new magazine, *Put* (The Way), which provided Berdyaev with another means of spreading religious ideas. It also undertook the publication of Berdyaev's books in their original Russian.

Many of the Russian émigrés in Germany were hostile to Berdyaev. These were arch conservatives who considered him too radical. When he moved to Paris, he encountered more opposition at the Academy of St. Sergius at the time the only remaining seminary for the Russian Orthodox Church. The professors and priests there remembered his article "The Quenchers of the Spirit" all too well, and had read passages in his books that denied the Church any special role in dispensing of God's grace. The faculty at St. Sergius were especially infuriated because Berdyaev had become the best known Russian thinker in the West, and was considered by many to be a spokesperson for the Church itself.

In some ways Berdyaev seemed to thrive on opposition. Most of his books have passages in which he attacks the enemies of freedom. Over half of his total output of thirty books were written in exile. Indifferent to literary style, he rarely proofread his books. As a result, they tend to be repetitive. Each of them, however, contains insights into the subjects which preoccupied his interest. Whether his metaphysics are tenable depends on the temperament of the individual reader, but his thoughts cannot fail to offer genuine enlightenment on the human condition.

Overview of Biographical Sources

While he continues to have readers, academic interest in Berdyaev and his philosophy was most intense from the late 1940s through the 1960s when Existentialism was enjoying its greatest vogue. In 1950, three biographies were published: O. F. Clarke, *Introduction to Berdyaev*; George Seaver, *Berdyaev*; and Matthew Spinka, *Nicholas Berdyaev: Captive of Freedom*. The first two, while useful, are in no sense definitive studies. Spinka's book is a much fuller account of Berdyaev's life, and provides a good analysis of his philosophy.

In the 1960s, Donald A. Lowrie wrote the definitive biography, *Rebellious Prophet: A Life of Nicolai Berdyaev*. Lowrie, an official with the Y.M.C.A., knew and worked with Berdyaev twenty-four years. *An Apostle of Freedom: The Life and Teaching of Nicholas Berdyaev* (1960), although a less scholarly work, is interesting because its author, Michael A. Vallon, fought in the French Underground during World War II and brings a special perspective to the biography.

Some books give brief accounts of Berdyaev's life along with an analysis of his philosophy. V. V. Zenkovsky's well-known *A History of Russian Philosophy* (1953) presents a rather negative analysis of both Berdyaev and his philosophy. In 1968 three studies of Berdyaev appeared that also dealt with his life: C. S. Calian *Berdyaev's Philosophy of Hope: A Contribution to Marxist-Christian Dialogue* explains why Berdyaev was attracted to Marxism and continued to admire Marx as a thinker; George L. Kline, *Religious and Anti-Religious Thought in Russia,* places Berdyaev in the tradition of Dostoevsky, Solovev and other Russian religious thinkers; and David Bonner Richardson, *Berdyaev's Philosophy of History: An Existentialist Theory of Social Creativity and Eschatology* examines the philosopher's views of history and aesthetics.

In 1978 a colloquium was held at the Paris Institute of Slavic Studies during which certain less familiar aspects of Berdyaev's thought were treated in a number of papers. The essays were published soon afterward, entitled *Colloque Berdiaev* (Paris: Institut d'Etudes Slaves, 1978). In 1982, Douglas Kellog Wood in *Men Against Time: Nicolas Berdyaev, T. S. Eliot, Aldous Huxley, and C. G. Jung* places Berdyaev first in a book which shows how these authors tried to transcend time through their mystical beliefs.

Evaluation of Principal Biographical Sources

Calian, C. S. *Berdyaev's Philosophy of Hope: A Contribution to Marxist-Christian Dialogue.* Minneapolis, MN: Augsburg, 1968. (**A**) The book's purpose is to reveal the significance of eschatology in Berdyaev's thought. Communism is a mixture of truth and falsehoods. Russian communism is a distortion of the Russian messianic idea. Berdyaev believed that light from the East was destined to enlighten the bourgeois darkness of the West. Calian explains the initial attraction of Marxism for Berdyaev and why he never completely repudiated Marx.

Clarke, Oliver Fielding. *Introduction to Berdyaev.* London: Geoffrey Bles, 1950. (**G**) A brief survey of Berdyaev's life and thought, this book presents the philosopher as a very fair-minded critic of Russian communism by someone convinced that it was also a divine judgment on the failures of the old regime. Argues that the greatness of Berdyaev is that he sees both the inevitability of the Soviet period and at the same time its transcendence in the name of God and human freedom.

Copleston, Frederick C. *Philosophy in Russia.* Notre Dame, IN: Search Press, University of Notre Dame, 1986. (**A**) Argues that the failures of the Russian Orthodox Church to apply Christian principles to contemporary problems formed part of the background of the renaissance of religious philosophy at the turn of the century, and that Berdyaev was part of this movement. Copleston, a noted Jesuit scholar, says that Berdyaev is a thoroughly Russian thinker who often refers to his country's history and tries to explain the Russian mind for the benefit of Western readers unfamiliar with the traditions of the Eastern Church. Includes a good bibliography.

Davy, M. M. *Nicholas Berdyaev: Man of the Eighth Hour.* London: Geoffrey Bles, 1967.(**G**) A sympathetic treatment of Berdyaev's thinking by someone who agrees with his mystical outlook. Davy states that Berdyaev can be understood only by a person who is willing to turn his being "toward the Light."

Edie, James M., James P. Scanlan, and Mary-Barbara Zeldin. *Philosophers in Exile.* Book 8. Vol. 3 of *Russian Philosophers.* 3 vols. Chicago: Quadrangle Books, 1965. (**A, G**) An anthology as well as a survey, this book provides the essentials on Berdyaev's life and a generous selection from his writings, including a portion of his first book *Subjectivism and Individualism in Social Philosophy.* Includes a brief bibliography.

Kline, George L. *Religious and Anti-Religious Thought in Russia.* The Well Lectures. Chicago: University of Chicago Press, 1968. (**A, G**) A noted authority on Russian thought and the translator of Zenkovsky's *History of Russian Philosophy*, Kline stresses the influence of Nietzsche on the Russian Existentialists. He is not overly impressed with Berdyaev's philosophy, dismissing much of it as posturing.

Lowrie, Donald A. *Rebellious Prophet: A Life of Nicolai Berdyaev.* New York: Harper and Brothers, 1960. (**A, G**) Lowrie is principally concerned with

Berdyaev's politics, which is apropos for an Existential philosopher who claimed that his experiences were always the criteria as to whether he accepted or rejected ideas from books. His interpretation of the philosopher's books are very illuminating. He shows how Berdyaev's thought controlled his life from school days onward. The definitive biography by a scholar who had a long association with Berdyaev. Good notes and bibliography.

Richardson, David Bonner. *Berdyaev's Philosophy of History: An Existentialist Theory of Social Creativity and Eschatology.* The Hague: Martinus Nyhoff, 1968. (**A**) Among Existentialist philosophers only Karl Jaspers shares Berdyaev's intense interest in history. Richardson analyzes the role history plays in Berdyaev's thought in such books as *The Philosophy of History* (1936) in which he emphasizes the subject. He agrees with Berdyaev's insistence that history is messianic, a process leading to salvation. The goals of history are realized at its conclusion. Richardson is struck by the "clarity of his insights" in books Berdyaev devotes to the subject. Richardson believes that Berdyaev, far form being the superficial philosopher he has been called, is a very profound thinker when his philosophy is seen in its entirety.

Seaver, George. *Nicolas Berdyaev.* London: Clarke, 1950. (**A, G**) Considered by some reviewers as a relatively difficult commentary. In 122 pages both Berdyaev's life and thought are covered. Seaver accepts most of Berdyaev's philosophy. The Russian thinker follows the tradition established in the nineteenth century by such philosophers as Alexander Herzen, who began by criticizing Russia by western European standards and who finally returned to theories developed in Russia itself. Offers a thorough treatment of its subjects.

Spinka, Matthew. *Nicholas Berdyaev: Captive of Freedom.* Philadelphia, PA: Westminster, 1950. (**A, G**) The first part of Spinka's book furnishes the most complete account of Berdyaev's life prior to Lowrie's definitive biography. The second part is a commentary on his thought. An authority in the Russian Orthodox Church and fluent in Russian, Spinka translated passages of Berdyaev's book which had not appeared in English at that time. He does not agree with all of Berdyaev's ideas, but feels grateful because "he has helped me to understand the significance of human destiny—the greatest service a human being can render to his fellows.'' His chief concern is to expound Berdyaev's basic faith and he succeeds admirably in doing so. The bibliography is good and includes a list of Berdyaev's articles dating from 1900, mostly in Russian, something Lowrie does not provide.

Vallon, Michel Alexander. *An Apostle of Freedom: The Life and Teachings of Nicolas Berdyaev.* New York: The Philosophical Library, 1960. (**A, G**) A veteran of the French underground during the Second World War, Vallon in his introduction surveys both Russian history and Russian thought. Vallon maintains that Berdyaev began ''as a stranger in the world, and never managed (indeed, nor ever even tried) to achieve any other status.''

Wernham, James C. S. *Two Russian Thinkers. An Essay on Berdyaev and Shestov.* Toronto: University of Toronto Press, 1968. (**A, G**) The two subjects of this essay were both natives of Kiev, Existentialist philosophers, and close friends before going into exile. Wernham says that the thinking of both of them is built on the works of Feodor Dostoevsky. Good notes and bibliography.

Wood, Douglas Kellog. *Men Against Time: Nicolas Berdyaev, T. S. Elliot, Aldous Huxley, and C. G Jung.* Lawrence: University of Kansas Press, 1982. (**A, G**) Berdyaev says in his autobiography: ''The conquest of the deadly flux of time has always been the chief concern of my life.'' All of the writers in this work believed they could project themselves out of time into eternity through their religious practices. Berdyaev, born in the period when faith in materialistic progress was at its height (1870-1900 as Wood sees it), rebelled against it as an adolescent. Like the others, World War I completed his disillusionment with the spirit of the age. A good sketch of Berdyaev's life with a good annotated bibliography.

Zenkovsky, V. V. *A History of Russian Philosophy.* Vol. II. New York: Columbia University Press, 1953. Translated by George L. Kline. (**A**) Zenkovsky, a professor and archpriest at St. Sergius Theological Institute (where Berdyaev was disliked by most of the faculty), admits that while Berdyaev had philosophical ability, his romantic impulses prevented him from thinking his ideas through. Superficially brilliant, Berdyaev's writing ''grows dim when one analyzes his ideas.'' However, he credits Berdyaev with valuable individual ideas, "brilliant bon mots,'' and genuine moral concern.

Overview and Evaluation of Primary Sources

There is not a complete edition of Berdyaev's works in English. Lowrie cites many letters in his biography, but a volume of Berdyaev's letters has not been published. Berdyaev's autobiography, *Self-Knowledge, An Essay in Philosophical Autobiography*, was published in 1949. An abridged and heavily edited English translation of *Dream and Reality* (London: Geoffrey Bles, 1950) followed. Despite its repetitiveness, something it has is common with all of Berdyaev's books, it makes fascinating reading. He is primarily interested in his development as a philosopher, and only secondarily in the historical events he witnessed. Little information is provided on his relationships with his contemporaries, and personal events such as the date of his wedding are omitted. The work focuses almost exclusively on his spiritual development.

Geoffrey Bles, a British publisher who became interested in Berdyaev's works in the 1930s, printed English translations and distributed them throughout the British territories. Parallel editions were published in the United States prior to and after World War II. Berdyaev's works thus have been more widely disseminated in English than in any other language. Early in his exile, Berdyaev became editor-in-chief of the Y.M.C.A. Press, and the Russian editions of his books have been published by this press ever since. Two anthologies which provide generous selections from his writings as well as brief biographies are Will Herberg's *Four Existentialist Theologians: Jacques Maritain, Nicolas Berdyaev, Martin Buber, and Paul Tillich* (Garden City, NY: Doubleday/Anchor, 1958) and James M. Edie, et al., *Philosophers in Exile*, Book 8, Vol. 3 of *Russian Philosophers* (3 vols. Chicago: Quadrangle Paperback, 1965).

Museums, Historical Landmarks, Societies

Berdyaev's Home (Clamart, France). Pilgrims continue to visit this house described by Lowrie in his biography.

The Nicolas Berdyaev Society (Paris). Founded by his sister-in-law Eugenie Rapp after his death, this society was formed to perpetuate his memory, and to encourage study of his philosophies. Membership is open to anyone interested. The address is 29 hue St. Didier, Paris 1be.

Other Sources

Berdyaev, Nicolas. "The Crime of Anti-Semitism," *Commonweal* 24 (April 21, 1934): 706-709. Written a year after the National Socialists came into power in Germany, this article expresses Berdyaev's opposition to them and their problems.

————. "My Attitude Toward the Revolution." *Commonweal* 42 (September 28, 1945): 570-572. As he had done frequently since 1917, Berdyaev explains that the Russian Revolution was both a necessity and a curse for his native country.

Heinemann, F. H. "The Mystical Anarchist." *Existentialism and the Modern Predicament.* New York: Harper/Torchbooks, 1958. Heinemann admires Berdyaev's personality and his passionate defense of freedom but considers his mystical philosophy "a wonderful youthful slogan, but not a ripe and considered viewpoint."

Karl Avery

Ingmar Bergman
b. 1918

Chronology

Born Ernst Ingmar Bergman on July 14, 1918, in Uppsala, Sweden, son of Erik Bergman, curate at Hedvig Eleonora Church in Stockholm, and Karin Akerblom Bergman, a trained nurse; *1918-1924* raised in relatively comfortable surroundings in Stockholm and in the country at the home of his grandmother Anna Akerblom near Dalarna; suffers from a number of ailments anticipating the persistent nervous stomach and chronic insomnia which plague him in adulthood; *1926* attends first film, *Black Beauty*; *1927* receives his first movie camera as a gift; *1928* makes first "film" by cutting and rearranging used celluloid strips; *1928* trapped in the mortuary of Royal Hospital where his father is chaplain, an incident that recurs as an image in films where "the dead cannot die but are made to disturb the living;" *1930* visits backstage at a production of Swedish playwright August Strindberg's *Dream Play*, during which he experiences "the magic of acting;" *1934* spends a month in Germany where he learns about the music of Kurt Weill and Bertold Brecht, introducing the concept of rhythmical patterns as the basis for a dramatic style; *1935* makes a commitment to theatrical life after seeing Olof Molander's influential production of Strindberg's *Dream Play*; *1937* graduates from Palmgrenska School with top grades; *1938* serves briefly in the military before being released due to stomach problems; enrolls in Stockholm University; for Master-Olofsgorden youth group, stages Sutton Vane's *Outward Bound* and Strindberg's *Lucky Peter's Journey*; *1939* hired as production assistant at the Stockholm Opera; *1940* convinces the Swedish national library to sponsor a company under his direction to perform children's plays; leaves Stockholm University without a degree; *1941* directs Strindberg's *The Ghost Sonata* and William Shakespeare's *A Midsummer Night's Dream* with an experimental repertory company; *1942* hired as script writer for Svensk Filmindustri under the direction of Carl Dymling, the head of the studio; produces Else Fisher's *Beppo The Clown* at Student Theater and writes his first play, *The Death of Punch*; *1943* marries Else Fisher, with whom he has one child; begins producing the anti-Nazi allegory *U-Boat 39*; *1944* first screenplay (for *Torment*) filmed by noted Swedish director Alf Sjoberg; begins work with Helsingborg City Theater, staging Shakespeare's *MacBeth*, Brita Von Horn's *Lady Ascheberg of Widtskövle* and Carl Erik Soya's *Who Am I*; *1945* produces his second play, *Scapin, Pimpel, and Kasper*; starts filming *Crisis*, a sentimental Danish comedy, his initial effort as a director; divorces Else Fisher and marries Ellen Lundstrom, with whom he has four children; *1946* directs second film, *It Rains on Our Love*; joins Gothenburg City Theater as director, staging Albert Camus's *Caligula* as his first production; withdraws from political activity, refusing to vote, read, or listen to speeches in reaction to revelations of the Holocaust, a decision he regrets in retrospect; *1947* writes several scripts; produces plays; directs films, including the obscure *A Ship Bound for India* and *Music in Darkness*; *1948* directs *Prison* for independent producer Lorens Marmstedt, his first film from his own screenplay; directs radio production of Strindberg's *Mother Love*; continues to mount productions for Helsingborg City Theater; collaborates with Gustaf Molander on screenplay of *Eva*; *1949* stages Tennessee Williams's *A Streetcar Named Desire*; films *To Joy* and *Thirst*, his first production with the cinematographer Gunnar Fischer; travels to Paris for three months with his future third wife Gun Hagberg; *1950* short fiction is serialized in the leading Swedish literary quarterly *Bonniers Litterära Magasin;* stages Brecht's *The Threepenny Opera* in Stockholm and Hjalmar Bergman's *A Shadow* and Jean Anouilh's *Medea* as a double bill at Intima Theater, Stockholm; *1951* shoots nine one-minute commercial spots for television during a studio strike in Sweden; after his divorce from Ellen Lundstrom marries Gun Hagberg, with whom he has a son; *1952* appointed to direct the Malmö City Theater; films *Summer With Monika* starring Harriet Andersson, who becomes his lover; stages Strindberg's *The Virgin Bride* at Malmö; *1953 Summer with Monika* premieres, which is praised by French New Wave filmmaker/critics; films *Sawdust and Tinsel* and *A Lesson in Love*; stages Luigi Pirandello's *Six Characters in Search of an Author*; *1954 Sawdust and Tinsel* savaged by critics; films *Dreams*; stages Strindberg's *The Ghost Sonata* at Malmö; writes script for *Painting on Wood* for radio broadcast, the first version of his later film, *The Seventh Seal*; *1955* films *Smiles of a Summer Night*, which becomes a tremendous success; begins relationship with actress Bibi Andersson; stages Jean-Baptiste Molìere's *Dom Juan* at the Intima Theater *1956 Smiles of a Summer Night* wins Special Jury Prize at the Cannes Festival; films *The Seventh Seal* in thirty-five days during summer; *1957 The Seventh Seal* wins Special Jury

Prize at Cannes; *1958 Wild Strawberries* wins the Golden Bear award at the Berlin Festival; *Brink of Life* wins special prize for its three leading actresses at the Cannes Festival; *1959* appointed director of the Royal Dramatic Theater of Stockholm; after his divorce from Gun Grut marries Käbi Laretei, with whom he has a son; *1960* as "Frenchman" Ernest Riffe, attacks his own film work in the Swedish film journal *Chaplin*; *The Virgin Spring* and *The Devil's Eye* premiere; produces Strindberg's *First Warning* for television; *1961* stages highly acclaimed version of composer Igor Stravinsky's opera *The Rake's Progress* for Stockholm Opera; appointed Artistic Advisor at Svensk Filmindustri; *The Virgin Spring* wins Academy Award for Best Foreign Film; *1962 Through a Glass Darkly* wins Academy Award for Best Foreign Film; *1963 The Silence* premieres to mediocre reviews but arouses controversy due to some mild censorship; appointed Head of Royal Dramatic Theater; *Winter Light* premieres; stages Strindberg's *A Dream Play* for television; stages American playwright Edward Albee's *Who's Afraid of Virginia Woolf?* at Royal Dramatic Theater; *1964 All These Women*, his first color film, premieres; stages Henrik Ibsen's *Hedda Gabler* at Royal Dramatic Theater; *1965* becomes ill with viral infection; begins relationship with actress Liv Ullmann, with whom he has a daughter; shares Erasmus Prize (established in Holland in 1958 to honor contributions to European culture) with *Chaplin* magazine; stages Albee's *Tiny Alice* at Royal Dramatic Theater; *1966 Persona* premieres with distribution by United Artists, which pays $1,000,000 for rights and option on next film; stages French dramatist Jean-Baptiste Molìere's *The School for Wives* at Royal Dramatic Theater, then resigns as its head; *1967* stages Pirandello's *Six Characters in Search of an Author* at National Theater, Oslo; *1968 Hour of the Wolf* premieres; establishes Swedish production company Cinematograph; *1969 Shame* nominated as Best Foreign Film at the Academy Awards; films *The Fårö Document*, a depiction of his island retreat; *The Ritual* shown on television; *A Passion,* his first use of color in film, premieres; stages Georg Büchner's *Woyzeck* at Royal Dramatic Theater; *1970* wins National Society of Film Critics' Award; stages a radically simplified, chamber-play adaptation of Strindberg's *A Dream Play* at Royal Dramatic Theater; *1971* receives Irving Thalberg Memorial Award at the Academy Awards; *The Touch* premieres to severe critical reaction; after divorce from Käbi Laretei marries Ingrid Karlebo; *1972* stages an innovative production of Ibsen's *The Wild Duck*; *Cries and Whispers* premieres in the United States in December to tremendous enthusiasm; *1973* stages Strindberg's *The Ghost Sonata* in definitive modern production at Royal Dramatic Theater; *Scenes from a Marriage* shown in weekly episodes on Swedish television; *1975* receives an honorary doctorate from Stockholm University; *1976* arrested on charges of tax fraud; leaves Sweden for voluntary exile in Munich, Germany, after presenting his defense; receives the Goethe Prize in Frankfurt; accepts a position at Residenztheater in Munich; *The Serpent's Egg* premieres; *1978* celebrates sixtieth birthday on Fårö with all his children in attendance; *Autumn Sonata* premieres; *1979* stages Molìere's *Tartuffe* and Ibsen's *Hedda Gabler* at Residenztheater, Munich; officially exonerated in tax case; *1980 From the Life of the Marionettes* premiers in Oxford; *1981* stages Ibsen's *A Doll's House* and Strindberg's *Miss Julie* at Residenztheater, and his own play *Scenes From A Marriage* also in Munich; fired from Residenztheater in June, and reinstated in December under new management; *1982 Fanny and Alexander* premieres; announces retirement from filmmaking; *1983* stages controversial reinterpretation of Jean-Baptiste Moliere's *Dom Juan* at Salzburg Festival; complete five-hour version of *Fanny and Alexander* shown on Scandanavian television during Christmas holidays; *1984 Fanny and Alexander* wins four Academy Awards; film version of *After The Rehearsal*, his forty-fourth and final feature film, shown at the Cannes Festival against Bergman's wishes; stages Shakespeare's *King Lear* at Royal Dramatic Theater; *1985* stages Ibsen's *John Gabriel Borkman* at Bavarian State Theater, Munich, his final work in Germany; returns permanently to Sweden; *1986* works on his autobiography, *The Magic Lantern*; stages several plays, including Shakespeare's *Hamlet*, at Royal Dramatic Theater which opens to a storm of controversy; *Karin's Face* premieres; *1987* publishes his autobiography; *1988* stages American playwright Eugene O'Neill's *Long Day's Journey Into Night* at Royal Dramatic Theater, his eightieth major stage production; *1989* stages innovative production of *Hamlet* (in Swedish) in New York; works on screenplay for *The Best Intentions*, a film about his parents; stages Japanese writer Yukio Mishima's *Madame de Sade* (1965) at Lilla scenen; *1990* works on *Images*, an account of his impressions of his film work; publishes Swedish edition in October; *1991* selects Danish director Bille August (*Pele The Conqueror*) to make *The Best Intentions*; stages *The Bacchae* (Euripides) as a music-drama at the Royal Opera in Stockholm; *1992 The Best Intentions* opens in the United States; writes script of *Sunday's Children,* depicting his own childhood as a boy who loves and fears his father, to be directed by his son Daniel; 1993 stages *Madame de Sade* and *Peer Gynt* at the Brooklyn Academy of Music; publishes *The Best Intentions* (translated by Joan Tate) as mix of screenplay, novel and memoir; publishes *Images* in an English edition.

Activities of Historical Significance

Until his dynamic, startling productions of *Hamlet* (1989) and *Peer Gynt* (1993) were presented in the United States at the Brooklyn Academy of Music, Ingmar Bergman's reputation as a filmmaker considerably exceeded his accomplishments as a theatrical director for most Americans, but once critics and audiences in the U.S. were able to see what Bergman has been capable of achieving on the stage for more than four decades, the full range of his abilities as a dramatic artist finally became clear on both sides of the Atlantic. This is an appropriate widening of appreciation, since Bergman's work on film and in the theater is connected in many areas, and although he has been "retired" from filmmaking since the mid-1980s, he has maintained contact with the world of film through scripts prepared for other artists, and in his recollections and memoirs of his career, while continuing to mount new stage productions with no diminution of energy or invention.

Bergman once remarked in characteristically sardonic fashion that "film is my mistress, theater my loyal wife," but as astute critics have noted, the actual situation is more like a *ménage a trois* where various elements seem to co-exist amiably and simultaneously. While his films may remain as a more permanent historical record of his artistic vision, Bergman began his career as a theatrical director and plans to conclude it that way as well.

At the heart of his pleasure in his work, Bergman has consistently cited his work with actors, an aspect of his craft crucial to both realms, and it is this emphasis on the actor that is at the core of his philosophy as a director.

The primacy of the actor owes something to Bergman's origins as the son of a clergyman trained in the brooding Protestant theology of Northern Europe, in his education in the reflective tradition of philosophical inquiry located in the writing of August Strindberg (Bergman's spiritual mentor), and in the religious commentaries of Søren Kierkegaard. From this perspective, Bergman has examined, particularly in his films, the agony of what he describes as "two people whose lives could not be peaceful together but who could not live apart." In this statement, one of the central paradoxes of "modernism" has been presented, and it is Bergman's penetrating insights into the full range and psychological complexity of human relationships that have been placed at the foundation of his finest productions. Accordingly, he has called upon the actors, many of whom he has been working with for decades, to be the focal point for probing the exigencies of existence. Bergman has made a point of studying and assimilating the reality of past styles, and his work depends on and is an excellent expression of his knowledge of the history of the theater. He has no single directorial theory, regarding each play as a distinct and new situation, and while he claims that he is always faithful to the inner spirit of the playwright's text, he seems himself as an interpreter or re-creator, and has defended his imaginative staging by saying "absolute word fidelity is trumpery in the theater. The text is not a prescription but raw material, a frequently hidden path into the writer's consciousness." As the American critic Robert Brustein notes, "Bergman's recent treatment of classical writers almost amounts to co-authorship," and while this is undeniably a controversial position, it is a much more bold route toward theatrical reality that even the most precise, professional reproduction of a previous setting. The playwrights Bergman has been most interested in—Strindberg, Henrik Ibsen, and Jean-Baptiste Molière—remain fresh, exciting and engaging for audiences and for Bergman himself as he stages the "same play in new productions" in succeeding decades.

In his theatrical productions, Bergman draws on both his cinematic and dramaturgic expertise. For instance, in his third production of Molière's *Dom Juan* (1664) in Salzburg in 1983, he brought the play's twenty-two short scenes "together in a swift, uninterrupted flow of juxtaposed images" using an "utterly flexible setting" which could be moved around "at will by costumed servants-stagehands or the actors themselves." This effect was something like the "shifting, colliding images" that are at the heart of the cinematic method of organization known as "montage." His production of Molière's *Misanthrope* of 1957 in Malmo, which starred Max Von Sydow who had just come to prominence as the questing knight in the film *The Seventh Seal,* emphasized the theatrical artificiality of the comic style of the play by placing the actors at the front of the stage rather than amidst the scenic environment of a more naturalistic setting, a method akin to the filmmaker's closeup. This type of close observance has been a particularly important device for Bergman in his films as a means of probing the specific psychological configuration of a character.

Bergman's command of theatrical technique has permitted him to locate innovative solutions to the problems presented by the international masterpieces he has worked with, often freeing them from the glacial rigidity they had assumed due to the accumulated conventions established by previous celebrated productions. He moves beyond a reliance on technical proficiency toward what he considers the most vital component of theatrical art, namely the relationship between the actors and the audience. As his long-time collaborator Von Sydow has said, Bergman's aim is to "simplify complicated plays and complicated pieces of action in plays and make them crystal clear." As with Bertold Brecht, his clarity derives from an awareness on the part of the audience of a dramatic device that nonetheless transcends that awareness. The audience knows that it is subject to the ministrations of the magician/director—nonetheless, the "magical transformation" occurs, an idea that Bergman returns to often, notably in the film *The Magician* (1958). "It is in their hearts," Bergman says of the audience "in their imaginations that the performance takes place," and after utilizing the full power of theatrical manipulation, Bergman has moved in the latter stages of his career to a direct confrontation between the audience and the actor, using the words the actor speaks and the active responses of the audience as his instruments.

Bergman's attitude toward the audience is effectively illustrated by the way in which he has modified Brecht's well-known concept of "alienation." Using the German word *verfremdung,* Bergman contends the common understanding of alienation is a misconstruction because ideally the spectator is "always involved and always outside, at one and the same time." This parallels his view that the "world" is a stage, and the "stage" is an image of the world, a fusion designated by the term *teatro mundi.* Thus, the line between performance and actuality is always shifting and blurred, as Bergman moves toward a "style cleansed of everything that would dissipate or detheatricalize the hypnotic presence and power of the performer" so that the audience can be drawn toward a place of magical transformation.

Bergman's attitude toward theatrical possibility stands as a major part of his contribution to the dramatic arts and which makes him, in the twilight years of his extraordinary career, "the ideal interpreter of Ibsen and Mishima as well as Strindberg, O'Neil and much of Shakespeare," as Brustein puts it, a director who "has found the undiscovered country where one culture merges gracefully with another . . . to merge periods and centuries . . . along his artistic path with high confidence and total dedication."

At the same time, although his filmmaking career essentially ended with the production of *Fanny and Alexander* in 1982, the finest films that he directed have lost none of their power to move and involve an international audience. The retrospect that history affords confirms the supposition that Bergman was a part of a post-World War II Golden Age of the Cinema, and among other great directors like Federico Fellini, François Truffaut, Akira Kurosawa, and Jean-Luc Godard, his individual style and technical resourcefulness—not to mention his celebrated skill with actors—enabled him to leave a body of work that is part of the ''New Wave'' of cinematic brilliance that transformed the medium from a kind of poor relation to the theater into what many commentators consider the ultimate art form for the latter part of the twentieth century.

Compared to Godard, whose extraordinary innovative genius seemed somewhat more striking in its originality when both directors were releasing films concurrently during the 1960s, Bergman's work appears to be more traditional, but in his use of more familiar cinematic conventions, he may have established a deeper foundation than Godard or other more flashy practitioners. While *Summer with Monika* (1953) and *Sawdust and Tinsel* (1954) caught the attention of the more astute critics, *The Seventh Seal* (1957) was Bergman's breakthrough to an international audience. Bergman completely imagined the ethos of the plague-ridden, fear-driven medieval society controlled by religious bigots, zealots and fanatics in which a tormented crusading knight and an innocent, life-relishing family struggle to survive. The film's epic grandeur, its visions of conflicting historical forces, and its meditations on the nature of existence carry it beyond its fully realized tableau of medieval Europe into universal time.

Following *The Seventh Seal*, Bergman directed and wrote or co-wrote a stunning series of films that were universally acclaimed. *Wild Strawberries* (1957) examined the value of an individual's life. *The Magician* (1958) explored the nature of the artist's methods of creating reality by comparing the artist to a magician. *The Virgin Spring* (1960) is a meditation on the nature of Evil, reflecting Bergman's deep concern with the horror of the holocaust. *A Glass Darkly* (1961), *Winter Light* (1963) and *The Silence* (1963) depict the spiritual agony resulting from the vast emptiness of the late-twentieth century. *Persona* (1966) and *A Passion* (1969) are penetrating psychological studies of the relationships that develop between two people who are attempting to fill this void with some kind of love. *Cries and Whispers* (1973) is an expression of the compassion and empathy human beings are capable of in moments of pain and need. *The Magic Flute* (1975) utilizes the director's sensitivity to the structural possibilities of tempo and rhythm in building a dramatic foundation. Bergman's body of work is so varied and compelling that not only the films themselves but the mind and spirit of the man who made them have become a standard-bearer of modern cinematography.

Overview of Biographical Sources

Because so much of Bergman's work, especially his film work, is drawn from incidents in his own life, biographers have been particularly interested in establishing the connections between biographical fact and a scene, image, or place in his movies. In his autobiography, *The Magic Lantern* (1988), Bergman offers a number of occasions where he turned his life into art, such as the third part of *Scenes from a Marriage* (1973) which is based on a dramatic discussion with Ellen Lundstrom just before the breakup of their marriage.

Bergman, while not exactly reluctant to offer information about his background, has been generally reserved in his comments in interviews, preferring to present his thoughts in his films or plays, and then willing to discuss them after a production has taken place. Consequently, information has appeared in a fragmented fashion, with many incidents reported in differing accounts that have been gradually verified or shown to be false. This has led to some speculation, which seems to amuse Bergman, who has either permitted an erroneous account to remain uncorrected if it didn't irritate him or occasionally contributed to an inaccurate description, perhaps as a reflection of his wry, sardonic sense of humor.

An interest in the factual matters of Bergman's life on more than a local level began in the 1950s, when his films started to reach audiences outside Sweden. An article in the noted French journal *Cahiers du Cinéma* 13, 74 (September 1957: 19-28) by Jean Béranger examined Bergman's work as a dramatist and screenwriter with references to his use of childhood and his depiction of women, making some speculative suggestions about the director's life. During the next year, Béranger conducted an interview with Bergman in which Bergman mentioned the importance of his father's personality and of the religious motifs in his life in *Cahiers du Cinéma* 15, 88 (October 1958: 12-30). Other journal articles followed, providing additional scraps of information, and early books such as Corrado

Farina's *Ingmar Bergman* (Torino: n. p., 1959), offer an analytic overview of Bergman's career, concentrating primarily on his work but containing some biographical material as well. The first lengthy study of Bergman in English is Peter Cowie's chapter on the filmmaker in *Antonioni, Bergman, Renais* (New York: A. S. Barnes, 1960: 51-121), in which themes and patterns of narration are presented, with some references to the director's life. Cowie's *Ingmar Bergman: A Critical Biography* (New York: Charles Scribner's Sons, 1982) is the first full-length biography in English, although as the Bergman scholar Birgitta Steene observes, "the book is more of a chronological presentation of [Bergman's] work in the cinema and on stage than an in-depth attempt to place the subject of the biography in a cultural context." Cowie's accurate, detailed "Bergman Chronology" appears in the *The Magic Lantern*.

The first Swedish book to reach the public abroad was Jorn Donner's *The Devil's Face*, published in the United States as *The Films of Ingmar Bergman* (1964. Reprint. New York: Dover, 1972) translated by H. Lundberg. Donner has been one of Bergman's strongest supporters both as a film critic and as a producer at Svensk Filmindustri, and the book's merits and limitations stem from his personal acquaintance with the filmmaker. The biographical information is not detailed but covers important elements of Bergman's life with respect to his work prior to *Persona* (1966).

Marianne Höök's *Ingmar Bergman* (Stockholm: Wahlström & Widstrand, 1963) provides an examination of the director's productions through *Winter Light* (1963). The director was irritated with Höök's personal tone, but the material on Bergman's family background and his relationships with his cast and crew is revealing. The book has not been translated.

Although not a biography in any traditional sense, director Vilgot Sjoman's (*I Am Curious: Yellow*) diary, which he kept during the production of *Winter Light*, was published as *L136: Diary With Ingmar Bergman* (Ann Arbor, MI: Karoma, 1978). He includes conversations, dialogue, observations, and considerable information about Bergman's life at the time of the film's production, and offers a considerable amount of biographical information circa the early 1960s.

Robin Wood's *Ingmar Bergman* (New York: Praeger, 1969) discusses the films of the 1960s with considerable insight and emphasizes psychological and psychoanalytical approaches that depend on some biographical information, which he provides. Steene's study, *Ingmar Bergman* (2d ed. New York: Twayne, 1978) has a very clear, accurate biographical section that presents the essential facts of the director's life while indicating how key episodes have been integrated into his creative activities.

Vlada Peric's compilation *Film and Dreams: An Approach to Ingmar Bergman* (South Salem, NY: Redgrave, 1981) gathers papers given at an international film conference on Bergman at Harvard in 1978 and includes a chronology of Bergman's life and work by M. Duda. The actress Liv Ullmann's memoir, published in English as *Changing* (New York: Alfred A. Knopf, 1977), offers some thoughts about Bergman's life during the time that the two were working (and living) together. In his autobiography, Bergman remarks that "On the whole, her testimony is, I think, affectionately correct."

Two of the most ambitious, and in some ways, most idiosyncratic studies of Bergman have ventured into the field of psycho-biographical speculation, a direction that is likely to be pursued by future efforts. They are Vernon Young's *Cinema Borealis* (1972) and Frank Gado's *The Passion of Ingmar Bergman* (1986), both of which follow to some extent the first book-length biography of Bergman—Fritiof Billqvist's *Ingmar Bergman: Man of the Theater and Filmmaker* (Stockholm: Natur och kultur, 1959). Although Steene, in her comprehensive study of Bergman criticism, *Ingmar Bergman: A Guide to References and Resources* (Boston: G. K. Hall, 1987) notes that none of Billquist's extensive quotations from interviews, conversations, and anecdotes are referenced, and that many seem apocryphal, thus making the entire project "virtually worthless," there is probably enough accurate material to guide other biographers toward many interesting areas of exploration. Gado, for instance, uses quotes from Billqvist tellingly in several places. Works such as Billqvist's "Maud Webster's" series of articles on Bergman in the magazine *Vecko-Journalen* 8, 15, 22 and 29 (April 1970) under the title "Ingmar Bergman Today", and the autobiography *Schein, Schein* (Stockholm: Bonniers, 1980) of Harry Schein, a friend of Bergman's and the former head of Svensk Filmindustri, present material that must be examined further to form a comprehensive biography of the director.

Evaluation of Principal Biographical Sources

Gado, Frank. *The Passion of Ingmar Bergman.* Durham, NC: Duke University

Press, 1986. (**A**) By far the most penetrating Bergman biography to appear so far, Gado follows the pattern established by initial biographical efforts in linking the life with the work, but goes much further in his specific analysis of themes, images, motifs and ideas in Bergman's films. His identification of thematic patterns derived from the experiences of Bergman's life is probing, incisive, and challengingly speculative. One of his major contributions is to use the manuscript of a novel by Bergman's sister, Margareta Bergman Britten Austin, (1985) and information gained through correspondence with Else Fisher-Bergman, Bergman's first wife. He also has a list of recurrent names in Bergman's work, a filmography and an index.

Young, Vernon. *Cinema Borealis: Ingmar Bergman and the Swedish Ethos.* New York: David Lewis, 1971. (**A**) Young's study is so idiosyncratic that it has been routinely dismissed by academic critics as biased, wrong-headed, and almost perverse. Its lack of standard scholarly apparatus has led Steene to categorize it as "practically worthless," although she does suggest that Young's acerbic style and cultural commentary make it interesting reading. Comparisons with other sources will help to clarify the "facts" of some matters, and Young's interpretation of various events and their consequences is worth considering, if carefully.

Overview and Evaluation of Primary Sources

Bergman's films, screenplays for other directors, radio plays, and stories all include, to varying degrees, material drawn from his life. Bergman's sister, Margareta Bergman Britten Austin, has published *Karin: A Novel* (London: 1985, **G**), which she says is a work of fiction, but which contains characters very similar to the Bergmans. Ingmar Bergman's autobiography, *The Magic Lantern* (New York: Viking, 1988, **G**) is a fascinating, episodic, powerfully emotional, and often very revealing if selective account of his life, written with verve and a distinctive style. It includes discussions of his formative years and crucial early experiences with women, art, nature and his family, including his close kin. The veracity of Bergman's accounts, however, should be corroborated since all of his reflections on his life have been designed as an artistic means of seeking the "truth" of an incident or a relationship by exploring its psychological ramifications for him through the lens of his artistic imagination. Caryn James, a reviewer for the New York Time, has called *The Magic Lantern* "the most overtly autobiographical of all his quasi memoirs, though hardly a conventional life story." His accounts are not attempts to deceive or distort but ways of understanding which often involve interpretive or symbolic positions. This approach may also be seen in his screenplay for the film *The Best Intentions* (New York: Arcade, 1993), that James calls "a kinetic mix of screenplay, novel, and memoir" in which Bergman seems to be playing a game "with readers as well as with his own imagination." The forthcoming publication of *Sunday's Children,* a screenplay directed by his son Daniel which depicts Bergman as a small boy, and of *My Life in Film* (1993), in which he discusses the origins and development of his films with respect to crucial moments in his life, continue his presentation of selective details, often highly charged and provocative, from his life and times.

Bergman's autobiographical novel, *The Best Intentions* (1993), a single work with novelistic narration and pages also designed as a screenplay, follows his parents' courtship and early marriage. In the novel Bergman's father is a poor, proud divinity student and his mother is a bourgeois nursing student. That Anna's parents oppose the marriage lends fuel to the fires of their passions, drawing them into a flawed, complicated marriage. Though the facts of the novel may be disputed, the work is valuable for documenting Bergman's emotions about his parents as he considers the past late in his life.

Fiction and Adaptations

There are two films about Bergman that add to the available biographical data. Stig Björkman made *Bergman* during the shooting of *The Touch* in 1971 for Svensk Filmindustri, and Jorn Donner produced *The Bergman File* from conversations with Bergman in December, 1975 and January, 1976. In that film, Bergman talks about his childhood, adolescence, some of his films and in particular, *The Fårö Document.*

Other Sources

Björkman, Stig; Torstens Manns; and Jonas Sima. *Bergman on Bergman.* Stockholm: Norstedt, 1970. The text is in Swedish but is available in English in Paul

Britten Austin's translation (New York: Simon and Schuster, 1973). It includes interviews with Bergman over an eighteen-month span, covering all of his films through the making of *The Fårö Document.*

Bragg, Melvin. *The Seventh Seal.* Bloomington: Indiana University Press, 1993. A finely written appreciation of Bergman's complex film.

Cohen, Hubert I. *The Art of Confession.* New York: Twayne, 1993. Cohen analyzes the structure,character, plot, pacing, lighting and sound of all Bergman's films, providing insight into the motivation, psychology, and artistic development of the director.

Jones, G. William, ed. *Talking With Ingmar Bergman.* Dallas, TX: Southern Methodist University Press, 1983. Contains a record of a visit Bergman made to the SMU campus to receive an award for excellence in the arts. Bergman participated in several seminars and was very forthcoming in response to questions from students and Professor Jones. The book also has some good photographs and a handsome filmography, as well as a list of Bergman's principal stage productions.

Kakutani, Michiko. ''Ingmar Bergman Summing Up a Life in Film.'' *New York Times Magazine* 26 (June 1983): 24. A much more placid view of Bergman.

Marker, Lise-Lone, and Frederick J. Marker. *Ingmar Bergman: A Life in the Theater.* Cambridge: Cambridge University Press, 1992. While this is basically a close analysis of Bergman's most important stage productions, the fact that his life and work are so closely connected make it an indispensable text for anyone interested in Bergman's artistic achievements. It is clearly written, comprehensive, sensitive to Bergman's ambitions and goals and well illustrated with photographs and diagrams. It also contains some informative interviews with people who have worked with Bergman and a very nicely annotated chronology from 1944 to 1991.

Samuels, Charles Thomas, ed. *Encountering Directors.* New York: Putnam, 1972. Contains an interview with Bergman in which the filmmaker is in a combatative, boisterous mood sparring with a prickly, somewhat egotistic interviewer. The result is entertaining and erratically informative.

Simon, John. *Ingmar Bergman Directs*. New York: Harcourt Brace Jovanovich, 1972: 11-40. Contains some interesting interview information, as well as many perceptive critical thoughts.

Leon Lewis
Appalachian State University

Henri Bergson
1859-1941

Chronology

Born Henri-Louis Bergson on October 18, 1859, in Paris, son of Michael Bergson, a musician and composer of Polish Jewish descent, and Katherine Levinson, of English Jewish descent; *1859-1878* grows up in Paris, where he shows ability in the sciences and humanities at the Lycée Condorcet; *1878-1881* studies at the École Normale Supérieure in Paris, reading Greek and Latin classics, science, and philosophy; considers career in mathematics; influenced by Herbert Spencer and John Stuart Mill; writes essay on a problem in Pascal's geometry; *1881-1883* appointed professor of philosophy at the lycée at Angers; *1883-1888* teaches at the Lycée Blaise Pascal in Clermont-Ferrand; has ''intuition'' that leads to first philosophical book; *1888* moves back to Paris where he teaches in lycées during the next decade; *1889* receives his doctorate with essay published that year, *Time and Free Will: An Essay on the Immediate Data of Consciousness*, a rejection of the primacy of mechanistic theories and an attempt to define duration (that is, psychologically lived time rather than time measured mechanically) and to distinguish between consciousness and extension in space; *1890* begins eight-year period of teaching in the Lycée Henri IV in Paris; *1891* marries Louise Neuburger, cousin of Marcel Proust, with whom he has a daughter; begins study of literature on memory, especially on aphasia, the partial or total loss of the ability to articulate ideas in any form; *1896* publishes *Matter and Memory: An Essay on the Relation of the Body to the Spirit*, which defines essential characteristics shared by mind and body; *1898* begins to lecture at the École Normale Supérieure; *1900* publishes *Laughter: An Essay on the Meaning of the Comic*, a study of laughter as a social phenomenon by which society responds to the mechanistic, inelastic, and socially threatening in human behavior; awarded a chair at the Collège de France, the most prestigious academic institution in France, and becomes famous for his brilliant lectures; *1903* publishes *An Introduction to Metaphysics*, defining a theory of knowledge with intuition having central role and first using the terms ''intuition'' and ''analysis''. although both concepts are implied in earlier works; *1907* publishes *Creative Evolution*, his most famous book, using his intuitive method and critiquing theories of biological evolution, especially neo-Darwinism; *1911* lectures in Oxford and Birmingham; publishes *The Perception of Change*, based on two lectures delivered at Oxford University, proposing intuition rather than rationalism or empiricism as a philosophical method and examining the nature of change; *1912-1913* lectures at Columbia University in New York; *1914* retires from active duties at the College de France; elected to the French Academy, although he is not received into the Academy until the end of the war in 1918; *1916* gives a number of addresses in Madrid on his philosophy and on relations between France and Spain; *1917* makes a diplomatic trip to the United States to persuade the U.S. government to join the war against the Central Powers; begins to discuss the possibility of a League of Nations; *1919* publishes *Mind-Energy*, a collection of essays and talks, especially on the mind-body relationship; *1921* retires from his chair at the Collège de France; *1922* publishes *Duration and Simultaneity*, a criticism of Einstein's theory of relativity; active in the establishment of the International Commission for Intellectual Cooperation (later, UNESCO), becoming the first president of the organization; discusses, with Madame Curie and others, the creation of an international bibliographic index; *1927* receives Nobel Prize for Literature; *1929* writes that he is so ill (insomnia, headaches, rheumatoid arthritis) that he can work only minutes each day; *1932* publishes *The Two Sources of Morality and Religion*, viewing the Judeo-Christian tradition as a culminating point in human ethics and religion; *1934* publishes *La Pensee et le mouvant* (translated as *Creative Mind*, 1946), including only two new essays; *1937* writes his last will in which he says he would become a baptized Roman Catholic except that he anticipates increasing anti-Semitism and wishes to remain among the persecuted; forbids publication of his manuscripts, letters, or notes; *1940* crippled by arthritis, leaves the sickbed he has occupied for years to register as a Jew in accordance with regulations of Vichy government; *1941* dies on January 4 in Paris.

Activities of Historical Significance

Henri Bergson was born the same year, 1859, that Charles Darwin's *On the Origin of Species by Means of Natural Selection* created a storm of controversy;

he thus grew up in a world concerned with the theory and meaning of evolution. Bergson himself rejected a materialistic and mechanistic view of the universe. He resisted what he saw as the confined and confining world of thinkers like Auguste Comte, Immanuel Kant, and Ernest Renan. For Bergson, reality is grasped by intuition, not by analysis of static, spatial, externally related bits. A world of fluidity, spontaneity, creativity, and freedom exists for the individual.

A chronological approach to Bergson's writings reveals that his essays reflect the gradual development of his thinking, including reconsideration of concepts and changes in the use of terms. In addition, his prose is eloquent, frequently digressive and unpredictable, and highly metaphoric. Thus, a single essay may be somewhat misleading when read out of the context of his other works. The fact that Bergson supervised the translations into English of all of his works except *Duration and Simultaneity* does offer assurance to the English-speaking reader that he was satisfied with the representation of his thought in these translations.

Three ideas lie at the core of Bergson's thought: his belief in intuition as a philosophical method and his concepts of duration and *élan vital*. Bergson himself, in 1915, argued that his concept of duration preceded his concept of intuition and was more fundamental to his philosophy. Intuition, to Bergson, is not a simple feeling or inspiration but immediate knowledge, without the learning or intellectual operations of analysis. Intuition is holistic, grasping reality as a whole and as dynamic process, that is, a continuity of durations. Duration, the special object of intuition, is inner, psychological time. It is qualitative, not quantitative, heterogeneous rather than homogeneous, dynamic rather than static. Each human self exhibits one "tension" of duration in a universe of differing sorts of duration. The goal of both philosophy and science is the study of reality, or the all-inclusive continuity of durations. Reality has no fixed structure but continually evolves, in a creative, not mechanistic, process; it continually develops and generates new forms. Reality, then, is an *élan vital*—an impetus, momentum, vigor.

Bergson's major contribution to the thought of his day was his attempt to establish an empirical foundation for a belief in the reality of spirit. His works were enthusiastically acclaimed for their denial of an exaggerated determinism and mechanism. William James, who became a close friend, was especially excited by *Matter and Memory*.

Bergson's first major work, *Time and Free Will* (1889) contains most of the themes elaborated in his subsequent studies. It emphasizes his distinction between outer experience, which is quantitative and spatial (the purview of science), and inner, psychological experience (duration). In addition, the final section addresses the question of human freedom and asserts that the self is not determined by forces acting on it from outside but by psychological states, the very forces that comprise the self. Thus, humans have free will; they are self-determined. Further, some people do not simply choose between possibilities but actually create possibilities. Thus, Bergson began to articulate for his excited readers and listeners a philosophy that restored faith in the potential of man at a time when scientific rationalism, materialism, and determinism dominated French intellectual life.

Matter and Memory (1896), Bergson's most difficult book, reflects five years of study and continues his assertion of the remarkable capacities of being with his theory of "la memoire par excellence," that is, "pure memory," which preserves the totality of an individual's past. Bergson distinguishes between physiological or habit memory, that is established by the deliberate storing of details in the present, and a very different kind of "memory": spontaneous recollection, which recalls a past unconsciously stored. All of a person's past is stored up even though, under normal conditions, the brain releases only those memories relevant at a particular moment. Consciousness, then, is "pure memory" and is independent of the body.

The potential of man was further supported by Bergson's *Introduction to Metaphysics* (1903), that distinguishes between two ways of knowing: analysis, which uses static concepts and quantitative methods, and intuition, which is immediate knowledge. For Bergson, the goal in philosophy is to use intuition methodically to discover the nature of reality.

It was *Creative Evolution*, however, in 1907, that introduced Bergson's most celebrated concept, the *élan vital*. Combining a belief in reality as process and a belief in evolution as creative rather than mechanistic, Bergson argues that the single cosmic principle is the *élan vital*, a driving life-force of process and creativity. This study appears to see God as creativity or superconsciousness, although *The Two Sources of Morality and Religion* (1932) suggests a transcendental God independent of the world he created.

Among Bergson's minor works, *Laughter* (1900) has been the most influential, probably the most famous of his works after *Creative Evolution*. This study proposes that laughter is a function of intelligence, that some emotions are inconsistent with laughter, that laughter's chief target is human automata, and that laughter is social in nature, often having a socially corrective function.

Bergson's thinking, especially his emphasis on intuitive knowledge and reality as process, has influenced innumerable thinkers and artists. Among the better known are William James, Jacques Maritain, George Santayana, Alfred North Whitehead, Henri Delacroix, Jean Piaget, Marcel Proust, Bernard Shaw, Claude Monet, and Claude Debussy.

Bergson's political and moral influence has also been considerable. During World War I, he put aside his scholarly work to assist in political and international affairs, participating, for example, in diplomatic missions to Spain and the United States. In the last years of the war, he supported the idea of a League of Nations; immediately after the war, he was active in the International Commission for Intellectual Cooperation (which later became UNESCO). Among the issues he was concerned with were international cooperation to preserve archeological treasures, world libraries, international bibliographic libraries, an international bibliographic index, and the advantages and disadvantages of an artificial international language.

Bergson's courage during the early years of World War II made him an international symbol. He publicly refused to accept the German government's offer to exempt him from the rule that Jews could not hold educational posts and renounced any honors associated with the Nazi regime. Two weeks before his death, he got up from his sickbed to register as a Jew.

Overview of Biographical Sources

Although commentaries on Bergson's work were numerous in the early 1900s, his philosophy was most popular after the publication of *Creative Evolution* in 1907. He was one of the most prominent philosophers of the early twentieth century, with most of the era's eminent thinkers, writers, literary critics, religious leaders, statesmen, and journalists addressing his tenets and insights. Bergson's prestige and influence waned, however, after World War II. He left no school of philosophy, with disciples to carry on his work. Only in the last two decades have scholars again begun to examine his legacy.

Three early, sympathetic studies were E. Le Roy's enthusiastic *The New Philosophy of Henri Bergson* (1912. Reprint. New York: Henry Holt, 1913), Jacques Chevalier's *Henri Bergson* (1970) and Vladimir Jankelevitch's excellent *Henri Bergson* (Paris: Presses Universitaires de France, 1959).

The strongest of Bergson's critics was the French rationalist Julien Benda, whose writings on Bergson have not been translated into English. These include *Le Bergsonisme ou one philosophie de la mobilité* (Paris: Mercure de France, 1912); *Une Philosophie pathétique* (Paris: Cahiers de la Quinzaine, 1913); and *Sur le succès du Bergsonisme: précédé de une réponse au défenseurs de la doctrine* (Paris: Mercure de France, 1914). Another critical study, from a rationalist viewpoint, was Bertrand Russell's *The Philosophy of Bergson* (Cambridge: Bowes and Bowes, 1914), that includes a reply by H. W. Carr. Jacques Maritain's Thomist criticism, *La Philosophie bergsonienne* (1914), was more sympathetic. George R. Dodson's *Bergson and the Modern Spirit* (1914. Reprint. London: Lindsey, 1976), and John A. Gunn's *Bergson and His Philosophy* (1920. Reprint. New York: Dutton, 1976) are early studies still highly valued by Bergson scholars. J. Guitton's *La vocation de Bergson* (Paris: Gallimard, 1960) and M. Barlow's *Henri Bergson* (Paris: Editions Universitaires, 1966), both in French, are valuable for biographical details.

A number of recent studies of Bergson's tenets and influence have appeared in English: P. A. Y. Gunter, *Bergson and the Evolution of Physics* (Knoxville: University of Tennessee Press, 1969); Idella J. Gallagher, *Morality in Evolution: The Moral Philosophy of Henri Bergson* (The Hague: Nijhoff, 1970); Milic Capek, *Bergson and Modern Physics* (Dordrecht: Reidel, 1971); A. E. Pilkington, *Bergson and His Influence* (1976); Shiv Kumar Kumar, *Bergson and the Stream of Consciousness Novel* (1962. Reprint. Westport, CT: Greenwood, 1979); Leszek Kolakowski, *Bergson* (1985); Paul Douglas, *Bergson, Eliot, and American Literature* (Lexington: University Press of Kentucky, 1986); A. C. Papanicolaou and P. A. Y. Gunter, ed., *Bergson and Modern Thought* (1987); Ellen Kennedy's *Freedom and the Open Society: Henri Bergson's Contribution to Political Philosophy* (New York: Garland, 1987); Tom Quirk, *Bergson and American Culture: The Worlds of Willa Cather and Wallace Stevens* (Chapel Hill: University of North Carolina Press, 1990); and Mark Antliff, *Inventing Bergson: Cultural Politics and the Parisian Avant-garde* (Princeton, NJ: Princeton University Press, 1993).

An excellent reference source is P. A. Y. Gunter's *A Bibliography of Bergson* (1974. 2d ed. Bowling Green, OH: Bowling Green State University, 1986).

Evaluation of Principal Biographical Sources

Chevalier, Jacques. *Henri Bergson*. Paris: Plon, 1926. Translated by Lilian A. Clare. 1928. Reprint. Freeport, NY: Books for Libraries, 1970. (**A, G**) An enthusiastic study of Bergson's philosophy. Includes a chapter entitled "The Man and the Work," one of the few biographical essays in English on Bergson's life. Chevalier attended Bergson's lectures at the College de France for two years and was a friend and disciple.

Kolakowski, Leszek. *Bergson*. Oxford: Oxford University Press, 1985. (**A, G**) Excellent brief examination of the development of Bergson's thought. Cites the split in Bergson's thinking between the romantic praise of human creativity and the attempt to assimilate modern science and Christianity. Suggests that although Bergson's beliefs may be true, his metaphysics requires an act of faith. Argues that although there are no Bergsonians among philosophers today, few philosophers "could boast of having been entirely beyond Bergson's direct or indirect field of influence."

Lacey, A. R. *Bergson*. London: Routledge, 1989. (**A, G**) A recent examination of Bergson's main arguments, steering "between unsympathetic rejection and uncritical overestimation." Lacey classifies Bergson as a "process philosopher," like Heraclitus, the Stoics, Hegel, and Whitehead.

Maritain, Jacques. *Bergsonian Philosophy and Thomism*. 1914. Translated by Mabelle L. Andison and J. Gordon Andison. New York: Greenwood, 1968. (**A**) A vigorous criticism, toned down in subsequent editions. Argues that Thomas Aquinas's views are superior. Maritain was one of Bergson's students.

Papanicolaou, A. C., and P. A. Y. Gunter, eds. *Bergson and Modern Thought*. New York: Harwood Academic Publishers, 1987. (**A, G**) Emphasizes that Bergson anticipated many modern theories, especially in physics, psychology, and parapsychology.

Pilkington, Anthony Edward. *Bergson and His Influence: A Reassessment*. Cambridge: Cambridge University Press, 1976. (**A**) Examines the intellectual relationship between Bergson and four of his contemporaries—Charles Peguy, Paul Valery, Marcel Proust, and Julien Benda. Discussion of Benda's attacks on Bergson is especially helpful. Suggests that much of Bergson's thought anticipates contemporary philosophical concerns, e.g., the role of time, the nature of perception, the emphasis upon the experiential.

Solomon, Joseph. *Bergson*. 1912. Reprint. Port Washington, NY: Kennikat, 1970. (**G**) A brief and sketchy summary of Bergson's views on change, life, evolution, thought, intelligence, and knowledge.

Wilm, Emil Carl. *Henri Bergson: A Study in Radical Evolution*. New York: Sturgis and Walton, 1914. (**A, G**) Accurately self-characterizes itself as "a brief and comparatively non-technical statement of Bergson's philosophy" despite the "profusion" and "extreme complexity" of Bergson's thought.

Overview and Evaluation of Primary Sources

The definitive edition of Bergson's major works is *Oeuvres* (Paris: Presses Universitaires de France, 1959), with seven studies by Bergson, an introduction by Henri Gouhier, and annotations by Andre Robinet. It does not include, however, such works as *Introduction to Metaphysics* and *Duration and Simultaneity*.

Harold A. Larrabee's *Selections from Bergson* (New York: Appleton-Century-Crofts, 1949) is very valuable to the English reader, offering Bergson's 1911 lecture entitled "Philosophical Intuition" and carefully selected passages from seven of his major works: *An Introduction to Metaphysics*, *Time and Free Will*, *Matter and Memory*, *Creative Evolution*, *Mind-Energy*, *The Creative Mind*, and *The Two Sources of Morality and Religion*.

The English translations of his major works authorized by Bergson are also available in many libraries. P. L. Pogson, trans., *Time and Free Will* (1889. Trans. 1910. Reprint. New York: Harper, 1960. Reprint. London: G. Allen and Unwin, 1970); Nancy Margaret Paul, and W. Scott Palmer, trans., *Matter and Memory* (1896. Trans. 1911. Reprint. Garden City, NY: Doubleday, 1959. Reprint. London: G. Allen and Unwin, 1970); Cloudesly Brereton, and Fred Rothwell, trans., *Laughter* (1900. Trans. 1911. Reprint. London: Macmillan. 1935); Mabelle L. Andison, trans., *Introduction to Metaphysics* (1912. Trans. New York: Philosophical Library, 1961); Arthur Mitchell, trans., *Creative Evolution* (1907. Trans. 1911. Reprint. New York: Modern Library, 1944. Reprint. London: Macmillan, 1954. Reprint. Westport, CT: Greenwood, 1975. Reprint. Lanham, MD: University Press of America, 1983); R. Ashley Audra, and Cloudesly Brereton, trans., *The Two Sources of Morality and Religion* (1932. Trans. 1935. Reprint. Garden City, NY: Doubleday, 1954. Reprint. Westport, CT: Greenwood, 1974. Reprint. Notre Dame, IN: University of Notre Dame Press, 1977); Mabelle L. Andison, trans., *The Creative Mind* (1934. Trans. 1946. Reprint. Totowa, NJ: Littlefield, Adams, 1965. Reprint. New York: Greenwood, 1968); Leon Jacobson, trans., *Duration and Simultaneity* (1922. Trans. Indianapolis: Bobbs-Merrill, 1965).

Other Sources

Fourastié, Jean. "Reflections on Laughing." *Diogenes* 121 (Spring 1983): 126-141. Notes that Bergson's *Laughter* is the most famous and most read book on laughter in the world; its incorrect thesis, however, has prevented other serious considerations of laughter. Defines a very different concept of laughter.

Gidley, Mick. "The Late Faulkner, Bergson, and God." *Mississippi Quarterly* 37 (1984): 377-383. Suggests that Faulkner's and Bergson's concepts of God were similar.

Gunter, Pete A. Y. "Bergson's Philosophical Method and Its Application to the Sciences." *Southern Journal of Philosophy* 16 (1978): 167-181. Argues that intuition and intelligence form a dialectic. Bergson's method applies today in thermodynamics and chronobiology.

Hall, Dorothy Judd. "The Height of Feeling Free: Frost and Bergson." *Texas Quarterly* 19 (1976): 128-143. Discusses influence of Bergson on Frost, especially in "The Grindstone," "West-Running Brook," and "Kitty Hawk."

Johnson, Richard E. *In Quest of a New Psychology: Toward a Redefinition of Humanism.* New York: Human Sciences, 1975. Suggests a model for psychology based on Bergson's tenets. Argues that humanistic psychology will fail because it lacks a scientific base.

Mitchell, Timothy. "Bergson, Le Bon, and Hermetic Cubism." *Journal of Aesthetics and Art Criticism* 36 (1977): 175-183. Explains the importance of Bergson's philosophy to the development of Cubism.

Roche de Coppens, Peter. "The Rediscovery of Bergson's work. Its Implications for Sociology in General and the Sociology of Religion in Particular." *Revista Internacional de Sociologia* 34 (1976): 133-160. Stresses the importance of Bergson's philosophy for an understanding of human nature. Describes Bergson's influence on William James, Carl Jung, Arnold Toynbee, and Mircea Eliade, among others.

Rosalie Murphy Baum
University of South Florida

George Berkeley
1685-1753

Chronology

Born George Berkeley on March 12, 1685, near Dysert Castle in County Kilkenny, Ireland, the eldest son of William Berkeley, a gentleman and a commissioned officer; raised at Dysert Castle; *1696* enters Kilkenny College; *1699 or 1700* enters Trinity College, Dublin; *1704* receives bachelor of arts degree from Trinity; *1707* named a Fellow of Trinity; publishes *Arithmetica and Miscellanea Mathematica*, probably as part of fellowship requirements; *1709* serves as librarian as Trinity; ordained as a deacon; publishes *An Essay Towards a New Theory of Vision*; *1710* ordained as a priest; publishes *Treatise Concerning the Principles of Human Knowledge*; *1710-11* serves as junior dean of Trinity; *1712* publishes *Passive Obedience*; *1713* publishes *Three Dialogues Between Hylas and Philonous*; serves as chaplain on a year-long embassy to Sicily with Charles Mordaunt, 3rd Earl of Peterborough; *1715* publishes *Advice to the Tories Who Have Taken the Oaths*; *1716-20* travels to Italy as tutor to George Ashe, son of the Bishop of Clogher; *1721* publishes *De motu* and *Essay Towards Preventing the Ruin of Great Britain*; *1724* appointed Dean of Derry; publishes *A Proposal For the better Supplying of Churches*; *1728* marries Anne Forster, daughter of the Chief Justice of Ireland, with whom he has five children; sets sail for the American colony of Rhode Island, where he lives for three years and plans the establishment of a missionary college in Bermuda; *1731* abandons plans for college and sails for London; *1732* publishes *Alciphron, or the Minute Philosopher*; *1733* publishes *The Theory of Vision, or Visual Languages . . . Vindicated and Explained*; *1734* appointed Bishop of Cloyne; publishes *The Analyst, or a Discourse Addressed to an Infidel Mathematician*; *1735* publishes *A Defense of Free-Thinking in Mathematics*; *1735-37* publishes the three-volume *The Querist*; *1737* elected to the Irish House of Lords; *1744* publishes *Siris*; *1752* attempts to resign his bishopric; moves to Oxford, England, to be near his son at Christ Church College; *1753* dies suddenly at Oxford on 14 January of unknown causes.

Activities of Historical Significance

George Berkeley, born in the closing decades of the seventeenth century, was educated in a philosophical milieu that had recently undergone profound changes brought on in a large part by the emergence of experimental science. An age that included such luminaries as Italian scientists Galileo Galilei and Evangelista Torricelli, British scientists Sir Isaac Newton and Robert Boyle and French philosophers Rene Descartes and Blaise Pascal, the seventeenth century saw the founding of the Royal Society in London and the increased influence of a new metaphysical worldview known variously as "the modern philosophy," "the corpuscularian philosophy," and "the atomical hypothesis."

It is common to divide Berkeley's intellectual career into three broadly defined periods. The early stage coincided roughly with his tenure at Trinity, beginning with 1704, when he completed his degree, and ending around 1713, when he left Ireland for the first time to serve as chaplain on the Earl of Peterborough's embassy to Sicily. To this early stage belong the works that record the results of Berkeley's metaphysical investigations. He examined visual distance, sight, touch, magnitude, and the senses, ultimately rejecting material substance, material causes, and abstract genral ideas as a means to truth.

The second period involves Berkeley's travels to London, Italy, France, and the American colonies—travels during which he published a number of philosophical discussions, including *De motu* (1721) and *The Theory of Vision* (1733). Berkeley's final period of intellectual activity began in 1734 with the appearance of *The Analyst, or a Discourse Addressed to an Infidel Mathematician* and ended with his death in 1753. His philosophical aims were to undermine skepticism and atheism by refuting materialism, to demonstrate God's existence and immateriality, to show the immortality of the soul, and to clarify current scientific and philosophical confusion.

During the Trinity years, Berkeley produced the works upon which the greater part of his fame rests. Beginning with *An Essay Towards a New Theory of Vision* (1709), in which he wrestled with the visual apprehension of distance and the size and the relative position of objects and came to the conclusion that the real objects of sight were within the mind, Berkeley went on in 1710 to produce his *Treatise Concerning the Principles of Human Knowledge*. This work contains three sections, the first of which rejects the existence of tangible matter, claiming instead that the existence of an object lies in its ability to be perceived by a mind—*esse est percipi*, or "to be is to be perceived." The second section contains Berkeley's attempts to answer objections that he knew would be raised to his ideas; the third and last section discusses the consequences—both epistemological and theological—of his new principles. In 1713, Berkeley published *Three Dialogues Between Hylas and Philonous*, which was aimed at a wider readership, and re-presented the ideas of the Principles in a simpler and more attractive format.

The Trinity years also saw Berkeley's ordination first as a deacon in 1709 and then as a priest in 1710. He also served the college as a librarian in 1709, as a junior dean from 1710 to 1711, and as a lecturer in Greek and Hebrew; on occasion he preached at services in the Trinity College chapel.

Berkeley left Ireland in 1713 for London, where he quickly joined Jonathan Swift's circle, which included such literary figures as Alexander Pope, Joseph Addison, and Sir Richard Steele, in whose periodical *The Guardian* Berkeley published fourteen essays. Two trips to the Continent followed, the second of which is vividly recorded in Berkeley's journals. On his return to England in 1721, Berkeley published *De motu*, in which he argued against Sir Isaac Newton's ideas on space, time, and motion as absolute measurements of the material world. Shortly thereafter, Berkeley returned to Dublin and Trinity and once more took up his duties, this time as a senior fellow and lecturer in divinity.

In 1724 Berkeley was elected Dean of Derry, thus ending his long association with Trinity College. Although appointed and in possession of a rather lucrative preferment there, Berkeley never became a resident of Derry. He did visit the city to take possession of the deanery and to arrange for the care of his property holdings, but his energy was largely devoted to developing his idea of building a college on the British island of Bermuda for the education of both the sons of colonial planters and a select group of American Indians. The venture was made possible when Berkeley received a surprise legacy from Esther Vanhomrigh—whom Swift had immortalized in his "Vanessa"—who had, upon her death, left to Berkeley half her extensive property. When the British Parliament approved a substantial grant for the college, Berkeley sailed for America in 1728 with his wife, Anne Forster Berkeley. Settling in Newport, Rhode Island, the Berkeleys bought land and built a house while they waited for the money from Parliament. When word arrived that the funds would not be sent as promised, the Berkeleys returned to England in 1731.

The Newport sojourn produced *Alciphron, or The Minute Philosopher*, a defense of Christianity and theism combined with attacks on deists and free-thinkers. Published in 1732, *Alciphron*, with its appended essay on vision, provoked attack from an anonymous writer as well as replies from a number of contemporary thinkers, including Berkeley's former teacher Peter Browne. Berkeley countered with *The Theory of Vision, or Visual Language . . . Vindicated and Explained* (1733). He followed with *The Analyst, or a Discourse Addressed to an Infidel Mathematician* in 1734, provoking another long controversy among himself and eminent mathematicians and scientists. Berkeley eventually replied with *A Defense of Free-Thinking in Mathematics* and *Reasons for Not Replying*, both published in 1735 after the third phase of Berkeley's career had already begun.

Nominated to the bishopric of Cloyne in 1734 and consecrated to that office a few months later, Berkeley returned to Ireland, where he took up residence at the bishop's manse at Cloyne. The principal writings of the Cloyne period are *The Querist*, which was issued in three parts from 1735 to 1737, and *A Chain of Philosophical Reflexions and Inquiries* (1744), which sold out immediately and was reissued a short time later as *Siris*. *The Querist* is a discourse on economics—banking, currency, trade, industry—and the poverty of Ireland; Siris contains a substantial discussion and explanation of the medicinal properties of tar water, followed by a reflection on the infinite Mind.

In 1752 Berkeley resigned his bishopric with the intention of finding ''a quiet retreat'' in which to spend his old age. However, George II of England refused to accept the resignation, announcing that Berkeley could live where he wished but that he should die a bishop. Accordingly, Berkeley arranged for his brother, Dr. Robert Berkeley, and the bishop of Cork to perform his duties. The Berkeleys then traveled to Oxford, where their son George was attending Christ Church. Berkeley spent the last five months of his life in a house on Holywell Street in Oxford, where he died quietly.

Overview of Biographical Sources

It is interesting that Samuel Johnson, that skilled if opinionated biographer, wished to write a life of George Berkeley, a philosopher whose theories of immaterialism Johnson sought to refute by kicking a rock. The Berkeley family

withheld permission, with the consequence that in the decade immediately following Berkeley's death at least two unofficial and largely inauthentic biographies
appeared, portraying Berkeley as a well-meaning but absent-minded philosopher,
as an amiable and eccentric gentle soul singularly lacking in common sense. The
first of these spurious biographies, published in the *British Plutarch* and misspell-
ing the bishop's name among other errors, created the caricature of Berkeley that
was to persist in the learned public's imagination for generations.

In 1766, an unsigned article in *Biographia Britannica* became the first semireliable account of Berkeley's life. Although the article contains a number of
factual errors, it is clear that its author had access to some information from the
Berkeley family, and tried as well to acquire other authoritative information instead
of relying on hearsay.

To counteract the general misperceptions and to correct the inaccuracies of
earlier accounts, Robert Berkeley, younger brother of George, provided a written
account of his older brother's life and work for Joseph Stock, then a Trinity
Fellow, who published *An Account of the Life of George Berkeley* . . . in 1776.
Although still marred by errors, this work was reissued in a number of editions
with changes, and was finally published in the second edition of the *Biographia
Britannica.* Berkeley's widow, Anne, criticized the Stock biography, publishing in
the third volume of the *Biographia* a number of corrections and additions.

Other attempts at an accurate life of Berkeley were produced by Eliza Berkeley,
widow of Berkeley's son George, in 1797 and by A. Chalmers in 1812, but not
until A. C. Fraser's *Life and Letters of George Berkeley, D.D.* (Oxford: Clarendon,
1871) was an extensive and—for the time—exhaustive account of Berkeley's life
produced. Published before the discovery of Sir John Percival's collection of
Berkeley's correspondence, Fraser's account provides an incomplete portrait of the
bishop.

Two modern accounts must be mentioned: J. M. Hone's and M. M. Rossi's
Bishop Berkeley (New York: Macmillan, 1931), and John Wild's *George Berkeley*,
(1962). Both of these are accurate, but because they combine a discussion of
Berkeley's philosophy with an account of his life, the essential man comes through
only sketchily, although his ideas are lucidly and thoroughly presented.

A. A. Luce's *The Life of George Berkeley, Bishop of Cloyne*, the first carefully
researched genuine biography of George Berkeley (and still the definitive work),
appeared in 1949 and was reissued in 1968. Luce carefully points out in the

preface that his intention is to make all philosophical commentary subordinate to the biographical account of a complex and multi-faceted man, an attempt at which Luce succeeds admirably.

For an account of Berkeley's plans to create a university of Bermuda and his subsequent journey to America, see Benjamin Rand, *Berkeley's American Sojourn* (Cambridge: Harvard University Press, 1932); and Alice Brayton, *George Berkeley in Newport* (1954).

Evaluation of Principal Biographical Sources

Dancy, Jonathan. *Berkeley: An Introduction.* Oxford: Basil Blackwell, 1987. (**A, G**) A good introduction to Berkeley's *Principles* and *Three Dialogues.* The lucid text is aimed toward general readers and those new to the study of Berkeley's ideas.

Engle, Gale W., and Gabriele Taylor. *Berkeley's Principles of Human Knowledge: Critical Studies.* Belmont, CA: Wadsworth, 1968. (**A, G**) A collection of essays designed as an introduction to one of Berkeley's classical texts.

Hicks, G. Dawes. *Berkeley.* 1932. Reprint. New York: Russell & Russell, 1968. (**A, G**) Covers Berkeley's life, philosophy, and place in history in three extensive sections written both for the beginning student of philosophy and the more advanced scholar. Good bibliography of secondary material from the first part of the twentieth century.

Luce, A. A. *The Life of George Berkeley, Bishop of Cloyne.* 1949. Reprint. New York: Greenwood, 1968. (**A, G**) The definitive biography thus far, and the first biography to avoid lengthy discussion of Berkeley's works and their implications. The reprint adds a few newly discovered facts about Berkeley's family, and strengthens portions of the text. The work is authoritative, well-researched, and exhaustive. Appendices include information about the Berkeley offspring, about the purchase of the Rhode Island property, and about extant portraits of George Berkeley.

Pitcher, George. *Berkeley.* London: Routledge & Kegan Paul, 1977. (**A**) Considered by some Berkeley scholars to be one of the best available major studies of Berkeley's philosophy.

Urmson, J. O. *Berkeley.* Oxford: Oxford University Press, 1982. (**A, G**) A good objective introduction to Berkeley's life and works within the context of widely accepted philosophical and scientific beliefs of his age.

Warnock, G. J. *Berkeley.* Harmondsworth, U.K.: Penguin, 1953. (**A, G**) A brief treatment of Berkeley's ideas, concentrating chiefly on the major themes in the *Principles.* An excellent introduction to Berkeley's major doctrines.

Wild, John. *George Berkeley.* 1936. Reprint. New York: Russell and Russell, 1962. (**A, G**) A study of Berkeley's ideas in the context of his life. Wild states in his preface that Berkeley's thought cannot be separated from his life; this study thus covers a great deal of ground not only in its discussion of Berkeley's life but also in its elucidation of his philosophical theories.

Overview and Evaluation of Primary Sources

The most significant primary source is Berkeley's own four-volume notebook of ideas, memoranda, jottings, questions, and random thoughts written down intermittently from 1707 to 1709. Discovered among the Berkeley papers held by Archdeacon Rose, and initially published by Berkeley scholar A. C. Fraser in 1871 as the *Commonplace Book,* this collection of miscellaneous notes is important for its revelation of Berkeley's early intellectual development. The notebook, now known as *Philosophical Commentaries, Generally called the Commonplace Book,* edited by A. A. Luce (New York: T. Nelson, 1944), contains not only Berkeley's written reworkings of various ideas but also the records of his emotions as he contemplated the possible reactions to his theories.

The four notebooks containing Berkeley's travel diaries from his sixteen-month second journey to the Continent are in the British Museum, and they include detailed descriptions of cities and villages, terrain and natural scenery, and architecture and people. The diaries provide a portrait of an inquisitive and curious

Berkeley, of a friendly and accommodating traveler who was an indefatigable recorder and observer with the eye of an artist.

Also of interest are various letters by Berkeley and others in his wide circle of acquaintances and friends, available in the three major editions of Berkeley's collected works: an anonymously edited collection from 1784, the Fraser edition, *Commonplace Book* (1871), and the definitive nine-volume *The Works of George Berkeley, Bishop of Cloyne* (9 vols. Edinburgh: Nelson and Sons, 19481957), edited by A. A. Luce and T. E. Jessop.

In 1766, an unsigned article, "George Berkeley," in *Biographia Britannica* became the first semireliable account of Berkeley's life. Although the article contains a number of factual errors, it is clear that its author had access to some information from the Berkeley family and apparently tried to acquire other authoritative information instead of relying in hearsay and rumor. Robert Berkeley, younger brother of George, provided a written account of his older brother's life and work for Joseph Stock, then a Trinity Fellow, who published *An Account of the Life of George Berkeley* in 1776. Although still marred by errors, this work was reissued several times with corrections and was finally published in the second edition of the *Biographia Britannica*. Berkeley's widow, Anne Forster Berkeley, added a number of corrections and additions in the third volume of the *Biographia*.

Other attempts at an accurate life of Berkeley were produced by Eliza Berkeley, widow of Berkeley's son George, in 1797, and by A. Chalmers in 1812, but not until A. C. Fraser's *Life and Letters of George Berkeley, D.Div.* (1871) was an extensive and—for the time—exhaustive account of Berkeley's life produced. Published before the discovery of Sir John Percival's collection of Berkeley's correspondence, Fraser's account provides an incomplete portrait of the bishop.

Museums, Historical Landmarks, Societies

Brown University (Providence, RI). Sayles Hall has on display a portrait of Berkeley, copied from the original by an artist identified as "Pratt" from a group portrait by John Smibert entitled "The Dean and His Companions."

Hanwell Castle (Banbury, England). Houses a portrait of Berkeley painted in Rome by an unidentified artist.

Holywell Street (Oxford). Street on which Berkeley was residing at the time of his death.

Kilkenny College (Kilkenny, Ireland). Protestant boarding school attended by George Berkeley, Jonathan Swift, and William Congreve, among others.

Lambeth Palace (London). Houses a portrait of Berkeley by an unknown artist.

Massachusetts Historical Society (Boston). Has a painting of Berkeley made by Smibert during Berkeley's voyage to America.

National Gallery (Dublin). Contains a smaller version, said to be the work of Smibert as well, of the group portrait at Yale.

National Portrait Gallery (London). Houses a Smibert portrait, dated 1728.

Redwood Library and Athenaeum (Newport, Rhode Island). Owns yet another copy of the group portrait, this one by Alfred Hart.

Trinity Church (Newport, Rhode Island). Berkeley often preached from the pulpit here during his stay in America.

Trinity College (Dublin). Berkeley's alma mater. During his tenure here, he produced his major philosophical works. Regent House on campus has a portrait of Berkeley that may be by Vanderbank; the Fellows Common Room displays a Berkeley portrait by James Latham.

Whitehall (near Newport, RI). Berkeley's home during his American stay. Renovated and reopened to the public in 1980.

Yale University (New Haven, Connecticut). The library contains nearly a thousand volumes donated by Berkeley just before his return to England; the original of the painting, "The Dean and His Companions" (including Berkeley's wife Anne and son Henry), hangs in Trumbull Hall. The university still administers a fellowship that began as a bequest from Berkeley.

Other Sources

Bennett, J. F. *Locke, Berkeley and Hume.* Oxford: Clarendon, 1971. A comparative study of the three central themes of each philosopher, who are often grouped together as "empiricists."

Bracken, Harry. *Berkeley.* London: Macmillan, 1974. Places Berkeley's philosophy within their historical context.

Jessop, T. E. *A Bibliography of George Berkeley.* Oxford: Oxford University Press, 1934. Although dated, this is still a valuable guide to Berkeley's works and to the early secondary material. The bibliography has been updated to 1962 by C. M. Turbayne and R. Ware in the *Journal of Philosophy* (1963): 93-112.

E. D. Huntley
Appalachian State University

Hector Berlioz
1803-1869

Chronology

Born Louis-Hector Berlioz on December 11, 1803, in La Côte-St-André, in the *département* of Isère, France, the first of six children of Louis-Joseph Berlioz, a physician from an established and respected local family of professionals, and Marie-Antoinette Marmion Berlioz, daughter of a well-respected family from nearby Grenoble; *1813* attends, for a brief period, a seminary at La Côte; his father teaches him French and Latin literature and gives him instruction on the flute and the guitar; teaches himself basic music theory; *1819* submits a sextet and some songs to several Paris publishers and publishes his first composition, a romance entitled *Le dépit de la bergère*; *1821* receives his bachelor's degree at Grenoble; *1822* enrolls in medical school (against his wishes) at the École de Médecin in Paris; *1822-1823* publishes several romances; *1823-1825* publishes articles in *Le corsaire*; *1824* receives *baccalauréat de sciences physiques*; writes a mass (only the *Resurrexit* survives), which is performed at St. Roch; *1826* composes his opera *Les Francs-juges*; enters the Conservatoire de musique, putting himself at odds with his family over his failure to pursue medicine; *1827* enters competition for the Prix de Rome, for which he composes a cantata, *La mort d'Orphée*; meets Shakespearean actress Henrietta Smithson, whom he pursues passionately for the next few years; *1828* gives his first orchestral concert in Paris; awarded second prize in Prix de Rome competition; *1829* writes the *Waverley* overture and publishes *Huit scènes de Faust*, as opus 1; publishes first articles in *Berliner allgemeine musikalische Zeitung*; *1830* win the Prix de Rome for his cantata *La mort de Sadanapale* (most now lost); composes *Symphonie fantastique*; meets Hungarian composer Franz Liszt; proposes to Camille Moke; *1831* meets German composer Felix Mendelssohn in Italy; writes overtures the *King Lear* and *Rob Roy*; *1832* finishes *Le retour à la vie* (later renamed *Lélio*), the sequel to the *Symphonie*; publishes articles in *Revue européenne*; *1832-1842* devotes much energy to organizing and conducting performances of his music; *1833-1834* organizes a concert of his music, including *Symphonie* and *Lélio*; marries Henrietta Smithson, with whom he has one son; writes criticism for numerous musical and artistic periodicals; begins *Benvenuto Cellini*; composes *Harold en Italie* at the request of Italian violinist Niccoló Paganini; *1835-1836* continues writing for various periodicals; *1837* secures a commission for the *Grand Messe des morts*; *1838* writes for *Chronique de Paris*; *1839* composes *Roméo et Juliette*; *1840* receives government commission for *Grande symphonie funèbre et triomphale*, performed on July 28 to celebrate the anniversary of the 1830 revolution; *1841* composes piano version of the song cycle *Les nuits d'été*; begins work on a comprehensive study of the orchestration technique; *1842* leaves Paris, with singer Marie Recio, for a tour of Europe; meets with composers Robert Schumann, Mendelssohn, and Richard Wagner; his marriage to Henrietta dissolves; *1843* completes and publishes *Grand traité d'instrumentation et d'orchestration modernes*, opus 10; *1844* composes *Le carnaval romain*; writes *Voyage musical en Allemagne et en Italie*; *1845* performs in southern France, Germany, Austria, Bohemia, and Hungary; begins *La damnation de Faust*, which is based on his earlier *Scènes*; *1846* performs *La damnation*, to critical disapproval; *1847* tours England; *1849* composes *Te Deum*; *1850* begins his oratorio, *L'enfance du Christ*; *1852* publishes *Les soirées de l'orchestre*; *1854* Henrietta dies; marries Marie Recio seven months later; *1855* completes *Le chef d'orchestre: théorie de son art*; *Te Deum* performed at Exposition Universelle; first Paris performance of his oratorio *L'enfance du Christ*; *1856* begins *Les Troyens*; *1859* publishes *Les grotesques de la musique*; *1861* the first performance of *Les Troyens* at Théâtre-Lyrique is a failure; *1862* first performance of *Béatrice et Bénédict*; publishes *A travers chants*; *1864* a physical, spiritual, and emotional deterioration gradually causes him to retire from most activities; *1865* completes and revises his *Mémoires de Hector Berlioz* (published posthumously in 1870); *1869* dies on March 8, of complications due to physical deterioration, in Paris and is buried in the Cimetière de Montmartre.

Activities of Historical Significance

Hector Berlioz is the leading French musical figure of the first half of the nineteenth century. He made extraordinary contributions in many spheres of music and was one of the most intriguing and interesting musical personalities of all time. During his lifetime he achieved a reputation—though not the corresponding success—as a significant composer, author, music journalist, and conductor. A truly unorthodox, idiosyncratic individual with an erratic personality, Berlioz was sadly misunderstood during his lifetime; his music was unlike any then conceived, and most of his contemporaries struggled with his unique musical style. It can truthfully be said that even his immediate followers—with the exception of Robert Schumann, Camille Saint-Saens, and Nikolay Rimsky-Korsakov—for the most part failed to grasp his musical ideas, and thus they also failed to absorb and build upon them. Berlioz, therefore, stands as an isolated figure. Yet, in his music, his devotion to "the ideal," his expressiveness, audacity, and emphasis on the grandiose and bombastic, and his constant search for the means to express romantic ideals and attitudes, he represents the quintessence of romanticism for many people today. His intricate, imaginative, and evocative orchestrations, his attachment to the programmatic concept (which, in his own compositions, reflected the literary sources that he so loved), and his interesting, daring concepts of form all derive from his unconventional personality and attitudes about music.

Though Berlioz was a prolific composer, his principal contributions to the history of music lie in his brilliance at the art of orchestration and his important writings about music and musical life. His *Grand traité d'instrumentation* (1843) stands as the first significant work in this area, but it is his music that reveals most clearly his brilliant understanding of the orchestral palette. Ever anxious to employ the newest instruments, to explore new combinations and to extend the capabilities of all instruments, he filled his scores with an almost unbelievable array of highly evocative orchestral colors and effects. His scores abound with very specific "instructions" to the performer, even taking into account the importance of spatial placement of instruments and singers. In this attention to details of color and his belief that music should be properly fitted to its performance space, he stands as a precursor to twentieth-century thought. Integral aspects of his style include extreme care in the use of dynamic ranges and effects as well as careful use of rhythm and tempo. No composer before him and few after were as successful in creating "musical images."

His skill at orchestration has, perhaps unfortunately, caused many writers to pass over his other interesting and important innovations. Though he read widely and was very knowledgeable about the music of his predecessors and contemporaries, many new, "untried" ideas affected his musical style. Especially important are his interesting concepts of musical process and form. These include his exploration of cyclic form (the use of recurring musical material to lend cohesion to large, multiple-movement works), the skillful transformation of the character of a musical idea by lacing it in new harmonic or rhythmic contexts, his use of then-unconventional, chromatic key relationships between major sections of compositions, and his innovations in the processes by which musical ideas are developed or "worked out."

Berlioz also stands as the first important French music journalist and critic; his sophisticated, often humorous journalistic observations cover virtually every aspect of musical life in his time. His critical opinions and other writings, most later collected in *Les soirées de l'orchestre* (1852), *Les grotesques de la musique* (1859) and *A travers chants* (1862), appeared regularly in the most important Parisian journals, especially during the last decades of his life. He presented reviews and commentaries on concerts and the latest musical trends and wrote on both famous and new young musicians, music in other countries, new instruments, and aspects of the art of conducting. Indeed, no aspect of musical life escaped his eye, ear, or pen. A discerning and discriminating observer, he was dedicated to the highest musical ideals and was one of the first to advocate historically accurate performances of music, often railing against the "improvement" of earlier scores. If, as his biographers have noted, he failed to gain recognition during his lifetime (ironically, particularly in his own country) or even in the decades after his death, it appears that now, more than 100 years after his death, a full understanding and appreciation of the man and his music seems finally to be at hand.

Overview of Biographical Sources

The task of compiling a complete and thoroughly accurate account of Berlioz's life has fallen to the scholars of the twentieth century. Though a considerable amount of literature on Berlioz dates from his lifetime, much of it consists of brief commentaries. Also, a profusion of conflicting anecdotal material and "romanticized" writings (especially during the nineteenth century) inspired by Berlioz's popular reputation as a bizarre personality has clouded the picture considerably.

Except for Eugène de Mirecourts's *Berlioz* (Paris: Gustave Havard, 1856; **A**), no full biographical studies appeared until more than a decade after his death. These include Adolphe Jullien's *Hector Berlioz: la vie et le combat; les oeuvres* (Paris:

Charavay, 1882; **A**); *Hector Berlioz: sa vie et ses oeuvres* (Paris: Libraire d'Art, 1888; **A**); Edmond Hippeau's *Berlioz intime* (Paris: La Renaissance musicale, 1883; **A**); and *Berlioz et son temps* (Paris: Ollendorf, 1890; **A**).

The celebration of the centenary of his birth in 1903 produced several important biographical studies and also resulted in Charles Malherbe and Felix Weingartner's *Hector Berlioz Werke* (20 vols. Leipzig: Breitkopf und Härtel, 1900-1907; **A**). Primary among the works from this period are Jacques-Gabriel Prod'homme's *Hector Berlioz (1803-1869): sa vie et ses oeuvres* (Paris: Delagrave, 1904; **A**); Julien Tiersot's *Berlioz et la societe de son temps* (Paris: Hachette, 1904; **A**); and Adolphe Boschot's study, *L'histoire d'un romantique: Hector Berlioz* (3 vols. Paris: Plon, 1906-1908; **A**). Except for Walter J. Turner's *Berlioz: the Man and his Work* (1934) and Edward Lockspeiser's *Berlioz* (1939), no additional major studies appeared until Jacques Barzun's *Berlioz and the Romantic Century* (1950), which was revised as *Berlioz and His Century* (1982).

The centennial of Berlioz's death in 1969 produced many studies and resulted in Hugh Macdonald, ed., *New Edition of the Complete Works of Berlioz* (Kassel: Barenreiter, 1969-; **A**), in addition to the revision of Barzun's biography (cited above). Recent scholarship has added much to the knowledge of Berlioz's life and music and had corrected many inaccuracies in some earlier writings. Among these works are Hugh Macdonald's *Berlioz* (1982), and the same author's "Berlioz" entries in the *New Grove Dictionary of Music and Musicians,* reprinted and expanded in the *New Grove Early Romantic Masters* (1985). The most recent, and perhaps the most definitive, work is D. Kern Holoman's *Berlioz* (1989).

Evaluation of Principal Biographical Sources

Barzun, Jacques. *Berlioz and the Romantic Century.* Boston: Little, Brown, 1950. (**A, G**) First, but still an important biography of Berlioz in English, this study also contains excellent material on nineteenth-century culture and a detailed bibliography, despite numerous citation errors. It was revised in 1956 and again in 1969, and published under the title *Berlioz and his Century* (1956. Reprint. Chicago: University of Chicago Press, 1982).

Bennett, Joseph. *Hector Berlioz.* London: n.p. 1883. (**G, Y**) One of the better

English biographies dating from before the turn of the century; as such, it provides a good sense of Berlioz's position in the musical world at that time.

Clarson-Leach, Robert. *Berlioz: His Life and Times*. New York: Hippocrene Books, 1983. (**G, Y**) Part of a large series on famous composers, this is a brief but good, non-technical discussion of Berlioz's life with many illustrations.

Daniskas, John. *Hector Berlioz*. 1948. Reprint. Stockholm: Continental, 1949. Translated by W. A. G. Doyle-Davidson. (**G, Y**) An excellent, brief biography with many photos, facsimiles, and musical examples.

Holoman, D. Kern. *Berlioz*. Cambridge, MA: Harvard University Press, 1989. (**A, G**) The most recent and most important source in English. It provides not only the most complete biographical account of his life but also comprises the most revealing account of Berlioz's musical and social activity. Many illustrations and figures, and ample musical examples are included. The copious and annotated appendices include a list of performances of his own music by Berlioz (including dates, venues and performers), a list of the most important prose writings and a chronological list of compositions, including sources.

Lockspeiser, Edward. *Berlioz*. London: Novello, 1939. (**A, G**) One of the earliest studies in English, this includes a good, if brief discussion of the life and works of Berlioz.

Macdonald, Hugh. *Berlioz*. London: Dent, 1982. (**A, G**) One of the better English biographies, this volume includes a brief discussion of Berlioz's character and lifestyle as well as the standard biographical details. Most of the important works are discussed from a stylistic and historic viewpoint, incorporating quotes from Berlioz's writings. Many earlier biographical inaccuracies are corrected, and the appendices include a calendar of events and a list of important people in Berlioz's life.

————. "Berlioz." In *The New Grove Dictionary of Music and Musicians*, edited by Stanley Sadie. Vol. 2. London: Macmillan, 1980: 579-610. (**A, G**) A concise review of the major events in Berlioz's life as well as a listing of works, dates and venues of first performances, locations of sources, and a good basic bibliography.

—————. "Berlioz." In *The New Grove Early Romantic Masters 2: Weber, Berlioz, Mendelssohn*, edited by H. MacDonald, J. Warrack, and K-H Kohler. New York: Norton, 1985: 87-195. (**A, G**) This valuable addition to Berlioz literature expands upon the *New Grove Dictionary* article, and includes an updated list of his works and an expanded bibliography.

Turner, Walter J. *Berlioz: The Man and his Work*. 1934. Reprint. New York: Vienna house, 1974. (**G, Y**) A good, nontechnical discussion of Berlioz's music, which, though lacking musical examples or detailed musical analyses, does include a chronological list of major works and an essay on Berlioz as music critic. This is one of the best of the early biographies in English.

Overview and Evaluation of Primary Sources

There are two complete editions of Berlioz's musical works, Charles Malherbe and Felix Weingartner's *Hector Berlioz Werke* (20 vols. Leipzig: Breitkopf und Härtel, 1900-1907), and Hugh Macdonald's *New Edition of the Complete Works* (Kassell: Barenreiter, 1969-; **A**). This new edition of the complete works, known as the *NBE*, will comprise twenty-three volumes when completed.

Many of Berlioz's writings and letters exist in untranslated versions. Among the most important English translations are William Apthorp's *Hector Berlioz: Selections from his Letters, and Aesthetic, Humorous and Satirical Writings* (1879. Reprint. Portland, ME: Longwood Press, 1976; **A**); and Jacques Barzun's *New Letters of Berlioz: 1830-1868* (New York: Columbia University Press, 1954; **A**), which includes adjacent English translations, a checklist of unpublished Berlioz letters, and a chronology of Berlioz's domiciles. Humphrey Searle's *Hector Berlioz: a Selection from his Letters* (New York: Harcourt, Brace and World, 1966; **A**), offers a good general collection of the letters from 1819-1868.

Berlioz's treatises and other writings can be found in the following translations: J. Broadhouse, trans., *The Conductor: The Theory of His Art* (A translation of *Le chef d'orchestre* [1855]. Reprint. St. Clair Shores, MI: Scholarly Press, 1976; **A**);

David Cairns, *The Mémoires of Hector Berlioz* (New York: Norton, 1975; **A**), which is a translation of Berlioz's *Mémoires* (1865) that includes accounts of his travels in Italy, Germany, Russia, and England; M. C. Clarke, *A Treatise Upon Modern Instrumentation and Orchestration* . . . (1850. Rev. ed. New York: Novello, 1882; **A**), edited by J. Bennett, which is a translation of *Grand traité* . . . (1843); E. Evans, *Beethoven's Symphonies* (New York: Scribner's, 1914; **A**); *Gluck and his Operas* (London: Reeves, 1914; **A**); and *Mozart, Weber and Wagner* (New York: Scribner's, 1918; **A**), separate publications comprising translations of *A travers chants* (1862); and C. R. Fortescue, *Evenings with the Orchestra* (London: Penguin, 1963; **A**), which provides the most recent of three translations of *Soirées* . . . (1854).

Principal Works

Large instrumental works

Symphonie fantastique (1830)
Harold en Italie (1834)
Roméo et Juliette (1839)
Grande symphonie funèbre et triomphale (1840)

Overtures

Waverly (1826-1828)
Rob Roy (1831)
Rob Roy (1839)
Le carnaval romain (1843)

Operas

Les francs-juges (1826)
Benvenuto Cellini (1836-1838)
Les Troyens (1856-1858)

Vocal Works

La mort d'Orphée (1827)
Huit scènes de Faust (1828-1829)
Le retour à la vie [Lélio] (1831)
Grand messe des morts [Requiem] (1837)
Les nuits d'été (1841)
La damnation de Faust (1845-1846)
Te deum (1849)
L'enfance du Christ (1853-1854)

Prose

Grand traité d'instrumentation et d'orchestration modernes (1843. 2d ed., 1855)
includes *L'art du ched d'orchestre* (1855)
Voyage musical en Allemagne et en Italie (1844)
Les soirées de l'orchestra (1852)
Les grotesques de la musique (1859)
A travers chants (1862)
Mémoires de Hector Berlioz (1870)

Fiction and Adaptations

Berlioz has been the subject of a number of poems, including those by Jean Celle, "A Hector Berlioz" (1890); Charles Grandmougin, "A Hector Berlioz" (1878); Victor Roussy in "Le ménestrel" (1836); odes and other honoraria by G. Lefevre, "Ode à Berlioz" (1890); L. Nublat, "Gloire à Berlioz" (1903); L. Pocat "Hommage à Berlioz" (1903); and Meyerstein in *The Music Review* (November 1943). He is also the subject of *Berlioz: Piece in quatre Actes à dix-neuf Tableaux* (1927), a play by C. Mère, and *Symphonie fantastique* (Delta Productions, [n.d.]), a film. Berlioz, Wagner, and Rossini were the subjects of a satiric vaudeville presented in Paris in the mid 1850s. Selections from his music have been used in several films, most recently *Sleeping with the Enemy* (1990).

Museums, Historical Landmarks, Societies

Bibliothèque nationale (Paris). Manuscripts of his music, portraits, and other visual depictions of the composer are located here.

La Côte-St-André (Isère, France). Berlioz's birthplace is now a museum.

The Musée Instrumental Conservatoire Nationale Supérieur de Musique (Paris). This museum owns Berlioz's guitar, as well as many manuscripts and other memorabilia.

Portraits. Many painters have chosen Berlioz as a subject for their work. These include portraits by Dubufe (1830, the first "official" portrait); Gustave Courbet (1850, Louvre); and Honoré Daumier (1850-60, Musée de Versailles). There are also drawings by Alphonse Legros (Fitzwilliam Museum, Cambridge) and J. A. D. Ingrès (pencil sketch). Countless caricatures attest to Berlioz's flamboyance; especially notable are those by Horace Vernet (c. 1831), Gustave Doré (1850), and Carjat and Daumier (*Le charivari*, 1856). Berlioz was much-photographed, and of the many lithographs, Prinzhofer's (1845, Vienna) was thought a good likeness. Busts were cast by J.-J. Perraud (1875, Grenoble Bibliothèque municipale) and Carlier (1885, Paris Bibliothèque Opéra); statues by Basset and Lenoir (both melted for bronze during the German occupation), and Blatez (1948, Nice); and a death mask by Lami ([n.d.], Bibl. Opéra). His figure was on the 40c and 55c stamps of the Third French Republic in 1936, and medallions by Godebski (1884, on Berlioz's first Monument in the Cimetière de Montmartre) and Leverd (c. 1830), as well as a medal (1953, Bouret) issued by the French Hôtel de la Monnaie. His house on Montmartre has been the subject of paintings by Utrillo and one attributed to Van Gogh.

Statue (Square Berlioz, 9th arondissement, Paris).

Tomb (Cimetière de Montmartre, Paris). Location of Berlioz's remains.

Other Sources

Appert, Donald. "Berlioz, the Conductor." Dissertation, University of Kansas, 1985. Discusses Berlioz's importance in the historical development of orchestral conducting.

Barzun, Jacques. *Hector Berlioz: Critical Questions on Music and Letters, Culture and Biography, 1940-1980.* Chicago: University of Chicago Press, 1982. Examines major issues in Berlioz research.

Holoman, D. Kern, ed. *Catalog of the Works of Hector Berlioz.* Kassel: Barenreiter, 1987. The definitive catalog of Berlioz music and prose; it includes, in addition to the usual scholarly apparatus, lists of performances during Berlioz's lifetime, notations of Berlioz's borrowing or reuse of themes from early compositions in later works, as well as sketches and fragmentary scores of planned but never-completed works.

Hopkinson, Cecil. *A Bibliography of the Musical and Literary Works of Hector Berlioz, 1803-1869, With Histories of the French Music Publishers Concerned.* Edinburgh: Edinburgh Bibliographical Society, 1980. A good publication history that includes locations of manuscripts and a section on the French publishers of Berlioz's music.

Klein, John W. "Berlioz's Personality." *Music and Letters* 50, 1 (1969): 15-24. An interesting study of Berlioz's complex personality.

Langford, Jeffrey, and Jane D. Graves. *Hector Berlioz: A Guide to Research.* New York: Garland, 1989. The most recent bibliographic guide to writings by and about Berlioz, his life, his music (including a guide to literature on specific works), criticism, travels, and association with other musical figures. This is an indispensable tool for research at any level.

Murphy, Kerry. *Hector Berlioz and the Development of French Music Criticism,* Studies in Musicology, edited by G. Buelow, No. 97. Ann Arbor: University of Michigan Research Press, 1988. This book includes a complete list of the journalistic music criticism of Berlioz, in addition to treating his importance in the history of music criticism.

Wright, Michael. *A Berlioz Bibliography: Critical Writing on Hector Berlioz from 1825-1986.* Farnborough: St. Michael's Abbey Press, 1988.

William E. Melin
Lafayette College

Gian Lorenzo Bernini
1598-1680

Chronology

Born Gian Lorenzo Bernini on December 7, 1598 in Naples, Italy, to Pietro Bernini, a sculptor of some talent, and Angelina Galante Bernini; *1598-1604* family lives in Naples while his father pursues an unremarkable career; *1604-1605* the family relocates to Rome where Pietro begins work for the court of Pope Paul V; the boy's remarkable talents in sculpture begin to emerge, trained by his father and encouraged by members of the court; *1612* carves portrait bust of the surgeon Antonio Coppola; *1613-1614* carves *Boy with a Dragon*; *1615* first papal commission, *The Goat Almathea with the Infant Jupiter and a Faun*; *1616-1617* sculpts two statues of martyrs, St. Sebastian and St. Lawrence; *1619* produces *Aeneas, Anchises, and Ascanius Fleeing Troy*, his first major work, and two busts, the *Anima Beata* and *Anima Dannata*; *1620* finishes a large sculpture, *Neptune and Triton*, for which he is named president of the Academy of St. Luke; *1621* knighted by Pope Gregory XV; *1621-1626* produces *Pluto and Persephone*, the *Apollo and Daphne*, *David*, and the portrait busts *Monsignor Pedro de Foix Montoya* and *Antonio Cepparelli*, as well as a new facade for the Church of St. Bibiana and the full-length figure of the young martyr over the altar; *1627* studies painting under Andrea Sacchi; paints *Saints Andrew and Thomas*; *1627-1629* designs the *Barcacci Fountain* in the Piazza di Spagna; appointed Architect of St. Peter's at age thirty and begins to design the massive bronze structure, the *Baldachin*, with a studio of sculptors under his direction; carves the fourteen-foot high *St. Longinus* for the interior of the basilica; *1630-1632* carves bust of his foremost patron, Pope Urban VIII and continues design work on the interior of St. Peter's; *1632* carves bust of Cardinal Scipione Borghese, incredibly lifelike even by Bernini's standards; *1633-1636* produces a bust of King Charles I of England from a painting by Anthony Van Dyck, as well as a bust of the king's messenger, Thomas Baker; twin busts of the eccentric Duke of Bracciano, Paulo Giordano Orsini and his duchess, and an unusual portrait of his own mistress, Constanza Bonarelli, the wife of an artist working in Bernini's studio; *1637-1639* continues work on St. Peter's, particularly the bell towers on either side of the facade; becomes ill for some months and is urged to change his lifestyle; *1640* completes renovation of the Barbarini Palace, leaves Constanza and marries Caterina Tezio, with whom he has eleven children; *1641-1643* continues work on the bell towers, although cracks are beginning to appear in the foundations; work on a long-time project for Pope Urban, his tomb, progresses as the pope nears the end of his reign; *1643* completes a small but imaginative monument to the nun Maria Raggi; *1644* loses his greatest friend and patron upon the death of Pope Urban VIII; *1645* a new pope, Innocent X, discovers that Pope Urban had spent the Vatican almost into bankruptcy and is therefore not disposed favorably towards Bernini; *1646* the bell towers of St. Peter's are pulled down, a professional disaster for Bernini; there were many artists in Rome who had resented his near-monopoly on papal commissions and his critics had a field day with this misfortune; *1647* completes Pope Urban's tomb and begins work for the Cornaro family on a chapel which will contain a superb sculpture, *The Ecstacy of St. Theresa*; *1648-1650* finishes the interior design of St. Peter's; renovates the Montecitorio Palace; *1650* produces the portrait bust of the Duke of Modena, Francisco d'Este; *1651* wins over Pope Innocent with his design of the *Four Rivers Fountain* in the Piazza Navona; *1652* finishes the Cornaro Chapel; *1655* becomes closely associated with the papacy once more upon the beginning of Pope Alexander VII's reign; *1655-1657* renovates the Church of Santa Maria del Popolo, creating two sculptures of prophets: *Daniel* and *Habakkuk and the Angel*; *1656* begins the construction of the collonades around St. Peter's Square; *1657* begins work on the *Cathedra Petri* inside St. Peter's basilica, as well as on the outside colonnades and their crowning statues of saints, all of which would take eight years to complete; *1658* begins to design a chapel for the Jesuits, the Sant' Andrea al Quirinale, an eleven-year task; *1661-1663* creates full-length statues of St. Mary Magdalen and St. Jerome; *1664* designs the church of Santa Maria dell' Assunzione, a three-year-long project; *1665* leaves his country for the first time to work for Louis XIV in Paris for six months, producing an heroic portrait bust of the king as well as plans for the completion of the Louvre; *1666* back in Rome, seeing to the completion of the *Scala Regia*, a large and ancient private stairwell from the Pope's apartments in the Vatican to St. Peter's; it also contains a magnificent equestrian statue of St. Constantine on one landing; *1667* produces *The Elephant and the Obelisk*, a monument to Pope Alexander' in the Piazza della Minerva; *1668* begins to renovate the ancient bridge over the Tiber, the Pont Sant' Angelo, with a new balustrade and ten huge statues of angels to line it and carves a half-length statue of the physician Gabriele Fonseca at prayer; *1670* completes the chapel for the Jesuit novices on the hill Quirinale, Sant' Andrea; *1671-1673* designs the altar and tabernacle for the Chapel of the Blessed Sacrament in St. Peter's; *1674* produces the full-length portrait sculpture *The Death of the Blessed Ludovica Albertoni* for her tomb; *1675-1678* designs the tomb of Pope Alexander VII in St. Peter's; *1680* carves his last work, the *Salvator Mundi*, now lost, although two copies may exist; dies on November 28, 1680.

Activities of Historical Significance

Gian Lorenzo Bernini was the great artist of his age, but he lived in an age of ironies. Sculptor, architect, engineer, playwright and stage designer, even a composer of musical scores for his plays, he was able to fulfill his many-sided genius by the immense good fortune of being born into a sculptor's family and then being relocated to the artistic center of the Western world—the papal court of Rome. But, as he predicted, his popularity as an artist would go into a dramatic decline after his death, from which it has only recently begun to recover.

Bernini was recognized for his exceptional talent early in his life, and as a thirteen-year-old he was already making portraits that revealed remarkable skill, such as the bust of Antonio Cippola, evoking the dignity and fragility of the elderly surgeon whom young Bernini had never met; the portrait was begun weeks after the old man's death and was done only from a death-mask. At seventeen he received the first of many papal commissions, *The Goat Amalthea with the Infant Jupiter and a Faun*. In 1620 he finished a large sculpture designed for a cardinal's water garden. The *Neptune and Triton*, a work unlike any that he had produced before in the power and expressiveness of its composition—an angry god, weapon in hand, strides forward to command the mighty waters at his feet, his young son, blows a trumpet blast on a large conch shell, rising chest-high beneath him. In recognition of his work, the young sculptor was named president of the Roman Academy of St. Luke, and was honored for a portrait of Pope Gregory XV by being knighted the very next year into the Papal Order of Christ, allowing him to use the title *Cavaliere*.

Now twenty-three years old, Bernini began to produce revolutionary work. His

Pluto and Persephone, the *Apollo and Daphne*, and his own *David*, a biblical figure in the tradition of the giants of the Quattrocento, Michelangelo and Donatello, were foundations of a new style—the Baroque, which would eventually sweep Europe, and shape art and architecture even to the far reaches of St. Petersburg in Russia. Never before had flesh portrayed in marble seemed so pliant, or hair and limbs so free to express extremes or subtleties of emotion. But Bernini's desire to capture the attention of and draw in his audience did not end with freeing himself from working, as Michelangelo with whom he identified had, with a single block of stone whittled down to find a shape within. Bernini worked the stone from front to back, allowing new ideas to occur to him even as he carved; he joined several blocks of stone together as he needed them. More importantly, he used his sense of the theatrical to make the spectator part of the action represented by the statue. The struggling Persephone turns her head away from Pluto, who has just seized her, and towards the spectator, as if pleading for his help. David is poised to hurl his stone up at his enemy Goliath, as if the giant were standing just behind the viewer. Daphne is at her maximum of terror just as Apollo has caught up with her, as if she not yet aware of her beginning transformation into a tree.

With the ascension of his good friend Urban VIII to the papacy in 1623, Bernini's scope expanded to include papal commissions in architecture. His principal project would be the completion of St. Peter's, the central monument of Roman Catholicism to which many great artists had already contributed. The interior decoration of the basilica, which included the baldachin, or bronze canopy, over the grave of St. Peter under the dome, would occupy Bernini and a phalanx of assistants for nearly a decade.

While his studio executed his designs for St. Peter's, Bernini carried on with other commissions in other religious as well as secular sculpture. These began with the enraptured martyr *Saint Bibiana* (1624-1626), and includes the dramatic centurion-saint *St. Longinus* (1629-1638). But his most remarkable portrait yet was the lively bust of the corpulent Cardinal Scipione Borghese (1632), done with Bernini's exhaustive and particular method of following his subject throughout his normal routine for days at a time, making one drawing after another of unstudied poses, until enough information was gathered to make a sculpture with or without the subject present.

Bernini's fame as a portraitist of the first magnitude had spread to the rest of Europe by 1635, resulting in a commission from the Catholic king of England,

Charles I, based on Van Dyck's famous triptych painting. A private portrait bust of Bernini's mistress, the wild Constanza Bonarelli, was done about the same time; some critics think it a work ahead of its time in its sheer unvarnished naturalism.

The sculptor set the standard in Rome for monuments large and small; he transformed the plain geometric shapes of the typical Roman fountain into a spectacle of mythic fantasy with the *Triton Fountain* in the Barberini Plaza. A smaller but equally imaginative monument, the tomb of the nun Maria Raggi (1643) presaged the unveiling of the tomb of longtime friend and patron Pope Urban VIII later in the decade.

The year 1646 nearly saw the end of Bernini's architectural career in Rome with the destruction of St. Peter's bell towers, which had to be pulled down because of soggy foundations. An unsympathetic new pope, Innocent X, was disinclined to use Bernini's talents, and Bernini went without a new papal commission for several years. When Innocent X saw the *Four Rivers Fountain* (1651) in the Piazza Navona, he realized Bernini's genius, but Bernini was not completely restored to papal nepotism until Alexander VII became pope in 1655.

During the years between Urban VII and Alexander VII, Bernini invented a new style of "heroic portraiture" suited to an age of autocrats by creating a bust that has the young Duke of Modena surmounting a swirl of cloak and armor, a configuration destined to be linked to the more potent figure Louis XIV during the next decade. This worldly power contrasts with the great spiritual effect of the *Ecstacy of Saint Theresa* in the Cornaro Chapel, a design considered by many critics to be the best of Bernini's many sculptures.

With the ascension of Alexander VII to the papacy in 1655 Bernini returned to a close association with the papal court. In this decade he began to evolve a new, late style in his sculpture that would not become fully pronounced until the 1660s; his figures become more ethereal in expression and proportions, with longer limbs and more agitated drapery; his composition becomes more varied and asymmetrical. His architectural projects became widely known beyond the borders of his native country, particularly as the piazza in front of St. Peter's Church began construction. Also known as St. Peter's Square, where even today thousands gather to hear and be blessed by the pope from his balcony, it is defined by two immense colonnades that emerge from either side of the church facade, then curve outward to enclose the obelisk and two fountains at the center of the piazza in an ellipse. Atop the colonnades are huge statues, one hundred and forty in all, of the Apostles, popes, and bishops of the Catholic church.

The *Cathedra Petri* or Chair of St. Peter was conceived as a monument inside the church, encompassing and exalting the papal throne. It was to be the main focus of the church and symbolically, the center of the Christian world, a response to the Reformation. It was a project that needed to stand out among the many treasures of Rome and of the Vatican itself, that could visually compete with the work of Raphael and Michelangelo. Bernini's design included a marble altar topped by thirty-foot high bronze statues of two saints and two bishops in vigorous poses; just above them is a throne carved with the image of Christ and his apostles, and above all is a window with the image of a dove, the Holy Spirit, surrounded by radiance and a sculptural explosion of flying cherubim and seraphim in gilt bronze. It is as if Heaven itself is piercing the solid walls of the church to reach out to the pilgrim.

These massive renovations took nine years for the artist and a shop of talented assistants to accomplish, yet in the final months of construction, Bernini was not even in the country. With his son Paulo and another assistant he was engaged in the service of the formidable Sun King of France, Louis the XIV, for a short but significant time, as the French king was the first monarch to have the political leverage to pry loose such a prize from the papacy.

In the first six months of 1665 Bernini produced two items of greatest significance and influence: a heroic portrait of the king and drawings for the completion of the royal residence in Paris, the Louvre. While the portrait was an immediate success, the plans for the Louvre were never implemented. But the plans proved an inspiration to architects all over Europe. While a guest of the young diplomat de Chantelou, Bernini was having his own portrait made in the private diary of his host. It candidly but with affection documents the working methods that produced the bust of the king along with the purely human side of the artist.

By 1666 Bernini was back in Rome seeing to the completion of what he regarded as his most difficult technical challenge, the *Scala Regia*. This private papal stairway between St. Peter's and the Vatican had been in desperate need of redesign and renovation for many years. Bernini engineered a wider and safer stairway and an aesthetically pleasing passage as well, even including an equestrian statue of St. Constantine, first Christian emperor of Rome and builder of a basilica on the same site that predates the present St. Peter's.

In 1667 Bernini was at work on a new commission for a new pope, Clement IX:

the renovation of the ancient bridge across the river Tiber, the Ponte Sant' Angelo. In 1670 he completed a twelve-year project for the Jesuit order: the *Sant'Andrea al Quirinale*, a small church built on one of Rome's seven hills, for the devotions of Jesuit novices; it was one of Bernini's personal favorites. Its exterior is classical and subdued, but its interior is Baroque and a fine example of Bernini's late style. His late fascination with varicolored marbles and gilded figures here translates into an exuberant vision of heaven, towards which a large white marble statue of St. Andrew the apostle, high over the altar, is gesturing.

His last project for St. Peter's, the altar for the Chapel of the Blessed Sacrament, completed in 1673, shows a mixture of different-colored marbles and bronze with lapis lazuli, yet is more subdued in its use of gilt on white stucco. Two magnificent bronze angels kneel on either side of the tabernacle, a miniature temple in front of a large painting of the Trinity set back under a white and golden arch. The Baroque exuberance is here scaled back to provide a more restful effect conducive to quiet meditation.

Bernini was now seventy-five years old. In his old age his energy may have diminished, but his creativity did not. In the 1670s he continued to produce work of the highest quality. *The Death of the Blessed Ludovica Albertoni* is highly expressive and daringly naturalistic. The dying woman struggles to take her last breath, her body twisting up from her bed, fingers pressing into her side. In 1878, he completed the *Tomb of Pope Alexander VII*. A multi-colored marble shroud is held aloft by a bronze skeleton over a doorway; the shroud is flanked at its four corners by the allegorical figures of Justice, Truth, Prudence, and Charity. The skeleton holds an hourglass, pointing up towards the kneeling statue of the pope in prayer.

The following Age of Reason was not kind to Baroque artists, and Bernini's florid, highly colored style became closely associated with the royal and religious autocrats he served. While Bernini himself predicted a decline in interest in his work after his demise, such as had happened to other dominant artists as a reaction by the next generation, it is doubtful that he could have foreseen the negative reaction lasting three centuries. But the challenges of modern life have created a new need for faith and feeling, and the positive aspects of the artist's legacy are being re-discovered by a new generation of scholars and the public.

Overview of Biographical Sources

Bernini has been the subject of many books and articles from his own time to the present day. During his lifetime many anecdotes about him circulated in the Roman community; many of these are gathered in two works completed in the years immediately after his death, *The Life of Cavalier Gian Lorenzo Bernini*, by his son Domenico Bernini, and the *Life of Bernini* by Filippo Baldinucci. Scholars are still debating the primacy of one of these accounts over the other, as well as the authenticity of the contents of each.

A more valuable and cogent source of information about Bernini as a man and an artist is contained in a diary by a young French diplomat and courtier to King Louis XIV. Paul Fre'art de Chantelou was Bernini's host and interpreter during the artist's only trip outside his native Italy in 1665. Chantelou records in detail Bernini's daily itinerary and reactions to the French court, his projects, and the subject of the arts in general. Although Bernini did not make many friends in France, Chantelou seems to have regarded him affectionately. Excerpts from the diary exist in both the original French and in at least two English versions, although the original manuscript has been lost. *Diary of the Cavaliere Bernini's Visit to France* (1985) is well translated by Margery Corbett, and Cecil Gould's adaptation *Bernini in France* (1981) is the story of Bernini's travels with much additional historical information.

In succeeding centuries the treatment of Bernini is less kind. Art critics took potshots at him from various parts of Europe. Among the most influential was the German critic Johann Joachim Winckelmann, the "father of the Greek Revival" who in the mid-1700s led a movement for "noble simplicity and great quietness" in the arts, clearly in direct opposition to Bernini's complex and highly emotional style. John Ruskin, the English art critic who in Victorian times was held in the same high regard as Bernini was in his, was a champion of the Gothic as opposed to the classical influence in arts and architecture. Ruskin, a prolific writer of extraordinary eloquence, educated a generation on subjects from political economy to architectural criticism. Ruskin argued that art and particularly architecture affected the emotions and morality of the people who were exposed to them, either uplifting or degrading the human spirit. The Renaissance artists' rediscovery of the classical worlds of late Greek and Roman thought, he decided, had led to a debasement of their work—a debasement that had been passed on to the rest of

Europe to its detriment. Among the artists he denounced was Bernini, architect of the edifice Ruskin most detested, St. Peter's in Rome. Bernini's reputation was effectively buried under an avalanche of critical disdain for another century.

Not until the mid-twentieth century did the artist's international reputation begin to recover. He had not been forgotten by Italian historians; numerous books and articles have been written in Italian during this century about Bernini, nor could they easily forget him since his mark is everywhere on their national capital. Starting with Ernst Benkard's, *Giovanni Lorenzo Bernini* (Frankfurt am Main, Germany: Iris-Verlag, 1926), German critics began to take new notice of Bernini. But the pre-eminent German proponent of the artist's work has been Rudolf Wittkower, whose excellent books have been translated into English. *Gian Lorenzo Bernini: The Sculptor of the Roman Baroque* (1981) is a fine critical introduction to Bernini's works for both the scholar and layman. The text is not overlong and the book is illustrated with numerous full-page black and white photographs, as well as an extensive catalog of works with a commentary on each.

Following Wittkower's lead, British and American art historians published books on Bernini. Charles Schribner III's *Bernini* (1991) is written for the educated layman. It contains a good short biography and is illustrated by full-page color photographs of the most important works. Among books more widely available to the general public is *The World of Bernini 1598-1680*, part of the Time-Life Library of Art, published in 1970. Author Robert Wallace paints a sympathetic portrait of an artist and man born and nurtured to achieve remarkable things. The text is rambling and informal, almost gossipy in style, making it a comfortable read while still very informative. Significant space is devoted to descriptions of Bernini's contemporaries: brilliant architect and rival Francesco Boromini, Annibale Carracci a painter whom Bernini much admired, and an entire chapter to the strange, passionate, and short-lived painter Caravaggio. His patrons the popes, particularly the proud and complex man who became Pope Urban VIII, are described individually and realistically. Next to Bernini himself it is the city of Rome, depicted by beautiful full-page color and black and white photographs, which is the star of this book.

Another excellent book for the general reader is Howard Hibbard's *Bernini* (1966). Pocketbook size, it was obviously intended to serve the traveler as well as the student. Hibbert's compact but very literate style is used to advantage to discuss Bernini's most famous works as the visitor encounters them, pointing out how each engages the attention and the emotions to function as art and as, in the religious works, pious inspiration for those on pilgrimage. The book is illustrated with half- and full-page black and white photos.

Evaluation of Principal Biographical Sources

Baldinucci, Filippo. *The Life of Bernini*. University Park: Pennsylvania State University Press, 1966. (**A, G**) Translated from the Italian by Catherine Enggass. Foreword by Robert Enggass. An acceptable translation retaining the antique flavor of this short seventeenth-century biography, which collects the many anecdotes circulated about the artist during his lifetime. Includes two catalogs of the artist's works: sculptures and architecture.

Gould, Cecil. *Bernini in France: An Episode in Seventeenth-Century History*. London: Weidenfeld and Nicolson, 1981. (**A, G**) The story of Bernini's journey from Rome to Paris in the year 1665, and his six months in the French capital working for King Louis XIV. Based on the private journal of de Chantelou, a French diplomat who accompanied the artist and his assistants to France and in whose home Bernini was a guest during his labors, with much historical background added by the author. A good introduction to both the artist and his era, particularly for those without much familiarity with the history of the seventeenth century.

Hibbard, Howard. *Bernini*. Baltimore: Penguin Books, 1966. (**A, G**) A small but excellent guide to Bernini's life and work. Contains short but important commentaries and explanations of Bernini's many works, especially those which visitors to Rome are most likely to see. Photographs, mostly black and white, are included.

Schribner, Charles, III. *Bernini*. New York: H. N. Abrams, 1991. (**A, G**) Part of the Abrams Masters of Art series. A large book with a good, if short, biography of the artist, followed by forty-two beautiful color plates, each faced by a full page of commentary about the work shown.

Wallace, Robert. *The World of Bernini, 1598-1680*. New York: Time-Life

Books, 1970. (**G**) This large book contains a rambling but enjoyable long biography of the artist, with much information on his contemporaries who were extraordinary artists in their own right, and the influential men and women who were his friends and patrons. Superb photographs illustrate the artist's works, many full-page and in color.

Wittkower, Rudolf. *Gian Lorenzo Bernini: The Sculptor of the Roman Baroque.* 3d ed. Revised by Howard Hibbard, Thomas Martin, and Margot Wittkower. Ithaca, NY: Cornell University Press, 1981. (**A, G**) Short but influential biography, followed by a long illustrated section of commentary on individual works.

Primary Sources

A fine translation is available of Paul Fre'art de Chantelou's private diary, tucked away in his family archives for a century before its re-discovery, *Diary of the Cavaliere Bernini's Visit to France* (Princeton, NJ: Princeton University Press, 1985; **A, G**), edited, and with an introduction by Anthony Blunt; annotated by George C. Bauer; translated by Margary Corbett. Bernini is portrayed here with all his foibles and brilliance intact. A valuable source for the historian, the artist, the psychologist, or anyone interested by the subject of artistic genius.

Museums, Historical Landmarks, Societies

Chrysler Museum (Norfolk, VA) Location of a copy (by some claims, the original) of the last work of Bernini, the *Salvator Mundi*, Bust of the Savior.

Galleria Borghese (Rome). Location of several of Bernini's early sculptures, including the *Pluto and Persephone*, the *Apollo and Daphne*, the *David*, and the *Bust of Scipione Borghese*.

J. Paul Getty Museum (Malibu, CA). Holds *Putto with Dragon*, one of Bernini's boyhood sculptures and one of the very few works of the artist exhibited outside of his native country.

Metropolitan Museum of Art (New York City). Houses *Faun Teased by Cupids*, thought to have been produced in the artist's teen-age years.

Musée National de Versailles et de Trianon (Versailles, France). Display of the *Bust of Louis XIV*, a rare work produced outside the artist's native Italy.

Museo Nazionale (Florence, Italy). Display of the *Bust of Costanza Bonarelli*, Bernini's mistress until the time of his marriage. An unusually informal, private portrait.

National Gallery (London). Location of one of Bernini's few surviving paintings, *Sts. Andrew and Thomas*, produced about 1627 under the tutelage of master painter Andrea Sacchi.

Piazza Baberini (Rome). Site of the *Triton Fountain*, where Bernini transformed the standard geometrical mushroom shape into a figure of the sea-god seated upon a giant open clamshell, borne up by dolphins.

Piazza di San Pietro (Rome). Saint Peter's square in front of St. Peter's Church, seat of the Papacy, is bound on either side by immense colonnades, consisting of two hundred and eighty-four huge columns arranged four deep, and topped with over one-hundred giant statues.

Piazza di Spagna (Rome). Site of the *Barcaccia*, the fountain called "the Old Boat," symbol of the Catholic Church which, Bernini claimed, constantly took on water but never sank.

Piazza Navona (Rome). Site of the *Four Rivers Fountain*, a large four-sided edifice with an allegorical male figure standing for each of the four major rivers of the ancient world: the Ganges, the Danube, the Nile, and the Plate.

Piazza Santa Maria sopra Minerva (Rome). Site of the monument to Pope Alexander VII, the *Elephant and Obelisk*.

Ponte Sant' Angelo (Rome). An ancient bridge over the River Tiber, linking the Vatican to the rest of the city, redesigned by Bernini to give a more memorable view to the visitor to Rome.

San Francesco a Ripa (Rome). Site of the tomb portrait of *Blessed Ludovica Albertoni*, a dramatic late work depicting the subject in her last difficult moments of life.

San Lorenzo in Lucina (Rome). Location of the bust of Gabriele Fonseca, devout physician to Pope Innocent X.

San Pietro (Saint Peter's) (Rome). Site of numerous works of the artist, including the *Cathedra Petri*, the *Baldacchino*, the *Chapel of the Blessed Sacrament*, the *Scala Regia* with its equestrian statue of Constantine, the *Tomb of Pope Urban VIII*, the *Tomb of Pope Alexander VII*, and the statue of St. Longinus.

Sant' Andrea al Quirinale (Rome). A small church designed by Bernini, characterized by his late style in the choice of multi-colored marble and gilt for the interior, with a large marble figure of St. Andrew over the altar.

Santa Bibiana (Rome). Site of the statue of St. Bibiana, an early work, as well as a church facade redesigned by the artist.

Santa Maria del Polopo (Rome). Site of the statues of the prophets Daniel and Habakkuk.

Santa Maria della Vittoria (Rome). Site of the Cornaro Chapel, with its magnificent statue of the *Ecstasy of St. Teresa.*

Santa Maria di Monserrato (Rome). Location of the bust of the Spanish cardinal Pedro de Foix Montoya, one of Bernini's stunning early portraits.

Santa Maria Maggiore (Rome). Site of Bernini's tomb, where he is buried under the floor in a lead coffin, marked by a simple stone marker.

Santa Maria sopra Minerva (Rome). Site of the *Maria Raggi Memorial*, a simple work but marvelous in its conception.

Siena Cathedral (Siena, Italy). Site of the Chigi Chapel, which Bernini designed, with its statues of the repentant Mary Magdalen, and the scholar-priest Saint Jerome.

Thyssen-Bornemisza Foundation (Lugano, Switzerland). Location of the statue of the martyred Saint Sebastian, one of Bernini's earliest sculptures.

Victoria and Albert Museum (London). Location of the statue of Neptune and Triton, a transitional work of the young Bernini for a cardinal's water garden.

Other Sources

Bauer, George C., ed. *Bernini in Perspective*. Englewood Cliffs, NJ: Prentice-Hall, 1976. (**A**) A slim volume of essays on Bernini's work, both positive and negative reviews, covering the last three centuries.

Borsi, Franco. *Bernini*. Translated by Robert Erich Wolf. New York, Rizzoli International Publications, 1984. (**A**) A thick volume by one of Bernini's countrymen, this work emphasizes Bernini's architectural legacy, including the sculpture that adorns it. Good introduction that treats Bernini as a complex man with flaws of character as well as strengths. Profusely illustrated with full-page black-and-white photographs, illustrations and diagrams, as well as a small number of color photographs.

Magnuson, Torgil. *Rome in the Age of Bernini*. Atlantic Highlands, NJ: Humanities Press, 1986. (**A, G**) Two-volume history of Rome from the reign of Pope Sixtus V (1588) to Pope Innocent XI (1689) by a member of the Swedish Institute of Rome. Enjoyable, highly detailed history of the Eternal City and its political, artistic, and physical growth in the Baroque Era, from the intrigues of the powerful to the problems of the humble; its streets and palaces, villas and churches, from its great artists to its criminal classes.

Ruskin, John, *The Works of John Ruskin*. Volumes IX-XI. Edited by E. T. Cook and Alexander Wedderburn. London: George Allen, c.1912. (**A, G**) Volumes IX-XI contain *The Stones of Venice*, first published in 1853, which attempts to demolish an architectural aesthetic based on traditions formulated in the Italian Renaissance. Saint Peter's Church in Rome is singled out again and again as the prime example of the worst that the Renaissance architecture has to offer. Bernini's name seldom appears, but his work is described so thoroughly that anyone familiar with it would immediately recognize who Ruskin is denouncing.

Suzanne M. Munich

Annie Wood Besant
1847-1933

Chronology

Born Annie Wood on October 1, 1847, in London, daughter of William Burton Persse Wood, a businessman, and Emily Roche Morris; *1852* moves with her family to Harrow after her father dies; privately educated until age sixteen by Ellen Marryat, a teacher and family friend, with whom she lives; *1866* marries Frank Besant, a clergyman, with whom she has two children, and moves to Cheltenham College; *1871* moves to Sisby, where her husband serves as vicar; *1873* obtains a legal separation from Frank Besant; *1873-1885* serves as a leader of the National Secular Society, an atheist/free thought organization, and serves with social reformer Charles Bradlaugh as co-editor of its journal, the *National Reformer*; writes numerous pamphlets and delivers lectures on secularism and free thought; *1877* convicted, along with Bradlaugh, of publishing obscene literature in a trial central to the birth-control movement; publishes *The Gospel of Atheism; 1879* becomes one of the first women to attend the University of London and to study science; *1882* begins publishing her own literary journal, *Our Corner,* which runs for six years; *1885-1889* joins the Fabian Society, a socialist group, and severs most ties with the National Secular Society; becomes an influential socialist; gives speeches and writes pamphlets on socialism; publishes a political magazine, *The Link*; serves on the London School Board; *1888* leads the first successful strike by unskilled workers in Britain; *1889* converts to Theosophy and breaks completely with socialism and secularism; becomes a major leader in the Theosophical Society, a religious/philosophical organization; *1893* travels to India; *1898* founds and serves as president of the Central Hindu College for boys in Benares; *1904* founds Central Hindu Girl's School in Benares; publishes *Theosophy and the New Psychology; 1907* becomes president of the Theosophical Society; *1909* resigns as president of Central Hindu College and establishes a home in Adyar, India; *1914-1919* campaigns for home rule for India; publishes *New India,* a daily newspaper; *1916* begins the Home Rule League and travels throughout the country to establish local chapters; *1917-1919* serves as president of the Indian National Congress, the indigenous governing body; *1933* dies on September 20 in Adyar and is cremated.

Activities of Historical Significance

Annie Wood Besant was an influential leader of many important late-nineteenth- and early-twentieth-century social movements. Although she has never been noted as an original thinker, she was an important interpreter of atheism, socialism, feminism, theosophy, and Indian home rule through her gifted oratory, organizational skills, and numerous pamphlets, articles, and books. She was closely associated with many of the most famous intellectuals of her time, including Charles Bradlaugh, Edward Aveling, playwright George Bernard Shaw, leading theosophists Helena Petrovna Blavatsky and Henry Steele Olcott, and Indian leader Mahatma Gandhi.

Besant devoted herself to causes with passionate intensity that frequently bordered on martyrdom. As a young child, Besant was a deeply religious and devout Christian. An unhappy marriage combined with severe illnesses afflicting both her children and herself caused her to question seriously many of her religion's tenets. After joining the National Secular Society she devoted herself as ardently to atheism and free thought as she had to the church. She first gained notoriety in 1877 when she and Charles Bradlaugh published a pamphlet on birth control, *The Fruits of Philosophy* by Charles Knowlton, in an effort to take a stand on both free speech and the right to publish birth control information. They were brought to trial for publishing obscene literature and although found guilty and sentenced, the decision was overturned because of legal technicality. The trial attracted a great deal of publicity and was very important in the birth-control movement.

In the mid 1880s, Besant became drawn to socialism as a means to help the poor and downtrodden and consequently joined the newly-founded Fabian Society, which promoted the peaceful spread of socialism, in 1885. As a well-known social reformer, she was a tremendous asset to the fledgling organization and was instrumental in establishing it as an important socialist society. She was also instrumental in organizing labor movements, and in 1888, she led a successful strike of the women workers at the Bryant and May match factory and helped establish the Matchmakers's Union. Because it was one of the first successful strikes by unskilled workers in Great Britain, it became significant in trade union history and helped stimulate the founding of other unions for unskilled workers.

In 1889, Besant shocked many of her friends and colleagues by converting to Theosophy and breaking ties with socialism and secularism. Her earlier religiosity had reasserted itself, and she found lifelong satisfaction in Theosophy's blend of mysticism, occultism, and Indian Hinduism. She quickly became an important figure in the Theosophical Society, led by H. P. Blavatsky and H. S. Olcott. In 1907, she was elected president of the Theosophical Society, and she remained its principal leader until her death.

After Blavatsky's death in 1893, Besant traveled to India and came to believe that she had led previous lives in that country. For the rest of her life, she spent at least six months of each year there. With characteristic energy, she immersed herself completely in Indian life and culture and, in fact, came to regard herself as an Indian and a Hindu. Frustration with the lack of adequate education for Indians led her to establish schools for boys and girls at Benares. The Central Hindu College emphasized Hinduism and other Indian traditions. In 1909 she became embroiled in a controversy when she claimed that her adopted Indian son, Jiddu Krishnamurti, had been revealed to her as the embodiment of a world teacher, or Messiah. As a result, she resigned as president of the college and moved to Adyar, where she established the headquarters of the Theosophical Society. The Benares schools continued to thrive and formed the nucleus of the Hindu University, founded in 1916. After he grew up, Krishnamurti renounced his Messianic role in 1929 but became a sincere and insightful spiritual lecturer and teacher of world-wide significance.

At the outbreak of World War I, Besant became involved in Indian politics by agitating for Indian home rule. She began with lectures and articles and established the Home Rule League in 1916. During her travels, some governors refused to admit her to their provinces—in fact, the governor of Madras interned her in 1917, a move that only added to her popularity and power. For several years, she was a key leader in the movement; her activism was recognized with her election as president of the Indian National Congress in 1917. She was the first non-Indian and woman to serve in that office. In the years after the war the emotional tide turned against her as Indians began to resent a white person having a strong leadership role. Also, many abandoned her when she defended Britain's Rowlatt Act, which gave government the power to arrest without trial anyone suspected of sedition. By 1919, many of her former followers had become involved in Gandhi's civil disobedience movement, which became the central force in the campaign for home rule. But Besant continued her own effort; in 1925, she brought to England a "Commonwealth of India" bill, which was twice introduced into the House of Commons and supported actively by the Labour Party. She is generally regarded as having hastened the move toward home rule by several years. Her efforts earned her the title "Mother of India."

Overview of Biographical Sources

Several biographies, written by both British and Indian authors toward the end of Besant's life and soon after her death, are personal remembrances or general narratives. Although they are useful in assessing her reputation at that time, they are primarily non-critical tributes. The titles published in India are not available in many American libraries. These include: Bepin Chandra Pal, *Mrs. Annie Besant: A Psychological Study* (Madras: Ganesh, 1917); Geoffrey West, *Annie Besant* (New York: Viking, 1928); Gertrude Marvin Williams, *The Passionate Pilgrim: A Life of Annie Besant* (New York: Coward-McCann, 1931); and Sri Prakasa, *Annie Besant: As Woman And As Leader* (Madras: Theosophical Publishing House, 1941).

More recent biographies offer more objective and scholarly assessments of Besant. A good general work is Rosemary Dinnage's *Annie Besant* (1986). The most thorough biography is Arthur H. Nethercot's *The First Five Lives of Annie Besant* (1960) and his *The Last Four Lives of Annie Besant* (1963). Anne Taylor offers the most scholarly treatment of Besant's life in *Annie Besant: A Biography* (1992).

Several books and scholarly articles focus on specific aspects of Annie Besant's life. Her religious thought is thoroughly analyzed in Catherine Lowman Wessinger's *Annie Besant and Progressive Messianism, 1847-1933* (1988). Her work in India is discussed in Raj Kumar's *Annie Besant's Rise To Power in Indian Politics: 1914-1917* (1981), Joanne Stafford Mortimer's "Annie Besant and India 1913-1917" in the *Journal of Contemporary History* (1976), and Peter Robb's "The Government of India and Annie Besant" in *Modern Asian Studies* (1976). Roger Manvell's *The Trial of Annie Besant and Charles Bradlaugh* (1976) focuses on the obscenity trial after the publication of *Fruits of Philosophy*.

Works on atheism, free thought, the Fabian Society and the Theosophical Society should also be consulted for a thorough picture of Besant's life and work. Examples are: John Mackinnon Robertson, *A Short History of Freethought, Ancient and Modern* (New York: Arno, 1957); Bruce F. Campbell, *Ancient Wisdom Revived: A History of the Theosophical Movement* (Berkeley: University of California Press, 1980); A. M. McBriar, *Fabian Socialism and English Politics 1884-1918* (Cambridge: Cambridge University Press, 1962); and Norman and Jeanne MacKenzie, *The Fabians* (New York: Simon and Schuster, 1977).

Evaluation of Principal Biographical Sources

Besterman, Theodore. *Mrs. Annie Besant: A Modern Prophet.* London: Kegan Paul, Trench Trubner, 1934. (**A, G**) Besterman's biography is one of the more available of the early ones. He was a member of the Theosophical Society but was disillusioned with it when he write this work. His judgment of Besant is rather negative and biased. Although it is not objective, it does draw from her writings, interviews with associates and contemporary periodicals.

Dinnage, Rosemary. *Annie Besant.* New York: Penguin Books, 1986. (**G, Y**) Part of a series, "Lives of Modern Women," this is a non-scholarly, general biography. It will be primarily useful for young adults or general readers.

Kumar, Raj. *Annie Besant's Rise To Power in Indian Politics: 1914-1917.* New Delhi: Concept Publishing, 1981. (**A**) A very useful interpretation from the Indian point of view of Besant's participation in Indian politics. The author made extensive use of Indian archives.

Manvell, Roger. *The Trial of Annie Besant and Charles Bradlaugh.* New York: Horizon, 1976. (**A, G**) An account of the publication of *The Fruits of Philosophy* and the subsequent trial. Reprints the transcript of the trial at which Besant defended herself.

Mortimer, Joanne Stafford. "Annie Besant and India 1913-1917." *Journal of Contemporary History* 18 (1983): 61-78. (**A, G**) Focuses on Besant's entrance into

Indian politics and the beginnings of the Home Rule League. Mortimer discusses Besant's program for a free India which brought together religious, social, political, and educational reform and united diverse political groups. Besant was successful in broadening the Home Rule movement to include a much larger segment of the population.

Nethercot, Arthur H. *The First Five Lives of Annie Besant.* Chicago: University of Chicago Press, 1960. (**A, G**) To date, the Nethercot works are the most comprehensive biography of Besant. This is the first of two works, both of which are based on primary source material, including Theosophical Society archives. Besant's diaries and writings, as well as those by her many associates, publications of the many movements in which she participated, and interviews with her associates. Very readable as well as scholarly. This first volume covers her life through 1892, which Nethercot labels the "English" phase.

————. *The Last Four Lives of Annie Besant.* Chicago: University of Chicago Press, 1963. (**A, G**) The second volume in Nethercot's comprehensive biographical study, this work begins in 1893 when Annie Besant first traveled to India and covers the rest of her life or the "Indian" phase. Nethercot credits Besant with significant contributions to all of the movements in which she participated, especially birth control, women's rights, free public education, and Home Rule for India. These were advanced by several years because of heractivity according to Nethercot.

Robb, Peter. "The Government of India and Annie Besant." *Modern Asian Studies* 10 (1976): 107-130. (**A**) An in-depth analysis of the home-rule controversy from 1916 to 1919 with discussion of Besant's role. Robb suggests that Besant's internment and later release was a symbol of change in the government's policy in recognizing the Home Rule movement as political rather than a revolutionary force. This biography primarily analyzes Besant's public contribution to her various causes, especially free thought, birth control, socialism, and, to a lesser extent, theosophy and Indian politics.

Taylor, Anne. *Annie Besant: A Biography.* New York: Oxford University Press, 1992. (**A, G**) A scholarly and authoritative study of Besant that concentrates on the years in Britain more than those spent in India. Taylor made extensive use of Besant's personal correspondence as well as well as of the Theosophical Society archives in Adyar, personal papers of her associates, archives of the various movements with which Besant was affiliated, and contemporary periodicals.

Wessinger, Catherine Lowman. *Annie Besant and Progressive Messianism, 1847-1933.* New York: Edwin Mellen, 1988. (**A**) Wessinger provides a thorough analysis of Besant's religious thought from her early Christianity through Secularism and her ultimate immersion in Theosophy. She identifies millenarianism as central to Besant's Theosophical philosophy and traces elements of it in her early days as well, and she also explores how Besant's millennial dream affected her political and educational work in India.

Overview and Evaluation of Primary Sources

Besant was a prolific writer of books, articles, essays and pamphlets. Many of her lectures were also published. One collection of her pamphlets has been published: *A Selection of the Social and Political Pamphlets of Annie Besant* (New York: A. M. Kelley, 1970; **A**), edited by John Saville.

Bibliographies of her works are scattered among her biographies and among studies of the movements and organizations to which she belonged. The only compilation published *A Bibliography of Annie Besant* (London: Theosophical Society of England, 1924; **A**), edited by Theodore Besterman, includes her books and pamphlets through 1923. Leaflets, supplements to periodicals, and contributions to periodicals are excluded. Additional listings of her works may be located through usual library resources, such as the *British Library Catalog,* and the Library of Congress's *National Union Catalog,* and *Pre-56 Imprints.*

Besant published an autobiography in 1893 that covers her life to that point, *Annie Besant: An Autobiography* (London: Unwin, 1893; **A, G**). According to Nethercot, many of her later personal writings are lost.

Major archives include the national American headquarters of the Theosophical Society at Wheaton, Illinois, and the library of the international headquarters of the Theosophical Society at Adyar, India.

Museums, Historical Landmarks, Societies

Burial site (Adyar, India). The ashes of Annie Besant are buried in the Garden of Remembrance.

Statue (Marina, Madras, India). Statue by an unknown artist.

Bust (Benares, India). Outside the portico of the main hall of the Central Hindu College.

Other Sources

Biographical Dictionary of British Feminists. Vol. 1. 1800-1930: 21-23. New York: New York University Press, 1985.

Cole, Margaret. *Women of Today*. London: Thomas Nelson and Sons, 1938.

————. *Dictionary of National Biography, 1931-1940*: 72-74. Oxford: Oxford University Press, 1949.

Encyclopedia of Unbelief. Vol 1.: 57-59. Buffalo, NY: Prometheus Books, 1985.

Longford, Elizabeth. *Eminent Victorian Women*. New York: Knopf, 1981.

Twentieth-Century Literary Criticism. Vol. 9. Detroit: Gale, 1983.

Kathryn Moore Crowe
Jackson Library
University of North Carolina at Greensboro

Henry Bessemer
1813-1898

Chronology

Born Henry Bessemer on January 19th, 1813, in Charlton, Hertfordshire, England, son of Anthony Bessemer, an engineer and typefounder; *1813-1830* grows up in Hertfordshire and attends school; after leaving school before graduation, learns metalworking in his father's business; *1830* moves with his father to London, where he continues to study casting and electro-metallurgy; develops a successful process for embossing cardboard; *1833* develops an improved document stamp for the English government; *1838-1843* develops a mechanical saw for cutting plumbago (graphite) into leads for pencils; develops a process for compressing waste plumbago dust for use in pencils and sells the invention to an unnamed entrepreneur who brings it to success; develops a water-cooled vacuum casting machine for lead type; invents a typesetting machine for Scottish chemical industrialist James Young; develops a process for embossing Utrecht velvet and sells the equipment to a velvet weaver; *1840* marries; *1843* devises a process for producing bronze powder, which becomes his major source of income and support for other inventions; *late 1840s* visits Germany, where he is accused of attempting to buy bronze powder manufacturing secrets in Furth; invents a steam fan for mine ventilation, a centrifugal pump, and a machine for compressing and forming bituminous coal; also experiments with optical and sheet glass, sheet-glass polishing, and silvering mirrors; sells several patents, including one for producing sheet glass; *1849* turns his attention to the sugar industry and develops a successful sugarcane press that wins a gold medal; *1851* exhibits inventions at the International Exhibition in London that include a machine to separate molasses from crystallized sugar and a centrifugal pump; invents a simultaneous-acting hydraulic railway car brake that uses water; *1854* invents a system to rotate smooth-bore cannon projectiles, which is rejected for patenting; begins experiments to produce improved steel or iron for artillery that leads to his greatest success; *1855* files for patent on the process for manufacture of cast steel and for "Improvements in the Manufacture of Iron and Steel"; working on both an open-hearth furnace and a converter, successfully develops the converter; reads his now-famous "Cheltenham" paper, "The Manufacture of Iron Without Fuel" at a meeting of the British Association for the Advancement of Science; *1858* forms Bessemer and Company; builds a steelworks at Sheffield, England; receives the HB Telford gold medal from the Institution of Civil Engineers for his advances in steelmaking, and the HB Howard Quinquennial Prize; *1859* presents a paper at the Institution of Civil Engineers on "The Manufacture of Malleable Iron and Steel"; Bessemer tool steel becomes a common enough commodity to be listed in the *Mining Journal*; *1862* exhibits steel products produced with his process at the International (London) Exhibition; first Bessemer steel rail is laid; *1865* begins production of Bessemer steel in the United States in Troy, New York; develops ferro-manganese (a mixture of iron and manganese), which allows steelmakers to better control the carbon content of their steel; *1868* helps to found the Iron and Steel Institute; *1869* patents a design for a ship with a suspended cabin to reduce seasickness; forms the Bessemer Saloon Steamboat Company to test the idea; *1871-1873* serves as president of the Iron and Steel Institute; *1875* liquidates the Bessemer Saloon Steamboat Company after loss of his ship, largely ending his active business career; *1879* becomes a fellow of the Royal Society; receives knighthood for the invention of the movable stamp; *1879-1898* prepares drawings for his account of the invention of the Bessemer Process, designs machinery for diamond mills in Clerkenwell and experimental diamond cutting machines; publishes a number of papers; *1898* dies on March 15th at Denmark Hill, London.

Activities of Historical Significance

Sir Henry Bessemer is generally credited with developing the steel-manufacturing process that launched the Age of Steel. What became known as the Bessemer Process was the first low-cost and rapid method of manufacturing low-carbon malleable iron alloys (steel) from brittle high-carbon pig iron. This cost reduction led to the replacement of other materials, such as iron and wrought iron, that were much less suitable than steel for many applications, but had also been much less costly. The Bessemer Process was also much less labor intensive. The early Bessemer Process could produce up to five to ten tons of iron or steel per heat or batch, whereas the earlier processes of puddling and cementation produced less than half a ton per batch. Later converter capacities rose to twenty-five tons. The process was widely adopted by the English, American, and European steel industries. Mechanical innovations, such as the tilting converter, were most important. The new process required considerable development to become commercially feasible, but by the 1880s the older wrought iron and steel industries were dwindling. Although many others contributed to the success of the Bessemer Process, Henry Bessemer was the driving force behind it. Not until the early 1900s did the open-hearth process developed in the 1870s overshadow the Bessemer Process.

Although Bessemer claimed full credit for inventing the converter, it was actually first devised by William Kelly of the United States in the late 1840s. There is no evidence that Bessemer knew of Kelly's invention before patenting his own converter. Nevertheless, one critic, John Boucher argued in his self-published work, *William Kelly: A True History of the So-Called Bessemer Process* (1924) that Bessemer did steal Kelly's invention.

Bessemer was a prolific inventor in areas outside of iron and steel. These inventions included movable dies for embossing stamps, brass powders for painting, sugar processing equipment, and a ship with a stabilized compartment to protect passengers from seasickness. Some of these inventions were quite successful, and Bessemer became moderately wealthy from them, but the invention of the Bessemer converter was by far the main source of his fame and wealth.

Overview of Biographical Sources

Honored today as the inventor of the first process for mass production of steel, Bessemer or his converter is mentioned in all texts on the subject of steel. Nevertheless, information about the man himself is sparse. The most informative source is his autobiography, which provides almost all the available information about his early life and offers details of the development of the Bessemer Process. Obviously self-serving and replete with omissions, it remains the basic source of personal information. The contributions of other inventors who refined the Bessemer Process are detailed by more impartial authors. All authors but one (John Boucher) credit Bessemer with the success of the Bessemer Process, but point out that the contributions of inventors Robert Mushet, Sidney Thomas, and Percy Gilchrist were critical to his success.

Other works including information on Bessemer are almost exclusively devoted to his association with the development of the Bessemer Process or with the process itself. Significant sources are W. K. V. Gale, *Iron and Steel* (1964); Douglas Alan Fisher, *The Epic Of Steel* (1963); James M. Swank, *History of The Manufacture of Iron In All Ages* (1892; 1965); and Theodore A. Wertime, *The Coming of the Age of Steel* (1962).

Evaluation of Principal Biographical Sources

Boucher, John Newton. *William Kelly: A True History of the So-Called Bessemer Process.* Greensburg, PA: Published by the author, 1924. (**G**) This book contains the story of William Kelly's development of the converter process and the struggle between the holders of the Kelly and the Bessemer patents in the United States. The author claims to have been told by Mrs. Kelly that Bessemer or his agents worked for Kelly to learn Kelly's process and later patented it. Very few dates are given, making it difficult to corroborate the story in any way.

Butler, Joseph G. *Fifty Years of Iron and Steel.* Cleveland, OH: Penton Press, 1923. (**A, G**) Butler contends that Kelly and Bessemer only discovered how to remove silicon and carbon from pig iron. Robert Mushet found out how to make Bessemer steel by recarburizing the iron after it had been blown in a converter. Includes an Index, but no bibliography. Consists largely of the author's reminiscences, which include his recollections of William Kelly and development of the Bessemer Process in the United States.

Fisher, Douglas Alan. *The Epic Of Steel.* New York: Harper and Row, 1963. (**A, G**) Chronicles the development of iron and steel from antiquity. Synthesizes development of the Bessemer steel process and recognizes the contributions of Robert Mushet, Fredrik Goransson, Sidney Thomas, and Percy Gilchrist.

Gale, W. K. V. *Iron and Steel.* London: Longmans, Green, 1969. (**A, G**) Written from the perspective of iron and steel development in Great Britain. Gale points out that Bessemer created mild steel, not wrought iron as he was attempting to do. Provides a summary of the development of the Bessemer Process, including the roles of Mushet and Thomas. Also contains a select bibliography.

Swank, James M. *History of The Manufacture of Iron In All Ages*. 1892. Reprint. New York: Burt Franklin, 1965. Summarizes the development of the Bessemer Process in England, with emphasis on its application to steel manufacture in the United States. Describes the impact and interaction of Kelly and Bessemer patents in the United States. Also contains documentation, but no bibliography.

Wertime, Theodore A. *The Coming of the Age of Steel*. Chicago: University of Chicago Press, 1962. (**A, G**) The text focuses on the development of ferrous metallurgy in the iron industry and of the iron industry from 1400 to 1900. The author offers a good summary of the contributions of Henry Bessemer and others to the Bessemer Process. Wertime considers Bessemer's work after his first failure at making steel to be the first systematic effort to solve a metallurgical problem.

Overview and Evaluation of Primary Sources

Sir Henry Bessemer: An Autobiography (1905. Reprint. London: Institute of Metals, 1989), provides the most comprehensive source on Bessemer. The greater part is devoted to development of the Bessemer Process. It has, however, been criticized as one-sided and incomplete from the standpoint of the development of the Bessemer Process, which brings the truthfulness of the rest of the work into question. The work contains no bibliography or index.

Other Sources

Ashton, Thomas Southcliffe. *Iron and Steel in the Industrial Revolution*. New York: A. M. Kelley, 1968.

Baker, Elijah. *Introduciton to Steel Shipbuilding*. New York: McGraw Hill, 1943.

Bishop, Philip. *The Beginnings of Cheap Steel.* Washington, DC: Smithsonian Institution, 1959.

Carr, J. C. and Walter Taplin. *History of the British Steel Industry.* Cambridge, MA: Harvard University Press, 1962.

Chattin, A. E. "Bessemer—or Steelmaking Without Fuel." *Journal of the Iron and Steel Industry.* Vol. 183, 1956.

Fisher, Douglas A. *The Epic of Steel.* New York: Harper and Row, 1963.

Holbrook, Stewart Hall. *Iron Brew: A Century of American Ore and Steel.* New York: Macmillan, 1939.

Kitson, James. "British Contributions to the Metallurgy of Iron and Steel." *Transactions of the American Institute of Mining Engineers* XIX (1890-1891).

Lange, Ernest F. "Bessemer, Goranssen, and Mushet: a contribution to technical history." *Memoirs of the Manchester Literary and Philosophical Society* 57, 17 (1912-1913).

Lord, W. M. "The development of the Bessemer Process in Lancashire, 1856-1900." *Transactions of the Newcomen Society* 14-15 (1945-1947).

Osborn, Fred M. *The Story of the Mushets.* London: Nelson & Sons, 1952.

Russell, Clifford S. *Steel Production: Processes, Products, and Residuals.* Baltimore, MD: Johns Hopkins University Press, 1976.

Temin, Peter. *Iron and Steel in Nineteenth Century America: An Economic Inquiry.* Cambridge, MA: M.I.T. Press, 1964.

Loralee Davenport
Mississippi State University

Joseph Black
1728-1799

Chronology

Born Joseph Black on April 16, 1728, at Bordeaux, France, fourth of twelve children of John Black, a native of Belfast, Ireland, and merchant in the wine trade, and Margaret Gordon Black, whose father had come from Aberdeen, Scotland; educated by his mother; *1740* sent to Belfast where he attends private school; *1744* begins studies at the University of Glasgow (Scotland), where he eventually chooses to study medicine; comes under the influence of William Cullen, who had recently initiated lectures in chemistry in the medical faculty; Cullen regards chemistry as a science in its own right, rejecting the traditional university status of chemistry as an adjunct to medicine; captivated by Cullen's lectures and enthusiasm for chemistry, Black assists Cullen for three years and forms the basis of a lifelong friendship; *1752-1754* shifts medical studies to the prestigious University of Edinburgh, where he is pleased with the clinical experiences, but in letters to Cullen expresses disappointment with the inadequate role of chemistry in his medical instruction; *1754* receives his medical degree with a dissertation on "magnesia alba" (magnesium carbonate) which he had hoped would yield an effective agent for treating urinary stones; *1755* describes before the Royal Society of Edinburgh experiments performed before and after his dissertation that show a gas he calls "fixed air" (carbon dioxide) is a constituent of alkaline substances such as magnesia alba, lime (calcium carbonate), potash (potassium carbonate), and soda (sodium carbonate)—fixed air is released when these substances are heated or treated with acid; *1756* publishes these experiments, which break new ground in the conception of gases by demonstrating that fixed air is not identical with ordinary air; exposes the critical importance of his fixed air for understanding the difference between mild and caustic alkalis (carbonates and hydroxides) by showing that caustic alkalis become mild when they absorb fixed air; *1756-1766* Cullen comes to Edinburgh as Professor of Chemistry, and Black returns to Glasgow to replace Cullen; Black becomes an effective and popular teacher of chemistry while maintaining an active and demanding medical practice; *late 1750s* introduces his doctrine of "latent heat"—heat required to melt ice at the freezing temperature but not detectable by the thermometer; *early 1760s* conducts experiments to measure this latent heat of fusion; extends the concept of latent heat to include heat not detectable by the thermometer that is required to vaporize water at the boiling point; uses concept of latent heat to explain to James Watt, a young technician at the University of Glasgow, why such a large amount of cold water is required to condense the steam in the cylinder of a steam engine—Watt later credits Black with clarifying issues of concern to him, but insists that the invention of the separate condenser for the famous Watt steam engine did not arise directly from his interaction with Black; clarifies the concept of "specific heat" as the heat required to raise the temperature of a substance a specified number of degrees; initiates measurements of the specific heats of various substances in cooperation with Watt and William Irvine—the earliest specific heat measurements of which we are aware; *1766-1799* returns to Edinburgh to succeed Cullen as Professor of Chemistry, Cullen having assumed the position of Professor of the Institutes of Medicine at Edinburgh; remains at Edinburgh for the rest of his life, publishing virtually nothing and restricting his medical practice to a few close friends; concentrates on teaching chemistry during these years and is one of the primary reasons for the international reputation of the University of Edinburgh's medical instruction; never marries, but participates actively in the social and intellectual life of Edinburgh; with his friends Adam Smith, James Hutton, William Cullen, Dugald Stewart, John Playfair, and other scientific and industrial acquaintances, wins for Edinburgh a status second only to Paris as a leading center of scientific activity in the late eighteenth century; *1799* dies at Edinburgh on December 6 of unknown cause.

Activities of Historical Significance

Joseph Black contributed significantly to the evolution of modern chemistry and the growth of understanding about heat. His chemical innovations included the recognition that a gas he called "fixed air" (carbon dioxide) had distinct chemical properties, and its absorption or expulsion determined whether alkaline substances were mild or caustic. He introduced into speculations about heat the concepts of latent heat and specific heat, and he performed experiments and measurements to clarify and quantify these concepts.

His chemical achievements stand between important breakthroughs of the later seventeenth—early eighteenth centuries and the Chemical Revolution in France at the end of the eighteenth century. Up to the seventeenth century, chemical activity and speculation affected medicine, metallurgy, pharmacy, philosophy, and alchemy. But chemistry lacked an identity in its own right. Efforts to establish a science of chemistry are clear in the writings of Andreas Libavius, Robert Boyle and others in the early-to-mid 1600s. This was part of a broader movement—an essential dimension of the early-modern Scientific Revolution—to specify experimental method as the appropriate means to interrogate nature. Not only the incipient science of chemistry, but the experimental sciences of pneumatics, electricity, and magnetism emerged during this time. Experimental method transformed optics, physiology, and medicine. All of this resulted not merely from intellectual changes, but important socio-economic alterations that broke down previous barriers among technological, university, and magical-alchemical traditions in Western Europe. New institutional arrangements such as the Royal Society of London and the Paris Academy of Sciences aptly reflected these changes in the mid-to-late 1600s.

By the seventeenth century, the factual bases of chemistry had expanded enormously as a result of accumulating experiences within Hellenistic, medieval (Islamic and Latin), and early-modern technology, pharmacy, and alchemy. Yet people striving to establish a chemical science had not formulated a satisfactory theoretical foundation for it. Well into the eighteenth century, the traditional alternatives of a mechanical approach (particles combining by aggregation or attraction), the four-element theory (air, earth, fire, and water), and the doctrine of "powers" within substances (e.g., combustibility and volatility) remained influential in the somewhat chaotic speculations about an ever-increasing store of chemical information.

The "Chemical Revolution" of the late-eighteenth century essentially resulted from the formulation of a new operational definition of "chemical element." The idea that a chemical element should be a final product of chemical analysis—a substance that laboratory operations could simplify no further—appeared in the seventeenth century. But an operational criterion, based on laboratory operations and observations, for recognizing when the limits of chemical analysis were attained continued to elude chemists. Between the early 1770s and the early 1790s, Antoine Lavoisier developed an operational criterion in accordance with his radical reinterpretation of the phenomena of combustion. Rejecting previous opinions that combustion essentially involves the loss of a combustible principle from the material undergoing combustion, Lavoisier instead argued that the material undergoing combustion combines with a substance that he eventually termed "oxygen." The initial stimulation to this change of view was the recognition by numerous investigators by the early 1770s that heating a given weight of a metal invariably produced a "calx" that weighed more than the original metal. Emphasizing these weight relations, Lavoisier concluded that the traditional view of metals as compound substances, consistent with the prevailing view of combustion, was incorrect. He asserted that a metal was more simple than the calx formed from combustion. Using the criterion of weight relations even more generally, he identified a chemically simple substance by the inability to produce from a given weight of that substance two or more distinct substances whose weights add up to the weight of the original substance. By this criterion, a metal was identified as a simple substance and its calx as a compound substance (combination of the metal and oxygen). Water was exposed as a compound substance when Lavoisier was able to produce from a given weight of steam two gaseous substances (oxygen and hydrogen) whose weights added up to the original weight of the steam. Together with his French colleagues Guyton de Morveau, Berthollet, et al., Lavoisier instituted a new chemistry that rested upon the new operational definition of a chemically simple substance. Weight relations now assumed an importance in chemical theory that was unprecedented in the history of chemistry up to this late-eighteenth-century generation. Clearly, crucial eighteenth-century prerequisites for this operational definition of chemical element were recognitions that chemically distinct gases exist and that gases participate in chemical reactions quantitatively by weight: two of Black's chief accomplishments by the end of the 1750s.

The most important chemical invention of the eighteenth century—a crucial step in the sequence leading to the Chemical Revolution—was the "pneumatic trough" constructed by Stephen Hales in the 1720s. This device enabled Hales to collect gases by directing them through a tube bent into an inverted flask. Hales used the pneumatic trough to isolate gases obtained by heating many substances. He clearly conceived that gases were absorbed or "fixed" in many solid substances and were expelled and thus returned to their free "elastic" state by heating. But Hales believed that all gases were modifications of air. Indeed, he referred to all gases he collected as "airs." Hales missed what was to be a major discovery by

Black—that chemically distinct gases exist.

Before he left Glasgow in 1752, Black had begun experiments on "causticity" using chalk (calcium carbonate) and quicklime (calcium oxide). He had observed that quicklime, which is caustic or strongly alkaline when dissolved in water, absorbs "air" in becoming mild (calcium carbonate); at this time, he was not aware that the absorbed gas (our carbon dioxide) differed from atmospheric "air." He had discovered that roasting an ounce of chalk produces a calx (calcium oxide) that weighs less than the salt (calcium sulfate) resulting from treating an ounce of chalk with an acid (sulfuric acid). He had found that "fixed air" (air absorbed by a solid—in this case, our carbon dioxide) can be transferred from one substance to another when he reacted limewater (calcium hydroxide solution) with potash (potassium carbonate) to produce chalk (calcium carbonate). Finally, he recognized that the fixed air behaved like an acid in neutralizing the causticity of lime.

Black began his work with magnesia alba (magnesium carbonate) in late 1753, hoping to prepare from it a "new quicklime and limewater" analogous to the "common sort" (calcium oxide and calcium oxide dissolved in water to form calcium hydroxide solution). He hoped that the new quicklime and limewater would be more effective for dissolving urinary stones. Though his investigations of magnesia alba were not to produce a remedy for urinary stones, they proved successful in other ways. He prepared magnesia alba by reacting Epsom salts (magnesium sulfate) with potash (potassium carbonate). He noted that the magnesia alba effervesced strongly when treated with acids, a behavior similar to limestone and chalk (calcium carbonate). He wondered if the magnesia alba behaved like limestone in other ways. Would it form a product similar to quicklime (calcium oxide) when heated? If so, would a solution of this product be caustic and have the solvent power of limewater? Black heated magnesia alba and observed that, like quicklime (calcium oxide), the product that he termed magnesia usta (magnesium oxide) did not effervesce with acids. Unlike quicklime, magnesia usta was not readily soluble in water. But Black recognized that the magnesia usta weighed considerably less than the original sample of magnesia alba. He initiated one of the most systematic chemical determinations by use of the balance performed up to this time. Beginning with three ounces of magnesia alba (magnesium carbonate), he heated it, weighed the amount of magnesia usta (magnesium oxide) that remained, and concluded that the lost weight must have resulted from expulsion of "fixed air" from magnesia alba during the heating. To verify this, he combined the magnesia usta (magnesium oxide) with fixed air (carbon dioxide) to regenerate almost exactly the same weight of magnesia alba (magnesium carbonate).

By early 1754, Black had determined that the same salts formed when acid combined with magnesia alba (magnesium carbonate) and magnesia usta (magnesium oxide). Apparently the important difference between the two was that the magnesia usta had lost its fixed air before reacting with the acid, while the magnesia alba—containing fixed air—lost its fixed air when reacting with the acid.

In January, 1754, Black recognized that the fixed air in chalk had peculiar properties that differed from ordinary air. He produced the fixed air by treating chalk with acid at the bottom of a long cylindrical glass vessel. The fixed air rising to the top of the glass had a pronounced odor and immediately extinguished a candle. These experiments conducted in late 1753 and early 1754 were expanded within the following two years. Black now unequivocally referred to magnesia alba as "a compound of a peculiar earth and fixed air." He reasoned that chalk and magnesia alba became caustic when they lost their fixed air and returned to a mild condition when they recombined with fixed air.

In addition to exposing the crucial role of fixed air (carbon dioxide) in the change from a caustic to a mild alkali, Black also expanded his study of the fixed air itself. He observed that limewater became cloudy when exposed to fixed air. Noting that atmospheric air also clouded limewater, but at a much slower rate, he asserted that the fixed air was a trace component of atmospheric air. By blowing into a solution of limewater and observing the onset of cloudiness in the limewater, he demonstrated that fixed air was a component of exhaled air in respiration. Black found that the density of fixed air was greater than that of common air. Birds and animals could not survive in an atmosphere of fixed air. He discovered that fixed air formed during combustion of charcoal (carbon) in atmospheric air; moreover, when this fixed air was then absorbed by caustic potash, a residual gas remained. The more detailed study of the properties of this residual gas (nitrogen) would be carried out in the early 1770s by Black's student Daniel Rutherford, and independently by Joseph Priestley, Henry Cavendish, and Carl W. Scheele.

In these researches, then, Black showed that a gas chemically distinct from ordinary air participates quantitatively in a variety of chemical reactions. In the late 1760s and early 1770s, other British scientists isolated and studied gases. Henry Cavendish isolated hydrogen. Daniel Rutherford discovered nitrogen. Joseph

Priestley identified oxides of nitrogen and discovered the gas that Lavoisier eventually would call oxygen. Yet Black's direct influence on notable British "pneumatic chemists" such as Henry Cavendish and Joseph Priestley seems to have been minimal. Priestley, for example, was influenced far more in his research on gases by the writings of Stephen Hales than by Black's work. Of equal significance, Black exerted very little impact on French chemists up to mid-1772. His lone publication on his experiments had appeared only in English in an obscure Edinburgh journal. Lavoisier's experimentation leading to his later identification of oxygen and reconception of combustion was underway by 1773 without direct stimulation by Black or, for that matter, the work of the other British pneumatic chemists. Lavoisier did learn of and appreciate the significance of Black's work in 1773. But however important Black's achievements of the 1750s appear in retrospect, they did not arouse great excitement for well over a decade, even among his fellow British colleagues.

Of utmost importance, neither Black nor the other British pneumatic chemists attempted to reconstruct chemical theory using the information about gases that accumulated, beginning with Black's work of the 1750s. Black expressed to confidants such as John Robison his distrust of hypothetical explanations, inclining to the belief that the present state of chemistry was more appropriate to rigorous empiricism than theoretical conjectures. In his lectures, Black refrained from expressing an opinion about chemical "elements", though he admitted dissatisfaction with the traditional four-element theory. When he did interpret chemical phenomena, his explanations were hardly revolutionary. For example, his explanation of combustion remained traditional in its retention of the idea that an inflammable principle is lost during the combustion. As late as 1785, Black hesitated to accept the new chemistry of Lavoisier. After that, he began to include in his lectures references to the new interpretation of combustion and the new definition of element. But to the end of his life, Black resisted the accompanying changes in chemical terminology that the French chemists believed so essential to their new program. A proper assessment of Black's role in eighteenth-century chemistry would seem to be that he discovered important new facts about gases and their roles in chemical reactions, but he did not seek or foresee in these facts the path to a revolution in chemistry.

Black's interest in heat originated in 1754 when Cullen described to him how evaporation of a volatile substance such as ether produces extreme cold. At about the same time, he became aware of an observation by German physicist G. D. Fahrenheit that undisturbed water can be cooled below the freezing temperature (32 degrees F), but if the water is shaken, it freezes immediately and the thermometer rises suddenly to 32 degrees. To Black, Fahrenheit's observation indicated that solidification or liquefaction demanded significant amounts of heat not detectable by the thermometer. The reality and importance of what he began to call "latent heat"—heat not detectable by the thermometer in changes of state— became more obvious to him as he reflected on the length of time snow requires to melt with its surroundings at temperatures well above the freezing point. By the late 1750s, he was including references to latent heat in his Glasgow lectures.

Black's experimentation on heat did not begin until 1760, when he verified that the scale of expansion of mercury was a reliable scale of temperature. Though not the first person to distinguish temperature from quantity of heat, he recognized the crucial significance of their separate identities and explicitly differentiated the methods of measuring each: temperature can be measured by the thermometer, while a quantity of heat transferred can be measured by the time necessary to warm or cool a body to a given temperature. By the summer of 1761, he was exploiting these ideas to measure the latent heat of fusion of water. He cooled a quantity of water to about 33 degrees F and then measured the time required to raise its temperature one degree. He then compared this time to the time required to melt an equal quantity of ice. Later in December, 1761, he compared the time necessary to lower a quantity of water one degree with the time necessary to freeze that same quantity of water completely. By the end of 1762, he had also determined the latent heat of vaporization of water.

As early as 1760, Black conceived that different substances have different "heat capacities." He was led to this conclusion by pondering the discovery by Fahrenheit that mixing equal quantities of mercury and water which are at different temperatures produces a temperature of the mixture far closer to the original temperature of the water than to the original temperature of the mercury. From this, Black concluded that water stores more heat than an equal quantity of mercury at the same temperature. Not until 1764 did Black begin systematic determinations of the specific heats of various substances—heats necessary to raise their temperatures a specified number of degrees.

At that time, James Watt had been hired by the university as a technician and was preparing apparatus for Black's experiments. Watt asked Black why so much cold water was needed to condense the steam in the cylinder of the Newcomen steam engine. Black explained the phenomenon to Watt by reference to his concept of latent heat. At least partly due to Watt's interest and curiosity, Black again turned to heat investigations. Under his direction, William Irvine and Watt worked to attain a more accurate value for the latent heat of steam. Watt also initiated measurements of the specific heats of various substances. Black and Irvine soon took this up as well, determining specific heats by measuring the heats transferred to water by different solids. Thus, by using as a standard the heat necessary to change the temperature of a specified quantity of water by a specified number of degrees, Black, Irvine, and Watt undertook the first systematic measurements of specific heats. Though these results were known to his acquaintances and included in his lectures, Black never published them. Because he did not publish, as in the case of his chemical innovations, Black was not as powerful an influence in the development of a science of heat as he might have been. By the 1770s, specific heat determinations were proceeding independently elsewhere in Britain and in Scandinavia. In addition, Black did not want to commit himself strongly to a theory about the nature of heat. He knew that some of his predecessors such as Bacon, Boyle, and Newton had associated heat with motion and that the current view—particularly in France—interpreted heat as a weightless elastic fluid. Though favoring the fluid theory, he placed much greater importance on the activities of experiment and measurement in the investigations of heat.

Overview of Biographical Sources

Only one full-length biography of Black has been published—by the chemist William Ramsay in 1918—but it does not meet late-twentieth-century scholarly standards of professional historians of science. Several dependable biographical sketches are available in science dictionaries and encyclopedias along with articles and chapters of books that deal with specific aspects of Black's chemical investigations and researches on heat. Biographical material on Black written in the mid-to-late twentieth century has tended to reduce his stature in the Chemical Revolution of the late-eighteenth century. While recognizing the quality of his mid-eighteenth century experimentation and the important role he filled as a chemical educator at the University of Edinburgh, contemporary scholars of the period also note that he published very little and seems to have been a minor influence on the French chemists who initiated the Chemical Revolution in the early 1770s.

The most important early biographical sketch of Black is Adam Ferguson's "Minutes of the Life and Character of Joseph Black, M.D.," in *Transactions of the Royal Society of Edinburgh* 5 (1805: 101-117). Ferguson was a cousin and close friend of Black. John Robison, another close friend of Black, edited Black's lectures on chemistry and included biographical material in his "Editor's Preface" to *Joseph Black, Lectures on the Elements of Chemistry* (Edinburgh, 1803). In 1830 Thomas Thomson added somewhat to the information found in Ferguson's and Robison's accounts in chapter 9 of his *History of Chemistry* (London, 1830). Lord Henry Brougham, a student of Black, wrote a chapter on Black in his *Lives of Philosophers of the Time of George III* (London and Glasgow, 1855: 1-24). In the early twentieth century, William Ramsay studied the life and work of Black, first publishing *Joseph Black, M.D., A Discourse* (Glasgow, 1904) and then his *Life and Letters of Joseph Black, M.D.* (1918). Another important shorter treatment of that time is Henry Riddell's, "The Great Chemist, Joseph Black, His Belfast Friends and Family Connections," in *Proceedings of the Belfast Natural History and Philosophical Society* 3 (1919-1920: 49-88). J. G. Crowther provided a lengthy account of Black's contributions in his *Scientists of the Industrial Revolution* (London: The Cresset Press, 1962: 9-92). More recently, Henry Guerlac composed an excellent biographical sketch in the *Dictionary of Scientific Biography* (1970). Arthur Donovan's *Philosophical Chemistry in the Scottish Enlightenment: The Doctrines and Discoveries of William Cullen and Joseph Black* (1975) described the relation and influences of Black and his teacher. A. D. C. Simpson edited a symposium on Black (1982) that depicts important aspects of Black's scientific work and interaction with contemporaries.

Evaluation of Principal Biographical Sources

Donovan, Arthur. *Philosophical Chemistry in the Scottish Enlightenment: The Doctrines and Discoveries of William Cullen and Joseph Black.* Edinburgh: Edinburgh University Press, 1975. (**A, G**) Stresses the effects of Scottish university reform, eighteenth-century natural philosophy, the Edinburgh medical/natural philosophic environment, moral philosophy, and technology on Cullen's view of chemistry. Argues that Cullen's investigations of the uses of lime in bleaching and agriculture stimulated his particular interests in calcareous substances and the theory of causticity. Black's initial interests in causticity and work leading to discovery of fixed air's chemical role derived from his association with Cullen. Donovan interprets Black's work on latent heat as part of an effort to conceive a satisfactory general theory of chemical phenomena. Material on Black deals primarily with technical aspects of Black's science.

Guerlac, Henry. "Joseph Black." In *Dictionary of Scientific Biography*, II. New York: Scribner's, 1970: 173-183. (**A, G**) The outstanding biographical sketch of Black which contains a full bibliography of primary and secondary sources, including the known manuscript versions of Black's lectures and their current locations.

Ramsay, William. *Life and Letters of Joseph Black, M.D.* London: Constable, 1918. (**A, G**) This is the only full-length biography of Black. It references an autobiographical sketch, as well as other of Black's letters and papers. Discusses his major scientific achievements. By standards of recent scholarship does not adequately relate Black's work to frameworks of eighteenth-century physics and chemistry; lacks insight into the social, economic, and cultural contexts of Black's activities.

Simpson, A. D. C., ed. *Joseph Black, 1728-1799: A Commemorative Symposium.* Edinburgh: Royal Scottish Museum, 1982. (**A, G**) Papers on the background to Black's philosophy of nature, his work on heat, experimental science in Glasgow during Black's time, his medical activities, relation to Lavoisier's chemistry, interaction with John Robison, and manuscripts of his chemical lectures.

Overview and Evaluation of Primary Sources

An English translation of Black's medical dissertation of 1754 by A. Crum Brown appears in *Journal of Chemical Education* 12 (1935: 225-228, 268-273). A more recent translation of Black's dissertation, translated by Thomas Hanson, was published in English as *On Acid Humor Arising from Foods, and On White Magnesia* (Minneapolis, MN: Bell Museum of Pathobiology, 1973). Black's most notable chemical publication was "Experiments Upon Magnesia Alba, Quicklime, and Some Other Alcaline Substances," in *Essays and Observations, Physical and Literary. Read Before a Society in Edinburgh* 2 (1756). It was reprinted as *Alembic Club Reprint* 1 (Edinburgh, 1898). Black's chemical lectures at Edinburgh were published by John Robison in *Lectures on the Elements of Chemistry,* (2 vols. Edinburgh, 1803; American ed. 3 vols. Philadelphia, 1806-1807).

Museums, Historical Landmarks, Societies

Andersonian Library, University of Strathclyde (Glasgow, Scotland). Contains two ink sketches of Black by Thomas Cochrane that were included in his notes of Black's lectures in 1767-1768 at Edinburgh. Reproduced by Douglas McKie in *Annals of Science* 1 (1936): 110.

University of Edinburgh (Edinburgh, Scotland). Owns an oil painting by David Martin (c. 1770), reproduced by Henry Guerlac in *Isis* 48 (1957); and a portrait of Black by Henry Raeburn showing Black at about age sixty. Reproduced in the frontispiece of Robison's edition of Black's lectures. At about the same time as the Raeburn portrait, John Kay made some sketches of Black that were eventually published in *A Series of Portraits and Caricature Etchings by the Late John Kay* (Edinburgh, 1837; Part 1: 52-57). Ramsay's biography contains reproductions of the Kay sketches.

Other Sources

Barnett, Martin. "The Development of the Concept of Heat From the Fire Principle of Heraclitus Through the Caloric Theory of Joseph Black." In *Scientific Monthly* 42 (1946): 165-172, 247-257. Discusses Black's role in the history of ideas concerning heat.

Clow, Archibald, and Nan L. Clow. *The Chemical Revolution.* London: Batchworth, 1952. Includes references to Black's interests in industrial applications of chemistry.

Crosland, M. P. "The Use of Diagrams as Chemical 'Equations' in the Lecture Notes of William Cullen and Joseph Black." In *Annals of Science* 15 (1959): 75-90. Discusses Black's teaching symbols.

Davis, Audrey and Jon Eklund. "Joseph Black Matriculates: Medicine and Magnesia Alba." In *Journal of the History of Medicine and Allied Sciences* 27 (1972): 396-417. Describes the context of Black's work with magnesia alba in the 1850s.

Donovan, Arthur. "Pneumatic Chemistry and Newtonian Natural Philosophy in the Eighteenth Century: William Cullen and Joseph Black." In *Isis* 67 (1976): 217-228. Discusses the thoughts of Cullen and Black about the relation of Newtonian physical theory and the chemistry of gases in the eighteenth century.

————. "James Hutton, Joseph Black, and the Chemical Theory of Heat." In *Ambix* 25 (1978): 176-190. Traces connection between Hutton's theory of the earth and the research tradition of eighteenth-century Scottish chemistry.

————. "Toward a Social History of Technological Ideas: Joseph Black, James Watt, and the Separate Condensor." In *The History and Philosophy of Technology*, George Bugliarello and Dean Doner, eds. Urbana: University of Illinois Press, 1979: 19-30. Asserting that Watt merely applied Black's theory of latent heat to the steam engine, argues that Black and Watt at Glasgow illustrate a union of theory and practice (science and engineering) in a "happy integration of technology, society, and culture."

Guerlac, Henry. "Joseph Black and Fixed Air." In *Isis* 48 (1957): 124-151, 433-456. Describes Black's early chemical researches.

McKie, Douglas, and Niels H. de V. Heathcote. *The Discovery of Specific and Latent Heats*. London: Arnold, 1935: 1-53. Describes Black's work on heat.

Partington, J. R. *History of Chemistry, III.* New York: Macmillan, 1962: 131-143. A rendition of Black's work in chemistry.

Perrin, Carleton. "A Reluctant Catalyst: Joseph Black and the Edinburgh Reception of Lavoisier's Chemistry." In *Ambix* 29 (1982): 141-176. Assesses Black's cool response to the new chemistry of Lavoisier.

————. "Joseph Black and the Absolute Levity of Phlogiston." In *Annals of Science* 40 (1983): 109-137. Analyzes Black's interpretation that phlogiston possesses absolute levity. This was motivated by efforts to relate physical and chemical phenomena and, in Black's view, was drawn from his critical appraisal of experimental evidence. The notion persisted in his lectures for about fifteen years until he quietly dropped it in the early 1780s.

Robert K. DeKosky
University of Kansas

William Blackstone
1723-1780

Chronology

Born William Blackstone on July 10, 1723, in Cheapside, London, the posthumous son of Charles Blackstone, a silk merchant and Mary Bigg, the daughter of a wealthy landowner in Wiltshire; 1735 becomes an orphan and grows up in the care of his mother's brother, a London surgeon; *1735-1738* attends Charterhouse School; *1738* attends Pembroke College, Oxford University, where he studies the classics, deepens his love for literature and turns to the study of law with some reluctance; *1741* enters the Middle Temple to study law; *1743* writes a comprehensive but unoriginal treatise on the elements of architecture, which circulates widely and foreshadows his later talent as a writer of a textbook on the laws of England; *1744* accepts a fellowship at All Souls College at Oxford, where he demonstrates his talent more as an administrator than as a lecturer; *1745* receives his Bachelor of Civil Law degree from Oxford; *1746* called to the bar and begins to practice law; *1749* succeeds his uncle as recorder, the chief judicial magistrate, of Wallingford, Berkshire; *1750* receives his doctorate of civil law; during the 1750s helps to complete the Codrington Library at All Souls; *1746-1753* serves as college bursar; *1749* begins ten-year position as the steward of its manors; and occasionally serves as legal representative; *1753* initiates lectures on English law for the first time in a British university, Oxford; *1755-1756* receives appointment as one of the delegates to direct Oxford's Clarendon Press, where he magnificently improves its efficiency and the quality of its typography; *1756* resumes his law practice before the courts at Westminster; *1758* at All Souls wins first appointment to first endowed chair of English law; *1759* revives his legal career and begins a political one; *1761* becomes a King's Counsel and member of Parliament for the pocket borough (a constituency whose parliamentary representatives were controlled by a prominent family because the number of voters were few and easily influenced) of Hindon, in his parents' native county of Wiltshire; because Fellows then had to be unmarried, resigns his fellowship at All Souls after marriage to Sarah Clitherow, with whom he has nine children; obtains principalship of New Inn Hall at Oxford, which he attempts to convert into a separate college for students of English law; *1763* receives appointment as solicitor-general to Queen Charlotte, wife of King George III; *1766* resigns principalship and professorship at All Souls owing to his waxing legal practice and waning health; *1765-1769* publishes his lectures in the first edition of the *Commentaries of the Law of England*, his four-volume master-piece and best-selling textbook; *1770* resigns from Parliament and recordership for Wallingford to become a justice of the Court of Common Pleas; *1780* dies in London on February 14, possibly from a lack of exercise, which contributed to the dropsy that killed him.

Activities of Historical Significance

William Blackstone's place in English legal history is as a writer of a textbook that was an elegant and accessible, comprehensive and comprehensible, elementary summary of the Laws of England intended to entice gentlemen to know their own laws. Blackstone's statement of these laws was mostly an encomium that comfort-ed the complacent and a target that unwittingly displayed fuzzy thinking and abuses in the law against which reformers might blast their remonstrations and recommendations. In this textbook, the laws of England were celebrated so clearly that by other minds an innumerable host of specific legal presumptions, attitudes, statutes, and practices could be—and were—more readily questioned than ever before. In this way, Blackstone's *Commentaries* were at once a memorial to the laws of his own time and a cradle for those measures of the future which were to abolish so many of them.

"Law was the point where life and logic met." So goes the legal historian Frederic Maitland's justly famous dictum. But whose life and what sort of logic? Blackstone's logic was the discourse of a mostly, though not completely, apologet-ic and complacent celebrant of the general structure of society and the politics of his time and place—a wealthy commercial country dominated by a landed gentry and aristocracy whose honors flowed from a monarch whose actual political sov-ereignty was ever diminishing under the corrupting demands for the control of administrative places and the principled attacks of politicians in Parliament, many of whom feared the residual constitutional powers of the king whom they served and the nascent political and social claims of the people, both the few voters and the many non-voters, whom they claimed ultimately to represent. However, Blackstone did show a humane inclination toward the reform of criminal law, where the work of the Italian philosopher and jurist Cesare Beccaria exerted its influence on the strategy of punishments and in which Blackstone collaborated after 1776 with English prison reformer John Howard and English statesman William Eden for the reform of prisons. Apology and complacency also informed his work as a politician and a legist (such is the judgment of almost all scholars who have studied it), but only during the past sixty years has anyone tried to go deeper to grasp and articulate the precise philosophical, sociological, and historical grounds of the many opinions that Blackstone advanced.

Blackstone also wanted to prove the advantages of the English common law as a national law, thereby deterring an exaggerated appreciation of the Roman law, as well as to encourage more university-educated gentlemen to join the bar, thereby improving the social quality and mental capacity of barristers. In this third goal, Blackstone was demonstrably and markedly successful—a gentle-born laity was systematically introduced to the substance of the law and a greater number of them were persuaded to learn more about it and even to practice it.

Although Blackstone was not the first author of a textbook of English law, his *Commentaries* was the most accessible and comprehensive statement of its substantive rules. Blackstone may not have regarded this work as an authoritative statement of the law, but it nonetheless became an important interpretation of English law—often cited as an authority in court decisions and lawyers' briefs—until the twentieth century. The *Commentaries* was reissued scores of times in revised working editions by various eminent editors until the early twentieth century, when the effort to make it ever-up-to-date was suspended. The influence of the *Commentaries* on the European continent and elsewhere, through whole and partial translations in French, German, and Italian, remains largely unexplored.

It is well known, however, that Blackstone's influence in nineteenth-century America was especially great because legal education at that time was so poor. Blackstone was used consciously by relative "conservatives" such as James Kent, an American lawyer who used Blackstone's Commentaries as the basis for his own classic, *Commentaries on American Law* (1826-1830); by U.S. Supreme Court Justice Joseph Story to try to contain democratic impulses; and by others through revision, including Thomas Jefferson's friend and legal thinker, St. George Tucker, to Americanize and republicanize the former colonies' inheritance of English common law. By exposing and expounding English legal principles, Blackstone's systematic understanding of the spirit and reason of those principles encouraged nineteenth-century writers of specialized legal treatises as well as judges to be more self-consciously philosophical legists. Blackstone's educational monument, however meritorious or flawed in its particulars, helped not only to nurture the growing juristic spirit in his nation and its cousins, but also to maintain the structure of the English common law and all that it tended to support. Here, in the architecture of the law, new function followed upon his form.

English social and legal reformer Jeremy Bentham's attack on Blackstone in *A Fragment on Government* (1776) was the first popular and lasting expansion of that new juristic spirit and served as the first systematic critique of the common law that Blackstone had encapsulated so comprehensively.

There are many particular judgments in the *Commentaries* that deserve to be better illuminated against the long historical background of earlier English, civil, and canon laws as well as political theory. For example, in the famous contested election of 1754 for knights of the shire from the county of Oxford, an objection was made to admitting to the right of voting "customary freeholders," who were a distinct species of copyholder that held land not at the will of the lord of the manor. Such copyholders existed in other counties as well, and all had for some time exercised the franchise as if they were regular freeholders. Blackstone was retained as counsel for the Tory interest that denied the right of customary freeholders to vote. He argued that they and all other copyhold titles were originally vested in bondsmen, and the taint of villeinage so persisted that this peculiar species of tenure still could not be deemed a freehold. Although Blackstone's opinion rested on eminent authorities going back to Sir Edward Coke's *Compleat Copyholder,* section xxxii, he never really wrestled with the principal legal argument of his opponents, *viz.* that "customary freeholders" had acquired their franchise by right of prescription. From the early seventeenth century on, after the case of *Goodwin v. Fortescue* (1604), the House of Commons, sitting as a court in judgment of electoral returns, had frequently expanded the franchise on the basis of prescriptive right. With the tendency in the eighteenth century to narrow the franchise, a tendency supported by Blackstone in his *Commentaries* despite a pious proclamation seemingly to the contrary, the prescriptive acquisition of the franchise was abandoned. His brief, published in 1758 as a pamphlet, *Considerations on Copyholders*, was instrumental in obtaining an enactment that declared all copyholders to be incapable of voting (31 Geo. II, cap. 14).

In 1769, Blackstone figured prominently in another famous case affecting the franchise. John Wilkes, who had been convicted in absentia in 1764 for seditious libel and contumacy, returned to England in 1768 and was elected a member of Parliament for Middlesex, which availed him of parliamentary privilege to escape imprisonment. The House of Commons expelled Wilkes in 1769 on the ground that he was still an outlaw. Wilkes was elected and expelled two more times. Finally, after his fourth electoral success, the Commons declared Wilkes ineligible to stand for election and elected his nearest rival, who had polled only 296 votes to Wilkes's 1,100. In this complex constitutional crisis, where it seemed that the Crown could influence the Commons in practice to expel those members of Parliament deemed undesirable and thus virtually to nominate its own members—a process of corporate co-optation reminiscent of restricted English municipalities and continental regimes—Blackstone asserted in parliamentary debate and in his pamphlet, *The Case of the Late Election of the County of Middlesex*, that Wilkes was disqualified to sit and consequently could not be chosen by the electorate. George Grenville noted that the list of causes for disqualification in the *Commentaries* contained none that applied to Wilkes. Blackstone's essential argument, that the very act of expulsion of a member rendered him incapable of re-election, was and has long been jeered. Indeed, in 1782, Wilkes's expulsion was expunged from the Commons's *Journal* and thus eliminated as a legal precedent. But Blackstone's legal point, however disagreeable to democrats and however insufficiently explored by scholars, was that the House of Commons, sitting in judgment of electoral returns and requiring that power to preserve its vaunted "independence," was at that time supreme in its jurisdiction and free to be arbitrary in its decision, and that a long tradition of juristic thought supported that position. Blackstone altered later editions of the *Commentaries* to include the legality of Wilkes's expulsion and thereby better reveal the quasi-corporatist quality of the House of Commons.

Blackstone made only one other comparable and notable revision to his classic text. In the earliest editions of the *Commentaries*, he doubted that Protestant dissenters were any better subjects than were papists. He had to alter this illiberal judgment as a result of hostile pamphlets written in 1769 by Joseph Priestley, nonconforming minister, theologian, scientist, man-of-letters, and reformer, and in 1770 by Philip Furneaux, author, non-conforming minister, and reformer, but he continued to defend the laws which discriminated against those whose religious status was non-Anglican.

Blackstone's *Commentaries*, which were so relatively adequate and attractive as a summary of the substantive rules of English law, became an icon to be adored by the politically satisfied and to be smashed by the politically discontented, because political theory is would-be law, and law is institutionalized political theory, and a judge's decision is both. These two sects established themselves over two hundred years ago; only the precise words of their respective creeds, not their spirit, have been altered in the passage of time.

Overview of Biographical Sources

Little is known about Blackstone the man—he was alleged to have been languid and hot-tempered and compulsively orderly—and few letters of personal revelation have been located by scholars. Scholarly interest in Blackstone has been primarily confined to understanding his principles of law and the influence that he exerted upon the legal system of his own day and during the nineteenth century.

Beginning in 1781 with his brother-in-law, James Clitherow, and continuing on into the twentieth century with such legal luminaries as Rupert Cross, Harold Hanbury, W. S. Holdsworth, and S. F. C. Milson, as well as W. B. Odgers, David Lockmiller, and L. C. Warden, Blackstone's apologists have presented him as a relatively accurate and supremely graceful describer of the substance of English law as it stood in his time. Although Blackstone was complacent about the English common law, his defenders note correctly that he was also critical on many particular points; and with respect to the criminal law and prisons, he was a genuine reformer.

From some eighteenth-century Whigs and Benthamite "radicals" to twentieth-century historians, dispassionate philosophers, liberals and leftists, Blackstone's conception of rights seemed to abridge the rights that they felt were due to Englishmen and perhaps even to all people; to obviate the need for "natural" rights on which positive ones may be founded; and to lead to that legal positivism where arbitrary will, not right reason, is the ultimate justification of any law. Broadly speaking, such is the general tendency of the arguments of Burns, Hart, Lucas, McKnight, and Rinck; while, Finnis and possibly Lieberman find in Blackstone a supporter of natural law.

Blackstone's critics could easily dispute his defenders, not only because in many instances they may have had different political agendas, but also because the arguments and very structure of the entire four volumes of the *Commentaries* seem incoherent and riddled with internal contradictions. In 1776 Jeremy Bentham, in *A Comment of the "Commentaries"*, mounted the most memorable examination of the arguments and structure of the *Commentaries*, and he did so as a utilitarian opponent of natural rights, which Blackstone seemed at times to support.

The philosophical description and explanation of the social intention and tendency of the structure of the *Commentaries* has been significant because the walls of a legal structure include and exclude different legal content, just as the form of a building shapes the character of the activities that may go within it. Blackstone's critics have not been consistent or clear in examining his legal architecture. Daniel Boorstin, *The Mysterious Science of the Law* (1941) simply arranged a grab-bag of quotations from noted authors to demonstrate that Blackstone's law is an agreeably mysterious composite of common eighteenth-century platitudes. Duncan Kennedy, "The Structure of Blackstone's *Commentaries*" (1979) describes the contradictory claims of individual and state under a nascent liberal and capitalist regime. David Lieberman, *The Province of Legislation Determined* (1989), presents the conflict between the common-*cum*-natural law, which Blackstone favored, and a statute law of which he was wary. Michael Lobban, *The Common Law and English Jurisprudence* (1991), analyses the form of Roman law versus the content of English common law. All conclude that the contradictions in the *Commentaries* are caused by its structure. Although John W. Cairns, "Blackstone, an English Institutionalist" (1984) and Alan Watson, "The Structure of Blackstone's *Commentaries*" (1988) prove through careful, broad-ranging, and deeply historically minded scholarship that Blackstone adopted the structure of the *Commentaries* from Roman civil law models, they do not explore the philosophical intentions and social tendency of his choice.

In addition to the arguments of "rights" and "structure," there is a third viewpoint in interpreting the *Commentaries*, under which "rights" can be rhetorically subsumed and "structure" becomes potentially irrelevant. On fundamental issues Blackstone was often content to vanquish his difficulties by an appeal to expediency and public policy. Ultimately, he argued, expedience, convenience, and the necessity of achieving happiness was the first, last, and "right" principle of societal power. Such appeals were not peculiar, but common in his time; there were more versions of utilitarianism in eighteenth-century England than just Bentham's. Paul Lucas, "Essays in the Margin of Blackstone's *Commentaries,*" (1963), reveals Blackstone's utilitarianism, which is later expanded, albeit unwittingly, by Kennedy and by Gerald Stourzh, "William Blackstone: Teacher of Revolution" (1970). The legal positivism and utilitarianism of the *Commentaries* may therefore be seen as a precursor to Bentham, as Albert V. Dicey recounts in "Blackstone's *Commentaries*" (1930). Unlike the individualism of Bentham's utilitarianism, Blackstone's was focused on the privileges due to and social benefits derived from the primacy of status within his English version of a corporative *Ständestaat*, a society and state founded more upon legally privileged status groups than upon legally equal individuals who freely contract their relationships with each other. Kahn-Freund's brilliant exposition (1977) of Blackstone's anti-liberal position in the history of the contract of employment, Posner's article (1976) on Blackstone as a sociological legist (probably derived from Montesquieu), and Willman's interpretation (1983) of Blackstone as the defender of an idealized aristocracy can all be incorporated within this third, and possibly more comprehensive, focus of interpretation.

Evaluation of Principal Biographical Sources

Clitherow, James. "The Life of Sir William Blackstone, Knight." Preface to Blackstone's *Reports of Cases*. 2 vols. 1781. 2d ed. London, 1828; and to John Bell's edition of Blackstone's *Commentaries* 1 (London, 1813): 7-26. (**A**) First and fundamental narrative by Blackstone's brother-in-law.

Doolittle, I. G. "Sir William Blackstone and his *Commentaries on the Laws of England:* a Biographical Approach." *Oxford Journal of Legal Studies* 3 (1983): 99-112. (**A**) The beginnings of a thoroughly scholarly biography. Tries to understand Blackstone in his historical context as a practical man of business, but neglects Blackstone the wrestler with law.

Douglas, D. *The Biographical History of Sir William Blackstone*. 1782. New York: Augustus Kelley, 1971. (**A**) Bloated repetition of Clitherow's life. Corrects a few minor errors. Includes a bibliography of Blackstone's works.

Hanbury, Harold G. *The Vinerian Chair and Legal Education.* Oxford: Blackwell, 1958. (**A**) Three chapters defending Blackstone's legal education.

—————. "Blackstone as a Judge." In *American Journal of Legal History* 3 (1959): 1-27. (**A**) More explanation about Blackstone's legal background.

Lockmiller, David A. *Sir William Blackstone.* Chapel Hill: University of North Carolina Press, 1938. (**A**) Better of the two modern biographies, but superficial. Lists with photographs and locations the major portraits and statues of Blackstone.

MacDonnell, G. P. "Sir William Blackstone." In *Dictionary of National Biography.* Vol. 2: 595-602. New York: Macmillan: 1921-1922. (**A**) The best brief nineteenth-century account.

Odgers, William Blake. "Sir William Blackstone." *Yale Law Journal* 27 (1917): 599-618; 28 (1919): 542-566. (**A**) Like most biographies of Blackstone, this is full of information but lacks a profound understanding of its subject.

Philip, Ian Gilber. *William Blackstone and the Reform of the Oxford University Press in the Eighteenth Century.* Vol. 7. Oxford: Oxford Bibliographical Society Publications, 1957. (**A**) The only full account of the subject.

Sutherland, Lucy. "William Blackstone and the Legal Chairs at Oxford." In *Evidence in Literary Scholarship: Essays in Memory of James Marshall Osborn.* René Wellek and A. Ribeiro, eds. Oxford: Clarendon, 1979: 229-240. (**A**) Proves that the idea of lecturing on common law at Oxford was initially entirely Blackstone's.

Warden, Lewis C. *The Life of Blackstone.* Charlottesville, VA: Michie, 1938. The second of the two modern lives. Even more superficial than Lockmiller.

Overview and Evaluation of Primary Sources

Manuscript copies of Blackstone's lectures on the law are listed, located, and analyzed in Holdsworth, *A History of English Law* XII (London: Methuen, 1938-1952: 747-750). Other, but not all, manuscripts and letters are listed in Lockmiller, (see above). Microfilm copies of the letters in the Lansdowne manuscripts are to be found at Washington University, St. Louis, Missouri. Letters by Blackstone are at the British Museum, London; the New York Public Library; the Greater London Record Office; the Law School of Harvard University; the Hampton L. Carson Collection of the Free Library of Philadelphia. The Newdigate manuscript is in the Warwickshire County Record Office. Blackstone's letters in the Folger Shakespeare and Huntington Libraries are of significance only for his signature. There are unquestionably other letters in private collections.

Misleading characterizations of and excerpts from Blackstone's correspondence with Lord Shelburne are in Edmund Petty, Lord Fitzmaurice, *Life of William, Earl of Shelburne* (2 vols. 2d rev. ed. London: Macmillan, 1912). (See microfilms of originals in Washington University, St. Louis.) For letters in the Carson Collection, see Howel J. Heaney, ed., "The Letters of Sir William Blackstone in the Hampton L. Carson Collection of the Free Library of Pennsylvania," *American Journal of Legal History* 1 (1957): 363-378. Blackstone's famous letter of 1745, about his life as a reluctant student of the law, to his uncle, Seymour Richmond is in the *Harvard Law Review* 32 (1919): 975-976. For Blackstone's letter to John Eardley Wilmot, see Wilmot's *Memoirs* (London, n.p., 1802: 71-72) and *The University of California Chronicle* 12 (1910): 346-347.

Selected Poems and Translations, 1736-1744 are in the Law Library of the University of California, Berkeley. Blackstone's marginalia, which may be revealing, are in annotations to books and MSS in the Library of All Souls College, Oxford.

There are two significant modern reprints of the four volumes of the *Commentaries*. The first edition (London, 1765-1769) was reprinted by the University of Chicago Press, 1979; the 9th ed. (London, 1783), which was the last corrected by Blackstone, was reprinted by Garland Publishing, 1978. There is no variorum edition of the *Commentaries*, but changes made in the second edition are in a *Supplement to the First Edition; containing the most Material Corrections* (n.p., 1766) in the Clark Memorial Library of the University of California at Los Angeles and in the Los Angeles City Law Library.

Evaluation of Selected Critical Sources

Bentham, Jeremy. *A Comment on the "Commentaries"* and *A Fragment on Government*. J. H. Burns and H. L. A Hart, eds. Atlantic Highlands, N.J.: Humanities Press, 1977. (**A**) First and most powerful critique of Blackstone's general view of law. The *Fragment* was first published in London in 1776; the *Comment*, of which the *Fragment* was part, first appeared in 1928. This is the best and most recent edition.

Boorstin, Daniel J. *The Mysterious Science of the Law: An Essay on Blackstone's Commentaries*. 1941. Reprint. Boston: Beacon, 1958. (**A**) Clever and witty. Illuminates the *Commentaries* as a potpourri of selections from seventeenth- and eighteenth-century books, largely non-legal. The work obscures Blackstone as the disciplined follower of any legal tradition, buries any originality in and understanding of Blackstone's opinions, and does not read Blackstone's text closely.

Burns, Robert P. "Blackstone's Theory of the 'Absolute' Rights of Property." *University of Cincinnati Law Review* 54 (1985): 67-86. (**A**) More evidence of Blackstone's artful devotion to the primacy of positive, not natural, law.

Cairns, John W. "Blackstone, an English Institutionalist: Legal Literature and the Rise of the Nation State." *Oxford Journal of Legal Studies* 4 (1984): 318-360. (**A**) The structure of Blackstone's *Commentaries* follows Roman civil law models to establish the English common law as a national law. Sets Blackstone in a comparative European context and includes a learned critique of Duncan Kennedy's article.

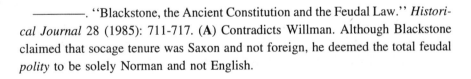

————. "Blackstone, the Ancient Constitution and the Feudal Law." *Historical Journal* 28 (1985): 711-717. (**A**) Contradicts Willman. Although Blackstone claimed that socage tenure was Saxon and not foreign, he deemed the total feudal *polity* to be solely Norman and not English.

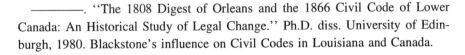

————. "The 1808 Digest of Orleans and the 1866 Civil Code of Lower Canada: An Historical Study of Legal Change." Ph.D. diss. University of Edinburgh, 1980. Blackstone's influence on Civil Codes in Louisiana and Canada.

Cross, Rupert. "Blackstone v. Bentham." *Law Quarterly Review* 92 (1976): 516-527. (**A**) Argues that Blackstone, as a pluralistic thinker, could not escape internal contradictions in his presentation of the common law; Bentham, a monist, could, but often did not, and inexcusably often misrepresented Blackstone's meanings. One of the best of the apologies because it grasps the difficulty of recasting the common law into logical coherence and satisfying all interests in society, which is the aim of most reformers and critics of Blackstone.

Dicey, Albert V. "Blackstone's *Commentaries.*" *Cambridge Law Journal* 4(1930): 286-307. (**A**) Places Blackstone in the context of the state's attempt to control social behavior according to the principles of Benthamite Utilitarianism.

—————. *Lectures on the Relation Between Law and Public Opinion in England during the Nineteenth Century.* 1905. Reprint. London and New York: Macmillan, 1962. (**A**) Classic critique of Blackstone placed in the context of the progress of the utilitarian intervention by the state to control social behavior according to the principles of Benthamite utilitarianism.

Finnis, John M. "Blackstone's Theoretical Intentions." *Natural Law Forum* 12 (1967): 163-183. (**A**) Asserts that Blackstone supported natural law, if one understands natural law and its relation to positive law from what seems to be a Straussian, Thomistically neo-conservative viewpoint. To be doubted.

Hart, H. L. A. "Blackstone's Use of the Law of Nature." In *Butterworth's South African Law Review* 3 (1956): 169-174. (**A**) Foundation of modern, close, scholarly examinations of the text of Blackstone's passages on the law of nature; model of thoughtfulness and brevity.

Holdsworth, William S. *A History of English Law.* Vols. 11-13. London: Methuen, 1938-1952. (**A**) Best and briefest introduction to the Blackstone problem, especially volume 12: 702-737; fairest and most judicious of all the apologies.

Kahn-Freund, Otto. "Blackstone's Neglected Child: the Contract of Employment." In *Law Quarterly Review* 93 (1977): 508-528. (**A**) This learned, sensitive, and untendentious piece asserts that Blackstone and the common law tradition could not see statute and common law as a whole. Notes that on issues of master and servant, Blackstone, unlike continental Roman lawyers, resisted the progress of individual contract to maintain a regime of status.

Kennedy, Duncan. "The Structure of Blackstone's *Commentaries.*" In *Buffalo Law Review* 28 (1979): 205-382. (**A**) The most profoundly, elaborately, and tortuously reasoned of all modern commentaries on Blackstone. Kennedy attempts to show, in accordance with the method of the school of critical legal studies, that the internal and philosophical structure of the text of the *Commentaries* reflects a oneness with an allegedly single, dominant trend of political thought of his times. He argues that Blackstone wanted to legitimatize the common law and prove it consistent with incipient liberal political theory: substance and function, therefore, logically follow from form and structure. Although Cairns (1984) and Watson (1988) prove that the structure of the *Commentaries* was historically guided by earlier civil lawyers, the question of the nature of the philosophical integrity and social intention of that structure remains moot. Kennedy argues that there is no logical coherence in Blackstone, for he failed to reconcile the rights of the individual with those of society. By denying and disguising that contradiction within an analysis of the mediation of legal rights, Blackstone realized, if not his intention, then his social tendency to defend ideologically the "possessive individualism" of capitalism and liberalism in their will to power. But Kennedy assumes that there was only one kind of legal liberalism—mediation between individuals and between them and society by means of an appeal to rights. One utilitarian form of liberalism, by which Benthamites in England undermined Blackstone's common law in the nineteenth century, is evidence in curious support of Kennedy's view. Blackstone reflected, however, another type of utilitarianism, similar to William Paley's. Blackstone's rhetoric about the defense of the rights of individuals seems so individualistic that Kennedy, like Roscoe Pound in *The Spirit of the Common Law* (Boston, 1923) can indict him on that count as well as for not adequately defending all individuals. But the overarching structure of the *Commentaries,* especially in the first volume, is actually an assertion of the rights of statuses; and Blackston'e ultimate arguments, which Kennedy recognizes in part, are usually from "convenience" and "necessity", not from "rights"; thus Blackstone really leans, with contradictions, toward a utilitarian, corporatist defense of a *Ständestaat,* which is one argument of Lucas (1962; 1974) and Cairns (1984).

Lieberman, David. "Blackstone's Science of Legislation." In *Journal of British Studies* 27 (1988): 117-149. (**A**) Reprinted in *Law and Justice* 98/99 (1988): 60-74; 100/101 (1989): 31-45.

―――――. *The Province of Legislation Determined.* Cambridge, England: Cambridge University Press, 1989. (**A**) Argues that Blackstone is best understood as a defender of active courts, the law-finding organ of the common law, and as an opponent of overly active and necessarily inept law-making by parliamentary statute. States that Blackstone was confused about sovereignty and not about natural law: Blackstone's natural law was, like all law, historical, not metaphysical. Explains that the metaphysical version of natural law had to be limited by a strong sovereign, but that in practice Blackstone urged that parliamentary legislation be restrained because it was less wise than the common law. If one believes that the legislative sovereign can truly be comprehensive and equitably wise, then Benthamism was the remedy for Blackstonism. Cites, but does not really argue with, other explanations of the structure of law set forth in the *Commentaries*.

Lobban, Michael. "Blackstone and the Science of Law." *Historical Journal* 30 (1987): 311-335. (**A**) Explains structure of the *Commentaries* as a conflict between two methods of thought: the deductive theoretical structure of Roman law and the inductive, detailed, dynamic, practical description of the English common law. Also discerns Hobbesian, positivist leanings in Blackstone's jurisprudence.

―――――. *The Common Law and English Jurisprudence, 1760-1850.* Oxford: Clarendon Press, 1991. (**A**) Restates and expands earlier article.

McKnight, Joseph. "Blackstone, Quasi-Jurisprudent." *Southwestern Law Journal* 13 (1959): 339-411. (**A**) Doubts that Blackstone fully supported natural law.

Milsom, S. F. C. *Studies in the History of the Common Law.* London and Ronceverte, WV: Hambledon Press, 1985: 197-208. (**A**) The most thoughtful apology for the *Commentaries* as a layman's textbook of substantive rules of law related closely to life as Blackstone saw it, ungnarled by the diffusion of rules in scores of law reports and digests and alphabetical abridgements, and unburdened by an account of legal procedures to enforce them. States that the commentaries spawned a new juristic spirit that enabled others in the nineteenth century to transform the law because they did not like what Blackstone had described.

Nolan, Dennis R. "Sir William Blackstone and the New American Republic: a Study of Intellectual Impact." *New York University Law Review* 51 (1976): 731-768. (**A**) Essential, but neither the first nor the last word on the subject.

Posner, Richard A. "Blackstone and Bentham." *Journal of Law and Economics* 19 (1976): 569-606. (**A**) Brilliant defense of Blackstone as a sociological jurisprudent who presented English law as a "functioning social system." Anticipates Lieberman on the roles of courts and statutes for Blackstone and Bentham.

Rinck, Hans-Justus. "Blackstone and the Law of Nature." *Ratio* 2 (1960): 162-180. (**A**) Well-argued, close textual analysis of the flaws in the logic and structure of the *Commentaries*. Argues that Blackstone undermines natural law by failing to link it to common and statutory law. Blackstone deemed will, not reason, to be the foundation of law; this article supports, therefore, the view that Blackstone leaned towards legal positivism.

Waterman, J. S. "Thomas Jefferson and Blackstone's Commentaries." In *Essays in the History of the Early American Law*. D. H. Flaherty, ed. Chapel Hill: University of North Carolina Press, 1989. (**A**) One of the best accounts of part of the influence and use of the *Commentaries* in America.

Watson, Alan. "The Structure of Blackstone's *Commentaries.*" *Yale Law Journal* 97 (1988): 798-821. (**A**) Superb, historical critique of Kennedy. Structure of Blackstone's *Commentaries* follows the civilians, especially Dionysius Gothofredus (1549-1622); but Watson does not adequately consider Blackstone's philosophy and social intentions in adopting the structure he chose; does not, therefore, succeed in totally refuting Kennedy.

Willman, Robert. "Blackstone and the 'Theoretical Perfection' of English Law in the Reign of Charles II." In *Historical Journal* 26 (1983): 39-70. (**A**) Discusses the fact that Blackstone distinguished a "good" Anglo-Saxon "feudalism" from a "bad" Norman version and synthesized the good feudalism with the "ancient constitution'' to avoid the notion that the Glorious Revolution of 1688 interrupted the continuity of the English constitution and to maintain the constitutional function of an idealized aristocracy. Although refuted by Cairns (1985), can be used to support a corporatist understanding of Blackstone's work.

Other Sources

Barker, Ernest. *Essays on Government*. Oxford: Clarendon, 1960: 120-153. (**A**) Best introduction on the subject; much matter in few words.

Dictionary of National Biography 2: 601-602. (**A**) A handy, but abbreviated, list of materials in the catalogue of the British Museum, pamphlets and other printed works of Blackstone, foreign translations of his work, and pamphlets by other authors critical of his opinions.

Dunoyer, Luc Henry. *Blackstone et Pothier*. Paris: Rousseau, 1927. (**A**) Limited, but comparative, study of Blackstone from a French perspective.

Jones, John W. *A Translation of all the Greek, Latin, Italian, and French Quotations which Occur in Blackstone's Commentaries* 1823. Reprint. Woodbridge, CT: Research Publications, 1984. (Nineteenth-Century Legal Treatises; microfiche no. 2847-2848). (**A**) For those who need help in translation of foreign phrases in Blackstone.

Lucas, Paul. ''A Collective Biography of Students and Barristers of Lincoln's Inn, 1680-1804: A Study in the 'Aristocratic Resurgence' of the Eighteenth Century.'' In *Journal of Modern History* 46 (1974): 227-261. (**A**) Offers statistical evidence of Blackstone's success at recruiting more students of law from the higher stations of society.

————. ''Blackstone and the Reform of the Legal Profession.'' *English Historical Review* 77 (1962): 456-489. (**A**) Suggests that one motive of Blackstone was to entice university-trained gentlemen to join the ranks of barristers, and to discourage the obscure from entering the law.

————. "*Ex parte* Sir William Blackstone, 'Plagiarist': a Note on Blackstone and the Natural Law." In *American Journal of Legal History* 7 (1963): 142-158. (**A**) Argues that Blackstone was almost Hobbesian in his understanding of natural law; therefore, Blackstone was closer to Austin and legal positivism than one would think. Unaware of earlier articles by McKnight and Rinck when he wrote it, but offers new evidence.

————. "Essays in the Margin of Blackstone's *Commentaries*." Ph.D diss. Princeton University, 1962. (**A**) One essay, "The Indelible Villeiny of Copyholders," is an analysis of Blackstone's argument respecting the Oxfordshire election of 1754; another, "In the Breast of Parliament," is an examination of Blackstone and the election of John Wilkes in 1769.

Mersky, Roy M. "A Bibliography of Articles on Blackstone." *American Journal of Legal History* 3 (1959): 78-87. (**A**) Extremely valuable, especially for fugitive nineteenth-century pieces, but not annotated and not complete.

The Pantheon: A Vision. London: Dodsley, 1747. (**A**) Thirty-two pages of religious poetry ascribed to Blackstone by Horace Walpole in his copy in the Houghton Library of Harvard University.

Postema, Gerald J. *Bentham and the Common Law Tradition.* Oxford: Clarendon, 1986. (**A**) Insights into Blackstone scattered *passim*.

Stourzh, Gerald. "William Blackstone: Teacher of Revolution." *Jahrbuch für Amerikastudien* 15 (1970): 184 ff. (**A**) Very learned, but confused and ill-argued. Observes correctly that Blackstone, as a true Hobbesian, justified the Revolution of 1688 with the utilitarian argument from the safety and necessity of self-preservation, which influenced certain American revolutionists in the 1770s; but misses the crucial point that this argument was also Lockeian and historically typically "Tory" after 1688 and opposed to "Whiggish" arguments for Revolution from this and especially other natural and contractual rights. Where Professor Blackstone wrote "powers of society," his colonial students scribbled "rights of society." Stourzh wisely makes no serious effort to regard Blackstone as the spiritual grandfather of the right-ridden, popularly sovereign, American Declaration of

Independence from the King-in-parliament. Condensed version of article is in chapter I of Stourzh, *Alexander Hamilton and the Idea of Republican Government.* Stanford, CA: Stanford University Press, 1970.

Paul Lucas
Clark University

Jean Bodin
ca. 1529/1530-1596

Chronology

Born Jean Bodin ca. 1530 in Angers, France, son of Guillaume Bodin, a well-to-do master tailor, and Catherine Dutretre, who may have been descended from Jewish refugees from Spain; *ca. 1544-1548* after entering the Carmelite order, which his mother's brother headed in Angers, sent to Paris to study, under the patronage of Gabriel Bouvery, bishop of Angers; while in Paris, probably attends lectures by Pierre Ramus at College de Presle of the University of Paris to hear Ramus's radical criticism of Aristotelian philosophy; *1548* summoned before the Parliament of Paris for heresy, but is released, possibly through the good graces of his bishop-patron, Bouvery; *1552* leaves Carmelite order; possibly stays briefly in Geneva, Switzerland, where records show the marriage of a Jean Bodin de Saint-Amand to a Typhaine Reynaude, widow of a suspect arrested with Bodin four years earlier who had been executed for heresy; *ca. 1550s* studies law in Toulouse, in an atmosphere of fervent Protestant evangelism and legal humanism; *1555* publishes a translation of Oppian's *De Venatione* (On Hunting), which he dedicates to Bouvery; composes *Table of Universal Law*, a survey of basic principles of jurisprudence and natural law; *1559* publishes "Oration to the Senate and People of Toulouse Concerning the Education of Youth in the Republic," in which he calls for the creation of an academy for adolescent education in Toulouse and stresses the importance of moral education to civic life; *1562* after moving to Paris to practice law, takes an oath of fidelity to the Catholic faith before the Parliament of Paris as religious wars break out; *1566* publishes *Method for the Easy Understanding of History*, which becomes his major contribution to the theory of history; *1568* publishes *Response to the Paradoxes of Monsieur Malestroit*, arguing that the "price revolution" of the sixteenth century is due to the influx of New World bullion; *1569* made attorney general for Poitiers; arrested as a suspected Protestant and spends the next year and a half in prison; *1570* released during a temporary truce between Catholics and Protestants; *1571* appointed secretary and counselor to the king's younger brother, François, duc d'Alençon, who becomes head of a party of Catholics and Huguenots who become known as the ''Politiques''; *1574* named as a conspirator in an abortive plot to establish the duc d'Alençon as the next king after the death of Charles IX; *1576* goes to the Estates-General at Blois as a representative for the third estate for Vermandois; publishes *Six Books of the Republic*, the foundation-stone of absolutist political thought in France, which he dedicates to friend Guy du Faur de Pabrac, an emerging figure in the Politique movement; marries the Catholic widow of royal official in Laon; *1578* presides in a trial for witchcraft of a Joanna Harvilleria, whom he finds guilty and condemns to death; *1580* publishes *Demonmania*, a treatise on witchcraft and the role of spirits and demons in divine cosmology; *1581* accompanies Alençon to England, where he is warmly received by both Secretary Walsingham and Elizabeth I, with whom he discusses his theory of climate determining political constitutions; writes a letter to Queen Elizabeth protesting the hanging of Jesuit father Edmund Campion; *ca. 1580* composes *Colloquium of the Seven Secrets of the Sublime*, a plea for universal religious tolerance and harmony, which remains unpublished until the nineteenth century; *1584* death of Alençon; retires permanently from politics to his wife's home town of Laon; *1587* succeeds his brother-in-law as attorney for the Crown in Laon; interrogated by lieutenant governor of Laon for religious unorthodoxy, but cleared; *1589* declares himself supporter of the ultra-Catholic League, as France moves toward the climax of two-and-a-half decades of civil war; *1590* accusations of witchcraft stemming from his *Demonmania* lead to a search of his house and the public burning of certain of his books; *1591* completes a religious work, the *Paradox*; *1594* in a political *aboutface*, flees Laon and declares his support for the Catholic League's nemesis, Henri IV; *1596* publishes *Theater of Universal Nature*, and *Paradoxon*, which, like the *Method* and the *Republic*, are placed on the Catholic Church's Index of Prohibited Books; dies on June 7 and is buried at Church of the Franciscans in Laon.

Activities of Historical Significance

The basic facts of Jean Bodin's early life remain obscure, and much of how we interpret his ideas turns on what we accept as true of those first three decades of his life. He almost certainly served as a novice in the Carmelite religious order: an exposure to Carmelite mystical theology and spirituality, of illumination of the soul by divine grace leading to prophetic perfection, would help to explain something of his conception of God in his later religious works. While in Paris he may also have attended the lectures of the preeminent intellectual iconoclast of the period, Pierre Ramus, and he may be the Carmelite Jean Bodin who was arrested for heresy in 1548. Whether we accept all or part of these accounts as factual, they do suggest that Bodin was active in the intellectual ferment of the 1540s, when French Renaissance humanism merged with the Reformation.

This same intellectual ferment evidently led him to take up legal studies at Toulouse. Here the Bodin biographer is on firmer ground. The University of Toulouse had become an important center of legal humanism in France, in the use of philological and historical method for the study of civil law, as well as French customary law. The leading representative of the *mos Gallicus* or "French school" of jurisprudence, was Jacques Cujas: his magisterial influence at Toulouse from 1547 on created a thriving environment of legal and historical scholarship. Bodin's major works, the *Method for the Easy Understanding of History* (1606) and the *Republic* (1576), grew out of this legal humanism. However, his first published work, the translation of *De Venatione*, shows a different influence: that of Cujas's rival, Étienne Fourcadel (1520-1576). Fourcadel insisted in going beyond Cujas's textual and philological criticism, and promoted the study of law in light of all that was known about the ancient world. Fourcadel was interested in how the structure of daily and religious life in the ancient world affected the development of law and political institutions. This would be a decisive influence on the development of Bodin's own work.

An important aspect of the French school, at Toulouse and elsewhere, was its anti-Roman bias. The criticism of civil law sources had the inevitable effect of undermining the authoritative claims of Roman law as a coherent system of universal justice and of canon law as the embodiment of papal authority. It is hardly surprising that so many of the legal humanists flirted with Protestantism: Bodin's mentor Fourcadel faced accusations of heresy, and scholars such as François Baudouin and François Hotman had to flee to Geneva to escape religious persecution. John Calvin himself had once been a student of the "French school," as well as his leading French disciple Theodore Bèze.

Did Bodin cross the same line? Here the evidence of his earlier bout with heresy becomes crucial: the possible Ramus influence, which was closely associated with Protestantism (Ramus himself died in the St. Bartholomew's Day massacre in

1572) and his possible residence and marriage in Geneva suggest so. Conversion to Calvinism would explain his troubles with Catholic authorities during the wars of religion (although not his allegiance to the Catholic League in 1589). But why did he leave Geneva in 1553, after only one year? That year had been a turning-point for Calvin's Geneva because of the trial for heresy and burning at the stake of Michel Servetus. Servetus had been the exponent of religious syncretism and rejection of doctrinal differences between Christianity, Judaism, and other religions. Many saw in this "true religion" a sane alternative to the violence and confessional struggles of the Reformation. Servetus's trial made it clear that, as far as *true* religion was concerned, Calvin's Geneva was a dead end. Other syncretists fled from Geneva that same year. Assuming that Bodin was in Geneva, and assuming that he left for the same reasons, it would indicate that Bodin was already inclined toward the syncretism and natural religion of his last works.

Whether we accept the residence in Geneva or not, the years of study in Toulouse probably also contributed to Bodin's unusual, not to say heterodox, religious beliefs, as revealed in his Oration of 1559. These tended toward a conviction that differences in religious beliefs, between Catholic and Protestant, between Christian and Jew, were unimportant and of no theological consequence. Which denomination one accepted, therefore, was only a matter of political convenience. This position allowed him to take the oath of loyalty to the Catholic faith while in Paris in 1562 and to begin his legal work and studies unmolested.

Bodin, like many other young legal humanists, had felt a growing dissatisfaction with the narrow critical approach to the study of law taken by the old French school. Bodin and others like him came to believe that the comparative study of law could reveal hidden, universal principles by which the entire study of law could be systematically reorganized. The *Method for the Easy Understanding of History* of 1566 was part of this reconstruction of juristic science on the basis of universal history, in which, as he put it, "the best part of universal law lies hidden."

Bodin later completed the shift from the study of comparative law to a comparative history of nations and customs. In looking for the natural causes of the rise and decline of political systems, Bodin developed his theory that climate, geography, and the motions of the planets determine the form of governments. In the early part of the twentieth century, this part of Bodin's theory of universal history was treated with contempt. However, since the rise of the *Annales* school and their own form of geographic determinism and *histoire structurelle*, Bodin's approach cannot be so lightly ignored. The key to Bodin's approach to climate, geography, and history, however, is his religious frame of reference. Bodin's God reveals himself in time through nature, rather than through grace or revelation, and establishes a divine order beyond Christianity, as it were, but imbedded in history. It is this divine direction through nature that the student of universal jurisprudence discovers.

Like other neo-Bartolists, Bodin was insistent that these universal principles have a practical relevance and application, which he explained through his presentation of the principles of the French constitution. In light of Bodin's later absolutism, it is interesting to note that in the *Method for the Easy Understanding of History* Bodin accepted traditional constitutional checks on monarchical authority, such as the Parliament of Paris, the Estates General, and the royal coronation oath. For Bodin, the oath was in effect the king's promise to obey the laws of the land.

If Bodin had hoped that these constitutional restraints might prevent France from descending into the chaos of civil war, he soon learned his mistake. He observed the effects of religious "non-indifference" first hand: he narrowly escaped death for his unorthodox religious views more than once. It was in the service of the duc d'Alençon, and in his renewed acquaintance with his old law school friend Guy du Faur de Pibrac and his circle at Court, that he would come in contact with those who shared his views on the futility of religious civil war. The Politiques, as they were called, looked to a political solution to the kingdom's troubles, without reference to religious differences. The movement, which began to gather momentum after 1577, provided a convenient sounding-board for Bodin's own views.

As a work of political theory, the *Six Books of the Republic* (1576) was the culmination of Bodin's study of comparative history and law laid out in the *Method for the Easy Understanding of History* ten years earlier. But now it also answered an urgent, practical need, that of political order and harmony. Bodin was repudiating those authors who used their legal-historical scholarship to justify political chaos and anarchy and armed rebellion against the king. Bodin found the solution to the kingdom's problems in a new definition of sovereignty. He rejected the traditional, Aristotelian classifications and instead proposed that sovereignty was merely the power to command; it, and the corresponding obligation to obey, is found in every political community. Sovereignty is, in short, the power to coerce others, and Bodin had a keen appreciation of the important role of coercive force in politics. However, Bodin insisted that this power to coerce was legitimate, because it was natural. It is in order to discover the principles of this natural sovereign power that Bodin relied on the patriarchal family as the template of the natural political community. Scholars have always remarked on Bodin's patriarchalism; however, it seems fair to point out that Bodin did not use his patriarchalist arguments to give absolute monarchy a cloak of legitimacy. In his mind, this was not necessary. Instead, his point was that this paternal power is inherent in any exercise of political authority. Regardless of the type of government or constitution, sovereignty is absolute, whether it is held by the king or the people.

In many ways, the *Republic* was the culmination of his neo-Bartolist program and pointed to a new understanding of natural law. However, Bodin understood that the direction of the laws of nature were not in human hands; instead, they were determined by the will of God. Small wonder, then, that Bodin willingly abandoned the field of political theory in order to pursue his inquiries into the God of nature and man's relationship with Him.

His religious works, the *Demonmania*, the *Paradox*, *Colloquium Heptaplomeres*, and the *Theater of Universal Nature*, form a whole and share the assumption that God is the God of Nature, who has endowed humans with knowledge of nature's laws and with free will to serve as the basis of religious faith. Bodin's religion is not based on the Augustinian doctrine of grace: instead, humankind's faith in God rests on revelation through nature and illumination through prophecy, which serves to reinforce that faith. Bodin's religious writings show the influence not only of Renaissance Neoplatonism, but also of Jewish cabalistic and Platonic sources, specifically Philo and Maimonides.

The *Colloquium* is the key to his religious thought. Constructed as a dialogue between men of seven different religious faiths and perspectives, the *Colloquium* reveals a God who is known through his creative influences, especially through the workings of nature. This is also the main theme of the *Theater* as well, that God is only truly known from the effects of his works, in the wealth of experience in a universal nature. It is these effects in nature, and their uniform causes, that leads to a natural, and de-Christianized, "true religion" (*vera religio*) of the *Colloquium* and the *Paradox*. The *Demonmania*, on the other hand, shows how demons and angels take their places in Bodin's syncretist religion, as emissaries, and intermediaries, between the realm of God and pure spirit and the natural world of man.

It is hardly surprising that Bodin would not allow the *Colloquium* to be published in his lifetime, and the *Theater*, as well as the *Method for the Easy Understanding of History* and the *Republic*, were placed on the Catholic Church's Index of Prohibited Books. Bodin's great, overriding passion was his desire for religious harmony and *concordia*, which was associated with the political harmony described in the Sixth Book of the *Republic*. Bodin's "true religion" grasps the harmonious unity underlying the multiplicity of religious sects. However, Bodin's allegiance to the Catholic League suggests that it is a mistake to see him as a religious liberal. Bodin believed in religious unity, just as he believed in unity of sovereignty; he wanted to construct this unity on a new basis, not that of doctrinal uniformity, but harmony with God's will, whether revealed through prophecy (as in the case of the League or later, Henri IV) or through nature.

One of the characters in the *Colloquium* makes the remark that: "Natural things do not happen by chance, at random, or in blind sequence but proceed uniformly according to the same laws, so that given the cause the effect follows, unless they are kept from doing so by the divine will in all things." This might be the motto not only of his religious works, but of the *Method for the Easy Understanding of History* and *Republic* as well. In this way the study of man's work in politics and law, and God's works in nature, is the same.

Overview of Biographical Sources

Bodin has the distinction of being, with the occasional exceptions of Machiavelli and Sir Thomas More, the one sixteenth-century author to become part of the canon of the history of political theory. Most of the older scholarship has concentrated on him as the great exponent of absolutism, where he is often conjoined with Thomas Hobbes. American scholars such as Beatrice Reynolds and William F. Church made an important break from this "canonical" approach, in showing how Bodin changed from an exponent of limited monarchy to an absolutist theorist. Church, in particular, revealed Bodin's context to be not that of seventeenth-century absolutism, but of the French "legist" tradition of Charles du Moulin and Louis Le Roy. In their very different ways, Kenneth McRae and Pierre Mesnard also helped to locate Bodin in the intellectual milieu of the mid-sixteenth century.

More recent scholarship, led by Julian Franklin and others, sees Bodin as an important figure in the "methological revolution" in legal and historical scholarship in sixteenth-century France. Not only does this approach put the "legist" tradition in a somewhat different light, as part of the reaction to legal humanism, but it also helps to explain Bodin's place among the generation of legal humanists such as François Baudouin, François Hotman, and Étienne Pasquier, who lived through the agonies of civil war and attempted to persue their learning to find a solution to violence and anarchy. Thanks to scholars like Franklin, Donald Kelley, and John Salmon in H. Dentzer, ed. *Jean Bodin* (1973), we now have a much better grasp of the ideological context of Bodin's work on politics and law.

Even more recently, there has been a renewed interest in his works on religion and witchcraft, which scholars preoccupied with his political ideas tended to ignore (with the important exception of Pierre Mesnard). M. L. D. Kuntz's edition of the *Colloquium Heptaplomeres* (1975; see below), and Paul Lawrence Rose's examination *Bodin and the Great God of Nature: The Moral and Religious Universe of a Judaiser* (1980) of Bodin's espousal of *vera religio* or "true religion," have added another dimension to Bodin's thought, that of the religious syncretism of Giovanni Pico, Guillaume Poste, and the Hermetic tradition of the Late Renaissance. What impact these ideas had on his political doctrines seems to be the next task for Bodin scholarship.

Evaluation of Principal Biographical Sources

Chauviré, Roger. *Jean Bodin, Auteur de la République*. 1914. Reprint. Geneva: Slatkine, 1969. This is still the only comprehensive biography of Bodin, although much of the interpretation is now outdated. Available only in French.

Church, William F. *Constitutional Thought in Sixteenth Century France*. Cambridge, MA: Harvard University Press, 1941. Contains an important discussion of Bodin's *Republic*, showing his move away from traditional, constitutionalist thought to absolutism of the French "legist" tradition.

Franklin, Julian. *Jean Bodin and the Sixteenth Century Revolution in the Method for the Easy Understanding of Historiology of Law and History*. New York: Columbia University Press, 1963. Puts Bodin's approach to comparative law firmly in the context of the legal humanist treatment of legal and historical sources. A concise and important book.

————. *Jean Bodin and the Rise of Absolutist Theory*. Cambridge: Cambridge University Press, 1973. Contrasts Bodin's discussion of the French constitution in the *Method for the Easy Understanding of History* with the theory of sovereignty in the *Republic*.

King, Preston. *The Ideology of Order*. London: Allen and Unwin, 1974. Presents the absolutism of Bodin and Hobbes as a discourse on "order" and a covert defence of the status quo. A good example of where a narrow, unhistorical reading of Bodin can lead.

McRae, Kenneth D. "Ramist Tendencies in the Thought of Jean Bodin." *Journal of the History of Ideas* 24 (1955): 306-323. Although Ramus was clearly not the dominant influence on Bodin's Method for the *Easy Understanding of History,* the affinities between the two thinkers are clearly set forth.

Rose, Paul Lawrence. *Bodin and the Great God of Nature: The Moral and religious Universe of a Judaiser*. Geneva: Librairie Droz, 1980. The most comprehensive treatment of Bodin's religious and ethical views. Clearly demonstrates the intellectual roots of Bodin's doctrines of natural religion and *vera religio*, although the claim that Bodin's "mental world revolves around a vision of Judaism" seems to go a bit far.

————. "The Politique and the Prophet: Bodin and the Catholic League 1589-1594." *The Historical Journal* 21 (1978): 738-808. Argues that Bodin's temporary allegiance to the Catholic League was consistent with his earlier religious views.

Ulph, Owen. "Jean Bodin and the Estates General of 1576." *Journal of Modern History* 19 (1947): 289-296. Best account of Bodin's activities as deputy in the Estates General, based on his manuscript diary. However, should be supplemented by Martin Wolfe, "Jean Bodin on Taxes: the Sovereignty-Taxes Paradox" [*Political Science Quarterly* 83 (1968): 268-284], which shows that Bodin's opposition to taxation in the Estates General was not inconsistent with his views on absolute sovereignty.

Overview and Evaluation of Primary Sources

Pierre Mesnard's *Oeuvres philosophiques de Jean Bodin* (Paris: Presses Universitaires de France, 1951; **A**) contains Latin texts and French translations of important early works, including the *Oration to the Senate of Toulouse* (1559) and the *Method for the Easy Understanding of History for the Easy Comprehension of History* (1566). G. A. Moore's *The Response of Jean Bodin to the Paradoxes of Malestroit* (Washington, D.C.: Country Dollar Press, 1947; **A**) is a translation of the 1578 edition of Bodin's only contribution to political economy, published with a translation of Malestroit's *Paradoxes*. Beatrice Reynolds translation of the *Method for the Easy Comprehension of History* (2d ed. New York: Archon Books, 1965) is the most reliable in English.

Curiously, there is no modern French edition of the *Six Books of the Republic*, but there are two available in English: M. J. Tooley *Six Books of the Commonwealth* (New York: Macmillan, 1955; **A**), which is an abridged edition that includes material of interest to the modern political scientist, if not necessarily the student of Bodin's thought; and Kenneth D. McRae's *The Six Bookes of a Commonweale* (Cambridge, MA: Harvard University Press, 1962; **A**). McRae's is a facsimile edition of the English translation of 1606 and has the advantage of being a complete edition of Bodin's work, rendered into the political idiom of his English contemporaries. It includes critical apparatus, and useful synopsis of contents.

M. L. D. Kuntz's *Colloquium of the Seven about Secrets of the Sublime* (Princeton, NJ: Princeton University Press, 1975; **A**) is a translation of the *Colloquium Heptaplomeres*, with a very useful introduction to the context of Bodin's religious thinking.

Jonathan Pearl of the University of Toronto is compling an annotated edition and the translation of the Démonmanie, which will be published by the University of Toronto Press.

Other Sources

Dentzer, H., ed. *Jean Bodin*. Munich, 1973. Contains many valuable articles, most notably Donald Kelley, "The Development and Context of Bodin's Method for the Easy Understanding of History'' (pp. 123-1950); Ralph Giesey, ''Medieval Jurisprudence in Bodin's Concept of Sovereignty'' (pp. 167-1686); and J. H. M. Salmon, ''Bodin and the Monarchomachs'' (pp. 359-378).

Mesnard, Pierre. ''La 'démonmanie' de Jean Bodin.'' In *L'Opera e il pensiero di G. Pico della Mirandola*, Vol. II. Florence, 1965: 333-356. An important starting point for an understanding of Bodin's life and thought by one of the most important Bodin scholars of this century. Unfortunately, his work is available only in scattered articles and has not been translated into English.

Mosse, G. L. ''The Influence of Jean Bodin's 'République' on English Political Thought.'' *Medievalia et Humanistica* 5(1948): 73-83. Discusses the influence of Bodin's theories of legislation and sovereignty on the conflict between king and Parliament in early seventeenth-century England. Should be supplemented by J. H. M. Salmon's *The French Religious Wars in English Political Thought* (Oxford: Oxford University Press, 1959).

Arthur Herman

Niels Bohr
1885-1962

Chronology

Born Niels Henrik David Bohr on October 7, 1885, in Copenhagen, Denmark, son of Christian Bohr, a physician, and Ellen Adler; *1903* graduates from Gammelholm Latin-og Realskole; studies physics at the University of Copenhagen; *1907* receives the Gold Medal of the Royal Danish Academy of Sciences and Letters for his essay on the determination of the surface tension of liquids; *1909* receives his master's degree in physics; *1911* receives his doctoral degree; *1911-1912* works as a researcher at the Cavendish Laboratory at Cambridge University with physicist J. J. Thomson; *1912* works as a researcher at the University of Manchester under the inspiring leadership of Ernest Rutherford, with whom he develops a close, lifelong friendship; returns to Copenhagen and marries Margrethe Nørlund, with whom he has four children; writes three essays on the constitution of atoms and molecules that delineates his ground-breaking theories on the hydrogen spectrum; *1913* quantum theory essays published in England; lectures at the University of Copenhagen; *1914-1916* lectures at the University of Manchester; *1916* accepts a position as professor of theoretical physics, a post expressly established for him by the University of Copenhagen; *1917* becomes a member of the Royal Danish Academy; applies for government funding for the establishment of his own laboratory; *1921* establishes the University Institute for Theoretical Physics in Copenhagen with considerable financial support from the Carlsberg Foundation, a foundation supporting research in arts and sciences funded by the Carlsberg Breweries (officially renamed the Niels Bohr Institute in 1965); *1922* explains the periodic system of the elements; his son Aage Niels is born (who later wins the Nobel Prize in physics in 1975); receives the Nobel Prize in physics for his work on atomic structure and other contributions in his field; *1923* receives honorary doctoral degrees from the universities of Cambridge and Liverpool, the first two of thirty such awards; *1927* gives a speech presenting his theory of complementarity, which analyzes for the first time the difficulty of making observations in nuclear physics; *1931* offered the Carlsberg Foundation's honorary residence which became for more than twenty-five years a center of Danish intellectual life and culture; *1933* publishes in Dutch, together with the Belgian physicist Léon Rosenfeld, the epoch-making paper *Zur Frage der Messbarkeit der elektromagnetischen Feldgrössen* (The Problem of Measurement in Quantum Electrodynamics); *1936* develops the liquid-drop model of the atomic nucleus; *1939* becomes president of the Royal Danish Academy; collaborates with American physicist John A. Wheeler on a theory of nuclear fission based on Bohr's drop model, described in "The Mechanism of Nuclear Fission"; *1943* escapes to Sweden during the German occupation of Denmark; travels to England and then to the United States; *1943-1945* works on the British-American nuclear energy project at Los Alamos Atomic Scientific Laboratories under the name Nicholas Baker; *1945* returns to Denmark; *1950* writes "Open Letter to the United Nations" urging scientific and political openness and cooperation between all countries; *1955* serves as chairman of the Danish Atomic Energy Committee; *1957* receives the Ford Foundation's Atoms for Peace Award; *1962* dies on November 18 at his Carlsberg honorary residence and is buried in Copenhagen.

Activities of Historical Significance

Between 1913 and 1945 Niels Bohr was a central figure in the development of nuclear physics. During the 1920s and 1930s, his modest Institute for Theoretical Physics in Copenhagen became the most important training center for many of the world's nuclear physicists, such as Nobel Prize winners George de Hevesy, Werner Heisenberg, Paul Dirac, and Erwin Schrödinger.

Bohr was not only a highly gifted scientist; he was also an inspiring teacher and a unique human being who personified the classic ideal of the citizen of the world. The foundation for Bohr's humanist orientation was laid during his philosophy studies at the University of Copenhagen, and it later came to permeate his research, teaching, and writing.

Bohr's first decisive contribution to the development of modern physics occurred during his tenure at the University of Manchester. Building on the atomic model of colleague Ernest Rutherford, Bohr presented the evolution of his own atomic theory in three papers published in England during 1913. According to the ideas of classical physics, electrons move around the nucleus of an atom, emitting light as their orbits gradually deteriorate towards the nucleus, which eventually absorbs them. Bohr proposed that, instead of being absorbed by the nucleus, the electrons circle around the nucleus in certain so-called stationary orbits, as proposed by classical physics, in which they can continue orbiting without losing energy. He also proposed that light, which, according to the traditional view, was produced when the electrons move around the nucleus of an atom, is actually emitted when an electron jumps from a stationary orbit with high energy to another with lower energy until it comes to a state of rest. The frequency, and thus the wavelength, is definite and can be expressed by a means of oscillations of the light emitted by the atom. In subsequent years Bohr continued to refine his atomic model and to develop his theory of the relationship between the elements in the periodic system.

Bohr was first and foremost a theorist, but he always based his theoretical speculations on experimental data. However, Bohr always recognized both the limitations of the methods employed and the incomplete data on which his theories were based. To address this issue, Bohr devised the "correspondence principle," which says that any new theory must be in accordance with the laws of classical physics when these laws appear to correspond to the theory in question.

When Bohr received the Nobel Prize in Stockholm in 1922, he presented a lecture on the structure of the atom, in which he took stock of the pioneering period of nuclear physics that had begun with Rutherford's discovery of the nucleus in 1911 and Bohr's own contributions to electron theory. In keeping with his characteristically speculative mind, Bohr also pointed to a number of unsolved questions regarding the inner structure of the nucleus.

Bohr's lecture ended with a sensational announcement of the discovery of a previously unknown element. The night before the lecture at Bohr's institute in Copenhagen, the Hungarian physicist George de Hevesy had discovered the element that Bohr had predicted would have the chemical properties corresponding to atomic number 72 in the periodic table. The element was named Hafnium, after the Danish name for the city in which it was discovered.

During the 1920s, with such revolutionary discoveries as Max Planck's quantum theory and Albert Einstein's theories of relativity, scientists became increasingly aware that many of the physical properties observed by modern physics could be described in two seemingly conflicting ways. On the basis of experimental evidence, Einstein, already in 1905, had shown that light, which had been considered a form of electromagnetic waves, must also be thought of as a series of moving particles called photons. Now, researchers found that electrons, which until then had been conceived only as material particles, also displayed wave properties such as wavelength and frequency under certain circumstances. This meant that a complete description of some phenomena, such as light or gravity, required the combination of data from two completely opposite viewpoints, a synthesis that Bohr in 1928 labeled complementarity. This theory implied, according to Bohr, "the impossibility of a sharp distinction between the behavior of atomic objects and their interplay with the measuring instruments that serve to define the conditions under which the phenomena occur." In other words, it is impossible to observe both the wave and particle aspects simultaneously. Together, however, they present a fuller description than either of the two taken alone.

When he first proposed it, Bohr's concept of complementarity met with some resistance, primarily from Einstein, who, contrary to Bohr, believed it was possible to find unambiguous, non-contradictory explanations for the causes of the atomic phenomena. However, in 1930, at an international conference in Belgium, Bohr, on the basis of Einstein's own theory of relativity, was able to convince him of the validity of the theory, and complementarity has since become a permanent component of the conceptual repertoire of modern physics. Bohr himself extended its use to other branches of science, in particular psychology and biology, and he saw this concept as an aid to obtaining greater mutual understanding between cultures and nations.

The Rutherford/Bohr atomic model implied the presence of very large quantities of energy in the individual atom. A number of discoveries, such as James Chadwick's finding of the neutron in 1932, caused Bohr in 1936 to develop his so called "liquid drop theory" about the composition of the nucleus, also helped him to formulate an explanation of why different elements behave in different ways when they are bombarded with neutrons. His atomic theory was applied to the successful splitting, or fission, of uranium atoms, which in turn led to the release of nuclear energy. In 1939, together with American physicist J. A. Wheeler, Bohr published a detailed description of the various processes of fission pointing out that ordinary uranium-238 could not be used for the needed chain reaction. Only a rare, lighter isotope, uranium-235, would trigger the reaction. Thus, nuclear research in England and the U.S. was initiated by Bohr's theories. The transuranic elements neptunium and plutonium (nos. 93 and 94 respectively in the periodic table) that Bohr had predicted, were discovered, and in 1941 the Austrian Otto Frisch and the German Rudolf Peierls, both in England, issued a memorandum which suggested the feasibility of a bomb based on fast neutrons—as foreseen by Bohr—if at least ten kilograms of uranium-235 could be produced. This document became the starting point for the Anglo-American nuclear project.

In September 1943, during the German occupation of Denmark, Bohr escaped to Sweden and joined, in the United States, the distinguished group of scientists who later that year developed the atomic bomb. Realizing the disastrous potential in the nuclear science he had helped to create, Bohr sent a letter dated July 3, 1944, urging President Franklin Roosevelt's cooperation with the Soviet Union in the peaceful utilization of nuclear energy. His initiative was supported by a number of distinguished American and British scientists, but was met with strict rejection by Winston Churchill. Bohr never took part in any military discussions and he had left the U.S. before the test bomb was exploded in July 1945. Neither was he informed beforehand that the bomb would be used against Japan. Privately and later also publicly he expressed profound regret at this event which he saw as a threat against civilization. For the rest of his life, Bohr tirelessly spoke out in favor of international scientific collaboration in the hope of avoiding future nuclear catastrophes. His open letter of 1950 to the United Nations was prompted by the tensions of the Cold War. It is the stirring appeal of a true humanist for greater international cooperation in order to prevent military abuse of scientific inventions.

In the post-war years the Niels Bohr Institute continued as an international research center. Bohr himself—in his last years burdened with high honors—continued as an active scientist refusing to slow down. He took an active part in the establishment in 1952 of the European Centre for Nuclear Research in Geneva (CERN), whose theoretical group was attached to his institute until 1957. In September 1962 he discussed plans for an international conference to be held in July 1963 on the fiftieth anniversary of the publication of his first paper on atomic structure, and one month later he began to write a history of atomic theory which was destined never to be finished.

Upon his death, Victor Weisskopf, CERN's director-general, said at a ceremony honoring Bohr's memory: "He was a great man. What is greatness? A great man is one who creates a new period, a new way of thinking, and truly he and his life correspond to this definition. The influence of what he started is seen in every aspect of our life."

Overview of Biographical Sources

Apart from a laudatory essay by his colleague Léon Rosenfeld, *Niels Bohr: An Essay Dedicated to Him on the Occasion of His Sixtieth Birthday October 7, 1945* (Amsterdam: North-Holland Publishing, 1961), no major biographical study was published in English (or in any other language) during Bohr's lifetime. However, shortly after Bohr's death two book-length biographies were published in the United States: Robert Silverberg's *Niels Bohr: The Man Who Mapped the Atom* (1965) and Ruth Moore's *Niels Bohr: The Man, His Science, and the World They Changed* (1966). A third English-language biography, Poul Dam's much-shorter *Niels Bohr (1885-1962): Atomic Theorist, Inspirator, Rallying Point* (1985) is a translation from the Danish. All three works take a journalistic approach and are basically intended for a general audience. They focus primarily on Bohr's life, career, and interaction with family, friends, and other colleagues.

In-depth English-language analyses of Bohr's achievements as a nuclear physicist are found in an essay collection edited by Wolfgang Pauli, *Niels Bohr and the Development of Physics: Essays Dedicated to Niels Bohr on the Occasion of his Seventieth Birthday* (1955); in an anonymous memorial by the American Physical Society, published in *Physics Today* 16 (1963: 21-64); and in an article by Léon Rosenfeld in *Dictionary of Scientific Biography,* vol. 2 (1970: 239-254). *Niels Bohr: A Centenary Volume,* A. P. French and P. J. Kennedy, eds., (Cambridge: Harvard University Press, 1985), includes a bibliography and short biography.

Accounts of various periods of Bohr's life as well as his scientific achievements can be found in the essay collection *Niels Bohr: His Life and Work as Seen by His Friends and Colleagues* (1967), edited by Stefan Rozental, a translation of the 1964 Danish edition, and in Peter Robertson's *The Early Years: The Niels Bohr Institute 1921-1930* (1979).

Not until 1985 was the definitive biography on Bohr published in Danish, *Harmoni og enhed. Niels Bohr. En biografi,* written by Niels Blædel. The work was translated in 1985 as *Harmony and Unity: The Life of Niels Bohr.*

Evaluation of Principal Biographical Sources

Blædel, Niels. *Harmony and Unity: The Life of Niels Bohr.* 1985. Trans. Chesterbrook, CT: SciTech, 1988. (**A, G**) The most recent and definitive scholarly treatment which includes an abundance of illustrations. Blædel obtained information directly from Bohr's sons and utilizes hitherto unpublished correspondence with members of Bohr's family and colleagues, as well as family memoirs. The volumes contain an inventory of busts and paintings of Bohr, his bibliography (not in correct chronological order), and a list of secondary sources.

Dam, Poul. *Niels Bohr (1885-1962): Atomic Theorist, Inspirator, Rallying Point.* Copenhagen: Royal Danish Ministry of Foreign Affairs, 1985. (**G**) A brief, informational, and well-written treatment enhanced by excellent illustrations. Dam does not provide new facts about Bohr's life and career but focuses on his later years and his involvement as a humanist who was deeply concerned with the future of nuclear technology.

Moore, Ruth. *Niels Bohr: The Man, His Science, and the World They Changed.* New York: Alfred A. Knopf, 1966. (**A, G**) A highly readable, at times exciting, account of Bohr's career and scientific discoveries. Strong emphasis is placed on Bohr's years in the United States as well as his interaction and collaboration with English and American scholars and statesmen, based on original research. The volume concludes with an excellent index.

Pais, Abraham. *Neil Bohr's Times: In Physics, Philosophy, and Polity.* Oxford: Oxford University Press, 1991. (**A, G**) Written by a former physics professor who studied with Bohr in the late 1940s. Presents exacting information on Bohr's life, on developments in physics during his lifetime, on the work of other important figures of the time, and on the broader social and political events of the period.

Robertson, Peter. *The Early Years: The Niels Bohr Institute 1921-1930.* Copenhagen: Akademisk Forlag, 1979. (**A, G**) A fascinating account of the pioneering years of Bohr's institute, his inspirational leadership, teaching, and relationships with other scientists.

Rozental, Stefan, ed. *Niels Bohr: His Life and Work as Seen by His Friends and Colleagues.* Amsterdam: North-Holland, 1967. (**A**) This collection of essays contains fascinating accounts by Bohr's Danish and foreign colleagues as well as essays by two of his sons, one of whom, Aage Bohr, was awarded the Nobel Prize in physics in 1975. Most valuable are the often very personal insights into Bohr's work as a scientist given by such outstanding nuclear physicists as Léon Rosenfeld, Werner Heisenberg, and Otto Frisch.

Silverberg, Robert. *Niels Bohr: The Man Who Mapped the Atom.* Philadelphia, PA: Macrae Smith, 1965. (A) A rather wordy biography containing much irrelevant, often anecdotal material. Although it portrays Bohr quite vividly, it only superficially discusses his scientific achievements. Written in an entertaining, captivating style but contains errors and must be read with caution.

Overview and Evaluation of Primary Sources

Most of Bohr's scientific discoveries and analyses were published in over 150 essays and papers in scholarly journals in Denmark and abroad, primarily in English. Several of these essays and papers were published separately in the volumes *The Theory of Spectra and Atomic Constitution. Three Essays* (Cambridge: Cambridge University Press, 1922; **A**); *Atomic Theory and the Description of Nature* (Cambridge: Cambridge University Press, 1934; **A, G**); and *Essays 1958-1962 on Atomic Physics and Human Knowledge* (New York: Interscience Publishers, 1963; **A, G**). The contents of the last two works are not limited to strictly scientific matters but deal with a number of philosophical questions as well. Of a planned 11-volume edition of Bohr's *Collected Works* (Amsterdam/New York/Oxford: North-Holland Publishing, 1972-; **A, G**), volume eight was published in 1987. Bohr's papers are housed in The Niels Bohr Archives at the Niels Bohr Institute in Copenhagen.

Museums, Historical Landmarks, Societies

Portraits. There are eighteen known portraits of Bohr. One by Karen Trier Frederiksen (ca. 1960) hangs in The Niels Bohr Library, New York. Nine busts of Bohr have been made. Several copies of that by Harald Isenstein (1955) have been placed in several American universities; a bust by Jørgen Gudmundsen-Holmgreen

(1959) was installed in front of the University of Copenhagen and another is in The Niels Bohr Library, New York. Niels Bohr is portrayed on two Danish stamps from 1963 and 1985.

Niels Bohr Institute (Copenhagen). Houses the Niels Bohr Archives with Bohr's papers and an extensive collection of books and periodicals.

Other Sources

Frisch, Otto Robert. *What Little I Remember.* Cambridge: Cambridge University Press, 1979. Contains personal notes about the author's stay at the Niels Bohr Institute in Copenhagen in the 1930s.

Heisenberg, Werner. *Schritte über Grenzen. Gesammelte Reden und Aufsätze.* Munich: Piper Verlag, 1971: 52-70. Heisenberg tells of his collaboration with Bohr from 1922-1927.

Blædel, Niels. *Harmony and Unity: The Life of Niels Bohr.* Madison, WI: Science Tech Publishers, 1985.

Sven Hakon Rossel
University of Washington

Margaret Grace Bondfield
1873-1953

Chronology

Born Margaret Grace Bondfield on March 17, 1873, at Furnham, near Chard, Somerset, England, the daughter of William Bondfield, a lace factory foreman, and Ann Taylor Bondfield, the daughter of a Methodist minister; *1887* becomes an apprentice in a draper's shop in Brighton; *1894* moves to London, finds work, joins the National Union of Shop Assistants and is elected to the London District Council; *1896* joins the Independent Labour Party (ILP); *1898-1906* serves as assistant secretary of the Union; *1908-1910* works as a free-lance lecturer in England and the United States; *1911* becomes organizing secretary of the Women's Labour League; *1913-1921* serves on the executive committee of the ILP; *1918* is elected to the Parliamentary Committee of the Trades Union Congress; *1919* is a delegate to the Congress of the American Federation of Labor, to the Socialist International Conference at Berne, and to the International Labour Conference in Washington; *1920* joins the British Labour delegation to Russia; *1921* becomes the chief woman officer of the National Union of General and Municipal Workers and serves in that position until 1938; *1923* appointed the first woman chairman of the Trades Union Congress and is elected to Parliament from Northhampton; *1924* appointed parliamentary secretary to the Minister of Labour; *1926* elected to Parliament from Wallsend; *1929* appointed Minister of Labour, the first woman Cabinet officer and receives an honorary L.L.D. from Bristol University; *1930* receives the freedom of Chard; *1931* loses her seat in Parliament; *1939-1949* serves as vice-president of the National Council of Social Service and chair of the Women's Group on Public Welfare; *1948* appointed Champion of Honor; *1953* dies June 16 at Sanderstead, Surrey of unknown causes.

Activities of Historical Significance

Margaret Bondfield was a significant leader of women's trade unions in late nineteenth and early twentieth-century Britain and one of the first women actively involved in Labour politics. Her public career began when she moved to London in 1894 when she joined the Shop Assistants Union and quickly began an important leader. She wrote for the Union's journal, *Shop Assistant,* and in 1898 raised protest when she wrote an article portraying the ideal couple as one where both went out to work and shared household tasks. After becoming Union secretary in 1898, the membership rose from 3,000 in 1898 to 7,500 in 1900, as a result of her tireless efforts to recruit women to join. Bondfield became involved with wider industrial and political issues as well. In 1899 she was her union's delegate to the Trades Unions Congress (the only woman delegate) where she strongly advocated alliance between the trade unions and socialists and supported independent labor representation.

Bondfield also participated in other women's organizations and issues. Beginning in 1896, she conducted a two-year study of women's shop work for the Women's Industrial Council, a socialist research organization. This research was widely used by reformers, most especially Lord Avebury, who was largely responsible for the Shop Hours Act of 1904. She was also active in the Women's Trade Union League, where she collaborated with leading trade unionist Emilia Dilke and Gertrude Tuckwell, who helped found the League. There she met Mary MacArthur, who had served as president of the Shop Assistants' Union's Scottish District Council and who became one of her closest friends and associates. In 1906, she assisted MacArthur in founding the National Federation of Women Workers, the first general trade union for women. Also in 1906, she helped Margaret McDonald (the wife of Ramsey McDonald, the first Labour Prime Minister), found the Women's Labour League, an organization of Labour women who worked for women's suffrage and other reforms for women. Bondfield disagreed with many socialist women who supported immediate suffrage for women on a limited basis. Instead, she advocated working for universal adult suffrage. Bondfield was also very active in the Women's Cooperative Guild, an organization for the wives of higher-paid working class men. She was largely responsible for its report that secured maternity benefits in the 1911 National Insurance Bill.

In the years just before World War I, Bondfield became more directly involved with the Labour Party. In 1910 and 1913 she stood unsuccessfully as the Labour candidate for the London County Council for Woolwich. Bondfield opposed

Britain's involvement in World War I and joined other socialists in public demonstrations and conferences for peace. During the war, she concentrated her efforts on seeking decent working conditions for women war workers through her membership in the Central Committee on Women's Employment.

After the war, she turned her attention to political office while still continuing her trade union work. She became more conservative in her later years and alienated the left wing of her party. In 1927, she was criticized for signing the Blanesborough Committee Report which advocated some lowering of benefits and contributions to workers. As Minister of Labour in 1929, she became more unpopular when she introduced an unemployment insurance bill that was unsatisfactory to the left wing. Also in 1931, she accepted a Bill that deprived some married women of unemployment benefits. These actions, along with rising unemployment, led to her defeat in the General Election of 1931 and again in 1935.

In 1938 Bondfield retired from full-time trade union work. She spent her remaining years lecturing both at home and abroad in the U.S. and Canada and conducting social research through the National Council of Social Service and the Women's Group on Public Welfare.

Overview of Biographical Sources

There is only one biography of Bondfield: Mary Agnes Hamilton, *Margaret Bondfield* (1925). Because it was written during her lifetime by a close associate, it cannot be considered a complete study.

Most of the general books on British trade unions and the Labour Party do not include much discussion on Bondfield, except for A. Fox, H. A. Clegg and A. F. Thompson, *History of British Trade Unions Since 1889* (New York: Clarendon, 1964). There are several useful sources, however, on women's trade unions and participation in Labour politics. Contemporary works include Barbara Drake, *Women in Trade Unions* (London: G. Allen & Unwin, 1920), and Marian Phillips, ed., *Women in the Labour Party* (New York: B. W. Huebsch, 1918). There are several recent sources on women in trade unions and women in the labor movement in England: Sheila Lewenhak, *Women and Trade Unionism* (1977); Norbert Solden, *Women in British Trade Unions 1894-1976* (1978); Lucy Middleton, ed., *Women the Labour Movement* (1977); Angela V. John, *Unequal Opportunities:*

Women's Employment in England (New York: Basil Blackwell, 1986); Christine Collette, *For Labour and for Women: The Women's Labour League, 1906-1918* (1989).

Evaluation of Principal Biographical Sources

Bellamy, Joyce M., and John Saville, eds. *Dictionary of Labour Biography*. Vol. II. Clifton, NJ: Augustus M. Kelley, 1974: 39-45. (**A, G**) A most useful encyclopedia article, it provides an excellent starting point for research on Bondfield. Her early trade union activities and collaboration with Mary MacArthur are especially praised here. Her post-war participation in Labour government and shift to the right are awarded less credit. It is the only source that includes a bibliography of her articles and pamphlets.

Collette, Christine. *For Labour and for Women: The Women's Labour League, 1906-1918*. Manchester, England: Manchester University Press, 1989. (**A**) Bondfield was one of the founders of the Women's Labour League along with Margaret McDonald and Mary Middleton. She served as secretary after these two women died in 1911. Her contributions as a leader are discussed here as are her dispute with other League leaders over the suffrage issue.

Hamilton, Mary Agnes. *Margaret Bondfield*. New York: Thomas Seltzer, 1925. (**A, G**) This book is more of a tribute than a biography, but does provide a contemporary account of Bondfield's life. Hamilton particularly discusses Bondfield's contributions to the Shop Assistant's Union and the Labour Party. Her activities in the international Labour movement are mentioned as well. Hamilton viewed Bondfield's election to Parliament and her Cabinet appointment as major victories for women.

Lewenhak, Sheila. *Women and Trade Unions*. New York: St. Martin's, 1977. (**A, G**) A survey of women in the British trade union movement from the eighteenth century to the mid-twentieth century. It covers Bondfield's work in trade unionism especially with the Shop Assistant's Union, the Women's Trade Union League, and the National Federal of Women Workers. Her post-war activities with the Trades Union Congress are discussed as well. Although Lewenhak acknowledges her importance to women's trade unionism, she suggests that Bondfield was more interested in her own political career than improving the situation for women workers.

Middleton, Lucy, ed. *Women in the Labour Movement.* Totowa, NJ: Rowman and Littlefield, 1977. (**A, G**) Several of the essays in this collection are about the various organizations to which Bondfield contributed. Lucy Middleton, in "Women in Labour Politics" discusses the Women's Labour League and the participation of women in the Labour Party after World War I. Anne Godwin, in "Early Years in the Trade Unions," covers the formation of the Women's Trade Union League and the National Federation of Women Workers. Jean Gaffin in "Women and Cooperation," provides a brief history of the Women's Cooperative Guild.

Solden, Norbert. *Women in British Trade Unions, 1874-1976.* London: Rowman and Littlefield, 1978. (**A**) In addition to Lewenhak, this is the other major source on women in British trade unions. It concentrates on the nineteenth and twentieth century and covers Bondfield's significance to the movement. One entire chapter focuses on her work with Mary Macarthur for the NFWW and the WTUL.

Overview and Evaluation of Primary Sources

Bondfield published an autobiography that covers her most active years, *A Life's Work* (London: Hutchinson, 1949; **A, G**). In addition to selections from her diaries and letters, she used relevant public documents and newspaper articles. Of the many organizations in which she participated, only the records of the Women's Labour League have been published (Harvester Press Microfiche).

Museums, Historical Landmarks, Societies

Manchester City Art Gallery (Manchester, England). Contains a black chalk drawing by Colin Gill.

National Portrait Gallery (Washington, DC). Contains a Miniature by W. M. Knight (1937).

Other Sources

Biographical Dictionary of British Feminists. Vol 1. 1800-1930. New York University Press, 1985: 30-32.

Dictionary of National Biography, 1951-1960. Oxford University Press, 1971: 122-123.

Kathryn Moore Crowe
University of North Carolina at Greensboro

Dietrich Bonhoeffer
1906-1945

Chronology

Born Dietrich Bonhoeffer on February 4, 1906, in Breslau, Germany (now Poland), sixth child (and fourth son) of Karl Bonhoeffer, professor of psychiatry and neurology, and Paula von Hase Bonhoeffer; grows up in comfortable middle class surroundings in Breslau; *1912* moves to Berlin, where his father becomes director of Charité Clinic, University of Berlin, most prestigious position in his field in Germany; mingles with families of leading German academicians, including Max Planck, Adolf von Harnack, Hans Delbrück; *1918* older brother Walter dies in World War I; *1923-1927* studies theology at the universities of Tübingen and Berlin; is increasingly attracted to theological writings of Karl Barth; *1927* completes doctoral thesis, *Sanctorum Communio*; *1928-1930* spends a year as assistant pastor at the German church in Barcelona, Spain; upon return to Germany, completes and publishes *Act and Being,* acceptance of which qualifies him as university lecturer in theology; *1930-1931* undertakes advanced study at Union Theological Seminary in New York; *1931-1932* appointed to a position on theological faculty at University of Berlin; ordained into the ministry; as part of his pastoral duties, works as student chaplain at Berlin Technical University, and is assigned the tough responsibility for the confirmation of working-class boys from Belrin-Wedding, which he handles successfully; becomes involved in an ecumenical movement; voices concern at rising threat of Nazism; *1933* broadcasts talk (which is cut off before he is finished) implicitly criticizing the concept of a Führer two days after Hitler becomes chancellor; expresses opposition to ideas and church politics of Nazi-oriented "German Christians"; speaks out against Nazi anti-Semitism, becoming one of the few Protestant figures to challenge persecution of Jews on biblical grounds; writes pamphlet criticizing application of "Aryan Clause" to the church; supports efforts of Pastors' Emergency League to stem the tide of Nazification of churches carried out by German Christians; *1933-1935* serves as pastor of two German Protestant congregations in London; begins long ecumenical association with Anglican Bishop George K. A. Bell; becomes deeply involved in ecumenical activities; actively supports Barmen Declaration and establishment of Confessing Church, separate from and opposed to the official German Christian-dominated National Church; *1935-1937* heads illegal Confessing Church preacher's seminary, first located in Zingst, shortly moved to Finkenwalde, near Stettin, which continues to function until closed by the Gestapo in 1937; right to serve as university lecturer withdrawn; publishes *The Cost of Discipleship*; *1938-1939* establishes initial contacts with resistance forces; continues seminary efforts, in rural Pomerania, in a period of "collective pastorates"; visits England in a period of intense personal uncertainty, and converses with Bishop Bell; visits the United States on the eve of outbreak of World War II, where he resists pleas of his friends not to risk his life by returning to Germany; publishes *Life Together*; *1940-1942* employed by Abwehr (military intelligence) as cover for increasing resistance activities; takes numerous trips abroad in attempt to sound out, via ecumenical contacts, Allied response to post-Nazi Germany should resistance succeed in overthrowing Hitler; *1943* becomes engaged to Maria von Wedemeyer; arrested and incarcerated in Tegel military prison, Berlin, where he remains for the next eighteen months, and where Gestapo interrogation fails to create substantive evidence against him; resumes theological writing; *1944* implicated by Gestapo discovery of compromising Abwehr files in wake of unsuccessful attempt to kill Hitler; transferred to Gestapo prison; *1945* transferred to concentration camp at Buchenwald; taken subsequently to the concentration camp at Flossenbürg where, after the formality of trial and condemnation, he is hanged on April 9, at age thirty-nine; *Ethics* (1949) and *Letters and Papers from Prison* (1951) published posthumously.

Activities of Historical Significance

Dietrich Bonhoeffer's short life has come to epitomize the relatively rare conjunction between theology and political activism in the preponderantly secular twentieth century. Bonhoeffer's early career was something of a paradox. After spending a year at the University of Tübingen, he completed his formal education within the liberal theological environment of the University of Berlin, dominated for many years by Adolf von Harnack. However, he gradually came under the influence of Karl Barth, whose more orthodox theology—vigorously challenged by von Harnack—was in part a response to the intellectual uncertainty of post-World War I Europe. Barth, convinced that the liberals had forsaken their roots, sought to restore to theology what he considered its essence: the overpowering majesty of God. Bonhoeffer never fully resolved the liberal-conservative dichotomy in his own theology, with the result that interpretations of his influence since his death in 1945 have frequently been at odds.

The rise of Nazism, and particularly Hitler's assumption of power in 1933, obliged Bonhoeffer to take active interest in politics to which, as an academic theologian and Lutheran pastor, he was not naturally inclined. The rapid ascent of the pro-Nazi Protestant group known as the German Christians, paralleling the Nazi regime's effort to unify the disparate Protestant churches in Germany, encouraged counter-movements in defense of traditional Christian values. Bonhoeffer strongly supported these movements, which culminated in 1934 with the creation of the Confessing Church as an alternative to the National (Reich) Church dominated by the German Christians. He also spoke out early and consistently against Nazi anti-Semitic racism and the persecution of the Jews. Furthermore, he aggressively opposed the application to the churches of the so-called ''Aryan'' legislation, intended to eliminate the allegedly pernicious influence of Christians whose background was Jewish. Later, during the war, although he could not affect the deportations, he did help to spirit a few German Jews to safety in neutral Switzerland.

During the 1930s Bonhoeffer was drawn into the ecumenical movement, and gradually became more deeply involved. From 1933 on, he took an active interest in the World Alliance for Promoting International Friendship through the churches and other ecumenical organizations which formed the nucleus of the later World Council of Churches. Through his acquaintance with such prominent personalities as George K. A. Bell, the Anglican Bishop of Chichester, and Willem A. Visser't Hooft, he made contacts that later became important to his work on behalf of the German resistance. Within the ecumenical movement, he ceaselessly advocated the recognition and the representation of the Confessing Church in preference to the official National Church backed by the Nazi regime. At the same time, he expressed growing frustration at the short-sightedness of the Confessing Church in its desire to accommodate itself to the Nazi state, and in particular the church's failure to speak out on such issues as the persecution of the Jews and the growing threat of war.

Theologically, Bonhoeffer was firmly Christocentric. Even in his earliest writings one finds the gist of such mature themes as Christian community and the relationship of Christians to their secular environment, ideas that were reinforced by his exposure to American theology, his ecumenical and anti-Nazi perspectives, and his experiences with the Confessing Church seminary at Finkenwalde. Ultimately, in the prison letters to his friend and later biographer Eberhad Bethge, he developed such concepts as the world's "coming of age" and the much-misunderstood "religionless Christianity." The former referred to the intellectual "maturity" of the modern world and the "profound this-worldliness" of Christianity that this necessitated. Historically, the world, and individual Christians, had existed in a condition of childlike dependence on the institutional church, but the world had by now outgrown this tutelage and Christianity had to acknowledge the new reality. "Religionless" meant placing Christ once again at the center of the world, devoid of the formal trappings of the institutional church which have often obscured him. Bonhoeffer found "religion" as traditionally understood—with its stress on what he called "pietism," other-worldliness, and individual salvation—inappropriate to the needs of the modern human community. In short, Christianity must come to terms with the world. The theological implications of this position were potentially quite radical.

Bonhoeffer's evolving theology dovetailed nicely with his growing commitment after 1938 to the anti-Nazi resistance within Germany. Indeed, his political attitudes and his theological outlook appear to have been mutually reinforcing. Two events—the intensification of the Jewish persecutions and the startling collapse of France in 1940—seem to have forced his hand. But his heightened political involvement confronted him with a moral dilemma: how can a convinced Christian, committed to love and peace, justify actions that as a practical necessity mandate the rejection of these values? Specifically, Bonhoeffer's deepening incorporation into the anti-Hitler conspiracy forced him to accept the Fuhrer's assassination as a logical requirement. He eventually concluded that the absolute evil of Nazism obliged a truly patriotic German to resist the regime by any means available. Only a handful of people, and virtually no other churchmen, could bring themselves to endorse this view.

Since his execution by the Nazis in 1945, less than a month before the end of the war, Bonhoeffer has become a "heroic" figure. Some contemporary theologians have distorted his concept of "religionless Christianity" as a means of justifying their secularized views. Others, while acknowledging the revolutionary implications of his ideas, have pointed out that Bonhoeffer's thinking contains much that is conservative and traditional. Since the theological writings from the last two years of his life are fragmentary and not fully developed, many scholars are wary of easy interpretations. But most would agree that Bonhoeffer died a martyr, convinced to the end that, as a Christian and a German, he had acted justly.

Overview of Biographical Sources

Given Bonhoeffer's comparatively recent death in 1945 and the time it took for the English-speaking world to discover him (mainly after the publication of *Letters and Papers from Prison*), it is hardly surprising that biographical interest in him dates only to the mid-1960s.

Eberhard Bethge's *Dietrich Bonhoeffer* (English ed., 1970) is the standard against which all other biographies of Bonhoeffer are measured. Virtually all biographers since (and even before) the publication of Bethge's massive volume have acknowledged their indebtedness to its author. But Bethge has never sought to monopolize the Bonhoeffer story. Indeed, both E. H. Robertson and Mary Bosanquet, authors of briefer, less technical Bonhoeffer biographies, have noted Bethge's generosity in sharing both his sources and his knowledge of the subject.

Evaluation of Principal Biographical Sources

Bethge, Eberhard. *Bonhoeffer: Exile and Martyr.* New York: Seabury, 1975. (**A, G**) While not strictly a biography, this volume, based on a series of lectures delivered by Bethge in South Africa in 1973, provides useful biographical and especially interpretive perspectives. It is in essence a thematic analysis of Bonhoeffer's ideas and activities inextricably tied to the events of his life. The book is particularly insightful with regard to Bonhoeffer's attitudes on race and the "Jewish question," his ecumenism, and his political involvement in the conspiracy against Hitler.

————. *Costly Grace: An Illustrated Introduction to Dietrich Bonhoeffer.* New York: Harper & Row, 1979. (**A, G**) This brief, well-illustrated account by Bonhoeffer's official biographer is largely intended for general readership. Organized chronologically, with a final chapter devoted to Bonhoeffer's thought, the book's primary focus is on the events of Bonhoeffer's life, but it effectively integrates the development of his main theological ideas into the broader biographical context. Bethge's overview of the theology is successful as it relates to Bonhoeffer's better-known concepts, less so in terms of those which, as Bethge acknowledges, are "almost incomprehensible except to the specialist." While at times the biographical section seems to assume familiarity with the overall history of the period, this is probably unavoidable given its comparative brevity. It does, however, provide useful insights unavailable in other shorter biographies—insights which perhaps only Bethge himself could furnish—and is therefore valuable. Many of the pictures do not appear in other standard books about Bonhoeffer and complement the text nicely.

————. *Dietrich Bonhoeffer: Man of Vision, Man of Courage.* New York: Harper & Row, 1970. (**A**) Unquestionably *the* biography of Bonhoeffer. Bethge was Bonhoeffer's closest friend during the last ten years of his life, married Bonhoeffer's niece, Renate Schleicher, and was given carte blanche by the Bonhoeffer family to research and write this volume. Despite the author's close personal ties to Bonhoeffer, the book is not uncritical. Parts of it, especially those dealing with theological issues, will be difficult for the layperson, but no better or more comprehensive biography exists. It is a fundamental research tool for anyone examining Bonhoeffer's career, a monograph which, because Bethge himself participated in many of the events he discusses, is in effect a primary source.

Bosanquet, Mary. *The Life and Death of Dietrich Bonhoeffer.* New York: Harper & Row, 1968. (**A, G**) This well-written, descriptive biography presents an understandable summary of Bonhoeffer's life and the essential features of his theology. It makes Bonhoeffer accessible as a historical figure to the non-professional. The reader should be wary of Bosanquet's tendency to be somewhat superficial in dealing with political events, but since this is not her major purpose it does not seriously detract from what is overall a well-balanced book. Contains extensive quotations from Bonhoeffer's published and unpublished writings, as well as from recollections of friends, associates, and family members.

Leibholz-Bonhoeffer, Sabine. *The Bonhoeffers: Portrait of a Family*. New York: St. Martin's, 1971. (**A, G**) A moving family biography by Dietrich's twin sister. Combines a recollection of the author's parents and siblings with a somewhat longer account of her family life after her marriage to Gerhard Leibholz (including their voluntary exile in England after 1938). Particularly valuable are the liberal quotations from the correspondence of friends and family members, especially Dietrich.

Robertson, Edwin H. *Dietrich Bonhoeffer*. Richmond, VA: John Knox, 1966. (**G**) This is the earliest, the briefest, and the least useful of all the Bonhoeffer biographies. Its brevity was no doubt mandated by the editors of the makers of Contemporary Theology series of which it is a part, but by the author's own subsequent acknowledgement that it is only a sketch of Bonhoeffer's life and ethological concepts. Its superficiality is evidenced by the amount of space devoted to Bonhoeffer's life as well as by numerous factual inaccuracies.

————. *The Shame and the Sacrifice: The Life and Martyrdom of Dietrich Bonhoeffer*. New York: Macmillan, 1988. (**A, G**) Robertson's more recent biography, based largely on published sources and the author's own anthologies of Bonhoeffer's writings, is fuller than the earlier volume. But some Bonhoeffer scholars are wary of Robertson's methodology, and this book shows why. While the coverage of certain parts of Bonhoeffer's life is thorough, other aspects are dealt with very superficially. Moreover, there are frequent examples of factual misstatements or inaccuracies that raise broader questions about Robertson's research. While the quotations are helpful, on balance the book should be used with some caution.

Wind, Renate. *Dietrich Bonhoeffer: A Spoke in the Wheel*. Grand Rapids, MI: Eerdmans, 1992. (**A, G**) Wind, a German pastor and teacher, has put together the most recent brief, popular biography of Bonhoeffer. It is well-written and easily comprehensible by those intimidated by the more difficult theological concepts discussed in Bethge's works. Wind stresses Bonhoeffer's search for himself, from an upper middle class Berlin childhood characterized by rather strained relations with a distant father to his final days in prison. She also notes the logical connection between Bonhoeffer's active involvement in the world—for example, his ecumenism, his illegal church activities, and his political resistance—and his belief in the "this-worldliness" of Christianity.

Overview and Evaluation of Primary Sources

The German edition of Bonhoeffer's collected writings, *Gesammelte Schriften*, (6 vols. Munich: Chr. Kaiser Verlag, 1958-1974; **A**), is comprehensive, but difficult. English translations of some of these writings, under the general editorship of Edwin H. Robertson, have appeared under the following titles: *No Rusty Swords: Letters, Lectures, and Notes, 1928-1936* (New York: Harper & Row, 1965); *The Way to Freedom: Letters, Lectures, and Notes, 1935-1939* (New York: Harper & Row, 1966); and *True Patriotism: Letters, Lectures, and Notes, 1939-1945* (New York: Harper & Row, 1973; **A, G**). Most of Bonhoeffer's theological writings have been translated, but the reader unversed in theology may find them daunting. They include his doctoral thesis, *Sanctorum Communio*, published in the United States as *The Communion of Saints* (New York: Harper & Row, 1963; **A**); *Act and Being* (New York: Harper & Row, 1961; **A**); *The Cost of Discipleship* (New York: Macmillan, 1959; **A**); *Life Together* (New York: Harper & Row, 1954; **A**); and *Ethics* (1949. Translated 1955. New York: Macmillan, 1962; **A**), edited by Eberhard Bethge from Bonhoeffer's posthumously preserved papers. The best known, and most accessible, of Bonhoeffer's writings in English translation is *Letters and Papers from Prison* (1951. Translated 1955. Enlarged ed. New York: Macmillan, 1971; **A, G**), edited by Eberhard Bethge, the original publication of which aroused intense public interest in Bonhoeffer's life and the circumstances of his death. Also of interest are fragments of a play and a novella he wrote while in Tegel prison; they appear, together with an introduction and a critical commentary, in *Fiction from Prison: Gathering Up the Past* (Philadelphia, PA: Fortres, 1981; **A, G**), edited by Renate and Eberhard Bethge, with Clifford Green in the English edition. A very useful and interesting source is a brief anthology, *I Knew Dietrich Bonhoeffer* (New York: Harper and Row, 1966; **A, G**), edited by Wolf-Dieter Zimmermann and Ronald Gregor Smith. It consists of a series of mostly short vignettes written by family members, students, and other contemporaries of Bonhoeffer, and is arranged chronologically.

The most recent anthology is *A Testament to Freedom: The Essential Writings of Dietrich Bonhoeffer* (San Francisco: Harper, 1990; **A, G**), edited by F. Burton Nelson and Geoffrey Kelly, a selection of Bonhoeffer's lectures, sermons, letters, and excerpts from his published books. It contains a splendid historical introduction. Noteworthy also is the appearance of the first volumes of a multi-volume critical edition of Bonhoeffer's writings; the publication of the entire set is expected to be complete by the end of the decade. It is a joint effort of German publisher Chr. Kaiser Verlag, Munich, and the English language section of the International Bonhoeffer Society.

Fiction and Adaptations

Donald Goddard's *The Last Days of Dietrich Bonhoeffer* (1976), is a fictionalized account of Bonhoeffer's life from his arrest in 1943 to his execution two years later. Based on a careful study of the biographical sources, it is an imaginative reconstruction. By his own admission, Goddard has invented the dialogue—including in particular Bonhoeffer's interrogation by the Gestapo, little of which has survived. The result, however, is an authentic and readable story, stressing the personal and political side of Bonhoeffer's last years.

Dietrich Bonhoeffer: Memories and Perspectives (Trinity Films, 1982) is an excellent documentary that traces Bonhoeffer's career through stills, film clips, and extensive interviews with his biographer and friend Eberhard Bethge, his sister-in-law Emmi Bonhoeffer, and several students and associates.

A Third Testament: Bonhoeffer, 1906-1945 (Canadian Broadcasting Corporation, 1974) is part of a series of films about six theological figures, narrated by Malcolm Muggeridge, which served as the basis for a book by the same title (1976). Muggeridge's opinionated, personal narration tends to obscure the intended subject of the film.

Road Signs on a Merry-Go-Round (CBS, 1968) attempts to assess the impact of Bonhoeffer and two other twentieth-century thinkers—Martin Buber and Pierre Teilhard de Chardin—on contemporary society.

Museums, Historical Landmarks, Societies

Bonhoeffer Archive and Research Center, Union Theologial Seminary (New York City). Supported by the Seminary and the International Bonhoeffer Society. The Bonhoeffer Room, formerly known as the Prophets' Chamber, is a memorial to Bonhoeffer who stayed there while doing post-graduate work at the seminary during 1930-1931.

Bonhoeffer family home, Marienburger Allee (Berlin). The second home in Berlin of Bonhoeffer's parents, where Dietrich frequently stayed and where he was arrested by the Gestapo in 1943. Now a meeting place and a memorial to Bonhoeffer.

Flossenbürg Church (Flossenbürg, Germany). Contains a memorial to Bonhoeffer; near the site of the concentration camp where he was hanged.

German Church, Sydenham (London). One of the two churches where Bonhoeffer served in London from 1933 to 1935; rebuilt as a memorial to him after having been destroyed during the war.

International Bonhoeffer Society, English Language Section (Philadelphia, PA). One of several language sections. The Society sponsors international symposia approximately every four years, and works with related scholarly organizations in holding conferences and encouraging research.

Other Sources

Conway, John S. "Dietrich Bonhoeffer." In *Encyclopedia of the Holocaust.* Vol. 1. New York: Macmillan, 1990: 230-231. Emphasizes Bonhoeffer's opposition to the Nazi persecution of the Jews.

Green, Clifford J., and Wayne W. Floyd, Jr. *Bonhoeffer Bibliography: Primary and Secondary Sources in English*. Hartford, CT: International Bonhoeffer Society (English Language Section), 1986.

Hamilton, Kenneth. *Life in One's Stride: A Short Study in Dietrich Bonhoeffer.* Grand Rapids, MI: Eerdman's, 1968. An introduction to Bonhoeffer's theology.

Schoenherr, Albrecht. "Dietrich Bonhoeffer: The Message of a Life." *Christian Century* 102 (November 27, 1985): 1090-1094. A recollection of Bonhoeffer by one of his Finkenwalde students, written to commemorate the fortieth anniversary of his death.

Zerner, Ruth. "Dietrich Bonhoeffer and the Jews: Thoughts and Actions, 1933-1945." *Jewish Social Studies* 37 (Summer/Fall, 1975): 235-250.

Eugene W. Miller, Jr.
Pennsylvania State University, Hazleton

Nadia Boulanger
1887-1979

Chronology

Born Juliette Nadia Boulanger on September 16, 1887, in the Montmartre district of Paris, France, daughter of Henri Alexandre Ernest Boulanger, a professor of singing at the Paris Conservatory, and Princess Raissa Ivanova Mychetskaya, a tutor and singer; studies music with her father; *1895* begins lessons in piano and solfège with Mlle Laure Donne; *1896* enters the Conservatoire national to study solfège; takes private lessons in organ with Louis Vierne, the great Parisian organist at Notre Dame; *1897* places third in solfège competition at the Conservatoire; *1898* enters August Chapuis's harmony class, religious instruction in the Catholic faith at église de la Trinite; *1899* acts as substitute organist for Gabriel Fauré at the Church of the Madeleine; *1900* enters *classe d'accompagnement au piano*; *1901* studies composition with André Gedalge; *1903* wins first prize in harmony competition; takes private organ lessons with Alexander Guilmant; studies composition with Gabriel Fauré; *1904* during her final year at the Conservatoire, studies music history with Louis-Albert Bourgault-Ducoudray and takes private piano lessons with Alphonse Duvernoy; takes first prize in organ, *accompagnement au piano*, and fugue at the Conservatoire; moves with family to 36 rue Ballu, where she lives until her death; becomes protegee of Raoul Pugno, renowned pianist, organist, and composer; begins teaching career; *1905* gala inauguration of her rue Ballu Cavaillé - Coll organ; debuts in official public concert; spends first full summer in summer home, Gargenville; *1906* acquires first American pupil, Marion Bauer; performance of her composition, the song *Versailles*, in a chamber music concert at The Grand Palais des Champs-Elysées launches her as a serious composer; first joint concert with Raoul Pugno; *1907* reaches final round of the Prix de Rome competition; appointed to position of teacher of elementary piano and *accompagnement au piano* at the Conservatoire Femina-Musica; wins Second Grand Prize in Prix de Rome competition, her composition being the contata *La Sirène*; besieged by women's publications for interviews: *Femina, La Vie Heureuse, La Petite Republique, Le Monde Musical*; *1909* appointed assistant

to conservatoire national harmony professor, Henri Dallier; premiere of compositions *Elégie* and *Soleil couchant* by Concerts Lamoureux; premiere in Paris by the
Concerts Colonne of her cantata *Dnégouchka*; *1910* premiere of compositions
Larme solitaire and *Pour toi in Paris*; *1911* finds first patron in Miki Piré, an
heiress, who provides Nadia a living allowance; *1912* debuts as a conductor under
auspices of the Société des Matinées Musicales; performance of *Les Heures claires*
in recital at the Salle des Agriculteurs in Paris; chooses "the joys of a life dedicated to art" rather than "the joys of a family"; premier of *Rhapsodie variée* for
piano and orchestra at Deutscher Lyceum-Club in Berlin; *1913* completes opera *La
Ville morte* in collaboration with Pugno; directs orchestra in Nice in performance
of her composition, *Fantaisie*; *1914* gains fame as a teacher with when she presents her first child prodigy, Jacques Dupont; formation of the Nadia Boulanger
Society; conducts her sister Lili's composition, *Faust et Hélène* at the Presidential
Palace; publishes transcriptions for cello and piano of three organ pieces; plays as
organist at Grande Salle des Fêtes of The Palais du Trocadéro for the inaugural
program of the Association des Grands Concerts; *1915* premieres *Airs populaires
flamands* for solo organ; forms, with sister Lili, the Comité Franco-Américain du
Conservatoire National de Musique et de Déclamation under patronage of American architect Whitney Warren; accompanies her composition *Cantique* in concert
for war relief at the Chapel of the Château of Versailles; edits, with Lili, the
Gazettes des classes de composition du Conservatoire; *1917* premiere in Paris of
her latest work *Vie Nouvelle*, later published as *Vers la vie nouvelle*; joins the
mass evacuation of Paris because of German shelling; *1918* sister Lili, winner of
the Prix de Rome and composer extraordinaire, dies at the age of twenty-five of
Crohn's disease; plays as organ soloist in the Saint-Saëns symphony under conductor Walter Damrosch; makes plans, with Damrosch, to establish a music school for
Americans; acts as liaison between the French and Americans, acting in a bilingual
capacity as secretary of the Comité Franco-Américain; *1919* appointed to faculty
of École normale de musique to teach harmony, counterpoint, organ and composition; writes as part-time music critic for the magazine *Monde Musical*; accompanies Jacques Ibert's cantata when he wins the Prix de Rome; *1920* begins teaching
organ to American ex-doughboy Melville Smith from Boston; composes a series
of compositions based on Mauclair's poetry; *1921* becomes a full professor in
harmony when the Franco-American Conservatory opens its doors in the Louis XV
wing of the Palace of Fontainebleau; Aaron Copland is first student to enroll; *1922*

receives Cleveland premiere of her composition *Airs populaires flamands* by organist Douglas Moore, her student; *1923* embraces Stravinsky's music using his *Octet for Winds* as a model for its conciseness, wit, and use of jazz materials within a classical context; *1924* arrives in New York on the *Aquitania*; *1925* gives organ recital in Philadelphia's Wanamaker auditorium; debuts with the New York Symphony Society under Walter Damrosch; plays concerts in New York, Pennsylvania, Ohio, Minnesota, and Massachusetts; lectures at the Cleveland Institute; visits Ernest Bloch; premieres Copland's *Organ Symphony* in Boston under Serge Koussevitzky; lectures in Boston; gives organ recital at Harvard; *1928* chosen outstanding French woman in the arts by the magazine *Minerva*, being named "Princess of music"; *1930* after serving as chapelmaster to Prince Pierre of Monaco, who dies, is named chapelmaster to Prince Rainier; *1931* her student Jacques Dupont wins Premier Grand Prix de Rome; *1932* awarded the Légion d'Honneur rank of chevalier; conducts a master class for thirty American music teachers; gains prominent recognition in *Courrier musical* article on Jean Françaix, her French prodigy; *1934* begins teaching Rumanian pianist Constantin Lipatti; conducts the new Orchestre Philharmonique de Paris in Bach, Monteverdi, and Schütz; *1935* appointed chair of composition as co-professor with Igor Stravinsky at École normale; publishes a chart prepared with pupil Dieudonné illustrating the history of musical styles and forms from the Greeks to the twentieth century; *1936* lecture-recitals are broadcast from Broadcast House, London; *1937* secures three radio programs with NBC (National Broadcasting Company); lectures at Mannes College; receives honorary commission from French government to study music teaching methods in the U.S.; secures a major commission from Mrs. Robert Woods Bliss for Stravinsky; invited to teach at Radcliffe and Wellesley; asked to conduct the Boston Symphony; records a series of programs at the Schola Cantorum to be aired by BBC and Radio-Paris; records six-record album of Monteverdi and her interpretation of Monteverdi's *Lamento della ninfa* wins the Grand Prix du Disque in Paris; *1938* becomes first woman to conduct the Boston Symphony; broadcasts on New York's station WEAF; gives more than 100 lecture-demonstrations, recitals, and concerts on this tour; awarded an honorary doctorate of music by Washington College of Music; conducts world premiere of Stravinsky's *Dumbarton Oaks Concerto* which was dedicated to her; *1939* joins editorial board of the new *Revue internationale de musique*; plans 102 lectures in 118 days for U.S. tour; conducts the New York Philharmonic Symphony; shelters

Stravinsky when war is declared; takes Agathe Rouart-Valéry, then pregnant, to Brittany; *1940* accepts a three-year contract at the Longy School, Cambridge, MA in the U.S.; *1941* conducts a gala testimonial concert for Ignaz Paderewski at Carnegie Hall; appointed to teach in Newport at the Fontainebleau School; moves to the states because of the war; *1942* appointed to faculty of Peabody Conservatory; *1944* arranges joint recital with Stravinsky at Mills College; *1945* interviewed by Paul Strachan; devotes five concerts in Cambridge to Fauré's music; *1946* appointed full professor at the Conservatoire national; begins teaching Leonard Bernstein; writes music criticism for the *Spectateur des arts*; deplores the use of native and folk elements in the new compositions; emphasizes the primacy of the line to create the impression in performance of long, soaring, arching line; *1947* makes frequent forays into art, literature, ethics, and many other fields; observes that American and British students have insufficient training in the fundamentals; *1949* appointed technical director of the Conservatoire américain; *1950* organizes the gala festivities that accompany the coronation of Prince Rainier II; *1953* becomes director of the Conservatoire américain; *1954* tours Scandinavia; accepts composition students who are interested in serial composition and avant-garde trends; *1956* organizes and prepares the music for the marriage of Prince Rainier to Grace Kelly; tours Poland attending the First International Festival of Contemporary Music; *1958* arrives in U.S. as a Fellow of the Institute of Contemporary Arts in Washington, D.C.; conducts anniversary performance of Stravinsky's *Dumbarton Oaks Concerto* for the fiftieth wedding anniversary of Mr. and Mrs. Robert Woods Bliss; makes four films in Pittsburgh; *1962* conducts the English Chamber Orchestra in Stravinsky's *Violin Concerto* and Fauré's *Requiem*; invited to the White House by the Kennedys; awarded Yale's prestigious Howland Medal; lectures on music at Yale; *1966* invited by Soviet government to Moscow as juror for the Tchaikovsky competition; *1967* given an eightieth birthday party by Prince Rainier; awarded rank of commander of the French Légion d'Honneur; *1968* conducting appearances in England are well received; *1971* attends the fiftieth-anniversary celebration of the Conservatoire américain at Fontainebleau; *1973* begins going blind, but continues teaching; *1977* decorated with the Most Excellent Order of the British Empire eighteen days after the French government awarded her the Medaille d'or of the academie des Beaux-Arts of the Institut de France; awarded the grand officier of the Légion d'Honneur; *1979* dies on the morning of October 22; concelebrated Mass is held at the Trinité, her parish church, on October 26.

Activities of Historical Significance

Nadia Boulanger was in her thirties in the 1920s when American music students began flocking to her. From then until her death in 1979, she devoted her musical life to teaching performers and especially, composers. Most of her students were Americans who discovered her genius through the Conservatoire américain in Fontainebleau, France. More than any other teacher of composition in the twentieth century, Boulanger turned American composers away from their penchant for imitating the style of nineteenth-century German Romanticism. She encouraged and cultivated an American music of a more classically oriented style yet still remained eclectic and encouraged each student to develop a personal approach to composition.

The twentieth century has seen the evolution of a truly American musical art form of international import due to Boulanger's influence. Among her American students of notoriety in pedagogy, performance, or composition are the following: Marion Bauer, Aaron Copland, Douglas Moore, Virgil Thomson, Beveridge Webster, Walter Piston, Ross Lee Finney, Suzanne Bloch, Quinto Maganini, Roy Harris, Louise Talma, Theodore Chanler, Marc Blitzstein, Elie Siegmeister, Ruth Slenczynska, Yehudi Menuhin, Elliott Carter, Anthony Lewis, David Diamond, Irving Fine, Douglas Allanbrook, Leonard Bernstein, Julia Perry, Quincy Jones, Jay Gottlieb, James Harrison, Noel Lee, Serge Tcherepnin, Jeremy Menuhin, Robert Levin, Robert Xavier Rodriguez, and Philip Glass.

Overview of Biographical Sources

Biographers to date have given a thorough coverage of Nadia Boulanger's life, achievements, views on music, and influence as a pedagogue. Her biographers have not, however, delved deeply enough into the profound historical effect which she has had on twentieth-century style in American music.

Leonie Rosenstiel's *Nadia Boulanger: A Life in Music* (New York: W. W. Norton, 1982), covers her family background and her life as a world-renowned teacher, composer, performer and conductor. It includes some important photographs. Yet this biography seems biased with unsupported assumptions. For example, the book contains unsupported allegations of anti-Semitism and discrimination against non-whites and non-Catholics, as well as the unfounded assumption that Boulanger was envious of her sister Lili.

Suzanne R. Hoover's "Nadia Boulanger," in *The American Scholar* (Autumn 1977: 496-502) and Rose Keylbut's "The Meaning of a Musical Education," in *The Etude Music Magazine* (October 1937: 648-649), provide a valuable discussion of Boulanger's philosophy on teaching music. Irving Kolodin's "Music to My Ears: Nadia Boulanger and Her Dynasty," in *Saturday Review* (December 24, 1979: 46-47) states that Boulanger transformed serious American music from an apology to a source of pride. Kolodin points out that she brought a new perspective on music and composition to Americans in the twentieth century. Discusses the likenesses, but even greater dissimilarities, in the characteristic works of her students. Allen Shawn's "Nadia Boulanger's Lessons," in *The Atlantic Monthly* (March 1983: 79-85) also addresses her teaching methods.

Ellen Pfeifer's "Longy salutes 'Mademoiselle' Boulanger," in the *Boston Herald* (September 18, 1987), discusses the festivities surrounding the Longy School's celebration of the centennial of Boulanger's birth, which included an eleven day tribute in the form of concerts, symposia, and showings of a documentary film about her life.

Mark Swed's "A Tribute to the Late, Legendary Nadia Boulanger," in the *San Francisco Herald Examiner* (February 20, 1985: 66C13), discusses a program by the Los Angeles Philharmonic devoted to works by five of Boulanger's American pupils. Virgil Thomson's "Greatest Music Teacher, at Seventy-five," in the *New York Times Magazine* (February 4, 1962: 24), is an account by one of her students that discusses her approach to teaching and her influence on her foreign students. Thomson recalls her total understanding of any musical score she analyzed and her approach to analysis and teaching composition.

Obituaries and tributes in French include Maurice Fleuret's "La Grande Mademoiselle" in *Le Nouvel Observateur* 781 (October 29, 1979); J. Holingue's "Aspects de la France" in *Le Monde* (November 1, 1979); "Nous n'oublierons pas Nadia Boulanger" in *Le Quinzaine Literaire* 313 (November 1979): 16-30; and Anne Rey's "Nadia Boulanger" in *Le Monde* (October 24, 1979).

Evaluation of Principal Biographical Sources

Brody, Elaine. *Paris: The Musical Kaleidoscope, 1870-1925*. New York: George

Braziller, 1987. (**A, G**) Contains an outstanding section on Boulanger with quotes from her pupils. Pays tribute to Boulanger in stating that she "single-handedly trained and developed the foremost American musicians of the post-World War I era," and notes that Boulanger, along with Gertrude Stein, was one of the two women who reigned supreme in Paris of the 1920's.

Campbell, Don G. *Master Teacher: Nadia Boulanger.* Washington, DC: Pastoral, 1984. (**A, G**) Written by a Boulanger student, this work includes the author's impressions and reflections on "her mind, manners, and intentions." A sensitive coverage of her life, works, and writings. Contains exceptional photographs.

Kendall, Allan. *The Tender Tyrant: Nadia Boulanger. A Life Devoted to Music.* London: MacDonald and Janes, 1976. (**A, G**) Contains excellent material on Boulanger's attitudes and values toward music and reveals her genius as a teacher.

Monsaingeon, Bruno. Translated by Robyn Marsack. *Mademoiselle: Conversation with Nadia Boulanger.* Carcanet, 1985. (**A, G**) This look at Boulanger's life and achievements contains a tremendous amount of material gained from her discussion of her views on teaching, on students, and on composing.

Spycket, Jerome. *Nadia Boulanger.* 1987. Stuyvesant, NY: Pendragon Press, 1992. Translated by M. M. Shriver. (**A, G**) The most accurate source in English or French published to date. There are 190 pages that include unique photographs, valuable reproductions of letters from Debussy, Rauel, Poulenc, Dukas, Pagno, Pierne, Gershwin, Copland, Bernstein, Milhaud and others, and a full page reproduction of the homage written to her for her sixtieth birthday by Stravinsky.

Museums, Historical Landmarks, Societies

Boulanger's correspondence, personal papers, or compositions may be found in the following libraries in Paris. *Archives of the Academie des Beaux-Arts; Archives Nationales; Bibliotheque Nationale; Conservatoire National; Miki Paronian Collection; Nice Nadia Boulanger Collection.*

Other Sources

Walters, Teresa. "Nadia Boulanger, musician and teacher: her life concepts and influences." Diss. Peabody Conservatory, 1981. Covers Boulanger's development as a performer, composer, conductor and pedagogue. It outlines her ideas on musical style, performance, composition, conducting, pedagogy, music history and music criticism. Analyzes Boulanger's success as a composition teacher. Most important, the appendix lists her compositions and those of her private students.

McKellar Israel
Sandhills Community College

Robert Boyle
1627-1691

Chronology

Born Robert Boyle on January 25, 1627, at Lismore Castle, Munster, Ireland, seventh and youngest son of Richard Boyle, first earl of Cork, and Catherine Fenton Boyle; *1627-1633* grows up in Ireland, receives private tutoring in French and Latin; *1635-1638* studies history, classical languages, and mathematics at Eton; *1639* resides briefly at his father's estate at Stalbridge in Dorset, England, studies under the private tutelage of Isaac Marcombes, a French Calvinist, and then embarks on a tour of Europe with his brother Francis and Marcombes; travels in France and Switzerland; *1641* travels to Italy and then to Marsailles, where he learns that the Irish rebellion has depleted his father's fortunes; Francis returns home to Ireland and Robert goes to live at Marcombes's home in Geneva, where he continues his studies in rhetoric, logic, mathematics, and theology; *1644* arrives at the London home of his sister, Katherine, Viscountess Ranelagh, where he meets leading figures of the day, such as poet John Milton, educational philosopher Samuel Hartlib, and medical author Kenelm Digby; *1646-1651* settles on his inherited estate at Stalbridge; becomes interested in agriculture and husbandry, reads extensively in natural philosophy, equips a laboratory for chemical experiments, and begins writing on primarily theological and moral topics; *1652* travels to Ireland and, aided by his brother Roger, Lord Broghill, who served under Cromwell, reclaims his inherited estates in Munster and Connaught; begins performing anatomical dissections with William Petty, physician-general to the Parliamentary Army at Dublin; *1655* moves to Oxford and takes a room in the home of an apothecary; joins the weekly meetings of a group of scholars, including Seth Ward, John Wallis, Thomas Willis, John Wilkins, Christopher Wren, Robert Hooke, and John Locke, who are interested in experimental studies of nature; also develops skills in Eastern languages and a knowledge of divinity through his association with Orientalists and linguists at Queens College Edward Pococke and Thomas Hyde; theologian/philosopher Samuel Clarke; and ecclesiastic Thomas Barlow, also Bodley's librarian and later bishop of Lincoln; *1658-1659* takes on Hooke as his assistant; they construct a device, called an air-pump, to create an artificial vacuum for experiments on the properties of air; publishes an anonymous essay "Inviting all True-lovers of Vertue and Mankind, to a Free and Generous Communication of their Secrets and Receits in Physick [medicine]"; *1660* travels frequently to London; involved with a plan to create a formal society for the study of natural philosophy; publishes his first book-length work, *Seraphic Love*, a theological treatise on the superiority of spiritual over physical love, and *New Experiments Physico-Mechanical*, which reports the results of his air-pump experiments; *1661* appointed to the Council for Foreign Plantations; publishes *The Sceptical Chymist*, in which he uses experimental results to call into question Aristotelian and alchemical theories of elements, and *Certain Physiological Essays*, in which he discusses experimental methods and the proper way to write up results in experimental essays; publishes another theological work, *Some Considerations Touching the Style of the Holy Scriptures*, on the proper way to interpret scripture; *1662* appointed by the King as the first Governor of the "Corporation for Propagating the Gospel in New England and the Parts Adjacent in America"; becomes a founding member of the Royal Society of London for the advancement of experimental learning; publishes a second edition of his *New Experiments Physico-Mechanical* with a *Defense of the Doctrine Touching the Spring and Weight of the Air* against the objections to his earlier work by philosopher Thomas Hobbes and Jesuit mathematician and missioner to England Francis Linus; *1663* publishes *Some Considerations Touching the Usefulness of Experimental Philosophy*, which combines his interests in science and theology by arguing that a knowledge of nature can increase one's admiration of God, its creator; *1664* elected into the Company of the Royal Mines; publishes *Experiments and Considerations Touching Colours*, a theoretical and experimental work on optics; *1665* nominated to the provostship of Eton College, which he declines; becomes an honorary Doctor of Physick at Oxford; publishes *Occasional Reflections*, a collection of essays on the lessons of morality to be learned from everyday occurrences, and *New Experiments and Observations Touching Cold*, a natural history on the properties and effects of cold combined with theoretical speculations about its production; *1666* publishes *A Hydrostatical Paradox* critically examining French philosopher and mathematician Blaise Pascal's work on the equilibrium of liquids, and *The Origin of Forms and Qualities*, which argues for the superiority of atomistic, corpuscular explanations of the qualities of bodies, in opposition to the Aristotelian theory of substantial forms; *1668* returns to London permanently and lives at the home of his sister Katherine; corresponds with and receives visits from some of the leading figures of the day, including English physicist and mathematician Isaac Newton, German philosopher and mathematician Gottfried Wilhelm Leibniz, and Dutch physicist and mathematician Christian Huygens; *1669* publishes *A Continuation of New Experiments Physico-Mechanical; 1670* publishes *Tracts about the Cosmical Qualities of Things*, that includes a "History of Particular Qualities," continuing his work on the forms and qualities of bodies, and *Tracts of a Discovery of the Admirable Rarefaction of the Air*, that includes "New Observations about the Duration of the Spring of the Air" continuing his work on the properties of the air; publishes a second volume of *The Usefulness of Experimental Philosophy*, which shows the practical benefits of the new learning; suffers a stroke and recovers from paralysis through a regimen of exercise and medicine; *1672* publishes *An Essay about the Origin and Virtues of Gems*, consisting of speculation about the growth of gems in the earth; and *Tracts Containing New Experiments Touching the Relation betwixt Flame and Air*, that also includes hydrostatic inquiries; *1673* publishes *Essays on the Nature of Effluviums*, which discusses how bodies too small to have an effect on the human eye can affect other bodies; *1674* publishes *Tracts Consisting of Observations about the Saltiness of the Sea*, which includes "A Sceptical Dialogue about the Positive or Privative Nature of Cold"; and *Tracts Containing Suspicions about Some Hidden Qualities of the Air*, which includes a critical examination of Hobbes's *Problemato de Vacuo*; also publishes *The Excellency of Theology*, arguing for the superiority of theological over natural studies, to which is appended "The Excellency and Grounds of the Corpuscular or Mechanic Philosophy"; *1675* publishes another theological work, *Some Considerations about the Reconcileableness of Reason and Religion*, showing that the truths of Christianity and natural philosophy need not conflict; *1676* publishes *Experiments and Notes about the Mechanical Origin of Particular Qualities* with a critical discussion of the chemists' doctrine of qualities; *1678* publishes *An Historical Account of a Degradation of Gold* on the possibility of the transmutation of metals; *1680* elected president of the Royal Society but declines because he prefers not to take the religious oaths required of the officeholder; publishes *The Aerial Noctiluca*, with observations about luminous bodies; *1681* publishes *A Discourse of Things above Reason*, which examines the problem of determining the truth of divinely revealed mysteries that defy human comprehension of reason; *New*

Experiments and Observations Made upon the Icy Noctiluca, to which is appended "A Chymical Paradox" about the transmutation of chemical principles; and a second *Continuation of New Experiments Physico-Mechanical* compiled by his assistant Denis Papin; *1684* publishes *Memoirs of the Natural History of Human Blood*, on how to determine its nature and function; and *Experiments about the Porosity of Bodies,* which discusses the spaces that exist between the particles that make up seemingly solid bodies; *1685* publishes *Short Memoirs for the Natural Experimental History of Mineral Waters*, including a discussion of their medicinal value; *An Essay of the Great Effects of Even Languid and Unheeded Motion*, arguing that the motion of the minute parts of matter is responsible for the visible effects produced in bodies; *Of the Reconcileableness of Specific Medicines to the Corpuscular Philosophy*, examining how the effects of chemical drugs can be explained in terms of matter and motion; and *Of the High Veneration Man's Intellect Owes to God*, a theological work on how the wisdom and power of God are revealed in nature; *1685-1686* publishes *A Free Inquiry into the Vulgarly Received Notion of Nature*, an extended argument against the view of nature as some type of entity capable of purposeful action that was being taught as part of the philosophy curriculum in the schools; *1687* publishes *The Martyrdom of Theodora and Didymus*, a juvenile work written as a literary allegory about standing firm in one's faith when faced with persecution; *1688* publishes *Receipts Sent to a Friend in America*, a collection of medical remedies; *A Disquisition about the Final Causes of Things* on the extent to which humans can discover the purposes of God in nature; and a two-page advertisement concerning the loss of some of his manuscript material; *1689* because of declining health and the need to repair the loss done to his manuscripts, has less communication with the Royal Society, resigns from the New England Company, and limits visitors to his home; *1690* publishes *Medicina Hydrostatica* on how to determine the genuineness of chemical substances by weighing them in water; and *The Christian Virtuoso*, Part I, on why there is no conflict between being a good Christian and a natural philosopher; *1691* publishes *Experimenta et Observationes Physicae*, a collection of previously unpublished observational and experimental reports, hastily assembled for press so as not to be lost; health continues to decline and, after a short illness, dies on December 30, seven days after his sister Katherine, and is buried near her in the Chancel of St. Martin's-in-the-Fields, London.

Activities of Historical Significance

Robert Boyle was born in the midst of scientific, religious, and political revolution. He described his position of birth as fortunate because, as the youngest son, he was able to avoid the political intrigues that often kept his older relations busy, and he declined the honors and titles that were offered to him on a number of occasions, in order to retain as much neutrality as possible. His fortunate position also gave him great wealth and the leisure to devote his life to the study of theology and natural philosophy, and his work in both these areas is of lasting historical importance. His books were popular and continued to be published after his death, along with some new works taken from his draft manuscripts.

Boyle was deeply concerned about how Christianity could be propagated throughout the world, and he spent a great amount of time and money having the Bible translated into the languages of the native peoples of New England, Ireland, and the East Indies. In his last will, he left funds to Harvard University and to the College of William and Mary for the furtherance of Christianity in the New World and established a lectureship in London for eight annual sermons on the proof of the truths of Christianity. Known as the "Boyle Lectures," they continue to be given to this day.

Even as he sought to promote Christianity in general, Boyle advocated tolerance among the various Protestant sects. His work in biblical interpretations led him to an appreciation of the difficulties involved in understanding scriptural passages, and he warned against dogmatically accepting the interpretations of particular religious groups because they were often prejudiced by the interests of those who proposed them.

Boyle also used his work in biblical hermeneutics (the science of scriptural interpretation) as a way to justify his pursuit of science. Many Anglican Church leaders feared that the new science was a threat to religious belief, and the atheistic tinge that was imposed upon it by philosophers such as Thomas Hobbes seemed to legitimize their fears. Boyle argued that both the book of Scripture and the "book of nature" were the products of the same divine author, and any seeming contradictions between the two were the result of human failure to understand them. In addition, he argued that the two books could not conflict because they were meant to deliver different messages. The Bible revealed God as savior and was meant to teach man spiritual lessons, whereas the book of nature revealed

God as creator, and was meant to teach man about His wisdom and power. Boyle believed that theology was the most important area of study; but paradoxically, the division that he helped to create between nature and the Scripture would be used by future generations as a way to devalue religious study as ''non-scientific.''

Boyle and his contemporaries, such as naturalist John Ray, argued that the study of nature would lead to an increased awareness of God's power in the design of the world and thus could supplement the religious truths learned through revelation. In the first Boyle Lecture of 1692, Richard Bentley used Newtonian science to argue that the complexity of the universe proved that it had been designed by the all-powerful God of the Christian religion. This tradition of ''natural theology'' reached its apex in the nineteenth-century work of William Paley, but by then the arguments drawn from nature were seen as sufficient grounding for one's faith. This was a somewhat unfortunate development, because the rise of Darwinian evolution, with its emphasis upon the role of chance variations, dealt a severe blow to the design argument in particular and natural theology in general.

Boyle's scientific works are of lasting historical significance not so much because of the specific theories that he developed but because of his successful promotion of a new way of thinking about nature and a new method for investigating physical processes. He championed the new corpuscular philosophy, which sought to explain the sensible qualities of bodies by reference to the motion of their minute parts, in opposition to the predominant Aristotelian philosophy taught in the schools, that sought to explain natural processes by reference to the essential forms and qualities supposed to be possessed by physical bodies. In addition, he advocated an experimental confirmation of corpuscular hypotheses in opposition to the deductive reasoning methods espoused by French philosopher Rene Descartes that predominated on the Continent. To popularize these views, Boyle wrote in English, although his works were quickly translated into Latin and were read by a wide audience in Europe, including Dutch philosopher Benedict de Spinoza, Christian Huygens, Gottfried Leibniz, Italian physician Francesco Redi, and Dutch physician and botanist Hermann Boerhaave.

Boyle's experimental work provided the factual basis upon which others built. ''Boyle's law'', which states that the volume of a gas is inversely proportional to its pressure, was actually discovered by Richard Townley, who first suggested the relationship to Boyle after reading his *New Experiments Physico-Mechanical*. The law was experimentally confirmed in Boyle's laboratory and first published by him in the second edition of *New Experiments*. In his *Experiments and Considerations Touching Colours*, Boyle suggested that the production of black and white could be explained by a particulate theory of matter, but it was Newton who developed a complete theory of optics that was able to explain the production of all colors. Boyle's experiments with the air-pump provided a great amount of information on the effects of the lack of air on the life of animals and on combustible substances, but it was French chemist Antoine Lavoisier a century later who developed a theory of oxygen to explain these experimental results.

Known as the "father of modern chemistry," Boyle deserves the title not for any specific contribution to chemical theory but for his efforts to make it a respectable area of study within natural philosophy. In works such as *The Sceptical Chymist* and *Certain Physiological Essays*, he discussed the many difficulties encountered in experimental practice. He appreciated the necessity of properly identifying the materials to be used in experimental trials and made a number of important methodological discoveries in this area, such as an indicator test for acids and bases—the precursor of today's litmus test.

Boyle's most important historical legacy is his contribution to scientific method. As Peter Shaw said in his 1725 abridgement of Boyle's works, Boyle was concerned with "showing philosophy [science] in action." His manner of writing experimental essays, in which he gave not merely the results of his trials but a detailed account of the methods used, became a model for the scientific report. And his strict adherence to the experimental confirmation of theory, which influenced the development of Locke's epistemology in *An Essay Concerning Human Understanding* (1690), became the standard for scientific objectivity in the modern world.

Overview of Biographical Sources

The earliest full-scale biography was published by Thomas Birch in volume one of *The Works of the Honourable Robert Boyle* (1744, 1772). Three twentieth-century biographies—Flora Masson's *Robert Boyle: A Biography* (1914), Louis Trenchard More's *The Life and Works of the Honourable Robert Boyle* (1944), and R. E. W. Maddison's *The Life of the Honourable Robert Boyle* (1969), follow the type of uncritical chronological account given by Birch, but are supplemented with material from the private documents and letters of Boyle, his relatives, and his associates.

When the history of science became a specialized academic discipline in the twentieth century, interest in Boyle's scientific work increased. The most detailed examination of his scientific and methodological ideas has been done by Marie Boas Hall in several books and articles, including *Robert Boyle on Natural Philosophy* (1965) and *Robert Boyle and Seventeenth-Century Chemistry* (1958). Her work, always scholarly and well-documented, can be relied upon as a guide for understanding Boyle's science.

Boyle's work has also been examined by historians interested in studying the social context within which past science was practiced. There has been considerable speculation about Boyle's political motivations, for example, by authors such as J. R. Jacob, *Robert Boyle and the English Revolution* (1977) and Charles Webster, *The Great Instauration* (1975). This literature tends to downplay Boyle's intellectual achievements in order to emphasize his social and political views.

The quantity and variety of Boyle's published writings has resulted in an extensive bibliography, a large portion of which has appeared in scholarly journals. There are differing interpretations of almost every facet of his thought. J. E. McGuire, for example, presented a nominalistic interpretation of Boyle's views on the laws of nature in his "Robert Boyle's Concept of Nature," *Journal of the History of Ideas* 33 (1972): 523-542. This was challenged by Timothy Shanahan in "God and Nature in the Thought of Robert Boyle," *Journal of the History of Philosophy* 26 (1988): 547-569. In another controversy, Larry Laudan argued that Boyle's methodological views can be attributed to the influence of Descartes in his "The Clock Metaphor and Probabilism," *Annals of Science* 22 (1966: 73-107), that Boyle's debt was actually owed to Bacon.

Evaluation of Principal Biographical Sources

Alexander, Peter. *Ideas, Qualities and Corpuscles: Locke and Boyle on the External World*. Cambridge: Cambridge University Press, 1985. (**A**) An interesting and thorough examination of Boyle's views on the experimental investigation of the corpuscular constitution of matter and of how his work influenced John Locke's theory of knowledge. Alexander focuses upon the details of Boyle's account of the mechanical philosophy, particularly on the subtle analysis that he offered of the distinction between the primary and secondary qualities of bodies. He argues that for Boyle these qualities were powers that objects actually possessed, distinct from the ideas and perceptions of humans which are caused by such qualities, and concludes that the well-known criticisms of the philosopher George Berkeley against the corpuscular philosophy were unfounded. Finally, Alexander traces how John Locke incorporated these notions into his philosophical theory of ideas in order to show that Boyle was the major intellectual source for Locke's epistemological views. While this work has little discussion of Boyle's personal life or scientific practice, it does provide a good account of the philosophical basis of his corpuscularianism.

Birch, Thomas. "The Life of Boyle." In *The Works of the Honourable Robert Boyle*. Vol. 1. 1772. Reprint. Hildesheim, Germany: George Olms, 1965. (**A, G**) Still an authoritative account of Boyle's life with some slight errors of interpretation and dating. Contains Boyle's autobiographical account of his youth up to 1642, as well as letters between Boyle, his family members, colleagues and business associates. Also includes accounts of Boyle's life from some of his contemporaries, such as the excerpts from Bishop Burnett's funeral sermon, as well as some draft material that survived among Boyle's manuscripts, and his last will and testament.

Hall, Marie Boas. *Robert Boyle and Seventeenth-Century Chemistry*. Cambridge: Cambridge University Press, 1958. (**A**) A detailed examination of Boyle's role in the chemical revolution of the seventeenth century. Hall describes how Boyle was drawn to the study of chemistry because he perceived that it would be useful for the improvement of natural philosophy and medicine. According to Hall, Boyle was able to produce an "original transformation of chemistry" because he was the first chemist to be truly conversant with natural philosophy, and his insights into the way in which chemistry could improve medical practice were right even though they did not prove to be fruitful in his own day. While this work provides an accurate account of the contributions that Boyle made to chemistry, and gives some details of the debt that Boyle owed to the earlier work of the alchemist van Helmont, Hall's generally dismissive attitude towards Boyle's interests in the more mystical elements of alchemy has been challenged by some of the essays in the

Hunter volume (see below).

—————. *Robert Boyle on Natural Philosophy: An Essay with Selections from His Writings.* Bloomington: Indiana University Press, 1965. (**A**) Contains a brief account of Boyle's life and intellectual development that includes his early relations with Samuel Hartlib and his associates and the role that Boyle played in the founding of the Royal Society of London for the advancement of the new learning. With the help of substantial excerpts from Boyle's published works, Hall then provides a detailed account of his chemical and air-pump experiments along with his theoretical speculations concerning the experimental results. She praises Boyle's achievements and originality, and notes that the great care that Boyle took in writing up his experiments for publication made them of lasting importance to alter scientists, such as Lavoisier, who were able to build significantly upon them. Although Hall has been criticized for her overly rationalist interpretation of Boyle's life and ideas, this remains a scholarly and well-documented work.

Hunter, Michael, ed. *Robert Boyle Reconsidered.* Cambridge: Cambridge University Press, 1993. (**A, G**) The most up-to-date collection of essays on various aspects of Boyle's life. A helpful introductory essay by Hunter discusses previous scholarship on Boyle and notes that in this collection an attempt has been made to provide a ''more nuanced, more detailed and more true to life'' account of Boyle than that usually found in earlier studies. Individual essays cover Boyle's early life and his political activities during and after the English revolution, his views on the rhetorical composition of scientific and theological works, and the intellectual and practical background from which he drew in the construction of his version of the experimental philosophy. A series of essays focus upon Boyle's chemical and alchemical interests and how these in part led him to incorporate some non-mechanical elements within his corpuscular philosophy. Boyle's theological beliefs are also discussed in detail. This volume is an excellent place to begin research because of the variety of topics covered, the effort that has been made to review and revise earlier accounts of Boyle's life and ideas, and the complete bibliography of all works published on Boyle from 1941 through 1993 that is appended.

Jacob, J. R. *Robert Boyle and the English Revolution.* New York: Burt Franklin, 1977. (**A**) A seminal work in the social studies of science genre. Jacob provides a good background on the general social and political climate of Boyle's day, and then speculates about the political motivations behind Boyle's scientific and religious views, based upon early manuscript material and the known political ambitions of some of Boyle's associates. Jacob claims, for example, that Boyle's piety was a response to the English revolution and that he cultivated the new natural philosophy because he thought it could be useful as a means to defend the established Anglican church. In opposition to earlier more rationalist accounts of Boyle's work, such as those offered by Hall, Jacob attempts to show that the new science represented an "aggressive, acquisitive, materialist, imperialistic ideology." Jacob's account has been criticized as being too speculative and too superficial in some of the essays in the Hunter volume (see above) and elsewhere.

Maddison, R. E. W. *The Life of the Honourable Robert Boyle*. New York: Barnes and Noble, 1969. (**A, G**) The most definitive life of Boyle; corrects errors in Birch's account and supplements it with material from the private papers of Boyle's relations. Maddison traces the family history of Boyle's ancestors as well as the major events in Boyle's life, and includes letters from leading figures such as Liebniz and Huygens either to or about Boyle. This is clearly the most reliable account of Boyle's life. It is carefully documented, yet, because it is written primarily as a chronology, it is not highly readable. It also tends to accept the largely laudable accounts of Boyle given by his contemporaries in an uncritical manner.

Masson, Flora. *Robert Boyle: A Biography*. London: Constable, 1914. (**A, G**) A more readable account than Maddison, it is less reliable and largely outdated. Masson tended to romanticize some of the events in Boyle's life and speculated, without documentation, about his private affairs. This work does provide an interesting account of the relation between John Milton and Boyle's sister Katherine, and is good on the details of his social relations in London, and the political intrigues of various members of his family, yet documentation for most of these details is sparse.

More, Louis Trenchard. *The Life and Works of the Honourable Robert Boyle*. London: Oxford University Press, 1944. (**A, G**) The most readable life of Boyle, this work draws upon Birch's account, some unpublished material, and accounts by Boyle's contemporaries, such as that by John Evelyn on Boyle's personal habits. Equal space is given to Boyle's scientific and theological views. Above all, More emphasizes what he sees to be the coherent interrelation that obtained between Boyle's interests in natural history, the mechanical philosophy, alchemy, and theology. A largely uncritical examination that is dismissive of Boyle's critics. Documentation is sometimes lacking.

Overview and Evaluation of Primary Sources

Boyle's works were reprinted many times, both in English and in Latin translation, and they can often be found in academic libraries. The best account of these various editions is John Fulton's *A Bibliography of Robert Boyle* (London: Oxford University Press, 1961; **A**). In 1744 Thomas Birch published a five-volume edition of *The Works of the Honourable Robert Boyle* that contained all of Boyle's published works, including those that had appeared as papers in the *Philosophical Transactions* of the Royal Society, together with letters, documents, and the previously unpublished parts of his *Christian Virtuoso*. *The Works* was reprinted in six volumes in 1772. The 1744 edition has been put on microfilm in the *Landmarks of Science* series, edited by Sir Harold Hartley and Duane H. D. Roller (New York: Readex Microprint, 1967-1976; **A, G**); and the 1772 edition has been reprinted in a facsimile edition (Hildesheim: George Olms, 1965; **A, G**), with a helpful introduction by Douglas McKie. A new annotated and corrected edition of Boyle's published works, in twelve volumes, is planned as part of *The Pickering Masters* series, edited by Michael Hunter and Edward B. Davis. In addition, two single volumes have been published: *Experiments and Considerations Touching Colours* (New York: Johnson Reprint, 1964; facsimile edition of the 1664 London edition; **A, G**) with an introduction by Marie Boas Hall; and *The Sceptical Chymist* (London: J. M. Dent, 1946; **A, G**) with an introduction by M. M. Pattison Muir.

Other works contain extensive excerpts from Boyle's writings. James B. Conant, *Robert Boyle's Experiments in Pneumatics* in *Harvard Case Histories in Experimental Science,* vol. 1. (Cambridge, MA: Harvard University Press, 1970; **A, G**) has an edited version of *New Experiments Physico-Mechanical* with a discussion of the methodological aspects of this work. Marie Boas Hall, *Robert Boyle on Natural Philosophy: An Essay with Selections from His Writing* (Bloomington:

Indiana University Press, 1965; **A, G**), presents selections pertaining to Boyle's general methodological views as well as his work in chemistry and pneumatics. M. A. Stewart, *Selected Philosophical Papers of Robert Boyle* (New York: Barnes and Noble, 1979; **A, G**), presents selections pertaining to Boyle's theoretical work in the corpuscular philosophy.

Boyle's unpublished works, housed at the Royal Society of London, include 46 volumes of manuscripts (mostly draft material of the finished works), seven volumes of letters, and 18 notebooks. This material has been put on microfilm as *The Letters and Papers of Robert Boyle* (Bethesda, MD: University Publications of America, 1992; **A**). A separate introduction and guide to the manuscript material has been prepared by Michael Hunter, *The Letters and Papers of Robert Boyle: A Guide to the Manuscripts and Microfilm* (Bethesda, MD: University Publications of America, 1992; **A**).

Some manuscript material not published in the Birch edition has appeared in journals: Marie Boas, "An Early Version of Boyle's *Sceptical Chymist*," *Isis* 45 (1954: 153-168); Margaret E. Rowbottam, "The Earliest Published Writing of Robert Boyle," *Annals of Science* 6 (1948-1950: 376-389); and Richard S. Westfall, "Unpublished Boyle Papers relating to Scientific Method I and II," *Annals of Science* 12 (1956: 63-73, 103-117). In addition, selections from Boyle's early ethical manuscripts have been published in *The Early Essays and Ethics of Robert Boyle* (Carbondale: University of Southern Illinois Press, 1991; **A**), edited by John T. Harwood.

Museums, Historical Landmarks, Societies

Ashmolean Museum (Oxford). Contains a drawing on vellum by William Faithorne of Boyle at the age of thirty-seven.

College of William and Mary (Williamsburg, VA). The library contains an oil painting derived from the portrait of Boyle by J. Kerseboom.

Kensington Palace (London). Houses a marble bust of Boyle by Joannes Michiel Rysbrack.

Museum of Science and Technology (London). Contains one of Boyle's early air-pumps.

National Portrait Gallery (London). Houses two portraits of Boyle derived from a portrait by J. Kerseboom.

University College (Oxford). A plaque marks the site of Boyle's lodgings.

Royal Society of London (London). Owns the two original portraits of Boyle by William Faithorne (c. 1665) and Johann Kerseboom (c. 1689).

Other Sources

Emerton, Norma E. *The Scientific Reinterpretation of Form.* Ithaca, NY: Cornell University Press, 1984. (**A**) A discussion of how the rise of modern chemistry revised, rather than replaced, earlier philosophical speculation about the composition of bodies, with particular emphasis on the role that Boyle played in this revision.

Frank, Robert G., Jr. *Harvey and the Oxford Physiologists.* Berkeley: University of California Press, 1980. (**A, G**) A detailed discussion of the social relations among the Oxford group with whom Boyle was associated, and the central role that the physiological work of William Harvey played in their experimental inquiries.

Hunter, Michael. *Science and Society in Restoration England.* New York: Cambridge University Press, 1981. (**A**) A detailed study of the membership and proceedings of the early Royal Society and Boyle's role in it. Contains a very helpful bibliographical essay on Restoration science.

Klaaren, Eugene M. *Religious Origins of Modern Science.* Grand Rapids, MI: Eerdmans, 1977. (**A**) The religious views of Boyle and his contemporaries are discussed in terms of how these views influenced their scientific inquiry.

van Leeuwen, Henry G. *The Problem of Certainty in English Thought: 1630-1690*. The Hague: Martinus Nijhoff, 1963. (**A**) Examines in detail the religious views of a number of Boyle's associates and how they influenced him theologically and scientifically.

Shapin, Steven, and Simon Schaffer. *Leviathan and the Air-Pump: Hobbes, Boyle, and the Experimental Life*. Princeton, NJ: Princeton University Press, 1985. (**A**) An account of a debate between Hobbes and Boyle on the proper interpretation of the air-pump experiments, designed to show the political implications of the debate. Some new historical information is presented on the problems associated with attempts to replicated Boyle's experimental results. Well-documented and interesting, but because the authors take Hobbes's side in the debate, it is not a complimentary account on Boyle.

Shapiro, Barbara J. *Probability and Certainty in Seventeenth-Century England*. Princeton, NJ: Princeton University Press, 1983. (**A**) An interesting account of the interrelation of religious, legal, literary, and philosophical ideas in Boyle's day, and how they all contributed to the acceptance of experimentalism in England.

Webster, Charles. *The Great Instauration: Science, Medicine and Reform, 1626-1660*. New York: Holmes and Meier, 1975. (**A**) Focuses primarily upon the social and political aspects of the rise of modern science and Boyle's role in its advancement.

Westfall, Richard S. *Science and Religion in Seventeenth-Century England*. Ann Arbor: University of Michigan Press, 1973. (**A, G**) A general account of the relation between theological and scientific study with a good discussion of Boyle's particular views on this subject.

Rose-Mary Sargent
University of Minnesota

Johannes Brahms
1833-1897

Chronology

Born Johannes Brahms on May 7, 1833 in Hamburg, son of Johann Jakob Brahms, professional double bass player, and Johanna Henrike Nissen; *1834-1838* spends early childhood increasingly attuned to music; *1839* attends the Privatschule of Heinrich Friedrich Voss in the Dammerthorwall; *1840* trains with his father for a career as an orchestra player; *1841* begins piano lessons with Otto Cossel; *1842* witnesses a great fire that destroys most of the old town; *1843* embarks on advanced study of piano with Eduard Marxsen; *1844* attends secondary school; plays a piano sonata of his own to Louise Japha; *1845* becomes exclusive pupil of Marxsen; *1846* studies theory and composition; *1847* gives first public concert; *1848* gives first solo concert, which includes a fugue by composer Johann Sebastian Bach; *1849* performs second solo concert, which includes Ludwig van Beethoven's *Waldstein Sonata*; *1850* meets Hungarian violinist Eduard Reményi; *1851* composes his *Scherzo in E flat minor* and *F sharp minor Piano Sonata*; *1853* tours Europe with Remenyi; meets violinist-composer Joseph Joachim in Hanover, Franz Liszt in Weimar, and Robert and Clara Schumann in Düsseldorf; praised by Schumann in October 28 issue of *Neue Zeitschrift;* *1854* meets Hans von Bülow in Leipzig; becomes close with the Schumanns, (particularly Clara after Robert attempts suicide and is confined to the Enderich Sanatorium); composes *Trio no. 1 in B major* for violin, cello, and piano, and *Variations on a Theme of Schumann;* *1855* lives in Düsseldorf; tours with Clara Schumann and Joachim as pianist and conductor; *1856* Schumann dies; composes the *C sharp minor Piano Quartet; 1857* spends four months in Detmold working as court pianist, chamber musician, and conductor in the court choir; *1858* composes the first *Hungarian Dances;* arranges folk songs; meets and falls in love with Agathe von Siebold; composes *Ave Maria* and *Begräbnisgesang; 1859* breaks off secret engagement with Agathe; performs *D minor Piano Concerto* in Hanover; composes *Serenade no. 2* for orchestra without violins; *1860 Serenade no. 1 in D major* premieres; together with Joachim, J. O. Grimm, and Bernhard Scholz, writes a manifesto dissociating himself from the aesthetic principles of the "New German School"; meets Fritz Simrock, who becomes his publisher; completes *Sextet no. 1 in B flat major*; *1861* finishes *Quartet no. 1 in G minor* and *Variations and Fugue on a Theme of Handel*; *1862* works on the *Magelone Lieder;* finishes *Quintet in F minor* for two violins, viola and two cellos (now lost in this form) and *Quartet no. 2 in A minor* for piano, violin, viola and cello; travels to Vienna, where he gives recitals and meets new friends, including Carl Tausig and Eduard Hanslick; *1863* completes solo piano work *Variations on a Theme of Paganini*; succeeds Ferdinand Stegmayer as conductor of the Vienna Singakademie; *1864* meets Richard Wagner at Penzing; conducts Bach's *Christmas Oratorio*; resigns from the Singakademie; *1865* mother dies; completes *Sextet no. 2 in G major*, *Cello Sonata no. 1 in E minor*, and *Trio in E flat major* for violin, horn, and piano; *1866* visits Switzerland with Joachim; works on *German Requiem* at Karlsruhe and Winterthur; *1867* tours Austrian provinces in the spring and autumn; *1868* tours Germany and Copenhagen with Julius Stockhausen; *German Requiem* premieres in Bremen Cathedral; settles permanently in Vienna; *1869 Rinaldo*, a cantata for tenor solo, chorus, and orchestra, premieres; visits Budapest with Stockhausen; composes the *Liebeslieder Waltzes* for vocal quartet and piano duet; *1870 Alto Rhapsody* premieres; attends performances of Wagner's *Das Rheingold* and *Die Walküre* in Munich; *1871* first part of his *Triumphlied* performed in Bremen; *Schicksalslied* premieres in Karlsruhe; *1872* father dies; completes *Triumphlied* in Karlsruhe; meets philosopher Friedrich Nietzsche at Baden; becomes Director of the Gesellschaft der Musikfreunde concerts; *1873* composes *Variations on a Theme of Haydn* for two pianos; *1874* meets Heinrich von Herzogenberg and wife; completes *C minor Piano Quartet*; *1875* resigns from his post at the Vienna Geschellschaftskonzerte; finishes his *Piano Quartet no. 3 in C minor*; *1876* visits Holland, Mannheim, Kollenz; after twenty years of work, finally completes *Symphony no. 1 in C minor*; *Symphony no. 1* premieres in Karlsruhe under Otto Dessoff; *1877* gives concerts in Leipzig; composes eighteen songs, Op. 69-72., the motet *Warum ist das Licht gegeben*, five of eight piano pieces of Op. 76 (Intermezzi and Capricii), and *Symphony no. 2 in D major*; *1878* vacations in Italy with Theodor Billroth; composes the *Violin Concerto in D major*; *1879 Violin Concerto* premieres in Leipzig; writes *Violin Sonata no. 1 in G major* and *Two Rhapsodies for Piano;* tours Hungary, Transylvania and Poland with Joachim; *1880* attends the unveiling of the Schumann Memorial in Bonn; spends summer at resort town Ischl, where he meets Johann

Strauss II and composes the *Tragic Overture* and *Academic Festival Overture*; *1881* tours Holland and Hungary, where he again meets Liszt; composes *Piano Concerto no. 2 in B flat major*, which he premieres with the Meiningen court orchestra; *1882* completes his *C major Piano Trio*, *F major String Quartet*, and *Gesang der Parzen* for chorus and orchestra; *1883* spends summer in Wiesbaden, where he meets Hermine Spies; completes *Symphony no. 3 in F major*; *1884* spends summer at Mürzzuschlag, where he begins *Fourth Symphony*; tours as a pianist and accompanist for Hermine Spies; *1885* completes *Symphony no. 4 in E minor* and conducts its premiere at Meiningen; *1886* summers in Hofstetten on Lake Thun, where he composes his *Cello Sonata no. 2 in F major*, *Violin Sonata no. 2 in A major*, and *Piano Trio no. 3 in C minor*; *1887* composes vocal quartet *Zigeunerlieder* and *Double Concerto in A minor* for violin, cello, and orchestra; *1888* meets composers Edvard Grieg and Peter Tchaikovsky; summers in Thun, where he composes *Violin Sonata no. 3*; *1889* dedicates his unaccompanied choral work *Fest-und Gedenksprüche* to his native city of Hamburg; receives Order of Leopold from Emperor Franz Josef; *1890* summers at Ischl; composes *String Quintet no. 2 in G major*; *1891* upon hearing the clarinettist Richard Mühlfeld play, writes *Clarinet Trio in A minor* and *Clarinet Quintet in B minor*; *1892* Elisabet von Herzogenberg and his sister Elise die; composes *Fantasias* for piano, Op. 116; *1893* shaken by the untimely death of Hermine Spies; composes the *Klavierstücke,* Op. 118 and 119; *1894* Billroth, Bülow, and Spitta die; summers at Ischl, composing the *Clarinet Sonatas nos. 1 and 2*; accompanist to Alice Barbi at her farewell concert; *1895* tours German cities with Mühlfeld; honored, with Beethoven and Bach, at the Meiningen Festival of the "three Bs"; *1896* conducts his piano concertos in Berlin with Eugen d'Albert as soloist; composes *Vier ernste Gesänge*; Clara Schumann dies; summers at Ischl, where he composes *Chorale Preludes* for organ; visits medicinal waters at Karlsbad to treat his own deteriorating health; attends funeral of composer Anton Bruckner; *1897* appears in public for the last time at a performance of his *Symphony no. 4* under Richter; dies on April 3 in Vienna of liver cancer and is buried on April 6.

Activities of Historical Significance

In a decidedly historicist age, Johannes Brahms was easily the most historically minded of composers. In the age of Romanticism he alone succeeded in bringing to life Renaissance and Baroque traditions and in incorporating them into a style that was in temperament Romantic while in formal terms Classical. In his own time Brahms was recognized as a practitioner of what had only recently come to be known as the classical style: The sum of those forms and conventions which, after centuries of development, came to maturity in the music of Franz Joseph Haydn, Wolfgang Amadeus Mozart, and Ludwig van Beethoven. This recognition elicited two diametrically opposed reactions: on the one hand there were those who extolled this quality as a breath of fresh air amidst the self-indulgent and soul-wrenching expressions of Romanticism; on the other there were those who bemoaned this "unimaginative" and (or so it seemed to them) obdurate conservatism.

These were, roughly speaking, the two poles of the so-called Brahms vs. Wagner debate. The "New German School," at first chiefly represented by Liszt and then increasingly by Wagner, exalted personal expression (and a much expanded personal expression at that), hailing those who found their source of inspiration or—in the *Gesamtkunstwerk* of Wagner—very means of attainment, was more often than not in art, myth, or literature. Hence the ascent of program music that was descriptively titled, that "told" a story or evoked moods and images in the listener, that corresponded to themes, motifs, or ideas in the arts or literature. In contrast to this was the "absolute" music of Brahms, music that bore no descriptive titles, was contained by forms long accepted by convention, and alluded not to mythic or literary figures but simply to other, sometimes much older, musical traditions.

Brahms was considered classical, and thus conservative, to adherents of the New German School in the nineteenth century, but in the twentieth century he has increasingly come to seem modern. Certainly this is in part due to his pervasive influence on the music of the early twentieth century and beyond, especially in the realms of *Lieder* (German art songs), piano, and chamber music. Composers who were particularly influenced by Brahms include Max Reger, Alexander Zemlinsky, Arnold Schoenberg, and in England, Edward Elgar and Ralph Vaughan Williams. The question of Brahms's modernism was first presented by Schoenberg in his seminal essay "Brahms the Progressive" in 1947, and it has gradually won acceptance ever since. What made Schoenberg's argument so original was its obvious implication that, at least in matters of harmony and thematic processes, Brahms was not Liszt's or Wagner's opposite but rather their kindred spirit. For, while never going so far as the New German School with its ultrachromaticism (chromaticism, by employing accidentals, tends to subvert tonality; ultrachromaticism takes this process as far as it will go), Brahms similarly explored ways of extending tonality (the major-minor system of Western music, based on the uneven division of the octave).

In his efforts to impart to his works an overarching flow and continuity, Brahms avoided symmetry and definite closures in both melody and harmony, and above all evenly pulsating rhythms. Blurring of the rhythmic contour is brought about by accentual shifts, syncopation, imitation at irregular intervals, and the superimposition of one meter upon another. There are even times when his rhythmic irregularities anticipate those of twentieth century composer Igor Stravinsky.

Brahms's early works are, naturally enough for a budding keyboard artist, mainly for the piano. In the three piano sonatas of 1852-1853, Op. 1, 2 and 5, one can find broad features of his mature style already in evidence: a preference for dense sonorities, frequent pedal points, opulent harmonies, and a propensity for syncopation and polyrhythms.

During the years 1854-1859, Brahms was kept busy as a pianist and conductor, yet he wrote only a few new compositions. Among these, however, was the epochal and perennially popular *First Piano Concerto*, which Brahms completed in 1858 after four years of arduous labor. It has an interesting and, given that Brahms was a perfectionist, by no means unusual history. It began as a two-piano sonata and was reconceived as a symphony before finally taking its familiar form. In 1859, the year of its premiere, the concerto struck audiences as an insufficient centerpiece for the soloist. Ignoring the imperatives of the concerto as it had come to be understood, Brahms eschewed all rhetoric in favor of an integrated sound, imaginative counterpoint, and rhythmic intricacies.

The early to mid 1860s were rich in chamber music, and during this period Brahms wrote his two string quartets, the first two of three piano quartets, a piano quintet, the first cello sonata, and a horn trio. In the realm of melody, textures and rhythm these works show the influence of Schumann; in that of large-scale structure they betray the influence of Schubert. The contrapuntal features of these works reflect Brahms's studies of the Baroque masters.

Over the next six years, Brahms wrote almost nothing but vocal music. During this period he completed some fifty-six *Lieder*, based on German folk songs, and a great deal of choral music; he also completed his most important composition of this period—*German Requiem* (1867). This work is so titled because the text is excerpted by Brahms himself from the Bible of Martin Luther. The vocal-instrumental fugue of the third and sixth movements recalls Bach and Handel; elsewhere the work evokes the music of the Renaissance.

By their very nature *Lieder,* which are texts put to music, no more constitute absolute or pure music in Brahms's case than in any other composer's. Indeed, even his piano accompaniment, usually simple and spare, is a far cry from being any kind of instrumental evocation of the text such as one hears in, say, Schumann or Hugo Wolf. The general absence of preludes and postludes makes Brahms much more akin to Schubert than Schumann as a song composer.

Not only did Brahms collect and adapt German folk songs, he was influenced by them, with the *Volkslied* impressing itself upon his original song compositions. Generally his *Lieder* are strophic or modified strophic in form, all the stanzas of the poem are sung to the same music. If in instrumental genres Brahms was generally concerned with large-scale structural problems, then in the sphere of *Lieder,* just the opposite tendency manifested itself. He was content to string together several poems by diverse authors, only once writing an interconnecting song cycle, the *Magelone* Romances (text by Ludwig Tieck).

In the early 1870s Brahms once again began to write instrumental music, including string and piano quartets and several symphonies. His first important work from this period was the *Variations of a Theme of Haydn* for two pianos (Op. 56b) and the slightly later version for orchestra (Op. 56a) of 1873. The Haydn theme on which this work is based came from the second movement of a little-known divertimento. Since Haydn himself referred to the theme as "the Chorale St. Antoni," there has long existed serious doubt if it was original with him or borrowed from some anonymous source. The piano quartet was a medium already out of fashion by the time Brahms wrote his variations, yet in its harmonic and tonal richness and ambiguity, it exhibits subtleties and depth justifying Schoenberg's praise of Brahms as a progressive. Brahms was a consummate master of variation writing, both in the narrow sense of the genre and as combined and integrated with sonata form. The prodigal freedom with which he treats the basic theme in all of its intricate permutations harkens back to Schumann, even to Beethoven. Yet Brahms's variations are ultimately less abstract than Beethoven's; their intricacy in the employment of received techniques is best understood by reference to Bach.

Encouraged perhaps by the critical and popular success of the *Variations on a Theme of Haydn*, Brahms returned to, and in 1876, finally completed, his *First Symphony* (a project some twenty years in the making). In large part because of its sheer complexity and monumentality, this symphony invited comparison with Beethoven. The *Symphony no. 2 in D major*, Op. 73, was written within two years of the completion of the *First Symphony*. As the *First Symphony* was compared to Beethoven's *Fifth Symphony*, so the *Second Symphony* was likened to Beethoven's *Sixth Symphony*, the *Pastorale*.

Brahms's compositions for solo piano were mainly written in the early years (1852-1864), when he himself was active as a pianist. Then, after decades of very sparse production, a sudden resurgence of solo piano works occurred from 1892 to 1893. The *Fantasias* Op. 116, the three *Intermezzi* Op. 117, and the *Klavierstucke* of Opp. 118 and 119 were all created during this brief two-year span. In these miniatures it is clear that Frédéric Chopin's influence on Brahms was also far from negligible. Brahms wrote *Lieder* in virtually every stage of his career, with the years 1884-1886 being the most prodigious song production period of his later life. These songs, about thirty-five in number, are set to poems by diverse—and on the whole distinctly minor—poets. His arrangements of German folk-songs, *49 deutsche Volkslieder,* were published in 1894. In the spring of 1896, Brahms made his final and best contribution to song writing, *Four Serious Songs.* As in the case of the *German Requiem,* Brahms himself compiled the texts from the Old and New Testaments in Luther's translation. Like the *Requiem,* and especially fitting in Brahms's penultimate year, the subject of *Four Serious Songs* is death.

Overview of Biographical Sources

It should come as no surprise that the first works on Brahms in English were translations from German. One such work, Albert Dietrich and J. V. Widmann's *Recollections of Johannes Brahms* (London: Seeley, 1899), translated by Dora Hecht, is in important respects a primary source, yet its anecdotes and personal recollections also qualify it as biography. A similar work in this regard is George Henschel's *Personal Recollections of Johannes Brahms,* (Boston: Richard G. Badger, 1907).

The first original work on Brahms in English was Florence May's two-volume opus, *The Life of Johannes Brahms* (1905). Like the two just mentioned, this early work includes personal recollections. Written in straightforward English, the book marks a significant breakthrough in Brahms scholarship. No Brahms biographies of note were published over the next two decades. This hiatus came to an end in 1929 with Walter Niemann's *Brahms*, translated by Catherine Alison Phillips. Niemann was one of the first to demonstrate systematically—though from today's vantage point, not always convincingly—the influence of Brahms on the music of subsequent generations.

By the mid-1930s, Brahms literature in English had appreciably proliferated. William Murdoch's *Brahms* (1933) and Robert Haven Schauffler's *The Unknown Brahms* (1933) is each in its own way an important work. Even so, the most significant work on Brahms in the 1930s, and indeed for several decades thereafter, was yet again a translation: *Brahms: His Life and Work* (1936), by Karl Geiringer. One of Geiringer's theses was that Brahms manifested both Romantic and Classical impulses. Unlike most earlier Brahms biographies, this work dispenses with anecdotal evidence and is mostly concerned with what is, after all, of primary importance: his music.

Peter Latham's *Brahms* (1948), an installment in the Master Musicians Series, gives generous space to the consideration of Brahms as pianist and conductor, but emphasis is naturally placed on Brahms the composer. It is precisely in this regard that Latham's work has become most dated, because in it Brahms is depicted, both implicitly and in no uncertain terms, as the last in a line of Classicists, anachronistic, belatedly summing up one age and leaving no legacy for the age(s) that followed.

Even with the publication of Schoenberg's provocative article "Brahms the Progressive" (1947. Reprinted in *Style and Idea*. New York: Philosophical Library, 1950), over fifteen years passed until the next notable biography appeared, again in a translation: Hans Gal's *Johannes Brahms—His Work and Personality* (1963).

In the 1980s the Brahms literature in both the fields of biography and musicology, grew to astounding new dimensions. In part this was due to the advent of new, alternative publishers, such as Amadeus Press in Portland, Oregon. The biographies of this period are remarkably sophisticated and well-researched. One of the best of these is Ivor Keys' excellent *Johannes Brahms*. By including in his book an exhaustive catalog of works—not merely a roster but a technical overview of each and every work (grouped according to genre)—Keys deftly avoids interrupting the flow of his biography with too detailed a musical analysis.

Evaluation of Principal Biographical Sources

Chissel, Joan. *Brahms.* London: Faber and Faber, 1977. (**G**) Concise biography depicting Brahms as a tender-hearted but tactless man-child, an unaffected genius. Careful to show the milieu in which Brahms grew up and developed. Well-written and informative. Illustrated.

Gal, Hans. *Johannes Brahms—His Work and Personality.* New York: Alfred A. Knopf, 1963. Translated by Joseph Stein. (**G**) Focuses on the problem of personality and the creative process. In addition to early standard sources, the author has also drawn on the reminiscences of his teacher, and one of Brahams's best friends, Eusebius Mandyczewski. Musical analysis of individual works is sparse. Contains an index, list of compositions, and selected bibliography.

Geiringer, Karl. *Brahms: His Life and Work.* Translated by H. B. Weiner and Bernhard Miall. London: G. Allen and Unwin, 1936. (**A, G**) A book that has undergone several revisions since its first appearance, but the original is still a classic. Well-written, incisive and delicately poised between biography proper and music history. Characterizes Brahms's personality as a battlefield between two elemental forces—an "urge to freedom" and a "desire for subjection." Illustrated, with bibliography, index, and plentiful music examples.

Holmes, Paul. *Brahms: His Life and Times.* Southborough, United Kingdom: Baton, 1984. (**G, Y**) Very light on musical analysis, this straightforward biography offers no new information or original points of view. Holmes's research seems mainly to have been limited to Brahms's correspondence. Illustrated, with select bibliography and selective listing of works.

Keys, Ivor. *Johannes Brahms.* Portland, OR: Amadeus Press, 1989. (**A**) An excellent work that is conveniently divided into two parts: a biography and an annotated catalog of works. The circumstances of the works (their dissemination, their audience, their reception) are treated in the first half; in the second, the works themselves are covered (every single one treated as a formal entity bearing certain distinctly musical characteristics). Illustrated, with general index and an index of compositions. Among the numerous music examples is a reproduction of an autograph score.

Latham, Peter. *Brahms.* London: J. M. Dent, 1948. (**A, G**) Though very much a biography, contains illuminating musical analysis as well. Offers the now rather dated view of Brahms as a conservative composer, "the very last of the classical Caesars." The author also discusses the English reaction to Brahams. Includes index, illustrations, and appendices.

MacDonald, Malcolm. *Brahms.* New York: Schirmer, 1990. (**A, G**) Written in clear and urbane prose, this account aims to show that Brahms foreshadowed much of twentieth-century music, his "conservatism" thus ultimately counting for more than Wagner's "progressivism." Looking to the past and to the future, argues MacDonald, Brahms ranks with the likes of Beethoven, Bach, Mozart, and Schubert. Contains illustrations (eight plates), general index, and several appendices, including a very useful calendar of events.

May, Florence. *The Life of Johannes Brahms.* London: E. Arnold, 1905. (**G**) The first original biography of Brahms in English, this early work includes personal recollections of the composer. Contains appendices on Op. 33, the Hamburger Frauenchor, and a general discussion of program music. This work is now of mainly historical significance.

Murdoch, William. *Brahms, with an Analytical Study of the Complete Pianoforte Works.* New York: Sears, 1933. (**A, G**) Early biography and analysis of Brahms. Divided into four principal parts: biography; Brahms as a man—his characteristics; pianoforte works; and pianoforte chamber music. The expertly musical analysis takes into account Brahms's historical position. Illustrated, with index of names, index of works, and bibliography.

Niemann, Walter. *Brahms.* New York: Alfred A. Knopf, 1929. Translated by

Catherine Alison Phillips. (**A, G**) Arguably the best Brahms biography prior to Geiringer, though what musical analysis there is tends to be impressionistic. The author, a devoted follower of Brahms, finds his influence in an array of composers. Contains index of names, index to works, and several useful appendices.

Schauffler, Robert Haven. *The Unknown Brahms. His Life, Character and Works.* New York: Dodd, Mead, 1933. (**G**) Discusses Brahms's historical position and incorporates previously unpublished information on Brahms's personality, including a psychological explanation of Brahms's attitude towards women. Sorely inadequate as a guide to Brahms's music.

Overview and Evaluation of Primary Sources

The complete scores of Brahms were first collected in a single work in the 26-volume *Johannes Brahms sämtliche Werke* (26 vols. Leipzig: Breitkopf & Hartel, 1926-1927; **A**), edited by Hans Gal and Eusebius Mandyczewski. *Thematisches Verzeichnis sämmtlicher im Druck erschienenen Werke von Johannes Brahms* (Berlin: N. Simrock, 1897; **A, G**), was the first exhaustive catalog of the works of Brahms. This was the definitive work and, with the aid of regular updatings, it has remained so. The latest edition is *Johannes Brahms: Thematisch-Bibliographisches Werkverzeichnis* (Munich: G. Henle Verlag, 1984; **A**), revised by Donald M. McCorkle and Margit McCorkle. Although the work is in German, it does contain a helpful introduction in English as well as in German. Of more use perhaps to the English reader is the *Thematic Catalog of the Works of Johannes Brahms* (New York: Da Capo Press, 1973; **A, G**), with Introduction (including addenda and corrigenda) by Donald M. McCorkle. Another work belonging here is Peter Dedel's *Johannes Brahms: A Guide to His Autograph in Facsimile* (Ann Arbor: Michigan Music Library Association, 1978; **A**), Number 18 in the MLA Index and Bibliographic Series. There is no comparable work of its kind, in German or in English. It contains several indexes for easy use.

Recollections of Johannes Brahms, by Albert Dietrich and J. V. Widmann (London: Seeley, 1899; **A, G, Y**), as previously noted under biographical sources, also deserves mention here. It contains letters between Brahms and Dietrich and his wife, and letters between Dietrich and other members of the Brahms circle. Of considerably more interest is *Johannes Brahms: The Herzogenberg Correspondence* (London: John Murray, 1909; **A, G, Y**), edited by Max Kalbeck and translated by Hannah Bryant. It contains the complete correspondence between Brahms and Henrich and Elisabet von Herzogenberg, spanning twenty-one years from 1876 to 1897. Of still more value is *Letters from and to Joseph Joachim* (London: Macmillan, 1914; **A, G**), translated by Nora Bickley. The correspondence between Brahms and Joachim provides a glimpse into Brahms's thinking on music and the problems of composing. Another important collection of correspondence is *Letters of Clara Schumann and Johannes Brahms, 1853-1896* (New York: Longmans, Green, 1927; **A, G, Y**), edited and translated by Berthold Litzmann, which contains nearly all of the correspondence between Brahms and Clara Schumann. Finally, there is *Johannes Brahms and Theodor Billroth: Letters from a Musical Friendship* (Norman: University of Oklahoma Press, 1957; **A, G, Y**), edited and translated by Hans Barkan. This excellent work is based on the following texts: Otto Gottlieb-Billroth's *Billroth und Brahms im Briefwechsel* (Berlin and Wien: Urban and Schwarzenberg, 1935); Fielding H. Garrison's "Medical Men Who Have Loved Music" in *Bulletin of the Society of Medical History of Chicago* 2,158 (October 1920: 158-176); Karl Geiringer's *Brahms—His Life and Work* (2d ed. New York: Oxford University Press, 1947); and Richard Litterscheid's *Johannes Brahms in seinen Schriften und Briefen* (Berlin: n.p., 1943).

Evaluation of Selected Critical Sources

Dunsby, Jonathan. *Structural Ambiguity in Brahms: Analytical Approaches to Four Works.* Studies in British Musicology. London: UMI, 1981. Provides in-depth analysis of the following works: *Variations and Fugue on a Theme of Handel*, the *C minor Piano Quartet* (first movement), *Symphony no. 4 in E minor* (first movement), and *Intermezzo*, op. 119, no. 1. This last analysis is interspersed with a critique of Arnold Schoenberg's views on Brahms as expressed in his 1947 essay "Brahms the Progressive."

Frisch, Walter, ed. *Brahms and the Principle of Developing Variation.* California Studies in 19th Century Music 2. Berkeley: University of California Press, 1984. Perhaps the most significant musicological study of Brahms. Employs and expands

Schoenberg's concept of developing variation to analyze eighteen works by Brahms. Traces a historical evolution through Brahms's works, not only in relation to each other but also in relation to significant compositions by Beethoven, Schubert, Schumann, and Liszt.

Hancock, Virginia. *Brahms's Choral Compositions and His Library of Early Music.* Ann Arbor, MI: UMI Research, c. 1983. Well-researched and buttressed with an abundance of music examples, this volume treats the subject of Brahms's interest in the music of the middle and late Renaissance and its impact on his own choral compositions. Contains several handy appendices, including a list of Brahms's printed library of early music.

Jacobson, Bernard. *The Music of Johannes Brahms.* London: Tantivy, 1977. Engaging study in accessible language. Makes the case that Brahms's interest in his predecessors—Schubert, Haydn, and Bach in particular, and also the earlier polyphonists—was more vital and seminal than the impact of Beethoven. Contains general index, index of works, and several useful appendices.

Musgrave, Michael, ed. *Brahms 2: Biographical, Documentary and Analytical Studies.* Cambridge: Cambridge University Press, 1987. On the whole, well-written and informative. Each chapter is written by a different scholar and devotes itself to a single aspect, work, or group of works by Brahms. Illustrated.

Musgrave, Michael. *The Music of Brahms.* London: Routledge & Kegan Paul, 1985. Exhaustive and penetrating survey of the whole of Brahms's oeuvre by one of the main authorities among today's Brahms scholars. Addresses itself to the music scholar as opposed to the general reader. Illustrated with index, list of works, calendar, and bibliography.

Principal Works

Orchestral Music

Four symphonies (1877, 1878, 1884, 1886)

Two serenades (1860)
Two piano concertos (1860, 1882)
Violin Concerto (1879)
Concerto for Violin, Cello, and Orchestra (1888)
Variations on a Theme of Joseph Haydn (1874)
Academic Festival Overture (1881)
Tragic Overture (1881)

Chamber Music

Three string quartets (1873, 1876)
Two piano quartets (1863, 1865)
Three piano trios (1854, 1883, 1887)
Three violin sonatas (1880, 1887, 1889)
Two string sextets (1862, 1866)
Two string quintets (1891)
Two cello sonatas (1887)
Two Sonatas for Piano and Clarinet (1866, 1895)
Piano Quintet (1865)
Horn Trio (Horn, Violin, Piano) 1866

Choral Music

A German Requiem
Rhapsodi (Alto Rhapsody)
Song of Fate
Song of the Fates
Song of Triumph

Keyboard (Piano and Organ) Music

Three Sonatas for Piano (1853, 1854)
Sixteen Variations on a Theme by Robert Schumann (1854)
Variations on a Theme by Handel (1862)
Variations on a Theme by Paganini (1866)

Fugue in A flat minor for Organ (1864)
Two Rhapsodies for Piano (1880)
Seven Fantasies for Piano (1892)
Eight Chorale Preludes (Posthumous, 1902)

Vocal Music

Liebeslieder Waltzes (1869)
Neue Liebeslieder Waltzes (1875)
Numerous Quartets, Motets, Lieder, Sacred Choruses, Canons, Songs and Romances for mixed voices with and without accompaniment (1864-1890)
Sixty-two songs and lieder for solo voice with piano accompaniment (1853-1877)
Seventeen Duets with Piano accompaniment (1861-1875)
Four Ballades and Romances for two voices (1878)

Fiction and Adaptations

Brahms has figured, either as the main subject or incidentally, in a few works of fiction. The first such work was Frederick Horace Clark's *Brahms Noblesse* (Berlin: n.p., 1912). It contains the author's reminiscences of Brahms and includes a discussion of the ethics of music that has relevance for Brahms's concept of *Menschenbild.* A couple of years later Ethel Notingham wrote a short sketch entitled ''Der Besuch bei Brahms'' (The Visit with Brahms), which appeared in the periodical *Die Musik* (February 1914). It depicts an historically credible Brahms in the context of an imaginary meeting with the composer in Bad Ischl.

''Die Stunde der Sterne'' (At the Hour of the Stars), written by Robert Hohlbaum and appearing in that author's volume *Himmlisches Orchester. Der Unsterblichen. Neue Folge. Novellen* (Leipzig: L. Staachman, 1924), is historical fiction at its best. Its central event is a dinner meeting between Brahms and Bruckner in the Rote Igel. In the story they come to understand each other as they never did in real life. The ''Brahms vs. Bruckner debate'' provides the inspiration for the tale. Hermann Richter's *Von ewiger Liebe* (Of Eternal Love) (Leipzig: Koehler & Amelung, 1929) sympathetically portrays the relationship between

Brahms and Clara Schumann from the time Robert Schumann was first admitted to the asylum in March of 1854 until his death in July of 1856. Kurt Arnold Findeisen's *Lied des Schicksals. Roman um Johannes Brahms* (The Schicksals' Songs) (Leipzig: Koehler & Amelung, 1929), is a novelization of Brahms's life from the 1836, year of Schumann's death, until his own death in 1897.

The American film *Song of Love* (1947), produced and directed by Clarence Brown, also belongs among the fictional treatments of Brahms. In this life story of Robert Schumann, the Johannes-Clara-Robert love triangle is depicted in the usual sentimental way of Hollywood the real Brahms is nowhere to be found. Finally, Brigid Brophy's ''Variations on Themes of Elgar and Brahms,'' in *The Adventures of God in His Search for the Black Girl* (London and Basingstoke: Macmillan, 1973), must be mentioned. In this imagined dialogue between Brahms and ''Polyhymnia'' on the subject of Elgar's *Concerto for Violincello and Orchestra*, Brahms is the exponent of ''absolute'' music.

Museums, Historical Landmarks, Societies

Brahms Memorial (Hamburg, Germany). Located at Peterstrasse 39. Dedicated in 1971. Two rooms of original Brahms dwelling reconstructed on site; on display are changing exhibits of Brahms memorabilia.

Brahms Memorial (Meiningen, Germany).

Brahms Memorial (Vienna).

Brahms Memorial Room (Vienna). Located in the Haydn-Haus. Contains items from Brahms's Karlsgasse residence.

Brahms Monument (Vienna). Located at Resselpark.

Brahms Museum (Gmunden, Austria). Replica of the Bad Ischl house where Brahms stayed.

Brahms Society (Baden-Baden, Germany). Located in the Brahmshaus at Maximilianstrasse 85. Publishes newsletters, organizes concerts and conferences.

Brahms Society of Vienna (Vienna). Publishes newsletters, organizes concerts and conferences.

Brahms-Saal (Hamburg, Germany). Located at Rosenstrasse 16. Concert hall named after Brahms.

Brahms-Saal (Vienna). Located at Dumbastrasse 3. Concert hall named after Brahms.

Brahmshaus (Baden-Baden, Germany). Located at Maximilianstrasse 85. The only home of the composer that has been preserved in Germany. The inscription on a memorial tablet on the door reads: ''Brahms lived here 1865-1874 . . .'' The house contains two display rooms for changing exhibitions of Brahmsiana.

Brahmshaus (Lichtenthal, Germany). Memorial house.

Gravesite (Vienna). Located at Zentral Friedhof XI, 234 Simmeringer Hauptstrasse.

Plaque (Dusseldorf, Germany). Marks Brahms's home from 1856-1857, located at Haroldstrasse 14 (formerly Portstrasse 32).

Plaque (Gottingen, Germany). Marks the house where Joachim and Brahms stayed in 1853.

Plaque (Hamburg, Germany). Marks the spot of Brahms's birthplace.

Plaque (Vienna). Marks Brahms's Viennese residence.

Other Sources

Becker, Heinz. ''Johannes Brahms.'' In *The New Grove Late Romantic Masters*

(London: Macmillan, 1985: 77-201). An exhaustive chronological study of Brahms's music together with a fairly detailed biographical account, first published in *The New Grove Dictionary of Music and Musicians* (1980). Though availing itself of all Brahms literature up to the mid-1980s, it does not entirely abandon the notion of Brahms as an "end-of-the-line" Classicist. Contains illustrations and musical examples.

Frisch, Walter, ed. *Brahms and His World.* Princeton, NJ: Princeton University Press, 1990. Outstanding collection of essays on Brahms, his music, and his milieu; some biography, some musicology, some sociology. Contains index of Brahms's works, index of names, music examples and an appendix, "Dedicated to Johannes Brahms," which lists works dedicated to Brahms by other composers, authors and artists.

Pascall, Robert, ed. *Brahms: Biographical, Documentary and Analytical Studies.* Cambridge: Cambridge University Press, 1983. Presents different aspects of Brahms's musical character, each treated by an able musicologist, biographer, or cultural historian. Specific works, such as the *Tragic Overture* and the *Fantasien* Op. 116, are also discussed. Illustrated, with music examples.

Quigley, Thomas. *Johannes Brahms: An Annotated Bibliography of the Literature through 1982.* Metuchen, NJ: Scarecrow Press, 1990. With a foreword by Margit L. McCorkle. The definitive bibliography on Brahms literature, conveniently divided into more or less distinct categories. Contains personal name index, titles, series and institutions index, newspaper and magazine index, and several useful appendices.

Gregory L. Nehler

John Bright
1811-1889

Chronology

Born John Bright on November 16, 1811, at Green Bank on Cronkeyshaw Common, Rochdale, England, the second child of Jacob Bright, a Quaker mill-owner, and Martha Wood Bright; attends the school of William Littlewood; *1822-1823* enrolls in the Friends' School at Ackworth where his father had studied; influenced by how his Dissenter ancestors had suffered under the discriminatory penal laws; *1823-1827* attends William Simpson's new Quaker school in York, which combines the moral and religious discipline of the previous school with a wider and more serious academic curriculum; enrolls in tiny school at Newton-in-Bowland on the moors between Lancashire and Yorkshire; *1827-1830* becomes clerk to his father and lives above the counting house; *1830-1833* becomes interested in reform politics during the 1830 election and visits London for the first time; delivers his first public speeches in support of temperance reform; *1833-1836* instrumental in founding the Rochdale Literary and Philosphical Society; travels extensively in western Europe and the middle east; *1834* enters public life in the anti-church rates agitations in Rochdale; *1836-1842* becomes more active in reform politics; attracts the notice of Richard Cobden; joins the newly formed Anti-Corn-Law League in 1838; *1839* marries Elizabeth Priestman of Newcastle; *1841* Elizabeth dies at Leamington, leaving an infant daughter; *1842-1847* helps to reorganize the now effective agitations of the Anti-Corn-Law League; elected M.P. for Durham as the League's free-trade candidate; repeal of the Corn Laws; *1847* marries Margaret Elizabeth Leatham; *1847-1854* organizes the Manchester Reform Association with Cobden and former Leaguers; elected M.P. for Manchester; *1854-1856* criticizes British involvement in the Crimean War; delivers his famous "Angel of Death" speech to try to persuade Prime Minister Palmerston to assume the role of peacemaker; *1856-1858* suffers from melancholia and exhaustion; rests in the north of England and Scotland; travels the Mediterranean; offers to resign his seat in Parliament; *1857* suffers crushing defeat at Manchester in the general election and announces his intention to retire from public life; returned for Birmingham without opposition in a by-election five months later; *1858-1860* returns to Parliament championing reform once again; helps organize the Financial Reform Association to advocate retrenchment; *1860-1865* sympathetic to the U.S. government's naval blockade of the South during the American Civil War despite the effect of the Lancashire cotton famine upon his own fortunes; *1865-1868* returns unopposed to Parliament from Birmingham; supports Gladstone's efforts to bring forward a reform bill; *1868-1870* re-elected for Birmingham and becomes President of the Board of Trade in Gladstone's first Liberal ministry and the first Dissenter in a British Cabinet; *1870* suffers nervous exhaustion and resigns from the Board of Trade after aiding Gladstone in disestablishment of the Church of Ireland and in the Irish Land Act, while opposing the Forster Education Act; *1872* returns to Parliament; accepts the office of Chancellor of the Duchy of Lancaster; *1874-1880* re-elected for Birmingham; remains prominent in Liberal politics during Disraeli Ministry, serving as an outspoken opponent of "Beaconsfieldism" in foreign policy and the Bulgarian atrocities in particular; *1878* death of second wife; *1880* re-elected yet again for Birmingham; resumes the Chancellorship of the Duchy of Lancaster in Gladstone's new administration; *1882* resigns in protest over the British bombardment of Alexandria in the Egyptian intervention; *1883* installed as Lord Rector of the University of Glasgow; *1884-1885* rejects both land nationalization and Home Rule for Ireland, though supportive of Irish tenant rights; insists on a redistribution bill to go along with further parliamentary reform and suffrage extension; *1886* refuses to support Gladstone in Home Rule for Ireland; *1889* dies at his home, One Ash, Rochdale on March 27, 1889, and is buried at the Friends' Meeting House in George Street, Rochdale.

Activities of Historical Significance

John Bright was the undoubted and abiding champion of free-trade radicalism in nineteenth-century Britain. As a Quaker and middle-class manufacturer from the industrial north in Lancashire, he advocated a wide variety of radical reforms, opposing all forms of monopoly, including what he saw as monopoly in trade and commerce, religion, political participation, and landholding. A powerful orator who drew on the Bible, literature, and poetry for his images, Bright, together with

Richard Cobden, was the leader and spokesman for the Anti-Corn-Law League (1838-1846) in a successful extra-parliamentary agitation against the restrictive Corn and Provision Laws.

Bright opposed what he often termed "aristocratic misrule," advocating broad extension of suffrage, adoption of the secret ballot, and redistribution of parliamentary representation on the basis of population. As a Dissenter he resented the establishment of the Anglican Church, imposition of church rates, and a host of other indignities which he felt Nonconformists had to endure. He was a staunch opponent of "landlordism," advocating tenant rights, compensation for improvements, and increased opportunities for peasant proprietoriship in landholding, especially in Ireland.

Bright became interested in politics in the Preston election campaign of 1830 between "Orator" Henry Hunt, a leading radical of the time, and Edward Stanley, the future earl of Derby. He made a series of temperance speeches that same year at Cately Lane Head, Rochdale, and Whitworth. The fight for the Reform Bill of 1832 captured his youthful imagination, and in 1834 he entered public life and drew attention to himself as an opponent of church rates in the bitter controversy at vestry meetings in Rochdale. In 1837 his anonymous pamphlet, *To the Radical Reformers of the Borough of Rochdale*, indicted the Tories for exaction of church rates, imposition of the Corn Laws, and demoralization of the people by drink.

National prominence came to Bright as the leading lecturer of the Anti-Corn-Law League. He solemnly pledged in 1841 not to rest until the Corn Laws were repealed. After the disastrous Northern Turnouts in 1842, Bright, Richard Cobden, and George Wilson helped reorganize the League into the best financed and most highly organized political pressure group in Britain. Bright stumped the country for repeal, wrote for a succession of League newspapers, and authored pamphlets, tracts, and circulars in the cause of free trade. To Bright, the Corn Laws were the keystone in the arch of "aristocratic misrule," the repeal of which would lead to far reaching reforms in church and state. With the League, Bright helped to create a political climate which forced Sir Robert Peel to suspend the Corn Laws when famine stalked Ireland in 1846.

Bright entered Parliament in 1843 when he stood as the League-sponsored free-trade candidate in the Durham by-elections. He lost the first poll, but results of this contest were invalidated after a successful League challenge on the basis of bribery by his opponent, Lord Dungannon. In the second election for a seat in the

House of Commons, Bright easily defeated Thomas Purvis, demonstrating the potential effectiveness of the League's new electoral strategy.

In Parliament, Bright supported a number of reform causes. He opposed the Game Laws as aristocratic privilege, but he remained a steadfast opponent of factory legislation as an infringement upon freedom of contract. He also opposed the permanent endowment of the Roman Catholic seminary at Maynooth in 1845 as tantamount to establishment of yet another denomination in Ireland. In 1847 and again in 1851, Bright was returned as an M.P., but on these occasions it was for Manchester, considered the capital of free-trade radicalism. He advocated provision of voluntary schools, fearing that state-sponsored schools would lead to control of education by the Church of England. Bright also favored reform of administration in India, believing that the East India Company ought to be replaced with a formal department of government with its own council and a minister of state.

A challenger to balance of power diplomacy, and of the long standing aristocratic control of the Foreign Office, Bright was an opponent of British involvement in the Crimean War. His speech to the Commons on February 23, 1854, warned of the loss in blood and treasure that was to come, saying: "The angel of death has been abroad throughout the land; you may almost hear the beating of his wings." Yet in a state of mental exhaustion, Bright withdrew from the public arena and offered to resign in a letter to his Mancunian constituents in January of 1857, but the offer was not accepted.

In the 1857 general elections, precipitated by the *Arrow* incident, Bright and other advocates of "Cobdenism" in foreign policy were overwhelmingly defeated. The *Arrow* was a small ship of British registry which was owned by a Chinese merchant from Hong Kong. It was boarded by Chinese officials who claimed to be searching for a pirate but who arrested and imprisoned a dozen crewmen of the technically British vessel instead. The Palmerston ministry demanded return of the imprisoned crewmen and an apology. When both were not forthcoming, a British naval squadron was ordered to bombard Chinese forts. Palmerston was severely criticized by Bright and other Cobdenites who succeeded in defeating the government on the issue in the House of Commons and thereby forced them to appeal to the country.

In despair after his defeat in Manchester in the ensuing general elections, Bright determined to retire and left for Florence to recuperate. A few months later he was persuaded to allow his name to be placed before the electors of Birmingham on the condition that he would not take his seat, if elected, for six months so as to complete his recovery from the pressures of public life. On August 10th Bright was returned in absentia and without opposition for Birmingham in a by-election, and he represented that midlands borough constituency for the next thirty-two years. When he re-entered the House of Commons a few months later he was greeted by the triumphant cheers of his colleagues in the house.

In 1858, Bright resumed his campaign for parliamentary reform, including advocacy of rate-payer suffrage and curtailment of the power of the House of Lords. When Gladstone introduced a substantial suffrage extension bill in 1866 he found a ready supporter in Bright who, alluding to the Bible, denounced opponents of the proposal as refugees of the Cave of Adullam, thus adding ''Adullamites'' to British political lexicon.

In the Gladstone ministry that followed upon enactment of the 1867 Reform Act, Bright was invited to become head of the India Office, but he declined to do so on pacifist grounds; he felt the position would associate him with military administration. He became instead the first Nonconformist to serve in a British Cabinet, serving as president of the Board of Trade. The queen, looking past her antipathy toward Bright, did not offend his Quaker sensibilities by requiring him to kneel as he became one of her Privy Councillors. During this time, Bright pushed for disestablishment of the Church of Ireland and for Gladstone's Irish Land Act of 1870, but he remained consistent in his opposition to state schools and spoke against Forster's Education Act of 1870.

Bright served in Gladstone's second Liberal ministry beginning in 1880 as Chancellor of the Duchy of Lancaster. However, he resigned in protest over British bombardment of Alexandria in the Egyptian Crisis of 1882. At the time of the Third Reform Act in 1884, which contained the general suffrage extension provisions Bright had long championed, Bright insisted upon a Redistribution Bill and called for an end to the veto power of the House of Lords. The former became the Distribution Act of 1885; the latter had to wait for the Parliament Act of 1911. Although he was a longtime supporter of tenant rights in Ireland, Bright denounced proposals for what amounted to nationalization of land in Ireland in 1884. He also opposed those who advocated Home Rule as a solution to the Irish Question, and in 1886 refused to support Gladstone's announcement of his conversion to Home Rule.

An enduring champion of reform, he embodied the laissez-faire doctrines of the

Manchester School of economic thought and the Dissenter tradition in nine-teenth-century political life, promoting middle-class political participation, free-trade radicalism, and Liberalism as the creed of a political coalition which to a considerable extent dominated Victorian Britain.

Overview of Biographical Sources

John Bright's public life was so thoroughly intertwined with the free-trade movement and career of his close friend and political ally, Richard Cobden, that it is difficult to separate these subjects when examining Bright's life. Biographies of Richard Cobden should not, therefore, be overlooked. Biographies of Bright appeared even while he was still living, and he has proven a valuable and important subject of study as well as the object of fresh interpretation throughout the twentieth century.

The early biographies are lengthy, much biased in favor of Bright, and contain long excerpts from his letters, diaries, and especially his speeches. William Robertson's two-volume work *Life and Times of the Rt. Hon. John Bright, M.P.* (1877) appeared during the Disraeli Ministry when Bright and the Liberals were out of office and the admission of a Quaker to the Cabinet and Privy Council seemed his crowning achievement. R. Barry O'Brien's study, *John Bright: A Monograph* (1911) first appeared after Bright's death, and evidences an Irish point of view. In 1911, the issues of Home Rule and reform of the House of Lords were particularly prominent, and emphasis is given in O'Brien's book to Bright as critic of Irish policy, opponent of the governing classes, and champion of free-trade and parliamentary reform.

The first really modern biography of Bright was George Macaulay Trevelyan's *The Life of John Bright* (1913). This Whiggish interpretation was for many years the standard work on Bright. Trevelyan is sympathetic to "the great agitator," relying extensively on Bright's speeches but also aided by his private letters and the recollections of contemporaries. Bright is portrayed as Cobden's faithful lieutenant in the Anti-Corn-Law League who emerged during the Crimean War as his equal. Trevelyan presents Bright as the more thorough-going radical of the two, one who went on to champion justice and further reform, without regard to party or personal popularity, to influence British statute books more than any other public man.

The mid-twentieth century witnessed a continuation of the interpretation of Bright as the quintessential radical of his time. Two book-length biographies appeared that did not substantially change the view of Bright's contribution to nineteenth-century British political life. J. Travis Mills's two-volume study, *John Bright and the Quakers* (1935), places Bright in the context of Dissenting tradition. The pervasiveness of Bright's Quaker upbringing and the extent to which it shaped his view of the world is evident in this work. Margaret Hirst's *John Bright: A Study* (1945), has the advantage of being brief and readable, but does not expand on the understanding of Bright which Trevelyan had earlier established. Asa Briggs's classic, *Victorian People* (1955), includes a chapter on Bright, "John Bright and the Creed of Reform," in which he calls the Quaker from Rochdale "the most important figure in the history of mid-Victorian radicalism." Briggs emphasizes free trade, retrenchment, changes in laws relating to the holding of land, suffrage extension and redistribution of seats according to population, and a cheaper and more pacifist foreign policy as the central lines in Bright's radical creed.

The 1960s and 1970s witnessed much renewed attention to Bright as radical reformer. Herman Ausubel offers a fresh interpretation of Bright in *John Bright: Victorian Reformer* (1966). Relying on manuscript sources far more than upon printed speeches, Ausubel portrays Bright as a figure who entered politics in the 1830s as an "angry young man"—who went on to become an "angry middle-aged man" and later an "angry old man." Ausubel's John Bright is at once the champion of middle-class radicalism and one of its most formidable critics, especially in what he perceived as its deference to the landed classes. Donald Read's *Cobden and Bright: A Victorian Political Partnership* (1968), is an excellent comparative study of these two well-known free-trade radicals. Drawing from a very wide reading of manuscript sources, Read suggests that Bright's radicalism has usually been overplayed by historians, that Bright's views were not always identical with Cobden's, and that in certain respects it was Cobden who was the more thoroughgoing democrat of the two. Bright's colonial views were taken up in James L. Sturgis's *John Bright and the Empire* (1969). The most recent biography of Bright is Keith Robbins's *John Bright* (1979). Robbins finds a consistency of principle in Bright's character, and notes that the Quaker traditions that he internalized and radical views that he developed in his youth remained the guiding principles of his life; thus, the ''Conservative vein'' detected by Bagehot in the 1870s was not inconsistent with his variety of radicalism. The great reform advocate of so many radical causes could also oppose factory legislation on free-trade libertarian grounds, Home Rule as an innovation which was inconsistent with cardinal constitutional principles, and British intervention in Egypt on pacifist and anti-imperialist lines. Robbins concludes that Bright remained his own man, consistent in principle and strong in character, regardless of consequences.

In the 1980s, Bright received attention in several shorter studies of free-trade radicalism. Paul Adelman devoted chapters to ''Radicalism and the Anti-Corn-Law League'' and to ''The Age of Bright'' in *Victorian Radicalism: The Middle-Class Experience 1830-1914* (1984). Adelman aptly observes that free trade was a broader and more exalted doctrine to Bright and middle-class Manchester radicals than a simple creed of economic liberalism; it had far reaching reform implications. Bright and the Manchester School consistently felt they were battling aristocratic privilege and monopoly. Three recent articles by Richard Spall have considered the privilege and monopoly which Bright and his League friends opposed: ''Landlordism and Liberty: Aristocratic Misrule and the Anti-Corn-Law League,'' *Journal of Libertarian Studies* (Summer 1987: 213-236); ''Free Trade, Foreign Relations, and the Anti-Corn-Law League,'' *International History Review* (August 1988: 405-432); and ''The Anti-Corn-Law League's Opposition to English Church Establishment,'' in *Journal of Church and State* (Winter 1990): 97-123. In each of these the prominent role of John Bright as opponent of aristocratic misrule, class legislation, and monopoly in all its variations is considered.

Evaluation of Principal Biographical Sources

Adelman, Paul. *Victorian Radicalism: The Middle Class Experience 1830-1914.* London: Longmans, 1984. (**A, G**) A recent, reliable, and fact-filled account of the range of middle-class radical activity in the nineteenth century, and a useful addition to the plentiful literature on working-class radicalism during the period. Some familiarity with the subject is required to keep from being overwhelmed. Two chapters are devoted to bright's political activities.

Ausubel, Herman. *John Bright: Victorian Reformer.* New York: Wiley, 1966.

(**A, G**) A superb, accurate, and readable interpretation utilizing Bright's private papers and letters to a great extent. Ausubel pointed out that despite being seen as influential by previous historians, Bright rarely derived a sense of success from his political efforts and was often overwhelmed by a sense of failure, discovering repeatedly throughout his career that he spoke only for himself or for an insignificant portion of the British public. Lacks a bibliography.

Briggs, Asa. "John Bright and the Creed of Reform." In *Victorian People: The Interplay of Men, Ideas and Events at the High Noon of Victoria's Reign.* Chicago: University of Chicago Press, 1955. (**A, G**) A wonderful collection of interpretative essays on major mid-Victorian figures and the interplay between personalities and events. Lacks documentation but is reliable.

Hirst, Francis W. *John Bright as Statesman and Orator.* London: Belvedere, 1911. (**G, Y**) A brief biographical sketch with excerpts from several speeches and letters illuminating Bright's views on nearly a score of issues.

Hirst, Margaret E. *John Bright: A Study.* London: Headley, 1945. (**G**) A brief and fairly readable introduction which relies on letters and diaries to examine Bright's life topically as politically active citizen, officeholder and statesman, opponent of aggressive foreign policy, and practicing member of the Society of Friends.

Mills, J. Travis. *John Bright and the Quakers.* 2 vols. London: Methuen, 1935. (**A, G**) Considered important for both the Quakers and Bright. Examines Bright in the context of his Quaker upbringing and religious principles, presenting him as a "political Quaker" who was much interested in temperance, religious equality, education, disestablishment, humanitarianism, and peace.

O'Brien, Richard Barry. *John Bright.* Boston: Houghton Mifflin, 1911. (**G**) A readable, popular biography with extensive quotations from Bright's speeches and letters, including some facsimiles.

Read, Donald. *Cobden and Bright: A Victorian Political Partnership.* London: Arnold, 1968. (**A, G**) A splendid comparative biography, solid in scholarship and quite readable. The best single volume on these two free-trade radicals, it argues that Bright has too often been portrayed as more of a radical than he really was and that Cobden was the more far-reaching in his application of anti-monopoly free-trade views.

Robbins, Keith. *John Bright*. London: Routledge and Kegan Paul, 1979. (**A, G**) The most recent biography, it combines synthesis and original scholarship. Robbins considers some of the apparent contradictions in Bright's radicalism and reconciles them in an interpretation of consistency of character. It is well organized, engagingly written, and utilizes widely scattered manuscript sources. The best single volume available; contains a good, albeit brief, bibliography.

Robertson, William. *Life and Times of the Rt. Hon. John Bright, M.P.* 2 vols. London: Cassell, 1877. (**A**) A rather dated contemporary biography published during Bright's lifetime.

Sturgis, James L. *John Bright and the Empire*. London: Athlone, 1969. Considers the imperial and colonial aspects of Bright's free-trade radicalism.

Trevelyan, G. M. *The Life of John Bright*. London: Constable, 1913. (**A, G**) A wonderfully written, engaging, and highly favorable biography by the great Whig historian. Drawn from speeches, letters, Bright's diaries, and recollections of contemporaries, the book is still readable and useful for its lengthy extracts from primary sources. It is chronological in organization, narrative in style, and yet still analytical in approach. Extensively indexed and in certain respects still a place where the serious student may begin.

Overview and Evaluation of Primary Sources

Manuscript sources pertaining to Bright are widely scattered and include mainly correspondence. Bright's letters are generally found in the papers of those to whom he often wrote, including Richard Cobden, George Wilson, and the Anti-Corn-Law League; these collections may be found in the Archives Department of the Manchester Central Reference Library. The Additional Manuscripts collections of the British Library and the West Sussex Record Office in Chichester contains an extensive collection of Bright's letters in the Cobden Papers. The Bright Papers in the Additional Manuscripts collection of the British Library and the John Bright Correspondence in the Archives Department of the Manchester Central Reference Library include many letters to Bright from his radical allies and others. The papers of Joseph Sturge and William Gladstone in the British Library also contain many of Bright's letters. Many family letters are contained in the John Bright Correspondence in the Ogden Manuscripts of the Archives Department of University College, London; other family correspondence makes up part of the archive of C and J Clark, Street, Somerset. (**A**)

Published sources pertaining to Bright abound. Bright kept a journal for fifty years, and in *The Diaries of John Bright* (1931. Reprint. New York: Kraus, 1971; **A**), edited by R. A. J. Walling, the selections cover the period from 1837 to 1887. A forward by Bright's son, Philip, is included. There is relatively little on the Anti-Corn-Law League era, presumably as Bright was most active at that time and did not record much. Bright's speeches before the House of Commons are found in *Hansard's Parliamentary Debates* (London: Hansard, 1803-; **A**), but several volumes of his speeches have been published elsewhere. A two-volume collection of speeches, *Speeches on Questions of Public Policy by John Bright, M.P.* (1869. Reprint. New York: Kraus, 1970; **A**), edited by James E. Thorold Rogers, includes addresses, in and out of Parliament, concerning the colonies, foreign relations, Ireland, and reform. Bright's *Speeches on the American Question* (1865. Reprint. New York: Kraus, 1970; **A**) were published at the conclusion of the American Civil War. After Bright's death, some of his letters on public issues were collected and published as *The Public Letters of the Rt. Hon. John Bright* (1895. Reprint. New York: Kraus, 1970; **A, G**), edited by H. J. Leech, in which the full range of his reform interests is displayed. The official organs of the Anti-Corn-Law League, *The Anti-Corn-Law Circular*, *The Anti-Bread-Tax Circular*, and *The League* (complete collections available at Columbia University and the University of Illinois at Urbana-Champaign) contain many accounts of Bright's activities and extended excerpts from his speeches in Parliament, before public gatherings, and upon the hustings. Many unsigned articles in these newspapers were probably written by Bright, but only a handful of these may be identified with certainty.

Fiction and Adaptations

There is a collection of *Punch* cartoons on Bright, who was the frequent object of the magazine's humor, in *The Rt. Hon. John Bright, M.P. From the Collection of 'Mr. Punch'* (London, 1878; **A, G**).

Museums, Historical Landmarks, Societies

Albert Square (Manchester). Contains a statue by W. Bruce Joy. Taken from a face mask made shortly after Bright's death.

Birmingham Art Gallery (Birmingham). Includes a statue from the Joy death mask.

Dunford House (Midhurst, West Essex). Cobden's home contains some of the library collection previously housed at Bright's home, One Ash, which no longer stands.

Free Trade Hall (Manchester). Here, on the very site of the Peterloo Massacre, was where the Anti-Corn-Law League erected several structures named Free Trade Hall. The current one is a restoration of the 1853 version which was heavily damaged by German bombing in World War II.

Friend's Meeting House Cemetery (Rochdale). Bright is buried in the cemetery of the meeting house in George Street.

Local History Library (Salford). Holds a collection of engravings featuring Bright.

National Liberal Club (London). Copy of a bust reported in the *Dictionary of National Biography* to have been in the private possession of J. Thomasson (Bolton), which is most likely that now housed in the conservatory of Dunford House.

National Portrait Gallery (London). Contains a statue by Hamo Thornycroft; unveiled by John Morley in 1894, and a painting by W. W. Ouless completed in 1879.

Ordsall Hall Museum (Peel Park, Salford). Bright was depicted prominently in J. R. Herbert's painting, "Mr. Cobden Addressing the League Council," which hung in League headquarters and was later donated to this museum. The painting was extensively damaged and had to be destroyed, but black and white photographs of it have been preserved at Ordsall Hall.

Palace of Westminster (London). Houses a statue after Joy's in Birmingham.

Portraits. There also portraits in private collections by Lowes Dickinson, Sir John Everett Millais, and W. B. Morris.

Reform Club (London). Houses a bust by G. W. Stephenson, and a portrait by Frank Holl.

Town Hall (Manchester). Holds a statue of Bright after Joy.

Other Sources

Longmate, Norman. *The Breadstealers: The Fight Against the Corn Laws, 1838-1846*. London: Temple Smith, 1984. (**G**) A recent popular account of Anti-Corn-Law League activity, not extensively documented but with a good bibliography and many fine illustrations. Longmate's focus is on the agitation of the League including its lecturers, election tactics, pre-scripted conferences, and establishment of local associations, but he does not consider the wider political context in which Bright and the Anti-Corn-Law Leaguers operated.

McCord, Norman. *The Anti-Corn-Law League, 1838-1846*. London: Allen and Unwin, 1953. (**A, G**) The standard work on League activity and organization, thorough and reliable in its scholarship. Uses the League's—and its most prominent members'—publications and papers. Emphasizes the central roles of Richard

Cobden, John Bright, and George Wilson in the formulation of the League's methods of proselytization and propaganda, its modes of fund-raising, and its electoral and parliamentary tactics.

Richard Francis Spall, Jr.
Ohio Wesleyan University

Benjamin Britten
1913-1976

Chronology

Born Edward Benjamin Britten in Lowestoft, Suffolk, England on November 22, 1913, son of Robert Victor Britten, a dentist, and Edith Rhoda, an amateur soprano and pianist; *1918* receives informal piano lessons from his mother and produces his first compositions; *1923* begins viola lessons with Audrey Alston; studies at South Lodge, a preparatory school; *1924* attends the Norwich Festival, where his music attracts the attention of composer Frank Bridge, who agrees to take him as a private student, and whose influence on Britten's early development is profound; *1927* again attends the Norwich Festival; *1928* attends the Gresham School in Holt, Norfolk, where he is adept at mathematics, the sciences, cricket, and tennis; *1930* receives a scholarship to the Royal College of Music, where he studies piano with Harold Samuel and Arthur Benjamin and composition with John Ireland and Frank Bridge; *1932* awarded the Cobbett Prize for his *Phantasy in F minor*; makes his compositional debut in London at the Macnaghten-Lemare concerts, playing three two-part songs for women's voices, based on texts by Walter de la Mare, and the *Phantasy in F minor;* 1933 performs his first published piece, *Sinfonietta*, at the Macnaughten-Lemare concerts; *1934* meets tenor Peter Pears during BBC Singers' rehearsal for his choral variations, *A Boy Was Born*; *1934* learns of the music of Austrian composer Alban Berg when he hears a performance of *Wozzeck;* his *Phantasy Quartet for Oboe and Strings* represents England at the festival of the International Society for Contemporary Music at Florence; *1935-1939* works at the Government Post Office Film Unit writing music for plays and documentary films; works with W. H. Auden, the script writer for the plays; *1936* his *Suite for Violin and Piano* is performed at the International Society for Contemporary Music in Barcelona; *Our Hunting Fathers* is performed at the Norfolk and Norwich Festivals; *1937 Variations on a Theme of Frank Bridge* is performed at the Salzburg Festival; introduced to Peter Pears, with whom he forms a lifelong relationship; acquires the Old Mill, Snape, which later becomes the site of the Aldeburgh festivals; *1938* begins recital partnership with Peter Pears, writing music for, and accompanying, Pears's vocal performances; *1939* writes *Violin Concerto*; dissatisfied with the political climate in England, relocates to New York City; *1940* works with Auden on an opera entitled *Paul Bunyan*; gives recitals with Pears; *1941* Frank Bridge dies; *Paul Bunyan* is performed at Columbia University; receives the Library of Congress Medal for Services to Chamber Music; *1942* receives a commission from the Koussevitsky Foundation for an opera, *Peter Grimes,* the first opera to be commissioned by the new foundation; returns to England with Pears, and both register as conscientious objectors and are exempted from military service; continues composing and giving wartime recitals with Pears under the auspices of the Council for the Encouragement of Music and the Arts as a condition of their exemption from military service; *1945 Peter Grimes* staged at Sadler's Wells Theater, London, and all performances are sold out; visits Bergen-Belsen and other concentration camps while serving as piano accompanist to American violinist and conductor Yehudi Menuhin; *1946* composes *The Young Person's Guide to the Orchestra*; first screening of *Instruments of the Orchestra,* a film designed to accompany the variations; composes *The Rape of Lucretia*; *1947* with Eric Crozier and John Piper, forms the English Opera Group to present experimental chamber operas; conducts the first performance of *Albert Herring* with the English Opera Group at Glyndebourne; moves to Crag House in Aldeburgh with Pears; *1948* guarantees the money necessary to establish the Aldeburgh Festival; conducts the first performance of *The Beggar's Opera* at the Arts Theatre, Cambridge; the first Aldeburgh Festival of Music and the Arts is held; *1949 The Little Sweep* is produced; *1951* conducts the first performance of *Billy Budd* at the Royal Opera House, Covent Garden; *1952* Imogen Holst, who will become his collaborator and biographer, joins Britten as his music assistant; *Billy Budd* is produced by NBC in the United States, the first television production of a Britten opera; *1953* named a Companion of Honour in the Coronation Honours list; the opera, *Gloriana* is first performed at Covent Garden as part of the celebration for the Coronation of Queen Elizabeth II; *1954* conducts the first performance of *The Turn of the Screw* with the English Opera Group at Teatro la Fenice in Venice; *1955* departs with Pears on a world tour, visiting Austria, Yugoslavia, Turkey, Singapore, Indonesia, Japan, Macau, Hong Kong, Thailand, India and Sri Lanka; *1956* returns to England; *1957* conducts the first performance of *The Prince of the Pagodas* at Covent Garden; becomes an honorary member of the American Academy of Arts and Letters and of the National Institute of Arts and Letters in New York; *1958* with Imogen Holst, publishes *The Story of Music*; directs the first performance of *Noye's Fludde* in Orford Church; *1962* conducts the first performance of the *War Requiem* for the festival of consecration of the restored St. Michael's Cathedral at Conventry; receives the Honorary Freedom of the Borough of Aldeburgh medal; *1963* participates in the Festival of British Music in the U.S.S.R.; for his fiftieth birthday, *Gloriana* is performed at the Royal Festival Hall; a new production of *Peter Grimes* and a collection of "tributes" to Britten from colleagues is published by Faber and Faber; *1964* the *Cello Symphony* performed in Moscow; becomes the first recipient of the Aspen Award for contributions to the advancement of the humanities; awarded the Royal Philharmonic Society Gold Medal after traveling to the U.S.S.R. on tour with the English Opera Group; *1965* visits India; awarded the Order of Merit; *1965-1972* tours and gives recitals throughout Europe, Scandinavia, and North America; *1972* gives the last Britten-Pears recital; increasing heart trouble curtails his activities; *1973 Death in Venice* is his final composition; it is first performed on June 16 at Bedford, Snape Maltings; undergoes partially successful open heart surgery, but never fully recovers; *1976* dies on December 4 at Red House, Aldeburgh, and is buried at the Aldeburgh parish church.

Activities of Historical Significance

Much of Benjamin Britten's music, whether for solo voice, instrumental groups, or the stage, may be described as music written for chamber groups. He rarely used the larger performing bodies normally associated with orchestral or operatic genres. Britten preferred smaller chamber groups, the members of which combined to produce a transparent, almost sparse, texture. These reduced and concentrated forces were mirrored by an equal concentration of the musical material. Melodic lines and musical structures were constructed from small cells or motives that were combined and stacked to produce the result desired by the composer. The economy of musical materials and performing means resulted in music that was stylistically compact and economical.

Perhaps the most characteristic of all Britten's pieces are those written for the voice. He explored all vocal mediums, including solo voices, choral groupings, and operatic textures. It is in his songs and operas that his melodic and poetic gifts are most apparent. He set more than one hundred songs, a number that made him one of the most prolific composers for the solo voice in the twentieth century. Much of this output was a result of his relationship with the tenor Peter Pears, whom he accompanied during numerous recital tours. These settings were often conceived as cycles consisting of seven or nine pieces; these cycles were not meant to be broken into component parts, a fact that now severely limits performance of the songs in recital. The songs are also made difficult by Britten's conception of the settings in terms of particular vocal timbres and abilities. Based on his experience with Pears, he assumed a certain level of literary sensibility on the part of the performer, making these songs especially difficult for many performers.

Britten set to music a wide range of texts chosen from both English and foreign poets. A common element in his choices, however, is that the text offers some significant message. Britten used his songs to convey feelings about social and political issues, as well as to illuminate themes concerning the human community. The first cycle, which was heavily influenced by the works of W. H. Auden, was *Our Hunting Fathers* (1939), in which the poet addressed man's relations with the animal world.

Britten's operas have been considered his most significant contribution to the history of twentieth century music. These operas were the first native English operas produced in several generations and opened the way for such composers as Michael Tippet and Ralph Vaughan Williams, establishing a significant twentieth-century English school of opera. The operas became Britten's favorite vehicle for the expression of his ideology. They deal with the themes of the betrayal of innocence, and with parodies of cruelty and compassion. A number of the pieces center on the theme of alienation, often providing an outlet for Britten's outrage against social taboos.

As in his instrumental works, Britten used limited resources in his operas, often writing for no more than a chamber group of musicians and the number of soloists absolutely essential to the plot. In addition to the practical and economic reasons for such restrictions, the operas reflect Britten's fundamental philosophy of producing chamber works in every medium. Though the number of performers are small enough to categorize the operas as chamber, they are full-length, lasting as long as the larger operas of the late nineteenth century.

Britten's instrumental music was limited to the beginning and end of his career and is generally considered of secondary importance to his dramatic and vocal works. In his instrumental music, Britten's knowledge and understanding of instruments was thorough and practical. Each of the solo and duet pieces, as well as his string quartets, is carefully constructed to highlight each player's talents. Players are treated as individuals, whether in a chamber group or in an orchestra, creating a texture that is transparent and clear. The earlier instrumental works, with the exception of the cello sonata, are set either as variations or suites.

Later in his career Britten turned to more traditional genres, such as the string quartet. Much of his instrumental music exhibits the same characteristics as the vocal music: they were written with particular performers in mind. Perhaps the most notable of these associations was with the cellist Mstislav Rostropovich, for whom he wrote a cello sonata, three cello suites, and a cello symphony. Finally, a number of his instrumental works are based on literary models. Among these are *The Young Apollo* (1939), *Sinfonia da Requiem* (1940), *Lachrymae* (1950), and *Six Metamorphoses after Ovid* (1951).

Among the most famous of Britten's works are those written for children and amateurs. He was interested in music that would give pleasure to nonprofessional musicians, no matter what age, and would, at the same time, challenge and expand their abilities. Among these are several dramatic works, including *St. Nicolas* (1948), in which Britten used both professional and amateur forces in a complementary manner that exploited the strengths of each group. In *The Little Sweep* (1949), children are given the operatic roles, and the adults in the audience function as the opera chorus. The opera is presented after the staging of a play in which the adults and the children collaborate on the musical drama to follow. The most often performed work from this category is the piece now commonly known as *The Young Person's Guide to the Orchestra*. Written originally to accompany a film on the instruments of the orchestra, the piece is now performed both as an independent concert work and as a teaching aid to accustom the non-musician to the various sounds produced by the instrumental families of the orchestra.

Though not the first notable twentieth-century British composer, Britten was the first to establish a reputation outside his native homeland. His refusal to be completely nationalistic through his use of foreign texts and subjects set him apart from the insular attitude that often marked British music of the period. The driving force of the last half of his life, the Aldeburgh Festival, became the impetus for the composition of much of his music, and a forum for the production of that music as soon as it was written.

Overview of Biographical Sources

Britten's life, both private and professional, was well-documented through letters, reviews, and analytical/biographical articles and monographs. His biographies are all similar accounts of his life and works, differing only in the amount of personal reminiscence or the technical level of the analytical overview of his compositions. There are three sources in which extensive bibliographies are to be found: the article on Britten in *The New Grove Dictionary of Music and Musicians* (New York: Macmillan, 1980); *A Britten Source Book* (Aldeburgh: The Britten-Pears Foundation, 1987), edited by John Evans, Philip Reed and Paul Wilson; and *Benjamin Britten: A Commentary on his Works from a Group of Specialists* (London: Rockliff, 1952), edited by Donald Mitchell and Hans Keller. The earliest bibliography is in the *Commentary* and is reasonably complete for its relatively early date. The one included in the *Grove* article is divided into subjects and places heavy emphasis on periodical articles, particularly reviews of new works. In addition to biographical details, there is discussion of Britten's stylistic development and of the place of the composer's works in his various style periods. The article in the *Source Book* is the most recent and complete and includes broadcasts and writings about Britten from the days of the earliest reviews, Britten's prose writings, articles, theses, books, record-jacket notes, and broadcasts involving his works. The items are listed in chronological order, allowing the reader ready access to materials from any stage of Britten's career.

The two most common types of Britten biographies are those combining accounts of his life and works, and those which are personal accounts of friendships and working relationships. In the more objective category, Peter Evans's *The Music of Benjamin Britten* (1979), focuses on Britten's personal and professional development from 1952, the year of a symposium devoted to the music of Britten and documented by Mitchell. This biography was written for the well-informed amateur as well as for the music student wishing further information on Britten's music. The work is brief, but positive, highlighting social, political, and personal influences on his works. Also a must in any biographical survey is Eric Walter White's *Benjamin Britten: His Life and Operas* (1948). The operas are considered in light of his life; all discussions include performance histories and analyses. These analyses are musicological rather than theoretical, tending at times toward the superficial.

The personal reminiscences are of limited value to the scholar, but they provide interesting windows into the composer's personality, even though they are subjective and often emotionally colored. Among the more interesting of these volumes is that of Alan Blyth, *Remembering Britten* (1981). In many cases other individuals are identified and quotes concerning Britten are included in the synopsis. Anthony Gishford's *A Tribute to Benjamin Britten on his Fiftieth Birthday* (1963), consists of contributions by persons closely associated with Britten. The entries are unique; they may be as far removed as a portion of an unfinished novel by E. M. Forster, or as personal as a remembrance of a particular event. A third important compilation is Donald Mitchell's *Britten and Auden in the 30s: the Year 1936* (1981), which emphasizes the working relationship of Britten and Auden. The volume is a reprint of Mitchell's Eliot lecture of 1979, a series based on Britten's diaries and letters from 1928-1938 in which Mitchell explores the entire length of their working relationship, including the difficulties between the two at the end of their time together.

Among the biographies written by friends is Ronald Duncan's *Working with Britten: A Personal Memoir* (1981). As Britten's librettist and friend, Duncan gives opinions and judgments only. He makes no claims to musical expertise or analytical competence and characterizes his observations as biography colored by gossip. He reveals what it was like to have worked with Britten and the composition process from the poet's point of view. His remarks give valuable insight into the composer's personality, as far as memory can be trusted.

There are also a number of biographies intended for a general audience and which contain no analysis of Britten's works. Some are more valuable than others for the depth of information they impart. Among the more reliable of these are Michael Kennedy, *Britten* (Master Musician's Series; London: J. M. Dent, 1981); Imogen Holst, *Britten* (London: Faber and Faber, 1966); and Michael Hurd, *Benjamin Britten* (Biographies of Great Musicians; London: Novello, 1966). All are brief and border on the superficial and popular. They are of little use to the music specialist, though they are informative for the general reader.

Evaluation of Principal Biographical Sources

Blyth, Alan. *Remembering Britten.* London: Hutchinson, 1981. (**G**) Identifies the important figures in Britten's life and career, sometimes with reminiscences by the people themselves. Included are Peter Pears, Imogen Holst, Sir Michael Tippet, Rosamond Strode, and Mstislav Rostropovich.

Carpenter, Humphrey. *Benjamin Britten: A Biography.* New York: Scribner, 1993. Having access to papers from the estate of Britten enabled Carpenter to write a comprehensive, probing and objective study that focuses on Britten's homosexuality and how it influenced his work.

Duncan, Ronald. *Working with Britten: A Personal Memoir.* Devon, United Kingdom: Rebel Press, 1981. (**G**) A personal recollection by one of Britten's librettists. Includes anecdotal reminiscences, as well as insight into Britten's character and attitudes. The appendix includes a brief chronology.

Evans, Peter. *The Music of Benjamin Britten.* Minneapolis: University of Minnesota Press, 1979. (**A, G**) The works are covered chronologically and generically. Evans gives emphasis to the works written after 1952, discusses the reception of the first operas, and evaluates scholarly works about the composer. The biography is descriptive and brief but positive, listing influences, both social and political, and people who were important in his life.

Holst, Imogen. *Britten.* London: Faber and Faber, 1966. (**G**) Though one of the persons most closely connected with Britten, Holst has produced a book that is for the general reader. Her tone is reminiscent, relating incidents and biographical facts from a personal perspective.

Hurd, Michael. *Benjamin Britten.* Biographies of Great Musicians. London: Novello, 1966. (**G**) Brief and superficial; outlines the composer's life with little attention to the individual works.

Kendall, Alan. *Benjamin Britten.* London: Macmillan, 1973. (**G**) An iconographical account of Britten's life, complete with a catalogue of works and some discussion of Britten's political and social theories.

Kennedy, Michael. *Britten.* Master Musician Series. London: J. M. Dent, 1981.

(**G**) A superficial biography intended for the general reader with an interest in the composer. The works are listed chronologically and are briefly examined.

Mitchell, Donald, and Hans Keller. *Benjamin Britten: A Commentary on his Works from a Group of Specialists.* London: Rockliff, 1952. (**A, G**) A collection of articles dealing with various aspects of Britten's life and career. The list of works and the bibliography were the most complete in print at that time and form a valuable resource for earlier sources, many of which were omitted from later works.

White, Eric Walter. *Benjamin Britten: A Sketch of his Life and Works.* New York: Boosey and Hawkes, 1948. (**G**) Focuses on the biographical details, though there is some discussion of works. The approach is popular in tone, intended for the general reader. It has become somewhat obsolete in light of later publications.

Young, Percy M. *Britten.* London: Ernest Benn, 1966. (**G**) This general biography includes only the most basic of descriptive analysis. There is little or no documentation of facts and no bibliography is included. Aimed at the general and young adult reader.

Overview and Evaluation of Primary Sources

Britten letters and memorabilia are now housed in the Britten-Pears Library in Aldeburgh, which includes a working collection of books and music assembled by Benjamin Britten and Peter Pears during their professional lives. There is also a large collection of letters, photographs, and printed programs, as well as a sound and video archive. Britten's manuscripts are also housed here, including those owned by the British library and on permanent loan to the Aldeburgh collection. The library is now part of the Britten-Pears Foundation. Britten's letters are found scattered throughout numerous biographies and articles on his works. An article that centers on his correspondence is M. Boyd, "Benjamin Britten and Grace Williams: Chronicle of a Friendship," *Welsh Music* 6, 6 (1980; **A, G**). Britten's letters and portions of his diaries have been edited by Donald Mitchell, *Letters from a Life: The Selected Letters and Diaries of Benjamin Britten, 1913-1976* (2 vols.

Berkeley: University of California Press, 1991; **A, G**). Mitchell also includes a number of photographs from the Britten-Pears Library.

There are a number of publications that give insight into Britten's professional attitudes and opinions, including the reviews, record-jacket notes, and articles written by him or in collaboration with Peter Pears. A complete list is given in the *Britten Source Book*. The program books from the Aldeburgh Festival offer material on the works of Britten and other contemporary composers, and the articles contained in them have extensive materials on the pieces that were performed and on the festival itself, including retrospectives on past festivals. These are a valuable source of contemporary commentary on Britten's compositions and are available at the Britten-Pears Library.

Britten's books and articles should be consulted by anyone studying his life. They include "An English Composer Sees America," *Tempo I* (April 1940; **A, G**); "On Behalf of Gustav Mahler," *Tempo II* (February 1942; **A, G**); *The Story of Music*, with Imogen Holst (London: Rathbone Books, 1958; **G, Y**); "On Realizing the Continuo in Purcell's Songs," in *Henry Purcell: 1659-1695*, edited by Imogen Holst (London: Oxford University Press, 1959; **A**); "On Receiving the First Aspen Award," (London: Faber & Faber, 1964; **G**); and "Frank Bridge (1879-1941), *Faber Music News* (Autumn 1966; **G**).

Britten also gave numerous speeches, some of which were preserved and published. Most are in acceptance of an award or honor, and center on his feelings about the occasion. The most important of these concerns the first Aspen Award in 1964. This speech appeared first in *Saturday Review* (August 22, 1964), and was later reprinted by Faber Music in London that same year.

Interviews with Britten also provide an important source of information on his life and works. They range from those given in the early stage of his career to one that appeared posthumously in the *Britten Companion* in 1984. These cover a wide range of topics, including Britten's personal outlook, his thoughts on contemporary composers, and his expectations for the future of Aldeburgh. The following are the most comprehensive: "Interview," *Tempo I* (February 1944; **A, G**); "Profile: Benjamin Britten," *Observer* (October 27, 1946; **A, G**); "An Interview," *The London Magazine* 3 (October 1963; **A, G**); M. Schafer, *British Composers in Interview* (London: Faber and Faber, 1962; **A, G**); "Benjamin Britten Talks to Edmund Tracey," *Sadler's Wells Magazine* (Autumn 1966; **A, G**); *Contemporary Composers on Contemporary Music* (New York: Holt, Rinehart & Winston, 1967;

A, G), edited by E. Schwartz and B. Childs; "Communicator, an Interview with England's Best-known Composers," *Opera News* 31, 16 (1967; **A, G**); "Interview with E. Forbes," *Opera News* 31, 16 (February 11, 1967; **A, G**); "Aldeburgh and the Future (Interview with H. Rosenthal)," *Opera* 18 (Autumn 1967; **A, G**); "An Interview with R. Mercer," *Opera Canada* 9, 4 (December 1967; **A, G**); "No Ivory Tower: Benjamin Britten Talks to *Opera News*," *Opera News* 33, 23 (April 1969; **A, G**); and "Mapreading: Benjamin Britten in Conversation with Donald Mitchell," in *The Britten Companion* (London: Faber, 1984; **A, G**), edited by Christopher Palmer.

The Britten Source Book, edited by John Evans, Philip Reed, and Paul Wilson (Aldeburgh: The Britten-Pears Foundation, 1987; **A**), was commissioned by the Britten-Pears Foundation to make public materials and facts previously available only in scattered form or known only to those with access to the composer's private papers and compositional manuscripts. The volume includes a chronology of his life and works; a catalogue raisonné of the incidental music, a list of the recorded repertoire, and a select bibliography. There is a detailed list of juvenilia that is unavailable elsewhere, an up-to-date survey of music for film, theater, and radio, and an extensive bibliography that includes writings and broadcasts relating to Britten from the earliest years to the date of publication. The entries include Britten's prose writings, articles, theses, books, record-jacket notes, and broadcasts. The items are listed in chronological order. The scores for Britten's records have been published by Boosey and Hawkes, Faber Music, and Oxford University Press, all listed in *Benjamin Britten: A Complete Catalogue of His Published Works* (London: Boosey and Hawkes, 1973; **A, G**).

Other Sources

Brett, Philip. *Benjamin Britten: Peter Grimes.* Cambridge Opera Handbooks. Cambridge: Cambridge University Press, 1983. One of a series of books detailing the conception of an opera and the various stylistic aspects of the music. The discussion is detailed and technical, aimed at the more informed musician or listener.

Gishford, Anthony. *A Tribute to Benjamin Britten on his Fiftieth Birthday.*

London: Faber and Faber, 1963. Gishford collected reminiscences from people important in Britten's life. There are thoughts on *The Turn of the Screw* by Auden, and an unfinished novel by E. M. Forster, as well as a variety of that articles deal directly with Britten.

Howard, Patricia. *Benjamin Britten: The Turn of the Screw.* Cambridge Opera Handbooks. Cambridge: Cambridge University Press, 1985. Howard presents a complete overview of the opera, including analyses of the music and libretto, as well as a plot synopsis, notes on the original performance and staging, and performance history and discography.

Mitchell, Donald. *Benjamin Britten: A Death in Venice.* Cambridge Opera Handbooks. Cambridge: Cambridge University Press, 1987. Follows the same format as the others in the series, covering all aspects of the opera's music and production.

Palmer, Christopher, ed. *The Britten Companion.* Cambridge: Cambridge University Press, 1984. A series of articles by those who knew Britten best (Donald Mitchell, Imogen Holst, Rosamund Strode, John Culshaw, Christopher Palmer, Wilfred Mellers, and Peter Pears) that deal with various aspects of Britten's life and career.

White, Eric Walter. *Benjamin Britten: His Life and Operas.* 2d ed. Berkeley: University of California Press, 1983. Provides biographical data and analyses of the operas and their performance histories. The analysis is musicological rather than theoretical; at times it seems a bit descriptive and superficial. There is a chronological list of publications and information on the first performances of each work. In the case of vocal music this includes the names of the first performers.

Karen M. Bryan
Georgia State University

Pieter Bruegel the Elder
c.1525/1530-1569

Chronology

Born Pieter Bruegel some time between 1525 and 1530 in or near Breda, northern Brabant, in the Provinces of the Netherlands; *1545?-1550* may have been apprenticed to celebrated painter Pieter Coecke van Aelst, who died in Brussels in 1550; *1550-1551* works in the shop of Claude Dorizi in Mechelen with the painter Pieter Baltens on a now lost altarpiece for the Cathedral of Saint Rombouts; *1551* becomes a free master and a member of the Guild of Saint Luke, the Artists' Guild in Antwerp; possibly works with Hieronymus Cock, an Antwerp engraver and publisher of prints, whose shop, The Four Winds, opened about 1550; *1551-1552* travels to Italy through France; *1552 or 1553* reaches southern Italy; visits Reggio di Calabria, Messina, Naples, and Palermo, where he probably sees the fresco of the *Triumph of Death*; *1553* visits Rome; collaborates with miniaturist Giulio Clovio, possibly painting landscape backgrounds for Clovio's figures; completes *Landscape with Christ Appearing to the Apostles at the Sea of Tiberias*, his earliest known (signed and dated) painting; *1553 or 1554* returns to Antwerp through the Alps, drawing mountain landscapes along the way; *1555-1556* works on "Large Landscape Series" of twelve prints and the *Great Alpine Landscape*, which Cock has engraved for publication; *1556-1562* executes additional landscapes; for Cock's engravers, produces didactic, satirical, or religious figure compositions, many of which, such as *Big Fish Eat Little Fish* (1556), are in the style of Dutch painter Hieronymus Bosch; *1556* begins two series: *Seven Deadly Sins*, and *Seven Cardinal Virtues*, which are printed between 1557 and 1560; *1557* paints *Landscape with the Parable of the Sower*; *1557-1558?* paints two versions of *Landscape with the Fall of Icarus*; *1559* paints *The Netherlandish Proverbs* and *The Fight Between Carnival and Lent*; changes the spelling of his name from Brueghel to Bruegel; *1560* paints *Children's Games*; friends and patrons in Antwerp who may have influenced Bruegel's art likely include the geographer and humanist Abraham Ortelius, Jan Cornelisz Vermeyen, the German merchant Hans Franckert, and Niclaes Jonghelinck, who once owned sixteen paintings by Bruegel;

possible contacts with the moral and religious ideas of a circle of Erasmian Catholics who sought to practice humility and toleration in an age of intolerance and violence; *1562* completes at least three large apocalyptic works in the style of Bosch: *The Dulle Griet,* also known as *Mad Meg, The Fall of the Rebel Angels,* and *The Triumph of Death,* as well as *Two Monkeys;* probably paints *The Suicide of Saul; 1562-1563?* visits Amsterdam and draws the city's walls and towers; *1563* settles in Brussels, where he remains until his death; marries Mayken, daughter of celebrated painter Pieter Coecke van Aelst and his wife, the watercolorist Mayken Verhulst Bessemers; patronized by Cardinal Antoine Perrenot de Granvelle, president of the Netherlands Council of State, who amasses a fine collection of his paintings, including *Landscape with the Flight into Egypt* (1563); paints two versions of *Tower of Babel; 1564* birth of his son, Pieter; paints *The Procession to Calvary, The Adoration of the Kings,* and *The Death of the Virgin; 1565* receives from Niclaes Jonghelinck, a commission for a series based on the months of the year, five paintings of which survive: *The Hunters in the Snow, The Gloomy Day, Haymaking, The Corn Harvest,* and *The Return of the Herd;* paints *Winter Landscape with Skaters and a Bird-Trap, Christ and the Woman Taken in Adultery,* and, possibly, *The Massacre of the Innocents; 1566* paints *The Census at Bethlehem, The Sermon of Saint John the Baptist,* and *The Wedding Dance in the Open Air; 1567* mentioned in author Ludovico Guicciardini's *Descrittione;* paints *The Adoration of the Kings in the Snow, The Conversion of Saul, The Wedding Banquet, The Peasant Dance* (also known as *The Kermess*), and *The Land of Cockaigne; 1568* son Jan is born; paints *Head of an Old Peasant Woman, The Peasant and the Bird Nester, The Cripples, The Misanthrope, The Parable of the Blind,* and *Landscape with the Magpie on the Gallows; 1569* paints *The Storm at Sea;* works on paintings commissioned by the Brussels City Council to commemorate the digging of the Willebroeck Canal linking Brussels with Antwerp; *1569* dies on September 5th or 9th in Brussels and is buried in Notre Dame de la Chapelle; left two sons who became painters in their father's tradition, Pieter Brueghel the Younger (1564-1638), known as "Hell Brueghel", and Jan Brueghel the Elder (1568-1625), nicknamed "Velvet Brueghel," both of whom were raised and probably trained as painters by their grandmother, Mayeken Verhulst Bessemers.

Activities of Historical Significance

Pieter Bruegel the Elder ranks today as the greatest Netherlandish painter of the sixteenth century, and he is usually placed in the company of such undisputed masters as Jan van Eyck, Peter Paul Rubens, and Rembrandt van Rijn. His total body of work includes more than 150 drawings, numerous prints done after his original work, and an extensive body of paintings, of which some forty-five authenticated pieces survive. Precise knowledge of Bruegel's professional life is lacking, but many scholars believe that his paintings were commissioned by rich patrons, cosmopolitan men who appreciated both his artistic talents and his moral vision. The frequently used sobriquet of "Peasant Bruegel" is accordingly misleading. Instead, Bruegel was an artist of great insight, sophisticated thought, and ethical complexity. And, his work, like that of any creative genius, cannot be easily sorted into tidy categories or characterized with facile generalizations.

Bruegel is probably renowned as much for his depictions of peasant weddings and fêtes as for his landscapes with peasants at work or resting from their labors. But the very popularity of these widely-reproduced paintings, coupled with the notion of Bruegel as a peasant painter of peasants, has resulted in a public conception of his work that is both one-sided, and impoverished. For, in addition to his peasant paintings, Bruegel executed epic landscapes, compelling biblical paintings, occasional mythological scenes such as *Landscape with the Fall of Icarus* (c.1557-1558?), illustrations of Netherlandish proverbs and folk sayings, allegorical pictures in the nightmarish tradition of Hieronymus Bosch, and miscellaneous images such as *The Fight Between Carnival and Lent* (1559) or the so-called ''naer het leven'' (from life) drawings, which fascinate even as they defy classification. These latter drawings include studies of peasants and the daily lives of common people as well as the popular *The Painter and the Connoisseur* (1565), which may be a self-portrait. Even if not, it is certainly a droll meditation on the uneasy relationship between artist and patron.

Examination of Bruegel's images of peasant life dispels any notion that he painted unsophisticated genre scenes. For example, the five paintings that he completed during 1565, which include *The Hunters in the Snow*, *The Corn Harvesters*, and *Haymaking*, derive from a medieval tradition and portray not only human's dependence on the endlessly repeated cycles of nature but also the varying degrees of harmony that may exist between the natural world and men and women engaged in physical labor. The three often-admired female figures in *Haymaking* suggest a sort of Golden Mean, the simple joy that results from a balance of hard work and deserved rest. In contrast, the crudely sleeping peasants in *The Corn Harvest* represent the consequences of overly hard work and overindulgence in food and drink. Similarly, the paintings of peasant weddings and festivals seem initially to celebrate the occasional pleasures of peasant life, but a closer look reveals admonitions against excess of any sort, whether of food, drink, anger, or lust. The Vienna *Peasant Dance* (1567 or 1568?), for example, depicts peasants dancing and drinking, kissing and fighting, their backs to a distant church and seemingly oblivious of an image of the Virgin Mary. Wich such paintings and drawings, as indeed with all of his work, Bruegel demonstrates his empathic understanding of the fallen human condition and his moral vision, two qualities that ensure his continuing appeal.

In more than half of his known paintings, Bruegel used familiar subjects from both the Old and New Testaments, but he treated them with an originality that raises them above their overtly didactic character. Of the Old Testament scenes, the most compelling are the two extant versions of the *Tower of Babel* (1563 and c. 1564), set, like all of Bruegel's biblical paintings, amidst the rich secular life of the sixteenth-century Netherlands. Although meditations on the theme of pride and the futility and transitory nature of human endeavor are hardly original, Bruegel's depiction of the Tower elevates it from a conventional symbol into an image in which both the overall conception and the details illustrate rather than merely represent the moral. By setting this massive but useless tower in the immediate foreground of the painting, Bruegel reduces to insignificance man and the world made by men, the nearby village and the harbor, and indeed, all of nature. At the same time, the hundreds of ant-like figures at work on the tower and the extraordinary details of contemporary building techniques suggest not only the magnitude of human self-delusion but also a gross misuse of human talents and energies.

Among the incidents from the life of Christ painted by Bruegel are *The Procession to Calvary* (1564) and *The Census at Bethlehem* (1566). Like *The Tower of Babel*, both are set in the Netherlands of Bruegel's day, and the biblical scenes are all but obscured by anecdotal details depicting types of human behavior. In *The Procession to Calvary*, which incidentally depicts the horrifyingly festive character of contemporary executions, soldiers drag Simon of Cyrene from a curious but largely indifferent crowd of onlookers to carry the cross as his wife attempts to pull him back. In *The Census at Bethlehem*, Mary and Joseph arrive in a wintry village, and, amidst details redolent of peasant life, they approach an inn before which a crowd of people waits to pay their taxes. By representing traditional biblical scenes in contemporary situations, Bruegel reflects on the fate of Christianity, suggesting that although the Christian message is ever present, humankind is too caught up in the minutiae of daily life to even perceive it, let alone grasp its meaning.

Bruegel earned his reputation as a second Bosch with such apocalyptic paintings as *The Fall of the Rebel Angels* (1562), *Dulle Griet* (c.1562), and *The Triumph of Death* (c.1562) and with moralistic drawings made into popular prints. Although the paintings display the unmistakable influence of Bosch, Bruegel's style was hardly imitative of his predecessor's, and paintings such as *The Triumph of Death* display the fiendish inventiveness of Bruegel's imagination. In this vast panorama of death and destruction, no cruelty ever devised by man appears to have been omitted, and the work may actually allude, as some scholars suggest, to the Spanish exploitation of the Netherlands in the sixteenth century. Bruegel's allegorical compositions include two series, *The Seven Deadly Sins* (1557-1558) and *The Seven Cardinal Virtues* (1559-1560), both of which catalog human foibles in the tradition of philosophers Desiderius Erasmus and Sebastian Brant. Likewise, in drawings such as *Big Fish Eat Little Fish* (1556), *Elck* (Everyman) (c. 1558), and *The Alchemist* (1558), in which a chemist neglects his family while expending his energy and wealth on the search for instant riches, human folly results from the absence of self-knowledge and the ease with which humankind is misled by greed. Paintings by Bruegel that illustrate contemporary proverbs and folk wisdom include both those in which the intent is obvious, such as *The Netherlandish Proverbs* (1559), *The Land of Cockaigne* (1567), or *The Parable of the Blind* (1568), and those in which the allusion is less overt, such as *Winter Landscape with Skaters and a Bird Trap* (1565) or *The Landscape with the Magpie on the Gallows* (1568). In this last picture, ironically one of Bruegel's loveliest landscapes and a painting specifically bequeathed to his widow, the magpies symbolize gossips, according to Carel van Mander, Bruegel's first biographer, and the gallows may represent the consequences of malicious and thoughtless gossip. *The Netherlandish Proverbs* is a panel crowded with hundreds of figures in a contemporary Netherlandish village setting, acting out some 100 proverbs that depict a surfeit of human foolishness.

Although Bruegel drew numerous mountain scenes, some of which were later engraved for Hieronymus Cock, no pure landscape paintings are known. But given the importance accorded the landscape in his paintings, he nonetheless represents, according to Bruegel biographer Walter Gibson, the culmination of the great Flemish tradition of the world panorama pioneered by the artist Joachim Patinir. Bruegel's landscapes were not drawn directly from nature, however, and in these constructed landscapes emerges one of the persistent themes in his art—the contrast between sinful and fallen humankind and an unsullied and serene nature independent of humans. Indeed, this profoundly pessimistic view of human nature is evident throughout Bruegel's work, and it led him to attack, through his art, human sinfulness, shortcomings, folly, selfishness, greed, and materialism.

The appeal of Bruegel's art, during his lifetime no less than for the modern world, derives first from the immediate charm of his brilliantly structured panoramic landscapes and from the robust animation that courses through his figures. Bruegel's uncanny ability to recreate nature awed Carel van Mander, his earliest biographer, who wrote that during Bruegel's visits to the Alps ''he had swallowed all the mountains and cliffs'' and that after his return home ''he had spit them forth upon his canvas and panels.'' Equally compelling are the figures populating Bruegel's paintings and drawings, for just as he recreated nature in his epic panoramas, so he created panoramas of human nature and activity in the scenes of peasant life. Whether depicting an entire village engaged in the minor pleasures of daily life, as in *Winter Landscape with Skaters and a Bird-Trap* (1565), or clusters of uninhibited peasants frolicking at some village fête, or individuals such as the three weary hunters trudging home through the snow in *The Hunters in the Snow* (1565), Bruegel combined acute observation of human activity with intuitive insight into the human condition and indeed human nature itself. Even in his moralizing prints and his Bosch-like allegories, these same qualities are apparent. Like all great art, the work of Bruegel invites and rewards close scrutiny, and the extraordinary details of everyday life, comic as well as tragic, found in his paintings and drawings delight as they instruct.

Bruegel's influence on artists of his day and subsequent generations is unquestionable. Copies of his paintings and drawings were common; for example, there are four known versions of *The Painter and the Connoisseur*, some twenty reproductions of *The Massacre of the Innocents*, and countless imitations of his peasant scenes. According to van Mander, he had pupils, but nothing of their work is known. Nevertheless, he greatly influenced Dutch and Flemish art during the next century and beyond, inspiring the so-called Bruegel Dynasty, made up of his sons, Pieter and Jan, his grandsons and great-grandsons, and his granddaughter's husband, David Teniers the Younger. Other artists for whom he was a source of inspiration range from Roelant Savery, Adriaen Brouwer, and Lucas van Valckenborch to Joos de Momper and Peter Paul Rubens.

Overview of Biographical Sources

References to Bruegel by contemporary writers are scarce, but they indicate that his works were known and prized, and not just his satirical, moralizing, or fantastic prints in the style of Hieronymus Bosch, which had great appeal in the sixteenth century, but also his landscapes and his compositions with human figures. Both Ludovico Guicciardini (*Descrittione di tutti i Paesi Bassi,* 1567) and Dominicus Lampsonius (*Pictorum aliquot celebrium Germaniae inferioris effigies,* 1572) characterize Bruegel as a second Bosch, stressing his inventiveness and the bizarre but often witty fantasies that poured from Bruegel's clever imagination. Later writers, such as Giorgio Vasari, who in the second edition of his *Vite de'piu eccellenti pittori, scultori e Architettori* (1568) drew on these accounts, also linked Bruegel with Bosch. In contrast, Bruegel's friend Abraham Ortelius makes no mention in his *Album Amicorum* of Bruegel's humorous inventiveness, praising the artist rather for his ability to render nature faithfully no less in his landscapes than in his human figures.

Much of what is known about the life and personality of Pieter Bruegel comes from Carel van Mander's *Het Schilderboeck,* first published in 1604. Van Mander characterized Bruegel as taciturn but also witty, with a predilection for devilish pranks. Astute reflections on Bruegel's paintings, at least a dozen of which are described, led him to observe that, although Bruegel worked in the tradition of Bosch, he merited the epithet ''Pieter the Droll'' because his fantastic prints made even the most serious viewer laugh. Van Mander also lauded Bruegel's ability to reproduce nature convincingly. He claimed, further, that Bruegel disguised himself as a peasant and went into the countryside to observe and sketch rural dress, manners, customs, and behavior, especially at weddings and fairs, and van Mander praises the accuracy of these images. In descriptions of specific paintings, van

Mander notes the trifling details that give them life and humanity. Such anecdotes recorded by van Mander, together with his appraisals of Bruegel and his works, have not only provided the key elements of his biography, they have also done much to establish the stereotype of the "droll and peasant Bruegel" which still retains its force, despite the corrective efforts of modern scholars.

For the next three centuries, Bruegel's fame would depend on these few literary sources and on the many prints of his drawings and paintings, especially the landscapes, which won frequent praise from writers, including Johann Wolfgang von Goethe in his *Landschaftliche Malerei* of 1832. During these years, most of Bruegel's great paintings were inaccessible to the public, either in the Habsburg Collection in Vienna, where nearly a third of the authentic Bruegel's still hang, or in private hands. In 1809, the emperor Napoleon removed several Bruegel's from Vienna for display in Paris, including *The Corn Harvest*. Interest in Bruegel began to revive because of romantic interest in the so-called primitive painters of the early Netherlandish School, but for most of the nineteenth century, the humorous and Bosch-like character of Bruegel and the literary qualities of his work predominated, attracting admirers like Charles Baudelaire, who appreciated the hallucinatory and diabolical elements in Bruegel.

Only in the late nineteenth century did serious study of Bruegel begin. Scholars sought not only to establish a catalogue raisonné of his works but also to place him in the history of Flemish and European art. Although turn-of-the-century European scholars, such as Henri Hymans and Axel Romdahl, made contributions to this endeavor, the first comprehensive catalogue raisonné was compiled by Georges Hulin de Loo, and it appeared in René van Bastelaer's influential *Peter Bruegel l'ancien, son oeuvre et son temps* (Brussels: G. van Oest, 1907; **A**). Writing in an age of assertive nationalism, Bastelaer saw Bruegel as a national artist, minimizing any possible influence of Italian art, and he stressed the attention paid popular beliefs, customs, and proverbs.

Other notable Bruegel scholars include Gustav Glück, who, in his *Peter Bruegels des Aeltere Gemälde im kunsthistorischen Hofmuseum zu Wien* (Brussels: G. van Oest, 1910; **A**) and later influential works, contended that Bruegel was of urban not peasant origins. Max J. Friedländer agreed, and he viewed Bruegel within the traditions of the early Netherlandish School. In contrast, Max Dvořák's *Pieter Bruegel der Aeltere* (Vienna: E. Hölzel, 1921; **A**) emphasized Italian influences, describing Bruegel as a northern Mannerist and attributing to him sophisticated concepts of man and nature, a tradition carried on by Charles de Tolnay. Scholars who study the formal aspects of Bruegel's paintings include Hans Sedlmayr and Fritz Novotny, both of whom raise questions as to the actual relation between nature and Bruegel's landscapes.

Recent works, it should be noted, such as Walter S. Gibson's *Bruegel* (1977), stress Bruegel's place in Flemish landscape art, demonstrating his ties with the world panoramas of Joachim Patinir and the influence of local traditions on his work. Other valuable recent studies of Bruegel include those by Fritz Grossmann (1973) and Wolfgang Stechow (1969), both of which supplant the widely available study by Gustav Glück, *Peter Bruegel the Elder*, first published in German in 1932. Many paintings attributed to Bruegel by Glück are no longer considered authentic. Both Grossmann and Stechow emphasize Bruegel's moral vision, basing their interpretations on thoughtful readings of his paintings and drawings and on studies of the intellectual milieu in which the artist may have worked.

Pieter Bruegel was a painter of great talent, sophistication, and complexity who lived during a most difficult and violent era in European history and, as this assessment of Bruegel scholarship makes clear, many questions concerning his life and work have been raised but few have been satisfactorily answered. Given the few extant documents and the absence of a definitive catalogue raisonné of his work, arguments are likely to continue concerning the authenticity of unsigned works, the nature of Bruegel's art, and his place in the history of European art.

Evaluation of Principal Biographical Sources

Delevoy, Robert L. *Bruegel: Historical and Critical Study*. Translated by Stuart Gilbert. Geneva: Skira, 1959. (**A**) Well-illustrated biographical and analytical study that offers symbolic readings of the paintings, some of which are interpreted as representing the brutal wars between Spain and the Dutch. Also included are translations of contemporary documents.

Foote, Timothy. *The World of Bruegel*. New York: Time-Life, 1968. (**G**) Well-written and illustrated introduction for the general reader. It provides an overview of the Italian and Northern Renaissance, reflections on the nature of Flemish painting and the influence of Bosch, a biographical sketch of Bruegel's life, consideration of the influence of the Spanish wars on Bruegel's art, and an interpretation of the peasant pictures as a mirror of sixteenth century Flemish life. Major paintings are reproduced and discussed, and there is an adequate bibliography.

Friedländer, Max J. *Pieter Bruegel.* Vol. 14. *Early Netherlandish Painting.* Translated by Heinz Norden. 1937. Reprint. Leyden: A. W. Sijthoff, 1976. (**A**) Classic study by one of the great Bruegel scholars of this century. With notes and comments by Henri Pauwels. It contains a brief biographical sketch and discussions of individual paintings. More recent scholarship has questioned the attribution of some of these works to Bruegel. Friedländer compares Bruegel to William Shakespeare, arguing that he, like Shakespeare, wished to depict every aspect of human life on Earth, while tempering it with a sense of pessimism.

Gibson, Walter S. *Bruegel.* New York: Oxford University Press, 1977. (**G,Y**) An easily accessible biographical and critical study that is clearly written and organized. Gibson balances his view of Bruegel's humanity and his "visual imagination" against those scholars who advance sophisticated philosophical and iconographical interpretations. Relating Bruegel to his social, political, and artistic milieu, Gibson argues that he painted subjects of universal significance from a uniquely Flemish point of view. Numerous paintings and drawings are reproduced, some in color, and there is an adequate selected bibliography.

Glück, Gustav. *Peter Bruegel the Elder.* New York: Braziller, 1936. (**G**) Originally published in 1932 and reprinted often, Glück's volume contains the most extensive catalogue of Bruegel's paintings; the attribution of some paintings to Bruegel is questioned by more recent scholarship.

Grossmann, Fritz. *Pieter Bruegel: Complete Edition of the Paintings.* 3d ed. New York: Phaidon, 1973. (**A**) An authoritative introduction to Bruegel's life and career, with a critical survey of literature on Bruegel from the sixteenth century to the 1970s. Reproductions, most in color, of paintings Grossmann accepts as Bruegel's, extensive notes, and commentary on each painting make this volume attractive. The catalogue raisonné and the collection of early documents relating to his life and work promised in the original 1955 edition have yet to appear.

Lavalleye, Jacques. *Pieter Bruegel the Elder and Lucas van Leyden: The Complete Engravings, Etchings, and Woodcuts.* New York: Abrams, 1967. **(A, G)** Although the Lebeer volume listed below is the most authoritative catalogue of Bruegel's prints, this brief, accessible study in English offers excellent reproductions of 173 prints.

Lebeer, Louis. *Catalogue raisonné des estampes de Bruegel l'ancien.* Brussels: Bibliothque Royale Albert Ier, 1969. **(A)** Brings up to date the pioneering catalogue of Ren van Bastelaer, *Les estampes de Peter Bruegel l'ancien* (1908). With the exception of one print actually executed by Bruegel, the *Rabbit Hunt* (1566), these prints are by other artists after drawings by Bruegel. The prints are clearly reproduced and detailed notes accompany each plate. Excellent bibliography.

Marijnissen, Roger H., and Max Seidel. *Bruegel.* New York: Harrison House, 1984. **(A, G)** An attractive overview of Bruegel's life and work, together with a catalogue of his paintings and extensive notes; photographs, many in color, of the details of the paintings make this volume a valuable supplement to the standard catalogues. Especially useful is the chapter, "The Work of Pieter Bruegel," which reminds one that the interpretation of Bruegel's art requires a knowledge of his world and its ways and methods of thought.

Münz, Ludwig. *Bruegel: The Drawings.* London: Phaidon, 1961. **(A)** Brief authoritative study and catalogue of more than 150 drawings; separate essays focus on the landscape drawings, the *naer het leven* studies, and the compositions for engravers, with an emphasis on Bruegel's draftsmanship. Reproductions are outstanding, and there are detailed notes for each plate and bibliographical entries. It updates Charles de Tolnay, *The Drawings of Pieter Bruegel the Elder, with a Critical Catalogue* (New York: The Twin Editions, 1952), a revised version of a work originally published in 1925.

Stechow, Wolfgang. *Pieter Bruegel the Elder.* New York: Abrams, 1969. **(A, G)** Much-indebted to Grossmann, it includes a brief biographical overview, consideration of the influence on Bruegel's paintings of Bosch, Joachim Patinir, and others, a sketch of Bruegel's view of human nature and the natural world. Excellent color reproductions of Bruegel's paintings, with notes and commentary on each plate. The text is illustrated with reproductions of drawings and prints.

Van Mander, Carel. "Pieter Brueghel of Brueghel." In *Dutch and Flemish Painters*. Translated by Constant Van de Wall. New York: McFarlane, Warde, McFarlane, 1936. (**G**) Invaluable biographical sketch, originally published in 1604, and the source for many details of Bruegel's life; almost all Bruegel scholars have subjected this account to minute and searching analysis.

Overview and Evaluation of Primary Sources

Documents pertaining to the life of Bruegel are scarce and difficult to interpret. They consist, for the most part, of brief mentions, such as the appearance of his name on the membership rolls of the Guild of Saint Luke in Antwerp, passing references in letters, and his marriage documents. Two contemporary writers on painting, Guicciardini in 1567 and Vasari in 1568, mention Bruegel not long before his death. The earliest biographical sketch, that of Carel van Mander in *Het Het Schilderboeck* (1604), appeared some thirty-five years after his death. Meticulous analysis of van Mander, combined with documents contemporary to Bruegel's life and his signed and dated drawings, prints, and paintings, have allowed scholars to create a conditional biographical outline.

Bruegel's paintings, drawings, and prints must accordingly be considered primary biographical sources as well as works of art. But to make matters difficult, there is as yet no definitive catalogue raisonné for Bruegel, and those in search of Bruegel's oeuvre must consult several studies. For the paintings, there are numerous tentative catalogues. Of particular usefulness are those by Fritz Grossmann, Wolfgang Stechow, and Roger H. Marijnissen; for the drawings, see the studies of Charles de Tolnay and Ludwig Münz; and for the prints, see the work of Louis Lebeer. Close examination of these books reveals a core of about forty-five paintings and some 156 drawings, many of them either signed, dated, or both and almost universally accepted as Bruegel's. In addition, there are other works said to be by Bruegel, but the attribution remains controversial.

Principal Works

Landscape with the Parable of the Sower (1557)

Landscape with the Fall of Icarus (Two versions, c.1557-1558?)

The Fight Between Carnival and Lent (1559)

The Netherlandish Proverbs (1559)

Children's Games (1560)

The Fall of the Rebel Angels (1562)

'Dulle Griet' ("Mad Meg") (c.1562)

The Triumph of Death (c.1562)

The Suicide of Saul (1562)

Two Monkeys (1562)

The Tower of Babel (Two versions, 1563 and c.1564)

The Procession to Calvary (1564)

The Adoration of the Kings (c.1556)

The Massacre of the Innocents (Two versions, c.1565)

The Hunters in the Snow (1565)

The Gloomy Day (1565)

Haymaking (1565)

The Corn Harvest (1565)

The Return of the Herd (1565)

Winter Landscape with Skaters and a Bird Trap (1565)

The Census at Bethlehem (1566)

The Sermon of Saint John the Baptist (1566)

The Wedding Dance in the Open Air (1566)

The Land of Cockaigne (1567)

The Conversion of Saul (1567)

The Adoration of the Kings in the Snow (1567)

The Wedding Banquet (1567 or 1568)

The Peasant Dance, or The Kermess (1567 or 1568)

The Misanthrope (1568)

The Parable of the Blind (1568)

The Peasant and the Bird Nester (1568)

Landscape with the Magpie on the Gallows (1568)

The Cripples (1568)

Fictions and Adaptations

Felix Timmermans' once popular biographical novel, *Droll Peter* (1930), owes more to the author's lively imagination than to fact. Timmermans reconstructs a fanciful version of Bruegel's life from the account by van Mander and from the content of his paintings. Bruegel's paintings have inspired literary works, most often in the form of poetry. For "Musée des Beaux Arts," (1940), W. H. Auden selected details from two Bruegel paintings, the disappearance of Icarus's legs into the sea as the plowman goes on with his work in the *Landscape with the Fall of Icarus* and the skating children in *The Census at Bethlehem*, to illustrate his theme that great human suffering often occurs unnoticed amidst the mundane activities of daily life. William Carlos Williams's *Pictures from Brueghel* (1962), which was originally published in the *Hudson Review* of 1960 and which earned Williams the Pulitzer Prize for poetry in 1963, is a cycle of ten poems, each inspired by a painting Williams believed to have been painted by Bruegel. Williams's "The Dance" (1944) also owed its origin to a Bruegel painting, *The Peasant Dance*, which he saw in Vienna in 1924. Williams's poems after Bruegel, together with excellent notes, may be found in the second volume of *The Collected Poems of William Carlos Williams* (2 vols. New York: New Directions, 1986-1988). A more recent poem is Michael Hamburger's "Lines on Bruegel's Icarus." Gert Hofmann's *The Parable of the Blind* (New York: Fromm International, 1986), which takes its title from the painting of the same name, is a novel in which blind characters imagine themselves as they are painted by Bruegel. Also inspired by Bruegel's works were Bertolt Brecht and Michel de Ghelderode.

Museums, Historical Landmarks, Societies

Alte Pinakothek (Munich, Germany). Contains two paintings, including *The Land of Cockaigne* (1567).

Bibliothèque Royale Albert Ier (Brussels). Houses a major collection of Bruegel prints.

Eglise Notre-Dame-de-la Chapelle (Brussels, Belgium). A side chapel contains the tomb erected by Pieter Brueghel for his father; it is adorned with a copy of a painting by Peter Paul Rubens; the original was sold in 1765.

Hessisches Landesmuseum (Darmstadt, Germany). Contains *Landscape with the Magpie on the Gallow* (1568).

Institute of Arts (Detroit). Contains *The Wedding Dance in the Open Air* (1566).

Kunsthistorisches Museum (Vienna). With fourteen works, this museum has the largest collection of paintings by Bruegel. Among the most famous are: *The Fight between Carnival and Lent* (1559); *Children's Games* (1560); *The Suicide of Saul* (1562); *The Tower of Babel* (1563); *The Procession to Calvary* (1563); *The Hunters in the Snow* (1565); *The Gloomy Day* (1565); *The Return of the Herd* (1565); *The Massacre of the Innocents* (1565-1567?); *The Conversion of Saint Paul* (1567); *Peasant Wedding* [The Wedding Banquet (c. 1567?); *The Peasant Dance* [The Kermess] (1567?); *The Peasant and the Bird Nester* (1568); and *The Storm at Sea* (1569).

Metropolitan Museum of Art (New York City). Contains *The Corn Harvesters* (1565).

Museum Boymans-van Beuningen (Rotterdam, Netherlands). Contains *The Tower of Babel* (c. 1563?)

Musée du Louvre (Paris). Contains *The Cripples* (1568).

Musée Mayer van den Bergh (Antwerp, Belgium). Contains *The Dulle Griet* (Mad Meg) (1562).

Museo Nazionale (Naples). Contains *The Misanthrope* (1568) and *The Parable of the Blind* (1568).

Museo del Prado (Madrid). Contains *The Triumph of Death* (c. 1562).

Musées Royaux des Beaux-Arts (Brussels). Contains four works by Bruegel, including *Landscape with the Fall of Icarus* (c. 1557-1558); *The Adoration of the Magi* (c. 1556); *The Fall of the Rebel Angels* (1562), and *The Census at Bethlehem* (1566).

National Gallery (London). Contains *The Adoration of the Magi* (1564).

National Gallery (Prague). Contains *Haymaking* (1565).

Staatliche Museen (Berlin-Dahlem, Germany). Contains two paintings, including *The Netherlandish Proverbs* (1559).

The Timken Art Gallery (San Diego). Contains *Landscape with the Parable of the Sower* (1557).

For the location of additional paintings, see Fritz Grossmann's *Pieter Bruegel* (1973). Institutions with collections of Bruegel drawings include: the *Graphische Sammlung Albertina* (Vienna); the *British Museum* (London); the *Kupferstich-kabinett, Staatliche Museum* (Berlin-Dahlem); the *Rijksmuseum* (Amsterdam); and the *Museum Boymans-van Beuningen* (Rotterdam, Netherlands).

Other Sources

Benesch, Otto. *The Art of the Renaissance in Northern Europe: Its Relation to the Contemporary Spiritual and Intellectual Movements.* Rev. ed. London: Phaidon, 1965. Sets Bruegel clearly in the context of contemporary developments in art, literature, and scientific thought.

Bianconi, Piero. *The Complete Paintings of Bruegel.* New York: Harry N. Abrams, 1967. (**A, G**) Paintings are reproduced in color, with close-up views of important details. Also included is a review and critical bibliography of nineteenth and twentieth-century scholarship, a compendium of key quotations from Bruegel scholars from the sixteenth century to the present, an outline biography, a family tree, and a catalogue of the Bruegel's art, with extended commentary on each work reproduced.

Bruegel. Une dynastie de peintres. Brussels: Palais de Beaux-Arts, 1980. (**A**) Exhibition catalogue containing essays on the historical situation of Flanders in the sixteenth century, the life of Bruegel, Bruegel and the critics, the drawings and prints, and the Bruegel children and followers like David Teniers, the Younger. Illustrations of rarely seen drawings and prints are included, as is an excellent bibliography.

Conarroe, Joel. "The Measured Dance: Williams' 'Pictures from Bruegel.' " *Journal of Modern Literature* 1 (May 1971): 565-577. Brief study of how particular Bruegel paintings inspired Williams.

Gibson, Walter S. *"Mirror of the Earth"*: *The World Landscape in Sixteenth-Century Flemish Painting.* Princeton, NJ: Princeton University Press, 1989. Detailed and scholarly study of Flemish landscape painting. It begins with the founder of the world landscape, Joachim Patiner, whose massive world landscapes reveal a new relationship with and interest in the physical world, and ends with Pieter Bruegel the Elder, who Gibson sees as the "culmination of this tradition." Contains excellent notes, bibliography, and a large number of black-and-white reproductions.

Grossmann, Fritz. "Pieter Bruegel the Elder." In *Encyclopedia of World Art.* Vol. 2: 632-651. Provides a concise but masterful sketch of Bruegel's life, a critical catalogue and chronology of his works, a discussion of the style and character of his art, and an overview of scholarly studies. Excellent comprehensive bibliography of nineteenth- and twentieth-century works in the major European languages, it is arranged by subjects.

Kay, Marguerite. *Bruegel.* London and New York: Paul Hamlyn, 1969. (**G, Y**) In addition to a brief biographical sketch, there is an essay on "Bruegel the Artist," which emphasizes his indebtedness to northern European traditions. Bruegel is viewed as a link between the Middle Ages and the seventeenth century. Generous selection of color plates, each with commentary.

Klein, H. Arthur. "Pieter Bruegel the Elder as a Guide to 16th-Century Technology." In *Scientific American* 238, 3 (March 1978): 134-140. (**A, G**) Focuses on

Bruegel's detailed knowledge of contemporary machinery, such as the cranes in the two Tower of Babel paintings; also notes that modern physicians can diagnose at least five types of blindness from the images in *The Parable of the Blind.*

Marlier, Georges. *La Renaissance flamande: Pierre Cock d'Alost.* Brussels: Editions Robert Finck, 1966. Authoritative study of the painter to whom Bruegel was supposedly apprenticed.

Riggs, Timothy. *Hieronymus Cock, Printmaker and Publisher.* New York: Garland, 1977. Comprehensive study of Cock's career, with a catalogue of prints, including those by Bruegel, printed and sold at Cock's The Four Winds.

Rocquet, Claude-Henri. *Bruegel, or the Workshop of Dreams.* Chicago: University of Chicago Press, 1991. (**A, G**) In this hybrid of biography, historical study, and fiction, Rocquet supplies fascinating details about sixteenth-century Flanders, creates conversations between Bruegel and his contemporaries, and meditates on links between Bruegel's character and his works. Some critics have found this experiment more annoying than satisfying. Nevertheless, it draws on the extant primary material concerning Bruegel and his art.

Sullivan, Margaret. "Bruegel's Proverbs: Art and Audience in the Northern Renaissance." *Art Bulletin* 73, 3 (September 1991): 431-466. A learned and revisionist essay that describes the contemporary context from which Bruegel drew for the proverbs used in his art and analyzes a selection of prints and paintings that visually represent proverbs, especially the *Netherlandish Proverbs.* Sullivan concludes that Bruegel used not just Flemish proverbs and folklore but also Latin proverbs and humanistic ideas.

Robert W. Brown
Pembroke State University

Martin Buber
1878-1965

Chronology

Born Mordecai Martin Buber on February 8, 1878, in Vienna, Austria, son of Carl Buber, an agronomist, and Elise Wurgast Buber; *1881-1887* after the divorce of his parents, is sent to live with his grandparents, Solomon Buber, a wealthy banker and respected scholar, and Adele Buber, a brilliant, mostly self-educated woman, who live on an estate near Lemberg, Poland; privately tutored until age ten; comes in contact with Hasidism by attending prayer meetings at nearby village of Sadagors; *1888-1896* attends school in Lemberg, learning several languages including Polish, German, Yiddish, Greek, and Latin; *1892* goes to live on father's estate, also in Lemberg, and attends Francis Joseph Gymnasium; *1893* reads works of Emmanuel Kant; *1895* reads works of Friedrich Nietzsche; *1896* returns to Vienna; spends two semesters at the University of Vienna studying German literature, art history, and philosophy; *1897-1898* studies at the University of Leipzig; joins the "Ethical Culture Society" and delivers his first lecture, "Individualistic and Socialistic Ethics" on Ferdinand Lasalle, charismatic leader of German socialism, whom he admired at the time; reads Mathias Acher's *Modern Judaism*, which converts him to Zionism; founds a Zionist chapter and a union of Jewish students; *1899* attends a Zionist convention in Cologne as representative of the Leipzig chapter; studies philosophy, art history, literature and psychology at the University of Zurich; meets future wife Paula Winkler in Munich during a seminar at the University of Zurich; speaks at the Third Zionist Congress in Basel; studies at the University of Berlin under philosopher Wilhelm Dilthey and philosopher/ sociologist Georg Simmel; *1900* becomes a member of the New Community (Neue Gemeinschaft) led and taught by the socialist Gustav Landauer, one of the great formative influences in Buber's life; writes his first major essay, "Old and New Community"; founds a department for Jewish art and science within the Zionist movement; *1901* marries Paula Winkler; appointed editor of *Die Welt*, the official publication of the Zionist movement; experiences bitter conflicts with Theodor Herzl, founder of the movement; plays central role at Fifth Zionist Congress in

Basel where the "Democratic Fraction" successfully opposes Herzl in its demand that the importance of cultural Zionism be recognized; proposes that plans be formulated for a Jewish university in Jerusalem to foster Jewish culture in the homeland; enters the University of Vienna to work on a doctorate in philosophy; is influenced by the writings of Christian mystics Nicholas of Cusa and Jacob Boehme; *1902* founding of the Judischer Verlag (Jewish Press) under editorship of Buber and Berthold Feiwel, another member of the Democratic Fraction; *1903* writes pamphlet on founding a Jewish university with Feiwel and Chaim Weizmann, an old friend of Buber's and later the first president of the state of Israel; *1904* withdraws from the Zionist movement after the death of Herzl; discovers the writings of Israel ben Eliezer (Baal Shem Tov), founder of the Hasidic movement, and devotes his time to the study of Hasidism; receives his doctorate of philosophy from University of Vienna; *1905-1906* lives in Florence, Italy, and writes his first book on Hasidism, *The Stories of Rabbi Nachman*; *1908* publishes *The Legend of the Baal Shem*, his second Hasidic collection; becomes active in the Zionist movement again, determined to establish communities in Palestine in the spirit of Hasidism; joins student movement in Prague, the Bar Kochba Union, where he lectures on the meaning of Jewishness in the twentieth century; *1911* publishes his speeches to the Bar Kochba as *Three Speeches on Judaism*; *1913* publishes *Daniel*, five dialogues which anticipate Buber's philosophic masterpiece, *I and Thou*, in their insistence that "holy insecurity" is the predicament of man in this world; *1914* rejected for military service due to medical reasons and his age; meets Franz Rosenzweig and Florenz Christian Rang, two men who will later be among his close friends and strong influences on his thought; abandons mysticism; *1916* moves to Heppenheim near the forest of Odenwald in the Necker Valley; founds the journal *Der Jude,* which he edits until 1924; writes the first draft of *I and Thou*; *1918* revolutions break out in Germany as World War I ends; *1919* grieves murder of his good friend Gustav Landauer, an official in Kurt Eisner's short-lived Bavarian Republic; cooperates in founding of Judische Volksheim, an adult education institute in Berlin specifically for Jewish immigrants; *1919-1921* becomes member of Hapoel Hazair, an organization advocating a revolutionary colonization of Palestine; continues to insist that the Zionist movement take steps to establish good relations with the Arabs in Palestine; *1921* withdraws from involvement in practical politics of Zionism after his proposals for communal socialism and cooperation with Palestinian Arabs are watered down by the Zionist leadership;

renews acquaintance with Franz Rosenzweig and joins him at the Freis Judisches Lehrhaus in Frankfurt, where he teaches courses on Judaism; *1923* publishes *I and Thou,* his major opus and the expression of his mature philosophy; appointed honorary professor of religious science at the University of Frankfurt; *1924* convinces planners of the proposed Hebrew University to include a land-folk school in the structure of the university; *1925* unable to attend opening of the proposed Hebrew University in Jerusalem; begins a translation of the Bible, collaborating with Franz Rosenzweig; *1926* publishes *Die Kreatur* (The Creature), a journal devoted to Jewish-Christian dialogue; *1927* visits Palestine; *1929* death of Franz Rosenzweig; continues work on his translation of the Bible until 1961; *1930-1933* growing influence of National Socialists culminates in Hitler's appointment as chancellor of Germany; resigns his professorship; writes a number of essays protesting the barbarity of Nazi policies—among them "The Jewish Person Today," "The Children," and "In the Midst of History"; serves as director of the Central Office for Jewish Adult Education at Frankfurt; *1935* prohibited from lecturing after delivering his lecture "The Power of the Spirit" at Frankfurt Lehrhaus; surprised when Nazis allow the publication of his essay "The Question to the Single One," which in its praise of individuality attacks the very foundation of totalitarianism; continues his educational work and attempts to promote Jewish-Christian dialogue; *1938* offered the Chair of Social Philosophy at the Hebrew University and reluctantly leaves Germany for Jerusalem; campaigns in Palestine against terrorist methods used by Jewish political extremists; publishes an essay, "Against Betrayal," in which he urges his fellow Jews to oppose extremist organizations and to work for closer relationships with the Arabs; writes a series of papers explaining his philosophical anthropology, collectively entitled "What is Man?" which is published later in his anthology *Between Man and Man* (1947); *1939* establishes, with Judah Menges, the Ihud, an organization opposing the creation of the Jewish state as advocated by David Ben-Gurion and to work for a binational (Jewish-Arab) state; storm of opposition to the Ihud arises both in Palestine and in Jewish communities abroad; *1942* writes and publishes in Hebrew an important book of Biblical exegesis, *Prophetic Faith,* considering such questions as why is a benign and omnipotent deity presiding over a universe in which suffering is a constant experience; *1943* publishes his only novel, *Gog and Magog,* which explores issues such as the problems of evil and redemption; *1944* writes article "Silence and Outcry" as news of the Holocaust begins to reach the Jews in Palestine; *1947* as Arab armies converge on Jerusalem, works on draft of *Two Types of Faith*, his study of the interpenetration of Jewish and Christian traditions; writes *Paths in Utopia*; completes his studies of Hasidic folklore which make up *Tales of the Hasidism: The Early Masters*, and *Tales of the Hasidism: The Latter Masters*; *1948* retires from his Chair at the Hebrew University; *1951* makes his first visit to the United States and lectures at American universities; receives the Hanseatic Goethe Peace Prize from the University of Hamburg on the basis of his work *The Eclipse of God,* consisting of several important essays issued to coincide with his visit to the U.S.; completes his Biblical drama "Elijah"; continues to oppose the policies of David Ben-Gurion, especially on the Arab-Jewish issues; *1957* protests reprisal action against the Jordanian village of Kibjain where sixty men, women and children are killed, attacks Israeli rabbinate for keeping silent on the incident; *1956* returns to the United States to lecture at the Institute of Psychiatric Medicine in Washington, D.C.; attends seminar with psychiatrists at the University of Michigan where he holds formal dialogue with American psychologist Carl Rogers, founder of the "client-centered" approach to psychotherapy; protests the killing of forty-seven Arabs in an ambush at Kafr Kassem; protests the invasion of the Sinai by French, British and Israeli forces; takes up the cause of Palestinian refugees on several occasions; issues a paper,"Israel's Mission to Zion," questioning Ben-Gurion policies; *1958* returns to America for his last lecture tour; wife Paula dies; *1961* edits a collection of his wife's stories for posthumous publication; completes his German translation of the Old Testament; *1962* denounces the trial and execution of Adolph Eichmann in Jerusalem, for which he is vilified in the Israeli press; *1963* receives the Erasmus Prize which he accepts with the provision that three-fourths of the prize money go to the Leo Baeck Foundation for a scholarly anthology on "Judaism and the European Crisis" in the Hitler era; *1965* dies on June 13 from complications after breaking his leg in a fall, and is buried in the "Hill of Rest" at the place reserved for professors from Hebrew universities.

Activities of Historical Significance

Probably no single small work on Existential philosophy has had such influence as Martin Buber's *I and Thou.* While most of the Existentialists, especially

Nietzsche, Kierkegaard and Sartre, were deeply pessimistic about human nature, Buber espoused the world-affirming spirit of Judaism, and purported that philosophy is not abstract speculation but assistance to the individual in achieving selfhood through resolute decisions. Claiming to be neither a theologian nor philosopher, Buber's eloquent voice and poetic prose affirmed for the despondent post-World War I generation the possibility of giving meaning to life through an I-Thou encounter.

Buber reached maturity at a time when thoughtful Jews began to realize how precarious their existence in Europe had become. Pogroms in eastern Europe had driven thousands of Jews out of Russia and Poland during the final decade of the nineteenth century. Theodor Herzl, who had been in France when the Dreyfus Affair (in which a Jewish army officer was wrongly imprisoned for treason) aroused such bitter anti-Semitism, had become convinced that Jews could be safe nowhere in Europe, and that the only answer was a Jewish homeland. Herzl started the modern Zionist movement in 1897. Buber joined the movement in 1898 while still a student, and except for brief intervals, he was active in Zionism for the rest of his life, first in helping to establish a Jewish homeland in Palestine, and afterwards by trying to make Israel fulfill his ideological expectations. World War I was of critical importance in forging Buber's philosophy of dialogue, and his influence on the Jews of Western Europe was strongest during the first five years of Nazi Germany. After World War II, Buber was not content to merely persuade the citizens of Israel to fulfill their destiny as an ideal community; indeed, he also became a spokesman against universal injustice.

While a university student, Buber was more interested in art and poetry than in religion and politics. He was particularly influenced by Nietzsche's opposition to the barren intellectual landscape of the times and the blind acceptance of convention; life should be lived unconditionally, and it was possible for men of heroic stature to create and transcend themselves. Buber was quite aware that European Jews did not measure up to Nietzschean standards. As a teenager Buber had become enthusiastic about the aesthetic aspects of Nietzsche's philosophy. Initially, Nietzsche's role as social critic, apart form his attack on the parochial philistinism of German society, was ignored by Buber. Later Nietzsche's warnings about the corruption in Western culture, and his exhortations for the spiritual renewal of man would form the basis of Buber's social and political philosophy. It was Nietzsche's critique of barren intellectuality and his call for the type of man who in his strivings transcends himself that caused Buber to turn to the Zionist movement. For the perseverance of Jewish culture a homeland was required; only in a homeland could the Jews revitalize themselves and become again the heroic figures seen in their history. In the summer of 1898, after reading Mathias Acher's *Modern Judaism*, he became converted to Judaism, and interested in the cultural and spiritual traditions of his people.

Buber was also influenced by socialism early in his student years, and by 1900 had joined Gustav Landauer's Neue Gemeinschaft (New Community). Gustav Landauer's influence is pervasive in Buber's thought. The Marxists, in Landauer's opinion, were not radical enough. They sought to reform industrial society by a revolution that would merely transfer power form one set of owners to another. A true revolution would basically alter human nature itself through dedication and will into a truly socialistic community. Neither Buber nor Landauer accepted the centralist socialism of Marx with its emphasis on man as an instrument of production, but rather insisted that an education for socialism should involve the development of spiritual values, especially those of Erlebnis mysticism, which insisted that union existed with all things in time and space. Buber's first important essay "Old and New Community" makes this same distinction between the two socialisms, and insists that a new order of creativity will grow out of the hearts of initiates in the new community. Buber wanted the new homeland in Palestine to be founded on these ideals.

Before entering the Zionist movement, Buber already had his own ideas about the kind of country the Jews should establish in Palestine. As a young man he had made a favorable impression on Theodor Herzl, who gave Buber the editorship of the official journal of the Zionists, *Die Welt*. Soon, however, it became apparent to Buber that Herzl, who had many admirable qualities of leadership, had no interest in promoting the ancient cultural and spiritual traditions of Judaism. Herzl's idea was to establish a state similar to those in Europe. Supported by his close friend Chaim Weizmann, Buber was able to successfully promote his ideas for the new homeland despite Herzl's opposition and the politically minded Zionists at the Fifth Zionist Congress at Basel in 1901. Herzl and his followers finally accepted the Buber group's proposals, entitled "The Democratic Fraction," which marked a turning point in the history of the Zionist movement. An immediate result was the establishment of the Judischer Verlag, a publishing press directed by Buber and a colleague, Berthold Feiwel, with a goal of establishing a Jewish university in Jerusalem. In 1903, the Judischer Verlag published the plans for establishing the university.

Buber's discovery of Israel ben Eliezer's work in 1904 introduced to him a form of Jewish religion, Hasidism, which would become a lifelong study. Called Baal-Shem-Tov (Lord of the Name) by his followers, Eliezer founded Hasidism around 1750 in the Ukraine as a reaction against the rigid formalism of the synagogue. Buber interpreted Hasidism as a religion devoted to this world and to the believer's relation to it and to his fellow men. Baal-Shem-Tov taught that Talmudic learning was less important than joyous communion with God and that this communion could be accomplished anywhere, since God was omnipresent in his creation. Buber's two books on the subject, *The Stories of Rabbi Machma* (1906), and *The Legend of the Baal Shem* (1908), literary adaptations of some of the materials he had read, introduced Hasidic lore for the first time to western Europeans.

In 1908, Buber returned to his work with the Zionist movement. After moving to Prague, he joined the Bar Kochbar Union, and in a series of lectures taught his ideals for Judaism and for the colonization of Palestine to student members. Although he had not been orthodox in his beliefs since his early teens, Buber wanted to see Judaism revitalized, for he believed the early Hasidic movement had reawakened Judaism by returning to the religion's roots. He became the spokesman and teacher for a generation of younger Jews as well as older believers who had returned to Judaism. In *Three Speeches on Judaism* (1911), Buber explains his developing philosophy as a desire to see a renewal of Judaism as well as the religious and social honing of humans. In the five dialogues of *Daniel: Dialogues on Realization* (1913), Buber uses Plato's method of bringing the reader to grips with the forces with which any individual must cope and the decisions one must make. The method is based on Plato's Socratic dialogues. In these dialogues Daniel applies the question/answer technique in five conversations (five separate dialogues). The experiences range from mystic ecstasy to existential ''angst,'' Buber's ''holy insecurity.'' For example, in the first dialogue a man and a woman are contrasted in the directions each instinctively takes, she the way of the Earth, he, upward. Buber is making use of the myth of woman as ''Earth mother.'' His man is a striver in the Faustian manner. The love of man and woman becomes a symbol of all inclusive love. While *Daniel* is not specifically Jewish in its presentation of the human situation, Buber is interested in showing the West examples of wisdom in ecstatic visions. *Daniel*, in its insistence that "holy insecurity" is the inevitable predicament of man as he tries to realize himself in this world, is both in example modern existentialism, and a precursor in many of its presentations of *I and Thou* (1923).

In the autumn of 1914, an event occurred which caused him to renounce his mysticism. One morning after he had spent some time in mystic contemplation, a young man came to him asking questions. Buber received him amiably enough, but did not give him his full attention; the young man died as a soldier at the front in World War I a few weeks later. Buber learned that this young man, Mëhe, was trying to learn from him insights into the meaning of life. Feeling he had let down another human in his hour of need, Buber resolved to always be available to others, and to always be ready for such meetings. The Mëhe incident was a sort of catalyst in that it made Buber aware of how self-centered a person experiencing mystic raptures really was. He had already come to the conclusion that the most important sphere for humans was that of interpersonal relationships between other humans and on another level with God. "Meeting" the God-head rather than unison with Him was the only true relationship.

By 1916, Buber had finished the first draft of *I and Thou*. The hopes of the Zionists were raised by the Balfour Declaration of 1917 only to be disappointed after the war when it was learned that the British had also made promises to the Arabs. The Balfour Declaration proclaimed the willingness of the British government to allow the Jews to have a national home in Palestine provided that this did not prejudice the civil and religious rights of the non-Jewish people already living there. Buber had long since lost faith in the type of revolution which Kurt Eisner began in Bavaria as the war ended in 1918. His friend Gustav Landauer, however, committed himself completely to the idea, and remained in Bavaria as an official in the revolution. Buber, to a great extent Landauer's disciple on political matters, believed his friend sacrificed his ideals by joining this revolution. He pinned his hopes on a state rather than on interpersonal human relations. The brutality of Landauer's murder (he was kicked to death after falling into the hands of a band of counter-revolutionaries) following the year of war shocked Buber. It seemed to him that Europe had fallen into the abyss he had described in *Daniel*, and that genuine dialogue between men was becoming more difficult. Working on a revision of his draft of *I and Thou*, he found that this latest tragedy also influenced his thinking. Even before the war had ended in 1918, anti-Semitic literature had been distributed accusing the Jews of being responsible for Germany losing the war. Buber as editor of *Der Jude*, a journal he had helped found in 1916, countered the charges.

Buber had insisted for years that the Arabs in Palestine should be made partners with the Jews in the establishment of a nation there, but at the Twelfth Zionist Congress in 1921, others bitterly opposed his proposals because Jewish settlers in Palestine were being savagely attacked by Arabs. After his suggestions had been watered down by the Zionist leadership, Buber withdrew from practical politics again for a time, but he repeated the same ideas at the Sixteenth Zionist Congress in 1929 at Zurich, appealing for concrete action to encourage an understanding between the Jewish settlers and the Arabs. On the day following the Congress the worst riots in Palestine broke out.

Isolated from the Zionist leadership, Buber became even more active as an educator in the 1920s. He taught courses on Judaism at Franz Rosenzweig's Freis Judisches Lehrhaus in Frankfurt. He completed his final draft of *I and Thou* in 1922, and the work was published the following year. This book, considered Buber's masterpiece, details his philosophy a person becomes an "I" only in the process of dialogue with another, a "thou." Buber intended this work and the ones that followed (especially his sequel, the 1929 essay "Dialogue") as a means of closing the distance between men, and ultimately, God. God can be addressed as Thou, but is also present if the I-Thou relationship of man is fully realized.

Paradoxically, Buber's educational ideas and his rather unorthodox variety of Judaism had their greatest influence after the Nazis came to power in Germany in 1933. His home at Heppelheim became a refuge for Jews bewildered by the events that had made them non-persons in a country where their families had lived for centuries. He helped to establish folkschools, which taught adults and young people about their Jewish heritage, and how they could remain firm in their convictions. The schools had become a necessity since the Nazis had forbidden Jewish children to attend state schools. In the summer of 1933 Buber wrote an essay "In the Midst of History" in which he indirectly alluded to Hitler as "the demon of the hour" who wished to destroy the Jewish people. In January 1934 he delivered an address at the Frankfurt Lehrhaus, "The Jew in the World" on the seemingly hopeless situation for the Jew in Germany.

As director of the Central Office for Jewish Adult Education in Frankfurt, much of Buber's time was spent planning community eduction. He lectured on the need to foster traditional values. After several Gestapo officers heard his lecture "The Power of the Spirit" at the Frankfurt Lehrhaus, in which he attacked the neo-paganism in the twentieth century, contrasting it with the spiritual grandeur men were capable of achieving, the Nazis decided they had to silence the man they called the "arch Jew." Although he was not arrested or molested, Buber was forbidden to lecture in public after February 21, 1935.

He continued to attack the Nazi order, however. His essay "The Question to the Single One" (1936) attacked the very basis of Fascist philosophy in its defense of the sacredness of individual human. Finally in March of 1938 Buber and his wife Paula left Germany for Palestine where he had been offered the Chair of Social Philosophy. Shortly after his appointment, he wrote a series of lectures on his philosophical anthropology, collectively titled "What is Man?", in which he traces the development of his beliefs and analyzes the influences which had shaped them. These lectures as well as his paper, "The Education of Character," are included in his anthology *Between Man and Man* (1947).

Buber was soon plunged into controversy once again when he protested the terrorist methods used by some Jewish extremists against Arabs and British soldiers. His essay "Against Betrayal" urged right-thinking Jews to oppose the use of methods so similar to those of the Gestapo, and tried to convince them to work for a closer relationship with the Arabs. In 1939, he and Judah Menges founded the Ihud organization with the objective of creating a bi-national state. Buber had opposed extreme nationalism for years, pointing to the Fascist states as examples of how far from genuine communal organizations such states were. He had hoped that the new Jewish country in Palestine might fulfill the Biblical destiny of Israel as an example among the nations.

Buber also worked tirelessly for the Ihud, writing essays, making speeches and associating as much as possible with the Arab section of Jerusalem called Dir Abu Tor, for which he won great respect from his neighbors. He became an opponent of the powerful Israeli statesman-politician, David Ben-Gurion, attacking his policy of favoring unlimited Jewish immigration into Palestine, promoting instead a more gradual immigration made up of Jews educated to appreciate their role in ushering in the Kingdom of God. He was convinced that the Kibbutzim could become the model for the socialistic and religious communities he had long favored. After the United Nations decided on November 29, 1947, to partition Palestine into two states—one Jewish, one Arab—the war Buber had worked hard to avoid became inevitable. When Jerusalem was under siege by the United Arab armies, he and his wife stayed in their home and continued to associate freely with their Arab neighbors. After it finally became impossible for the couple to stay, some of these neighbors guarded the Buber home even after Arab armies had invaded, destroying most other Jewish homes. Until the outbreak of war, Buber had continued to defend his belief that bi-nationalism was the only visible form for the new nation, but the United Nations had not even considered this option.

During the last seventeen years of his life, Buber continued to write prolifically, and to be a gadfly to the rulers of Israel. Despite the eloquence of his pleas and the soundness of his arguments, he and the Ihud generally did not prevail. In comparison to the influence he had on German Jews from 1933 to 1938, he was now highly unpopular. Though his writings were honored and much discussed abroad, they were generally ignored by Israelis. Three lecture tours to the United States increased Buber's popularity there in the 1950s, even though in the 1940s many members of the American Jewish community had called for Buber's dismissal from his university post because of his bi-national politics.

Much honored beyond the borders of Israel, Buber's motives were misunderstood in Israel when he accepted the Hanseatic Goethe Peace Prize in 1951. Israel's most influential newspaper, *Ha-aretz*, accused him of impure motives and also criticized the University of Hamburg for honoring him with the award. Buber donated the prize money to *Ner*, the Ihud's official journal. Though he remained controversial, Buber could say in his final years that he was "surfeited with honors," as his eightieth birthday and those following were celebrated in many countries. His last major award was the Erasmus Prize in 1963, most of the proceeds of which he donated to a research project on Jews in Nazi Germany. These acknowledgements of his work must have partially compensated for Israel's failure to live up to its responsibility, as he saw it, as the land of the "chosen" people, in his view chosen to make real on Earth the kingdom of God in true community.

Overview of Biographical Sources

An immensely popular and influential religious thinker, Martin Buber is the subject of a vast and growing bibliography. Books about Buber began appearing in the later 1920s, the first, by Wilhelm Michel, a German Protestant, was *Martin Buber's Path to Reality* (Frankfurt aum Main: Rütten and Loening, 1926), which appeared two years before his fiftieth birthday. The next biography was Hans Kohn's *Martin Buber: His Life and Times* (Cologne: Joseph Melzer Verlag, 1930), the first thoroughly scholarly account of the development of Buber's thought in the context of his times. Neither book has been translated into English.

Up until the end of World War II, *I and Thou* was the only one of Buber's works translated into English. Following the war other titles were made available, and in the 1950s and 1960s, Buber's broad popularity as a religious thinker was firmly established. His lecture tours in Europe and America aroused further interest in his work. His popularity has become a problem in itself, with writers on Buber often being accused of excessive reverence in their treatments, making him a sort of secular saint. Buber himself tried to discourage this hero-worship, maintaining that he was just another man poised, ''on a narrow ridge between the gulfs where there is no sureness of expressible knowledge but the certainty of meeting what remains undisclosed.'' Despite Buber's own disclaimers, the hagiographical attitudes have persisted.

Buber has also received some negative criticism, notably from Gershom Scholem, the famous authority of Jewish religion, who accused him of reading his own philosophy into Hasidic legends. The late Walter Kaufmann, a professional academic philosopher and the translator of *I and Thou* (1970), maintains that Buber's philosophy does not always stand up to critical analysis, a view shared by Bernard Susser in his *Existence and Utopia: The Social and Political Thought of Martin Buber* (1981).

Despite Maurice Friedman's three-volume biography of Buber, *Martin Buber's Life and Work* (1983), no definitive biography has yet been written. Friedman explains why in the ''Preface'' to Volume III of *Martin Buber's Life and Work*, noting the very limited access he was allowed to Buber's voluminous correspondence, held in the Buber Archives of the Jewish and National Library in Jerusalem. Friedman also cites the lack of cooperation from some of Buber's close friends such as Ernst Simon, who did not give him the full story of their lifelong relationship. Likewise, during her lifetime, Buber's reticent wife Paula did not give many details either about her life with Buber, or about her own career as a writer. Like most of the other biographers, Friedman has also been accused of not being sufficiently critical of Buber and his work.

Additional books containing biographical material on Buber are Grete Schader's *The Hebrew Humanism of Martin Buber* (1973); Lawrence J. Silberstein's Martin Buber's *Social and Religious Thought: Alienation and the Quest for Meaning* (1989); Paul Mendes-Flor's *From Mysticism to Dialogue: Martin Buber's Transformation of German Social Thought* (1989); Bernard Susser's *Existence and Utopia: The Social and Political Thought of Martin Buber* (1981); and Paula Vermes's *Buber* (1988).

Evaluation of Principal Biographical Sources

Friedman, Maurice. *Encounter on the Narrow Ridge: A Life of Martin Buber.* New York: Paragon House, 1991. (**A, G**) This book is based on Friedman's *Martin Buber's Life and Work.* In addition to condensing the material from the three-volume biography, Friedman used material previously not available, particularly letters from the Martin Buber Archives of the Jewish and National University Library at the Hebrew University, Jerusalem. The title is based on Buber's favorite metaphor describing the position of the human individual who lives "on the narrow rocky ridge between the gulf where there is no sureness of expressible knowledge but the certainty of meeting what remains undisclosed." Buber's philosophy has as its main emphasis the idea of meeting, or encounter, whether with other existing humans, living things in nature or God. For Friedman, most biographies distort the lives of their subjects by presenting one-sided accounts of what are really dialogical events. He tries to avoid this as far as possible by presenting the events in Buber's life as two-sided dialogues. No footnotes are provided, but there is a useful annotated bibliography of Buber's books in English translation.

————. *Martin Buber's Life and Works.* 3 Vols. New York: E. P. Dutton, 1983. (**A, G**)

Vol. I. *The Early Years.* Friedman shows how the events of the first forty-five years of Buber's life led to his writing *I and Thou* (1923), based on his insistence that real living is "meeting" yourself, others, and God, a philosophical outlook that his subsequent works would elaborate. The loss of his mother was the first *Vergegnung* (mismeeting) of his life. His grandparents provided the love which helped offset the loss. His reactions to later events he said were conditioned by the first "mismeeting." His Zioinist activities would enable him to work with some individuals on the level of *begegnung* (real meeting). His involvement with mysticism and his discovery of Hassidism were also steps in formulating his mature philosophy. World War I and the murder of Gustav Landauer demonstrated the spiritual problems with which twentieth century man had to cope. *I and Thou* is the initial blueprint of a way of life that might help modern man to attain some integrity, which because of the industrial age, he had lost.

Vol. II. *The Middle Years 1923-1945*. During these years Buber collaborated with Rosenzweig on his life-long task of translating the Hebrew Bible into German. In 1925 the Hebrew University in Jerusalem opened, a project he had worked on since 1901. His efforts also caused the Zionist organization to include a land-folk school within the structure of the university. This volume focuses on the role Buber played when the Nazis came to power, and his effective use of education to resist them. The volume ends with Buber's first seven years in Palestine, and the decline of his influence among Jews because of his position on Jewish-Arab relations.

Vol. III. *The Later Years 1945-1965*. Friedman describes Buber's international prestige during these years, his growing criticism of the Zionist intolerance of Arabs, his opposition to David Ben-Gurion and to the execution of Adolph Eichmann, and to the controversy created by his accepting the Goethe Prize of the University of Hamburg.

—————. *Martin Buber: The Life of Dialogue*. New York: Harper and Row, 1960. (**A, G**) Friedman's first book on Buber is an excellent introduction to his philosophy. For many years it was the only comprehensive guide available. Friedman focuses on the development of Buber's philosophy of dialogue. He also emphasizes Buber's thinking about the problem of evil in the course of that development, and his confidence that all evil will eventually be redeemed through the meeting of human personalities and that of God. Individual chapters are devoted to aspects of Buber's philosophy, its implications for Christianity, education, ethics, and social philosophy. Good bibliography.

Mendes-Flohr, Paul. *From Mysticism to Dialogue: Martin Buber's Transformation of German Social Thought.* Detroit, MI: Wayne State University Press, 1989. (**A**) Stresses the influence of Georg Simmel, one of Buber's teachers, on his social thought. Simmel's concern with relationship is quite close to Buber's *I and Thou* concept. Belief in God for Simmel did not mean a rational acceptance of His existence, but a definite inner relationship with Him, a relationship analogous to that between human individuals and to certain objects of nature. Buber, however, developed these concepts much more thoroughly than Simmel. Contains much of biographical interest as the origin of Buber's social philosophy is traced.

Schaeder, Grete. *The Hebrew Humanism of Martin Buber.* Translated by Noah J. Jacobs. Detroit, MI: Wayne State University Press, 1973. (**A**) Schaeder believes that Buber's thought, despite the strong influence of nineteenth-century German philosophy, owes more to his Hebrew roots than to anything else. As a member of a community rather than as a closed individual, a person opens to God and his fellow humans. Israel should be the model community completely open to humanity to fulfill its messianic destiny. This is the ideal Buber tried to persuade his fellow Israelis to follow after he settled in Palestine. The book provides an excellent study of Buber's works with biographical notes.

Silberstein, Lawrence J. *Martin Buber's Social and Religious Thought: Alienation and the Quest for Meaning.* New York: New York University Press, 1989. (**A**) Silberstein attempts to defend Buber against the charges of some contemporary philosophers that his thinking is obscure and ambiguous. Some contemporary British and American philosophers are especially prone to take this attitude. These thinkers consider Buber more of a literary man than a philosopher, and his work does appear in many literary forms. (*I and Thou* is considered by many as a kind of prose poem, and Buber also wrote some excellent poems in German). This book explores many of the ambivalent responses to Buber's writings, and provides an explanation of his responses to them. Silberstein believes that Buber's concern with alienation has been neglected by commentators of his work, and tries to compensate for this neglect. He presents Buber's ideas of community as a means of countering this alienation. Buber's views on Hasidism have been particularly controversial, especially after Gershom Scholem, the highly respected expert on Jewish mysticism, challenged them. Silberstein makes Buber's views on this subject clear. He also shows how Buber, because he was a university student at the time, is at least partially a product of *fin de siècle* Vienna.

Simon, Charlie May. *Martin Buber: Wisdom in Our Time: The Story of an Outstanding Jewish Thinker*. New York: E. P. Dutton, 1969. (**G**) Simon, who has written a number of popular biographies, presents one of the simpler accounts of Buber's life and thought. This book serves as a good introduction to the period in which Buber lived. The first chapter has a photograph of some typical Polish Jews at the time when he lived in Lemberg, and explains the kind of education young Jews received six days a week in synagogue schools. Other equally helpful illustrations and photos provide glimpses of German university life and show Buber and some of his contemporaries, Theodor Herzl for example, at the turn of the century and in later life. This is a good introduction for younger readers. Includes chapters on the development of Buber's philosophy of dialogue, the rise of Adolf Hitler, and a brief bibliography.

Smith, Ronald Gregor. *Martin Buber*. Richmond, VA: John Knox Press, 1967. (**G**) A noted Presbyterian cleric, Smith in his translation of *I and Thou* was much closer to Buber's way of thinking than Walter Kaufmann. After a brief chapter devoted to Buber's life, he explains the many facets of the Jewish thinker's philosophy. Buber's more formal terms can be difficult, but he is trying to explain how "we may not only understand but also live in the spirit" (p. 29). This is the section in which Smith explains Buber's meaning of the term "the interhuman," which Buber had coined in the early 1920s to describe the sense of mutual understanding arrived at in a true dialogue during which human beings may experience one another as living events, not as objects. The concluding chapter, "Relations to Christianity," explains the implications for followers of Jesus of Buber's thinking. Jesus pointed the way through which any person may say "Father" to God and be accepted by Him as a child.

Susser, Bernard. *Existence and Utopia: The Social and Political Thought of Martin Buber*. East Rutherford, NJ: Fairleigh Dickinson University Press, 1981. (**A**) Susser insists at the outset that Buber has become, thanks to his popularity, an "out-of-focus public image that is as blandly benign as it is inaccurate (introduction, xi). He believes that Buber's eloquence and theoretical skills as a stylist are partly responsible for this distorted picture of him. Wishing to present the real Buber, he concentrates on Buber's role as a social thinker, but this cannot be done without presenting his thought in its entirety. Buber saw his work as a unity. His philosophy can be conveniently seen from two perspectives: his existentialist view of the human individual and his idealistic, or utopistic, faith in that individual's ability to form a much finer community than has been realized before. This is possible only if a group of individuals have realized their full potential in dialogue. Susser in chapter 4, "The Prophet and the Apocalypse," gives a detailed comparison of the social theories of Buber and Karl Marx, who wanted to produce the same results Buber hopes for, but became confused by his own materialism. In criticizing Buber, Susser is not simply being a debunker. He presents a towering human being who was a greater man than he was a thinker. Includes a good bibliography.

Vermes, Paula. *Buber.* New York: Grove Press, 1988 (**A, G**) Another valuable and brief book on Buber that attempts to properly identify the man. Buber denied that he was either a philosopher or a theologian. Biblical specialists do not accept him as one of their own. He admitted only to being a Hebrew thinker and a writer, which was probably a deliberate oversimplification of his work. The book offers biographical information and good insights into Buber as a writer. His subtle use of language is demonstrated on pp. 97-98 as Vermes shows the distinction between two terms, one Greek, "Pistis," and one Hebrew, "emunah," both being types of faith, but the first meaning a mental assent, and the second an acceptance of the divine will as seen in the everyday life of the believer. Both forms of faith have been eclipsed in modern life. Good notes and bibliography.

Overview and Evaluation of Primary Sources

Buber was a recognized stylist in the use of literary German and an acknowledged master of oratory, and his works form an impressive bibliography. But they are not always easily accessible. As Bernard Susser, the author of *Existence and Utopia: The Social and Political Thought of Martin Buber* (1981; see above), has noted, his works present a challenge to the student because some essays are reprinted in several volumes, and some differ from the form in which they were presented as speeches when later published in the essay format. The fact that Buber wrote in two languages, German until he was about sixty, and German and Hebrew afterwards, further complicates matters when trying to approach some of the primary sources.

Though there is yet to be published a complete edition of Buber's works, a three-volume collection of his most important works, *Werke*, was published in German (Munich: Kosel-Verlag, 1962-1964; **A, G**). The first volume features Buber's philosophical writings, the second, his writings on the Bible, and the third, his writings on Hasidism.

A volume of Buber's writings on Judaism, *Der Jude und Sein Judentum* (Cologne, Germany: J. Melzer, 1963; **A**), has not been translated. Buber's letters, based on Ms. Schaeder's three-volume edition in German and other languages has been published, *The Letters of Martin Buber: A Life of Dialogue* (New York: Schocken Books, 1991; **A, G**), edited by Nahum N. Glatzer and Paul Mendes-Flor and translated by Richard and Clara Winston. Most of the over 40,000 letters Buber wrote in his lifetime remain untranslated. Buber's letters tend to be brief and they generally deal with important public issues. The longest letter and certainly one of the most interesting is No. 523 dated February 24, 1939 to Mohandas K. Gandhi written after Ghandi had published a statement in his weekly magazine *Harijan* which was very unsympathetic to Zionism. Palestine belonged to the Arabs. He advised that the Jews remain in Germany and pursue "satyagraha"—passive non-violent resistence even unto death. Buber tries to explain how different the Nazis were in comparison to the British officials with whom Ghandi had struggled.

Most of Buber's thirty or so books have been translated into English and published in the U.S. and England. *I and Thou* has been published in two translations, the first by Ronald Gregor Smith (1937. Reprint. New York: Charles Scribner's, 1955; **A, G**). The second is by Walter Kaufmann (New York: Charles Scribner's, 1970; **A, G**). Some authorities on Buber, notably Maurice Friedman, say that Smith's translation is closer to the spirit of Buber's original work. Smith also translated *Between Man and Man* (1947. Reprint. New York: Macmillan, 1965; **A, G**). This collection includes "Dialogue," "The Question to the Single One," "Education," "The Education of Character," and "What is Man." Buber says in his "Foreword" that these essays further develop his thoughts in *I and Thou*. The 1965 edition has a brief introduction by Maurice Friedman and an

"Afterward: The History of the Dialogical Principle" by Buber.

Though Buber did not write an autobiography, he provided what he called "Autobiographical Fragments" for Paul Arthur Schilpp and Maurice Friedman, eds., *The Philosophy of Martin Buber* (Vol. 12 in Library of Living Philosophers; La Salle, IL: Open Court, 1967; **A**), an important study of Buber's philosophy written by many who knew him well. This work also contains Buber's reply to his critics, and a good bibliography compiled by Friedman.

Buber's "Autobiographical Fragments" was later reprinted along with a wealth of other material about influential events in Buber's life, in Maurice Friedman, ed., *Meetings* (La Salle, IL: Open Court, 1973; **A, G**). The work features short accounts of significant meetings in Buber's life, including his reactions to his absent mother after his parent's divorce, a "vergegnung," or mismeeting, as he terms it (see the comments on Volume I of Friedman's 3-volume biography above); and his failure to understand the plight of the young man, Mëhe, the subject of the section he calls "Conversion."

Maurice Friedman has also translated *Tales of Rabbi Nachman* (Bloomington: Indiana University Press, 1962; **A, G**), *The Legend of the Baal Shem* (London: East and West Library, 1955; **A, G**), *The Original and Meaning of Hasidism* (New York: Horizon Press, 1960; **A**), *The Knowledge of Man* (New York: Harper and Row, 1966; **A**), *The Eclipse of God* (New York: Humanities Press, 1972; **A, G**), and *Pointing the Way: Collected Essays* (New York: Harper Brothers, 1957; **A, G**). Will Herberg published an anthology, *The Writing of Martin Buber* (New York: New American Library, 1956; **A, G**), including selections from *I and Thou*, *Between Man and Man*, and *The Eclipse of God*. Herberg also wrote a perceptive introduction for the book.

The most recent bibliography of Buber's works, complete up to 1978, is the one by Margot Cohen and Rafael Buber (Buber's son), *Martin Buber: A Bibliography of his Writings* (Jerusalem: The Magnes Press, 1980; **A**). Useful as well is W. Moonan's "Writings about Martin Buber in English: A selective Bibliography," *Bulletin of Bibliography* 32 (June, 1975): a8-31.

Museums, Historical Landmarks, Societies

Grace Cathedral (San Francisco). Buber is featured in a stained glass display of "Secular Saints," alongside Albert Einstein, John Glenn, and Thurgood Marshall.

International Council of Christians and Jews (Heppenheim, Germany). In 1975 plans had been made to tear down Buber's house in Heppenheim so that a freeway could be built. Under pressure, the Federal State of Hessen changed its plans, and the house was saved and has become the council's headquarters. A meeting room in the building is dedicated to Buber, in an effort to keep his memory and ideas alive.

Martin Buber Center for Adult Education and Continuing Education (Mount Scopus Campus, Hebrew University, Jerusalem). Opened in 1972, this building has a Martin Buber room in which Buber's study is preserved exactly as it was in his house in Talbiyeh, his last residence in Jerusalem. In addition to Buber's personal effects there is a portrait of Buber painted by his granddaughter, Barbara Golschmidt. The portrait is considered to be an excellent work.

Martin Buber Forest. (Galilee). Planted in his memory in 1970 at Kibbutz Hazorea, funded by a group of German admirers.

Martin Buberstrasse (Berlin). The street on which Buber lived in the Zehlendorf Borough of West Berlin was renamed after him in 1966 on the first anniversary of his death.

Other Sources

Barlow, R. M. ''Buber Looks at Nature.'' *Contemporary Philosophy* 12 (July/ August 1988): 5-11. The relevance of Buber's thinking to ecology is examined in this article, which discusses Buber's philosophy that ''Human respect for nature is included within human duty to the God who has been encountered.''

Rollins, E. William, and Harry Zohn. *Men of Dialogue: Martin Buber and Albrecht Goes.* New York: Funk and Wagnalls, 1969. Albrecht Goes, a German novelist, had known Buber before he moved to Palestine. After the war the two men met again, and their dialogues and lives are described here.

Karl Avery

Edward Coley Burne-Jones
1833-1898

Chronology

Born Edward Coley Burne-Jones in Birmingham, England, on August 28, 1833, the son of Edward Richard Jones, a craftsman who operates a frame and carving shop, and Elizabeth Coley, who dies of complications following his birth; *1845-1853* attends King Edward's Free School, where he receives an excellent education in classical grammar, history, and geography; develops intense friendships with classmates Richard Dixon, who introduces him to the works of Keats, and Cornell Price, with whom he explores the "Ossianic" poems (rhythmic works attributed to a legendary Gaelic poet) and works of German Romantics; spends summers with relatives in Leicestershire, where he visits a Cistercian monastery and develops High Church aspirations; *1849-1852* attends night classes at the government school of design and visits London frequently to explore the sculpture collections in the British Museum; *1852-1853* matriculates Exeter College, Oxford; unhappy with student life until he meets William Morris, another freshman who has similar idealistic, artistic, and intellectual leanings and who becomes a major figure in the history of the decorative arts; *1854* discusses with Morris plans for forming a celibate monastic brotherhood to be called "the Order of Galahad"; reads cultural and social theory of John Ruskin and becomes acquainted with the works of the Pre-Raphaelite Brotherhood, a group of artists and poets who take their inspiration from the period in art history that precedes the style of Italian Renaissance painter Raphael; *1855* attends London exhibit by Pre-Raphaelite painters John Everett Millais, Ford Madox Brown, and Holman Hunt; embarks with Morris on a walking tour of French cathedrals during his college vacation; *1855-1856* decides to commit his life to art rather than religion, and with Morris starts a magazine in imitation of *The Germ,* a Pre-Raphaelite publication, called the *Oxford and Cambridge Magazine*; leaves Oxford without taking a degree and becomes an apprentice to poet and artist Dante Gabriel Rossetti, a founder of the Pre-Raphaelite movement; moves into lodgings with Morris in Red Lion Square; *1857* returns to Oxford along with Arthur Hughes, Val Prinsep, Spencer Stanhope, and Morris to execute murals on the walls of the Oxford Union under the direction of Rossetti; *1857-1860* commissioned to make stained glass windows for White Friars Company; *1859* goes to Italy to study Renaissance painters such as Titian, Botticelli, and Tintoretto; *1860* marries Georgiana MacDonald after a four-year engagement; *1860-1862* helps form ''The Firm'' (as it became known) of Marshall, Morris, Faulkner & Co. (later known as Morris & Co.; William Morris was a poet, artist, and socialist philosopher; Marshall and Faulkner were financial backers); *1862* travels with Ruskin to Italy to see Giotto frescoes in the Arena Chapel; enlarges his circle of artistic associates to includes American painter James McNeill Whistler, George Du Maurier, and Edward Poynter, whose influences weaken his dependence on Rossetti; *1864* exhibits at the Old Watercolor Society; *1865* moves to Kensington Square; *1867* illustrates Morris's *The Earthly Paradise,* for which he makes over one hundred designs from classical subjects, marking a turn in his development as an artist; moves from the city to ''the Grange'' in Fulham, a rural suburb of London; *1869* enters into a three-year affair with Maria Zambacco, a Greek model; *1871* returns to Italy; tours the Sistine Chapel and the Vatican; *1873* reorganizes ''The Firm,'' making himself the chief glass designer; *1876* completes *The Beguiling of Merlin*, a work that has occupied him for three decades; *1877* exhibits *The Mirror of Venus* at the Grosvenor Gallery, a private art gallery established in 1877 by Sir Coutts Lindsay to rival the Royal Academy of Art and provide a place for modern English artists to exhibit their work; *1878* completes *Pan and Psyche*; *1881* buys a house at Rottingdean in Sussex to escape the pressures of city life; *1882* receives a commission to decorate the American Protestant Church in Rome with mosaics; *1884-1886* exhibits *King Cophetua and the Beggar Maid* and *The Depths of the Sea*; *1889* becomes a Chevalier of the Legion of Honor; *1891* founds with Morris the Kelmicott Press; *1894* receives a baronetcy; *1898* dies on June 14 from a heart attack.

Activities of Historical Significance

Although Edward Coley Burne-Jones was not a man of action and played no significant part in the real world of practical affairs, he is nevertheless an important figure in the cultural and intellectual history of the last half of the nineteenth century. His whole artistic output can be seen as an aesthetic challenge to the materialism of Victorian society. As a boy in Birmingham, he was exposed to the urban blight of one of England's largest industrial cities. The sight of squalor did not arouse his social consciousness, however. Instead, the awareness of these evils only created a desire in him for the more permanent and perfect order that he found in tales of medieval chivalry and classical romance. He declared that his pictures were intended to create ''a beautiful romantic dream of something that never was or never could be—in a light better than any light that ever shone—in a land no one can define or remember, only desire.''

After he renounced his intended vocation in the clergy and dedicated his life to art, he enlisted his services in the cause of the Pre-Raphaelite movement, which in 1855 was starting to disband as Holman Hunt and John Everett Millais went their separate ways, and became a disciple of Dante Gabriel Rossetti, working as his assistant, and, at first, modeling his own work after Rossetti's. In his choice and treatment of subject matter he was influenced by the literary and artistic circle that included Rossetti, Robert Morris, and poet Algernon Swinburne. His main source was that storehouse of medieval Arthurian legend, Sir Thomas Malory's *Morte d'Arthur*. Chaucer, the lives of the saints, and the Bible were important inspirations as well. Later he used Morris's *Earthly Paradise* (1868-1870), a valuable three-volume compendium of classical and romantic lore from which he took many images for his paintings.

In his pictures, Burne-Jones intended no moral meanings, and there is in all of his work an aura of unreality. His designs for pictures are usually flat; the surface does not recede to a horizon, and objects appear in relationships to one another that are deliberately unrealistic. As art critics have noted, dying and sleeping are recurrent themes in his work. The figures in his paintings exist in worlds without actions or agitation. Burne-Jones preferred subjects without specific meaning that offered ambiguity and invited the viewer to dream and meditate. These characteristics remained the same throughout his career, and none of his pictures seems to have any relation to the times in which he lived nor to his own actual experience. He was the ultimate practitioner of the unearthly style of Pre-Raphaelitism.

Generally, Burne-Jones's paintings lack the social purpose that informs the art work and writings of his contemporaries Morris and John Ruskin, a renowned art critic; but as a craftsman who designed stained glass, furniture, mosaic tiles, book illustrations, and even musical instruments, he made an important contribution to the arts and crafts movement. This movement was a reaction to the mechanization and acceleration of production that came as a result of the industrial revolution. The perception of thinkers like Ruskin and creative individuals like Morris and Burne-Jones was that the assembly line had not only killed off the artistic quality of the goods produced but was killing the spirit of the workers as well. They believed that the conditions of work and of the worker could be elevated by a return to the means of manufacture used by artisans in the Middle Ages.

The model for integration between the worker and the finished product was "The Firm" which aimed to unite all the visual and the decorative arts. The wallpaper, furniture, glass, and tapestries created by the craftspeople employed by Morris, Marshall, Faulkner, & Co. were a practical success. Unfortunately, supply could not keep up with demand due to the lengthy production process, and the high prices that resulted put the goods created by The Firm beyond the means of the ordinary people whose lives were supposed to be enriched by the skillfully crafted products. Nevertheless, the efforts of the artists and craftspeople saved from oblivion the historic means and customs of producing artifacts while instructing an industrial society about the value of quality over convenience or quantity.

The creations of Burne-Jones, the designs of Morris, and the writing of Ruskin were without question the animating force behind the Aesthetic movement that valued beauty and craftsmanship in England and later in America. Their ideas for reform in the arts and crafts introduced a concern for honest construction and fidelity to the principles of artistic creation into every aspect of public and domestic life from the mid-1870s to the turn of the century. Artists like Burne-Jones did not radically change the world, but they made it a more beautiful place to live and also cultivated an appreciation for art in all facets of everyday life.

Overview of Biographical Sources

To date there is only a handful of full-length biographical studies of Burne-Jones and these are now badly dated. Furthermore, many of the early records were left by family members, who omitted details about his intimate life and work habits they deemed too unseemly, and therefore are of limited value. The standard work on his life and work is Malcolm Bell's *Edward Burne-Jones: A Record and Review* (1892); it also contains a chronological catalogue of his finished pictures and stained glass designs. Another important source is Georgiana Burne-Jones's two-volume *Memorials of Burne-Jones* (1904) in which his widow provides an intimate but highly selective account of her husband's life and work. Val Prinsep's "A Chapter from a Painter's Reminiscences: The Oxford Circle: Rossetti, Burne-Jones, and William Morris" published in *The Magazine of Art* 2 (1904), includes an account of Rossetti, Morris, and Burne-Jones during the Oxford phase of their relationship.

More recently there has been an increasing candor in full-length treatments. The nearest to being a definitive biography is Penelope Marcus's *Burne-Jones* (London: Michael Joseph, 1975). Lord David Cecil's *Visionary and Dreamer* (Princeton: Princeton University Press, 1969), discusses both Burne-Jones and Samuel Palmer as visionary artists. Martin Harrison and William Waters' *Burne-Jones* (1973) is mostly a discussion of the work but also gives some of the essential biographical facts. Francis Spalding's *Magnificent Dreams: Burne-Jones and the Late Victorians* (1978) examines the life and works in the context of the end of the nineteenth century, showing how the shared interest in myths and use of the art of the past are not coincidental but due to the close sympathies among the Pre-Raphaelites and their circle. Both Jan Marsh's *The Pre-Raphaelite Sisterhood* (New York: St. Martin's, 1986) and Gay Daly's *The Pre-Raphaelites in Love* (New York: Ticknor and Fields, 1989) are good sources for readers who want to know more about Burne-Jones's relationship with his models and wife; each author devotes a chapter to the artist's marital problems, which became complicated by his love affairs with Mary Zambaco and May Gaskell.

Evaluation of Principal Biographical Sources

Bell, Malcolm. *Sir Edward Burne-Jones: A Record and Review*. London: George Bell, 1892. (**A**) One of the earliest studies of Burne-Jones's life and work, but erroneous in many details and scanty in documentation.

Burne-Jones, Georgiana. *Memorials of Edward Burne-Jones*. 2 vols. London: Macmillan, 1904. (**A**) The most important source for biographical information because the author was the artist's wife. She is a very capable writer who is totally sympathetic to her subject, despite just cause to be otherwise. The "memorial" aspect of this volume is obvious throughout. Its great value as a source is due to the immediacy of the record. Burne-Jones collected the material six years after her husband's death and thus included vivid contemporary accounts and reminiscences.

Carr, J. Comyns. *Coasting Bohemia*. London: Macmillan, 1914. (**A, G**) Includes an interesting essay on Burne-Jones from the perspective of someone on the fringe of the community of avant-garde artists that included Whistler, Beardsley, and Yeath senior.

Fitzgerald, Penelope. *Edward Burne-Jones: A Biography*. London: Michael Joseph, 1975. (**A, G**) Traces the daily life of her subject in what is to date the definitive biography of Burne-Jones. Based on new materials, Fitzgerald's study is much more comprehensive than earlier biographies. Her research draws on private papers and unpublished letters and notebooks as well as public documents. The book is fully documented with notes to the text and contains a valuable appendix that locates works by Burne-Jones in museums and private collections. Includes a useful index as well.

Harrison, Martin, and William Waters. *Burne-Jones*. New York: G. P. Putnam, 1973. (**A**) Another more recent and scholarly approach that undertakes an examination of both the life and works of the artist. Handsomely illustrated with over two hundred plates, many of them in color, the authors are particularly good in their analysis of Burne-Jones within the context of the Aesthetic movement and his contributions to the later phases of Pre-Raphaelitism. A useful book for understanding the various phases of Burne-Jones's technical developments as an artist and what his works reveal on a deeper, psychological level. The appendix lists the subjects and locations of stained glass windows designed by Burne-Jones and itemizes the contents of public galleries with holdings of his works.

Spalding, Francis. *Magnificent Dreams: Burne-Jones and the Late Victorians*. New York: E. P. Dutton, 1978. (**A, G**) Considers the paintings of Burne-Jones with some commentary on his life. This book shows how close all the art of the final decades of the nineteenth century in England is in terms of shared interest in the past, particularly the Middle Ages and classical Greece. The similarities among the paintings is discussed, but Spalding, who is an art historian, also connects the painters with one another in the social context in which they lived. Amply illustrated with seldom-seen pictures, this is a vivid account of the London art scene at the end of the Victorian era.

Waters, William. *Burne-Jones: An Illustrated Life of Sir Edward Burne-Jones, 1833-1891.* Aylesbury, Buckshire: Shire Publications, 1973. (**G**) Provides a brief, readable account of the career of Burne-Jones, emphasizing how his life epitomized the dilemma of nineteenth-century artists, who, like Burne-Jones, were faced with the problem of accommodating zealous religiousness on one hand, with new scientific materialism on the other. The author supplements the text with engravings, photographs, and illustrations.

Overview and Evaluation of Primary Sources

With few exceptions the letters, notebooks, and manuscript collections are in England. Much of the material is unpublished and in family or private hands. Such is the case with Burne-Jones's Italian notebooks, which are owned by Mary Chamot; likewise, the Burne-Jones and MacDonald papers are in the possession of Celia Rooke. The major public collection of Burne-Jones's letters is in the British Museum and contains his correspondence with Lord Balfour, William Morris, and Dante Rossetti and Georgiana's letters to him. Important letters to others in the circle are in the Victoria and Albert Museum and in the University of Texas and Harvard University libraries. The materials from which Georgiana compiled her *Memorials* are in the Fitz William Museum at Cambridge.

To date there are no published editions of any of these materials, and one must use the *Memorials* for the primary sources they contain. The only letters to have been collected are edited by W. Graham Robertson in *Letters to Katie* (London: Macmillan, 1925), which is the series of lighthearted letters he wrote to Katie Lewis, a little girl of six, for whom he sketched comic animal pictures in the margins.

Fiction and Adaptations

Director Ken Russell's 1968 film *Dante's Inferno* is a fictional biographical account of the life of Dante Gabriel Rossetti and also features those in his circle, including Morris, Ruskin, Swinburne, and Burne-Jones. In addition, the movie provides a superb recreation of the period's atmosphere. Although Russell takes liberties with the facts, he remains true to the spirit that infused these young artist-rebels in their lives and loves.

Museums, Historical Landmarks, Societies

Ashmolean Museum (Oxford University). Contains many fine examples of Burne-Jones's art, such as *The Building of the Brazen Tower*.

British Museum Prints Room (London). Houses numerous drawings and water colors, including the original designs for *The Flower Book*.

City of Birmingham Museum and Art Gallery (Birmingham, England). Houses over two hundred studies and drawings for many of Burne-Jones's most important works. In addition, the museum owns the *Pygmalion* series and *Cupid and Psyche,* as well as other good examples of his painting.

Fogg Art Gallery (Harvard University, Cambridge, Massachusetts). Owns the most important American collection of Burne-Jones's work—*The Death of the Sea, Pan and Psyche*, and *The Brazen Tower*—are among the most impressive.

Kelmscott Manor (outside London). Houses many of the products designed by The Firm, including some of Burne-Jones's stained glass and tiles.

Lady Lever Art Gallery (Port Sunlight, England). Owns two important oil paintings: *Merlin and Vivian* and *Phyllis and Demophoon*, as well as many good-quality late pencil drawings.

Tate Gallery (London). The most representative collection of Burne-Jones's works may be seen in this gallery, including *King Cophetua and the Beggar Maid* and nearly fifty other paintings.

Victoria and Albert Museum (London). Contains a wide variety of drawings, sketches, notebooks, painted furniture, stained glass and some late unfinished works, *The Garden of Vices*, *The Car of Love,* and *Feast of Peleus.*

William Morris Gallery (Walsham, London). Has drawings and studies from a wide range of subjects and two important paintings, *The Lament* and *St. George and the Dragon* in addition to many cartoons for glass and tiles.

Other Sources

Ash, Russell. *Sir Edward Burne-Jones.* New York: Abrams, 1993. Forty plates, many full page, are accompanied with commentary on facing pages. Ash's introduction sketches the artist's life and melancholy personality.

Bateman, Arthur B. "Edward Burne-Jones (1833-1898)." In *London Quarterly Review* 158 (October 1933): 447-452. Published as a centenary tribute, the author discusses Burne-Jones's special genius for creating a world of romance in the midst of commercial crassness.

Hallman, G. S. "From a Burne-Jones Sketchbook." In *Harper's Magazine* 141 (November 1920): 719-774. Contains valuable discussion of the studies for *The Mirror of Venus* and *The Romaunt of the Rose.*

Ironside, Robin. "Burne-Jones and Gustave Moreau." In *Horizon* 1 (June 1940): 406-424. Traces the influences of the artist on continental painters of the symbolist school.

Hallman Bell Bryant
Clemson University

Saint Frances Xavier Cabrini
1850-1917

Chronology

Born Maria Francesca Cabrini on July 15, 1850, in Sant'Angelo Lodigiano at Lombardy, Italy, the thirteenth child of Agostino Cabrini, a farmer, and Stella Oldini, a housewife; *1859-1868* attends the private school of the Daughters of the Sacred Heart at Arluno; granted a teacher's diploma and a teacher's certificate; applies for admission into the order but is refused by the mother superior, who considers her too weak for such a life; *1870* between February and December both parents die; *1871* attends the Pedagogical Training Courses at Lodi; *1872* contracts smallpox and is nursed back to health by her sister, Rosa; begins teaching at Vidardo, and decides to become a missionary; applies again for admission to the Daughters of the Sacred Heart and is rejected; applies to the Canossian Sisters in Crema and is refused; *1874-1876* appointed to head an orphanage in need of reform; *1877* takes vocational vows and is appointed superior of the House of Providence; *1880-1886* advised by Bishop of Lodi to found a missionary order; *1880* opens a convent with seven other sisters in the town of Codogno; acknowledged as "Mother Cabrini" by members of the Institute of the Missionary Sisters of the Sacred Heart of Jesus (M.S.C.); draws up the rules of the institute, establishing November 14 as its founding date; *1882-1885* opens four houses in Italy; *1887* leaves Milan for Rome to obtain papal approval of her institute and seek permission to open a house in the city; meets Giovanni Battista Scalabrini, bishop of Piacenza, who has just published *L'emigrazione italiana in America* (The Italian Emigration to America); *1888* returns to Rome and reports to Pope Leo XIII; desires to work in China, but the pope advises her: "You must not go to the East but to the West. Your mission will be in America"; *1889* embarks for New York, where within four months she founds the Asylum of the Holy Angel to house four hundred destitute children; *1890* takes possession of a former Jesuit property, Manresa, at West Park-on-the-Hudson, for her orphanage; *1891* establishes the novitiate; returns to Italy and opens a training college in Rome; plans to expand her missionary work into Central America; embarks with twenty-nine sisters for

Nicaragua, where she opens a school in December; *1892* leaves Nicaragua for New Orleans, where she establishes a mission to assist Italian immigrants; asked to manage the Italian hospital in New York; the hospital experiences serious financial difficulties which lead to foreclosure; founds Columbus Hospital; returns to Rome and meets several times with Pope Leo XIII; *1893* the sisters are expelled from Grenada by a revolutionary government and move to Panama; *1894* returns to New York with fifteen sisters; to ease crowding at Columbus Hospital, purchases the old Post Graduate Hospital; *1895* tours New Orleans, Panama City, and Buenos Aires; journeys by mule across Cordillera of the Andes from Chile to Argentina; arrives in Buenos Aires and establishes a home on Christmas Day; *1896* opens the Academy of St. Rose in Buenos Aires with fifty students; institutes training for Spanish- and Portuguese-speaking Catholic sisters; sails for Spain where she opens a house to "help in the work in Spanish America"; returns to Italy; *1898* visits the pope, who calls her a "saint"; visits Paris, where she opens a boarding-house for women; the first paying guest of the boarding-house, Countess Spottiswood Makin, is influential in securing an invitation for the missionary sisters to come to Spain under the patronage of Queen Maria Cristina; visits England to establish an orphanage for Italian children; *1899* returns to New York to establish various schools and missions for Italian children; opens schools in several U.S. cities; visits Spain and Italy where she establishes schools, orphanages, and convents; meets the pope, who commissions her to carry the spirit of God "to the whole world"; *1900* returns to Buenos Aires where she establishes more educational institutions; *1901* returns to Genoa in poor health; *1902* visits the Italian convents and travels to Spain, France, and England; returns to the U.S. in August; founds new houses, schools, and orphanages in Denver and other cities; *1905* founds Chicago's Columbus Hospital in the old North Shore Hotel in Lincoln Park; founds orphanages and schools in Oregon and California; celebrates the silver jubilee of her congregation; *1907* visits Italy, France, Spain, and England; awarded the "Grand Prix" by the queen of Italy in recognition of her work among the Italian immigrants; visits Argentina and Brazil; *1909* visits American cities; becomes an American citizen in October; *1910* returns to Italy and is made superior general of the congregation for life; travels to Paris and London; *1911* resides in Rome; *1912-1917* returns to the U.S., where she continues to establish new orphanages and hospitals; *1917* dies on December 22 in Chicago at age sixty-seven and is buried at West Park, New York; *1928* introduction of the cause for beatification begins in Chicago and continues in Lodi and Rome in 1929; *1931* the Ordinary Process is completed when the Congregation of Rites gives favorable opinion to the introduction of the Apostolic Process and submits its results to the pope for his approval; *September 1933* in Chicago, a Catholic Church tribunal headed by Cardinal Mundelein hears testimony regarding the virtues and miracles of Mother Cabrini; *October 3, 1933* she is pronounced Venerable; as part of the canonization process, her body is exhumed form her grave at West Park for identification; the body is reburied in the chapel of the Mother Cabrini High School, 701 Forth Washington Avenue; two miracles, attributed to her and regarding Sister Delfina Grazioli of Seattle and Peter Smith of New York, a 12-year-old boy, miraculously healed through Mother Cabrini's intervention, are examined; *1937* the Congregation of Sacred Rites, attended by the pope, recognizes the heroic virtues of Mother Cabrini and the formal announcement is made on July 31, 1938; in September Mgr. Salvatore Natucci of Rome, Procurator General of the Congregation for the Propagation of the Faith arrives in New York to take a relic from the coffin containing her body for the official ceremony of beatification; *1941* the Congregation of Rites, headed by Cardinal Alessandro Verde, takes over the case of Canonization; *1943* the Congregation of Rites, under the presidency of Pope Pius XII, approves two miracles proposed for her canonization; *July 7, 1946* declared a saint by Pope Pius XII.

Activities of Historical Significance

Saint Frances Xavier Cabrini was the first American citizen to be elevated to sainthood by the Catholic Church. In her missionary work Mother Cabrini established schools, orphanages, convents, and hospitals throughout Europe, the U.S., and Latin America. Recognized as a vital force for social and spiritual change by the leadership of the Catholic Church, she gave her time and energy unselfishly, bolstered by a simple but powerful faith. At her death, she left behind a legacy of sixty-three foundations of the Missionary Sisters of the Sacred Heart of Jesus (M.S.C.) with a membership of nearly thirteen hundred missionary sisters. Missions established in her honor in China, Australia, and Canada serve the social and spiritual needs of the young and the impoverished through education and the provision of orphanages, health-care facilities, rest homes, and retreat houses.

By Catholic church law, at least fifty years must pass after a candidate's death before he or she may be considered for sainthood. In Mother Cabrini's case, however, Pope Pius XI waived this requirement and the process was initiated in 1928. In September 1933 a church tribunal examined testimony in Chicago regarding Mother Cabrini's virtues and miracles. Two miracles of healing were attributed to her, and miracles have been attributed to her since her canonization.

On November 13, 1938, an official ceremony of beatification for Mother Cabrini was held in St. Peter's Basilica in Rome. At that time the pope extolled her life as a "poem of holiness, activity, intelligence and charity." On December 14 five thousand people gathered at St. Patrick's Cathedral in New York to celebrate the beatification of Blessed Mother Frances Xavier Cabrini.

On July 7, 1946, in St. Peter's Basilica, Pope Pius XII declared Mother Cabrini a saint, the highest honor conferred by the Catholic Church, and in 1950 he proclaimed St. Francis Xavier Cabrini the patroness of all emigrants.

Overview of Biographical Sources

The literature on Mother Cabrini's life and missionary work has grown in both quantity and quality since her death, although none of the current biographies can be considered definitive. Two studies are of particular value: Theodore Maynard, *Too Small a World* (1945), and Giuseppe dall'Ongaro, *Francesca Cabrini, La suora che conquisto' l'America* (1982).

Evaluation of Principal Biographical Sources

Borden, Lucille Papin. *Francesca Cabrini: Without Staff or Scrip.* New York: Macmillan, 1945. (**A, G**) Borden's study is overburdened by excessive biblical digressions which "submerge" the life and career of Mother Cabrini. Borden gives inadequate attention to Mother Cabrini's founding of the Missionary Sisters of the Sacred Heart of Jesus, which was the cornerstone of her missionary work.

Cotter, Marie. *Westward by Command.* Cork: Mercier Press, 1947. (**A, G, Y**) This straightforward and "unadorned presentation" of Mother Cabrini's life story is accurate and well-organized. Suitable for those with little historical or theological background.

Dall'Ongaro, Giuseppe. *Francesca Cabrini, La suora che conquisto' l'America* (Mother Cabrini, the Nun Who Conquered America). Milan: Rusconi, 1982. (**A, G**) Based on extensive research, Dall'Ongaro's biography is notable for a thorough analysis of Mother Cabrini's life within its socio-historical context. The author blends Cabrini's thoughts, ideas, travels, and commitments with the events of the Italian *Risorgimento.* Published only in Italian.

De Maria, Francesca Saverio. *La Madre Francesca Saverio Cabrini, Fondatrice e Superiora Generale delle Missionarie del Sacro Cuore di Gesú, Per una dell sue e figlie.* Turin: Societa' Editrice Internazionale, 1928. (**A, G**) Written by Cabrini's fellow sister and personal secretary, the biography traces Mother Cabrini's life and career from archival sources. Descriptive and useful, although Theodore Maynard uncovers some inaccuracies. Translated into English and published by the Missionary Sisters of the Sacred Heart (Chicago, 1984).

Di Donato, Pietro. *Immigrant Saint, The Life of Mother Cabrini.* New York: McGraw-Hill, 1960. (**A, G**) Di Donato, author of *Christ in Concrete* (1937), writes a laudable biography of Mother Cabrini. Despite its "syrupy prose," the book is a serious attempt to show how the work of this Italian-American missionary expresses the soul of the Italian-American immigrant.

Martignoni, Angela. *Madre Cabrini: La Santa delle Americhe* (Mother Cabrini, the Saint of the Americas). New York: Vatican City Religious Book Company, 1945. (**A**) A comprehensive biography. Includes Mother Cabrini's pensieri and fioretti, and discussions of her popes, beatification, and canonization. Recommended for scholars and researchers.

Maynard, Theodore. *Too Small a World.* Milwaukee, WI: Bruce Publishing, 1945. (**A, G**) Given access to the documents and sources used by the Catholic Church during the beatification process, Maynard's well-written study is highly recommended for scholars and students. Translated into Italian by M. Santi and published by Longanesi in Milan (1971) and by the Missionary Sisters of the

Sacred Heart (1987).

Ravetto, Sister Joan Mary. *"Mother Cabrini" by a Daughter of St. Paul.* Boston, MA: St. Paul Editions, 1977. (**G, Y**) This concise but comprehensive biography is intended for students and the general public. As the author states in her short introduction, it is a "humble attempt to depict her most outstanding achievements."

Vian, Nello. *Madre Cabrini* (Mother Cabrini). Brescia, Italy: Morceliana, 1938. (**A, G**) Traces the life and career of Mother Cabrini, giving special attention to her activities among Italians abroad. Published only in Italian.

Museums, Historical Landmarks, Societies

Cabrini College (Radnor, PA). A coeducational, four-year, liberal arts college, affiliated with The Catholic University of America.

Mother Cabrini League (Chicago, IL). Established on February 14, 1938, and located at 434 W. Deming Plaza, the league has over 50,000 members. Among many other commitments, it is responsible for the maintenance of the room where Mother Cabrini died, which is located in the Chapel of Saint Frances Xavier Cabrini in Columbus Hospital, Chicago, and is open daily to visitors.

Mother Cabrini Monument (Sant'Angelo Lodigiano, Italy). Erected in 1987 outside the place of her birth.

Motherhouse of the Missionary Sisters of the Sacred Heart (Rome). Located at Viale Cortina d'Ampezzo 269, the motherhouse is the custodian of part of Mother Cabrini's archives.

St. Cabrini Shrine (Denver, CO). Exhibits videotapes documenting her life.

St. Frances Cabrini Chapel (New York). Mother Cabrini is interred in the chapel of the Missionary Sisters of the Sacred Heart, 701 Fort Washington Ave.

Other Sources

Acta Apostolicae Sedis (Vatican City Archives, Vol. 30, 1938; Vol. 38, 1946) Contain the Vatican official acts of Mother Cabrini's beatification and canonization.

Cicognani, Amleto Giovanni. *Addresses and Sermons, 1938-1942*. Paterson, NJ: St. Anthony Guild Press, 1942. Contains the sermon delivered at the saint's tomb in New York on November 13, 1928, the day of Cabrini's beatification, by Cicognani, the apostolic delegate to the U.S.

DiGiovanni, Stephen Michael. "Mother Cabrini: Early Years in New York." *Catholic Historical Review* (January 1991): 56-77. The article deals with Mother Cabrini's early apostolate among Italian immigrants in New York City. First-hand sources from the Vatican Archives and those of the Congregation of Propaganda Fide reveal the reasons for the coming of Mother Cabrini to the United States.

Lorit, Sergio C. *Frances Cabrini*. New York: New City Press, 1970. Lorit's biography ends with Mother Cabrini's death in 1917, and adds little new information.

Molinari, Paolo, S. I. "Madre Cabrini E Gli Emigrati." *Civilta' Cattolica* 2 (1968): 555-564. Written on the fiftieth anniversary of her death, the article draws abundantly on Mother Cabrini's notes, travels, letters, and diaries, and underlines her missionary work among Italian immigrants.

Sullivan, Mary Louise. "Mother Cabrini: Missionary to Italian Immigrants." *U.S. Catholic Historian* 6 (Fall 1987): 265-279. This article, an extract from the author's dissertation, deals with Mother Cabrini's missionary work among the Italian immigrants in the U.S.

Pellegrino Nazzaro
Rochester Institute of Technology

John Calvin
1509-1564

Chronology

Born Jean Cauvin July 10, 1509, in Noyon, Picardy, about sixty-five miles northeast of Paris, the son of Gérard Cauvin, or Calvin, a lay official in the local cathedral, and Jeanne Lefranc, whose family was in the city council; *1514-1515* mother dies; *1520-1523* goes to Paris to study Latin at Collège de la Marche and then moves on to Collège Montaigu for art courses; *1528* receives M.A. from University of Paris and then, following his father's advice, begins the study of law at Orléans and then Bourges; *1531* after father's death devotes himself to studies of literature and philosophy; *1532* publishes first work, a commentary on Roman philosopher/statesman Seneca's *De Clementia*; *1529-1534* converts to Protestantism; *1533* leaves Paris for Angoulême after his friend and newly installed rector of the University of Paris, Nicholas Cop's, controversial address, which Calvin coauthors; *1534* resigns as chaplain of La Gesine; *1535* flees to Basel, Switzerland; *1536* publishes first edition of the controversial *Institutes of the Christian Religion*; returns briefly to France to sort out family affairs; on the way to Strasbourg is invited by Guillaume Farel to help with the reformation of Geneva; presents *The Confession of Faith*, which outlines a system of beliefs for a proposed New Testament church to the Genevan Councils, the main governmental bodies of the city, the chief of which—the Petit Conseil—consisted of twenty-four male members; *1537* presents *Articles on the Organization of the Church*, which outlines the new structure for the church; *1538* banished from Geneva over argument as to whether the church or town has the right to excommunicate; called by German Protestant reformer Martin Bucer to the French refugee church in Strasbourg— Bucer provides authority and guidance to Calvin; *1539* publishes *Commentary on Romans*, the first of his biblical commentaries, and a greatly enlarged Latin edition of *Institutes;* *1540* marries Idelette de Bure, a widow with two children; *1541* again settles in Geneva and publishes a French translation of *Institutes;* Genevan Councils enact his *Ecclesiastical Ordinances*; *1542* son dies in infancy; *1546* as a result of Calvin's reformation activities, taverns in Geneva are shut down and the theater is suppressed; *1547* along with ministerial colleague, receives threats of violence; *1549* wife Idolette dies; *1553* at Calvin's urging, Spanish theologian Michael Servetus is burned at stake for opposing infant baptism and belief in the Trinity; *1555* Calvin's partisans are victorious in taking political control of Geneva from the followers of Ami Perrin, who opposed Calvin's ideas of ecclesiastical discipline; *1557-1564* works on commentaries on books of the Old Testament based on his lectures to students; *1559* Calvin becomes a Genevan citizen; founds Academy of Geneva with curriculum based on Christian humanism; *1564* vast expansion of Calvinist movement and definitive edition of *Institutes* published; dies on May 27, probably of tuberculosis and intestinal problems.

Activities of Historical Significance

The Protestant Reformation began in Germany in 1517 when Martin Luther (1483-1546) published *95 Theses* challenging traditional Catholic beliefs and practices such as purgatory and indulgences. Over the next century this challenge would lead to the end of papal supremacy in Western Christianity and the formation of Protestant churches.

Conditions which led to Luther's defiance had existed for several hundred years. Politically, popes and princes, especially the Holy Roman Emperor, fought for jurisdiction and power. European rulers resented the money which flowed from their countries into papal coffers and resented the interference of a distant and foreign pope in their affairs. Religiously, reformers like fourteenth century John Wycliffe and Jan Hus attacked the sale of indulgences and venality of the church. Within the church there were schisms, including two different popes reigning simultaneously in Avignon and Rome in the fourteenth century. Church officials were attacked for their greed, immorality and ignorance by writers like Dante and Chaucer. Educationally, the new humanist learning based on classical reading and freedom of inquiry and the invention of the printing press led scholars like Erasmus, Colet, More, Reuchlin and d'Etaples to look closely at church practices, work for better understanding of scriptural texts, and publish widely the results of their inquiry.

While Luther led the Reformation in Germany, Huldreich Zwingli opposed abuses of ecclesiastical authority in Switzerland. He instituted a simpler communion service and abolished celibacy. Zwingli was slain in the civil war between Protestants and Roman Catholics in 1531.

Luther and Zwingli were joined by others who formed the first generation of Reformers. Calvin, who worked on reform from 1534 until his death in 1564, was the greatest of the second generation of Reformers. Like Luther, he abhorred the excesses of the Catholic Church and desired a return to primitive Christianity, to communities of Christians living the simple life of the spirit rather than a hierarchy of wealth and power. Also like Luther, he helped shape his native language—French in Calvin's case—through his masterful prose style. But Calvin's work in many ways modified and went beyond Luther's.

Both Luther and Calvin subscribed to the views of the early Christian writer Augustine, who saw humans as sinful creatures who can do little without the help of God and yet who praised God for choosing to save some (like himself) to do God's work. Both Luther and Calvin emphasized the importance of God's grace in saving humankind and of God's election of certain people to do His work. Whereas Luther, particularly in his writings, deemphasized the importance of works—what people could do on their own, Calvin took the more moderate view that if one were chosen by God, this election would be manifest through one's works. One could never, of course, justify oneself before God, but doing good and working hard were signs that one had been blessed and chosen by God; the active life of industry and frugality became the life of religious devotion. Extrapolating this view, one could believe that work was salvation and that worldly success resulted from God's favor. Calvin himself, however, would not have accepted this extrapolation of his beliefs, as he himself emphasized spirituality and holy poverty and was suspicious of economic activity. In the seventeenth century, however, Calvinism became closely identified with the rise of urban areas, the middle class, and trade. All of these fed into the growth of capitalism in western Europe and later, the United States.

Another important difference between Luther and Calvin was the extent to which their religion depended upon the state. Luther's new religion could flourish only under the protection of German princes who were anxious to throw off the authority and economic dominance of the church, and Luther, particularly after the Peasant Rebellion, a war in which peasants, inspired by Luther's teachings, tried to improve their economic situation. Luther needed protection from papal power (he had been excommunicated and had had to live in hiding for several years) and disapproved of peasants' upsetting social and economic structures, so he wrote a pamphlet "Against the Murdering, Thieving Hordes of Peasants." In its struggles with the governing bodies of Geneva, Calvin's Protestantism developed so that it could operate independently from state support and even challenge civil authority. Part of its strength came from the church organization of pastors, elders, deacons and a consistory, which was a group of twelve lay elders selected annually by magistrates and of a varying number of pastors who maintained religious orthodoxy by means of a court and excommunication. Another strength was the personal and social moral discipline preached by Calvin. As Calvin's supporters triumphed in Geneva, his church, which had been so independent, became entwined with the state. Calvin, with his ideal of a theocracy, aspired to bring every aspect of Genevan life under God's law. His work brought about an independent church but also influenced republican ideas.

Calvin's *Institutes of the Christian Religion* not only detailed the requirements of a strong moral code but also provided Calvinism with a clear and coherent theology. Luther's writings had often sparked or been responses to controversy. As a result, his output was enormous but it did not follow any orderly pattern. Not until his *Institutes* did Calvin's writing become carefully planned and revised. In this work, Calvin tried to establish a unified Christian religion and define what was common to all Christians. The moral code and orderly theology of the work gave strength to the reform movement and helped Calvinism to spread when the growth of Lutheranism had slowed because of its dependence on sympathetic political authorities.

Besides his influence on the survival and expansion of Protestantism and capitalism and on the modern French language, Calvin's influence on education is also important. He founded the Academy of Geneva in 1559 with a Christian humanistic rather than scholastic program of study.

Calvin's theological and educational works transformed Geneva from a medieval provincial town to an international center—the headquarters of Reformed Christianity and the intellectual powerhouse of Calvinism. Not all Genevans were happy with Calvin's changes, of course: they watched their city of easy living and easy morals became a disciplined community. Visitors and trainees came to observe and study; and, in turn, Geneva sent out missionaries, graduates, and converts to Calvinist spread views. As a result, Calvin's influence became international whereas Luther's concentrated in Germany and Scandinavia. For example, Calvin trained more than 120 French refugee pastors who eventually returned to France. In 1559, they called a national synod in Paris to draw up a confession of faith and a rule of discipline based on the Genevan model. The next year, 1560, John Knox convinced the Scottish Parliament to draw up still another confession of faith and rule of discipline which followed Calvin's plan. In the main, however, Calvinism did not rely on governmental support. It had its own organization which was completely independent of the state and could resist state efforts to control or suppress.

Calvin's work thus has had broad theological, political, educational, and economic impact. He formulated an organized belief structure, moral code, and ministry for his church and a model for church-state interaction; he founded a new humanist academy and influenced his own native language; and his ideas, joined with the growth of middle class and urban areas, shaped our modern world.

Overview of Biographical Sources

The first view of Calvin's life was written in 1564 by his friend and successor Théodore de Bèze, who had worked closely with Calvin for a long time. Avowedly moralistic in its intentions, Bèze's biography has been charged with making Calvin a "god". Modern scholars have also characterized Bèze's work as lifeless and lacking in insight. It is, however, a most important source for information about Calvin.

The next biography of Calvin was published in 1565 by Nicolas Colladon, a lawyer and associate of Calvin's who also published an edition of the 1559 *Institutes* with brief marginal summaries. Colladon's biography is the source of our knowledge about Calvin's years in Paris, but Colladon's sources are unknown. Colladon's work is also a primary source for the dates of Calvin's preaching and lecturing. Colladon writes of Calvin's spending time before 1534 at the court of Marguerite of Navarre, an important patron of early evangelical French reformers.

Jerome Bolsec's biography (1577) is hostile in its treatment of Calvin. Bolsec had quarreled with Calvin in 1551 over predestination and election and had been banished from Geneva by the council. In his work, he accuses Calvin of homosexual and promiscuous heterosexual activity and labels him a boring and bloodthirsty demogogue. Bolsec's sources are very questionable—he cites oral reports from "trustworthy" but anonymous individuals.

Like Bèze's work, many modern biographies have made Calvin into a saint or icon, though more recently, attempts have been made to view him from a more historical perspective. Others have studied him in relation to his Platonic and Stoic influences, particularly since his first published work was a commentary on Seneca. Calvin, for example, saw Christian blessedness in the limited, stoic sense of freedom from fear and anxiety rather than a sense of joyfulness. A number of biographies focus on Calvin's early years and his conversion process. Perhaps the best of the recent biographies of Calvin is that by William J. Bouwsma, *John Calvin: A Sixteenth-Century Portrait* (1988), which focuses on Calvin's inner life as representative of the cultural crises of Calvin's time.

Evaluation of Principal Biographical Sources

Bouwsma, William J. *John Calvin: A Sixteenth-Century Portrait*. New York: Oxford University Press, 1988. (**A**) Though Bouwsma claims not to have written a psychological study, his work focuses on Calvin's inner life as representative of the cultural crises of Calvin's time. Bouwsma sees Calvin as an anxious and troubled man seeking a father figure in men like Guillaume Farel and Martin Bucer. The book is a "portrait" rather than a biography and spends little time on Calvin political struggles, especially those with Ami Perrin.

Ganoczy, Alexandre. *The Young Calvin*. 1966. Translated by David Foxgrover and Wade Provo. Philadelphia, PA: Westminster Press, 1987. (**A**) One of the freshest but also more controversial studies of Calvin. Focuses on his development, including questions about his conversion, the influence of Luther and Swiss reformer Huldrych Zwingli on Calvin and on Calvin's prophetic call. Specifically, Ganoczy examines Calvin's account of his conversion to find out how it relates to Calvin as a Churchman. He also criticizes the idea that Calvin was heavily influenced by the Scottish theologian John Mair. One of the strengths of the book is Ganoczy's analysis of Calvin's strong belief that he had been called by God. Ganoczy uses documents contemporary with Calvin at a particular time in his life as his main sources rather than later statements by or about Calvin.

McGrath, Alister E. *A Life of John Calvin: A Study in the Shaping of Western Culture.* Oxford: Basil Blackwell, 1990. (**A**) A general survey of Calvin's life and times. McGrath dismisses the pictures of Calvin as a dictator or enemy of intellectual progress to discuss his cultural legacy. Traces the influence of Calvin's ideas upon Western culture including capitalism, the natural sciences, American civil religion and natural human rights, and provides a glossary of technical and historical terms. McGrath also traces the influence of existing Genevan economic and political concerns and beliefs on Calvin's thought.

Mullett, Michael. *Calvin.* London: Routledge, Chapman, and Hall, 1989. (**G**) Part of the Lancaster Pamphlets series, which offer concise accounts of major historical topics for introductory courses at universities, this short study explains Calvin's historical importance, his theology as presented in the *Institutes,* his relationship with Geneva, and his influence. Mullett explains how Calvin compensated for certain problems in Luther's Protestantism and made the Reformation a powerful force for change. A good introduction to Calvin and his times.

Parker, T. H. L. *John Calvin: A Biography.* London: J. M. Dent, 1975. (**G**) Excellent sympathetic and concise biography. Like Ganoczy, Parker emphasizes Calvin's early life, particularly as a university student. He also sees Calvin as a doctor of the Catholic Church and thus focuses on Calvin's Biblical work and preaching. Calvin, to Parker, is a man of peace and unity who was born into a world of disorder and conflict. Parker has also published books on Calvin's preaching, his doctrine of the knowledge of God, and his commentaries on the Old and New Testament.

Overview and Evaluation of Primary Sources

Unlike Luther, Calvin was a very private man who wrote little about his personal experiences. His letters are a main source of information about his life and particularly about his views of other Reformation figures. Jules Bonnet has edited a compendium of Calvin's letters (4 vols. 1858. Reprint. New York: Burt Franklin, 1972-1973), and these remain the standard version. A more condensed volume of Calvin's letters is *Letters of John Calvin* (Carlisle, PA: Banner of Truth Trust,

1980), which contains seventy of Calvin's letters (about one-tenth of Bonnet's collection).

Some of Calvin's theological works also provide information about his life. His Preface to the *Commentary on the Book of Psalms* written in 1557 is important in that it reflects on his life in general, his conversion, and his feelings of similarity to David the Psalmist and the trials that David endured. (Calvin, like David the shepherd boy who became king, felt chosen by God, and his life was forever changed. What had seemed true belief and worship to him before now seemed superstitious creations of men.) The introduction to Calvin's *Sermons on Ephesians* gives Calvin's views on preaching. Calvin's will and his parting address to the magistrates of Geneva were printed in Beze's biography, *Vie de Calvin* (1564), and in *Ioannis Calvini Vita,* vol. 21 in the Corpus Reformatorum edition, *Ioannis Calvini Opera quae supersunt omnia,* edited by G. Baum, E. Cunitz, and Ed Reuss (59 vols. Brunswick and Berlin, 1863-1900). The preface, will, and address can also be found in *John Calvin: Selections from His Writings* edited by John Dillenberger (Garden City, NY: Anchor Books, 1971). *Sermons on Ephesians* has been published by The Banner of Truth Trust (Carlisle, PA, 1973).

Museums, Historical Landmarks, Societies

Monument de la Reformation (Geneva). The cornerstone of the Monument de la Reformation or Reformation Monument was laid on July 10, 1909, to commemorate the 400th anniversary of Calvin's birth. The monument is a 100-yard long stone wall built along a sixteenth-century rampart beneath the walls of the old town on the promenade des Bastions. It faces the Place Neuve and is opposite the main building of the University of Geneva. The wall is engraved with religious texts in several languages, and features group statues of the leaders of the Reformation. The major group consists of Calvin, de Beze, Farel, and John Knox. Other statues depict Oliver Cromwell, the Pilgrim fathers, Luther, and Zwingli.

Musee Historique de la Reformation (Geneva). Located in the Bibliotheque Publique (Salle Lullin), the museum houses important collections on the Reformation.

Temple de l'Auditoire (Geneva). The Calvin Auditorium is the gothic church in which Calvin preached and is next door to the Cathedrale de Saint-Pierre. It was restored in 1959 to commemorate the 450th anniversary of Calvin's birth.

Other Sources

Bainton, Roland H. *The Reformation of the Sixteenth Century.* Boston: Beacon Press, 1985. The foremost twentieth-century authority on Luther gives a good overview of Reformation activities for general readers.

Battles, F. L., et al. *John Calvin.* Abingdon, UK: Sutton Courtenay Press, 1965. Collection of eleven essays which are helpful in understanding Calvin's theology. Battles has also translated the *Institutes.*

Gamble, Richard C., ed. *The Biography of Calvin.* Vol. 1. New York: Garland, 1992. Thirteen reprinted articles on Calvin's life from major Calvin scholars. The earliest (1909) by Benjamin B. Warfield looks reverently at Calvin as a theologian, while more recent articles looks at his life in the context of sixteenth century social and historical movements.

George, Timothy, ed. *John Calvin and the Church: A Prism of Reform.* Louisville, KY: Westminster/John Knox Press, 1990. Fourteen articles with Calvin as central focus for discussion of various disciplines and scholarly approaches in Protestantism today. Subjects include Calvin and his time, theology, ecclesiology, scriptural interpretation, and worship and preaching.

Reid, W. Stanford. *John Calvin: His Influence in the Western World.* Grand Rapids, MI: Zondervan, 1982. A collection of essays on Calvin's influence. Essays include discussions of Calvinism in Switzerland, France, the Netherlands, Germany, Hungary, England, Scotland, the United States, Canada, Australia, and South Africa.

Weber, Max. *The Protestant Ethic and the Spirit of Capitalism.* 1905. New York: Scribner's, 1958. This seminal work argues that Calvinism strongly influenced the tenor of modern capitalism as opposed to medieval capitalism: its rationality, ethical basis, and personal asceticism rather than opportunistic, decadent, "adventuring" capitalism.

Wendel, François. *Calvin: The Origins and Development of his Religious Thought*. London: Collins/Fontana Library of Theology and Philosophy, 1963. Translated by Philip Mairet. A biography and standard work on Calvin's beliefs. Wendel is also the author of *Calvin et l'humanisme* (Paris, 1976).

Ann W. Engar
University of Utah

Caravaggio
1571-1610

Chronology

Born Michelangelo Merisi somtime between September and December 1571 in Milan or nearby Caravaggio just south of Bergamo in Lombardy, Italy, son of Fermo Merisi, the majordomo and possible architect for the Marquis of Caravaggio, and Lucia Aratori, his father's second wife; *1584* apprenticed for four years to Milanese painter Simone Peterzano, a follower of Titian; *1592* inherits money from his parents and presumably sets off for Rome; *1593-1594* completes *Boy with a Basket of Fruit* and *The Boy with a Garland of Ivy*; *1594-1596* completes *The Boy Bitten by a Lizard* and *Concert of Youths*; *1597* mentioned in the will of the Abbot of Pinerolo, who bequeaths to his nephew Caravaggio's painting of St. Francis variously called *St. Francis in Ecstacy* or *The Stigmatization of St. Francis,* marking the first recorded reference to his fame as a painter; *1598-1599* paints *Judith and Holofernes,* gruseomely depicting the precise moment of Judith decapitating Holofernes; *St. Catherine of Alexandria* and *The Conversion of the Magadelen,* which represents one of the first instances of the artist's employing strong contrasts of light and shade (chiaroscuro) to contribute a visual dimension to a spiritual conversion; *1599* receives commission to paint *The Calling and Martyrdom of St. Matthew* on the side walls of the Contarelli Chapel in the Church of San Luigi dei Francesi in Rome; *1600* completes the Contarelli paintings, and the sensation they create makes his name resound throughout Italy; his name also appears for the first time in police records when he is accused of unprovoked assault; *1605-1606* completes *Madonna of the Serpent,* one of his least successful mature paintings because the figures are stiff and inundated by darkness; completes *St. Jerome Writing,* painted for Pope Paul V's nephew Cardinal Scipione, who rapidly becomes an avid collector of Caravaggio's work; paints *The Death of the Virgin* using a prostitute as a model; *1606* kills an opponent in a tennis game on May 29, and two days later flees Rome; *1606-1607* hides out in Paliano, Palestrina, and Agarolo to the east of Rome, locating finally in Naples, where he paints feverishly; *1607* in pursuit of the coveted honor, the Cross of Malta, appears on the island of Malta, where he paints two portraits of the French Grand Master of the Order Alof de Wignacourt (1547-1622); *Death of the Virgin* is purchased by the Duke of Mantua in 1607 on the advice of Rubens and later belongs to King Charles I of England before passing to the Louvre; *1608* escapes north to Sicily, where is commissioned by the Senate of Syracuse to paint an altarpiece commemorating the burial of the Sicilian saint, Lucy; receives the Order of the Knights of Malta, but is soon afterwards expelled from the Order for an unknown crime "as a corrupt and foul member"; *1609* suffers wounds when attacked at the entrance of an inn in Naples; *1610* dies on July 18 on a beach in the Spanish enclave of Porto Ercole on the southern border of Tuscany as a result of fever and his wounds.

Activities of Historical Significance

Few artists in history have exerted as remarkable an influence as the short-lived but impassioned Caravaggio, nor are there very many revolutions in art quite so easy to document. Reacting against both the eccentricities of the Mannerist style, denoting the artistic period mainly in Italy between Renaissance and Baroque, approximately 1520-1600 which emphasized an artist's intellectual preconception over a more direct visual perception and the archeological romanticism of the Classicists—those devoted to the study and imitation of art from ancient Greece, which by definition is classic—Caravaggio infused Italian art with the theatrical intensity of realism and the innovative technique of introducing light as an active element of composition. Certainly Leonardo da Vinci and Michelangelo Buonarroti had explored the possibilities of chiaroscuro (the artistic effect created by the interplay of light and shadow in a painting) before him, but it was Caravaggio who adopted chiaroscuro as a religion. It was his name that became associated with it as it spread throughout Europe that included such painters as Andrea Vaccar, Massimo Stanzioni and Mattia Preti.

More than technique, however, he offered painting a new attitude of liberation. Like the scientists of the Renaissance, Caravaggio cherished reality and sought to cut through appearances to the essence of things. Because he wished to restore corporeal density to the unstable figures of Mannerism, he eschewed models of formal aristocratic perfection, choosing instead for his subjects average people and everyday things. His vision of mythological and biblical incidents is straightforward: Bacchus is a street kid with curly black hair, the executioners of Saint Peter are thugs, the grave-diggers of Saint Lucy are clumsy peasants, and in *Death of the Virgin*, the body of Mary is already swollen by decomposition.

In addition, Caravaggio stands out from his Mannerist and Renaissance predecessors because he executed most of the detail in his paintings without the help of assistants and painted directly on the canvas without first making tentative sketches. His oeuvre, produced within a span of twenty years, consists of some forty works and approximately twenty attributions or copies. But this number is still expanding because works previously thought to be copies are continually being certified as authentic. Their recovery is due as much to modern techniques of cleaning and restoration as to the discerning scrutiny of dedicated scholars.

Within Italy his direct influence was primarily felt by his follower and imitator, the Mantuan Bartolommeo Manfredi, and Giovanni Battista Caracciolo and the Neapolitan School that included such painters as Andrea Vaccaro, Massimo Stanzioni, and Mattia Preti. Another Italian, Orazio Gentileschi, spread "Caravaggism" farther afield when he was invited to paint for the royal courts of France, Spain, and England. Ultimately the influence of Caravaggio on European painting was considerable, plainly manifest in such artists as José Ribera, Diego Velazquez, and Bartolomé Murillo in Spain; Peter Paul Rubens in Flanders; Adam Elsheimer in Germany, and Maurice-Quentin de La Tour and the Le Nain brothers, Antoine, Louis, and Mathieu, in France. Even artists opposed to the Caravaggesque approach, such as Guido Reni, who was devoted to "ideal" beauty and to the loftiness of his own role as an artist, owe to him the technique of slanting light so as to emphasize the model.

Overview of Biographical Sources

Caravaggio was popular during his own lifetime and for a decade or so thereafter; but following that, he was forgotten. It was not until about 1900 that interest in his work began to revive, partly because of a renewed appreciation of Baroque art, the style that followed Mannerism and lasted well into the eighteenth century, which emphasized illusionism, color, light, and movement in order to overwhelm the spectator, and because of a new sympathy for the ideas that informed his art.

A great deal has been written about him since that time, including some works that contain exaggerations and nonsensical claims (some of the roles claimed for him in the history of art are not even mutually compatible). But Caravaggio has not by any means been exhausted as a subject for research, because certain important aspects of his character and career remain shrouded in mystery.

Monographs by Roger Hinks (1953) and Walter Friedlaender (1955) became obsolete shortly after their publication because they were not able to incorporate the newly and definitively established chronology of Caravaggio's early works by Denis Mahon in a series of articles for the *Burlington Magazine* 93 (1951: 202-204; 223-234; 286-292) and 94 (1952: 3-23). Two decades later they were rendered even more obsolete by Mia Cinotti's important research on the painter's birth, youth, and background presented in the *Immagine del Caravaggio* (Milan: Cinisello Balsamo, 1973), the catalogue of an exhibition held in Bergamo, Caravaggio, and Brescia during the quatercentenary of Caravaggio's birth in 1973. Works by John Gash (1988), Micheal Kitson (1967) and Alfred Moir (1989) are art books primarily aimed at explicating the paintings, and Howard Hibbard's *Caravaggio* (1983) is therefore left as the major sourcebook for Caravaggio studies.

Among foreign-language works are *Il Caravaggio* (2d ed. Milan: Aldo Martello, 1968) by Roberto Longhi, the scholar generally acknowledged as the pioneer of Caravaggio studies; Hugo Wagner's *Michelangelo da Caravaggio* (Bern: Eicher, 1958); and René Jullian's *Caravage* (Paris: Editions IAC, 1961), which Michael Kitson has called the most complete catalogue of the artist's works available in any language.

Evaluation of Principal Biographical Sources

Friedlaender, Walter F. *Caravaggio Studies*. Princeton, NJ: Princeton University Press, 1955. (**A, G**) Divided into four parts: a biography, a catalogue raisonné, a section of translations of the original documentation, and sixty-six black-and-white plates of Caravaggio paintings. Cogently argues that Caravaggio was influenced by St. Philip Neri's campaign to encourage Catholics to seek more direct contact with the mysteries of God; and demonstrates how indebted Caravaggio was to the traditions of Northern Italian painting, which had always tended to prefer realism and the dramatic use of light to the more stylized conventions current in sixteenth-century central Italy.

Gash, John. *Caravaggio*. London: Bloomsbury Books, 1988. (**G**) The initial eighteen pages of extremely useful biography are followed by a concise chronology, an up-to-date bibliography, and sixty-eight black-and-white plates with substantial commentary.

Hibbard, Howard. *Caravaggio*. New York: Harper & Row, 1983. (**A, G**) Currently the standard authority on Caravaggio for the English-speaking public, Hibbard assembles everything that is known about the painter, revealing his thematic preoccupations, his creative response to his sources, and the response of critics to his art. Psychological interpretations are suggested but not insisted upon. There is a bibliography and two appendices, one treating paintings attributed to Caravaggio and one including nine "old reports" on his life, including all six cited in the Primary Sources section of this article.

Hinks, Roger. *Michelangelo Merisi da Caravaggio: His Life, His Legend, His Works*. New York: Beechhurst Press, 1953. (**A, G**). As indicated in the subtitle, Hinks's aim is to enumerate the facts of the painter's life, to examine the impact of his works upon his contemporaries, and to establish a canon in historic sequence of the works recognized as authentic.

Kitson, Michael. *The Complete Paintings of Caravaggio*. New York: Harry N. Abrams, 1967. (**G**) Depending for its illustrations and some of its documentary material on the Italian edition by Angelo Ottino della Chiesa, Kitson has here supplied an outline biography, an invaluable listing of museums and churches that own the various paintings of Caravaggio worldwide, and his own chronology for the sixty-four color plates.

Moir, Alfred. *Caravaggio*. New York: Harry N. Abrams, 1989. (**G**) Like Gash and Kitson, this is an art book cum text rather than an academic study of Caravaggio's life. There are forty color plates with additional black-and-white plates, and the text explains the events of his times, the patrons who housed and supported him, and his influence on subsequent European painting.

Overview and Evaluation of Primary Sources

Caravaggio scholars customarily regard six biographical commentaries from the century following Caravaggio's death as basic sources. These are Giulio Mancini, *Considerazioni sulla Pittura*, written about 1620 and published in a two-volume edition by Adriana Marucchi and Luigi Salerno (Rome: Accademia nazionale dei Lincei, 1956-1957); Carel Van Mander, *Het Schilder Boeck* (Haarlem, the Netherlands, 1604); Giovanni Baglione, *Le Vite de' Pittori, Scultori, ed Architetti* (published 1642 with facsimile edition by Valerio Mariani, Rome: Istituto d'Archeologia e storia dell'arte, 1935); Giovanni Pietro Bellori, *Le Vite de' Pittori, Scultori e Architetti Moderni* (1672. Edited by Evelina Borea, Turin: Einaudi, 1976); Joachim von Sandrart, *Academie De Bau-, Bild- Und Mahlerei-Kunste Von* (1675. Edited by A. R. Peltzer, Munich: G. Hirth, 1925: 275-277); and Francesco Susinno, *Le Vite de' Pittori Messinesi* (manuscript dated 1724. Published and edited by Valentino Martinelli, Florence, 1960).

The earliest sources are the manuscripts of the collector Giulio Mancini, a physician practicing in Rome. Although he may not have known Caravaggio personally, they had mutual acquaintances. Mancini is more detailed about the early life of Caravaggio than are other primary sources, and in recent years his credibility has risen. Baglione, a fellow painter, is the only one of the early biographers who actually knew Caravaggio, but because he initiated a long drawn-out libel suit against Caravaggio in 1603 for writing and disseminating abusive verses about him and his work, his assessment of the artist is negative.

Similarly the work of Bellori, also a fellow painter, is equally disapproving, but Bellori was particularly interested in works by Caravaggio done outside Rome, and so his writings, the earliest reliable source on the subject, focuses on paintings rendered in Naples, Malta, and Sicily. It is from Susinno's much later account that we have knowledge of Caravaggio's apprenticeship in Rome with a Sicilian painter Mario Minnitti, who may have helped the painter get his commission from the municipality of Syracuse for his big altarpiece, *The Burial of St. Lucy of Syracuse* in 1608 now at the Church of Santa Lucia al Sepolcro at Syracuse.

All six of these "old reports" are included as appendices in Hibbard's biography, in both their original languages (Italian, Dutch, German) and in English translation. All except Susinno are included in Friedlaender's *Caravaggio Studies*. Documentation regarding his youth and family background is included in Mia

Cinotti's catalogue *Immagine del Caravaggio*, prepared for what was assumed to be the quatercentenary of the artist's birth in 1973. This catalogue was republished with additions in *Novità sul Caravaggio* (Milan: Regione Lombardia, 1975).

Fiction and Adaptations

Robert Payne's novel *Caravaggio* (1968) emphasizes the artist's alleged homosexuality and the giddy succession of patrons, lovers, and intrigues that characterized the later years of his short life. In *The Dark Fire* (1977), however, art historian Linda Murray gives Caravaggio a mistress and two illegitimate children. Murray is hostile to the legend of homosexuality that has grown up around the artist because, as she asserts in the introduction to her novel, it is based on one scant reference to his *bardassa*, or "kept boy," in the libel suit brought by Baglione in 1603. A study in the form of a two-act play by Michael Straight, *Caravaggio* (1979) suggests that relationships with others, men and women, may not have been so important to someone as intensely egocentric as Caravaggio. Straight's play, which begins with Baglione assuring the audience that he knew Caravaggio as he really was, proceeds to show the development of the artist at various critical stages of his life, and finally offers a new theory about his trial and escape from Malta.

Derek Jarman, who produced his 1985 film *Caravaggio* in a London warehouse, preferred to envision for Caravaggio a bizarre menage à trois in which the artist is simultaneously involved with both Lena and her lover Ranuccio. Refusing to film any of the original paintings, Jarman instead used posed tableaux of models standing stock-still as well as copies by Christopher Hobbs of the Caravaggio originals.

Museums, Historical Landmarks, Societies

Galleria Borghese (Rome). Holds more Caravaggio paintings than any other single museum: *Boy With Basket of Fruit, David With the Head of Goliath, The Madonna of the Serpent, St. Jerome Writing, St. John the Baptist,* and *The Sick Bacchus.*

Galleria Nazionale d'Arte Antica (Rome). Holds three Caravaggio paintings: *The Madonna and Child, Narcissus,* and *St. John The Baptist.*

Kunsthistorisches Museum (Vienna, Austria). Holds three Caravaggio paintings: *Christ Carrying the Cross, The Crowning of Thorns,* and *The Madonna of the Rosary.*

Museo Nazionale (Messina, Sicily, Italy). Holds four Caravaggio paintings: *Adoration of the Shepherds, The Incredulity of St. Thomas, The Supper at Emmaus,* and *The Raising of Lazarus.*

Other Sources

Mariani, Valerio. "Caravaggio." In *Encyclopedia of World Art.* New York: McGraw-Hill, 1960. Substantial biographical treatment that includes in-depth criticism of the masterpieces and a bibliography especially attentive to works written in Italian, French, and German.

Murray, Peter, and Linda Murray. "Caravaggio." In *Dictionary of Art and Artists.* 2d ed. Peter and Linda Murray, eds. London: Penguin, 1973. Succinct treatment of the author's life and influence.

Moir, Alfred. *The Italian Followers of Caravaggio.* 2 vols. Cambridge, MA: Harvard University Press, 1967. Traces the dissemination of Caravaggio's paintings throughout Italy and analyzes the Caravaggesque work of painters by region (e.g., Giovanni Battista Caracciolo and Bernardo Cavallini from Naples, Mario Minnitti and Pietro Novelli from Sicily).

Posner, Donald. "Caravaggio's Homo-erotic Early Works." *The Art Quarterly* (Metropolitan Museum of Art) 34 (1971): 301-324. Addresses the problem of the effeminate nature of the youths of his early work and concludes that the androgynous character of the figures is central to the artist's intended aesthetic statement. He bases his conclusion on the word *bardassa* ("kept boy") from the Baglione libel suit and on a rumor recorded by Susinno that Caravaggio's sudden departure from Messina in 1609 was precipitated by suspicion aroused by his unnatural interest in a group of schoolboys at play.

Jack Shreve
Allegany Community College

Thomas Carlyle
1795-1881

Chronology

Born Thomas Carlyle on December 4, 1795, in the village of Ecclefechan, Annandale, in Dumfriesshire, Scotland, second child and eldest son of James Carlyle, a stonemason, and Margaret Aitken Carlyle; receives tutoring and attends Annan Academy in preparation for the Protestant ministry; *1809-1814* studies classics and mathematics at the University of Edinburgh, completing the arts program; abandons divinity study after reading sceptics Gibbon and Hume; *1814-1818* teaches mathematics at Annan, then at Kirkaldy; falls in love with Margaret Gordon, who will be the model for Blumine in one of his most important essays, *Sartor Resartus*; *1818-1821* gives up teaching and returns to Edinburgh; learns German and works as a tutor; relationship to Margaret Gordon ended by her aunt; *1821* begins a courtship by correspondence with Jane Baillie Welsh; *1822* experiences a spiritual crisis later immortalized in *Sartor Resartus*; *1824* translates Adrien Legendre's *Geometry* and Goethe's *Wilhelm Meister's Apprenticeship*; meets Samuel Taylor Coleridge in London; starts a philosophical novel, *Wotton Reinfred*, published in 1892; *1825* publishes *Life of Schiller* and begins correspondence with Goethe; *1826* marries Jane Welsh; *1827* translates *German Romances*, including Goethe's *Wilhelm Meister's Travels*; *1828-1831* moves for economic reasons to Jane's isolated family farm, Craigenputtoch, in Dumfriesshire; writes ''Sign of the Times,'' a witty argument that modern progress has created a mechanical society, and ''Characteristics,'' which identifies spiritual troubles and a new morality; befriended by John Stuart Mill; *1832-1834* father dies; publishes autobiographies on Goethe and Diderot; visited by Ralph Waldo Emerson; publishes *Sartor Resartus*, a philosophical, autobiographical narrative; *1834-1837* settles in London; writes, with Mill, *The French Revolution: A History*, which receives popular and critical success; publishes ''The Diamond Necklace''; *1839* publishes *Chartism*; *1841* publishes and lectures on *On Heroes, Hero Worship, and the Heroic in History*, showing that social order and constructive change require divinely inspired leaders; publishes *Past and Present*, which contrasts medieval monastic life and the injustices of the present, and calls for a New Aristocracy to bring about social justice; publishes a sympathetic account of Oliver Cromwell in *Oliver Cromwell's Letters and Speeches*; *1848-1851* defends colonial slavery in an article later reprinted as *The Nigger Question*, provoking a scathing response from Mill; begins friendship with future biographer James Anthony Froude; publishes *Latter-Day Pamphlets*, a bitter anti-democratic critique of social problems and contemporary institutions, which harms his reputation; writes *Life of John Sterling*, a tribute to a friend; *1852-1866* mother dies; travels to Germany; helps persuade Alfred, Lord Tennyson, John Ruskin, and Charles Dickens to back Governor Eyre of Jamaica against charges of cruelty in suppressing a slave revolt; publishes his third major historical work, *History of Friedrich II of Prussia, Called Frederick the Great*, an ambitious portrait of a heroic leader that helps revive Carlyle's reputation; elected by students as rector of the University of Edinburgh; learns of the sudden death of his wife; *1866-1871* write *Reminiscences*; annotates *Letters and Memorials of Jane Welsh Carlyle*; denounces the second Reform Bill and democratic trends in "Shooting Niagara: and After?"; *1871-1874* defends Prussia's annexation of Alsace-Lorraine in a letter to the London *Times*; supervises publication of the People's Edition of his works; accepts the Prussian Order of Merit; *1875-1876* has difficulty writing due to a weakness in his right hand; publishes *The Early Kings of Norway*, with "An Essay on the Portraits of John Knox"; *1881* dies on February 5; buried according to his wish in the Ecclefechan family plot.

Activities of Historical Significance

Thomas Carlyle, biographer, historian, social critic, and self-appointed prophet, guided Britain's transition from a Romantic to a Victorian sensibility. Using non-fiction prose, he popularized themes ranging from hard work and social conscience to reverence for the spiritual and admiration for heroes. He influenced every tier of English intellectual life. In 1855, novelist George Eliot declared: "There is hardly a superior or active mind of this generation that has not been modified by Carlyle's writings; there has hardly been an English book written for the last ten or twelve years that would not have been different if Carlyle had not lived." Such influence had pragmatic consequences, as Francis Espinasse noted in 1851: "Practically no useful scheme or measure has been carried out of late years, from the founding of the London Library to the repeal of the Corn-Laws, which does not owe something to him.''

As a critic, Carlyle promoted a moral aesthetic of sincerity and truth, and he even set the career pattern for the Victorian sage: from concerns for the aesthetic, to the social, and finally to concerns for the private, and from an outlook of enthusiasm to that of disillusionment. In his major writings, Carlyle offered memorable historical portraits, incisive social critiques, profound insights into spiritual problems, deeply felt sympathy for the poor, and positive values for which to strive. His message drew power not only from his moral intensity, but also from his literary faculties: dramatic presentation of events and ideas, striking characterizations, creative manipulation of genres, and an energetic, original prose style.

By insisting that modern institutions neglect human spirituality and therefore must be reformed, and that individuals should search for the facts behind appearances, Carlyle was the quintessential early Victorian, appealing to Christians as well as agnostics, and liberals as well as conservatives. For intellectuals, Carlyle's essays and translations revealed the wealth of recent German literature, especially Goethe and Johann von Schiller. In *Sartor Resartus* (1836), a complex philosophical fiction influenced by Sterne's *Tristram Shandy*, an ''editor'' pieces together writings by philosopher Diogenes Teufelsdröckh. The autobiographical center is a prototype for Victorian crisis of faith narratives; the hero, after turning outward from the self and passing through the ''Center of Indifference,'' is guided by the secular spirituality to ''annihilation of self,'' awakening to ''a new Heaven and a new Earth,'' and reaching the ''Everlasting Yea'' of secular faith in moral order and virtuous action. While material science observes surfaces, the philosopher recognizes the truth of miracles (''natural supernaturalism'') and declares that outworn institutions and symbols must be cast off so the phoenix of the future can rise from their ashes.

Implications of these ideas reached a wide audience in Carlyle's powerful essays, where he illuminated contemporary social conditions, railed against materialism, refuted optimism about progress and laissez-faire capitalism, and suggested sweeping reforms. ''Signs of the Times'' (1829) and ''Characteristics'' (1831) argued that under industrialization people are worse off, materially and spiritually, than in organic rural economies.

Carlyle's early social themes found their most powerful and influential expression in historical writings with moral overtones, contributions to the 1840s climate of historical debate inspired by Benjamin Disraeli's "Young England" in politics, the Oxford movement in religion, and the Gothic revival in architecture. As he transformed the public's interpretation of historical events and persons, Carlyle warned of the terrifying consequences of poor government and offered alternative models of wise leadership and new social relations. In his first biography, *The Life of Schiller* (1825), Carlyle treated the great German poet and dramatist as a model for overcoming obstacles and as a moral guide. *The French Revolution* (1837), which established Carlyle's reputation, interpreted the event as divine retribution for irresponsible, morally bankrupt leadership. Rich in quotation and paraphrase from primary sources, Carlyle's narrative places readers directly into the excitement and confusion of the revolution, using an epic structure and conventions. *On Heroes, Hero Worship, and the Heroic in History* (1841), told an uncertain age the "the History of the World is but the Biography of great men," who can defeat chaos and provide social order, constructive change, and guidance. *Past and Present* advances a medieval institution as a model for a new British aristocracy, exhorting factory owners to become concerned "Captains of Industry," and suggesting that Parliament legislate improved working and living conditions. The book drew critical fire, but influenced reformers from Disraeli to Ruskin and William Morris. In *Oliver Cromwell's Letters and Speeches* (1845), his second work of epic scale, Carlyle honored a political and religious hero who, in a "practical world based on Belief in God," exercised needed leadership.

On the strength of works produced in a decade and a half, Carlyle was, by 1845, an established public figure. But after the 1848 revolutions, and to the dismay of friends like John Stuart Mill, he became what Matthew Arnold termed a "moral desperado" who took determined stands against popular causes. Carlyle argued in "Occasional Discourse on the Negro Question" for colonial slavery to make indolent slaves work harder on the sugar plantations, and railed against misguided institutions in *Latter-Day Pamphlets* (1850), in which Britain is a rudderless ship and Europe is a house about to collapse. Though the pamphlets eloquently denounce economics as "the Dismal Science," expose genuine follies such as "model prisons," which had conveniences denied the working poor, neither Carlyle's denunciations of liberalism and educational "cant," nor his proposals for harsh punishment and forced labor, appealed to most mid-Victorians.

Mitigating Carlyle's declining reputation as social analyst were works in other genres. In *The Life of John Sterling* (1851), a sympathetic tribute to an essayist, poet, and close friend, Carlyle shared personal experiences. In *Frederick the Great* (1865), his most ambitious historical work, Carlyle traced the eighteenth-century Prussian king's education, narrated his military campaigns, glorified Frederick's determined pursuit of his objectives in complex situations, and gave tragic grandeur to his stoicism. Lively in style, although less entertaining than the early histories, *Frederick the Great* was a major impetus for the recognition Carlyle received in later years, including the position of rector at the University of Edinburgh and the Prussian Order of Merit.

Carlyle's influence was acknowledged even by those who disliked his style and questioned his ideas, including churchmen who found him unorthodox, or reformers expecting practical suggestions. As prophetic teachings, Carlyle's writings and ideas were sometimes spared the scrutiny because they were embedded in historical or literary genres. Liberal theologians and Christian socialists like Frederick Denison Maurice welcomed his insistence that beliefs be expressed in actions; American transcendentalists embraced his anti-materialism. Carlyle's ideas had significant impact on his contemporary writers and thinkers: poets Tennyson and Robert Browning, social prophets Arnold, William Morris and Ruskin, and above all, Victorian novelists, most prominently Dickens, adapted subjects, ideas, and literary techniques from Carlyle. His early writings were embraced in France by the Saint-Simonians; Americans who drew on his work ranged from Emerson and Herman Melville to Mark Twain and Walt Whitman.

Overview of Biographical Sources

The autobiographical hero of Carlyle's *Sartor Resartus* says: "The Man is the spirit he worked in; not what he did, but what he became." Although biographers have established and argued the facts of his uneventful life, and have pondered the spirit that shaped his complex personality and creations, no definitive biography of Carlyle exists. Biographical and critical sources up to 1973 were analyzed by G. B. Tennyson, both in a detailed essay (in *Victorian Prose: A Guide to Research*, 1973), and in an entertaining survey (in *Fielding and Tarr*, 1976); much of the following overview is derived from these texts.

Carlyle's "popular image" as a teacher and prophet shaped both favorable and unfavorable responses to his work during his lifetime and for a few years beyond, as is documented in Jules Paul Siegel's *Thomas Carlyle: The Critical Heritage* (1971). After his death, Carlyle as friend and conversationalist came to life in his own reminiscences and in those of Scotsman David Masson, *Carlyle, Personally and in His Writings* (1885. Reprint. Philadelphia, PA: R. West, 1977); his literary powers and spiritual influence were acknowledged, with reservations about tone and doctrines, by Leslie Stephen and Richard Holt Hutton (1881), and Carlyle as prophet-hero was featured in biographies by Richard Herne Shepherd, *Thomas Carlyle* (New York: Harper, 1882) and Moncure D. Conway, *Thomas Carlyle* (1881. Reprint. Folcroft, PA: Folcroft Library, 1977).

A product of this period, which foreshadowes the second phase of Carlyle studies were writings by fellow historian and trusted friend James Anthony Froude. Froude's four volume *Thomas Carlyle* (1882, 1884) is a life study on a grand scale, drawing on personal papers and a thirty-year friendship. In this classic literary biography, Froude captures the spirit of Carlyle well enough to remain, in most respects, the standard biographer. Froude richly presented and thoughtfully analyzed Carlyle as both a brilliant man of letters and a complex, profoundly gloomy human being who is in public an eloquent and inspired moral sage but in private often a self-centered, irritable individual. Froude also published *Letters and Memorials of Jane Welsh Carlyle* (1882) and Carlyle's *Reminiscences* (1883), letting his subjects speak for themselves and avoiding the usual bowdlerizing, thus making public Carlyle's less attractive personal qualities.

After 1885, the second, "reactionary" phase debated Carlyle's qualities with little serious evaluation. Lasting a half century, this reaction was fed by both the Victorian spirit of the modernists and by a debate termed the "Froude-Carlyle Controversy." On one side were those who, with Froude as an unintentional example, felt free to criticize Carlyle, not only as a difficult person but also as a misguided, conservative denouncer of modern life. On the other side were defenders of Carlyle, who built up his image by criticizing Froude and charging him with injudicious editing and the invention of Carlyle's faults. Among the latter were Charles Eliot Norton, publisher of a "corrected" edition of the *Reminiscences* (1887), as well as Carlyle's nephew Alexander Carlyle, editor of *New Letters and Memorials of Jane Welsh Carlyle* (1903). Among Carlyle's critics and Froude's defenders were Froude's children, who published Froude's 1887 manuscript *My*

Relations with Carlyle (1903), with its notorious comment by Jane Carlyle's friend Geraldine Jewsbury that Carlyle was impotent and his marriage was never consummated. Alexander Carlyle, with physician Sir James Crichton-Browne, countered with *The Nemesis of Froude* (1903). Waldo Hilary Dunn's detailed *Froude and Carlyle: A Study of the Froude-Carlyle Controversy* (London: Longmans Green, 1933) cleared Froude of many charges, but Carlyle scholars still find fault with Froude. As these controversies raged, biographers of Carlyle picked up their themes; among short works, John Nichol, *Carlyle* (1892. Reprint. New York: AMS Press, 1968), supported Froude. R. S. Craig, *The Making of Carlyle: An Experiment in Biographical Explication* (London: E. Nash, 1908), was pro-Carlyle; while Norwood Young, *Carlyle: His Rise and Fall* (London: Duckworth, 1927) was hostile to Carlyle. Outside the controversy were Richard Garnett's short biography, *Life of Thomas Carlyle* (1887. Reprint. New York: AMS, 1979), still respected for its literary criticism, and Frenchman Louis Cazemian's uneven study of social themes, *Study of Social Theories* (1913. Reprint. Hamden, CT: Shoe String Press, 1966). But the lasting products of this phase were editions, collections of letters, and guides for reading Carlyle by Bliss Perry, *Thomas Carlyle: How to Know Him* (1915. Reprint: Folcroft, PA: Folcroft Library, 1977); Augustus Ralli, *Guide to Carlyle* (2 vols. London: Allen and Unwin, 1920); Isaac Watson Dyer's bibliography of works by and about Carlyle, *A Bibliography of Thomas Carlyle's Writings* (Portland, ME: Southworth, 1928); and the second major Carlyle biography, *Life of Thomas Carlyle* (6 vols. London: Kegan Paul, Trench and Trubner, 1823-1834), by David Alec Wilson. Wilson thoroughly researched these six volumes and incorporated many new facts, but his uncritical defense of Carlyle all but precluded significant new insights.

Mid- and late-twentieth-century biographers and critics of Carlyle, benefiting from rising standards of scholarship and rehabilitation of Victorian studies, produced works that are both scholarly and critical. Most modern scholars intelligently, if often narrowly critique events and themes on Carlyle's life, and on issues unlikely to provoke controversy. Carlyle's relationship to the social and the intellectual currents of his age is central to Emery Neff's biography *Carlyle* (1932); Neff's comparative study *Carlyle and Mill* (New York: Columbia University Press, 1924); Basil Willey's essay on Carlyle's philosophy in his *Nineteenth-Century Studies* (1949. Reprint. Cambridge: Cambridge University Press, 1980); and Eloise M. Behnken's *Thomas Carlyle: "Calvinist Without the Theology* (Columbia:

University of Missouri Press, 1978). Carlyle's personality interests biographer Julian Symons (1952), while formative influences are important in Charles Frederick Harrold's, *Carlyle and German Thought, 1819-1834* (1934. Reprint. New York: AMS Press, 1978), Hill Shine's *Carlyle's Early Reading to 1834* (1953), and G. B. Tennyson's *Sartor Called Resartus* (1965). Other studies focus on Carlyle as historian, especially Louis M. Young's *Thomas Carlyle and the Art of History* (Philadelphia: University of Pennsylvania Press, 1939), and John D. Rosenberg's *Carlyle and the Burden of History* (Cambridge: Harvard University Press, 1985); on his medievalism, Alice K. Chandler's *A Dream of Order: The Medieval Ideal in Nineteenth-Century Literature* (Lincoln: University of Nebraska Press, 1970); on his religious concerns, Ruth Roberts's *The Ancient Dialect: Thomas Carlyle and Comparative Religion* (Berkeley: University of California Press, 1988); and on his anticipation of modernist themes, Alfred J. La Valley's *Carlyle and the Idea of the Modern* (New Haven, CT: Yale University Press, 1968). Literary qualities especially engage modern critics, mostly within broader studies: rhetoric and symbolism in John Holloway, *The Victorian Sage* (London: Macmillan, 1953); fictional devices in nonfiction in George Levine, *The Boundaries of Fiction* (Princeton, NJ: Princeton University Press, 1968); religious typology in Herbert L. Sussman, *Fact into Figure* (Columbis: Ohio State University Press, 1979); literary realism in John P. MacGowan, *Representation and Revelation* (Columbia: University of Missouri Press, 1986); and experiments with genre in Mark Cumming, *A Disimprisoned Epic* (Philadelphia: University of Pennsylvania Press, 1988). The explosion of biographical and critical material on Carlyle makes it understandable that the latest scholarly biographer, Fred Kaplan, in *Thomas Carlyle* (1983) eschews criticism and offers simply a detailed narrative with some psychological analysis.

Modern biographers and critics place Carlyle into two broad categories: the inspired radical who wrote entertaining, incisive social critiques and histories until the mid-1840s, and the embittered reactionary railing against democracy and social change while promoting despotism. The first group of critics, such as Philip Rosenberg, in *The Seventh Hero: Thomas Carlyle and Radical Activism* (Cambridge, MA: Harvard University Press, 1974) stop with the publication of *Past and Present* (1843) so as to ''rescue'' a radical Carlyle who saw all men as heroes. Ian Campbell's short biography *Thomas Carlyle* (1974) identifies four themes in Carlyle's work: faith in a higher order, ethic of action and hard work, support for social order against anarchy, and respect for "heroes." The second group of critics examine the entire body of work and often denounce Carlyle as an intolerant forerunner of facism, or psychoanalyze him as sadistic and paranoid as in James L. Halliday's *Mr. Carlyle, My Patient: A Psychosomatic Biography* (1949. Reprint. New York: Haskell, 1974). For John Holloway, Carlyle's core is "anti-mecha-nism,"; for G. B. Tennyson (in *The Victorian Experience: The Prose Writers*, edited by Richard A. Levine, 1982), everything derives from Carlyle's "conviction of the transcendent reality of God," whose spiritual force Carlyle sought in vain in the world around him but recreated for himself and his contemporaries through the power of his words.

Evaluation of Biographical Sources

Campbell, Ian. *Thomas Carlyle*. London: Hamilton, 1974. (**A, G**) A sympathetic, concise, readable account of Carlyle's life (not works) based on primary sources, showing how Carlyle responded to his Scottish family and family background, and the places he lived. Good starting point for general readers. Also useful is Camp-bell's entry in the widely available reference work, *Dictionary of Literary Biogra-phy, Vol. 55: Victorian Prose Writers Before 1867*, edited by William B. Thesing (Detroit: Gale Research, 1987: 46-64).

Clubbe, John, ed. *Carlyle and His Contemporaries: Essays in Honor of Charles Richard Saunders*. Durham, NC: Duke University Press, 1976. (**A**) A wide range of essays about Carlyle's topicality and reception, Froude as biographer, and relationships between Carlyle and Scottish religion, Goethe, the Saint-Simonians, Mill, Arnold, George Lewes, Anthony Trollope, Ruskin and George Meredith.

Froude, James Anthony. *Thomas Carlyle: A History of the First Forty years of His Life, 1795-1835*. 2 vols. London: Longmans, Green, 1882. *Thomas Carlyle: A History of His Life in London, 1834-1881*. 2 vols. London: Longmans, Green, 1884. (**A, G**) Froude's work remains the most respected biography of Carlyle and a classic literary biography. Froude presents Carlyle sympathetically yet honestly, identifying weaknesses such as his insensitivity to his wife. Extensive quotations from primary materials, often inaccurate.

Froude's Life of Carlyle. Abridged and edited by John Clubbe. Columbus: Ohio State University Press, 1979. (**A, G**) With this well annotated abridgment that omits mainly letters and includes forty-eight illustrations, Froude's biography becomes accessible to modern readers. The introduction defends Froude and analyzes his approach to biography, showing how literary models shaped his interpretations of the Carlyles and their marriage.

Kaplan, Fred. *Thomas Carlyle.* Ithaca, NY: Cornell University Press, 1983. (**A**) Now the standard modern academic biography, although it omits criticism of works and offers no coherent interpretation. A substantial, well-written narrative of Carlyle's life, integrating primary sources and modern scholarship; precise with dates. Interprets Carlyle and his psychology in his terms; slights some influences and contradictions. The book contains forty-nine illustrations and a detailed bibliography, notes, and an index, but does not have a conclusion.

Le Quesne, A. L. *Carlyle.* New York: Oxford University Press, 1981. Past Masters Series. (**G**) A brief introduction to Carlyle's life and works, emphasizing Carlyle's importance to his own nation and age. Contains a short bibliography.

Neff, Emery. *Carlyle.* New York: Norton, 1932. (**A, G**) A reliable, concise critical biography, valuable on the social, historical, and economic context of Carlyle's work, including his Scottish heritage and the reception of his major works. Less useful on the literary qualities and Carlyle's later life and works.

Sanders, Charles Richard. *Carlyle's Friendships and Other Studies.* Durham, NC: Duke University Press, 1977. (**A**) Mostly biographical essays by the co-editor of Carlyle's letters. Subjects include Carlyle's travels and his friendships with Mill, Leigh Hunt, Tennyson, and Thackeray.

Seigel, Jules Paul. *Thomas Carlyle: The Critical Heritage.* New York: Barnes and Noble, 1971. (**A**) A critical anthology of reviews and writings by British and American contemporaries. Introduction and forty-five annotated selections from 1835-1881, with a chronology and a bibliography of secondary sources.

Shepherd, Richard Herne. *Memoirs of the Life and Writings of Thomas Carlyle.*

2 vols. London: Allen, 1881. (**A, G**) Next to Froude's this is the most important among the biographies by Carlyle's contemporaries.

Symons, Julian. *Thomas Carlyle: The Life and Ideas of a Prophet.* London: Gollancz, 1952. (**A, G**) The most recent critical biography. Explains how Carlyle's works illuminate their time. Some psychoanalysis, at times condescending. Few exact dates; very brief on the later years. Bibliography, no notes.

Tennyson, G. B. *Sartor Called Resartus: The Genesis, Structure, and Style of Thomas Carlyle's First Major Work.* Princeton, NJ: Princeton University Press, 1966. (**A**) A study of Carlyle's literary apprenticeship and German reading, as well as a critical analysis of the structure and style of Carlyle's *Sartor Resartus.*

Waring, Walter. *Thomas Carlyle.* New York: Twayne, 1978. (**G**) Brief overview of life and works, with a chronology and an annotated bibliography. Views Carlyle as a biographer, and is critical of his ideas.

Wilson, David Alec. *Life of Thomas Carlyle.* 6 vols. London: Kegan Paul; New York: Dutton, 1923-1934. (**A**) The second substantial biography, marred by its polemical argument for Carlyle, against Froude, and its ponderous style. Still a valuable source for scholars for its research, documentation and indices; a few volumes have been reprinted separately.

Overview and Evaluation of Primary Sources

Detailed analysis of primary and secondary sources through 1972 can be found in G. B. Tennyson's bibliographical essay in *Victorian Prose: A Guide to Research,* edited by David De Laura (New York: Modern Language Association, 1973). Bibliographies of Carlyle's writings are Isaac Watson Dyer, *A Bibliography of Thomas Carlyle's Writings* (1928. Reprint. New York: Hippocrene Books, 1967), which also lists and annotates secondary sources to 1928, and Rodger L. Tarr, *Thomas Carlyle: A Descriptive Bibliography* (Pittsburgh, PA: University of Pittsburgh Press, 1989). Secondary sources are listed in Tarr's *Thomas Carlyle: A Bibliography of English-Language Criticism, 1824-1974* (Charlottesville: University of Virginia Press, 1976), updated by annotated bibliographies in the *Carlyle Newsletter*. The *Carlyle Newsletter* also published compilations by R. W. Dillon, *A Century Bibliography of Carlyle Studies: Supplement I, 1975-1980* (1985); *Supplement 1981-1985* (1988).

Among autobiographical writings by Carlyle the *Reminiscences* were first published, with editorial license, by Froude (1881); soon after Charles Eliot Norton published the "corrected" edition (1887. Reprint. London: J. M. Dent, 1972). Other personal accounts were published as *Reminiscences of My Irish Journey in 1849* (London: Low, Marston, Searle and Rivington; New York: Harper, 1882); *Two Notes of Thomas Carlyle from 23rd March 1822 to 16 May 1832*, edited by Charles Eliot Norton (1898. Reprint. Mt Vernon, NY: Appel, 1972); and *Two Reminiscences of Thomas Carlyle*, edited by John Clubbe (Durham, NC: Duke University Press, 1974), which includes Carlyle's 1866 marginal comments on an early German biography by Friedrich Althaus.

The definitive source for letters will be, when completed, *The Collected Letters of Thomas and Jane Welsh Carlyle*, meticulously edited by Charles Richard Sanders, Kenneth J. Fielding, Clyde de L. Ryals, John Clubbe, and others (Durham, NC: Duke University Press, 1970-); completed by 1987 were volumes 1-15, covering 1812-1842. Collections worth consulting until this edition is complete are listed in G. B. Tennyson's bibliographical essay. Correspondences between Carlyle and major figures of his time are published in *Correspondence Between Goethe and Carlyle*, edited by Charles Eliot Norton (London: Macmillan, 1887); *The Correspondence of Emerson and Carlyle*, edited by Joseph Slater (New York: Columbia University Press, 1964), and *The Correspondence of Thomas Carlyle and John Ruskin*, edited by George Alan Cate (Stanford, CA: Stanford University Press, 1982).

The most complete and still standard edition of Carlyle's works is the thirty volume centenary edition, *The Works of Thomas Carlyle*, edited by Henry Duff Traill (1896-1899. Reprint. New York: AMS Press, 1980), to which Alexander Carlyle added Carlyle's *Historical Sketches of Notable Persons and Events in the Reigns of James I and Charles I* (1898). This collection includes literary translations and appendices of relevant documents as well as indices for each work; the introductions are brief and idiosyncratic. Works not in the standard edition, in addition to the reminiscences listed above, appear in *Last Words of Thomas Carlyle*, edited by Charles Eliot Norton (London: Longmans, Green, 1892), including the unfinished novel *Wotton Reinfred* (New York: Appleton, 1892), and three transcripts of an 1898 lecture series, including J. Reay Greene's *Lectures on the History of Literature, Delivered by Thomas Carlyle* (London: Ellis and Elvey, 1892). Other important collected works are those Carlyle published: the first in 1857-1858, followed by *Collected Works* (1869-1871), and the *People's Edition of Thomas Carlyle's Collected Works* (London: Chapman and Hall, 1871-1874), for which he revised some early works. After Carlyle's death appeared the Ashburton Edition (London: Chapman and Hall, 1885-1888), the Shilling Edition (London: Chapman and Hall, 1885-1888), several American editions, and an edition in German (Leipzig: Wigand, 1895-1919).

Collections for students and critical editions of individual works have reached a wider public. Among critical anthologies of Carlyle selections the most recent is *Selected Writings*, edited by Alan Shelston (Harmondsworth and Baltimore: Penguin, 1974, 1981). G. B. Tennyson's *A Carlyle Reader* (New York: Random House, 1969; Cambridge University Press, 1984) remains worth consulting for its balanced selection, bibliography, and introduction that summarizes Carlyle's life, works, and importance for our time. The standard annotated edition of *Sartor Resartus*, the most widely read of Carlyle's works, is that of C. F. Harrold (New York: Odyssey, 1937). Benefiting from the editor's own scholarship and the work of previous editors, Harrold's introduction explains Carlyle's historical context, literary practices, and moral vision, especially his theme of turning ideals into actions. He includes an annotated bibliography. Kerry McSweeney and Peter Sabor edited a less scholarly recent edition of *Sartor Resartus*. (Oxford: Oxford University Press, 1987) with introduction and notes. Arthur Montagu Hughes edited the standard annotated edition of *Past and Present*. (Oxford: Oxford University Press, 1918); Richard D. Altick provided an annotated edition of *Past and Present* for modern readers, explaining its topicality (1965. Reprint. New York: New York University Press, 1977). For the major histories, no standard scholarly editions exist. The annotated Oxford World Classics series includes K. J. Fielding and David Sorenson's edition of *The French Revolution* (Oxford: Oxford University Press, 1989), previously edited and annotated; *The French Revolution* is also available in three volumes, with plates, maps, and plans both by C. R. L. Fletcher (London: Methuen; New York: Putnam, 1902) and by John Holland Rose (London: G. Bell, 1902). John Clive edited a reprint of *History of Fredrich II of Prussia* (Chicago: University of Chicago Press, 1969). *On Heroes, Hero Worship, and the*

Heroic in History was reprinted with a brief introduction by Carl Niemeyer but no notes (Lincoln: University of Nebraska Press, 1966). Of short works, the only one in a modern annotated edition is *The Nigger Question*, published with J. S. Mill's response (Arlington Heights, IL: Harland Davidson, 1971), edited by Eugene R. August, whose introduction castigates Carlyle, citing dubious authorities.

Fiction and Adaptations

Carlyle's personal life was depicted in two short plays: "Firelighters: A Dialogue on a Burning Topic" (*London Mercury*, 1929) dramatized Mill's loss of *The French Revolution* manuscript; O. W. Firkin's "Two Passengers to Chelsea" comically evoked the Carlyles, Lady Harriet Baring, Alfred Lord Tennyson, and Garibaldi Mazzini. Longer treatments are *Speaking Dust* (1938), a novel by Elsie Thornton-Cook, and *Mrs. Carlyle: A Historical Play* (1950), by Glenn Hughes.

Carlyle's eccentric style has provided a ripe field for parodists, as G. B. Tennyson demonstrates in *Carlyle and His Contemporaries*; most important are passages by "Dr. Pessimist Anticant" in Anthony Trollope's *The Warden* (1855), and sections of the "Oxen of the Sun" chapter of James Joyce's *Ulysses* (1921). Historian John Clive parodied Carlyle's historical style in a *Times Literary Supplement* essay reprinted in his *Not By Fact Alone* (1989). Victorian scholar Lionel Trilling quotes Carlyle and imitates his style in his sympathetic portrait of a brilliant but incoherent young student in "Of This Time, of That Place," (1943) a much anthologized short story.

Carlyle's enduring contribution to fiction and to film has been through themes, techniques, symbols, and characters in Victorian social, historical, and autobiographical novels by Disraeli, Thackeray, Elizabeth Gaskell, Eliot, Meredith, and especially Charles Kingsley and Dickens. The Scottish mentor, Sandy Mackaye of Kingsley's hero in *Alton Locke* (1850) is modeled on Carlyle. Dickens, as studies by William Oddie (1972) and Michael Goldberg (1972) have shown, not only drew on Carlyle for style, historical vision, and opinions from materialism to Christmas, but adapted passages from Carlyle's works in several social novels, especially *Hard Times* (1854). Dickens's *A Tale of Two Cities* (1859) explicitly derives its portrayal of the ancien régime and the Revolution from Carlyle's *The French Revolution*; this historical classic also has been filmed most memorably by director

Jack Conway (MGM, 1935); and in 1989 Arthur Hopcraft adopted *The French Revolution* for television screenplays in England and France.

Museums, Historical Landmarks, Societies

Carlyle House (London). Located at 24 Cheyne Row in Chelsea, the house is now a museum managed by the National Trust. Rooms are furnished much as they were in Carlyle's lifetime. On display are mementos, photographs, medallions, sketches, letters, and paintings of the Carlyles, their friends, and their homes.

Carlyle Newsletter (Edinburgh). Founded in 1979, the newsletter publishes short articles and promotes the study of Carlyle.

Craigenputtoch (Dumfriesshire). Farmhouse residence of the Carlyles, maintained by the National Trust of Scotland.

Ecclefechan (Dumfriesshire). Carlyle's birthplace, the family home built by Carlyle's father and now called the Arched House, is a museum with furnishings and mementos. In the churchyard is Carlyle's family gravesite with a marker, and in the market place is a 1929 statue of Carlyle.

Glasgow Art Gallery and Museum (Glasgow). Holds a painting of Carlyle, "Arrangement in Grey and Black No. 2" (1873) by James McNeill Whistler.

Metropolitan Museum of Art (New York). Houses a photograph of Carlyle (c.1867) by Julia Margaret Cameron in the Alfred Stieglitz Collection.

National Portrait Gallery (London). Holds paintings of Carlyle by John Everett Millais (1877) and George F. Watts (1868).

Societies. The Carlyle Society of Edinburgh was founded in 1929 and issues publications, sponsors lectures and essay competitions and helps to support the *Carlyle Newsletter*. The Carlyle Society of London existed from 1897-1907, but it was small and not widely influential.

Statue (London). Located at the Chelsea Embankment, end of Cheyne Row, this statue is the work of Jacob Boehme (1881).

Other Sources

Ashton, Rosemary. *The German Idea: Four English Writers and the Reception of German Thought, 1800-1860.* Cambridge: Cambridge University Press, 1980. A chapter on Carlyle evaluates his writings, in chronological order, on German literature and responses by contemporaries.

Holloway, John. *The Victorian Sage: Philosophy and Rhetoric in the Work of Carlyle, Disraeli, George Eliot, Newman, Arnold, and Hardy.* London and New York: Macmillan, 1953. Chapters on Carlyle as philosopher and "prophet-historian." Includes close readings, revealing Carlyle's message and rhetorical strategies. A model for later studies of Carlyle's rhetoric.

La Valley, Albert J. *Carlyle and the Idea of the Modern: Studies in Carlyle's Prophetic Literature and Its Relation to Blake, Nietzsche, and Others.* New Haven, CT: Yale University Press, 1968. Connects Carlyle with modern views of the artist as seer. Discusses themes of the unconscious, alienation, multiplicity, and myth-making.

Levine, George R. *The Boundaries of Fiction: Carlyle, Macaulay, Newman.* Princeton, NJ: Princeton University Press, 1968. A classic study showing how effectively Carlyle, despite his concern for facts and reservations about the novel, used fictional techniques.

McGowan, John. *Representation and Revelation: Victorian Realism from Carlyle to Yeats.* Columbia: University of Missouri Press, 1986. Within a study of how Victorians tried to represent in language a "reality" that pre-exists language, McGowan shows that Carlyle, in early writings, especially by his theory of the symbol, both identifies and bridges the gap between experience and language.

Williams, Raymond. *Culture and Society, 1780-1950.* New York: Columbia

University Press, 1958. In this influential study of social themes in Victorian literature, the chapter on Carlyle shows how "Signs of the Times" introduced Carlyle's major social concerns to his age.

Monika Brown
Pembroke State University

Howard Carter
1873-1939

Chronology

Born Howard Carter on May 9, 1873 in Swaffham, Norfolk, England, son of Samuel John Carter, a draftsman and a watercolorist, and Martha Joyce Sandys; receives a basic education at home from hired tutors and receives training as a watercolorist according to his father's wishes; *1890* achieves a local reputation for his paintings; recommended by patron Lady Amherst to assist Percy E. Newberry, an Egyptologist at the University of Cairo; at Newberry's recommendation, takes a position at the British Museum; appointed official illustrator for the Egyptian Exploration Fund and leaves for Egypt; *1890-1898* works under Sir William Flinders Petrie, Newberry, and the Swiss Egyptologist Edouard Naville at Deir-al-Bahri; learns to read Hieroglyphs and becomes a competent Egyptologist; *1899* receives appointment from Egyptologist Sir Gaston Maspero to the post of inspector-in-chief of monuments in the Egyptian Antiquities Department; meets the American millionaire Theodore M. Davis and serves as his guide in the Valley of the Kings, Luxor; *1903* loses his position with the Antiquities Service; earns money by giving guided tours, selling watercolors, dealing in Egyptian antiquities; hired by British entrepreneur and amateur Egyptologist Lord George Carnarvon to find tombs in the Valley of the Kings; *1907* begins investigating a number of sites in the valley; *1912* publishes, with coauthor Carnarvon, *Five Years of Exploration at Thebes*; begins work in an area formerly explored by Davis; *1915* ceases work due to the outbreak of World War I; *1917* resumes work; *1921* informed by Carnarvon that this will be the last season of excavation because of financial difficulties; *1922* finds entrance to King Tutankhamen's tomb; with Carnarvon, tours the United States and Europe and lectures on the discovery; *1923* Carnarvon dies from infected mosquito bite, leading the press to speculate about whether the Tut tomb was cursed; *1925* returns to Egypt and works at the site for the next seven years; *1932* returns to England in deteriorating health; *1939* dies at home in London on March 2, after a six-year illness, and is buried in Putney Vale Cemetery.

Activities of Historical Significance

Howard Carter was a unique man among scholars and Egyptologists. Without a university education, he became a world-renowned expert on ancient Egypt. His success was based on courage, physical stamina, and resourcefulness, but he was at the same time often tactless and needlessly aggressive. However, he is, along with Heinrich Schliemann, who unearthed Troy, and Sir Arthur Evans, who discovered the ruins of Minoan society, one of the most recognizable names in the history of archaeology.

As a child, it seemed that Carter was destined to follow in his father's footsteps as a watercolorist. Indeed, by the age of seventeen, he had achieved a reputation in his region and was painting for local aristocrats, an activity that would supply him with his first opportunity in the world of Egyptology.

In the summer of 1890, a patron of Carter's who, along with her husband, was an avid amateur Egyptologist, recommended the young artist to Percy E. Newberry, a professor of Egyptology at the University of Cairo. Newberry was in the midst of creating a sketched recording of the ancient monuments at the Egyptian site of Beni Hassan. Impressed with the quality of Carter's drawings, Newberry found him a position with the British Museum where he worked for three months to perfect his skills at recording artifacts. He then became a full-fledged member of the Egyptian Exploration Fund, a private group, of which Newberry was a member, organized to explore archeological sites along the Nile.

From 1890-1898, Carter worked as the official artist and assistant to Sir William Flinders Petrie, one of the great Egyptologists, recording the paintings, reliefs, and inscriptions at the tomb of Queen Hatshepsut. During this work, Carter learned to read Hieroglyphs and mastered the fine points of Egyptology.

In 1899, Carter was offered by the great Egyptologist Sir Gaston Maspero the position of inspector-in-chief of monuments for Upper Egypt and Nubia in the Egyptian Antiquities Department. Three years later, he met American millionaire Theodore M. Davis, a lawyer and financier who had retired to study Egyptian civilization and archaeology. Davis hired Carter to teach him the techniques necessary for the exploration of the Valley of the Kings, and for a time he was known as a great excavator. In 1902, the two uncovered the mummy of pharaoh Thutmosis IV, and Carter later coauthored a book with other members of the Egyptian Exploration Fund. Carter, however, remained in obscurity during most of these years, because although Davis paid Carter for his services, he never acknowledged Carter's tutorial. The two men would later become rivals.

In 1903, Carter resigned from his position as inspector after a run-in with some drunken French tourists ran him afoul of the French authorities in Egypt. Now jobless, Carter scraped out a livelihood by giving guided tours, selling watercolors to tourists, and dealing in antiquities. His luck changed in 1907, however, when Maspero introduced him to George Herbert, Lord Carnarvon, a wealthy English aristocrat who was interested in acquiring a collection of Egyptian art and a knowledge of classical Egyptian civilization. Carter agreed to work with Carnarvon, and the two men set about planning their excavation strategy.

The two agreed to focus their attentions on the tombs in the Valley of the Kings, despite the general consensus among scholars that all of its important tombs had been plundered by ancient graverobbers. Carter, however, believed that one major tomb might still be intact somewhere in the valley near Thebes. He delved into the works of Giovanni Belzoni, an Anglicized Italian, and German archaeologist Karl Richard Lepsius, both of whom had done work in the Valley of the Kings during the early nineteenth century, for clues to possible excavation sites.

In 1907, with Carnarvon's financing and with permission from the Egyptian government, Carter began investigating a number of sites in the valley. During the next few years, he excavated sites in locations in Karnak, Luxor, and along the west bank of Nile. They mostly came up empty handed, but they did recover a tablet with Hieroglyphs and the empty tomb of pharaoh Amenophis I. In 1912, Carter and Carnarvon published *Five Years of Exploration at Thebes,* in which they chronicled their fruitless excavations.

Davis, Carter's protégé and rival, was also excavating in the area and was having considerably more success than Carter. But after several disappointing field seasons, Davis became convinced that there was nothing left in the valley and returned to America, selling his excavation rights to Carnarvon and Carter. In 1914, Carter moved his excavations to the area formerly explored by Davis and continued to work there for the next seven years, with a two-year interruption (1915-1917) following the outbreak of World War I. During the war years, Carter was put in charge of recruiting and overseeing teams of Egyptian laborers, and he thought nothing of taking a few small crews away from their duties for a few brief excavations at his own sites. In 1916, he and his crew took over from a group of grave robbers the site of the tomb of Queen Hatshepsut.

After the war, Carter resumed his search for the lost pharaoh's tomb, but again met with continued failure. By 1921, Lord Carnarvon was faced with financial stress and wrote to Carter that he wished to end the explorations. Carter, however, convinced Carnarvon to finance one last effort. He turned to a site that had drawn his attention many times before, close to the spot where a stele bearing Tutankhamen's seal, as well as items from his burial ceremony, had been unearthed.

On November 4, 1922, Carter finally found his quarry. That morning a young boy attached to Carter's crew was scraping in the sand as part of a game and unearthed a step. The area was subsequently excavated, revealing a flight of steps that led down to the door of a tomb. Some of the seals on the door had been broken, but new seals had been placed over them. However, Carter did not open the tomb, instead cabling Carnarvon in England and securing the tomb for his arrival. When Carnarvon did arrive, and a hole was made in the door, the men looked upon sites that they had never imagined. In the words of Carter, "As my eyes grew accustomed to the light, details of the room within emerged slowly from the mist, strange animals, statues, and gold—everywhere the glint of gold."

Further examination of the Hieroglyphs and the grave gods indicated that the tomb indeed belonged to Tutankhamen, who was pharaoh of upper and lower Egypt from 1361-1352 B.C. and who died at the age of nineteen. No intact tomb of a pharaoh had ever been found, so the objects and sites that Carter and Carnarvon encountered were virtually unknown to the modern world. Few of the pharaohs' tombs went unplundered for even a few decades after their burial—grave robbing was as lucrative a "business" in the ancient world as it is today.

Word of the find spread rapidly, and Carter and Carnarvon became celebrities almost overnight. The international press carried front page stories of the find for the next six months. Hordes of reporters and many important people rushed to the scene. The world was in the midst of the Roaring Twenties, and the circuslike atmosphere that reporters and curious onlookers created in the Valley of the Kings simply drew more reporters and curios onlookers. Carter, though gratified with the recognition after toiling in obscurity for so long, found the situation trying. He set up a laboratory at the site and analyzed and photographed the artifacts as they came out of the tomb. He wisely invited the foremost Egyptologists of the day—Sir Alan Gardiner and Professor James Henry Breasted—to assist in studying the tomb and to help him assess the historical significance of the objects. The world was anxious for details of "King Tut," and Carter, with fine slides and the finesse of a businessman and promoter, set out on a lecture tour of England and the U.S. He was an excellent speaker, mixing erudition with wit, and he made a considerable sum of money. Carnarvon sold exclusive rights to the story to the London *Times* and provided a series of articles on the progress of the excavations.

Carter and Carnarvon faced criticism for the commercial exploitation of their work. Local and European newspapers were furious at the restrictive atmosphere around the tomb, and Carnarvon made a handsome profit selling the rights to photograph and film the collection, with Carter making a handsome profit as Carnarvon's agent. Some of the criticism was justified—no complete catalogue of the contents of King Tutankhamen's tomb was made, and some have alleged that Carnarvon took some of the better objects home with him, although there is still debate as to whether some of these items did indeed come from the tomb.

When Carter returned to Egypt in 1923, he experienced difficulties with the Egyptian authorities, and for a time he and Carnarvon were denied access to the tomb. Carter responded by writing a bitter diatribe accusing the Egyptian authorities and eminent Egyptologists of unprofessional and unethical conduct. The ill-advised pamphlet was ultimately suppressed, but it cost him many friends. He apologized to the Egyptian authorities and was allowed again to continue his work in the Valley of the Kings.

The media furor and the stress of excavating, documenting, and transporting the vast amount of objects in the tomb eventually took their toll on the health of and the relationship between Carnarvon and Carter. The two had a falling out, and Carnarvon returned to England in failing health owing to an insect bite. Although he recovered briefly, he suffered a relapse and died on April 5, but not before he had reconciled with Carter and asked him to serve as executor for his collections. Carnarvon's strange death, combined with an earlier incident—a cobra (ancient symbol of the pharaoh's power) ate Carter's canary on the day the tomb was opened—sparked the legend of the "curse of King Tut" that has become associated with the excavation to this day. The popular press suggested that Carnarvon had invoked a curse inscribed on the entrance to the tomb by violating it and removing sacred objects from it.

After Carnarvon's death, Carter worked for seven years in the Valley of the Kings, analyzing the artifacts and writing his three-volume work, *The Tomb of Tut-ank-Amun.* He especially worked to reconstruct the life history of the young pharaoh, which was not an easy task as there were no written records of his life, death, or burial. All that was known was that he was the son or brother of the pharaoh Akhenaton, who had during his reign tried to replace the pantheistic religion of Egypt with a religion based on monotheism.

In 1932, Carter returned to England in failing health. By 1933 he had lost his strength and gave up any hopes of continuing his arduous work in the Valley of the Kings. He spent the last years of his life as an invalid, and died on March 2, 1939, a lonely man with few friends.

The significance of his work, however, has not diminished. His legacy lives in the careful and systematic excavation techniques that he employed and in the prominent place in the public mind that his work has given archeology. And the curse associated with the tomb, as well as the fascination with the occult and spiritualism that pervaded the era in which Carter lived, has resulted in the popular Hollywood treatments of cursed mummies rising from the grave to take their revenge on those who disturbed them in their rest, and of archaeologists such as Indiana Jones, who encounter supernatural beings and situations as they pursue their goals.

Overview of Biographical Sources

Ever since Carter's discovery of Tutankhamen's tomb, the world has been much more interested in the death of the young king than in the life of his discoverer, and all biographies of Carter are overshadowed by the mystery and romance of unearthing, virtually in tact, the most glorious representative of a lost civilization. One would think that Carter's meager beginnings into archaeology, his perseverance in the desert with feisty patrons, and his ultimate discovery of the tomb would make him an ideal subject for biographers, but it hasn't. The ancient Egyptians, not Carter, attracted the world's attention, and Carter died a lonely, mostly forgotten figure.

The few biographies that have been written tend to be more critical than laudatory. Carter and Carnarvon faced criticism for the commercial exploitation of their work and the restrictive atmosphere around the tomb. Carnarvon's strange death, combined with an earlier incident—a cobra (ancient symbol of the pharaoh's power) ate Carter's canary on the day the tomb was opened—that sparked the legend of the "curse of King Tut," which has resulted in Carter being treated more as popular legend than the serious study of archaeological methodology. There is certainly no definitive biography of this important archaeologist, partly because Carter eclipsed biographers by telling his own story of the discovery in his three-volume work *The Tomb of Tut-ank-Amun* (1923-1933).

Thomas Hoving's *Tutankhamen: The Untold Story* (1978) is the best work, a well-illustrated biography with a focus on Carter's contribution to Egyptology, offering insights into Carter's personality and "detective" work. The author arranged the Tutankhamen exhibit at New York's Metropolitan Museum of Art. Barry Wyne's *Behind the Masks of Tutankhamen* (1987) provides a straightforward biography of Carter. The book is well illustrated and the style is readable though often colloquial. Arnold Brackman's *The Search for the Gold of Tutankhamen* (1976) provides another straightforward biography that focuses on the excitement generated by Carter's discovery of King Tut's tomb.

Evaluation of Principal Biographical Sources

Brackman, Arnold C. *The Search for the Gold of Tutankhamen.* New York: Mason/Charter, 1976. (**G**) A popularized account of the search for, excavation of, and subsequent media furor surrounding Tutankhamen's tomb. Early chapters contain some information on Carter's early life, but most of the book is concerned with the Egypt years.

Hoving, Thomas. *Tutankhamen: The Untold Story.* New York: Simon & Schuster, 1978. (**G**) A fine, well-illustrated volume that contains much information on Carter's contributions to Egyptology, offering insights into Carter's personality and "detective" work. The author arranged an exhibit of Tutankhamen's treasures at New York's Metropolitan Museum of Art.

Wyne, Barry. *Behind the Masks of Tutankhamen.* 1972. Reprint. Guildford, CT: Ulverscroft, 1987. (**G**) Provides a straightforward biography of Carter. The book is well illustrated and the style is readable though often colloquial.

Overview and Evaluation of Primary Sources

Carter gives his own account of the discovery and excavation of the tomb in his three-volume *The Tomb of Tut-ank-Amun* (1923-1933. Reprint. New York: Cooper Square, 1963; **G**). He also published several articles on work in the region: "Report on the Robbery of the Tomb of Amenophis II, Biban-el-Moluk" (*Annals du Service des Antiquitiés de Égypt* 3 [1902]; **A**); "Report on the Tomb of Zesser-Ka-Ra Amenhetep I, Discovered by the Earl of Carnarvon in 1914" (*Journal of Egyptian Archaeology* 3 [1916]; **A**); and "A Tomb Prepared for Queen Hatshepsut and other Recent Discoveries at Thebes" (*Journal of Egyptian Archaeology* 4 [1917]; **A**).

Lord Carnarvon sold his story to the London *Times*, which published exclusive stories about the tomb and its contents almost daily from December 1922 to May 1923. The Egyptian art department in New York's Metropolitan Museum of Art has a file containing more than fifty documents relating to Carter, including letters and his unpublished pamphlet written after his difficulties in returning to the Valley of the Kings.

Museums, Historical Landmarks, Societies

Cairo Museum (Cairo, Egypt). Contains the bulk of the artifacts removed from Tutankhamen's tomb.

Metropolitan Museum of Art (New York). Upon his death, Carnarvon's estate sold his entire collection of Egyptian artifacts, art, and papyri to the museum, even though it had been promised to the British Museum.

Tutankhamen's Tomb (Valley of the Kings, Egypt). Open to the public for tours, it still contains the wall decorations that adorned it when Tutankhamen was first laid to rest.

Other Sources

Bennet, J. "The Restoration Inscription of Tutankhamen." *Journal of Egyptian Archaeology* 25 (1939). Deals with the scholarly issues of Carter's work.

Breasted, Charles. *Pioneer to the Past: The Story of James Henry Breasted.* New York: Scribner's, 1943. Biography written by the subject's son, of the great Egyptologists who worked with Carter in the Valley of the Kings. Provides many insights into the problems of assessing the artifacts and offers anecdotes that shed light on Carter's personality.

Hardinge, Sir Arthur. *The Life of Henry Howard Molneux Herbert, Fourth Earl of Carnarvon.* London: Oxford University Press, 1925.

Silverman, David. "The Treasures of Tutankhamen." *Archaeology* 29 (1976): 232-241. Provides a popular and well-illustrated account of the tomb.

Anthony Papalas
East Carolina University

Benvenuto Cellini
1500-1571

Chronology

Born Benvenuto Cellini on November 2, 1500, in Florence, Italy, son of Giovanni Cellini, a musician and instrument-maker, and Elisabetta Cellini; *1500-1515* grows up in Florence; wants to be a goldsmith, yet studies the flute at his father's insistence; *1515* apprentices himself to a goldsmith; *1517* goes to Pisa after a family argument and works for a goldsmith; *1518* returns to Florence; *1519* goes to Rome; *1522* returns to Florence; *1523* prosecuted and fined for sodomy; flees to Rome and is sentenced in absentia to four years' banishment after wounding two men in a fight; *1526* serves as papal gunner at Castel Sant'Angelo during the Sack of Rome; melts papal gold at the pope's request; *1527* takes refuge from the plague at Mantua; *1528* returns to Rome and again works for Pope Clement VII, making ornaments and designing papal coinage; *1529* brother fights with police, killing one, and mortally wounded by another, who in turn is sought out and killed by Cellini; *1532* flees Rome briefly, thinking he has killed a man in an argument; *1534* kills Pompeo, a rival jeweller who had damaged Cellini's reputation with the pope; flees to Florence until a pardon can be arranged; designs coinage for Duke Alessandro de'Medici; *1535* returns to Rome, receives a papal pardon, and works for Pope Paul III; commissions include a jeweled book cover, which he personally presents to Holy Roman Emperor Charles V; *1537* visits Paris and meets King Francis I; enroute makes medal of Pietro Bembo in Padua; *1538* imprisoned in Castel Sant'Angelo on a false charge of stealing papal gold during the 1526 siege; breaks his leg in escape; takes refuge with a friendly cardinal, but is eventually returned to custody; released upon entreaty of the king of France; *1540-1545* invited to France by King Francis I, makes gold Salt cellar, bronze lunette *Nymph of Fontainebleau*, his first large sculptured figures, and other works for the king; given French citizenship and a castle in Paris for his workshop; *1545-1571* lives in Florence; *1554* completes statue of Perseus; *1557* imprisoned after a fight; imprisoned again and tried for sodomy, pleading guilty; *1558-1562* writes *Autobiography*; *1562* marries his maid, Piera de Salvatore Parigi; *1565* sells marble crucifix; *1571* dies on February 13, of pleurisy, and is buried in the Church of the Annunziata in Florence.

Activities of Historical Significance

Benvenuto Cellini is important as both an artist and a writer. Born at the very end of the Italian Renaissance, Cellini is now ranked as one of the better artists among his contemporaries. Relatively few works survive from his long career as a goldsmith, jeweler, and sculptor in bronze, silver, and marble, but those that remain include masterpieces.

Probably his best-known work is the bronze statue of Perseus and Medusa, still where Cellini placed it in the Piazza della Signoria, Florence. Commissioned by Duke Cosimo de Medici and finished in 1554, the Perseus implicitly celebrates the triumph of the Medicis. The details of Cellini's considerable technical achievement in casting the piece are dramatically recounted in one of the best-known sections of his autobiography.

The gold Salt Cellar, made for Francis I of France, features the nude figures of Earth and Ocean, and is one of the world's most famous and beautiful gold objects. Cellini carved a magnificent marble crucifix now in The Escorial in Spain. His bronze lunette *Nymph of Fontainebleau* is also much admired. As Maestro della Stampe at the papal mint, and while working for the Medici in Florence, Cellini designed some superb coins. His medallic portraits, though few, place him in the first rank of the genre. His subjects include the great humanist Pietro Bembo, Francis I of France, and Pope Clement VII. Other portraiture includes bronze busts of Cosimo I and Bindo Altoviti.

Cellini's nineteenth-century English translator John Addington Symonds, among others, thought of him as a less-than-first-rate Renaissance sculptor. More recently, the sixteenth-century Mannerists, among whom Cellini is included, have been more appreciated. Sir John Pope-Hennessy's efforts on Cellini's behalf have also had their effect, thus aiding the continued growth of Cellini's artistic reputation.

Cellini influenced other artists not only by his artistic example, but also by his writings. His treatises on goldsmithing and sculpture, first published in 1568, were widely read, although unfortunately in a form heavily revised by the person to whom he entrusted them. They were not published in their intended form until

1857. Cellini claimed some technical innovations, such as his method for preparing colossal bronze statues, and there is little doubt he can claim preeminence as a goldsmith, jeweler and craftsman in metals, though little of his work is extant. Clearly, though, the technical methods he presents in the treatises (e.g., how to gild, strike medals, cast bronzes, set jewels in foils) are largely distillations and refinements of what he learned form others over the years.

Cellini's artistic stature is, however, exceeded by his literary prominence—ironically so, since he seems never to have formally studied letters. Although his autobiography remained in manuscript until 1728, it became immensely popular in the nineteenth century after translation into English, French, and German, and it has remained available in various editions since then. As George Bull has remarked, "The Life has won Cellini his immortality." Generally considered a landmark autobiography, it is one of the earliest treatments of the life of a person who was neither a saint nor a statesman. As such, it symbolizes the period wherein the notion of the artist as a heroic figure in his own right was developed to its full proportions. The colloquial style of the autobiography is striking, and its lively, intensely personal narration makes Cellini the most knowable figure of his time.

Finally, Cellini is of historical interest because of his active participation in events (detailed in his autobiography) during a colorful and important period of Italian history. A major artist, a papal gunner during the Sack of Rome in 1526, and the chronicler of a rich internal life, he also details his acquaintance with many of the rulers, statesman, and artists of his day.

Overview of Biographical Sources

Cellini is by far the best source on his life. His autobiography, composed from 1558-1562, tells of an extraordinary life. A flamboyant, extravagant account by a man who knew no false modesty, the book is nevertheless essentially accurate in all verifiable details. Cellini gives his reader a full narration, from his antecedents and birth through 1562, with attention not only to his artistic efforts and triumphs, but also the character and behavior of the popes, dukes, cardinals, other artists, workmen and rogues with whom he associated. In addition, he details such personal events as sexual liaisons, street fights, and moments of religious epiphany.

Not published in Cellini's day (though he clearly had publication in mind), it was first published in 1728. Later translated into various languages, it finally, in the nineteenth century, brought Cellini his present fame. Striking a sympathetic chord in the rising chorus of European Romanticism, the autobiography found its first German translator in Goethe; Louis Berlioz's opera *Benvenuto Cellini* appeared in Paris in 1838. Although efforts have been made, no biography of Cellini can equal his autobiography in liveliness and authority. Scholarly biographies or editions of the autobiography can, however, add corroboration from other sources, fill in background and—most importantly—provide illustrations and appreciations of Cellini's works, which are of major concern in the autobiography.

The manuscript of the autobiography, partly dictated to an amanuensis and partly written in Cellini's own hand, reappeared in an Italian bookshop in 1805 and is now in the Laurentian Library in Florence. All modern editions derive from that manuscript. Artistic works of Cellini still extant are indispensable to any full reading of his autobiography. They are for the most part on public display and (especially the major works) have been widely published.

Since its first publication in 1888, John Addington Symonds's translation of the autobiography has been considered the standard English version; it is the translation published by Modern Library.

Cellini's two treatises on goldsmithing and sculpture, published during his lifetime, supply important insights into his work. Additionally, they include a good number of significant autobiographical anecdotes, often illuminating episodes of the *Autobiography.* Various legal documents, letters, poems, and other archival materials also provide illuminating details of Cellini's life and work. Many of these are printed in the third volume of Tassi's edition of the *Autobiography.*

Although George Bull calls Charles Avery's *L'Opera completa del Cellini* (1981)"the best illustrated companion to the Life," American readers are more likely to encounter Sir John Pope-Hennessy's *Cellini* (1985). This large-format, one-volume work is actually a lavishly illustrated biography with sufficient pictures for all but the most assiduous scholar. This work plus Bull's modern (1956) translation of the autobiography makes a first-rate—and probably the most accessible—Cellini package for those who read only English.

The Italian literature on Cellini is massive and rich, but the list below covers mostly sources available in English.

Evaluation of Principal Biographical Sources

Bacci, Orazio. *Vita di Benvenuto Cellini.* Florence, 1901. (**A**) Pope-Hennessy calls this "the best Italian edition" of the *Autobiography.*

Bull, George, trans. *Autobiography of Benvenuto Cellini.* New York: Penguin, 1956. (**A, G**) In this most recent of the English translations, Bull seems to succeed rather well in his attempt to convey Cellini's extravagance and variety, and to show his charm as a writer of colloquial rather than scholarly Italian.

Cust, Robert H. H. *Benvenuto Cellini.* London: McClurg, 1913. (**G**) One of the Little Books on Art series, this slim volume includes many illustrations and a list of works in addition to the biography. However, it is of little added value to anyone with a copy of Bull, Symonds or Pope-Hennessy.

Plon, Eugene. *Benvenuto Cellini, orfevre, medailleur, sculpteur.* Paris: Plon, 1883. (**A**) In French, this remains an important source on Cellini's works.

Pope-Hennessy, Sir John. *Cellini.* New York: Abbeville, 1985. (**A, G**) In this splendid coffee-table size volume, one of the greatest authorities on Cellini narrates Cellini's life story (based upon the *Autobiography* plus ancillary documents). Charles Hope in the *New York Review of Books* calls this "certainly the best account of the subject that has been written." It also includes 155 plates, many full-page and in color, of essentially every extant Cellini work. Multiple views, including some very close-up details, are given for the more important works, such as the Salt Cellar, the bronze statue of *Perseus and Medusa*, the Crucifix, and the *Nymph of Fontainebleau.* A special excellence is that the plates adjoin, and are keyed to, the pertinent text passages. Pope-Hennessy also includes rather copious and very useful annotation, a lengthy bibliography and an index.

Symonds, John Addington, trans. *The Life of Benvenuto Cellini.* London: John C. Nimmo, 1888. (**A, G**) The classic translation into English, Symonds's remains well regarded, and is readily available as a Modern Library volume. A version with 500 black and white illustrations, and notes by John Pope-Hennessy (3d ed. Oxford: Phaidon, 1960) is also often encountered.

Tassi, F. *Vita di Benvenuto Cellini*. Florence: 1829. (**A**) The third volume of this edition includes many previously unpublished archival documents associated with Cellini, and remains useful for the scholarly researcher.

Thaddeus, Victor. *Benvenuto Cellini and his Florentine Dagger*. New York: Farrar and Rinehart, 1933. (**G**) Inevitably based on the *Autobiography*, this biography covers the period from 1500 (Cellini's birth) to 1554 (the casting of the Perseus). Telling Cellini's story with added background for the modern lay reader, this book has been described as "dull" and "inept".

Vasari, Giorgio. *Lives of the Most Eminent Painters, Sculptors, Architects*. 10 vols. 1912-1915. Reprint. New York: AMS Press, 1971. Translated by Gaston du C. de Vere. Vasari gives a brief treatment of Cellini's life, usually omitted from the more readily available condensed versions of the *Lives*. The brevity, Vasari says, is because he is aware Cellini has written his own autobiography. Additionally, Vasari mentions Cellini in a number of the lives of other artists.

Overview and Evaluation of Primary Sources

In addition to his *Autobiography*, or *Vita,* Cellini's manuscript account books from 1545 on, full of financial and personal details, are in the Riccardian Library in Florence. The originals of most other documents associated with Cellini are in various Italian libraries and archives. A large sample of this material is published in Tassi's edition, cited above.

Cellini's two technical treatises, on goldsmithing and sculpture, were published during his lifetime in a heavily edited edition. Cellini's original version remained unpublished until 1857. The best available edition in English is C. R. Ashbee's translation, *The Treatises of Benvenuto Cellini on Goldsmithing and Sculpture* (1898. Reprint. New York: Dover Press, 1966; **A, G**).

Principal Works

Marble Crucifix (El Escorial, near Madrid).

Gold Saltcellar (Kunsthistorisches Museum, Vienna, Austria). Made for Francis I of France.

Bronze Bust of Bindo Altoviti (Isabella Stewart Gardner Museum, Boston, MA).

Bronze Bust of Cosimo I (Museo Nazionale, Florence, Italy).

Nymph of Fontainebleau (The Louvre, Paris).

Bronze Statue of Perseus and Medusa (Piazza dei Signoria, Florence). The statue remains under the Loggia dei Lanzi, where Cellini erected it.

Fiction and Adaptations

Hector Berlioz's opera, *Benvenuto Cellini,* first produced in Paris in 1838, is a romanticized tale mingling fiction with elements of Cellini's life. It climaxes in the dramatic casting of the *Perseus*; in the opera, however, Cellini throws in not merely his pots and pans but works of sculpture.

Museums, Historical Landmarks, Societies

Castle Sant'Angelo (Rome). Originally the tomb of the Roman emperor Hadrian, this is the structure where Cellini served as a gunner and goldsmith in 1526, and where he was later imprisoned. It is open to tourists.

Palazzo Vecchio (Florence). Holds the one absolutely authentic portrait of Cellini, who appears as a background figure in Vasari's painting, *Cosimo I with His Architects, Engineers and Sculptors*, painted about 1563.

Santissima Annunziata Church (Florence). Cellini is buried here, beneath a marble slab.

Other Sources

Avery, Charles, and Susanna Barbaglia. *L'opera Completa del Cellini.* Milan: Rizzoli, 1981. One of the Rizzoli *Classici dell'Arte* series. Though a number of these (e.g., *Giotto, Raphael*) have been translated into English and republished as the Penguin Classics of World Art, the Cellini volume has not. In standard Rizzoli/Penguin format, contains illustrations of all known works, notes on location and provenance, and an annotated list of lost works and works formerly ascribed to Cellini. For most American readers, Pope-Hennessy's *Cellini* will be more useful and much more accessible.

Benvenuto Cellini Artista e Scrittore. Rome: Accademia Nazionale dei Lincei, 1972. A conference report including various papers on Cellini with, according to Bull, important reassessments.

"Cellini's Halo." In *Encyclopedia Britannica.* 15th ed. Chicago: Encyclopedia Britannica, 1987. Explains the physics of the halo Cellini believed he had received from God.

Pope-Hennessy, Sir John. *Italian High Renaissance and Baroque Sculpture.* New York: Vintage, 1985. Places Cellini in artistic context of his time.

C. Herbert Gilliland
U. S. Naval Academy

Paul Cézanne
1839-1906

Chronology

Born Paul Cézanne on January 19, 1839, at Aix-en-Provence, France, son of Phillippe Auguste Cézanne, originally a hatmaker and later a wealthy banker, and Honorine Aubert, one of his father's bank employees; *1844* under pressure from their families, his parents marry; *1844-1849* attends elementary school at Rue Epinaux; *1848* father becomes co-founder of the Cézanne and Cabanol banking firm; thereafter he neither has to worry about his future nor about having to earn a living; *1850-1851* studies at the Pensionnat Saint-Joseph; *1852* enters the Collège Bourbon; meets and forms a close friendship with writer Émile Zola, who was then living with his widowed mother in Aix, and befriends Baptistin Baille; they will play a major role in his early artistic development; with Zola and Baille, reads Victor Hugo and is influenced by the serious romanticism of his rhetoric; *1852-1855* joined by writer Numa Coste, the sculptor Philippe Solari, the writer and poet Henri Gasquet, the journalist and writer Marius Roux, these three move away from Hugo's romanticism to that of Alfred Musset; the *Contes d'Italie* and the *Contes d'Espagne* are their main poetic influences; influenced by poets Edward Young and Jean Paul Richter, he develops his artistic vocation, following the spirit and style of Romanticism; *1854* younger sister, Rose, is born; *1855* graduates with honors; begins a voluminous correspondence with Zola, which will later be published by art historian John Rewald in 1937; *1856* studies academic drawing with Joseph-Marc Gibert at the École de Beaux-Arts in Aix, despite his father's disapproval; masters the academic style in drawing; *1858* wins second prize for drawing; in December sends his famous poem, "Une terrible histoire," to Zola in Paris in which lines of verse are interspersed with drawings and watercolors; *1858-1861* at his father's request, studies at the Law School of the University of Aix, but simultaneously and with much greater enthusiasm, attends the Académie de dessin in Aix, where he studies painting; *1859* sets up his first studio in Jas de Bouffan, his father's new country house, deciding to dedicate himself to painting as a career; *1859-1860* meets frequently with sculptor Philippe Solari, who becomes a lifelong friend; also befriends painters Achille Emperaire and Antoine Fortuné and the critic Antoine Valabrègue; *1861* at the urging of Zola, who wants his friend Cézanne to join him in Paris, and through the aid of his mother and his older sister, secures permission from his father to move to Paris; settles in Paris at Rue des Feuillantines; without a teacher, studies and works at the free Académie Suisse, where he could, for a modest fee, work from a model without any supervision; meets painters Armand Guillaumin and Camille Pissarro, who introduce him to Impressionist painters Claude Monet and Auguste Renoir; studies Old Masters and others like Caravaggio, Rivera, Zurbaran and Velasquez at the Louvre; views the Salon of 1861; is attracted to painters Meissonnier, Cabanel and Gustave Doré; returns to Aix after failing the entrance exams to the École des Beaux-Arts, doubting himself, feeling that he has no real artistic ability; beset by this inner crisis, enters his father's banking business in September; remorsefully, begins again to think of painting; *1862* takes art lessons at the Académie de Dessin while working for his father; decorates the walls of the Jas de Bouffan with gay, not very original compositions; journeys to Paris in November and returns to the Académie Suisse; stays there for a year and a half, an important period for his development; *1863-1864* lives in Paris and socializes with many painters of the day; views the Salon des Refusés of 1863 in the Palais de l'Industrie; is attracted to Gustave Courbet's kind of realism and admires Édouard Manet's *Déjeuner sur l'herbe;* sees and is deeply impressed by the great Eugène Delacroix's anti-academic exhibition of 1864; meets with Pissarro for the second time; again fails to gain entrance to the École des Beaux-Arts because of his technical clumsiness; Zola's encouragement is of crucial importance; his failure to be admitted to the Beaux-Arts solidifies his determination to continue his training; *1864* returns to Aix; paints regularly; studies minor Baroque masters in the churches of Aix; studies the works of Provençal painters Émile Loubon, Paul Guigou, and Honoré Daumier; *1864-1865* sends pictures to various Salons, where they are promptly refused; *1865* meets Manet, who praises his still lifes; Zola dedicates his novel *La confession de Claude* to Cézanne and Baille; *1865-1870* paints works of his Romantic period, marked by harsh and vigorous contrasts of light and shadow, striking darkness of tone and rough vigor; *1867-1869* manner begins to lose some of its excessive heaviness, tones become lighter, pigments become thinner; colors, particularly the blues, now play a more important role, though the emphasis is always on light-dark contrasts; throughout this period he remains in obscurity;

experiences with first large figure, portrait-like compositions, and with dramatic, erotic subjects reminiscent of Delacroix; portraits and genre paintings like *The Abduction* and *The Rape* are still regularly refused by the official salons; again denied entry into the École des Beaux-Arts; *1866* revolts against the strictures of the French Academy of painting; sends his famous letter of protest against the jury system of the Salon to Nieuwekerke, the director of the Beaux-Arts; inspires Zola to write the novel *Mon Salon* in defense of Manet; *1866-1869* alternates his stays between his studio at Aix, at the Jas de Bouffan, and numerous residences in Paris; meets frequently with the young experimental Parisian painters of the Café Guerbois, the haunt of Manet, Degas, Bazille and above all Pissarro, those painters who are later called the Impressionists, but remains an outsider to this circle; his paintings continue to be refused by the Paris salons; *1869* meets and cohabits with a young model Marie-Hortense Fiquet; over the years Cézanne will paint thirty-three portraits of her, all entitled *Madame Cézanne*; *1870* fall of the Second Empire; during the Franco-Prussian War and the Paris Commune, lives with Fiquet in Aix and at the Estaque, a Provençal village on the Bay of Marseille; concentrates on landscape painting; first motif of Mont Sainte-Victoire in the background of the *Railway Cutting with Mont Sainte-Victoire;* creates over forty paintings on this theme; *1871* after the fall of the Commune, returns to Paris and renews and intensifies his friendship with Pissarro, who has again brought together the Impressionists; *1871-1877* creates paintings of his Impressionist period; *1872* at the invitation of Pissarro, moves to a hotel at Pontoise with Fiquet and their son Paul born that year; *1872-1873* associates daily with Pissarro and other Impressionists like Guillaumin, who are living in Pontoise, and begins working outdoors; without abandoning still life or figure compositions altogether, fully comprehends the value of open air and motif painting; is influenced by Pissarro's color researches and, on his advice, seeks to build form with color, rather than with strong tonal contrasts; *1873-1875* spends two years at Pontoise; also travels to nearby Auvers-sur-Oise with Pissarro; meets Dr. Paul Gachet, one of the few collectors of Impressionist and avant-garde paintings; paints important landscapes, including *La maison du pendu à Auvers*; creates numerous prints in the workshop in the home of Gachet; *1874* at the urging of Pissarro, exhibits at French photographer Paul Nadar's in the first Impressionist Exhibition; the show is a disaster and his work is especially ridiculed; meets Vincent Van Gogh; sells his first paintings to Count Doria; *1874-1877* reacts strongly to the failure of the exhibition; sends his paintings to the official salons even though he is certain they will be refused; continues to work at Pontoise and Auvers; receives support from collectors Victor Chocquet, a French customs officer, and Père Julien Tanguy, a humble dealer in artists' supplies and paintings; *1876* refuses to participate in the second Impressionist Exhibition, but continues to await an invitation to the famous Parisian Salon of Monsieur Bouguereau; *1877* shows seventeen still lifes and landscapes including both oils and watercolors at the third Impressionist Exhibition, again failing to obtain public or critical approval, with the exception of some favorable reviews from young critic Georges Rivière; thereafter, association with Pissarro, Monet and Guillaumin comes to a gradual end as he emancipates himself from Impressionism to develop his own independent style; *1878* relationship with his father deteriorates because of the latter's continued disapproval of his artistic endeavors and of his love relationship with Hortense Fiquet; receives financial aid from Zola; becomes more and more irritable; returns to L'Estaque; works in almost complete isolation; *1878-1887* creates the paintings of his post-Impressionist Constructivist period, during which he examines the constructive and structural dimensions of the natural world; *1879* returns to Paris but still remains aloof from friends; *1882* finally accepted in the Paris Salon as a pupil of Antoine Guillemet, one of his last advocates; but the salons of the succeeding years still refuse his works; returns to Provence; *1883* befriends French Impressionist painter Monticelli; *1883-1887* lives and paints in almost total seclusion at L'Estaque; paints his most celebrated landscapes, including views of Mont Sainte-Victoire and the Bay of Marseille, and subjects such as card players, still lifes, and figure compositions like *Chestnuts at Jas de Bouffan* that rank among the highest achievements of nineteenth century painting; paintings are again refused by the official salons of the mid-1880s; *1885* Paul Gauguin buys one of his paintings; *1886* marries Fiquet when their son is already fourteen years of age; father dies, leaving him a small fortune; breaks with Zola after the publication of the latter's *L'oeuvre*, which features an unflattering character that could have been modeled on Manet, but that is based more particularly on Cézanne; *1887* shows three paintings in Brussels at the avant-garde Groupe des XX exhibition; *1888* lives in Paris; meets with Van Gogh, Émile Bernard, and Gauguin; returns to Provence; *1888-1898* creates paintings of his Synthetic period, in which he simplifies his subject matter and achieves a new geometric and expressive order; the architectonic clarity of form and color radiance are then to be found equally in his landscapes, his still lifes, his portraits, or his series of *Card Players*;

begins painting his most important masterpieces, including *The Commode, The Blue Vase, The Card Players,* and *The Bathers; 1889* exhibits at the Exposition Décennale; *1889-1890* makes a few short trips to Paris but otherwise rarely leaves Provence; *1890* travels to Switzerland; *1891* begins suffering from diabetes; *1892* spends the summer months at Fontainebleau; *1894* spends the autumn and part of the winter with Monet at Giverny; meets sculptor Auguste Rodin, statesman Georges Clémenceau, and critic Gustave Geoffroy, who ties Cézanne's style to that of Gauguin and Van Gogh; *1895* first one-man show in Paris organized by gallerist and art dealer Ambroise Vollard at the request of Pissarro, Monet, and Renoir, receives a generally favorable response; two paintings acquired by the Luxembourg collection; *1896-1897* fame continues to grow in France and neighboring European countries; meets painter Louis Aurenche and poet and writer Joachim Gasquet, son of a childhood friend who becomes one of his greatest proponents; makes painting trips to Montbriant and Talloires; *1897* deeply anguished after his mother dies; the Berlin National Gallery buys two paintings; *1899* obliged to sell the Jas de Bouffon estate as part of the arrangements of inheritance settlement; splits from his wife and son; cohabits with his son's governess, Madame Brémond; exhibits three paintings at the Salon des Indépendants; the French public begins to show some interest; after Chocquet's death, seven of his paintings are sold for 17,660 francs; *1900* takes part in the Exposition Centennale in Paris; young French post-Impressionist painters like Émile Bernard, Maurice Denis and K. X. Roussel travel to Provence to seek his counsel; Symbolist Maurice Denis paints his celebrated *Hommage à Cézanne; 1900-1906* creates paintings and watercolors of his Late period, at which time his work becomes more and more abstract and geometric; *1901-1904* exhibits frequently in Paris, Brussels, Berlin, and Vienna; *1901* participates in the Salon des Indépendants; exhibits at the Libre Esthétique show in Brussels; prompted by Maurice Denis and other Symbolists, decides to set up his last studio in Aix; begins writing down his views about art; after having been, like Zola, a convinced anticlerical, begins to be attracted to Christianity; a new religious sense emerges in his art; *1902* paintings arouse much interest at the Salon des Indépendents; builds last studio at Les Lauves in Aix; Zola dies, affecting him deeply; *1904* spends some months in Paris and Fontainebleau; given a whole exhibition room at the Salon d'Automne, which definitely establishes his successful reputation; thirty-one works are shown; pleased by the impact and critical success of the exhibition; returns to Aix to work until his death; meets often with painter Émile Bernard; through critic Bernard Berenson, American collector Leo Stein sees his first Cézanne at the Galerie Vollard in Paris; purchases by Leo and Gertrude Stein include the famous *Portrait de Madame Cézanne; 1905* exhibits ten paintings at the Salon d'Automne and ten more at the Salon des Indépendants; finishes *The Large Bathers*, begun in 1898; *1906* again exhibits ten paintings at the Salon d'Automne; caught in a storm while painting outdoors and collapses; health deteriorates; dies on October 22 in Aix of pneumonia; *1907-present* numerous retrospective exhibitions mounted.

Activities of Historical Significance

Paul Cézanne was the precursor of the modern artistic movement and inaugurated a new era in the history of art. Both as an individual and an artist, he absorbed himself in a search for a new way of painting and strove for representational truth. Because of his stubborn, frantic and almost maniacal perfectionism, he was never satisfied by his results and remained forever frustrated and embroiled in a constant, despairing personal struggle for the complete redefinition and reconstruction of day-to-day life and of visual reality. This accounts for Cézanne's solitary life, his cantankerous personality, and his difficulties with women and with friends. His own troubled family life bore witness to a desperate attempt to finally find happiness with the woman he loved and married after the end of another tumultuous love affair. When this love relationship with Hortense Fiquet failed, he was distraught and very bitter, and remained so for the rest of his life. His intense friendship, then his breakup with Émile Zola—over his characterization in Zola's novel *L'oeuvre* (1886)—as well as the critical and public disapproval of his work, hardened his determination to spend his life in almost complete isolation in the south of France. Annoyed at first by the attention paid to him at the turn of the century by the young post-Impressionist painters like Maurice Denis, he finally seemed able to accept, appreciate and justly value his artistic success before his death.

Cézanne's renunciation of traditional illusory space set the stage for the revolution of taste that took place in the first decades of the twentieth century. From the hindsight of modernist criticism, he has often been interpreted as the founder of formal distortions and deconstructive and abstract styles. In this sense, Cézanne's contribution to modern and contemporary art is nothing less than a new concept of realist representation and pictorial form leading toward a predominance of formal and chromatic combinations.

Cézanne's art can best be understood as a transition between objectivity and subjectivity, figurative representation and abstraction. From the start, he conceived painting as being a matter of imaginative (re)construction rather than academic imitation. The significance of his art thus rests on its formal qualities, especially in the need to imagine a world of art distinct from that of nature. His mapping of the philosophical, perceptual, and optical concerns of the late nineteenth century and his studies of light and color, of planes and volumes, of space and its relation to the object are a link between Impressionism and Post-Impressionism, between seeing and knowing, between the post-Romantic vision of color and form and a harmonious formal equilibrium. In seeking to understand and explain the complexity of Cézanne's achievement, we realize that the lessons of his work go beyond the subsequent schools of Cubism, post-Cubism, or Formalism and are still valid today.

In his early youth, Cézanne developed his vocation within the framework of the Romantic spirit, moving away from the academic style and design of the École des Beaux-Arts. He revived Romantic sentiments about the transformation of reality via the artist's temperament originally put forth by Delacroix, was influenced by the emphatic gestures of Daumier, assimilated aspects of the local Provençal painters, and was also attracted to the realism of Courbet.

The paintings of this period are dominated by the use of thick, "juicy" paint, expressive brush work, and somber colors, and he regularly experimented with painting with his palette knife. But as he became more familiar with the work of the Impressionists, a radical change took place in his style—he began a lifelong effort to record his visual sensations of nature. Like the Impressionists, he turned to open-air landscape painting. The tight discipline of such work provided the key to organizing his emotional sensibilities, and he also lightened and simplified his palette. He began to build forms in his work with color rather than tonal contrasts.

By 1877, Cézanne had mastered the techniques of Impressionism and began to seek out and develop his own style. This marked the beginning of his constructivist period, in which he concentrated on landscapes, striving for ever-greater formal organization. The works of this period became increasingly abstract as

Cézanne attempted to capture the exact relationship between structure, organization, and color through the use of tilting planes to achieve volume and mass in his images. He also altered the perspective of his subjects, changing the relationship between near and far to express the abstract compositions of his paintings.

After a decade of development, Cézanne achieved all he could in the constructivist style and began to focus less on structure alone and more on the total space in a composition. This change marked the transition to his Synthetic period, in which he treated his subjects more and more abstractly. Houses, landscapes, and other subject matter were translated into cones, cylinders, and spheres as Cézanne sought to synthesize multiple planes of color and abstracted images. The most famous product of this period is *The Card Players* (c.1890-1892), and many of its stylistic techniques (along with those in other paintings of the period), such as peripheral distortions and size inconsistency, herald the further abstractions that marked Cubism.

Cézanne's Late period is characterized by forms created from interlocking color surfaces and the disappearance of the background. These developments anticipate the work of post-1945 American Abstract Expressionists such as Jackson Pollock and color-field painters such as Mark Rothko.

When analyzing all of Cézanne's work, his rejection of the Renaissance idea of perspectival space and his forays into pre-Cubist techniques stand out among his many contributions to twentieth-century art. Perhaps his greatest legacy to the history of modern painting is to be found in his mastery of structural planes, his synthesis of the abstract and the real, his emphasis on surface patterns, and his perspectival flattening of images. In contrast to the lyrical naturalism of his Romantic predecessors and to nineteenth-century Realism, Cézanne seemed to distort and manipulate three dimensional subject matter for the sake of the "pure form" of two-dimensional picture space. In this, he anticipated more recent trends in visual theory and the polemics of contemporary painting. He created a new sense of space in which the significance of the depicted images lies in their relationship to each other rather than to any external reality. In all these respects, Cézanne therefore brought to its culmination the revolutionary efforts of the avant-garde of the nineteenth century and set the ground rules for the debates of twentieth-century art.

Overview of Biographical Sources

Cézanne has been a popular subject of treatment for a number of critics, historians, and art specialists, and the biographical material is very extensive. Contemporary writings on Cézanne often downplayed the critical importance of his paintings—even his close friend Émile Zola, after dedicating his earlier novel *La confession de Claude* (1865) to his childhood companion from Aix, had grown cooler toward the Impressionists and finally changed his position from admiration to carping and unimaginative criticism. He thus presented a view of Cézanne as an aborted and pigheaded genius, albeit in the guise of the fictional character Claude Lantier in the novel *L'oeuvre*. When writing *Savage Paris* (1873), Zola had wanted to convey a sense of color in his descriptions of Les Halles and had evidently been inspired by Cézanne's art; now he dismissed him as a loser whom the critics constantly needled. In 1894, critic Gustave Geffroy reaffirmed this view in his anecdotal *History of Impressionism*, presenting Cézanne as a painter who was frequently unable to bring his pictorial conceptions to fulfillment because of his self-created troubled personal life. This concept of Cézanne as an artist who didn't finish things, a serious critical error promulgated by Zola and Geffroy, was further developed by many others, including critic Camille Auclair, who as late as 1905 in the fashionable magazine *Revue Blanche* of December 15, had the audacity to write that this "old man who paints for pleasure in the provinces" would remain one of the most memorable artistic jokes of the last fifteen years. This biased view was to persist for a long time in the critical assessment of Cézanne's work. The first to react to it was critic Thadée Natanson in a biographical article published in the *Revue Blanche* of 1895 on the occasion of the solo exhibition organized by Ambroise Vollard at his Paris gallery. Nevertheless, apart from George Rivière, who as a young enthusiast had already written in 1877 that Cézanne was a great painter, most Parisian art critics and commentators continued to deny the merit of the artist, even while they were duly chronicling his achievements.

In 1891, painter and friend Émile Bernard wrote one of the first accurate presentations of Cézanne's character in a short but informative and reliable biographical essay. Fifteen years later, Bernard chronicled Cézanne's life and aesthetic ideals in two lengthy magazine articles based on long interviews with the painter. He further developed his character study in the 1911 book *Remembrances on Paul*

Cézanne. On the other hand, Bernard as was also the case with Gaugin and with other Symbolists, Divisionists and Post-Impressionists, wished to feel that he derived from Cézanne, so Bernard distorted the meaning of Cézanne's life and work to suit his own purposes. Bernard saw in Cézanne what he himself wanted to express aesthetically and contributed to the tendency to see Cézanne as a classic restorer of order who was returning to a kind of literary symbolism which had nothing in common with modern, avant-garde art. Before his death, Cézanne became aware of this misconception and in the letters of his last years expressed his hostility to Bernard's theses, calling him an "intellectual stuffed with museum memories." Nonetheless, this interpretation that lacked any credibility was widely accepted in art history circles before and immediately after World War I.

Several monographs dedicated to Cézanne appeared in France and other European countries not long after his death. With the revolution in taste which took place between 1910 and 1930, the attention given to Cézanne increased. Just as some wished to see him as a classicist, others, while not diminishing the value of his own art, made him the precursor of the modern movement and the forerunner both of Cubism and of abstract art. Thus a number of laudatory monographs began to appear. Critic Georges Rivière and influential art historian Élie Faure each published volumes entitled *Cézanne* in 1910; both contained extensive biographical data and critical comments on his work. That same year, critic Julius Meier-Graefe also published one in Munich that represented an important critical contribution to an understanding of his life and his art. Four years later, Ambroise Vollard, Cézanne's gallerist and friend, published *Cézanne: His Life and Art*, which recounted Vollard's reminiscences of the painter's life and work. In 1919, famous Parisian critic Gustave Coquiot wrote an interpretative essay on Cézanne's art, *Paul Cézanne* (Paris: Ollendorff, 1919). In his theoretical writings on art published before 1920, Suprematist Russian painter Kazimir Malevich retraced the origins of his own Abstractionism to Cézanne in *De Cézanne au Suprematism* (Lausanne, France: L'Age d'homme, 1974). Many more studies, tributes, and monographs on Cézanne's life and work like the literary evocation of the artist by his close personal friend Joachim Gasquet in 1926, appeared during the next decade, and by the end of the 1920s, Cézanne was well known and admired in artistic and literary circles on both sides of the Atlantic. For example, the first serious systematic criticism and analysis of Cézanne's life and works was formalist British critic Roger Fry's *Cézanne: A Study of His Development* (1927), which drew attention to the formal values of Cézanne's paintings. Fry tried to reconstruct the personality of the painter through certain paintings, stressing their abstract expressive character. Apart from her self-centered *Autobiography of Alice B. Toklas* (New York: Harcourt-Brace, 1933), in which she documents her "discovery" of avant-garde French painters, including Cézanne, American patron Gertrude Stein published, "Cézanne," a gossipy and incomplete portrait of Cézanne's character and personality, in *Portrait and Prayers*. New York: Random House, 1934).

From 1936 onward, many notable contributions to the study of the life of Cézanne were published. Italian critic and art historian Lionello Venturi's successive essays on Cézanne and catalogue of his works, *Cézanne: son art, son oeuvre* (2 vols. Paris, 1936), as well as his later volume, *De Manet à Lautrec* (Paris: Gallimard, 1950), established a solid tradition of art history scholarship. Reacting against Fry's presumed formal biases, Venturi insisted on the necessity of taking Cézanne's personal experiences into account for his artistic development. Following in Venturi's footsteps, in 1937, Fritz Novotny and Ludwig Goldscheider examined Cézanne's emotions and his inner crises from the standpoint of these life/art relations in *Cézanne*. French art historian Réné Huyghe took the same approach in his biographical essay *Cézanne* (Paris: Plon, 1936), allowing us to follow not only the psychological life of the painter but also the evolution of his artistic personality. Also among the best biographies are art historian John Rewald, *Paul Cézanne, A Biography* (1939) with its numerous revised and enlarged editions to date, as well as his *Cézanne et Zola* (Paris: Editions Sedrowski, 1936); Gerstle Mack, *Paul Cézanne* (1942); art historian Bernard Dorival, *Cézanne* (1948); French sociologist of art Pierre Francastel, *Peinture et société* (Paris: Denoël-Gonthier, 1952), which documents through biography and art criticism the new spatial values put forward by Cézanne; and British Cézanne scholar Sir Laurence Gowing, *An Exhibition of Paintings by Cézanne* (London: Arts Council of Great Britain, 1954). Robert Neiss's *Zola, Cézanne and Manet: A Study of L'Oeuvre* (Ann Arbor: UMI Research, 1968), and Jack Lindsay's *Cézanne: His Life and Art* (1969) both explore and attempt to define the painter's stylistic evolution and the new aesthetics demonstrated in his later works within the framework of his personal friendships and dislikes. More recent authors, such as Francis Jourdain, *Cézanne* (Paris: Braun, 1950); Meyer Schapiro, "The Apples of Cézanne. An Essay on the Meaning of Still-Life" in M. Schapiro, *Modern Art: 19th and 20th Centuries* (New York: George Braziller, 1978); Theodore Reff, "Cézanne and Poussin," in

Journal of the Warburg and Courtauld Institute 23 (1960: 150-174); "Cézanne's Constructive Stroke," in *Art Quarterly* 25 (Autumn 1962): 214-227; and Richard Kendall, *Cézanne by Himself* (London: Atlas, 1968), have perpetuated and revived the biographical tradition, providing readers once again with the opportunity to follow in its historical context the complex life and artistic transformations of Cézanne. Moreover, in an effort to understand the sensuous man behind the rather impersonal artist, as well as the significance of his subject matter, art historians like Meyer Schapiro, *Paul Cézanne* (New York: Harry N. Abrams, 1952) and Kurt Badt, *The Art of Cézanne* (Berkeley: University of California Press, 1956), as well as Theodore Reff, "Cézanne, Flaubert, Saint-Anthony and the Queen of Sheba," in *The Art Bulletin* 44 (1962), have adopted a psychoanalytical approach based on Freud's theory that art sublimates sexual desires to highlight Cézanne's life crises, solitary personality, friendships, love affairs and break-ups. This biographical effort has aimed at conveying Cézanne's somber and introspective mood of solitude and meditation that has presided over his artistic innovations; also it has permitted us to re-examine Cézanne's relation to the Old Masters.

Evaluation of Principal Biographical Sources

Badt, Kurt. *The Art of Cézanne.* Translated from the German by Sheila Ann Ogilvie. London: Faber and Faber, 1965. (**A**) Contains reliable biographical and stylistic data. Of particular interest in this study of Cézanne's artistic endeavors is the author's authoritative interpretation of the word "realization," which the painter frequently employed in a variety of contexts. Badt argues that Cézanne gave the initial impetus to modern art by reconquering space, by constructing with color and by developing a new set of spatial values. He notes that Cézanne has continued to exercise an influence on younger artists in this century because he was the first modern painter to create a dynamic balance between depth and surface—that is between things as they appear in depth and the compelling reality of the canvas itself.

Dorival, Bernard. *Cézanne.* Translated from the French by H. H. A. Thackthwaite. Paris and New York: Tisné, 1948. (**G**) One of the most important introductory texts published before 1950. Contains an exhaustive chronology, a complete list of exhibitions, and numerous reproductions. Very reliable and informative. Dorival intertwines biographical data with aesthetic observations, stressing the important role played by his passionate perfectionism, forever frustrated until the last decade of the past century by a bad critical press. Dorival painstakingly reconstructs the personality of the painter, as well as the non-illusionistic, structural and abstract character of Cézanne's art.

Faure, Élie. *Paul Cézanne*. Translated from the French by Walter Pach. New York: Association of American Painters and Sculptors, 1913. (**A, G**) A classic study by one of the best known French art historians of the first half of the twentieth century. Faure was one of the first to look at the poetic significance of Cézanne's subject matter from an art history point of view. Faure's theses on the sensitive and poetic qualities of the artist's inner vision and resulting work set the standard for future French-language scholarship.

Fry, Roger. *Cézanne: A Study of His Development*. London: Chatto and Windus, 1927. Reprinted in part in Roger Fry, *Transformations*. New York: Doubleday, 1956. (**A**) Critical evaluation of Cézanne's art from a formalist point of view; first thorough study of Cézanne's artistic evolution. One of the founders with Clive Bell of the formalist school of literary and art criticism known as the Bloomsbury Circle that turned its back on impressionistic and imprecise subjective critical commentary, Fry drew attention to the formal values of Cézanne's work, stressing and emphasizing its "objective" structural and abstract character. The importance of Fry's study still lies in the fact that he was the first critic to reconstruct the personality of Cézanne through certain paintings, even though he made no attempt to consider all the paintings individually, as contemporary formalists have since undertaken. Fry's interpretative error lay however in neglecting the importance of Impressionism for Cézanne. Partly because of his formalist structural bias, he failed to see how Impressionism as luminous vibration had taught the painter to construct with color, and not just illusionistically. Art historian and critic Lionello Venturi reacted strongly against this critical mistake.

Gasquet, Joachim. *Cézanne*. Paris: Bernheim-Jeune, 1921. (**G**) Often-quoted French-language biography by a close friend of the painter and a passionate advocate of his art. Often inaccurate and not very reliable. Gasquet is prone to exaggerations and half-truths. His documentary data is obviously subjective and always biased in favor of the painter. Nonetheless, of interest for those who seek to understand the man behind the famous artist, with his passions, his friendships, his love relationships, his ups and downs in terms of personal happiness and artistic success. However, Cézanne's profound inner crises are never explained by Gasquet, who prefers to stress Cézanne's dynamic personality, rather than his more somber moods.

Lindsay, Jack. *Cézanne: His Life and Art.* London: Jupiter, 1969. (**A, G**) Critical biography that directly relates the painter's life to his art. Well researched, reliable, easy reading. The author brings out the underlying unity of Cézanne's life, work, and thought. Lindsay argues that Cézanne became converted to solitude after the painful break with Zola and that his inability to communicate on a human level, as well as his unending contest to have his art win the approval of either Zola or his father, explains in part his aesthetic intention to study objectively the structural interrelationships of forms, objects and colors. Lindsay's bio-cultural approach thus seeks to link Cézanne's psychological disquiet in the context of his formal distortions, as well as in the context of changing philosophical theories of his day. Lindsay draws connections and correlations between Cézanne's new artistic practice and contemporary scientific as well as physical theories of cosmic change, movement, field of force or tensions of symmetry and asymmetry.

Mack, Gerstle. *Paul Cézanne.* New York: Alfred A. Knopf, 1935. French edition, *La vie de Cézanne.* Paris: Gallimard, 1938. (**G**) Excellent critical biography containing a chronology, bibliography, and detailed index. First pre-World War II volume that chronicles Cézanne's life and artistic evolution. Does not gloss over, but presents a balanced view, providing foundations for future investigations. Important to American public acceptance of the painter.

Meier-Graefe, Julius. *Cézanne.* London: Thames and Hudson, 1927. (**G**) Important essay on Cézanne's life in art by a German specialist of the post-Impressionist movement. It had been earlier published in Munich in 1910 under the title *Cézanne und seine Ahnen*, one of the first interpretative critical essays on Cézanne as the source and impetus of modern art. This was followed by two books on his paintings and his watercolors, also published in Munich in 1919 and 1920. Meier-

Graefe argues that Cézanne's itinerary can best be understood as a transition between the concerns of the late nineteenth and early twentieth centuries. He is at his best when he tries to explain the complexities and the contradictions of Cézanne's achievements.

Murphy, Richard W. *The World of Cézanne*. New York: Time-Life, 1971. (**A, G**) Well-researched intellectual biography of the painter. Very informative, readable, and reliable; provides a vivid picture of French art and society during the late nineteenth century. Documents Cézanne's contribution to modern art in contrast to the lyrical naturalism of the Romanticists, the realism of Courbet, and the momentary visual sensations of the Impressionists. Also puts in context Cézanne's critical disapproval before 1895 and increasing fame during the later years of his life and after his death.

Novotny, Fritz, and Ludwig Goldscheider. *Cézanne*. New York: Phaidon, 1937. (**G**) Short biographical and stylistic commentary; includes more than one hundred color and black-and-white reproductions. A surprising pre-World War II book that provided a notable contribution to our knowledge of the painter, this volume is important for the pivotal question its authors raised of space relations in the work of Cézanne. Analyzing Cézanne's renunciation of traditional illusory space, they saw his art as leading toward a predominance of formal and chromatic combinations. This spatial problem that had not been investigated in depth before Novotny's and Goldscheider's reconstructions, is then examined both in its capacity for generating emotion on the picture surface as well as from the purely structural standpoint of perspectival effects.

Perruchot, Henri. *Cézanne*. Translated from the French by Humphrey Hare. New York: Grosset and Dunlap, 1963. (**G**) Easy-to-read, reliable biography; contains a chronology and bibliography. Perruchot parallels Cézanne's personal struggles and his artistic transformations through numerous documents which allow us to follow not only the troubled life of the painter but also the development of his artistic personality. A complex and fascinating portrait of Cézanne emerges that takes into account both his strong and his weak points, and that zeroes in equally on his moody character and on his remarkable inventiveness.

Raynal, Maurice. *Cézanne: Biographical and Critical Studies.* Geneva: Skira, 1954. (**G**) Remarkable color plates with short but valuable biographical and stylistic notes. For the general reader who seeks reliable and informative data on Cézanne's artistic evolution. Raynal does not argue in favor of a specific approach, formalist, psychological, cultural, etc., but prefers a more neutral common-sense discussion.

Rewald, John. *Paul Cézanne, A Biography.* 1937. Reprint. New York: Simon and Schuster, 1968. (**A, G**) The definitive biography; thoroughly researched and based on numerous documents, letters, and personal meetings with critics and friends of the painter. Contains an extensive bibliography and index. In various works from 1936 on (*Cézanne et Zola,* Paris: Sedrowski, 1936; *Cézanne, sa vie, son oeuvre, son amitié pour Zola,* Paris: Albin Michel, 1939; *Paul Cézanne, Geoffroy et Gasquet,* Paris: Quatre Chemins, 1959; *The History of Impressionism,* New York: MOMA, 1961; *Le Post-Impressionisme,* Paris: Albin Michel, 1961; *Les aquarelles de Cézanne,* Paris: A.M.G., 1984), art historian Rewald has provided in either French or English a major contribution to our knowledge of Cézanne's life and art.

Rubin, William, ed. *Cézanne: The Late Work.* New York: Museum of Modern Art, 1977. (**A**) Catalogue, published on the occasion of a landmark 1977 exhibition, that documents and chronicles Cézanne's last ten years of artistic production and examines the relevance of this work to Cubism and contemporary abstract art. Rubin emphasizes the formal significance of Cézanneism for the beginnings of Cubism, especially the influence of the various Bathers and landscapes on Picasso and Braque. From the hindsight of twentieth-century Modernism, Cézanne is thus interpreted by Rubin as a founder of "distortive" tendencies and specifically Cubist manipulations of three-dimensional subject matter for the sake of the pure form of the two-dimensional picture plane. Notwithstanding, other contemporary critics and art historians like Leo Steinberg and Rosalind Krauss have seen this as a reductivist, neo-formalist, overly simplistic reading of the art of a complex artist.

Venturi, Lionello. *Cézanne. Son art, son oeuvre.* 2 vols. Paris: Paul Rosenberg, 1936 (**A**) First comprehensive catalogue of Cézanne's paintings and drawings that provided the foundation for other aesthetic and art historical investigations. Necessary tool for specialists. Reproduced in Gaëtan Picon and Sandra Orienti, *Tout l'oeuvre peint de Cézanne* (Paris: Flammarion, 1975).

Vollard, Ambroise. *Cézanne: His Life and Art.* 1914. Translated from the French by Harold L. Van Doren, 1924. New York: Crown, 1937. (**A, G**) Popular biography written by the painter's first and only gallerist. Documents the relationships among Cézanne and the other members of the Paris artistic milieu at the end of the nineteenth century. Mostly anecdotal, not very reliable from an historical point of view, and of no scholarly value today. This laudatory biography can still be of some interest, however, to help document Cézanne's friendships or love interests and their influence on the evolution of his art.

Wechsler, Judith, ed. *Cézanne in Perspective.* Englewood Cliffs, NJ: Prentice-Hall, 1975. (**A, G**) Thoroughly documented contextual study of Cézanne's life and art. Valuable and reliable first- and second-hand information. Widely acclaimed reference work for art specialists and students of the humanities. Seeks to situate Cézanne's intuitive art and process of looking seeing and composing, as well as his new concept of realism and pictorial form, in the context of late nineteenth-century art practices.

Wechsler, Judith. *The Interpretation of Cézanne.* Ann Arbor, MI: UMI Research, 1981. (**A**) For specialists only. In this book, Wechsler discusses several different critical and historical approaches to Cézanne's work that have emerged in the last thirty years to explain Cézanne's achievements, including formalist, psychoanalytical, cultural, perceptual and phenomenological approaches. Contains up-to-date, methodological data and theoretical commentaries by Wechsler.

Overview and Evaluation of Primary Sources

Almost all of Cézanne's ideas on art are to be found in letters to friends, critics, and fellow painters, which were published in the English edition of John Rewald's *Paul Cézanne: Letters* (Oxford: Bruno Cassirer, 1941; **A, G**), translated by Marguerite Kay from the 1939 French edition published in Paris by editor Bernard Grasset. Although awkward and ungrammatical at times, this correspondence provides an invaluable insight into Cézanne's career and preoccupations. An earlier source is French poet and art critic Guillaume Apollinaire's article "Quatre lettres sur la peinture (from Cézanne to Camoin)" that was published before World War I in the magazine *Les soirées de Paris* 2 (1912). Several other authors on Cézanne include quotations or paraphrases of his ideas and statements.

Cézanne and French Symbolist painter Émile Bernard had a rather lengthy correspondence that was more abstract and systematic than the rest. The correspondence, which continued long conversations begun during visits, focuses on Cézanne's artistic theories and upon general aesthetic questions. This dialogue was later published by Bernard as two articles and by the Société des Trente as *Souvenirs sur Paul Cézanne* (Paris, 1911; **A, G**). The letters are at times biased, but they nevertheless remain a valuable source of information; they have not yet been translated.

Accounts of visits and talks with Cézanne by other friends and acquaintances include R. P. Rivière and J. F. Schnerb's "L'atelier de Cézanne" published in *La grande revue,* on December 25, 1907 (English translation reproduced in Judith Wechsler, ed., *Cézanne in Perspective*, Englewood Cliffs, NJ: Prentice-Hall, 1961); Maurice Denis's "Cézanne" in *L'Occident* (September 1907), English translation by Roger Fry, *Burlington Magazine* 16 (Part I, January 1910), and (Part II, February 1910); Charles Camoin's "Souvenirs sur Paul Cézanne" in *L'amour de l'art* [January 1921]; Joachim Gasquet's biography *Cézanne* (Paris: Bernheim-Jeune, 1921; **A, G**), in which this Symbolist author-painter purports to convey the worlds of the painter in a series of three long dialogues: before the motif, in the Louvre, and in the studio; and Léo Languier's *Le dimanche avec Paul Cézanne* (Paris: L'Édition, 1925; **A, G**). Much later, painter Louis Aurenche recounted his impressions of the artist in *Cézanne, Gefroy et Gasquet* (Paris: Quatre-Chemins-Editart, 1960; **A, G**). Michael Doran's critical edition of biographical and stylistic documents on Cézanne's last ten years, *Conversations avec Cézanne* (Paris: Macula, 1978; **A**), contains annotated excerpts from his correspondence and talks with, among others, Émile Bernard, Maurice Denis, Joachim Gasquet, Gustave Geffroy, and Ambroise Vollard. More recently, Richard Kendall has assembled previously unpublished documents by Cézanne on his late paintings and works on paper: *Cézanne by Himself* (London and Paris: Atlas, 1988; **A**).

Principal Works

Portrait of Paul Cézanne (1861-1862)
The Autumn (1860-1862)
The Spring (1860-1862)
Tête de vieillard (1865)
Landscape at Aix (1865)
Uncle Dominic (c.1866)
The Abduction (1867)
The Murder (1867-1868)
The Black Clock (1868-1871)
The Painter (1868-1871)
The Temptation of Saint-Anthony (1869)
La pendule noire (1870)
Portrait of Painter Guillaumin (1869-1872)
The Orgy (1869)
The Rape (c.1870)
Melting Snow at L'Estaque (1870)
The House of the Hanged Man at Auvers-sur-Oise (c.1873)
Vase of Flowers (1873-1875)
Auvers vue panoramique (1873-1875)
Landscape near Auvers (c.1874)
Hermitage at Pontoise (c. 1875)
The Sea at L'Estaque (1876)
Apple Still Life (c.1876)
The Enclosure Wall c.1876
Madame Cézanne in a Red Armchair (c.1877)
Victor Chocquet Seated (c.1877)
Le bassin du Jas de Bouffan (c.1878-1879)
Paysage près de Médan (1879-1889)
Madame Cézanne au jardin (1879-1882)
Le pont de Maincy (1879)
Leda and the Swan (c.1880-1882)
Houses at L'Estaque (1883-1885)
Bay of Marseille Seen from L'Estaque (1883-1885)

The Sea at L'Estaque (1885-1887)
Vase of Flowers and Apples (1883-1887)
Chestnuts at Jas de Bouffan (c.1885)
Mont Sainte-Victoire Seen from Gardanne (1885-1886)
The Blue Vase (c.1887)
Mont Sainte-Victoire (c.1887)
The Bridge on the Marne at Créteuil (1888)
Pierrot and Arlequin (1888)
L'Estaque (c.1888)
The Kitchen Table (1888-1890)
Madame Cézanne in the Greenhouse (1890)
The Card Players (c.1890-1892)
Portrait of Paul Cézanne (1890-1894)
Woman with a Coffeepot (1890-1895)
Mont Sainte-Victoire (1894-1900)
Still-life with Plaster Cast of Cupid (1895)
Château-Noir (1895)
Young Man with Red Jacket (c.1895)
Portrait of Gustave Geffroy (1895)
Still-Life with Skull (1895-1900)
Lake Annecy (1896)
Mont Sainte-Victoire Seen from Bibémus Quarry (c.1897)
Portrait of Ambroise Vollard (1899)
L'homme aux bras croisés (c.1899)
Dans le parc de Château-Noir (1900)
Portrait de paysan (1901-1906)
Mont Sainte-Victoire Seen from Les Lauves (1902-1904)
Château-Noir (1904)
Le jardinier (1904-1905)
Bathers (1904-1906)
Large Bathers (c.1906)

Fiction and Adaptations

Cézanne has appeared as a character in the writings of many of his acquaintances. His most notable such appearance is in Zola's 1886 novel *L'Oeuvre*, whose unsuccessful and suicidal artist-protagonist and antihero, Claude Lantier—the same painter who had appeared earlier among the vegetable stalls at Les Halles in Zola's other novel, *Le ventre de Paris,* in which the novelist had been inspired by Cézanne's color—is based on a bad-tempered Cézanne. He also appeared in American expatriate in Paris Gertrude Stein's romanticized account of her meetings with avant-garde painters, including Cézanne, *The Autobiography of Alice B. Toklas* (1933), and critic Walter Pacht's laconic commentaries on modern artists in *Queer Thing, Painting* (New York: Harper and Brothers, 1938).

The painter has been the subject of at least two French-language documentaries. *Les chemins de Cézanne* (Flag Films, 1964), directed by Robert Mazoyer, is an hommage to the painter's life and art that remains true to historical fact. It focuses on his intellectual relationship with Zola and Pissarro, and despite Cézanne's numerous affairs, stresses the importance of his wife and son in his life. *Le regard de Cézanne* (Institut Pédagogique National de France, 1962), directed by Adrien Toubout, is another faithful documentary account of Cézanne's artistic friendships and influences.

Museums, Historical Landmarks, Societies

Barnes Foundation Collection (Merion, PA). Owns nearly fifty paintings and watercolors, including many critically recognized masterpieces such as *Apple Still Life* (c.1876), *Three Bathers* (1875), *Man with Vest* (1876), *Portrait of Madame Cézanne* (1885), *Mont Sainte-Victoire* (1885), and *The Card Players* (1890-1892).

The Hermitage (St. Petersburg, Russia). Important collection of Cézanne's work (twelve paintings), including *L'ouverture de Tannhäuser* (1869-1870), *Le grand pin* (1885-1887), *Portrait de Cézanne à la casquette* (1873), and *Dame en bleu* (1900).

The Louvre (Paris). Contains more than thirty paintings and watercolors from all periods of the painter's life. Holdings include *La moderne Olympia* (1868), *The Kitchen Table* (1888-1890), and *La maison du pendu à Auvers* (1872).

Metropolitan Museum of Art (New York City). Contains a great collection of paintings from the early and mid-1880s (sixteen paintings), such as *La colline des pauvres* (1888), *The Bay of Marseille, Seen from L'Estaque* (1883-1885), *Mont Sainte-Victoire* (1885), and *The Card Players* (1892).

Musée d'Orsay (Paris). The second-largest collection of Cézanne (thirty-seven paintings), including *Tête de vieillard* (1865-1868), *Portrait d'Achille Emperaire,* (1866-1870), *Nature morte, pommes et oranges* (1890-1895), *Woman with a Coffeepot* (1890-1895, and *The Card Players* (1890-1895).

Musée de l'orangerie (Paris). Has fourteen paintings from the Guillaume-Walter collection, including *Pommes et biscuits* (1879-1882), *Madame Cézanne au jardin* (1879-1882), and *Dans le parc du Château-Noir* (1900).

Museum of Modern Art (New York City). Contains a complete selection of works by Cézanne, including *Portrait de Choquet* (1879), *View of Gardanne,* pencil on paper (1885-1886), *The Bather* (1885), *Sous-bois Provençal* (1900), *Still Life with Apples* (1890-1900), *Liquor Bottle* (1888), and *Montagne Sainte-Victoire* (1900).

National Gallery (Washington, DC). Has a collection of seventeen paintings, including *Le jardinier* (1904-1905).

Other notable collections are located in the Gemeente Museum in La Haye; the Kunsthaus in Zurich; the Albertina Museum in Vienna; the Museum of the Bâle, in Switzerland; the Pushkin State Museum of Arts, in Moscow; the Philadelphia Museum of Arts; the Courtauld Institute in London; the National Gallery in Berlin; the Museum of Fine Arts in Budapest; and the National Gallery in Oslo.

Other Sources

Badt, Kurt. *The Art of Cézanne.* Translated from the 1956 German Prestel Verlag edition. Berkeley: University of California Press, 1956. (**A**) Taking his cue from American art historian Meyer Schapiro, Badt adopts a psychoanalytical approach to understanding Cézanne's life and work, emphasizing their spiritual content.

Barnes, Albert C., and Violette De Mazia. *The Art of Cézanne*. Merion, PA: Barnes Foundation, 1939. (**A**) Complete catalogue of the famous Barnes Foundation collection in Merion, PA.

Bell, Clive. *The French Impressionists*. New York: Phaidon, 1952. (**A, G**) Presents a formalist view of Impressionism and its most important painters. Bell maintains that Cézanne was "the Christopher Columbus of a new continent of form," a point of view reiterated by contemporary American art critic Clement Greenberg in 1951 when he claimed that Cézanne was "the most copious source of what we know as modern art."

————. "The Debt to Cézanne." In *Art*. 1914. Reprint. London: Chatto and Windus, 1931. (**A**) One of the first formalist rereadings of Cézanne's work.

Brion-Guerry, Liliane. *Cézanne et l'expression de l'espace*. 1950. Reprint. Paris: Albin Michel, 1966. (**A**) Suggests that all of Cézanne's work constituted a search for a compositional equilibrium and for necessary formal distortions. Offers an in-depth pre-semiotic, art theoretical analysis of spatial relations in Cézanne.

Callen, Anthea. *Techniques of the Impressionists*. Secaucus, NJ: Chartwell, 1982. (**A, G**) Includes an analysis of three paintings by Cézanne from different stylistic periods.

Chappuis, Adrien. *The Drawings of Paul Cézanne: A Catalogue Raisonné*. 2 vols. London: Thames and Hudson, 1972. (**A, G**) Besides remarkable reproductions, contains a biographical essay on the painter.

Elgar, Frank. *Cézanne*. New York: Abrams, 1968 (**A**) Art history reference book by an American specialist of Cézanne and of the Post-Impressionists.

Fry, Roger. "The French Post-Impressionists." In *Vision and Design*. 1920. Reprint. London: Oxford University Press, 1981. (**A, G**) A formalist perspective on turn-of-the-century French art, including Cézanne's contributions.

Goldwater, Robert, and Marco Treves. *Artists on Art, from the XIV to the XXth Century.* New York: Pantheon, 1945. (**A, G**) Includes short but well-selected excerpts from Cézanne's writings to fellow artists and friends. Reliable and useful.

Gowing, Sir Laurence. *An Exhibition of Paintings by Cézanne.* Edinburgh: Edinburgh Festival Society; London: Arts Council of Great Britain, 1954. (**A, G**) Catalogue of the 1954 English exhibition by a world-renowned authority on the painter.

──────. *Cézanne: The Early Years, 1859-1872.* London: The Tate Gallery; Washington, DC: The National Gallery of Art, 1988. (**A, G**) Catalogue of the landmark 1988-1989 exhibition that was shown on both sides of the Atlantic. Documents Cézanne's relationship to Romanticism.

──────. "The Logic of Organized Sensations." In *Cézanne: The Late Work*, edited by William Rubin. New York: Museum of Modern Art, 1977. (**A**) An important essay on the key notion of sensation in Cézanne's art.

Loran, Erle. *Cézanne's Composition.* Berkeley: University of California Press, 1943. (**A**) Frequently quoted interpretive essay on Cézanne's art and pictorial technique. Perhaps the most sustained formalist interpretation of Cézanne's art. Loran provides extensive diagrams of what he sees as the formal structure of individual works and emphasizes surface structuring.

Protter, Eric, ed. *Painters on Painting.* New York: Grosset and Dunlap, 1963. (**A, G**) Collection of brief passages from artists on the subject of painting. Almost half the book is devoted to letters and statements by Cézanne and later artists. Reliable and informative reading.

Reff, Theodore. "Cézanne's Constructive Stroke." In *Art Quarterly* (Autumn 1962): 214-227. (**A**) Evaluates the reliability of Émile Bernard and other firsthand commentators on Cézanne's ideas on painting. Indispensable for students of Cézanne's aesthetic ideals.

Rewald, John. *The History of Impressionism.* 1946. 4th Rev. ed. New York: Museum of Modern Art, 1973. (**A, G**) Still an indispensable work of historical and critical value.

Rilke, Maria Rainer. *Lettres sur Cézanne.* Paris: Correa, 1944. (**A, G**) Poetic rereading and interpretation of Cézanne's work by a famous French writer of the turn of the century, who was also for a short time Auguste Rodin's personal secretary.

Rishel, Joseph J. "Paul Cézanne." In *Great French Paintings from The Barnes Foundation.* New York: Alfred A. Knopf, 1993. (**A, G**) Rishel, curator of European paintings and sculpture before 1900, Philadelphia Museum of Art, describes in this catalogue the Cézanne paintings exhibited in the Barnes Foundation international exhibition which opened in Washington, D.C. at the National Gallery of Art in May 1993.

Rousseau, Theodore, Jr. *Cézanne.* New York: Museum of Modern Art; Chicago: The Art Institute, 1952. (**A, G**) Exhibition catalogue.

Schapiro, Meyer. *Paul Cézanne.* New York: Harry N. Abrams, 1952. (**G**) Contains fifty color plates with annotations and an important introduction on the evolution of style in the art of Cézanne. Schapiro was the first art historian to look at the significance of Cézanne's subject matter from a psychological point of view. For instance, according to Schapiro, Cézanne treated the still life subject of fruit as sublimated female form. In a now famous article on Cézanne's apples, as well as the painter's peaches and pears, Schapiro argued for and demonstrated how such a sexual reference worked. For Schapiro therefore, Cézanne's quest to recreate motifs like Mont Sainte-Victoire was a testimony to his victory over his own passions as well as a conquest of the means of his art.

Schiff, Richard. *Cézanne and the End of Impressionism.* Chicago: University of Chicago Press, 1984. (**A**) Takes aim at recent aesthetic debates on Cézanne's work. Schiff argues that Cézanne should be understood more from a nineteenth-century point of view, that is in relation to Impressionism and the goal of truth to nature, especially because of his interests in atmospheric effects filtered through a temperament.

Stein, Leo. *Appreciation: Painting, Poetry and Prose.* New York: Crown, 1947. (**A, G**) Pertinent comments on Cézanne's importance. See also his autobiographical *Journey into the Self* (New York: Crown, 1950).

Venturi, Lionello. *Cézanne.* Geneva: Skira, 1978. (**A, G**) Superb reference book with numerous color plates.

Vollard, Ambroise. *Recollections of a Picture Dealer.* Boston: Beacon, 1936. (**A, G**) Easy going, subjective recollections by Cézanne's gallerist.

Wright, Willard Huntington. *Modern Painting: Its Tendency and Meaning.* London and New York: John Lane, 1915. (**A, G**) Outdated, but historically valuable. Interesting comments on Cézanne's increased fame and influence after his death by one of his contemporaries.

Marie Carani
Université Laval, Quebec

Jean François Champollion
1790-1832

Chronology

Born Jean François Champollion on December 23, 1790, at Figeac, France, son of Jacques Champollion, a bookseller, and Jeanne-Françoise Gualieu, a local merchant's daughter and an invalid; *1795* teaches himself to read by looking at passages he had memorized in his mother's missal and figuring out the phonetic system; *1799* a soldier in General Napoleon Bonaparte's Egyptian Expedition stationed at the old fort of Rosetta at the mouth of the Nile discovers a stele of black basalt that bears three inscriptions: a mutilated one in Hieroglyphs, a second in demotic characters (a simplified system of ancient Egyptian writing), and a third in Greek; the "Rosetta Stone," as it comes to be known, is moved to the Institute of Egypt in Cairo, where copies (rubbings) of the inscriptions are made and sent to France, then to Alexandria, Egypt, and finally to the British Museum in London; *1801* sees for the first time a copy of the Rosetta Stone at the home of mathematician Jean Baptiste Fourier, and is inspired to decipher it after he acquires all the linguistic tools he will need to do it; tutored in Latin by Dom Calmet, a Benedictine monk; instructed in Hebrew by his brother, Champollion-Figeac; *1804-1807* attends the Institution Dussert, then the Lycée of Grenoble, where he studies Latin; studies Greek and Coptic on his own; *1807* reads a paper at the Academy of Sciences, Letters, and Arts of Grenoble in which he outlines his future research in the field of Egyptian geography, religion, languages, writing, and history and is awarded a membership in the academy; sent to Paris by his brother, where he studies Farsi, Sanskrit, and Arabic with Marie-Alfred Silvestre de Sacy, the foremost French Orientalist and member of the Institute of France; begins compiling a Coptic grammar book and dictionary; *1809* named adjunct professor of history at the Faculty of Letters of Grenoble; *1812* promoted to full professor; *1811-1812* serves as adjunct librarian of the city library; publishes *Observations on the Catalogue of Coptic Manuscripts of the Borgia Museum*; *1814* publishes two volumes on geographical names of ancient Egypt, a feat that makes Silvestre de Sacy, whose interpretation of Hieroglyphs was rather conservative, wary of his twenty-three year old rival who would eventually prove him wrong; *1815* publishes his *Letter on the Coptic Gnostic Odes Attributed to Salomon*; supports the restoration of the Imperial government after Napoleon Bonaparte returns from exile; exiled to Figeac for two years, thereby losing his professorship for disloyalty to the crown after Louis XVIII is restored to the throne; *1816* continues his scholarly research in exile; *1818* returns to Grenoble and publishes a treatise on the Coptic language; resumes teaching history and geography; *1821* returns to Paris and publishes his essay *On the Hieroglyphic Writing of the Ancient Egyptians,* in which he contradicts English physician Thomas Young's theory that the script is alphabetic by asserting his opinion that the symbols represent ideas instead of letters, i.e. signs of things and not sounds; receives Young in Paris; makes a long sought-after breakthrough, realizing that the symbols are both ideographic and phonetic, depending upon their use; dictates his memoir on Hieroglyphic writing to his brother, who has it lithographed and sent to the President of the Academy of Inscriptions and Belle Lettres; *1822* reads his memoir to the Academy and publishes it in *The Journal of Savants* as "Letter to Monsieur Dacier," who directs the academy; announcement of his independent discovery of phonetic Hieroglyphs sets off an academic fracas on both sides of the English Channel about whether it is really the Frenchman Champollion or the Englishman Young who first made the great discovery; *1824* publishes *Précis of Hieroglyphs*, which reveals the secret of decipherment at greater length; ordered to Turin by King Charles X, who was interested in colonizing Egypt, to examine Bernardin Drovetti's collection of Egyptian artifacts, and to Leghorn, where he purchases a similar collection for the Louvre; visits Rome, where he had been hired by Pope Leo XII to study obelisks, Naples, Florence, and Genoa; *1826* appointed conservateur of the Louvre's Musée Egyptien, which opens in 1827 during the reign of Charles X; *1828* appointed with Tuscan orientalist Ippolito Rosellini by the Duke of Blacas to lead a French-Tuscan expedition of thirteen architects and artists on a tour of the Nile Valley through Egypt and Nubia in order to copy inscriptions on monuments; *1830* returns to Paris; honored for his accomplishments by election to membership in the Academy of Inscriptions; King Louis Philippe creates the Chair of Egyptology for Champollion at the Collège de France; *1832* suffers a series of strokes in Paris from January 13 until he dies on March 4th from another attack.

Activities of Historical Significance

Jean François Champollion was undoubtedly one of the most brilliant archaeologists who ever lived. The demotic inscription on the Rosetta Stone consumed his energy from the moment he laid eyes on it in 1801 at the age of eleven until he understood it twenty years later, and only after he had studied sixteen languages in order to do it. The Rosetta Stone, discovered by the French in 1799, was inscribed in two languages, Egyptian and Greek, and in three writing systems, Hieroglyphs, demotic (local form) script, and the Greek alphabet. Until the discovery of the Rosetta Stone, archaeologists had no clue as to how to decipher Hieroglyphs, which was the principal writing system of the ancient Egyptians. Learning to read Hieroglyphs would unlock the history of a lost civilization. An Englishman, Thomas Young, had determined that the cartouches (oval figures enclosing Hieroglyphs) were the names of royalty and discovered, based on the way the bird figures faced, how the hieroglyphic signs were to be read. But it was Champollion who first realized that the text was not written in an alphabetical system but in signs representing ideas. He then realized that this was a translation of the Greek text with word order only slightly inverted from logical order. By 1834 he had distinguished three categories of signs: those depicting actual objects, conventional symbols, and a classification of sounds of the spoken language. He was then able to establish an entire list of Hieroglyphs with their Greek equivalents, which made it possible to translate all future hieroglyphic texts. Champollion had unlocked the secret to understanding ancient Egyptian civilization that had been shrouded in mystery for thousands of years. This monumental achievement overshadowed his personal life, about which little has been written in English.

When Champollion was about eight years old, "Egyptmania" swept Europe. This fascination with the mystery of Hieroglyphs and a fad for Egyptian styles in clothing, furniture and the decorative arts, which originated in the Renaissance and was strongly present during the French Revolution. The influence of ancient Egypt on French culture especially, escalated as a result of the Directory's Egyptian Expedition (1798-1801). After the First Italian Campaign had ended in 1797, the French government decided to attack Britain indirectly by taking Egypt, which it hoped to make a colony. General Napoleon Bonaparte, who was charged with the French military expedition, dreamed even then of digging a canal at Suez to give the French merchant marine an advantage over the British fleet. Napoleon invited

157 "savants" along on the Egyptian expedition to explore, map and study the ruins of that unknown civilization. The savants worked even amid pitched battles between the French soldiers and the Mamluks. Among the ruins in the Nile Delta, they discovered the Rosetta stone, the key to understanding the ancient Hieroglyphs, which Champollion would later decipher from rubbings. The Rosetta stone was taken to England after the French were defeated in 1801.

While from a military standpoint the Egyptian Expedition failed totally, except for the propagandistic use Napoleon made of it to enhance his popularity, we see an example of how deeply it involved individuals through the life of Champollion. Dominique Vivant Denon, the courtier, scholar, artist, diplomat and traveler who later raided all the art collections in Europe to fill the Louvre for Napoleon I, and the other members of the Institute of Egypt who accompanied General Bonaparte's army produced the great encyclopedic *Description of Egypt*, a multi-volume collection of text and plates that opened up that ancient civilization to Europeans. Champollion's love for Egypt connected him with the Napoleonic dynasty, and his support of Bonaparte reappeared in 1830 when he lobbied for the removal to Paris of the obelisk of Luxor, which now stands in the center of Place de la Concorde, as a monument to the memory of the First French expedition of artists and archaeologists.

The Franco-Tuscan voyage to explore the Upper Nile Valley in 1828-1829 allowed Champollion to verify his theory that the hieroglyphic alphabet used on the Rosetta Stone was commonly employed throughout the region on numerous temples, inscriptions and monuments from the time of the pharaohs to the Romans and the Ptolemies. Champollion documented this trip in *Monuments of Egypt and Nubia*, which was published posthumously in 1845.

During the 1830s, public imagination was captivated by Champollion's discoveries, and he, like Napoleon I, was seen as a symbol of French glory. At the time of his death Champollion was thought to be the most important person in France. A statue was immediately commissioned by the government for his birthplace, Figeac, along with a portrait for the Louvre and a lifetime pension of 3,000 francs was voted into law for his widow. Throughout the history of France, few scholars have captivated the public mind as did Champollion during the age of Romanticism. His career proves that a life in archaeology does not necessarily have to be dry as dust, and may be challenging, even thrilling. Subsequent to Champollion's untimely death, the seventy-eight foot Luxor obelisk was indeed placed on the

Place de Concorde in the presence of the Orléanist monarch King Louis Philippe and a crowd of 200,000. It was as much a monument to Champollion's genius as to Napoleon's inspired creation of the Institute of Egypt through which France attempted to prove its intellectual supremacy to the world.

Overview of Biographical Sources

Unfortunately, not much has been published in English on Champollion, possibly due to fact that Europeans have been the leading archaeologists as well as the fact that experts in this field are multi-lingual. The only information available in English is found in sections in books on the generalized topic of archaeology and in the briefest sort of biographies in reference books. British authors tend to diminish Champollion's contributions in order to aggrandize those of their own countrymen, and French nationalism colors the French point of view and promotes his uniqueness.

The definitive book-length biography in any language is Hermien Hartleben's *Champollion, sein Leben und sein Werk* (2 vols. Berlin: Weidmann, 1906), which captures the drama and intensity of his life, describing his political and religious values, his circle of friends and enemies, and his love life.

Evaluation of Principal Biographical Sources

Clayton, Peter A. *The Rediscovery of Ancient Egypt—Artists and Travelers in the 19th Century.* New York: Thames and Hudson, 1982. (**A, G**) The first part of this richly illustrated scholarly book places Champollion in context among the travellers, scholars, artists, and collectors who made ancient Egypt known to modern Europeans. Select bibliography lists location of archival and manuscript sources, letters, and diaries, as well as secondary works published in English, French, Swedish, and German. List of illustrations tells location of and describes visual materials. Indexed.

Greener, Leslie. *The Discovery of Egypt.* New York: Viking, 1966. (**A, G**) Scholarly but interesting and full of human interest details, such as the history of the discovery of Egyptian antiquities from Herodotus to 1881. Chapter 15 discusses Champollion's achievement in comparison with contemporary archaeologists. Provides information on Champollion's precocious childhood and his preparations for his life's work, on how he solved the mystery of the stone, on his role in the erection of the obelisk of Luxor in Paris; and his advice to Pasha Mohammed Ali on stopping the export of antiquities to Europe and safeguarding them to promote tourism. Includes illustrations, bibliography, and index.

Vercoutter, Jean. *The Search for Ancient Egypt.* Translated from the French by Ruth Sharman. New York: Harry N. Abrams, 1992. (**G**) This visually attractive book clearly explains through text and colored illustrations how Champollion deciphered Hieroglyphs. It explains how pharaonic Egypt disappeared; about travelers through the ages, including the Crusaders; how eighteenth and nineteenth century scholars created Egyptology, including Champollion's biography; and how recently archaeologists and UNESCO rescued the remains of ancient civilization from the lake created by the Aswan Dam. A highly readable text suitable for younger and adult readers.

Overview and Evaluation of Primary Sources

Champollion's scholarly papers were published by the French government and published and edited by his brother: *Letters from Egypt and Nubia* (1833), *Monuments of Egypt and Nubia* (1835-1845), *Egyptian Grammar* (1835-1841) and *Egyptian Dictionary in Hieroglyphic Writing* (1841-1843). Some unedited notes still exist in the manuscript section of the Bibliothèque Nationale, Paris, France. For the most complete list of Champollion's numerous writings, including all editions and reprints, consult the authors' catalogue of the Bibliothèque Nationale. Hartleben, the German who published the biography cited above, edited 2 volumes of Champollion's letters: *Champollion le jeune. Lettres* (Paris, no pub. 1909). They are volumes 30 and 31 of the *Bibliothèque égyptien* published under the direction of Gaston Maspero.

Museums, Historical Landmarks, Societies

Les Champollion (Vif, Dauphiné). Family home that contains his private correspondence and numerous documents.

Collège de France (Paris). A statue of him standing on some fragments of Pharaonic columns, sculpted by August Bartholdi, is located in the vestibule near the room where he taught.

Grenoble. A street and a lycée for boys are named for the archaeologist.

Musée de Louvre (Paris). Contains his oil portrait painted by Léon Cogniet in 1831.

Other Sources

Byrd, Melanie. "The Napoleonic Institute of Egypt." Ph.D. dissertation. Florida State University, 1993. This important critical research discusses Napoleon's Egyptian Expedition of 1798-1801 and the discovery, publication, and interpretation of Egyptologists before Champollion, which provided the impetus for his discoveries and for the first time places his significance into intellectual context.

Daugherty, Charles Mitchell. *Great Archaeologists.* New York: Crowell, 1962. Chapter in an illustrated, 140-page book suitable for junior-high through adult readers.

Magic Films. *Champollion: Egyptian Hieroglyphics Deciphered.* Chicago: International Film Bureau, 1979.

June K. Burton
University of Akron

Frédéric Chopin
1810-1849

Chronology

Born Frédéric François Chopin on March 1, 1810 in Żelazowa Wola, Poland, son of Nicolas Chopin, a French émigré, and high school French teacher, and Tekla-Justyna Krzyzanowska, a poor relation of the noble Skarbek family; family moves to Warsaw; *1811-1815* family begins to accept boarders in the home, including many of Chopin's lifelong friends; *1816* begins piano lessons with Wojciech Żywny, a locally prominent musician; *1817* publishes G minor polonaise; *1818* gives debut performance, playing a concerto by Adelbert Gyrowetz; *1820* plays for the renowned soprano Angelica Catalani; *1821* composes A-flat Major Polonaise, his earliest extant manuscript; *1822* begins studies with Józef Elsner, head of the Warsaw Conservatory; *1823-1826* attends the high school receiving a thorough academic education; *1825* publishes his Opus 1, a Rondo in C minor; performs at a charity concert in June; demonstrates an organ-piano hybrid for Czar Alexander I; *1826* gives two benefit concerts for recent orphans while vacationing in Reinertz to restore his health; formally enters Conservatory for further studies with Elsner; writes Rondo à la Mazur, Opus 5; *1827* sister Emilia dies; writes Variations on "Là ci darem la mano", Opus 2; *1828* travels to Berlin; writes Opus 14, *Krakowiak* Rondo for piano and orchestra, a significant manifestation of his interest in Polish folk-tunes; *1829* government rejects his request for a travel grant; proceeds to Vienna on father's funds and is well-received at Kärntnertor Theater on August 11; falls in love with soprano Constancia Gladkowska upon his return to Warsaw; writes F minor Concerto, Opus 21; *1830* gives first major concert in Warsaw on March 17, playing F minor Concerto and *Fantasia on Polish Airs* to rave reviews; travels to Dresden, Breslau, and Prague; Poles rise against Russian oppressors; *1831* writes Grand Polonaise, Mazurkas Opus 6 and Opus 7; leaves Vienna for London via Paris, stopping in Munich and Stuttgart; Russians capture Warsaw; writes *Revolutionary* Etude, Opus 10, No. 12; *1832* makes Paris debut in February and quickly achieves prominence; enjoys society patronage as a piano teacher; *1833* participates in multi-piano performances with notable artists such as Franz Liszt and Stephen Heller; performs at Hector Berlioz's concert; publishes earlier works including the E minor Concerto and the Etudes, Opus 10; *1834* travels to Aachen for a musical festival where he meets Ferdinand Hiller and Felix Mendelssohn, publishes Bolero, Opus 19, and *Fantasia on Polish Airs*; *1835* performs at a benefit for Polish refugees on April 4 and is poorly received, as is his performance on April 26; travels to Germany, sees parents for the last time; returns to Paris via Dresden, where he renews his relationship with the Wodziński family and becomes smitten with sixteen year-old Maria; continues on to Leipzig and meets Robert and Clara Schumann; begins Opus 25 Etudes upon return to Paris: *1836* meets with Maria Wodzińska in Marienbad and Dresden; couple becomes secretly engaged at the instigation of Madame Wodzińska; publishes F minor Concerto, G minor Ballade, and Andante spianato; meets novelist George Sand (Aurore Dudevant) through an introduction from Liszt; *1837* engagement to Maria Wodzińska fails due to his poor health; travels to London for vacation and gives one private performance at the home of piano maker John Broadwood; writes Funeral March; publishes Etudes, Opus 25, Scherzo, Opus 31, and Nocturnes, Opus 32; increasingly attracted to George Sand; *1838* performs E minor Concerto in Rouen, his last public concert for a decade; affair with Sand intensifies; couple departs for Majorca in November along with Sand's children; finishes Preludes, Opus 28; publishes Waltzes, Opus 30, and Mazurkas, Opus 33; *1839* falls ill in Majorca, forcing a return to Marseilles; recovers in Nohant at Sand's country house; writes B-Flat minor Sonata, Opus 35 and F-sharp Major Impromptu, Opus 36; performs for the royal family in October along with Moscheles; *1840* actively teaches and composes in Paris; *1841* gives private concert at the Salle Pleyel in April; summers with Sand in Nohant; composes the A-flat Major Ballade, Opus 47, F minor Fantasie, Opus 49, and the Nocturnes, Opus 48; friend and copyist Fontana leaves for the United States; *1842* gives another private concert; returns to Nohant for the summer, moves to new lodgings at 9 Square d'Orléans upon his return to Paris; major works include the F minor Ballade, G-flat Major Impromptu, and the E Major Scherzo; *1843* health declines; makes no concert appearances and writes few compositions; *1844* father dies; enjoys visit with elder sister Ludwika during the summer months; writes B minor Sonata; *1845* begins Cello Sonata, Opus 65, the most successful of his pieces for instrumentation other than solo piano; *1846* relationship with George Sand begins to deteriorate; completes Cello Sonata, Barcarolle, Opus 60, and Polonaise-Fantasie, Opus 61; *1847* separates from Sand over the issue of her daughter's marriage; *1848* gives final Paris concert on February 16; revolution overthrows the bourgeois monarch, Louis-Phillipe; travels to England at the invitation of his pupil Jane Stirling; gives many private concerts, including a performance for Queen Victoria on May 15; makes public appearances in London, Manchester, Edinburgh, and Glasgow despite failing health; returns to Paris incapacitated by tuberculosis, relies on aid from Stirlings, as he is no longer able to work; *1849* lives as an invalid; spends summer in Chaillot; moves to 12 Place Vendôme upon his return to Paris in the early autumn; sister Ludwika and pupil Adolf Gutmann care for him until his death on October 17; funeral on October 30 at the Madeleine Church features rare performance of Mozart's *Requiem*; buried in Père La Chaise cemetery.

Activities of Historical Significance

Frédéric Chopin's life coincided with an era of tremendous change in European society. Phenomena as diverse as the growth of nationalism, the elevation of the artist as an individual, and the loosening of social norms are reflected throughout his career. Chopin was among the first composers who might be labeled "nationalist." This played out in three distinct ways in his life. Socially, Chopin thrived as a part of the Polish émigré community in Paris. In this environment, he made the acquaintance of aristocratic and artistic Poles who, like himself, had been forced from their homeland by the November Uprising of 1830. Many members of this circle enjoyed prominence in their own right, such as the noble Czartoryski family, and the poet Adam Mickiewicz. Yet as Chopin's fame grew, his association with this community enhanced the Polish cause. A fine example of this was his repeated appearances at concerts given for the benefit of his fellow countrymen. His prestige as a performer could focus public attention on their plight far better than leaflets and speeches.

Chopin also demonstrated his nationalist sympathies musically. He wrote mazurkas throughout his entire life, and some of his polonaises are among his finest works. The characteristic rhythms and accentual patterns of these dances easily betrayed their Polish origin. Early works like the *Fantasia on Polish Airs* and the *Krakowiak* exploited Polish folktunes as a source of musical charm and novelty. Chopin also found more subtle methods of expressing a Polish sound. His works featured both functional harmony, in the tradition of Mozart and Beethoven, and modal harmony, which is more characteristic of folk-music. This modal harmony did not imply the same types of motion as did the functional harmony. It imparted an exotic, unsettled, and restless feeling to the music. Chopin similarly used the intervals of the augmented fourth and the diminished second for expressive effect, since they appeared infrequently in the Western art music of his time.

Historically, Chopin's nationalist techniques were prescient. The real flowering of "nationalist" music came at mid-century and beyond, just after his death. The movement was more closely associated with figures like Smetana, Dvorak, and Grieg. These later composers imbued their music with the sounds of their respective homelands, while still working within accepted musical conventions. They found a model for this type of expression in Chopin's music, though their pieces were by no means derivative.

Just as the burgeoning nationalism of the 1830s and 1840s celebrated the individuality of Europe's ethnic groups, so too did society slowly begin to appreciate the individual talents of great artists and musicians. Their works were seen less as a commodity and more as a personal statement of lasting cultural value. While this trend had been noticeable in the field of music earlier, few composers benefitted from the growing cult of genius as Chopin did. Though not of high birth, he often found himself accepted into the highest social circles. He filled his years in Paris with visits to the salons of the wealthy and the noble. He performed frequently in these settings, but more as an alternative mode of conversation than as a spectacle for the other guests.

This background is significant as these intimate settings encouraged Chopin to cultivate the variety of smaller forms which were the essence of his oeuvre. Works such as ballades, nocturnes, and waltzes relied more on tone and careful expression than on brilliant virtuosity. This approach stood in stark contrast to that of his contemporaries. Liszt, Kalkbrenner, and Thalberg, among others, who favored vigorous double-note runs, crashing octaves, and flamboyant embellishments over his quiet artistry. Yet Chopin did not reject making technical demands in his pieces. He even elevated the etude to the level of a concert work, but he did so by subordinating the drive for technical perfection to the more fundamental quest for profound musical expression. Writing for his elite audience, Chopin also rejected the contemporary vogue for program music, or pieces with overt literary associations. He sought to move his listeners rather than to titillate them with suggestive titles or fanciful stories. Even in the Ballades he did not rely on a narrative outline, though that genre borrowed its name from literature. This concentration on absolute music, in an era typified by pieces like Liszt's evocative *Années de Pélèrinage*, linked Chopin to the traditions of his predecessors more closely than his contemporaries.

In becoming what might be termed a piano specialist however, Chopin tied his career very much to the present day. While musicians of the late 1700s and early 1800s generally produced works for a wide variety of ensembles, several composers active in the 1830s and 1840s elected to write almost exclusively for one medium. Examples of this trend included Paganini, who concentrated on the violin, Bellini, who wrote operas, and several pianists, including Kalkbrenner, Thalberg, and Chopin. Chopin certainly achieved the greatest fame among the latter group, largely by creating new standards of composition and performance. He understood the piano's unique ability to provide textural variety. Thus he used with equal ease simple, single-line melodies over running accompaniments, dual-voiced structures in which a counter-melody emerges from the accompaniment, and thick, chordal constructions. He matched his variety of textures with an extended harmonic vocabulary. His works exhibited modal harmonies in addition to piquant dissonances and frequent chromatic sequences. He often employed these sequences in such rapid succession that he momentarily abandoned a work's central tonality, creating what is referred to as a harmonic parenthesis. In refining these techniques, he laid an important foundation for the harmonic explorations of Liszt, Wagner, and eventually, Debussy. He also invested his works with a broad range of expression markings. He called upon the performer to produce every level of volume, to create feelings of languor or excitement through the control of tempo and intensity, and to evoke a lyrical tone through the careful use of the sostenuto pedal. He willingly broke with the conventional rules of fingering too. Believing that every finger had a special strength, he sprinkled unusual markings throughout his pieces, even calling for the same finger to play two or three consecutive notes. This latter innovation showed something of Chopin's didactic side. He earned a large portion of his living as a piano instructor to the wealthy of Paris. Thus he included many simple and expressive works among his oeuvre, which he marked carefully to ensure an amateur's success.

Outside of the realm of music, Chopin also achieved a certain fame by virtue of his personal life. He engaged in a nine-year liaison with the novelist George Sand

(Aurore Dudevant). The couple never sought the sanctity of marriage during this time, a rejection of contemporary mores. The union was well-known within their circle of friends, but Chopin long maintained a separate residence in order not to scandalize his wealthy pupils. The menage ended in bitterness over a dispute about the marriage of Sand's daughter, Solange, but not before these two artists served as mutual inspiration for many of their finest works. Sand wrote no fewer than fourteen novels between 1838 and 1847. Likewise, Chopin completed his sonatas, the later scherzos and polonaises, the *Fantasie in F minor,* and a host of mazurkas and nocturnes during this period. Though many biographers have focused on the unfortunate denouement of the relationship, censuring Sand as stubborn and a bit cruel, this impressive body of work stands as a testament to her valuable role in Chopin's life.

Overview of Biographical Sources

The first significant English-language biography of Chopin was Frederick Niecks's two-volume text *Frederick Chopin as a Man and Musician.* Originally published in 1888, this biography was the basis for Chopin scholarship for more than fifty years. This approbation finds justification in the author's attempt to rectify the inadequacies of earlier works. Niecks cites Franz Liszt's *F. Chopin* (French edition, 1852; English translation, 1877) as a valuable reminiscence, but takes pains throughout his own work to discuss Liszt's reliance on hearsay and the assumptions of contemporaries. Niecks prefers archival evidence, so he claims as his sources periodicals, letters, and books, with additional input from conversations and correspondence with Chopin's friends and former pupils. Niecks strays from the realm of a strict biography on three issues, though. Interspersed throughout the text are frequent digressions on topics like the state of music in Poland and the nature of French Romanticism, intended to provide the reader with context for the biographical information. Further, an extensive chapter in Volume Two discusses Chopin's works. As these discussions are largely descriptive, they present no real barrier to a non-musical reader, but Niecks's reliance on colorful language and the opinions of Chopin's rivals and interpreters does little to convey any real sense of Chopin's oeuvre. The final digression amounts to a brief biography of George Sand, again intended to provide context, but replete with opinion and judgement.

When writing *Chopin: The Man and his Music* (1900), James Huneker was clearly abreast of contemporary Chopin scholarship, as he includes a discussion of the controversy over Chopin's birthdate that Niecks never acknowledges. Nonetheless, he relies heavily on Niecks for his basic biographical information. He even assumes the reader's familiarity with the work, referring to it often and skimming over much of Chopin's early life. Huneker's more original accomplish-ment is his insightful discussion of Chopin's aesthetic achievements in a chapter entitled "Poet and Psychologist." Here he groups Chopin with many other artists, including Wagner, Flaubert, and Velasquez, in an effort to define the nature of Chopin's genius as it played out in the realms of emotional and formal control. Huneker devotes the second half of his book to an overview of Chopin's works. Arranged by genre, these discussions are both technical and poetic. Huneker uses many musical examples to illustrate his points about contemporary performance practice and editing, in addition to exploring some of Chopin's more innovative harmonic structures. When he moves beyond analysis though, Huneker indulges in describing the effect of Chopin's music in flowery, highly personal language.

Arthur Hedley's *Chopin* (1947) represents the first real English-language attempt to move away from Niecks's biography. Hedley relies on original sources whenever possible, most significantly including archival material from Poland. With regard to Chopin's early years, this new approach yields little more than a few additional anecdotes. The substantive change comes in his treatment of Chopin's relationship with George Sand. Hedley faults Niecks and Huneker for their spiteful moralism, which caused them to depict Sand as manipulative and domineering. He graciously acknowledges the role that Victorian mores played in helping them adopt this tone, but he counters their position with a picture of Sand as the source of Chopin's nurture, comfort and inspiration.

Casimir Wierzynski's *The Life and Death of Chopin* appeared in an English translation in 1949. As a fellow Pole, Wierzynski elaborates on Chopin's formative years with greater depth and sympathy than earlier biographers. He paints vivid scenes of the Chopins' domestic life and early nineteenth-century Poland. Many episodes must be viewed with skepticism though, as he implies that a general social scenario applied to Chopin specifically. Wierzynski also includes extensive quotations from the supposed correspondence between Chopin and Delfina Potocka. To date, no scholar has accepted all of these letters as authentic, and many sources repudiate them completely. Wierzynski nevertheless offers the material without obvious qualification, a further cause for the reader to use caution.

Some examples of more recent Chopin scholarship include Bernard Gavoty's *Frédéric Chopin* (1977), George Marek and Maria Gordon-Smith's *Chopin* (1978), and William Atwood's *Fryderyk Chopin: Pianist from Warsaw* (1987). While each presents the essentials of Chopin's biography, they do so with a distinctly different focus. Gavoty devotes much of his effort to Chopin's love life. His discussion of Chopin's youthful infatuation with Constancia Gladkowska is brief, but by contrast, Chopin's secret engagement to Maria Wodzinska and supposed entanglements with Delfina Potocka each warrant a separate chapter, filled with telling quotations from letters and Gavoty's pointed commentary on Chopin's personality. Similarly, he describes Chopin's later years almost solely in terms of his relations with George Sand and her children.

In their well-balanced biography, Marek and Gordon-Smith demonstrate equal respect for Chopin's Polish youth and French maturity. They also avoid adopting a specific position on the controversy over the Potocka letters, preferring to offer all available evidence and let the reader decide. The same evenhanded approach prevails with respect to the relationship between Chopin and Sand. They present facts, mostly drawn from letters, and acknowledge that people can change. Ironically, Gavoty claims this same open-minded approach, while maintaining a consistent bias against Sand.

Atwood focuses attention on Chopin as a pianist. He provides details about performances, halls, impresarios, and programs, creating a vivid picture of the many demands on a nineteenth-century performer. Atwood also discusses Chopin's personality and private life, but primarily as they pertain to his concertizing, such as describing the nervous anticipation which he felt prior to public appearances.

Evaluation of Principal Biographical Sources

Atwood, William G. *Fryderyk Chopin: Pianist from Warsaw*. New York: Columbia University Press, 1987. (**A, G**) One of the more recent publications on Chopin, this book uses his concert career as the focal point for biographical detail. Atwood's engaging style makes this accessible reading for the general public, while his inclusion of concert programs and contemporary reviews also reward the scholar's attention.

Gavoty, Bernard. *Frédéric Chopin.* Translated by Martin Sokolinsky. New York: Scribner's, 1977. (**G**) Initially presenting an interesting and straightforward biography, Gavoty eventually develops a fascination with Chopin's love life when describing his adulthood. This colorful approach leaves the reader with little concept of Chopin's musical achievements, a flaw not remedied by an appendix devoted to his compositions. Gavoty's "Chopin Calendar" is more useful, showing the composer's chronology in relation to world events.

Hedley, Arthur. *Chopin.* London: J. M. Dent, 1947. (**A**) A concise and well-balanced biography which also includes insightful remarks about Chopin's methods of teaching and playing the piano. Additionally, Hedley's comments about Chopin's works provide genuine analysis and criticism in place of poetic description. The very strength of this latter section may render it obscure for the general reader however. Hedley's appendices include a bibliography, works list, and chronology, as well as a glossary of names to acquaint the reader with Chopin's significant contemporaries.

Huneker, James. *Chopin: The Man and his Music.* New York: Charles Scribner, 1900. (**A, G**) Though Huneker presents a derivative biography, his discussion of Chopin's aesthetics and influence is worth noting as it links him to a broader community of artists. The section on Chopin's works is more rewarding for the student of late nineteenth-century performance practice, because of Huneker's remarks about current editions and performances.

Marek, George, and Maria Gordon-Smith. *Chopin.* New York: Harper and Row, 1978. (**A, G**) In addition to a readable and unbiased biography, this book offers some of the most intelligent evidence regarding the alleged correspondence between Chopin and Delfina Potocka in the form of a report from a handwriting analyst. The authors also provide a chronology and a thorough bibliography.

Niecks, Frederick. *Frederick Chopin as a Man and Musician.* 3d ed. London: Novello, 1902. (**A, G**) Long considered the English-language standard for Chopin scholarship, this text gives the reader an expansive view of Chopin's life and works. It remains of interest for its historical value as Niecks had direct contact with many of Chopin's pupils and contemporaries, but subsequent research has stripped it of its primacy as source material.

Orga, Artes. *Chopin: His Life and Times*. Tunbridge Wells, England: Midas Books, 1976. (**G**) Orga's work shines in the quality and variety of its illustrations. He includes watercolors, pencil sketches, portraits, and daguerreotypes of Chopin with his circle of friends, as well as other people, places, and objects that were prominent in his life. The actual biography is unremarkable, as Orga uses it solely to unite the illustrations.

de Pourtalès, Guy. *Polonaise: The Life of Chopin*. New York: Henry Holt, 1927. (**G**) A fanciful and romantic presentation of Chopin's biography. Pourtalès quotes extensively from letters without notes or documentation, and weaves in a Chopin legend whenever possible. He also paints a melancholy portrait of his life, focusing on themes of homesickness, illness and thwarted love.

Wierzynski, Casimir. *The Life and Death of Chopin*. Translated by Norbert Guterman. New York: Simon and Shuster, 1949. (**G**) Though noteworthy for what Wierzynski would call his Polish perspective, this book should be approached with caution. Wierzynski generalizes frequently, and relies on some unsubstantiated sources.

Overview and Evaluation of Primary Sources

Chopin left no authenticated diary detailing his most intimate thoughts, but he was a faithful and frequent correspondent with family and friends in both France and Poland. Over time though, many of his letters were lost or destroyed due to carelessness, vengeance, and war. Two other barriers complicate the search for primary sources. The first is the simple issue of language. Chopin wrote to his family in Polish, using many colorful idiomatic expressions. The earliest Chopin scholars were not accomplished in Polish, and thus reliable translations have only become available within the past fifty years. The second obstacle is that of authenticity. Controversy surrounds both the letters to Delfina Potocka and a diary fragment dating from the early 1830s, so researchers cite these materials sporadically.

Despite these difficulties, two modern editions of Chopin's correspondence are available in English. The first is Henryk Opienski's *Chopin's Letters* (Translated by E. L. Voynich. New York: Alfred A. Knopf, 1932). It includes all correspondence available at the time of publication. It is arranged in chronological order, at the discretion of the editor where dates are not substantiated by postmarks or other evidence. Though some of the letters dealing with business affairs, such as Chopin's publications or housing arrangements, are a bit dry, they are a valuable source of insight into the social history of his time. Arthur Hedley's *Selected Correspondence of Fryderyk Chopin* (New York: McGraw-Hill, 1963) is an expanded translation of an earlier work by Bronislaw Edward Sydow. He chooses to omit much of the more mundane correspondence. The inclusion of telling letters between Chopin's closest friends and pupils easily offsets whatever loss this may be to the reader. An appendix which deals with the Potocka letters and the findings of the Chopin Institute on their authenticity is also of interest.

For all their variety, Chopin's letters say very little about his compositions or his views on music. A direct examination of his works reveals far more. Editions of these works proliferate, but three sets warrant special consideration. The first of these, published by Breitkopf and Härtel (Leipzig) between 1878 and 1889, is of historical interest since many friends and contemporaries of Chopin, including Liszt and the cellist Franchomme, were among the editors. A later edition exhibits a similar connection. Carl Mikuli, one of Chopin's pupils, edited *Frédéric Chopin's Complete Works for the Piano* (Vols. 1-15. New York: Schirmer, 1934). This publication also features historical annotations by James Huneker, an early Chopin biographer. The most reliable and widely accepted edition is *Fryderyk Chopin Complete Works*, edited by Ignaz Paderewski. (Vols. 1-27. Warsaw: Instytut Fryderyka Chopina, 1949-1966). This set includes useful facsimiles of some of the manuscripts used to create the edition, as well as comprehensive discussions of editorial decisions.

Two thematic catalogs are worth mentioning as research aids for primary sources. *Chopin: An Index of His Works in Chronological Order* by Maurice Brown (London: St. Martin's Press, 1962) is the only source of this type in English. His entries generally include incipits, publication information, and manuscript locations. Brown also provides nine appendices, one of which is a brief bibliography. Krystyna Kobylanska offers a greatly expanded catalog in her German-language *Frederic Chopin Thematisch-bibliographisches Werkverzeichnis*

(Munich: G. Henle, 1979). She presents Chopin's works in opus-number order, again with incipits, publication information and manuscript locations. She supplements this with references to Chopin's corrections of early, printed editions, a work's appearance in a manuscript catalog, or the discussion of a piece in Chopin's letters or any of the titles listed in her comprehensive bibliography.

Principal Works

Twelve Grand Études, op. 10 (1829-1832)
Twelve Études, op. 25 (1832-1836)
Sonata in C Minor, op. 4 (1827)
Sonata in B Flat Minor, op. 35 (1839)
Sonata in B Minor, op. 58 (1844)
Twenty-four Preludes, op. 28 (1836-1839)
Fantaisie in F Minor, op. 49 (1840-1841)
Polonaise—Fantaisie, op. 61 (1845-1846)
Piano Concerto No. 2 in F Minor, op. 21 (1829)
Piano Concerto No. 1 in E Minor, op. 11 (1830)
Piano Trio in G Minor, op. 8 (1828-1829)
Sonata for Piano and Cello, op. 65 (1845-1846)
Seventeen Polish Songs, op. 74 (1855)

Fiction and Adaptations

Fictional treatments of Chopin's life display a marked tendency toward romantic sentimentality and outright fantasy. The earliest among these works stands as the only notable exception. George Sand's *Lucrezia Floriani* (Translated by Julius Eker. Chicago: Academy Chicago Publishers, 1985) presents the tale of Prince Karol de Roswald, a delicate and sensitive young man, and his love affair with the title character, an unconventional and passionate woman. It is evident to the informed reader that Chopin and Sand inspired these characters. It is also clear that Sand wrote the book near the end of the couple's relationship (1846), as she portrays de Roswald (Chopin) as an egoist, incapable of truly loving anything or anyone, while Floriani (Sand) shines in the role of a patient, loving martyr.

Jeanette Lee's *Unfinished Portraits: Stories of Musicians and Artists* (New York: Scribner's, 1916) attempts an air of authenticity by presenting episodes from Chopin's life in the form of diary entries. She also uses characters and locations consistent with his biography, such as George Sand and her estate at Nohant. However, she has Chopin express sentiments of the most sterotypically romantic sort. He professes his love for Jane Stirling in one entry, and later agonizes over the break-up with Sand in an uncharacteristic manner.

The Nightingale: A Life of Chopin, by Marjorie Strachey (New York: Longmans, Green, 1927) similarly uses Chopin's biography as the basis for its storyline. Strachey takes every known Chopin anecdote, beginning with his crying at the sound of the piano as a toddler and ending with his deathbed serenade by Delfina Potocka, and stitches them together with imaginative dialogue. The result is an engaging novel, best enjoyed by those familiar with the real characters and events.

Shelton Sackett's *Nocturne: A Chopin Play in One Act* (New York: Samuel French, 1927) offers a more focused treatment than the earlier works. This play is set during a summer evening in 1847, at the point of Solange Sand's elopement with the sculptor Jean-Auguste Clésinger. Solange's presence, however, serves merely as the pretext for reuniting Sand and Chopin. Sackett depicts Sand as an infatuated devotee of the Socialist cause and its leader, Pierre Leroux. She has little time for Chopin, who is still in love with her and filled with nostalgia for their happier days. This sentimentality makes Chopin appear quite desperate, particularly when he collapses at the end of the play.

Chopin in Space: A Play of Dis-location (New York: Dramatists Play Service, 1986) provides a more contemporary, though no less fantastic portrayal of Chopin. Author Phil Bosakowski unites Poland's great figures of the nineteenth and twentieth centuries, Chopin and Lech Walesa, in one continually evolving character. By making this combination, he draws parallels between the Russian oppression of Poland in the 1830s and the attempts to stifle the Solidarity movement in the 1980s. He implies that Chopin's music spoke for Polish freedom as strongly as Walesa's union activities.

The film *Impromptu*, written by Sarah Kernochan, produced by Stuart Oken and Daniel Sherkow, and directed by James Lapine (1990), mixes biographical facts with romantic fiction and a little comedy to tell the story of the early stages of George Sand's relationship with Chopin. The film portrays Sand, played by Judy

Davis, as an aggressive suitor who surmounts obstacles like obsessive former lovers, jealousy, intrigue, and misunderstanding to win the heart of a reluctant Chopin, played by Hugh Grant. Much of the action occurs at a patron's country estate during a visit by several prominent Parisian artists. This setting allows for scenes which emphasize Chopin's refinement and identification with the aristocracy, along with some vivid demonstrations of Sand's unconventional independence. Aside from underscoring these key personality traits, the film makes no profound points about the artists or their art. *Impromptu* is intended solely as entertainment, and in that, it succeeds admirably.

Museums, Historical Landmarks, Societies

Chopin Piano Festival (Nohant, France). At Nohant, Chopin was a guest of George Sand for seven years, 1839-1846, where he composed his major works. In 1992 a new Piano Festival was created in Nohant/LaChatre by Adam Wibrowski, known for his research on Chopin's music.

International Frédéric Chopin Foundation (Warsaw, Poland). Founded in 1934, this organization works to encourage Chopin scholarship through seminars and publications. It also operates the central Chopin Museum in Warsaw, and maintains a library of more than 13,000 volumes. Best known among the Foundation's activities is the quinquennial International Frédéric Chopin Piano Competition, most recently held in 1992.

Monument (Żelazowa Wola, Poland). Erected in 1894 through the efforts of the Russian composer Mili Balakirev, this monument stands in the garden at Chopin's birthplace.

Monument (Warsaw, Poland). A gathering spot for summer concerts in Warsaw's Lazienka Park.

Plaque (Reinertz, Germany). A commemoration of Chopin's benefit concerts at the spa in August, 1826. Erected in 1897 in the Kurhaus.

Sculpture (Paris, France). The work of Jean-Auguste Clésinger, this sculpture dates from 1850. It depicts a grieving figure with a broken lyre, and it stands at Chopin's grave in the Père La Chaise Cemetery.

Other Sources

Abraham, Gerald. *Chopin's Musical Style*. 1939. Reprint. Westport, CT: Greenwood, 1980. Abraham takes the interesting approach of looking at Chopin's oeuvre chronologically, dividing his career into three phases: evolving, mature, and late—showing the origins of Chopin's style—and tracing the path of its refinement through all genres simultaneously. Abraham incorporates many musical examples and terms in his discussion, aiming this book toward a musically-literate audience.

The Chopin Companion: Profiles of the Man and the Musician. New York: Norton, 1973. Edited by Alan Walker. A collection of essays by Chopin scholars, this work offers brief historical and biographical sketches before proceeding to several analyses of Chopin's works. The authors strike a careful balance as their analyses are informative, yet accessible to a broad audience. Of particular interest is the chapter on Chopin's songs. It includes text translations in addition to a discussion of the forms and structural features of this little-known body of work.

Kallberg, Jeffery. "Hearing Poland: Chopin and Nationalism." In *Nineteenth-Century Piano Music*. Edited by R. Larry Todd. New York: Schirmer Books, 1990: 221-257. An insightful presentation of precisely what constitutes the national elements in Chopin's mazurkas. Kallberg also examines the extent to which these were evident to his contemporaries through the inclusion of many quotations from nineteenth-century critics along with supporting musical examples.

Methuen-Campbell, James. *Chopin Playing From the Composer to the Present Day*. New York: Taplinger, 1981. In an attempt to examine the variety of approaches to performing Chopin's music, the author discusses the interpretations developed by the great pianists of the last one hundred fifty years. He uses recordings as the basis for much of his information; thus the book features a thorough discography.

Samson, Jim. *The Music of Chopin*. London: Routledge and Kegan Paul, 1985. A part of the Companions to the Great Composers series, this book offers the most thorough analytical discussions of Chopin's piano music to be found outside of specialized journals. Samson uses a variety of analytical methods, based on the qualities of the piece being examined. He also draws interesting parallels between Chopin's works and those of his predecessors to illustrate paths of influence. There are extensive footnotes, and a well-organized bibliography.

————, ed. *The Cambridge Companion to Chopin*. New York: Cambridge University Press, 1992. Contains twelve essays by Chopin scholars. The book is divided into three sections: "Growth of Style," "Profiles of the Music," and "Reception"—which deal with Chopin's reception in nineteenth-century Poland, Victorian attitudes to Chopin, and his influence.

Temperley, Nicholas. "Freyderyk Chopin." In *The New Grove Early Romantic Masters* I. New York: Norton, 1985: 1-96. This concise and well-written chapter features a brief biography which acquaints the reader with the pertinent facts about Chopin's life, as well as many of the areas of controversy in Chopin scholarship. Supplementing this are remarks on his style of composition and performance, and longer analytical sections discussing Chopin's use of harmony and conception of musical form. A works list is cross-referenced with the text, and the bibliography is exhaustive.

Ruthmarie Kelley
Bowling Green State University

Auguste Comte
1798-1857

Chronology

Born Auguste Comte on January 20, 1798, in Montpellier, France, son of Louis-Auguste Comte, a cashier in a tax office and staunch Catholic and Royalist, and Rosalie Boyer Comte, also of conservative sympathies; *1806-1813* attends school in Montpellier, where he excels in rhetoric, receiving first prize in elocution in 1813; *1814-1815* attends the prestigious École Polytechnique in Paris after finishing fourth place in a nation-wide competition; loses rank because of his unruly behavior; meets Napoleon Bonaparte, who visits the school on his return from exile on the island of Elba, and becomes involved in patriotic agitation; *1816* returns to Montpellier when the École Polytechnique is closed by the French government after Napoleon's defeat at Waterloo; becomes secretary of an alumni association formed by the former students of the Polytechnique; writes first essay in June; returns to Paris in July; *1817* meets Henri de Saint-Simon, who employs him as editorial secretary; *1818* has a child with his mistress, a woman of Italian origin known as Pauline; *1819* contributes anonymously to Saint-Simon's magazine, *Le Politique*; publishes articles under his own name for the first time in the *Censeur Européen*; contributes to the *Organisateur*; *1820* publishes anonymously his "Sommaire appréciation de l'ensemble du passé moderne" in the *Organisateur*; *1821* works on Saint-Simon's new journal, the *Système industriel*; *1822* publishes "Système de politique positive" in Saint-Simon's *Catéchisme des Industriels*; tensions and resentments come between Comte and Saint-Simon, and Comte breaks off relations; *1825* marries former prostitute Caroline Massin; publishes "Considérations philosophiques sur les sciences et les savants" in the *Producteur*; meets the scientist Félicité Robert de Lamennais, who is attracted to the originality of Comte's ideas; *1826* publishes his "Considerations sur le pourvoir spirituel" in the *Producteur*; begins a "Course on Positive Philosophy" at his home, which is well-attended but interrupted by his nervous breakdown; *1827* jumps off a bridge in Paris in a suicide attempt; *1828* completely recovers from his breakdown; publishes a series of articles on economics in *Le Nouveau Journal de*

Paris et des départements; *1829* publishes "Discours d'ouverture du Cours de Philosophie Positive" in *La Revue Encyclopédique*; *1830* publishes the first volume of his *Cours de philosophie positive*; founds the Association polytechnique pour l'instruction populaire; *1831* refuses to serve in the National Guard and is sentenced to three days in prison; *1832* named to the post of reader at the École Polytechnique; *1833* makes unsuccessful attempt to convince the government to create a chair of the history of science for himself at the Collège de France; *1835* contributes to the defense of those arrested during and after the insurrections of 1834 in Paris and Lyon; publication of the second volume of his *Cours de philosophie positive*; *1836* named examiner at the Polytechnique after being denied a regular teaching post; *1838* publishes third volume of the *Cours de philosophie positive*; *1839* publishes fourth volume of the *Cours de philosophie positive*; replaces the expression "social physics" with the word "sociology"; *1840* denied a teaching post at the Polytechnique; denounces the "reign of pedants" in the *Journal des Débats*; *1841* publishes fifth volume of the *Cours de philosophie positive*; begins correspondence with John Stuart Mill; *1842* publishes sixth and last volume of the *Cours de philosophie positive*; wins a court case against his publisher for adding an unflattering preface to his book; *1843* publishes *Traité élémentaire de géométrie analytique* but is not reappointed to his examiner's post at the École polytechnique; a government commission is created to investigate what appears to be a case of discrimination against him, and he is reappointed for a period of one year; *1844* publishes *Discours sur l'esprit positif*; governing council of the École Polytechnique votes not to reappoint him and, despite massive support, he loses the post and thus one-half of his income; John Stuart Mill begins a subscription in England in order to help him financially; meets his platonic love, Clotilde de Vaux; *1846* Clotilde de Vaux dies of tuberculosis; *1847* begins a public course on the evolution of humanity in which he prophesies the imminent establishment of a republican form of government in France; *1848* founds the Association libre pour l'instruction positive du peuple de tout l'Occident européen after the February Revolution; publication of his *Discours sur l'ensemble du positivism*; *1849* creates the Eglise Universelle de la Religion de l'Humanité in which he marries a proletarian couple; gives his course on the evolution of humanity wearing a hat modeled on the pope's; *1851* publishes first volume of his *Système de politique positive*; loses his post as reader at the École Polytechnique and thus the rest of his income; approves the coup d'état of Louis Napoleon Bonaparte, which overthrows the Second Republic; *1852* publishes second volume of the *Système de politique positive* and the *Catéchisme positiviste*; *1853* publishes third volume of the *Système de politique positive*; Harriet Martineau's translation of an edited version of the *Cours de philosophie* appears in England; *1854* publishes fourth volume of the *Système de politique positive*; *1855* draws up his will; *1856* publishes first volume of the *Synthèse subjective*; *1857* dies in Paris after contracting jaundice and is buried in the Père Lachaise cemetery.

Activities of Historical Significance

Auguste Comte appeared at a critical moment in the development of social thought. In the aftermath of the French Revolution, when the process of industrialization was beginning on the European continent and provoking important demographic changes and transforming social relations and political life, a great change in Western thought was in preparation. The convergence of speculations about the nature of historical change, new scientific discoveries and theories, and optimism about the possibilities of social change distinguished the intellectual atmosphere of the first half of the nineteenth century.

Comte was one of the greatest thinkers of this extremely fertile period. He possessed an ability to synthesize ideas in a systematic way, incorporating new thinking from every domain of human speculation. He was not as original a thinker as Georg Wilhelm Friedrich Hegel, Henri de Saint-Simon, Charles Fourier, or Karl Marx in explaining the dynamics of social organization and historical development, but he was clear and comprehensive; and his attempts to unify all knowledge were more accessible to the general reader, corresponding more completely to the sensibilities of the educated elite of his day.

Taking concepts from Robert Jacques Turgot, the Marquis de Condorcet, Henri de Saint-Simon and others, whose ideas were based upon an optimistic belief that the application of reason to social affairs would lead to the perfection of humankind and society, and applying his mathematical and scientific expertise, Comte attempted to determine how humanity had evolved intellectually and socially, and how this evolution could be influenced in a positive way. The two basic principles that he employed in this endeavor were the ideas that the different stages of human development were governed by laws of progressive classification and perfection of the different realms of scientific activity. His employment by Saint-Simon was obviously an enormous influence over his subsequent intellectual work, for the scientific training that Comte received at the École Polytechnique was applied to the social and political speculations undertaken by his mentor (forty years his senior). The fact that the 1820s were a politically agitated period during which the middle classes chafed under the reactionary regimes of the Restoration reinforced Comte's critical outlook and probably encouraged his later eccentricities. At this time, during the constitutional monarchies of Louis XVIII (installed in power by the allied leaders of the anti-Napoleonic forces) and Charles X, attempts to restore aristocratic privileges, and repression of civil liberties, alienated the middle classes. Those in the liberal professions and, especially, the sciences were prone to identify political democracy and social justice with the advancement of technological progress and the development of scientific thought.

Comte's work represented a shift from the philosophical preoccupations of the pre-revolutionary era of the Enlightenment to the practical social and political concerns of the post-Napoleonic period. For this reason, his achievement lies in the establishment of a conception of historical evolution in which policy means and goals are implied. The sheer comprehensiveness combined with the scientific and philosophical acumen evident in his writings produced a vision of human development that was as ideologically compelling as it was impressively erudite.

Comte's intellectual work can be generally seen as comprising two phases: first, his attempt to show how human civilization has progressed through three distinct stages of development, which he set forth in *The Positive Philosophy* (1830-1842); second, his effort to analyze social and political life in terms of his discoveries, presented in his *System of Positive Polity* (1851-1854). The two phases of Comte's intellectual activity were respectively distinguished by two words he coined. The first is "sociology," and *The Positive Philosophy* presents the bases of his science of society. The second term is "altruism," and it is in *System of Positive Polity* that he attempts to demonstrate that a harmonious society cannot be founded upon egoism or individualism.

In *The Positive Philosophy*, he presented his conclusion that every branch of knowledge passes successively through three different theoretical conditions: the Theological, the Metaphysical, and the Scientific. Each of these conditions is characterized by a peculiar way of apprehending reality, of understanding the world in all its complexity. In the Theological stage, fictions are created in order to account for natural phenomena. Here is the reign of religion and superstition. These fictions lose their explanatory force only gradually as discoveries are made and more rational explanations emerge. The Metaphysical stage is a transitional stage during which natural laws are sought in abstractions unfounded upon the scientific methods of observation, experiment, and classification. The Scientific stage emerges only when such methods have been consciously systematized and applied; this is the emergence of "positive" science.

Far from being a simplistic categorization of the emergence of what today we call the "Scientific Revolution" of the sixteenth and seventeenth centuries, Comte's explanation of this historical and intellectual process accounted for the ambiguities and anomalies involved. For example, in saying that the Metaphysical stage of historical development was transitional, he admitted that his conceptualization was essentially a heuristic device and analytical framework. He stressed that the different realms of human understanding tended to retain elements of all the stages through which they had progressed. The evolution of the sciences was therefore gradual, virtually never-ending. He reasoned that social and historical development could be analyzed in terms of the development of the individual mind, and vice-versa. Comte thus posited a phenomenology that was social and psychological; the individual was a product of general social forces, themselves rooted in historical processes.

Comte's system cannot be considered deterministic for he did not single-out any one determining causative factor. If, epistemologically, Comte's premises are philosophically and historically idealist—seeming to privilege ideals or knowledge over "material" factors—they are only implicitly so because he did not enter into the debate over historical philosophy associated with the works of Hegel and Marx. Although he maintained that, with clear methodological principles, a certain "historical prevision" was possible, such a prevision could never be very precise and could only "furnish preparatory indicators of the general direction of the contemporary progress."

Comte's political philosophy broke with the Enlightenment and revolutionary traditions. In contrast to the *philosophies* of the eighteenth century in France, he did not believe that giving free reign to liberty would automatically result in a rational, harmonious society. The ideas of Denis Diderot, Voltaire and Jean-Jacques Rousseau were abstractions born of political and intellectual frustration. Comte viewed the experience of the French Revolution as representing the danger of any attempt to change a polity and society radically, in a non-evolutionary way. He recognized that ideals such as individualism and liberty were not completely compatible in an integrated and interdependent society. He reasoned that "True liberty is inherent in and subordinate to order, human as well as external order. It will never be possible to represent as hostile to the liberty and dignity of man the doctrine which places on the surest basis, and gives freest scope to, his activity, intelligence, and feeling."

Just as the state of scientific knowledge reflects a particular stage of intellectual development, a given political situation corresponds to the productive system prevailing. The political order is merely a manifestation of the civil order, and the civil order is a part of a particular stage in the social development of humanity. True to the inspiration of Saint-Simon, for Comte positivism was part of the dawn of a new age in which rational principles of social organization would come to govern human relations. The watch-words of this development, he said, were "Order and Progress."

Order and progress are indeed central to Comte's positivism, and the two concepts represent a tension within the corpus of his thought that is fundamental to our age and civilization. The rational reorganization of social institutions was both the objective and the precondition of human liberation from the constraints of the past. But a question remains: how compatible was such a will to remodel society with the individual freedoms believed basic to human dignity and creativity? This is the problem taken-up by John Stuart Mill in his essay *On Liberty* (1859), written partly in reaction to his reading of Comte's work. This question remains a basic consideration because Comte's positivism not only laid the foundations of modern sociological speculation, but presaged the twentieth-century will to alter cultural patterns and political institutions in a planned, self-conscious manner. It is this kind of utopianism that finds its origins in Comte's work. It is a legacy that has been appropriated by all political tendencies.

The scientistic stress on objective, "positive" knowledge in Comte's system, and his faith in the ability of an elite of technocrats, are ideas that he assimilated from his mentor Saint-Simon. It has been seen as something of an anomaly that in his later life Comte turned to moral and spiritual questions in his surprising book, *The Positivist Catechism* (1854). This turn from historical, sociological and scientific concerns is frequently explained by the spiritual crisis he suffered following the death of the woman he revered, Clothilde de Vaux. In fact, his outline of a

"Religion of Humanity" is consistent with his previous work. Comte's positivism was always a philosophy designed to act on the real social world; the objective of this action was moral revolution. Mental and moral anarchy would be eliminated by establishing a new spiritualism based upon positive science. In effect, Comte wished to create a social and political consensus on an entirely different basis. Many subsequent sociologists would fully share this aspiration.

Although his writings are far less known today than those of Karl Marx, the other great social thinker of the nineteenth century, Comte's have been just as influential. Not only did he directly or indirectly influence later social thinkers, historians, and scientists, but vulgarizations of his ideas were assimilated by generations of working-class people. During the nineteenth century, the power of his ideas was such that some newly independent states in Latin America borrowed heavily from him. Brazil, for example, adopted his slogan, "Order and Progress" as its national motto. Comte himself, persecuted by jealous colleagues at the École Polytechnique, where he never obtained a regular teaching post and from which he was fired in spite of his international reputation, died a poor and bitter man. Unrewarded in his own lifetime, his accomplishments and impact tend to be underrated during our own.

Overview of Biographical Sources

The secondary literature on Comte has changed in character commensurate with the diffusion of his influence. During the nineteenth century his work was extensively commented upon as contemporaries explored its complexities and as translations appeared. Controversy over his ideas raged at this time, but did not continue into the twentieth century. Although Comte's premises were often accepted by the generation of social scientists that contributed to "classical sociology," these scholars did not generally wish to acknowledge his influence.

Nineteenth-century surveys of his work are of limited value today. Not only are they imbued with the prejudices and mental habits of the age, but they sometimes lack the perspective needed to understand Comte's ideas in their historical context and in terms of the filiation of ideas that preceded and followed them. Nevertheless, such studies often provide informed discussions that are more sympathetic than some recent offerings. In this category should be placed G. H. Lewes's

Comte's Philosophy of the Sciences (1885), and the analysis made by Harold Höffding in his *A History of Modern Philosophy,* vol. 2 (1900). Especially interesting is John Stuart Mill's *Auguste Comte and Positivism,* first published in the *Westminster Review* in 1865.

During the early decades of the twentieth century, the first generation of academic sociologists often turned to Comte as they explored the genesis of the perspective that led to the establishment of their discipline. Comte is often criticized, but in a respectful way, in works such as F. J. Gould's *Auguste Comte* (London: Watts, 1920) and William H. George's article, "Auguste Comte: Sociology and the New Politics," published in the *American Journal of Sociology* (1927). The general attitude expressed towards Comte is further explored in "A Comtean Centenary," also published in the *American Journal of Sociology* (1922).

Later sociologists were far less sympathetic to the man who coined the word "sociology." Throughout most of the twentieth century, Comte's work has been largely ignored. Since the First World War, his "positivism" has frequently been referred to as the naive expression of a prescientific mode of reasoning. This was the position taken by Talcott Parsons in his influential *Structure of Social Action* (New York: McGraw-Hill, 1937). The reaction against Comte and positivism was a subtle phenomenon that began, in fact, before the turn of the century. H. Stuart Hughes has discussed the trend in his *Consciousness and Society: The Reorientation of European Social Thought 1890-1930* (New York: Vintage, 1958). The effect of this evolution was that Comte became more of interest to historians than to sociologists. His works were deemed central to the emergence of modern attitudes, and thus of undeniable historical importance, but his formulations were no longer considered applicable in the social sciences. The irony is that, as sociology and related disciplines became more oriented towards empirical research and quantitative analysis, i.e. more "positive" in the Comtean sense, his sweeping syntheses and audacious theorizing were increasingly rejected.

Like other social theorists of the nineteenth century, Comte regained the attention of scholars in the 1960s. The social and political passions of that decade, which continued into the 1970s and beyond, inspired a general reconsideration of social theory. The expansion of higher education, the development of the social sciences, and increased numbers of university scholars in the humanities led to the publication of numerous studies in the historical development of social ideas. For these reasons, Comte is no longer forgotten or scorned in the academy. At a time when many assumptions about the physical and social world are sorely challenged, it may be expected that Comte's efforts to show how they are intertwined will continue to arouse interest.

Evaluation of Principal Biographical Sources

Alengry, Franck. *Essai historique et critique sur la sociologie chez Auguste Comte.* 1899. Reprint. Paris: Slatkine, 1984. (**A**) Republication of a thorough study of Comte's work by a student of the early French sociologists Alfred Espinas and Émile Durkheim. Unavailable in English translation, this work attests to the conceptual force of Comte's formulations and how the development of sociology in France is largely due to their elaboration.

Charlton, D. G. *Positivist Thought in France During the Second Empire 1852-1870.* London: Oxford University Press, 1959. (**A, G**) This is a valuable study of positivism as a general intellectual phenomenon and, indirectly, of the influence of Comte's ideas during the decades following his death. Charlton shows how positivist philosophy influenced many of the projects undertaken during the Second Empire of Louis Napoleon Bonaparte. Doctrines of order and progress buttressed by notions of scientific progress coincided with the authoritarian, innovative government of Napoleon II. From the redesigning of Paris, to the rudiments of the modern "welfare state," Comte's ideas were subtly and, in many cases, unconsciously applied in actual government and state planning.

De Coppens, Peter Roche. *Ideal Men in Classical Sociology: the Views of Comte, Durkheim, Pareto and Weber.* University Park: Pennsylvania State University Press, 1976. (**A**) General study of Comte's ideas as part of an exploration of the construct of the "ideal type" in the writings of these most prominent of the "classical" sociologists. The positing of a sociological ideal type, or model, emerged out of concrete, historical experience but was a necessary step in the working out of sociological method. Although fraught with subjective (normative) considerations, the ideal type represents a positive step towards achieving the objectivity (value-free knowledge) that is the ultimate goal of sociological inquiry.

Edgar, Henry. *Auguste Comte and the Middle Ages*. Presbourg, Hungary: C. Angermayer, n.d. (**A**) Published series of lectures given in Presbourg, Hungary, in 1884 by one of Comte's disciples. Comte is portrayed as a man whose genius will be recognized centuries from now, when humanity is more capable of grasping his ideas. This work is less valuable as scholarly comment than as evidence of how powerful an influence Comte worked on the social imagination in the nineteenth century.

Fletcher, Ronald. *Auguste Comte and the Making of Sociology*. London: Athlone Press, 1966. (**A**) Brochure containing the text of a lecture delivered at the London School of Economics on November 4, 1865. Fletcher discusses how Comte influenced succeeding generations of sociologists. He concludes that "Comte is almost a contemporary."

Gouhier, Henri. *La jeunesse d'Auguste Comte*. 3 vols. Paris: J. Vrin, 1933-1941. (**A**) A classic work that remains one of the most important works ever undertaken on the life and work of Comte. Must be consulted for any serious study because its biographical documentation of Comte the man (not just the thinker) deepened understanding of how his ideas emerged out of a rich and complex historical period just as they were related to his unusual life situation. By its example, Gouhier's work announced new trends in the writing of intellectual history that came to prominence in the post-World War Two period.

————. *La Vie d'Auguste Comte*. Paris: J. Vrin, 1965. (**A, G**) An excellent popularization of Gouhier's impressive research. Comte and his ideas are presented in a lively way that appealed to a new (and far more numerous) generation of French sociology students. As such, it participated in the postwar revival of interest in social theories of all types, especially those critical of prevailing institutions. Unfortunately, not available in English translation.

Hawkins, Richmond Laurin. *Auguste Comte and the United States (1816-1853)*. Cambridge, MA: Harvard University Press, 1936. (**A**) Interesting history of the reception of Comte's ideas in the United States before the American Civil War by Americans such as various protestant theologians in New England and authors like Edgar Allan Poe.

Kremer-Marietti, Angèle. *L'Anthropologie positiviste d'Auguste Comte*. Lille, France: Atelier de Reproduction des Thèses, 1977. (**A**) Detailed doctoral dissertation submitted to the Sorbonne (Université de Paris IV) in 1977 by one of today's leading Comte scholars. Interprets Comte's work from the standpoint of contemporary philosophies of social science.

Lenzer, Gertrud. "Introduction" to *Auguste Comte and Positivism: The Essential Writings*. New York: Harper and Row, 1975. (**A, G**) Lenzer's introduction is one of the most insightful analyses of Comte's ideas and their historical significance to appear in print. She lucidly summarized and explains his conceptions in terms of their internal logic and in relation to his historical environment and to other social thinkers. In addition, Lenzer comments on the contemporary relevance of Comte's work in light of the evolution of social thought, and in relation to the discipline of sociology and historical transformation since his time.

Manuel, Frank E. *The Prophets of Paris: Turgot, Condorcet, Saint-Simon, Fourier and Comte*. New York: Harper and Row, 1965. (**A, G**) This is an excellent overview of Comte and his thought within the context of French social thought from the late Enlightenment to the utopian thinkers of the early nineteenth century. Manuel tends to stress the irrationalist content of Comte's thought, implicitly accounting for it in terms of his "bouts of insanity." Placing Comte in broad historical context, he explains that, whereas the eighteenth-century thinker Turgot was almost pathologically afraid of uniformity, Comte had an equally obsessive fear of novelty and nonconformity. It was this fear, according to Manuel, that ultimately led to Émile Durkheim's notion of anomie (normlessness).

Marvin, F. S. *Comte: The Founder of Sociology*. 1936. Reprint. New York: Russell and Russell, 1965. (**A, G**) This is a general history aimed at the nonspecialist. It is a good synthesis of Comte's life and ideas that fully merited its re-edition thirty years after the first publication.

Mill, John Stuart. *Auguste Comte and Positivism*. 1865. Reprint. Ann Arbor: University of Michigan Press, 1961. (**A, G**) This classic work is now more of a primary source, but it remains an enlightening commentary on Comte's work. Mill wished to introduce British readers to Comte's highly systematic thought in order to counter the philosophically static and relatively historical cast of utilitarian thought in his country. Mills' brilliantly clear exposition of the essence of the positivist philosophy is revealing of how Comte's contribution to social and historical understanding transcended his often laborious prose style.

Simpson, George. *Auguste Comte: Sire of Sociology*. New York: Thomas Y. Crowell, 1969. (**A**) General overview of the man and his influence that gains interest from the fact that its author translated much of Émile Durkheim's most important work. The filiation between Comte and Durkheim is of great significance because Durkheim laid the foundations for twentieth-century sociology.

Thompson, Kenneth. *Auguste Comte: The Foundation of Sociology*. New York: John Wiley, 1975. (**A**) General academic study that stresses the part played by Comte in delimiting the subject matter of an autonomous discipline of sociology, his contribution to a sociology of knowledge, and his influence on the development of sociology through figures such as John Stuart Mill, Herbert Spencer, and Émile Durkheim.

Overview and Evaluation of Primary Sources

For the most easily found editions of Comte's works see *The Positive Philosophy* (Vols. 1-2. London: Kegan Paul, Trench, Trübner, 1893; **A**), or the same work reprinted with a short but excellent introduction by Abraham S. Blumberg (New York: AMS, 1975; **A**). *A General View of Positivism*, translated by J. H. Bridges (New York: Robert Speller, 1957; **A, G**) and *The Catechism of Positive Religion* (London: Trübner, 1883). Comte's lesser works, and much of his correspondence, began to be published later in the nineteenth century: *Appeal to Conservatives* (London, 1889); *Religion and Humanity: Subjective Synthesis*, or *Universal System of Conceptions Adopted to the Normal State of Humanity* (London, 1891); *Confessions and Testament of Auguste Comte and His Correspondence with Clothilde de Vaux* (Liverpool, 1910); and *Passages from the Letters of Auguste Comte*, selected and translated by John K. Ingram (London: Adam and Ch. Black, 1909; **A, G**).

The difficulty of obtaining Comte's work in English was overcome in the 1970s with the publication of Gertrud Lenzer's *Auguste Comte and Positivism; The*

Essential Writings (New York: Harper and Row, 1975; **G**). Not only has Lenzer presented important selections from Comte's major and lesser works from all periods of his literary production in this 500 page volume, but she has provided it with an extremely incisive introduction. In her opinion, Comte's ideas represented ''a major turning point'' in the developing struggle between socially conservative and socially critical modes of thought in Europe.

Recent French editions of Comte's work are generally available. See: *Ouvres d'Auguste Comte* (12 vols. Paris: Editions Anthropos, 1968-1971); and *Correspondance générale et confessions* (Paris and La Haye: Mouton, 1973-1982).

Museums, Historical Landmarks, and Societies

Centre de documentation et de recherche (Paris). Located in the apartment below the Comte Museum. Houses the largest collection of Comte's correspondence, his published works, letters exchanged between France and foreign positivists, and a large collection of works concerning Comte and positivism.

Les Amis de la Maison d'Auguste Comte (Paris). Supporters of the positivist legacy.

L'Association International. La Maison Auguste Comte (Paris). The organization that manages the museum and the documentation center located in it.

Musée Auguste Comte (10, rue Monsieur le Prince, Paris). The apartment where Comte lived from 1841 until his death in 1857, restored with its original furniture and library.

Rue Auguste Comte (Paris). This street, not far from Comte's apartment, simply carries the philosopher's name.

Other Sources

Cohen, David. ''Comte's Changing Sociology,'' *American Journal of Sociology*

71, 2 (September 1965): 168-177. Discusses the evolution of how Comte's thought has been apprehended.

Davis, Devra Lee. "Conceptualizations of Religion and Science and Some Writings of Immanuel Kant and Auguste Comte." Dissertation. Chicago: University of Chicago, 1972. Specialized study that focuses upon a central tension in Comte's work.

Lourau, René. "La question du sujet chez Auguste Comte." *L'Homme et la Société* 101 (1991). Claims that the question of the subject is an important theme in Comte's early work where the subjective method is inseparable from the objective method. However, Lourau maintains, Comte's disciples deformed his work by institutionalizing a myth of scientific objectivity in conformity with the social demands of the bourgeoisie following the repression of the Revolution of 1848 and the Commune of 1871.

Portis, Larry. "Scientific Conservatism: The Social Implications of French Positivism in Say, Cournot, and Durkheim." Thesis. Dekalb, IL: Northern Illinois University, 1970. Explains the historical development of positivism in terms of its "elasticity," its ability to adapt to changing political conditions.

Weinberg, Adelaide. *The Influence of Auguste Comte on the Economics of John Stuart Mill.* London: E. G. Weinberg, 1982. (A) A doctoral dissertation submitted to the London School of Economics in 1949 and published posthumously by the author's family. This work is focused so narrowly as to be of interest only to those studying the influence of Comte's ideas.

Larry Portis
American University of Paris

Ercole Consalvi
1757-1824

Chronology

Born Ercole Consalvi on June 8, 1757, in Rome, son of two members of the Roman aristocracy, Marquis Giuseppi Consalvi and Claudia dei Carandini; *1767-1776* studies at the seminary in Frascati but does not become a priest; *1776-1782* enters papal service and rises rapidly in the administration of the Papal State; *1796* appointed to organize defense against Napoleon's invading army; *1798* arrested and exiled by the French after their occupation of the Papal State; *1799-1800* as secretary of the conclave of Venice, arranges the compromise that breaks a long deadlock and leads to the election of Cardinal Chiaramonti as Pope Pius VII; *1800* appointed papal secretary of state and made a cardinal by Pius VII; *1800-1806* undertakes a reform program to modernize the Papal State but is stymied by opposition from conservative cardinals; *1800-1801* negotiates Concordat with Napoleon, which allows the revival of the Roman Catholic Church and papal authority in France; *1801-1805* initial good relations with France deteriorate because of Napoleon's demand that the papacy side with him in his war with England, asserting that the pope's religious duty is to remain neutral in wars between Christian states; *1806* forced to resign as secretary of state because of Napoleon's threats and pressure but retains great influence over Pius VII, who continues to refuse alliance with Napoleon; *1809* French arrest and imprison the pope and force Consalvi to leave Rome for Paris; *1810* refuses to attend Napoleon's wedding to Marie Louis of Austria because the emperor's marriage to his first wife, Josephine, is still valid in the eyes of the Church; arrested again; *1810-1813* imprisoned at Rheims; *1813* released; rejoins Pius VII and again becomes secretary of state; *1813-1815* carries out a diplomatic campaign to secure restoration of the Papal States at the peace settlement; *1814* visits London where his diplomatic skill and moderation win him the good will of the Allied leaders; works to secure emancipation of British Catholics and to align the papacy behind the drive to abolish the slave trade; *1814-1815* represents the papacy at the Congress of Vienna, securing the restoration of the Papal State; *1815-1823* seeks agreements to place church-state relations on a more modern basis that will give the church greater freedom from state control and allow its revival after the damaging attacks of the French Revolution; secures concordats with Bavaria (1817) and Naples (1818) and less formal agreements with other states but is unable to secure a concordat with the German Confederation or to loosen state control over the church in the Austrian Empire; resumes efforts to modernize the Papal State, introducing numerous reforms in the legal, financial, economic, and administrative fields and opening to laymen the civil administration posts formerly reserved for the clergy; fierce opposition from reactionary cardinals delays and weakens his foreign policy of cooperation with Austrian statesman Klemens Metternich, who supports the reform of the Papal State; *1820-1821* cooperates with Austrian suppression of the revolution at Naples; *1820-1823* opposes Metternich's plan to increase Austrian control over Italy as a means of preventing further revolutions, fearing that it will weaken Papal freedom of action, and takes the lead in defeating it; the death of Pius VII (1823) deprives him of his chief support; during the conclave that follows, tries to secure the election of a moderate pope, but instead the reactionary Leo XII is elected; *1824* dismissed; dies on January 24 at Anzio; buried in the Roman church of San Marcello.

Activities of Historical Significance

Ercole Consalvi took office at one of the darkest moments in modern papal history: Revolutionary France had occupied Rome, proclaimed the end of the Temporal Power, carried off Pope Pius VI to die in captivity, driven underground the Catholic Church in France and its conquered territories, and dealt heavy blows to papal spiritual authority that had already been undermined by the Enlightenment of the eighteenth century. Consalvi deserved much of the credit for the revival that began in reaction to this oppression. A pragmatic realist, he saw that only if the Papacy adapted to the new post-revolutionary world as far as its essential nature allowed could it hope to survive. His fundamental historical significance lies in his being the first to undertake the formulation of that transformation.

His first role of major importance came in 1799-1800 as Secretary of the Conclave held at Venice to elect a successor to Pius VI. He broke a long deadlock by arranging for the election of Pope Pius VII, whom he favored because of his known willingness to come to terms with the revolution at a time when most Catholic leaders were bitterly hostile to it. The new pope saw eye to eye with Consalvi on most questions, and throughout his reign gave him unwavering support in his efforts to modernize the Church. Immediately after his election, Pius VII appointed Consalvi Secretary of State, placing him in charge of both the religious and the political affairs of the Papacy.

In the religious field, his greatest achievement was the Concordat of 1801 with Napoleon. The Concordat was a break with the past by its very nature, for, by abandoning its sterile support for French monarchy, the Papacy came to terms with the new political order sprung from the revolution. It was also a break with the past in its provisions: the pope abandoned the traditional claim of Catholicism as the official state religion of France, accepted the principle of religious toleration, and recognized the loss of the church property confiscated during the revolution. In return, the Church once again became legal in France and public Catholic worship was allowed to resume. No longer handicapped by identification with the old regime nor subject to persecution by the state, the Church began to revive and gain renewed popular support.

The Concordat also laid the foundations for a great increase in effective Papal authority in France: Napoleon, distrusting the bishops nominated by the monarchy, insisted that the pope replace them all. The pope did so, an action without precedent that publicly established the supremacy of his authority over the French church. A similar concordat was signed with Napoleon's satellite kingdom of Italy in 1803.

Consalvi's willingness to adapt to the post-revolutionary world did not imply weakness where basic principles were concerned. This became apparent when Napoleon sought to force the Papacy to side with him in his ongoing war with England. In 1805, he demanded that the pope expel from the Papal State all citizens of states with which France was at war and close its ports to all English ships and commerce. The popes, however, had long since decided that as religious leaders it was their spiritual duty to remain neutral in wars between Christian states. As a result, Consalvi firmly rejected Napoleon's demands. The infuriated emperor forced his resignation in June, 1806, but Consalvi remained influential behind the scenes, and with his encouragement Pius VII continued to resist. Eventually, in 1809, Pius and Consalvi were arrested by Napoleon; but it was a price worth paying, for they had saved the Papacy from becoming a subservient tool of the emperor, preserving both its freedom from state control and its reputation for impartiality that was essential for it to perform its spiritual mission effectively.

In his own time, the achievement that won Consalvi the greatest admiration was his success in securing the restoration of the Papal States at the peace settlement after the Napoleonic wars. This was indeed the work of a diplomatic virtuoso, a success won against great odds, for most of the powers had their own plans for the Papal State. Thus it was only by skillfully maneuvering among these contending ambitions that Consalvi was able to emerge triumphant. Later, doubt was cast on the value of this diplomatic triumph, for the restored Papal State became a source of weakness and distraction for the Papacy. Papal rule, unprogressive and clerical, became bitterly unpopular, provoking revolutions in 1831 and 1848-1849 and undermining the Papacy's reputation in the eyes of world opinion. Consalvi, however, was not to blame for this outcome. Like most statesmen of his time, he believed that political independence was necessary for the Papacy to be able to carry out its spiritual mission without interference from secular powers. He had realized that the papal government needed public support if it was to survive, and he sought to win popular approval for the "Temporal Power" (the political authority of the Pope as ruler of the Papal State, as distinct from his religious authority as head of the Catholic Church) by modernizing it and making it responsive to the ideals of the post-revolutionary world. He made a start on reform during his first period in office, 1800-1806, but the opposition of conservatives among the Roman clergy and distraction by the struggle with Napoleon had prevented him from accomplishing much. On his return from the Congress of Vienna in 1815, he realized that reform was more urgent that ever. French rule in the Papal State had accustomed the people to efficient government and modern ideas; only if the restored papal government accepted and carried on this modernization could it hope to find the solid base of popular support that would allow it to survive.

Unfortunately, during Consalvi's absence at the Congress of Vienna, the *Zelanti* (zealots)—the reactionary party among the cardinals—had been in power at Rome, where they had swept away the innovations of the French in favor of a return to the old regime. The result was growing discontent among the people that threatened the survival of the Temporal Power. To avert that danger, Consalvi made an effort to reform the Papal State that was to occupy him for the rest of his career.

His ultimate goal was to create a modern state adapted to the needs and ideals of the post-revolutionary age; his immediate aims were an efficient administration, a financial system that would meet the needs of the state without unduly burdening the people or the economy, a legal system based on the revolutionary principles of rationality, equality, and humanitarianism, the abolition of feudal survivals, and the admission of laymen to most government posts, formerly a clerical monopoly.

His plans met with bitter opposition from the *Zelanti*, who considered any reform as a concession to the hated revolution. Their opposition prevented Consalvi from introducing all the reforms he had planned, and even the reforms he was able to introduce were often sabotaged in practice by the *Zelanti* who held many important government positions. Even so, his reforms helped modernize the papal regime and reconcile public opinion to it, as was demonstrated during the Italian revolutions of 1820-1821, when the Papal State remained quiet in contrast to most of the peninsula. Unfortunately, after the death of Pius VII, the *Zelanti* returned to power and abolished Consalvi's reforms in favor of a return to the old order. Discontent grew rapidly and public opinion turned to revolution as the only way to secure reform. The result was revolution in 1831 and 1848, and the final downfall of the Temporal Power in 1879—a result that Consalvi had foreseen and tried to avert with his reforms.

Consalvi had greater success in other fields during 1815-1823. In the religious field, he was able to work out concordats with Bavaria (1817) and Naples (1818), and less formal agreements with a number of other states, that continued the process of adapting Catholicism to the new conditions and paved the way for its renewal in the nineteenth century after a century of decline.

In the diplomatic field, the Austrian Empire, the leading Catholic state and the dominant power in Italy, was Consalvi's chief concern. During 1815-1820, he was able to make cooperation with Austria the basis of his foreign policy, for he and the Austrian Chancellor, Metternich, agreed that reform was the best hope of preventing the new revolutions they both dreaded. The revolutions of 1820, however, convinced Metternich that Austria must exert greater control over the Italian states to compel them to reform. Consalvi could not tolerate Austrian infringement upon Papal freedom of action, and he took the lead in defeating Metternich's plans at the Congress of Verona in 1822.

The death of Pius VII in August 1823 undermined Consalvi's position. In the election that followed, he led the moderate party among the cardinals, who wished to elect another moderate and open-minded pope like Pius VII. The Zelanti were too strong, however, and secured the election of a reactionary as Pope Leo XII, who dismissed Consalvi and revoked his reforms. This was the final blow for Consalvi, who had long been in bad health, and he died in January 1824.

Though his career ended in apparent defeat, he is today generally considered the greatest papal statesman of modern times. With diplomatic skill and realism he successfully guided the papacy through the dangers of the Napoleonic era. His willingness to make concessions where non-essentials were concerned allowed him to work out a concordat with Napoleon that gave up nothing vital for Rome, yet allowed the revival of the Catholic Church and papal authority in France; it became the model for such agreements for a century to come. Later, he demonstrated that flexibility did not mean weakness when he took the lead in rejecting Napoleon's efforts to dominate the Papacy and use it as a tool for his policies. In consequence, the prestige and independence of the Papacy stood higher at the time of Napoleon's fall than it had for two centuries. The achievement that most impressed his contemporaries was his success in regaining the Papal State at the Congress of Vienna. With hindsight, we can see that though this was a striking example of his diplomatic skill, it was transitory. His real greatness lay elsewhere—in his realization that the french Revolution had changed the world irrevocably, and that if the Papacy hoped to survive and flourish, it must adapt as far as its nature allowed to the post-revolutionary world. It was Consalvi who began that adaption; and if the short-sightedness of his opponents defeated his attempt to modernize the Papal State, thus sealing its doom, he was successful in the far more important religious field, where his policies and example laid the foundation on which the later revival of the Catholic Church was built.

Overview of Biographical Sources

Though a number of biographies of Consalvi have been written, none is fully satisfactory. Those written in the nineteenth and early twentieth centuries, such as Ernest Daudet, *Le Cardinal Consalvi* (Paris: Levy, 1866), or Engelbert Fischer, *Cardinal Consalvi* (Mainz: Herder, 1899), were superficial and uncritical, basically hagiographical in nature. Somewhat less unsatisfactory is Richard Winterich, *Sein Schicksal war Napoleon, leben und Zeit des Kardinalstaatsekretars E. Consalvi*

(Heidelberg, 1951), which is less hagiographical in tone, though still superficial, essentially a recital of events with little effort to explain their significance. The most recent biography, and the only one in English, is John Martin Robinson's *Cardinal Consalvi, 1757-1824* (1987). Stronger on narrative than analysis, based on limited sources, and stressing the dramatic aspects of his career rather than its deeper significance, this is not the definitive biography Consalvi deserves. Still, it is generally accurate in its facts, gives a good account of his career, and is written in a lively, anecdotal style; it is the best biography to date. Also worth mentioning is the entry for Consalvi in the *Dizionario Biografico degli Italiani* 28 (Rome, 1983: 33-34), a good short account of his life.

For a deeper understanding of Consalvi's achievements than is provided by his biographies, it is necessary to turn to the numerous studies on various aspects of his career. His key role in the conclave of 1800 is explained in Lajos Pasztor's "Ercole Consalvi prosegratario del conclave di Venezia," *Archivio della Societa Romana di Storia Patria* 83 (1960: 99-187). His struggle with Napoleon is thoroughly covered in Ilario Rinieri's *La Diplomazia Pontifici nel XIX secolo* (1901-1906), which despite its title covers only 1800-1815. His diplomacy at the peace settlement of 1813-1815 is the subject of Alessandro Roveri's *La Santa Sede tra Rivoluzione Francese e Restaurazione: Il Cardinale Consalvi, 1813-1815* (Florence: La Nuova Italia, 1975). The best guide to Consalvi's efforts to reform the Papal State are the works of Massimo Petrocchi: *La restaurazione, il Cardinale Consalvi, e la riforma del 1816* (1941), and *La Restaurazione romana* (1943).

Walter Maturi's *Il Concordato del 1818 tra la Santa Sede e le Due Sicilie* (Florence: Le Monnier, 1929) is valuable not only as a study of his concordat with Naples but for its insights into his religious policy as a whole. Consalvi's dealings with England are thoroughly examined in John Tracy Ellis, *Cardinal Consalvi and Anglo-Papal Relations* (1942). Consalvi's Austrian policy is studied in Alan J. Reinerman, *Austria and the Papacy in the Age of Metternich*. Vol. I: *Between Conflict and Cooperation, 1809-1830* (Washington, DC: Catholic University of America Press, 1979), which also gives insights into Consalvi's religious policy and his role at the Congress of Vienna.

Consalvi's failure to base his foreign policy on cooperation with Austria is explained in Alan J. Reinerman, "Metternich, Italy, and the Congress of Verona," *The Historical Journal* 15 (1971): 263-287. Joseph Brady, *Rome and the Neapolitan Revolution* (New York: Columbia University Press, 1937) examines Consalvi's skill in handling policy toward the Neapolitan revolution of 1820-1821, in light of the Papacy's position of being caught between the expansionist Neapolitan revolution to the south, and the Austrian determination to crush the revolution to the north. An overview of his policy toward the Greek Revolution of 1821 can be found in Alan J. Reinerman, ''Metternich, the Papacy, and the Greek Revolution,'' *East European Quarterly* 12 (1978): 177-188.

Evaluation of Principal Biographical Sources

Ellis, John Tracy. *Cardinal Consalvi and Anglo-Papal Relations.* Washington, DC: Catholic University Press, 1942. (**A, G**) This is a solid study of a relative minor aspect of Consalvi's diplomacy. The chief limitation of Ellis's work is its dependence on printed sources—his plan to work in the Roman and British archives was thwarted by the outbreak of World War II. This led him, for example, to exaggerate the degree of support which England gave Consalvi at the Congress of Vienna, which in reality, despite verbal assurances, was insignificant. Overall, however, this is a reliable study of its topic, which also gives perceptive insights into Consalvi's character and policies as a whole.

Petrocchi, Massimo. *La restaurazione, il Cardinale Consalvi, e la riforma del 1816.* Florence: Le Monnier, 1941. (**A**)

————. *La Restaurazione roman.* Florence: Le Monnier, 1943 (**A**) In these two important works, Petrocchi broke away from the traditional interpretation of this period, derived from nineteenth century liberal polemics against the Papacy, as a time of reaction and repression, to describe instead Consalvi's enlightened effort to reform the Papal State. His first volume focuses on 1816, when Consalvi laid down what he intended to be the foundation for a modernized and efficient government responsive to popular needs, which he correctly saw as the only way to prevent future revolutions. His second volume studies Consalvi's effort to carry his reforms to completion after 1816. His reforms met with fierce opposition from both ends of the political spectrum: from revolutionaries who wanted not reform but a revolution that would set up a republic, and from the reactionaries who were strong in the papal administration and who believed that reforms would be the first step towards the collapse of the papal regime. As a result, many of his reforms were rejected, while those passed into law were often ignored in practice by reactionary officials and were revoked by the next pope. The consequence, as Consalvi had feared, was growing popular discontent and the eventual downfall of the papal regime. Petrocchi's works, solidly based on research from the Vatican Archives, offer the best account of Consalvi's reforms.

Rinieri, Illario. *La Diplomazia Pontificia nel XIX secolo.* 5 vols. Rome: Civilta Cattolica, 1901-1906. (**A**) Despite its title, this work covers only the years 1800-1815; it has long been the standard work on the papal diplomacy of this period, and is still the most detailed and comprehensive. Based on intensive research in the Vatical Archives, it offers a clear account of Consalvi's diplomacy from the concordat with Napoleon to the end of the Congress of Vienna. It has, however, two weaknesses. First, it fails to consult the archives of other states, or, indeed, many sources of any type other than the Vatican Archives, which, invaluable though they are, do not in themselves tell the whole story. Second, Rinieri is determined to defend the Papacy against criticism; and though this attitude is understandable in view of the fiercely anti-papal tone of most Italian historians of his time, it often leads him to defend the Papacy where no defense is possible, e.g., the weaknesses of the papal regime, which Consalvi for one saw all too clearly. Nonetheless, this is still a valuable study, though it needs to be supplemented with later works.

Robinson, John Martin. *Cardinal Consalvi, 1757-1824.* New York: St. Martin's Press, 1987. (**A, G**) This is the most recent biography, and the only one in English. It gives a clear, readable narrative account of Consalvi's career from birth to death, including some description of his role in the artistic and scholarly fields which most historians have ignored. Unfortunately, its analysis of Consalvi's character, policies, and historical significance is superficial. Until a better biography is written, this is the best starting point for learning about the cardinal.

Overview and Evaluation of Primary Sources

Consalvi's official papers are in the Vatican Archives (Archivio Segreto Vaticano) in Rome, primarily in the Secretary of State collection. His private papers are in the Archives of the Congregazione de Propaganda Fide, also in Rome. Some collections of his papers have been published, but none have been translated into English. Particularly important are his memoirs, which he wrote while in exile at Rheims in 1812; they only cover his career up to that date, of course, and they were written when he did not have access to his official correspondence, so occasional errors crept in. Nevertheless, they give an excellent picture of his career up to 1812 and offer unrivaled insight into his mentality and character. They were first edited by J. Cretineau-Joly, *Mémoires du Cardinal Consalvi* (Paris: Plon, 1864), but the more recent edition, in the original Italian, by Mario Nasalli Rocca di Corneliano, *Memorie del cardinale Consalvi* (Rome: Signorelli, 1950), is more reliable.

Consalvi's correspondence with Rome during his mission at the Congress of Vienna has been published by Alessandro Roveri, *La missione Consalvi il Congresso di Vienna* (3 vols. Rome: Istituto Storico Italiano per l'Eta Moderna, 1970-1973). A selection of his correspondence with Metternich was published by Charles van Duerm, *Correspondance du Cardinal Hercule Consalvi avec le Prince Clement de Metternich* (Louvain: Polleunis and Ceuterick, 1899); it is of great value for understanding his foreign policy in general as well as his relationship with Metternich.

Museums, Historical Landmarks, Societies

Church of San Marcello (Corso, Rome). Consalvi's burial place is a marble tomb in the Roman church of San Marcello. As he wished, he was buried in the same tomb as his brother Andrea, who had died in 1807.

Monument (Pantheon, Rome). Consalvi's friends erected a monument to him in the Pantheon, his titular church. On the plinth is a relief showing him restoring the Papal States to Pius VII after the Congress of Vienna, and on the top is a bust of Consalvi by the noted Danish sculptor, Bertel Thorwaldsen.

Painting (Windsor Castle, Windsor, England). The best known painting of Consalvi was by Sir Thomas Lawrence which hangs today at Windsor Castle.

Other Sources

Chadwick, Owen. *The Popes and European Revolution.* New York: Oxford University Press, 1981. (**A, G**) A perceptive and stimulating synthesis by a leading historian of modern Christianity, this is a masterly account of the background against which Consalvi's career unfolded—the decline of the Papacy in the eighteenth century, and the beginning of its revival after 1800.

Hales, E. E. Y. *Revolution and Papacy.* Garden City, NY: Doubleday, 1960. (**A, G, Y**) A good short account of the same period as Chadwick's work, less detailed and scholarly, but readable; a good introduction to this period of papal history.

O'Dwyer, Margaret M. *The Papacy in the Age of Napoleon and the Restoration, Pius VII: 1800-1823.* Lanham, MD: University Press of America, 1985. (**A, G**) The most recent biography, and the best to date, of the pope with whom Consalvi worked so closely and about whom some knowledge is essential for an understanding of Consalvi's policies and achievements.

Alan J. Reinerman
Boston College

John Constable
1776-1837

Chronology

Born John Constable on June 11, 1776, in East Bergholt, Suffolk, England, the son of Golding Constable, a prosperous mill owner, and Ann Watts from a well-to-do London family; *1795* probably meets Sir George Beaumont, who encourages Constable's interest in art; *1796* meets the draughtsman and engraver J. T. ("Antiquity") Smith at Edmonton and draws cottages at his suggestion; *1798* meets Dr. John Fisher, later Bishop of Salisbury, who influences his art; *1799* arrives in London with a letter of introduction to Royal Academy member Joseph Farington and applies to the Royal Academy Schools; *1800* enrolls at the Royal Academy Schools, studying nude models and anatomical drawings; spends summer sketching in Lord Dysart's Helmingham Park; *1801* paints *Old Hall, East Bergholt* on commission for John Reade; tours the Peak District in Derbyshire; *1802* exhibits an unidentified landscape at the Royal Academy show; spends the summer at East Bergholt and buys a studio there; *1803* exhibits four landscapes at the Royal Academy; sails from London to Deal on the *Coutts*, a Dutch East India Company trading vessel, and draws numerous nautical scenes before returning to East Bergholt for the summer; *1804* paints the local farmers and their wives in East Bergholt; sees Flemish painter Peter Paul Rubens's *The Chateau de Steen* in the collection of the notable patron of art and literature Sir George Beaumont; *1805* enters another landscape at the Royal Academy; paints the altarpiece *Christ Blessing the Children* for Brantham Church; *1806* visits the Lake District in September and October, making studies of mountains and keeping records of the weather; *1807* copies portraits on commission; exhibits three Lake District scenes at the Royal Academy; *1808-1809* visits East Bergholt and returns in the fall of 1809; meets and falls in love with Maria Bicknell; *1810* paints the altarpiece *Christ Blessing the Bread and Wine* for Nayland Church in Suffolk; *1811* visits Salisbury and meets John Fisher, nephew of the bishop of Salisbury, who later becomes archdeacon, and who becomes a close friend; *1812* exhibits *Salisbury: Morning* at the Royal Academy; summers in Suffolk; *1813* exhibits two landscapes at the Royal Academy and spends much of the year in Suffolk; *1814* devotes time to outdoor sketching in Suffolk and Essex; *1815* exhibits five paintings and three drawings at the Royal Academy; mother dies and father becomes seriously ill; *1816* father dies; marries Maria Bicknell, with whom he has seven children; spends part of their honeymoon at Fisher's vicarage at Osmington, Dorsetshire; sketches Netley Abbey and the Weymouth Bay area; *1817* spends ten weeks at East Bergholt; exhibits four works at the Royal Academy; moves to Russell Square, London; *1819* rents a house in Hampstead; exhibits *The White Horse* at the Royal Academy and is elected Associate of the Royal Academy; *1820* visits John Fisher in Salisbury; settles his family at Hampstead; exhibits *Stratford Mill* at the Royal Academy; *1821* exhibits *The Hay Wain* at the Royal Academy; travels with Fisher in Berkshire and visits him again at Salisbury; *1822* exhibits *View on the Stour near Dedham* at the Royal Academy; meets French art dealer John Arrowsmith; *1823* exhibits *Salisbury Cathedral from the Bishop's Grounds* at the Royal Academy; spends August at Fisher's residence; stays in Leicestershire with Sir George Beaumont during October and November; *1824* exhibits *The Hay Wain, View on the Stour near Dedham*, and *View of Hampstead* at the Paris Salon; receives gold medal from King Charles X of France; visits his family in Brighton, where they are spending the summer; *1825* exhibits *The Leaping Horse* at the Royal Academy; exhibits *The White Horse* at Lille, France and receives a gold medal; *1826* exhibits *The Cornfield* at the Royal Academy; *1827* exhibits *Chain Pier, Brighton* at the Royal Academy; *1828* exhibits *Dedham Vale* and *Hampstead Heath* at the Royal Academy; wife dies at age forty from consumption; *1829* elected Royal Academician; exhibits *Hadleigh Castle* at the Royal Academy; twice visits the Fishers in Salisbury; with David Lucas, his young assistant, undertakes the mezzotint engravings that later become *English Landscape Scenery*; *1830* becomes member of the Royal Academy's Hanging Committee; publishes first two numbers of *English Landscape Scenery*; exhibits *Salisbury Cathedral from the Meadows* at the Royal Academy; publishes third and fourth numbers of *English Landscape Scenery*; *1832* exhibits eight works at the Royal Academy; publishes fifth number of *English Landscape Scenery*; long-time friend Archdeacon John Fisher dies on August 25; *1833* exhibits seven paintings at the Royal Academy; lectures on *Outline of the History of Landscape Painting* at Hampstead; *1834* visits Arundel and Petworth; *1835* visits Arundel and Worcester; *1836* exhibits *The Cenotaph* at the Royal Academy; gives four lectures under the title *History of*

Landscape Painting at the Royal Institution; lectures to the Literary and Scientific Society, Hampstead; *1837* dies on March 31 at home in bed of an apparent heart attack, and is buried at Hampstead Parish Church.

Activities of Historical Significance

Unlike many artists whose best work stemmed from personal lives filled with trauma and torpor, John Constable's life was a relatively placid one. He came from a comfortable family, settled on his vocation early, and exhibited at the Royal Academy for thirty-five years. He was well liked and enjoyed the friendship of cultivated people. The only tragedy in his life came when his wife of twelve years died of consumption in 1828. Together they had had seven children and this shattering of their happy family life affected his painting as no other event in his life did.

Constable's name endures for his outstanding contribution to the history of art. After almost a decade of apprenticeship work painting portraits and altarpieces, he discovered his calling in painting the pastoral scenes of his childhood. For the next twenty-five years he expressed his vision of English country life in canvases more powerful than those of any his predecessors. Constable painted his canvases directly form nature, giving them a freshness lacking in conventional classical depictions of landscape. What Constable did to shape attitudes toward nature had its literary counterpart in the great poems by his close contemporary, William Wordsworth. Among French painters, Théodore Géricault, in compositions like *Raft of the Medusa* and *The Village Forge,* probably owed much to Constable's example, as did another French Romantic artist, Eugène Delacroix, who studied Constable and other English landscape painters. The Barbizon school, a mid-nineteenth-century school of French landscape painters, reacted against the severe classical landscapes of their time and presented nature more directly in the style of Constable. French appreciation for his work preceded his full recognition in England, for it was not until 1829 that he was elected a Royal Academician.

One element of Constable's work that has been much praised by modern critics is the number of small oil sketches and drawings he produced in preparation for his large canvases. Although Constable apparently valued them mainly as means toward an end, these preliminary studies are now prized as considerable works in their own right.

Overview of Biographical Sources

Constable has been blessed with sympathetic and very able biographers. The earliest of note was C. R. Leslie's *Memoirs of the Life of John Constable Composed Chiefly from his Letters* (1843. Reprint. 1980), a work that remains invaluable. A fuller edition of the Constable-Leslie letters (for Leslie had heavily edited their correspondence) appeared in 1931, and is a good companion volume to Leslie's biography (see Primary Sources).

In 1965, one of the best modern studies of Constable's life and work appeared: Graham Reynolds's *Constable: The Natural Painter* (1965), a highly esteemed book that offers a good introduction to Constable. Reynolds, the pre-eminent Constable scholar, later published a number of exhibition catalogs and collections that include text on Constable's life as well as color illustrations. Among these are *Constable's England* (New York: Metropolitan Museum of Art, 1983), an exhibition catalog which focuses on his development; and the two-volume *The Later Paintings and Drawings of John Constable* (New Haven, CT: Yale University Press, 1984), which illustrates and evaluates Constable's later work.

Recent decades saw a flurry of new publications about Constable, in part thanks to a renewed interest brought about by new exhibitions of his work. At the crest of this new wave was Basil Taylor's *Constable: Paintings, Drawings, and Watercolours* (London: Phaidon, 1973), with a large selection of color illustrations and a biographical overview that reveals how the sad death of Constable's wife in 1828 affected his work. Soon to follow was Reg Gadney's *Constable and His World* (1976), a brief book which placed Constable's life in the context of his relationships with other artists and the art world in general. Two years later, there appeared a brief, heavily illustrated work that offers a good biographical overview: John Walker's *John Constable* (New York: Harry N. Abrams, 1978).

Other recent biographies include: Michael Rosenthal's *Constable, the Painter and his Landscape* (1983), which explores Constable's relationship with the land as a defining element in his painting; Ian Fleming-Williams and Leslie Parris's *The Discovery of Constable* (1984), which examines Constable's life and the changing landscape of his reputation after his death; and Malcolm Cormack's *Constable* (1986), a full-length biography and appraisal of Constable's artistic development.

Constable's life and work was examined in the context of other artists in James Heffernan's *The Recreation of Landscape: A Study of Wordsworth, Colderidge,*

Constable, and Turner (1985), a scholarly examination of Late Georgian poets and painters.

Evaluation of Principal Biographical Sources

Cormack, Malcolm. *Constable*. New York: Cambridge University Press, 1986. (**A, G**) This is an excellent study that blends an account of the life with fine commentary on the works. Includes copious, detailed notes and many plates.

Fleming-Williams, Ian, and Leslie Parris. *The Discovery of Constable*. New York: Holmes & Meier, 1984. (**A, G**) First examines Constable's life and artistic development, then focuses on the posthumous transformation of his reputation. Includes a series of fascinating appraisals of works by others (including those by forgers as well as pieces by his own son), that have been mistaken for Constable's work.

Gadney, Reg. *Constable and his World*. New York: Norton, 1976. (**G**) A basic, brief overview of Constable's life in the context of the art world. The lack of color illustrations is a drawback, but the text works well as an introduction to Constable's career.

Leslie, C. R. *Memoirs of the Life of John Constable Composed Chiefly of his Letters*. 1843. Reprint. Ithaca, NY: Cornell University Press, 1980. (**A, G**) This is one of several editions, including one by the Hon. Andrew Shirley in 1937 with 160 plates. It was composed mostly in Constable's own words; this edition was edited by Jonathan Mayne.

Peacock, Carlos. *John Constable: The Man and His Work*. London: John Baker, 1965. (**A, G**) Besides offering a set of plates and an essay entitled "Constable and the Sea," Peacock discusses "Constable and the Romantic Vision" and provides a useful forty-page introduction on Constable and his work.

Reynolds, Graham. *Constable: The Natural Painter*. 1965. Reprint. Chicago: Academy of Chicago, 1977. (**A, G**) The best of all modern works on Constable.

If one were to read only one reliable study on Constable's life and work, this would be the best choice.

Rosenthal, Michael. *Constable, the Painter and his Landscape*. New Haven, CT: Yale University Press, 1983. (**A, G**) A heavily illustrated biography that weaves together Constable's life and his relationship with the land into an invaluable portrait of the artist's world as it affected his work.

Overview and Evaluation of Primary Sources

The six-volume *John Constable's Correspondence*, edited by R. B. Beckett (Ipswich: Suffolk Records Society, 1962-1968; **A, G**), is a superb source of information about Constable's life and career. Also good is Beckett's *John Constable's Discourses* (Ipswich: Suffolk Records Society, 1970; **A, G**). The *Discourses* contains C. A. Leslie's notes from Constable's lectures on landscape painting, as well as Constable's contributions to the Constable-Lucas volume, *Various Subjects of Landscape Characteristic of English Scenery* (London: M. Constable, 1833; **A, G**).

Constable's *Letters to C. R. Leslie, 1826-1837*, edited by Peter Leslie (New York: R. R. Smith, 1931; **A, G**), is a revealing collection of the complete Constable-Leslie correspondence, from which Leslie drew his *Memoirs of the Life of John Constable Composed Chiefly of his Letters* (1843. Reprint, 1980). The letters, which had been heavily edited by C. R. Leslie for his biography, reveal a caustic man who is a harsh critic of other artists. The introduction by Sir Charles Holmes offers a good, brief biography of the painter and places the letters in the context of the times.

Leslie Parris, Conal Shields, and Ian Fleming-Williams edited *John Constable: Further Documents and Correspondence* for the Suffolk Records Society in 1975, making available eight volumes of letters and other important works.

Graham Reynolds's *Catalogue of the Constable Collection in the Victoria and Albert Museum* (London: H.M.S.O., 1960; **A, G**) describes and dates the largest and most comprehensive individual collection of Constable's works. All 597 items are reproduced in 310 black-and-white plates and one color plate.

Museums, Historical Landmarks, Societies

Art Institute (Chicago). Owns *Stoke-by-Nayland* (1830-1836); a similar view is depicted in the second number of *English Landscape Scenery.*

Lord Ashton of Hyde Collection (Moreton-in-Marsh, Gloucestershire). Its holdings include *Salisbury Cathedral from the Meadows* (1831), which was one of Constable's most controversial paintings because of its impressionistic qualities.

Cottesbrook Hall (Northamptonshire). Site of the Sir Reginald and Lady Macdonald-Buchanan Collection, which includes Constable's *Stratford Mill* (1820) (also sometimes known as *The Young Waltonians*).

Frick Collection (New York City). Owns *The White Horse* (1819), the first of his larger paintings, which was originally exhibited under the title *A Scene on the River Stour.*

Huntington Library and Art Gallery (San Marino, California). Owns *View on the Stour near Dedham* (1822). Constable himself called this painting *The Bridge*; it was exhibited along with *The Hay Wain* (1821) and one other work in Paris in 1824.

Lady Lever Art Gallery (Port Sunlight, Chester, England). Contains *Cottage at East Bergholt* (1835-1837).

Museum of Art (Philadelphia). Its holdings include *The Lock* (1824).

National Gallery (London). Holds *The Hay Wain* (1821), probably one of Constable's best-known works; *The Cornfield* (1826), which depicts the lane from East Bergholt toward Dedham, a path that Constable would have followed to school as a child; and *The Grove, Hampstead (The Admiral's House)* (1832), which may be the painting that was shown at the Royal Academy in 1832 under the title *A Romantic House at Hampstead.*

National Gallery of Art (Washington, DC). Contains *Wivenhoe Park, Essex* (1816).

National Gallery of Scotland (Edinburgh). Owns *Dedham Vale* (1828), which Constable considered one of his best landscapes.

Royal Academy of Arts (London). Contains *The Leaping Horse* (1825).

Tate Gallery (London). Owns *Malvern Hall, Warwickshire* (1809), a painting that depicts the residence of Henry Grewolde Lewis; *Flatford Mill on the River Stour* (1817), which includes the mill buildings that belonged to Constable's father, who was a corn merchant; *Chain Pier, Brighton* (1827) (also known as *The Marine Parade and Chain Pier, Brighton*, which was criticized for not depicting Constable's usual trees, streams, and other pastoral commonplaces); and *The Cenotaph at Coleorton* (1836), depicting the memorial to Sir Joshua Reynolds erected by Sir George Beaumont on his estate at Coleorton.

Victoria and Albert Museum (London). Its holdings include *Boat-building near Flatford Mill* (1815); *Dedham Lock and Mill* (1820), which also depicts Constable's father's mill; *Salisbury Cathedral from the Bishop's Grounds* (1823), which was painted on commission from Bishop John Fisher; and *Hampstead Heath: Branch Hill Pond* (1828), one of Constable's favorite topics.

The best historical landmarks of Constable's life are of course the settings that inspired his paintings, such as East Bergholt, Hampstead, Dedham Vale, and Salisbury.

Other Sources

Baskett, John. *Constable Oil Sketches.* New York: Watson-Guptill, 1966. Includes a brief but useful biographical sketch, a list of catalogues and exhibition material, and thirty-two full-page color plates with notes and commentary. The information is arranged very conveniently to make this a good guide to the oil sketches.

Clay, Beryl, and Noel Clay. "Constable's Visit to the Lakes." *Country Life* 83(1938): 393-395. An account of Constable's trip to the Lake District.

Constable, Freda. *John Constable: A Biography—1776-1837*. Lavenham, England: Terence Dalton, 1975. A short but readable life-and-works study with many accompanying plates, written by the wife of a descendent of John Constable.

Farington, Joseph, R. A. *The Farington Diary*. 8 vols. 1922-1928. Reprint. New Haven, CT: Yale University Press, 1978-1984. Edited by James Grieg, this volume contains the writings of this important personage at the Royal Academy; there are frequent references to Constable in the entries between 1793 and 1821.

Heffernan, James A. W. *The Re-Creation of Landscape: A Study of Wordsworth, Coleridge, Constable and Turner*. Hanover, NH: University Press of New England, 1985. Examines Constable in the context of other painters and poets of his time in whose work the natural world played a major role.

Holmes, Sir Charles J. *Constable and his Influence on Landscape Painting*. Westminster: A. Constable, 1902. Holmes provides the first full-length critical account of Constable's work, still reliable today.

Paulson, Ronald. *Literary Landscape: Turner and Constable*. New Haven, CT: Yale University Press, 1982. A specialized scholarly study. There is no separate bibliography, but the serious student of these painters would do well to comb through the copious notes.

Taylor, Basil. *Constable: Paintings, Drawings, and Watercolours*. London: Phaidon, 1973. An exceptionally useful work. Taylor provides a generous and graceful introduction, including a biographical overview that reveals how the death of Constable's wife in 1828 affected his work. This is followed by 177 plates, many in color, with informative notes describing the paintings.

Frank Day
Clemson University

Nicolaus Copernicus
1473-1543

Chronology

Born Nicolaus Copernicus on February 19, 1473, in Torún, Poland, the son of Nicolaus Copernicus, a merchant, and Barbara Waczenrode Copernicus; *1483* his father dies and his uncle Lucas Waczenrode supports the family; *1489* Waczenrode becomes bishop of Ermland; *1491* after attending school in Torún and the Cathedral School of Wloclawek, enrolls at the University of Cracow, where he studies astronomy; *1495* leaves Cracow without a degree to live in Frombork (Frauenburg) as canon, a post obtained for him by his uncle, which assures him a sinecure for life; *1496* moves to the University of Bologna to study law, because an advanced degree is expected of a canon; works at Bologna with a talented astronomer, Domenico Maria da Novara; *1498* his brother Andreas joins him to study canon law at Bologna; *1500* visits Rome and witnesses an eclipse of the moon; *1501* both brothers return to Ermland for their canonical installation ceremonies; attends the University of Padua where he studies medicine, learns Greek, and reads widely in ancient literature; *1503* takes doctor of Canon Law degree at the University of Ferrara; probably returns to live in the bishop's palace in Lidzbark (Heilsberg); *1507* receives an extra fifteen marks a year to tend to the health of his uncle, the Bishop; *c.1507* composes an outline of his heliocentric theory, *Nicolai Copernici de hypothesibus motuum coelestium a se constitutis commentariolus*; *1509* publishes in Cracow a Latin translation of the "Epistolae morales rurales et amatoriae," written in Greek by the Byzantine poet Theophilactos of Simocatta; *1510* leaves the bishop's castle and takes up canon's life in Frombork, being elected chancellor of the Varmia chapter; *1512* his uncle dies; his brother Andreas, disfigured by leprosy, is forced to leave the canon and goes abroad to die; *1516-1521* stays at the chapter's castle in Olsztyn (Allenstein) and plays an important role in the defense of the castle against the Teutonic Knights; *1522* writes a treatise on monetary reform for the Prussian Diet, arguing for a union of the many states coining their own money; *1524* writes *De octava sphaera, contra Wernerum*, a refutation of Johannes Werner's *On the Motion of the Eighth Sphere* (1522); *1530-*

1532 composes his great work, *On the Revolutions of the Heavenly Spheres, Six Books*; *1538* harassed by Johannes Dantiscus, the bishop of Ermland, for the presence in his home of his young housekeeper, Anna Schillings, which leads to her dismissal; *1539* a young Wittenberg professor, George Joachim de Porris, known as Rheticus, arrives in Frombork and urges the publication of *On the Revolutions of the Heavenly Spheres, Six Books*; Rheticus brings with him the Greek edition of Ptolemy published in Basel in 1538, and *De triangulis omnimodis* on geometry by Regiomontanus (Nuremberg, 1533), two works that facilitate revisions of *On the Revolutions of the Heavenly Spheres, Six Books*; little is known about Copernicus's life after this point; *1540* Rheticus publishes in Gdansk a "First Account," or summary, of *On the Revolutions of the Heavenly Spheres, Six Books*; *1542* Rheticus arrives in Nuremberg and the Petreius Press begins printing *On The Revolutions of the Heavenly Spheres, Six Books*; Lutheran theologian Andreas Osiander intervenes and forges a preface maintaining that *On the Revolution of the Heavenly Spheres* is merely a hypothesis, removes the introduction to book one, and edits the title to read *De revolutionibus orbium coelestium* (On the Revolutions of the Heavenly Spheres); not until the original manuscripts turn up in the nineteenth century is Osiander's authorship confirmed; *1543* his manuscript is published in March as *Nicolai Copernici Thoruniensis de revolutionibus orbium coelestium libri VI*; dies in Frombork on May 24 after a series of small strokes over the last years of his life; buried in cathedral at Frombork.

Activities of Historical Significance

To understand the importance of Copernicus's contribution to science, one must first understand the history of geocentric (Earth-centered) beliefs and the climate in which his discoveries were made. Long before Copernicus's time, common sense observation told Aristotle that the Earth was at the center of the universe, and he believed in a universe made up of spheres within spheres. Moving outward from the Earth (the central sphere), were spheres of water, air, and fire, followed by the Moon, Mercury, Venus, the Sun, Mars, Jupiter, and Saturn, and finally a sphere made up of the fixed stars. Beyond this outermost sphere was the Unmoved Mover that governs everything.

For Christians, the Unmoved Mover was clearly God, and in the Middle Ages they easily assimilated Aristotle's spheres into Christian theology by adding a Heaven just outside the sphere of fixed stars and placing Hell at the center of the Earth. Reason demanded that all of these spheres moved in perfect circles at constant speed.

Close observation, however, indicated that these speeds were not uniform, and heavenly distances were not constant. Ptolemy, an Egyptian astronomer of the second century, A.D., worked out a complicated system to account for perceived eccentricities in these movements. Ptolemy found that planets do not move around a circle that has the Earth at the center, but rather, around a point some distance from the Earth—and that the path that the planet follows, called its "deferent", is thus an eccentric circle. But Ptolemy's system still had the Earth playing a central role in planetary movement, defining when planets were either at their perigee (at the point nearest the Earth) or their apogee (at the point farthest from the Earth).

Copernicus simplified Ptolemy's theories considerably with his theory that all planets, including the Earth, moved in an orbit around the Sun. This heliocentric (Sun-centered) theory, in which the Earth itself behaved just like any other planet, was considered highly controversial because it took away the Earth's central role in the universe, and therefore possibly altered the placement of Heaven (and the Unmoved Mover, or God), in the universe.

Copernicus revealed his theories in the *Commentariolus* (Little Commentary), in which he furnished an outline for his calculations. At first, the work circulated only among his friends, in manuscript form. Then the German scholar Rheticus arrived from Wittenberg in 1539 to study Copernicus's work, and in 1540 Rheticus published *Narratio Prima* (First Account) to introduce Coppernicus's main ideas.

In 1542 Rheticus also published the chapters on trigonemetry that later became the last part of *On the Revolutions of the Heavenly Spheres*. This work, published just before Copernicus's death (the publication of which he was probably unaware), included a forged preface written by the Protestant Osiander, who had taken over when Rheticus had to leave Frombork. The preface, "To the Reader on the Hypotheses of This Work," exonerated Copernicus's theory as a simple mathematical strategy to facilitate calculations of the motions of the heavenly bodies. Its intent was to forestall theological disputes by explaining that the theory was never meant to represent reality. It was not until the nineteenth century that this preface—which almost surely did not represent Copernicus's intentions—was identified as having been written by Osiander.

The Copernican Revolution is pretty much summed up in the seven axioms laid down in the *Commentariolus*:

1. The heavenly bodies do not all move around the same center;
2. The Earth is the center of the Moon's orbit only and not of the whole universe;
3. The Sun, not the Earth, is the real center of the universe;
4. The Earth is comparatively close to the Sun compared to the distance of the fixed stars;
5. It is the Earth's rotation on its own axis that makes it seem that the whole universe is revolving daily;
6. The seeming annual motion of the Sun is the really attributable to the Earth's revolving around the Sun;
7. The so-called "stations and retrogressions" of the planets are also explained by the Earth's revolutions around the Sun.

Ironically, nowhere in his work does Copernicus indicate he rejects Aristotle's vision of heavenly spheres nesting one within another. Yet it was for just such alleged blasphemy that Copernicus's work was at first rejected by many theologians.

Copernicus used both his own and Ptolemy's figures in establishing the positions at different times of the heavenly bodies. The calculations revolved around three steps: Arriving at a mean or regular motion based on a body's completing a regular circle at a uniform speed; measuring a so-called irregular motion derived from observed circles; and then producing the apparent or true motion by comparing tables of regular motions with tables of irregular motions. This method is much like Ptolemy's and reveals the fundamental conservatism of Copernicus's methodology. In his use of mathematics to analyze bodies of empirical data, however, Copernicus stands at the threshold of modern approaches to understanding the natural world.

It is probably a mistake to interpret Copernicus's reluctance to publish his controversial findings as a fear of religious backlash by the Catholic Church, which held firm to its belief in the geocentric universe. Indeed, his theory had been pretty well circulated and he had been supported by several clergymen. It is more likely that he feared the ridicule of the public, and possibly of his peers;

thus, when Copernicus wrote the pope that he was concerned about being laughed at, he was almost certainly telling the truth.

Whatever the case, the theory was not immediately accepted by most thinkers. In 1551, Erasmus Reinhold of Prussia published some new astronomical tables based on Copernicus's tables; but Copernicus's work did not achieve a sure footing until another genius, Johann Kepler (1571-1630), used the precise measurements of Tycho Brahe (1546-1601) to demonstrate that the planets moved in ellipses with the Sun at the focus. Kepler's contribution, along with the support earned by Galileo (1564-1642) in his observations through the telescope, sealed the fate of Aristotle's spheres and Ptolemy's epicycles. The modern world was left to adjust to a Copernican universe in which man and his Earth played a much less central part than had previously been believed.

Overview of Biographical Sources

Perhaps because little is known about Copernicus's life after he wrote the *Commentariolus*, and because much of the promotion of his theories was left to his disciples, little biographical material appeared about him until this century. The earliest major work, still considered the definitive scholarly study, is Leopold Prowe's *Nicolaus Coppernicus* (1883-1884. Reprint. 1967). Prowe's work is in German, as is E. Zinner's *Entstehung und Ausbreitung der Coppernicanischen Lehre* (1943. Reprint. Munich: C. H. Beck, 1988). Scholarly works in Polish include L. A. Birkenmajer's *Mikolaj Kopernik* (Krakow: Nakladem Polskiej akademenji umiejetnosci, 1900) and *Stromata Copernicana* (Berlin: n.p., 1924).

Among English language works, Angus Armitage published two short books on Copernicus's life and work that are readable and informative: *Copernicus, the Founder of Modern Astronomy* (1931), and *Sun, Stand Thou Still* (1947), which offer both biographical and scientific background on Copernicus and his times. Hermann Kesten's *Copernicus and His World* (1945) is useful, if somewhat overblown in its style. And Arthur Koestler provides a readable account of Copernicus and his accomplishments in "The Timid Canon," in *The Sleepwalkers: A History of Man's Changing Vision of the Universe* (1959).

In 1975, the Smithsonian Institution published *The Nature of Discovery: A Symposium Commemorating the 500th Anniversary of the Birth of Nicolaus Coper-*

nicus, a lively collection of essays and discussions—many of them incorporating some level of biography—delivered by scholars at the symposium. This work helps place Copernicus in a broader context, showing how his theories affected the science of the times and that of the future. Another work which places Copernicus's in a broader perspective is Hans Blumenberg's *The Genesis of the Copernican World* (1974), which includes biographical information but focuses on the larger society and science of the times. Another work that approaches Copernicus from the larger viewpoint of how he changed the world of science are Thomas S. Kuhn's *Copernican Revolution: Planetary Astronomy in the Development of Western Thought* (1957). Michal Rusinek's *The Land of Nicholas Copernicus* (1973) is a photographic look at the people and places of Copernicus's time.

Edward Rosen's entry on Copernicus in volume three of the *Dictionary of Scientific Biography* (1971) is a good place to begin reading about Copernicus. There are also two worthwhile introductory books for young adult readers: David C. Knight's *Copernicus: Titan of Modern Science* (1965), and Henry Thomas's *Copernicus* (1960), both of which offer readable overviews for beginning students.

Evaluation of Principal Biographical Sources

Adamczewski, Jan, with Edward J. Piszek. *Nicolaus Copernicus and His Epoch*. Philadelphia and Washington: Copernicus Society of America, 1973. (**A, G**) Excellent both for its readable and informative text and for the wealth of photographs and other illustrations pertaining to Copernicus's life and travels. Provides insight into how Copernicus was shaped by his times, and how he in turn helped shape the future.

Armitage, Angus. *Copernicus, the Founder of Modern Astronomy*. London: Allen and Unwin, 1938. (**A, G**) More for astronomers than for the general reader, this biography is heavy on science. It opens with an introduction to pre-Copernican astronomy, which is helpful in placing Copernicus in the context of those who came before him. An interesting and useful scientific portrait.

—————. *Sun, Stand Thou Still*. New York: Henry Schuman, 1947. (**A, G**) Reprinted as *The World of Copernicus* in 1951. A readable and reliable publication by a British scholar, this work relates Copernicus's life to the changes he wrought with his heliocentric theory.

Kesten, Hermann. *Copernicus and His World*. New York: Roy Publishers, 1945. (**A, G**) A popular study, this is considered one of the most readable the Copernicus biographies. Kesten, a novelist, employs a broad style that makes the work palatable to those who prefer fiction to non-fiction. The final quarter of the volume is dedicated to "The Slow Triumph" of Copernicus's vision, and it discusses how the work of Giordano Bruno, Kepler, and Galileo helped legitimize Copernicus's theories.

Knight, David C. *Copernicus: Titan of Modern Science*. New York: Franklin Watts, 1965. (**Y**) A good introduction for young adult readers, designed for grades seven through ten. Part of the "Immortals of Science" series.

Koestler, Arthur. *The Sleepwalkers: A History of Man's Changing Vision of the Universe*. New York: Macmillan, 1959. (**A, G**) Koestler theorizes that scientists' greatest discoveries occur by accident. Exceptionally vivid and highly recommended, this work helps one understand why Copernicus may have not recognized the importance of his own great discovery, and his reluctance to promote it.

Prowe, Leopold. *Nicolaus Coppernicus*. 2 vols. 1883-1884. Reprint. Osnabrück, Germany: Zeller, 1967). (**A**) The standard biography, in German. Volume one is devoted to biography, and volume two reprints pertinent documents of the period. Still considered by scholars to be the pre-eminent work on Copernicus, despite the fact that it remains unfinished (a planned third volume never appeared), that it is somewhat out of date, and that its tone is one of fervent nationalism.

Rosen, Edward. *Copernicus and the Scientific Revolution*. Malabar, FL: Krieger, 1984. (**A, G**) An excellent, detailed account of biographical facts and controversies, told in clear but authoritative prose with attention to background issues. Contains valuable notes and bibliography. Probably the best of the modern biographies.

Rusinek, Michal. *Land of Nicholas Copernicus*. Translated by A. T. Jordan.

New York: Twayne and the Kosciuszko Foundation, 1973. (**A, G**) Although the text is brief, this volume includes 173 pages of excellent photographs by Magdalena Rusinek-Kwilecka, and a biographical sketch.

Thomas, Henry. *Copernicus*. New York: Julian Messner, 1960. (**Y**) A useful introduction to Copernicus and his science, designed for a younger audience.

Overview and Evaluation of Primary Sources

There are three English translations of *On the Revolutions of the Heavenly Spheres*: C. G. Wallis, trans., *Great Books of the Western World*, vol. 16 (Chicago: Encyclopedia Britannica, 1952; **A, G**); Edward Rosen, trans., *Nicolaus Copernicus Complete Works*, vol. 2 (London: Oxford University Press, 1974; **A, G**); and *On the Revolutions of the Heavenly Spheres* (New York: Barnes and Noble, 1976; **A, G**), a translation from the Latin, with an introduction and notes by A. M. Duncan. The latter is the most readily available edition, with a good introduction that includes a succinct biographical sketch.

Rosen's *Three Copernican Treatises* (New York: Columbia University Press, 1971; **A, G**) includes English translations of the *Commentariolus,* the *Letter against Werner,* and Rheticus's *Narratio Prima.* Rosen also provides a bibliography of articles about Copernicus, published between 1939 and 1970, and a useful biography.

The best available translation, along with an insightful analysis, of the *Commentariolus*, is Noel M. Swerdlow's "A Translation of the *Commentariolus* with Commentary" in *Proceedings of the American Philosophical Society* 117, 6 (1973): 423-512.

A facsimile of the original manuscript of *On the Revolutions* is provided in volume one of Rosen's edition of *Nicholas Copernicus Complete Works*. The manuscript itself is in the library of Jagiellonian University in Cracow.

Fiction and Adaptations

John Banville's novel *Doctor Copernicus* (1976), is an excellent work that dramatizes Copernicus's struggle vividly. The account of his death is especially memorable and moving.

Museums, Historical Landmarks, Societies

Copernicus Society of America (Philadelphia and Washington).

Monument (Warsaw). Unveiled in 1830, it stands in front of the Palace Staszica.

Monument (Cracow). Erected in 1900 in the library courtyard of the University of Cracow.

Other Sources

Beer, Arthur, and Kaj A. Strand, eds. *Vistas in Astronomy*. Vol. 17. London: Pergamon, 1974. Fifteen papers given at a Copernicus conference in Washington, D.C., in 1972.

Bienkowska, Barbara, ed. *The Scientific World of Copernicus*. Boston: D. Reidel, 1973. Eleven entries collected on the five-hundredth anniversary of Copernicus's birth. The ''Selected Copernican Bibliography'' by Jerzy Dobrzycki is useful, as is Bienkowska's ''Name and Geographical Index.''

Blumenberg, Hans. *The Genesis of the Copernican World*. Boston: MIT Press, 1987. Translated by Robert M. Wallace. Traces the evolution of the Copernican Revolution and the society in which it occurred.

Boorstin, Daniel. *The Discoverers*. New York: Random House, 1983. Boorstin gives a succinct account of Copernicus's ideas, stressing the influence on his thought of the Pythagorean number, mystics, and the medieval Neoplatonists.

Czartoryski, Pawel, ed. *Nicholas Copernicus' Complete Works: Minor Works*. Baltimore, MD: Johns Hopkins University Press, 1992. Translated and commentary by Edward Rosen with Erna Hilfstein.

Dobrzycki, Jerzy, ed. *The Reception of Copernicus's Heliocentric Theory. Proceedings of a Symposium Organized by the Nicolaus Copernicus Committee of the International Union of the History and Philosophy of Science.* Boston: D. Reidel, 1973. Eleven scholarly papers presented at a conference in Torún, Poland.

————., ed. *Nicholas Copernicus' Complete Works: On the Revolutions.* Translated and commentary by Edward Rosen. Baltimore, MD: Johns Hopkins University Press, 1992.

Drake, Stillman. *Copernicus. Philosophy and Science. Bruno-Kepler-Galileo.* Norwalk, CT: Burndy Library, 1973. An essay originally presented at the Smithsonian Institution.

Gingerich, Owen, ed. *The Nature of Scientific Discovery.* Washington, DC: Smithsonian Institution, 1975. A stimulating collection of the proceedings of a four-day symposium sponsored by the Smithsonian Institution and the National Academy of Sciences.

Hoyle, Fred. *Nicolaus Copernicus. An Essay on His Life and Work.* London: Heinemann, 1973. An astronomer's introduction, complete with mathematical formulas.

Koyré, Alexandre. *The Astronomical Revolution: Copernicus-Kepler-Borelli.* Translated by R. E. W. Maddison. Ithaca, NY: Cornell University Press, 1973. Includes a treatment entitled "Copernicus and the Cosmic Overthrow."

Kuhn, Thomas. *The Copernican Revolution. Planetary Astronomy in the Development of Western Thought.* Cambridge, MA: Harvard University Press, 1957. Besides offering an excellent study of the topic, Kuhn provides a valuable collection of "Bibliographical Notes."

Mekarski, Stefan. *Nicholas Copernicus (Mikolaj Kopernik) 1473-1543.* 1943. Reprint. Translated by B. W. A. Massey. London: Polish Cultural Foundation,

1973. Includes sixteen plates and a sixty-page survey of Copernicus's life and work.

Mizwa, Stefan P., ed. *Nicholas Copernicus: A Tribute of Nations*. New York: Kosciuszko Foundation, 1945. A tribute occasioned by the Copernican quadricentennial in 1943.

Royal Society of Canada. *On a Disquieting Earth. 500 Years after Copernicus*. Ottawa: Royal Society of Canada, 1974. Proceedings from the "Copernicus Celebration" at Ottawa on November 28, 1973.

Westman, Robert S., ed. *The Copernican Achievement*. Berkeley and Los Angeles: University of California Press, 1975. Nine essays from a 1973 conference at UCLA.

Frank Day
Clemson University

Marie Curie
1867-1934

Chronology

Born Marya Sklodowska on November 7, 1867, in Warsaw, Poland, the fifth and youngest child of Bronislawa Bojuska Sklodowska, the principal of a small girls' boarding school, and Wladyslaw Sklodowska, a physics teacher; *1876* becomes profoundly depressed after the death of her mother; *1883* wins gold medal upon graduation from the imperial gymnasium; exhausted by her studies, spends a year with relatives in the country; unable to enter the University of Warsaw which does not accept women, joins a "floating university" where the emphasis is on underground political movements and reform; *1885-1890* a lack of other opportunities forces her to take posts as a governess; *1891* leaves Poland for Paris, enrolls in the Faculty of Science at the Sorbonne, and adopts the French version of her name; *1893* places first in the master's examination in physics; *1894* places second in the master's examination in mathematics; *1895* marries Pierre Curie, with whom she has two children; *1897* completes work on magnetization and begins work on her doctoral dissertation on the nature of the radiation of uranium; *1898* discovers evidence of a powerful new radioactive element in pitchblende ores and begins collaboration with her husband to characterize and isolate the new element; further work reveals the presence of the new radioactive elements polonium and radium; *1900* appointed lecturer in physics at the Girls' Normal School in Sèvres; *1902* purifies radium and calculates its atomic weight as 225; *1903* completes doctoral thesis, "Researches on Radioactive Substances"; shares the Nobel Prize in physics with her husband and Henri Becquerel; *1906* upon her husband's sudden death, takes his place at the Sorbonne, becoming the first woman to hold such a position; continues research on radioactivity; *1910* publishes *Treatise on Radioactivity* and with André Debierne isolates pure radium in the metallic state; provides the Paris Bureau of Weights and Measures with twenty-two milligrams of pure radium chloride which serves as the international radium standard; *1911* receives the Nobel Prize in chemistry, becoming the first person to win two Nobel Prizes; *1914* becomes head of the Radium Institute in

Paris and first director of the French radiology service; assists the French war effort by developing mobile X-ray units and a radiological school for nurses; *1920* tells Marie Mattingly Meloney, an American journalist, that her greatest desire is a gram of radium; tours the United States after Meloney successfully raises money from American women; receives a gift of the radium from President Warren G. Harding; travels to Brazil, Spain, and other countries; *1922* becomes a member of the Academy of Medicine; *1925* returns to Warsaw to lay the cornerstone of the Radium Institute; *1925* makes a second tour of the United States; *1934* dies on July 4, in a sanatorium at Sancellemoz, Savoy, France, of pernicious anemia caused by radium poisoning, and is buried at Sceaux next to her husband.

Activities of Historical Significance

Marie Curie and her husband Pierre were the first to discover and isolate polonium and radium and recognize the nature of radioactivity. After developing her research skills through a study of the magnetic properties of tempered steel, she decided to base her doctoral research on Henri Becquerel's 1896 discovery of the mysterious penetrating radiation emitted by uranium. In an abandoned store-room at the School of Physics and Chemistry, she measured the conducting power of the rays from uranium compounds using an electrometer invented by Pierre and his brother Jacques Curie. She discovered that the intensity of the rays depended only on the amount of uranium present, not on temperature, pressure, or other environmental conditions. This observation is considered her most important contribution to science, although her advances with radium brought popular fame. Her discovery indicating that radiation energy was intrinsic to the atom itself was fundamental to further investigations of atomic structure.

Extending her investigation to a multitude of chemical elements, Curie found that thorium also emitted this form of radiation. Studying various mineral samples, she found that pitchblende was apparently more active than its uranium or thorium content would indicate, suggesting that the mineral contained a new radioactive element. Curie's preliminary note to the Academy of Sciences on April 12, 1898, reported the strong possibility that a new radioactive element was present in pitchblende ores, but in very minute quantities. This fruitful prediction was her original and independent idea; although the Curies collaborated closely and harmoniously, she was always careful to assert ownership of her ideas and work. She apparently knew that people would find it difficult to believe that a woman had done original work in physics and that they would try to ascribe her ideas to others.

As a result of years of intensive, collaborative work, the Curies discovered polonium in July 1898 and radium in December 1898. In a paper announcing the discovery of polonium, Curie first used the word "radioactivity" to describe the phenomenon that Silvanus Thompson had called "hyperphorescence." Laboriously processing tons of pitchblende ores under extremely primitive conditions, Curie finally obtained a minute amount of pure radium and made several increasingly accurate determinations of its atomic weight. In June 1903 she defended her doctoral dissertation before a distinguished panel of judges and was awarded a doctorate. In the same year the Curies shared the Nobel Prize in physics with Henri Becquerel, but they were too ill to attend the awards ceremonies in Stockholm. When Pierre Curie finally fulfilled the obligation to present the Nobel Prize lecture in Stockholm in 1905, she sat in the audience.

On April 19, 1906, while attempting to cross a busy intersection, Pierre Curie fell under a large horse-drawn cart and was killed. Only thirty-eight years old, Curie was left alone to continue their work and raise their two daughters. Within a month she was once again throwing herself into her work and the Faculty of Science offered her the professorship that had been created for her husband. Curie was the first woman in France to achieve professorial rank.

In 1911 Curie received the Nobel Prize in chemistry for her work in isolating pure radium and determining its atomic weight; she was the first person to receive a second Nobel Prize. Her research from this point can be seen as consolidating and improving previous work: she established the half-life of actinium; measured the range of alpha-particles from polonium; and extended work that supported her original observation that rates of radioactive decay were intrinsic to the atom and independent of external factors.

In 1912 she was named head of the Curie Institute of Radium. With the outbreak of World War I, her appointment as head of the radioactivity laboratory of the new Radium Institute in Paris was overshadowed by her work as first director of the radiology service established to assist the French war effort. She pioneered the deployment of mobile X-ray units, set up radiological services for hospitals, and established a radiological school for nurses. Accompanied by her daughter

Irene, she operated one of the radiological stations, often driving into war zones. The mobile units and hospital radiological services provided examinations for over one million wounded men. When the war ended, she resumed her research and devoted her energies to making the new Curie Laboratory one of the world's leading research institutes.

After World War I, Curie traveled widely and was awarded many honors by universities, civic institutions, and learned societies. Unfortunately, her last years were marked by long periods of illness and diminishing powers of recuperation. She finally succumbed to pernicious anemia, presumably the result of her work with radioactive materials. Although scientists had begun to take interest in the physiological action of radium rays by about 1903, few people, including Curie herself, worried about the effects of radioactivity on health. Tubes of radium preparations that she kept in a pocket produced irritating burns and a closed box containing radium salts produced the sensation of light on the retina when the eyelid was closed. Her fingers were chronically sore and cracked, apparently from handling purified radioactive substances. In later life, Curie was plagued by many illnesses, including failing eyesight due to cataracts in both eyes.

Throughout her life, her ideals remained those of the nineteenth century and her belief in "disinterested" pure science was part of the scientific age of innocence. Although the Curies struggled with poverty for most of their lives, she refused to take out patents for her methods of preparing radium. She believed that making money from practical applications of science was vulgar and that only pure science was significant. Her research was the starting point for fundamental insights into the nature of radioactivity and the atom.

Overview of Biographical Sources

In his examination of the use of female "role models" to interest girls in science, Stephen G. Brush, warns of the "Madame Curie Syndrome" in which woman's scientific work is portrayed as tedious. Popular science books and biographies typically portray her work as the very worst sort of drudgery which ultimately led to her death from radiation disease. Most biographies of Curie written for young readers and general audiences tend to follow this pattern and fail to elucidate the importance of her theoretical concepts, presumably because it is easier to depict the tedious chemical work than to explain theoretical physics. On the other hand, most of these biographies are extremely favorable in evaluating Curie's character, personality, and devotion to her family.

Madame Curie (1938), the comprehensive biography by her daughter Eve Curie, remains immensely popular and has served as a source of inspiration for many young women considering a career in science. Most of the short biographies written for young readers are based on this portrait. For an account of the "scandal" involving Curie's relationship with fellow scientist Paul Langevin, readers should consult more recent biographies, such as Robert William Reid's *Madame Curie* (1974) and Françoise Giroud's *Madame Curie. A Life* (1974). Taken together, these biographies provide a fairly complete account of Curie's life and work. The most recent biography of Curie is Rosalynd Pfaum's *Grand Obsession: Madame Curie and Her World* (1989). Eileen Bigland's *Madame Curie* (1957) provides an assessment of Curie's work that is appropriate for younger readers.

Evaluation of Principal Biographical Sources

Curie, Eve. *Madame Curie. A Biography*. Translated by Vincent Sheean. 1938. Reprint. New York: Da Capo Press, 1986. (**G**) Comprehensive, well-illustrated, intimate biography by Curie's younger daughter. Although it lacks scholarly apparatus, it is based on extensive research, documentary evidence, and personal knowledge. An appendix lists Curie's prizes, medals, and honorary titles.

Giroud, Françoise. *Madame Cure, A Life*. Translated by Lydia Davis. New York: Holmes and Meier, 1986. (**G**) Originally published in French as *Une femme honorable* (1981), this book lacks a table of contents, index, bibliography, and notes.

Pfaum, Rosalynd. *Grand Obsession: Madame Curie and Her World*. New York: Doubleday, 1989. (**G**) This is a very readable account of Marie Curie, her family, her work, and her social and intellectual milieu. In addition to providing a comprehensive biography of the Curie family, the book adequately covers a good deal of science. The book provides a selected bibliography and notes. Much of the material is based on the author's personal interviews of relatives, friends, and colleagues of the Curies and the Joliot-Curies.

Reid, Robert William. *Madame Curie*. New York: Saturday Review Press, 1974. (**A, G**) This well-researched biography provides notes and a selected bibliography. Analysis of the Paul Langevin scandal is a major focus of the book. Some questions left open by Reid's biography are discussed in a review by Lawrence Badash, "Decay of a radioactive halo," in *Isis* 66 (1974: 566-568); see also the reply by Reid in *Isis* 67 (1976: 103-104).

Evaluations of Biographies for Young People

Bigland, Eileen. *Madame Curie*. New York: Criterion Books, 1957. Written in a simple narrative style, this is a valuable account of Curie's life and work which does not insult the intelligence of young readers. The book is suitable for grades six to twelve.

Birch, Beverly. *Marie Curie: The Polish Scientist Who Discovered Radium and Its Life-Saving Properties*. Milwaukee, WI: Gareth Stevens, 1988. This entry in the People Who have Helped the World series is suitable for grades five to six.

Brandt, Keith. *Marie Curie: Brave Scientist*. Mahwah, NJ: Troll, 1983. This brief biography is intended for grades four to six.

Bull, Angela. *Marie Curie*. England and New York, NY: David and Charles, 1986. This volume in the Profiles series is suitable for grades four to eight.

Conner, Edwina. *Marie Curie*. New York, NY: Bookwright Press, 1987. This thirty-two-page volume in the Great Lives series is intended for students from kindergarten to sixth grade.

Farr, Naunerle C. *Madame Curie*. West Haven, CT: Pendulum Illustrated Biography Series, 1979. Comic book format with simple dialogue and definitions of special words; suitable for young readers in grades five through nine.

Greene, Carol. *Marie Curie: Pioneer Physicist.* Chicago, IL: Childrens Press, 1984. This volume in the People of Distinction series is intended for grades four and up.

Keller, Mollie. *Marie Curie.* New York, NY: Watts, 1982. This volume in the Impact Biographies series is suitable for grades seven and higher.

Sabin, Louis. *Marie Curie.* Mahwah, NJ: Troll, 1985. A brief illustrated biography for grades three to six.

Steinke, Ann. *Marie Curie.* Hauppauge, NY: Barron, 1987. This volume in the Solutions series is intended for grades three to six.

Overview and Evaluation of Primary Sources

Almost all of the Curie Papers are housed at the Bibliothèque Nationale, Paris, although some materials remain at the Laboratoire Curie, Paris. The original family letters quoted in Eve Curie's *Madame Curie* were destroyed in Warsaw during World War II. For a brief discussion of the papers published by members of the Curie family see Ignacy Stronki, "The Collected Papers of the Curie Family" (*Archives Internationales d'. Histoire des Sciences* 25 [1975]: 309-313; **A**). While Eve Curie's biography was translated into many languages, unfortunately the brief memoir, *Marie Curie, ma Mère* (*Europe* 108 [1954]: 89; **A**), by her older daughter, the Nobel Laureate Irene Joliot-Curie, is not available in English. Also of interest is Marie Curie's *La Radiologie et la Guerre* (Paris: Alcan, 1921; **A**). The text of a brief lecture presented by Curie at Vassar College in 1921 was published as *The Discovery of Radium* (Poughkeepsie, NY: Vassar College, 1921; **A, G**). A translation of Curie's thesis presented to the Faculty of Sciences of Paris was published in English as *Radioactive Substances* (New York: Philosophical Library, 1961; **A**). In less than one hundred pages, this book summarizes four years of research into the nature of radioactivity and the identification of the new, strongly radioactive element radium.

Curie was persuaded to publish a biography of Pierre Curie and an autobiographical essay in connection with American efforts to raise money for her research. She authorized the publication of *Pierre Curie* and *Autobiographical Notes* in one volume in the U.S. (Translated by Charlotte and Vernon Kellogg. New York: Macmillan, 1923. Reprint. New York: Dover, 1963; **A, G**). She later refused authorization for publication of her *Autobiographical Notes* in any other country.

Fiction and Adaptations

Part of the Prizewinners series, the film *Marie Curie—A Love Story* (1977) emphasizes the relationship between Marie and Pierre Curie, their love for each other and for their work. As a brief introduction to the discoverer of polonium and radium, this film is suitable for general audiences or for educational use in grades seven through college. Released by Centron, this thirty-two minute film stars Anna Calder-Marshall and Terrence Hardiman as the Curies.

Robert Reid's biography was the basis of *Marie Curie* (1978), a five part BBC miniseries, which documents the lives and research of Marie and Pierre Curie. It is suitable for a general audience or for educational use in grades nine through college.

Museums, Historical Landmarks, Societies

Curie Laboratory (Paris). The greatest monument to the work of the Curies.

Plaque (Warsaw). A plaque at the entrance of the house on Freta Street where Maria Sklodowska was born commemorates her birth.

Plaque (Paris). The house where the Curies lived during the period in which Curie isolated radium, at 108 Boulevard Kellermann, is no longer standing, but a small plague on a wall commemorates the years they lived there.

Other Sources

Barr, E. Scott. "The Incredible Marie Curie and Her Family." In *Physics*

Teacher 2 (1964): 251-259. Attempts to provide role models in its discussion of Marie Curie and Irene Joliot-Curie.

Brush, Stephen G. "Women in Physical Science: From Drudges to Discoverers." In *The Physics Teacher* 23 (January 1985): 11-19. Explores the "Madame Curie Syndrome" and the negative impact stereotypical descriptions of the work of women scientists may have on young women's aspirations.

Opfell, Olga S. *The Lady Laureates. Women Who Have Won the Nobel Prize.* Metuchen, NJ: Scarecrow, 1978. Valuable analysis of the work of Marie Curie ("Pale Glimmer of Radium: Marie Curie") and Irene Joliot-Curie ("Triumph and Rebuff: Irene Joliot-Curie").

Pycior, Helena M. "Marie Curie's 'Anti-Natural Path': Time Only for Science and Family." In *Uneasy Careers and Intimate Lives. Women in Science 1789-1979,* edited by Pnina G. Abir-Am and Dorinda Outram. New Brunswick: Rutgers University Press, 1987. Explores Curie's adaptations to the roles of scientist, wife, mother, widow, and single parent.

Weill, Adrienne R. "Marie Curie." In *Dictionary of Scientific Biography.* Vol. 3. New York: Scribner's, 1971. Provides a brief, modern, objective overview of the work of Marie Curie.

Lois N. Magner
Purdue University

Charles Darwin
1809-1882

Chronology

Born Charles Robert Darwin on February 9, 1809, in Shrewsbury, Shropshire, England, son of Robert Waring Darwin, a successful physician, and Susannah Wedgwood, daughter of the successful potter Josiah Wedgwood I, and grandson of Erasmus Darwin, noted eighteenth-century physiologist; *1817* sent to school in Shrewsbury, where teachers consider him a slow learner; *1818* enters Samuel Butler's Shrewsbury School, where, he later complains, he learns a "blank education of the classics, ancient history, and geography"; *1827* sent to Edinburgh University to study medicine; then to Cambridge University to prepare for a position as a clergyman in the Church of England; at Cambridge meets geologist Adam Sedgwick and naturalist John Stevens Henslow; *1830* geologist Charles Lyell publishes the first volume of his *Principles of Geology*, which argues that the earth is extremely old and has been shaped by natural processes over a long period of time; *1831* receives a bachelor's degree from Christ Church College, Cambridge University; *1831* notified by Henslow that a position is available as an unpaid naturalist on the H.M.S. *Beagle,* an Admiralty survey ship scheduled to visit the coasts of Patagonia, Tierra de Fuego, Chile, and Peru, as well as some Pacific Islands; *1831-1836* serves as ship's naturalist aboard the *Beagle* and reads Lyell's book; *1833* in Argentina receives a severe bite from the Benchuca bug, which may have infected him with Chagas' disease, a possible cause of his later frequent bouts of ill health; *1835* visits the Galápagos Islands off the western coast of South America, where his discovery that species differ from island to island contributes to his emerging thoughts on natural selection; *1839* marries his cousin Emma Wedgwood; *1837* begins scattered description of evolution in his *Notebook on Transmutation of Species*, speculating that the large number of similarities between different animal species could be explained if species had descended from common ancestors; *1838* reads Thomas Malthus's *An Essay on the Principle of Population* (1798), and uses Malthus's phrase "struggle for existence" in forming his ideas about evolution; *1839* publishes his *Journal of Researches* detailing discoveries during the voyage of the *Beagle*; *1842* writes a pencil sketch of his "species theory" and moves to Kent; *1856* describes his theory of natural selection to close friend Lyell, who urges him to write a book; *1856* begins writing the *Origin of Species*; *1858* receives a letter from the naturalist Alfred Wallace, who, on the basis of personal research in South America, details thoughts on evolution which are almost identical to Darwin's still-unpublished ideas on natural selection; *1858* reads the Wallace letter and his own paper on evolution to the Linnean Society of London; *1859* publishes *Origin of Species*, theorizing that evolution proceeds by "natural selection"; the first edition of 1,250 copies sells out on the first day of publication; *1860* his close friend Thomas Henry Huxley holds famous debate over Darwinism with Bishop Samuel Wilberforce at Oxford; *1865* Gregor Mendel, an Austrian monk, publishes important research into genetics, but neither Darwin nor other important scientists read these articles about the operation of heredity in pea plants; *1871* publishes *The Descent of Man*, which explicitly includes human beings in the evolutionary process, asserting that human beings and apes are descended from a common simian ancestor; *1876* writes autobiographical sketch; *1882* dies at Down House, Kent, on April 19; buried in Westminster Abbey on April 26 next to the tomb of Sir Isaac Newton.

Activities of Historical Significance

Charles Darwin did not invent "evolution," but he solved many of the frustrating mysteries surrounding the processes which caused evolution. In place of a divinely guided universe, Darwin portrayed a nature that acted blindly—seemingly without set goals or ends—but in ways that brought about progress. It was a vision that captivated many of Darwin's contemporaries, so much so that Darwinism became a byword in many late nineteenth-century writings on politics, literature, and society.

By Darwin's time, the existence of evolution was often assumed, even by some religious individuals. The ancient Greek philosopher Aristotle had implied evolution in his famous "Great Chain of Being," which ranked plants and animals in increasing order of complexity. In the seventeenth century, the French naturalist Georges Buffon had assumed that evolutionary change went both forward and backward—so that a horse, for example, might produce offspring which resembled pigs. The most famous scientific theory of evolution before Darwin came from the French naturalist J. B. Lamarck, who proposed in the early nineteenth century that animals were able to change their characteristics in order to adjust to their environment—and were able to pass on these "acquired characteristics" to their offspring by the process of heredity. Lamarck's theory of the "inheritance of acquired characteristics" was greeted with skepticism by most of his colleagues, however, and even ridiculed by the influential French biologist Georges Cuvier.

In order to produce a credible, scientifically respectable explanation of how evolution proceeded, Darwin needed to overcome numerous obstacles. The major problem was that the Earth did not appear old enough for evolution to have occurred. In the seventeenth century, an Irish bishop, Bishop James Ussher, attempted to calculate the age of the Earth by adding together the number of generations represented in the Bible. He insisted that the earth had been created in the year 4004 B.C.—at about noon. Even Lord Kelvin, a famous nineteenth-century physicist, concluded that the Earth was no more than one hundred thousand years old.

The evidence in favor of evolution, including fossils and similar anatomical structures among many species, was convincing enough that many writers before Darwin had attempted to produce their own versions of evolution. Many of these writers resorted to the doctrine of "Special Creation"—by which it was believed that God, after great catastrophes like the Flood, had recreated entire species. The idea of Special Creation was used in 1846 by the British writer Robert Chambers in his best-selling book, *Vestiges of Creation*. In Britain, the most widely quoted writer on evolution until 1859 was a philosopher, Herbert Spencer, who argued that all nature was evolving from the simple to the complex, from the "homogeneous" to the "heterogeneous."

Darwin seemed unlikely to become more famous than Chambers or Spencer; extremely shy, he did not impress his teachers in school. Darwin's father steered him first to the study of medicine and then to Cambridge University to prepare for a comfortable life as a country cleric. When Darwin, upon graduation from Cambridge, was told that a position was available as a ship's naturalist aboard the British survey and natural history ship the *Beagle,* he felt it necessary to ask his father's permission to go.

Although Darwin made important geological discoveries during the trip, the highlight of the six-year voyage was a stopover at the Galápagos Islands off the coast of Ecuador. There the amateur scientist discovered considerable variation in the same species from island to island. During the trip Darwin also read two significant books. One, by geologist and friend Charles Lyell, argued that the Earth's surface was less the result of sudden catastrophes than of extremely slow processes, like erosion, which had operated "uniformly" over very long periods of time. The implication of Lyell's "uniformitarianism" was that the earth was much older than previously thought. On the same trip, Darwin also read Thomas Malthus's *Essay on Population*, which argued that human beings are in a constant "struggle for existence" because human reproduction constantly threatens to overwhelm the food supply.

Darwin began the voyage believing that species were immutable, or unchangeable; by the end of the trip, he had concluded that species underwent frequent, and perhaps constant, change. Early signs of his theory of natural selection do not appear in his notebooks and diaries until the early 1840s. In fact, there was a twenty-year hiatus between his voyage on the *Beagle* and the appearance of his landmark book *Origin of Species*. Darwin was acutely aware that his emerging discoveries would outrage many people, particularly the religiously devout. During his life, he frequently complained of nervous stomach and lack of energy, traits some historians have interpreted as signs of nervousness over the controversies which he realized might result from his work. Only when a letter arrived in 1858 from a fellow naturalist, Alfred Wallace, did Darwin act. Wallace, on the basis of armchair philosophy and a trip to South America, had arrived at conclusions similar to Darwin's. In 1858 Darwin went before the Linnean Society in London to announce his theory of natural selection; he was characteristically generous in also giving credit to Wallace.

In 1859 Darwin explained his theory of natural selection more thoroughly in his *Origin of Species*. To support his conclusions, the *Origin of Species* cited Darwin's trip aboard the *Beagle* and his experience in breeding farm animals. The book argued that "variations" are constantly appearing in plants or animals. Nature tests ("selects") these new traits to determine if they help the animal survive and propagate. "Advantageous" variations, which help the animal fit into its environment, make it more likely that the animal will live longer and produce more offspring, thus perpetuating the new variations. The term "natural selection" actually described a number of selection processes which Darwin described in the *Origin of Species*. Darwin believed that it was impossible to say where all these variations were heading, since nature appeared to act mechanically and without set goals. But since natural selection produced species with an increased chance of survival, it represented "progress" by nature. Darwin accepted Malthus's term "struggle for existence" and Spencer's term "survival of the fittest" to describe his natural selection. Darwin could not, however, explain why the variations occurred.

Darwin did not believe that human beings were descended from apes, but he did conjecture that human beings and chimpanzees might share a common evolutionary ancestor. The distinction was too fine for many of his readers, however. In 1860 Samuel Wilberforce, a bishop of the Church of England, charged during a debate at Oxford University that Darwin had equated human beings with apes. Did Darwin believe, he taunted, that his grandfather was an ape? The occasion became memorable because Darwin's friend Thomas Henry Huxley, known as one of "Darwin's bulldogs" for his aggressive defenses of the shy Darwin, replied with his famous defense of the *Origin of Species*—asserting that he would not be ashamed to have an ape for a grandfather but that, if he were an ape, he should be ashamed to have as a descendant a bishop who spoke from ignorance and who obscured, rather than illuminated, important topics.

Darwin's book *The Descent of Man* appeared twelve years after the *Origin of Species*. Darwin had said little in the *Origin of Species* about human beings; in the *Descent of Man* he finally included human beings in evolution, asserting that: "Man in his arrogance thinks himself a great work worthy of the interposition of a deity. More humble and I believe it truer to consider him created from animals."

Although religiously devout as a young man, by the time of the *Origin of Species,* Darwin had, like many of his fellow prominent Victorians, become an agnostic, believing that the existence of God could be neither proved nor disproved. Although the religious implications of the *Origin of Species* gained the most attention in Darwin's lifetime, since his death more attention has been given to the so-called "Social Darwinians," writers who tried to draw lessons for politics and society from his books. A varied group, the "Social Darwinians" included writers who tried to justify colonialism or war. Examples were the American minister Josiah Strong, who believed that only the "Anglo-Saxon race" was prepared for the "final competition of races," and the Prussian historian Heinrich Treitschke, who believed that war helped identify the "fittest" by "separating the wheat from the chaff." Darwin knew very few of the Social Darwinians—most emerged after his death—and he could not control the uses, or misuses of his work.

Overview of Biographical Sources

Darwin's scientific work and writings engendered heated controversies, some of which continue to the present day. As a result, the biographical literature on Darwin is large, reflecting contemporary and historical reactions to the scientific merits of his work, to the theological questions raised by Darwinism, and to the Social Darwinians who claimed to find scientific meaning in his work for society and politics. In the four decades following the publication of the *Origin of Species*, biographers focused on questions of the scientific viability of natural selection and on the religious issues raised by Darwinian evolution. Huxley, who had remarked of the *Origin of Species,* "How extremely stupid [of me] not to have thought of that," concentrated on defending Darwin from theological critics in his *Evolution as to Man's Place in Nature* (1863). In the United States, Asa Gray, Darwin's major early supporter among American scientists, defended Darwinism and pre-dicted a major struggle, or "survival of the fittest," among pro- and anti-Darwin-ian scientists in *Darwiniana* (1876). Louis Agassiz, the Harvard naturalist who was a leading critic of Darwin's work, rejected Darwinism as much on religious as scientific grounds in his *The Structure of Animal Life.* (1896). On the continent of Europe, Darwin's leading popularizer, the zoologist Ernst Haeckel, attempted in his two volume *Evolution of Man* (1872) to make Darwinism into an overall philoso-phy of life, encompassing a rejection of Christianity, eugenics, and a new religion of science. Another prominent German scientist, the pathologist Rudolf Virchow, in *The Freedom of Science in the Modern State* (1878), accepted Darwinism as a theory but believed it lacked enough certainty to be taught in the schools. By the 1880s, Darwinism had gained widespread acceptance among European and Ameri-can scientists, and some religious writers had begun to insist that Darwinism did not necessarily contradict theology. The French writer Edmond de Pressennsé believed that Darwinism lacked "scientific demonstration" but added that it did not rule out "divine causes" in nature. He expressed these views in *A Study of the Origin* (1882).

Between 1890 and 1920 doubts about Darwinism emerged when early work on genetics and genetic mutations appeared to contradict parts of natural selection.

Eventually the work of the geneticists August Weismann, *Essays upon Heredity and Kindred Biological Problems* (1893), who read Mendel and discovered that genetic material, or "germ plasm" is passed from generation to generation largely unchanged, and Hugo De Vries, *Species and their Origins by Mutation* (1904), who discovered that parts of this germ plasm are changed from time to time by mutations, was seen as fitting in very well with Darwin's ideas. Mutations, in fact, explained the origin of the "variations" that were central to the theory of natural selection.

The early biographies of Darwin were generally uncritical studies which glorified him as a scientific revolutionary. Published five years after Darwin's death, G. T. Bettany's *Life of Charles Darwin* (1887) portrayed the naturalist as a scientific saint. Bettany's book used almost none of Darwin's correspondence and no personal notes by Darwin.

During the 1920s and 1930s, writers on Darwin were influenced by the famous Scopes trial, a trial of a high school zoology teacher accused of violating Tennessee law by teaching evolution. Gamaliel Bradford's admiring but generally superficial biography of Darwin, *Darwin* (Boston: Houghton Mifflin, 1926), accuses "fundamentalists" of attempting to limit a never-ending search for truth by scientists. A decade later, Geoffrey West's (H. G. Wells writing as Geoffrey West) detailed, anecdotal biography, *Charles Darwin: A Portrait* (New Haven, CT: Yale University Press, 1938), continued the tradition of "biographer as defender" of Darwin's reputation. Basing his book on Darwin's letters and notebooks, West saw Darwin as a great man with the "amazing achievements" of changing people's minds in his lifetime, but he predicted that scientists would advance beyond Darwinism.

In the years since World War II, biologists have come to believe that evolution has frequently been more rapid than Darwin's extremely gradual "natural selection," proceeding often by quick "genetic jumps." Postwar writers on Darwinism have shown increasing interest in "Social Darwinism" and in national differences in the reception and interpretation of Darwin. A conference of eminent scholars of Darwin and Darwinism led to the publication of Thomas F. Glick, ed., *The Comparative Reception of Darwinism* (Austin: University of Texas Press, 1974). The American historian Richard Hofstadter opened a whole new field of study in his book *Social Darwinism in American Thought* (Boston, MA: Beacon, 1979). Subsequent studies of the phenomenon of Social Darwinism include Robert C.

Bannister, *Social Darwinism: Science and Myth in American Social Thought* (Philadelphia, PA: Temple University Press, 1979); Alfred Kelly, *The Descent of Darwin: The Popularization of Darwinism in Germany, 1860-1914* (Chapel Hill: University of North Carolina Press, 1981); Linda L. Clark, *Social Darwinism in France* (Tuscaloosa: University of Alabama Press, 1984); and Adel A. Ziadat, *Western Science in the Arab World: The Impact of Darwinism, 1860-1930* (New York: St. Martin's, 1986).

   Darwinism has remained of interest to modern researchers studying the origins of human beings and the reasons behind human behavior. Recent work in anthropology appears to confirm Darwin's prediction that traces of the earliest human beings would be found in Africa. See, for instance, Richard E. Leakey and Roger Lewin, *Origins: What New Discoveries Reveal about the Emergence of Our Species and Its Possible Future* (New York: E. P. Dutton, 1977). Harvard professor of biology Edward O. Wilson has created considerable controversy by proposing in *Sociobiology: The New Synthesis* (Cambridge, MA: Harvard University Press, 1975) that all human and animal behaviors are patterns that helped earlier living beings survive; altruism, for example, may be motivated by a desire for preservation.

Evaluation of Principal Biographical Sources

   Barzun, Jacques. *Darwin, Marx, Wagner: Critique of a Heritage*. Garden City, NY: Doubleday, 1958. (**A, G**) A classic book which places Darwin in the context of nineteenth-century thought, comparing him to two prominent Europeans of his time.

   Clark, Ronald W. *The Survival of Charles Darwin: A Biography of a Man and an Idea*. New York: Random House, 1984. (**A, G**) This well-illustrated book by the biographer of Freud and Einstein discusses the logical problems and difficult questions Darwin had to consider in arriving at natural selection. The author's emphasis is upon Darwin's struggle for scientific credibility with a Victorian audience that did not want to hear that nature operated by "tooth and claw." The book has a large number of footnotes, many of them based on manuscripts at Cambridge University.

De Beer, Gavin. *Charles Darwin: Evolution by Natural Selection.* Garden City, NY: Doubleday, 1964. (**A, G**) A British view of Darwin, written by a scholar who has also published Darwin's *Journal.* Argues that Darwin was little honored in his own country. Contains a number of photographs of contemporaries, such as Robert Fitzroy, the captain of the *Beagle,* as well as photos of pages form Darwin's notebooks. Portions of Darwin's conversations and correspondence with other scientists, such as the geologist Charles Lyell, are included. De Beer sees Darwin as a scientific genius whose work in a variety of fields, including geology, made possible his "grand synthesis" of natural selection. Darwin returned form the voyage of the *Beagle,* the author asserts, a "true scientist" who rejected "undisciplined lines of thinking" and insisted on "objective evidence."

Gaylord, George Simpson, ed., *The Book of Darwin.* New York: Washington Square Press, 1982. (**A, G**) Publishes excerpts from Darwin's major writings and indicates where Darwin changed his mind after a first draft. Gaylord, in his excellent introduction to Darwin's books, calls the "struggle for existence" an "unfortunate choice" of words, because Darwin did not mean physical combat but rather "success in bearing progeny."

Himmelfarb, Gertrude. *Darwin and the Darwinian Revolution.* Garden City, NY: Doubleday, 1962. (**A, G**) An ambitious book which attempts to trace both the development of Darwin's concept of natural selection and the religious, political, and philosophical issues raised by Darwinism. More successful in achieving the former than the latter, although it also contains a good deal of biographical information, particularly about the reactions of Darwin's wife to his work. Includes chapters on the relationship of Darwinism to religion in his day and on what some contemporaries thought Darwinism signified for politics. The author argues that the Darwinian revolution was a "conservative revolution" in several ways, especially because, in the author's view, Darwinism did not prove to be an "implacable foe" of religion.

Huxley, Julian, and H. B. D. Kettlewell. *Charles Darwin and His World.* New York: Viking, 1965. (**A, G, Y**) Darwin as seen by two "NeoDarwinians," including a descendent of Darwin's close friend Thomas Henry Huxley. Argues that "Darwin was the greatest amateur of all time—an amateur naturalist who became a great scientist.'' The book quotes extensively from Darwin's notebooks and diary entries, noting that Darwin encountered a number of unexplained problems in nature that were later solved. Includes many illustrations of scientific figures and of plant and animal life Darwin studied particularly during his voyage on the *Beagle*.

Irvine, William. *Apes, Angels, and Victorians: The Story of Darwin, Huxley, and Evolution.* New York: McGraw-Hill, 1955. (**A, G**) An excellent introduction to Darwin's life and ideas, this book reads like a novel. Irvine concentrates on explaining how Darwin arrived at his theory of natural selection and on tracing the major popularizers and defenders of Darwin in Britain during Darwin's lifetime. Irvine's engaging style draws colorful pictures of Darwin and Huxley, explaining how their personalities affected their relationships as scientists. All of Darwin's major books are noted and explained, although sometimes briefly The large number of footnotes includes some unpublished material from Darwin's correspondence.

Moorehead, Alan. *Darwin and the Beagle.* New York: Harper and Row, 1969. (**A, G**) Beautifully illustrated with paintings of the young Darwin, the *Beagle,* and the sites which the ship visited, this book traces Darwin's life from the departure of the *Beagle* to the Huxley-Wilberforce debate at Oxford in 1860. Helpful in understanding how Darwin's visit to the Galápagos Islands influenced his ideas on evolution. Quotes liberally from his letters and his journals, and includes a large number of illustrations. Many of these are color plates of the plants and animal life Darwin studied, particularly during the voyage of the *Beagle.* An appendix gives a chronology for Darwin's observations on the islands where the *Beagle* sailed.

Overview and Evaluation of Primary Sources

Although Darwin's papers and correspondence are scattered throughout the world—the principal collections being at Darwin's Down House, the library of Cambridge University, the British Museum, and the American Philosophical Society in Philadelphia—many of Darwin's papers, including his correspondence, autobiography, and notebooks, have been published. His son Francis published

Darwin's most significant letters in Francis Darwin, ed., *The Life and Letters of Charles Darwin* (2 vols. New York: Appleton, 1887; **A, G**). The commercial success of that collection led to a second series, Francis Darwin and A. C. Seward, eds., *More Letters of Charles Darwin* (New York: Appleton, 1903; **A, G**). Frederick Burkhardt, Sydney Smith, David Kohn, and William Montgomery aimed to produce an "authoritative and comprehensive edition of Darwin's correspondence" in their four volume *The Correspondence of Charles Darwin* (Cambridge: Cambridge University Press, 1985; **A, G**), which includes a large number of previously-unpublished letters. These four editors have also cataloged more than thirteen thousand letters and listed their locations in *A Calendar of the Correspondence of Charles Darwin, 1821-1882* (New York: Garland, 1985; **A, G**). Guides to individual collections of Darwin's letters and other papers include the *Handlist of the Darwin Papers at the University Library* (Cambridge: Cambridge University Press, 1960; **A, G**) and, Whitfield J. Bell, Jr., and Murphy D. Smith, comps., *Guide to the Archives and Manuscript Collections of the American Philosophical Society* (Philadelphia, PA: American Philosophical Society, 1966; **A, G**). Works published during Darwin's lifetime are cataloged in R. B. Freeman, *The Works of Charles Darwin: An Annotated Bibliographical Handlist* (Folkestone, England: Darwon, 1977; **A, G**). Darwin's early works on natural history and a selection of his correspondence are included in Paul Barrett, ed., *Collected Papers of Charles Darwin* (2 vols. Chicago: University of Chicago Press, 1977; **A, G**). Barrett included an article by Darwin attacking his critics because he considered it unique: "Darwin generally avoided polemics which the publication of evolutionary theories unleashed throughout the world."

Darwin's autobiography, which furnishes clues as to the writers who influenced him most, such as Malthus and Lyell, was originally published in abridged form as part of *The Life and Letters of Charles Darwin*. The autobiography was republished in 1959 as *The Autobiography of Charles Darwin, 1809-1822: With Original Omissions Restored* (New York: Harcourt Brace, 1959; **A, G**) by Darwin's granddaughter Nora Barlow, who restored an estimated six thousand words which were originally omitted by Francis Darwin. Most of the deleted sections detailed Darwin's thoughts on religion. Barlow also edited Darwin's diary aboard the *Beagle: Diary of the Voyage of the H.M.S. Beagle,* (Cambridge: University of Cambridge Press, 1933; **A, G**). The diary has also appeared in other forms. The latest reincarnation has been published by a descendent of Darwin, Richard Darwin

Keynes, under the title *Charles Darwin's Beagle Diary* (Cambridge: Cambridge University Press, 1988; **A, G**). In 1952 a facsimile edition was issued of Darwin's book, originally published in 1839 and reprinted in 1845, entitled *Journal of the Researches by Charles Darwin into the Natural History and Geology of the Countries Visited during the Voyage of the H.M.S. Beagle.* There are two other editions, one with introductions by Darwin's modern biographer Gavin de Beer, *Journal of the Researches of Charles Darwin on the Beagle, 1856* (1856. Reprint. New York: Heritage Press, 1956; **A, G**) and another by Graham Cannon, *The Voyage of the Beagle* (1906. Reprint. London: Everyman's Library, 1969; **A, G**). In an introduction to his edition, de Beer asserts that the journal demonstrated Darwin's ability to extract "great universal natural truths" from "simple ingredients." Sandra Herbert found that one of Darwin's notebooks, published as *The Red Notebook of Charles Darwin* (London: The British Museum, 1989; **A, G**), indicated that he had believed that species were unchangeable before his voyage aboard the *Beagle,* undergoing a change of view by the end of the trip. Finally, correspondence within Darwin's own family has been published by Emma Darwin as, Henrietta Litchfield, ed., *A Century of Family Letters, 1792-1896* (2 vols. New York: Appleton, 1915; **A, G**).

There are a number of published selections of Darwin's works. Roger Jastrow, ed., *The Essential Darwin* (Boston: Little, Brown, 1984; **A, G**) includes sections from Darwin's autobiography, from the journal he kept while aboard the *Beagle,* from the *Origin of Species,* and from *The Descent of Man.* Darwin's biographer de Beer included a preliminary sketch Darwin wrote on evolution in 1842 and an essay written by Darwin in 1844 in a collection which he edited entitled *Charles Darwin: Evolution by Natural Selection* (Garden City, NY: Doubleday, 1964; **A, G**). One of the most unusual books for reading Darwin, Paul Barrett, Donald J. Weinshank, and Timothy J. Gottleber, eds., *A Concordance to Darwin's Origin of Species* (Ithaca, NY: Cornell University Press, 1981; **A, G**) enables readers to trace the use of key words which Darwin repeated throughout his book. Also useful is a collection of Darwin's speeches and essays, Stanley Edgar Hyman, ed., *Darwin for Today: The Essence of His Works* (New York: Viking, 1963; **A, G**). Francis Darwin's 1909 book, *Evolution by Natural Selection,* a condensation of the *Origin of Species,* was reprinted by de Beer because he believed that it made Darwin more accessible to the average reader (London: Nelson, 1963; **A, G**).

Evaluation of Critical Sources

Bowler, Peter J. *Evolution: The History of an Idea.* Berkeley and Los Angeles: University of California Press, 1984. (**A**) Written by one of the preeminent modern scholars of Darwinism, this volume traces concepts of evolution before Darwin, beginning with the Enlightenment of the 1700s; the book then uses this background to explain Darwin's originality and importance, arguing that the Darwinian revolution was as important as the "Copernican revolution" (which established that the Earth, rather than the sun, was at the center of the solar system) in determining cultural values. The last chapters of the book, which discuss how modern biologists' versions of evolution differ from Darwin's, are intended partly as a background for debates raging over the teaching of evolution in the schools.

Eiseley, Loren. *Darwin and the Mysterious Dr. X: New Light on the Evolutionists.* New York: E. P. Dutton, 1979. (**A, G**) Controversial book published two years after Eiseley's death. Argues that Darwin failed to acknowledge his debt to an earlier English naturalist, Edward Blyth, from whom, Eiseley charges, Darwin borrowed many ideas about natural selection. A questionable book based more on anomalies in Darwin's papers than upon substantial evidence. The book includes a series of essays which were written at different times. The result is that they are occasionally repetitious and do not always "mesh" well. Included is an essay on Blyth's life.

Greene, John C. *The Death of Adam: Evolution and Its Impact on Western Thought.* Ames: Iowa State University Press, 1959. (**A, G**) Considers the intellectual significance of Darwin's ideas, explaining the rise of evolutionary ideas in the two hundred years between Newton and Darwin. Concentrates on the historical and scientific developments which were preconditions for Darwin's work. Contains extensive footnotes.

Karp, Walter. *Charles Darwin and the Origin of Species.* New York: Heritage, 1968. (**G, Y**) Brief, highly readable introduction to Darwin which asserts that the Darwinian revolution was as significant as the Copernican revolution of the seventeenth century. Especially suitable for younger readers. For the average reader, this may be the clearest book in explaining what Darwin meant by "natural selection." Lavishly illustrated with pictures of Darwin's family, the animal life he studied, the areas of his voyages, and the England of his day.

Kohn, David, ed. *The Darwinian Heritage*. Princeton, NJ: Princeton University Press, 1985. (**A**) A large collection of essays covering the development of Darwin's ideas on evolution, controversies in Darwin's time, the reception of Darwinism in Europe and the United States, and views of Darwinism held by modern writers. Extensive notes and bibliography, but no illustrations.

Ruse, Michael. *The Darwinian Revolution*. Chicago: University of Chicago Press: 1979. (**A**) Written by one of the major modern historians of Darwin, and using scholarship which has accumulated during the last two decades, this book deals extensively with the scientific problems and mysteries Darwin coped with in arriving at natural selection. A major argument of this 400-page book is that the problems of deciphering evolution were more complex than is generally believed, and the author, to prove his point, traces evolutionary ideas in astronomy (the Kant-Laplace hypothesis for the beginning of the universe) and genetics (Mendel). Also discussed are predecessors of Darwin, such as the French naturalists Jean Baptiste de Lamarck and Georges Cuvier.

Russett, Cynthia Eagle. *Darwin in America: The Intellectual Response, 1865-1912*. San Francisco: W. H. Freeman, 1976. (**A, G**) Excellent, highly readable analysis of the response of American intellectuals to Darwinism. Explains how the reception of Darwinism was often colored by extra-scientific issues. Russett argues that Darwinism raised a number of questions that "are still with us," such as "What are the limits of scientific knowledge?" and "Is science the only road to real knowledge?" Includes a useful bibliography and a small number of illustrations, including cartoons and pictures from American life.

Fiction and Adaptations

Irving Stone, the author of numerous "biographical novels" on the lives of famous historical figures, researched much of the documentary evidence about Darwin before accurately recreating Darwin's life in *The Origin: A Biographical*

Novel of Charles Darwin (1980). The Scopes trial over the legality of teaching Darwinism in the schools was dramatized, with some historical liberties, in Jerome Lawrence and Robert E. Lee's eloquent play *Inherit the Wind*, which was performed on Broadway in 1955. The play presents the trial as being essentially a confrontation between the famous defense lawyer Clarence Darrow and the politician William Jennings Bryan. The play was made into a motion picture in 1960, directed by Stanley Kramer and starring Spencer Tracy, Gene Kelly, Harry Morgan, and Claude Akins, among others. A television adaptation was released in 1988. This version, not as critically acclaimed as the 1960 version, was directed by David Greene and starred Kirk Douglas and Jason Robards.

Museums, Historical Landmarks, Societies

American Philosophical Society (Philadelphia, PA). Contains Darwin's correspondence and manuscripts.

British Museum (London). The natural history section contains manuscripts of Darwin's books.

Cambridge University (Cambridge, England). The Botany School Museum houses Darwin's collection of plant and animal species; the university library contains the original manuscript of *Origin of Species*.

Down House (Downe, Kent, England). Much of Darwin's home for forty years has been opened to the public as a museum. Includes the manuscript of Darwin's journal aboard the *Beagle* and many of his personal possessions, original furnishings, and other memorabilia.

National Maritime Museum (Greenwich, England). Contains a painting of the *Beagle* in the harbor of Sydney, Australia.

National Museum of Natural History (Washington, DC). The Charles Darwin Foundation for the Galápagos displays of biological specimens from the Galápagos Islands. Also supports a research station on the islands.

Peabody Museum of Natural History (New Haven, CT). This museum at Yale University maintains collections and displays relating to animal evolution and the significance of fossils.

Society for Study of Evolution (St. Louis, MO). This society of biologists, within the department of biology, Washington University, publishes a bimonthly journal *Evolution*; it also awards the Dobzhansky Prize to recognize outstanding young evolutionary biologists.

Other Sources

Fay, Margaret A. "Did Marx Dedicate his *Capital* to Darwin?" In *Journal of the History of Ideas* 39 (1978): 133-146. Examines the controversy over whether some of the supposed Darwin-Marx correspondence was either written to, or by, others, a controversy caused by the lack of an addressee on many of the letters. The author, on the basis of both her own research and research conducted by others, challenges the belief that Karl Marx offered to dedicate his monumental book *Capital* to Darwin, and that Darwin declined. The letters in question, according to the author, were actually written between Darwin and Marx's son-in-law, who was writing a book on philosophic and scientific materialism.

Rogers, James Allen. "Darwinism and Social Darwinism." In *Journal of the History of Ideas* 33 (1972): 265-80. Asserts that Darwin, by associating his conception of natural selection with the "struggle for existence" of Malthus and the "survival of the fittest" of Herbert Spencer, facilitated the use of his theories by the so-called "Social Darwinians." Using both Darwin's books and his correspondence, this article particularly focuses on darwin's personal and intellectual ties to Spencer. It argues that the Social Darwinians did not distinguish between the biological evolution studied by scientists and the "social evolution" of human beings.

Zetterberg, J. Peter, ed., *Evolution versus Creationism: The Public Education Controversy*. Phoenix, AZ: Oryx Press, 1983. Includes articles for and against "creationism," including decisions by various state courts on the question of whether high school biology teachers must give equal time to "creationism" and evolution. Roughly half of the book includes defenses of evolution, largely by university professors such as the biologist Theodosius Dobzhansky, whose contribution is entitled "Nothing in Biology Makes Sense Except in the Light of Evolution." The other half examines "scientific evidence for creationism," discusses creationist views on fossils, and includes a detailed outline for a course in creationism."

Niles R. Holt
Illinois State University

Jacques-Louis David
1748-1825

Chronology

Born Jacques-Louis David on April 30, 1748 in Paris, France, son of Louis-Maurice David, a merchant, and Marie Geneviève Buron; *1757* father killed in a duel; raised by his two uncles; given a formal education in the classics at the Collège des Quatre Nations but his talent for painting becomes obvious early; begins to learn painting from his distant relative François Boucher; *1766* begins study with antiquarian painter Joseph Marie Vien; *1770* enters a competition of the Royal Academy of Painting and Sculpture but is not a finalist; *1771* enters a second competition and wins second prize for *The Combat of Mars and Minerva*; *1772* enters a third competition but again fails to qualify; *1773* wins a prize for a study of heads and expressions; *1774* wins a first prize for *The Loves of Antiochus and Stratonice*, which entitles David to continue his studies at the French Academy in Rome the following year; *1775* with Vien, visits Parma, Bologna, and Florence on his way to Rome; *1779* suffers from depression; changes the subject matter of his paintings from Renaissance to Classicism after visits to scholars in Naples; becomes the undisputed leader of the new Neo-Classical School of Painting; *1782* marries Charlotte Pécoul, daughter of a contractor in the Bâtimens du Roi (King's Building Construction and Maintenance Department); *1783* first son is born; joins the Academy of Painting as a full member, offering *Andromache Mourning Hector* as his reception piece; *1784* second son is born; paints a portrait of his in-laws, the Pécouls; returns to Rome; begins *Oath of the Horatii*, which symbolizes ancient Roman virtues; *1785* exhibits *Oath of the Horatii* in Rome and Paris; *1786* twin daughters are born; paints *Death of Socrates*; *1787* paints *The Death of Socrates;* *1788* invited to the salon of the Duke of Orléans, where he meets poet André Chénier, French statesman Charles-Maurice Talleyrand-Perigord and writer Madame Stéphanie de Genlis; paints chemist Antoine Lavoisier and his wife; *Death of Socrates* (1787) and *Paris and Helen* (1788) are criticized by fellow artists for their realism and style that was not in keeping with Rococo taste in painting at that time; paints *Brutus Condemning his Son*; *1789* paints *Brutus Condemning his Son,* and witnesses the Tennis Court Oath taken by the leadership of the Third Estate, which begins the French Revolution and which David will later paint; attends the storming of the Bastille on July 14 and draws the head of the Garrison Commander Delaunay, which was impaled on a pike after he surrendered the symbolic fortress; campaigns to change the rules governing the Academy of Painting; *1790* becomes the leader of the dissident painters; commissioned to paint the Tennis Court Oath; with other dissidents, organizes a new independent artists group, the Commune des Arts; *1791* witnesses the interment of French philosopher and writer Voltaire's remains in the Panthéon; lobbies for the right of all artists to be allowed to exhibit in official government-sponsored competitions; André Chénier dedicates his ode on ''The Tennis Court Oath'' to David in the autumn as the latter begins to paint the event; *1792* David presents a self portrait to his friend Maximillian Robespierre, one of the leaders of the Revolution; after nomination by radical newspaper editor Jean-Paul Marat, elected to the new revolutionary government, the Convention; the First Republic is officially begun; accepts membership in the Committee of Public Instruction and Commission on Monuments, where his talent for propagandistic pageantry is put to use; *1793* votes in favor of the execution of Louis XVI and signs the official death warrant; serves as the President of the Jacobin Club for one month; organizes a civic festival for the Champs de Mars; urges the Convention to democratize the intellectual and artistic community by abolishing all the academies; joins the Committee of General Security, one of the two bodies that manages the Reign of Terror, during which many of the French aristocracy and bourgeoisie are put to death; completes *Death of Marat,* which is displayed in his studio beside the actual bath tub in which Marat was murdered; signs the death warrant for Philippe Égalité, a member of the academy; sketches Marie Antoinette on her way to the guillotine; proposes crushing the statuary on the facade of Notre Dame cathedral and using the rubble as a pedestal for a monument to Revolution; *1794* serves as President of the Convention for thirteen days, during the height of the Reign of Terror; signs the death warrant for General Alexandre Beauharnais, husband of Josephine, future wife of Napoleon Bonaparte; divorces his wife, retaining custody of his male children; organizes the Festival of the Supreme Being, a spectacle that culminates with Robespierre as High Priest ascending an artificial mountain constructed on the Champs de Mars and includes a choir of 2,400 voices, floats, colossal statues of virtues, dancers, doves, flowers, and antique costumes; works on *Barras,* a painting of a martyred drummer boy in whose honor he also organizes a festival; feigns illness and stays home from Convention the same day that Robespierre falls from power; arrested by Robespierre's successors; while imprisoned, paints a self portrait and his only landscape—the view of Luxembourg Garden from his cell window; released after repeated demands for his freedom by his pupils; escapes execution because of his confused mental state, and his denunciation of Robespierre and their close friendship; *1795* new charges are filed against him by a group of artists; leaves the capital to seek refuge in the countryside; rearrested but released after two months; remarries his wife; completes portrait of *Dutch Envoys Jacobus Blauw and Monsieur Meyer;* *1797* meets Napoleon Bonaparte and begins a portrait of him, which is never completed; *1798-1799* attracts derision when he deliberately tries to cause artistic controversy with his *The Sabine Women,* which he exhibits after Napoleon's coup d'état overthrowing the Directory; *1800* declines Napoleon's request to become the new government's official painter; begins *Madame Récamier* but refuses to complete it because the sitter becomes uncooperative; begins *Bonaparte Crossing the Alps by the Saint Bernard Pass;* *1801* abandons the unfinished *The Tennis Court Oath;* *1803* named Chevalier (Knight) of the Legion of Honor; designs Napoleon's coronation set; *1804* named First Painter to the Emperor; commissioned to do a series of four propagandistic history paintings: *The Coronation of Josephine, The Enthronement of Napoleon, The Distribution of the Eagle Standards,* and *The Reception of the Emperor and Empress at the Hôtel de Ville;* *1805* paints a portrait of Pope Pius VII, who was brought to France for the coronation and kept prisoner at Fontainebleau Château; *1810* removes the figure of Josephine from *The Distribution of the Eagles* after the couple divorces; *1811* designs furniture for Napoleon; *1812* paints *Napoleon in his Study;* *1815* goes into exile in Switzerland for fear of arrest after Napoleon's defeat at Waterloo; *1816* after a brief return to France, seeks permanent exile in Brussels after a law is passed banishing all those who signed the king's death warrant; invited to Berlin as Minister of the Arts by the King of Prussia; *1820* sells *The Sabine Women* and *Leonidas at Thermopylae* to Louis XVIII for the Royal Collection; *1822* with his pupil Georges Rouget, completes a copy of *The Coronation of Josephine* as well as *Mars Disarmed by the Three Graces;* *1825* on the way home from the theater in February, trampled by a carriage; hands become paralyzed; dies on December 29 in Brussels; his funeral procession is refused entry at the French border, so he is buried in Brussels.

Activities of Historical Interest

Jacques-Louis David was one of France's greatest painters and the most important Neo-Classicist, the creator of a style that is termed variously as severe, calm, austere, grave, noble, and cold. But it is also a style that seems more real than reality because of its symbolic content, which frequently drew themes from ancient history. Despite its classical inspiration, the School of David saw forward to future trends in art as well, some of which were realized by some of David's most famous pupils, including François Gérard, Anne-Louis Girodet, Antoine-Jean Gros, Jean-Auguste Ingres, and even Eugene Delacroix.

David not only revolutionized French art with paintings such as *The Oath of the Horatii* of 1784, which predates the overthrow of the Bourbon dynasty—he artistically recorded passing events while at the same time becoming an important actor in the unfolding Revolutionary drama itself. In spite of the cowardly manner in which he defended himself when Robespierre and the First Republic were overthrown, David was a major figure in the revolutionary government and the subsequent Reign of Terror. He was masterful at marshalling the visual, aural, and oral arts to serve the State. Because his early artistic life had been made so miserable by the government-supported Academy, he sought revenge on its members by trying to free the arts from government control. In a way, he thus served as a forerunner of the equally innovative though relatively apolitical Impressionist art movement, whose members would have to relive his struggle against governmental influence during the 1860s-1880s.

Aside from Napoleon himself, David was most responsible for turning the First Empire (1804-1814) into the Age of Napoleon. His neo-classical style of the Revolution and Directoire (the French government between 1795-1799) became synonymous with Empire style in art, interior decor, furniture, and all other aspects of the decorative and the performing arts of the era. Drawing upon Napoleon's extraordinary career for inspiration and building upon Napoleon's patronage of the arts and manufacturing, David's talent masterminded the creation of a complete style, perhaps the last complete style in European civilization. Ironically, only the Nazis would be as adept at the exploitation of pageantry and subtle uses of the arts as propaganda.

Because his career was so closely intertwined with political events, first with the Republic and subsequently with the First Empire, much of his work was discredited during the Restoration and was quickly superseded by the schools of Romanticism and Realism. Yet his prolific portraits remained popular and he continued to make a living in this genre and by executing sweetened versions of classically inspired works with less political relevance after the turn of events forced him to leave his native country.

Overview of Biographical Sources

Works on David are far more extensive in French than in English, but there are adequate resources in English. Major studies of David's contribution to painting are more numerous than true biographies, but French Revolutionary scholars on both sides of the Atlantic have written on such aspects of his pageantry as the unrealized Hercules colossus or the meaning of his depiction of women in *The Sabines.*

Recent research not yet incorporated into any book-length biographies has begun to focus on David's role in the Revolution, which he understandably sought to minimize to escape execution. For example, annual volumes of the *Consortium on Revolutionary Europe Proceedings* often contain papers on David and the Revolution. See Stanley Mellon's "J.-L. David, Revolutionary: The Case Reopened" (1983: 364-380), which focuses on David's radical Jacobinism and involvement in Revolutionary politics; Warren Roberts's "David's *Horatio and Brutus* Revisited: Are They Prerevolutionary Paintings?" (1986: 510-528); Robert A. Schumann's "Virility and Grace: Neoclassicism, Jacques-Louis David and the Culture of Prerevolutionary France" (1986: 519-528), which plays up the eighteenth century setting of these works; David A. Wisner's "Jacque-Louis David and André Chenier: *The Death of Socrates, The Tennis Court Oath,* and "The Quest for Artistic Liberty, 1787-1791" (1983: 529-544), which discusses the long friendship between the influential poet and the painter and their attitudes toward artistic liberty, wherein Chenier's was temperate while David's was totally unrestrained. The 1989 *CRE Proceedings* contains articles on three of David's most famous paintings, regarding their origination, inspiration and effect on politics: David A. Wisner's "A Literary Source for David's *The Tennis Court Oath*: Andre Chenier and the Allegory of the Legislator" (1989: 62-66); Robert A. Schumann's "Perser *La Mort de Marat*" (1989: 67-75); Warren Roberts's "David's 'Bara' and the

Burdens of the French Revolution'' (1989: 76-81), followed by a commentary by Stanley Mellon. Roberts extends his discussion on the topic in his book *Jacques-Louis David, Revolutionary Artist: Art, Politics and the French Revolution* (Chapel Hill: University of North Carolina Press, 1989).

The best short, recent biographical sketch and assessment is James A. Leith's ''David, Jacque-Louis'' in *The Historical Dictionary of the French Revolution, 1789-1799,* edited by Samuel F. Scott and Barry Rothaus (Westport, CT: Greenwood, 1985; vol 1: 292-295). Leith, a distinguished Canadian historian of iconography, also incorporates his insights into the article to update the full-length older biographies annotated below.

Evaluation of Biographical Sources

Brookner, Anita. *Jacques-Louis David.* London: Chatto & Windus, 1980. (**A, G**) Intended as an introduction to a lengthier monograph, this apologia concentrates on David the painter. Full of interesting human interest details but minimizes David's role in the Revolution. Includes two chapters on eighteenth century history and artistic theories, thirteen pages of endnotes, a select bibliography, index, eight color plates of poor quality, and 112 black-and-white prints.

Dowd, David Lloyd. *Pageant-Master of the Republic.* 1948. Reprint. Freeport, NY: Books for Libraries Press, 1969. (**A**) Primarily concerned with David's character and the effect of his propagandistic activities for the Republic, especially the role of the plastic arts, such as the use of floats, doves, sound, fire, torchlight, and the waving of banners and branches, in the festivals; David's artistry is subordinated to the theme expressed in the title. Research was based on contemporary sources, archival documents, official papers, memoirs, journals, diaries, correspondences, pamphlets, almanacs, and over one hundred newspapers and periodicals plus David's sketchbooks. Contains a splendid fifty-page bibliographic essay on sources and information about David's sketchbooks and drawings.

Schnapper, Antoine. *David.* New York: Alpine Fine Arts Collection, 1982. (**G**) Richly illustrated coffee table book that describes David's relation to his times with the aid of his works, especially the drawings, many of which have never been previously published. David's powerful realism comes out in his numerous portraits. A one-page bibliography lists thirty-eight sources in chronological order from 1806 to 1978; includes an index.

Valentiner, W. R. *Jacques-Louis David.* New York: Frederic Fairchild Sherman, 1929. (**A**) Unlike most other biographers, Valentiner provides a different, critical, sometimes openly hostile view of David and Neo-Classicism. Whereas Watteau is today considered as a superficial forerunner of Neo-Classicism, Valentiner prefers his decadent work to David's moral purity, although he does concede that David contributed to making the profession of art a more democratic endeavor. He also sees more influence of Boucher than of Vien's training in David's work, which runs counter to the opinion of most critics since the young David spent so brief a time under his tutelage. Because he obviously does not like Napoleon I either, Valentiner, offers a negative opinion of the emperor's influence on art, in contrast to his support of the arts in the years 1789-1799 when he thought art was free of government censorship. Thus, Valentiner seems to offer a royalist corrective to the Bonapartist points of view taken by authors who praise the age of Napoleon.

Overview and Evaluation of Primary Sources

Documents on David's life are extensive, incomplete, and scattered, and all are in French. Miette de Villars edited his memoirs: *Mémoires de David, peintre et depute a la Convention nationales.* Paris: 1850. David's pupil Etienne-Jean Delécluze provides materials from which it is possible to reconstruct what went on in his studio in *Louis David, son école et son temps* (Paris: Souvenirs, 1855). His grandson, J. L. Jules David published three works: *Peintre Louis David. Souvenirs et documents Le Peintre Louis David* (1748-1825); *Souvenirs et Documents inédits* (2 volumes. Paris: 1880-1882), which includes memoirs and documents never previously published; and *Quelques observations sur les dix-neuf toiles attribuées à Louis David à l'exposition de portraits du siècle à l'Ecole des Beaux-Arts* (Paris: 1883), which concerns his paintings. Three exhibition catalogues are M. Florisome, *Catalogue de l'exposition David* (Paris: Musée de l'Orangerie, 1948); *Catalogue des tableaux de galerie et de chavelet, etudes, etc., de Louis David, premier peintre de l'empéreur Napoléon* (Paris: 1826 and 1835); and *David et ses élèves* (Paris: Petit Palais, 1913).

Fiction and Adaptations

Megahey, Leslie. *Jacques-Louis David: The Passing Show.* Volume 25 in the BBC-TV series "Portrait of an Artist" (RM Arts, 1986). Available on video cassette. Looks at both the life and works of David; recreates a replica of David's studio based on the description of daily activities in his workshop by his pupil Delécluze (supra); the director employs newsreel technique to show the dictator of the arts of his eara, and incorporates parts of David's public speeches. Excellent for high school or college courses.

Museums, Historical Landmarks, Societies

Many major art museums of the world contain works by David. The Louvre is the richest source for the major works, but other museums hold important paintings, including the New York Metropolitan Museum of Art, the Chicago Art Institute, the Cleveland Museum of Art, the Fogg Art Museum at the University of Cambridge and the Musée royal des Beaux-Arts in Brussels.

Eglise Sainte-Gudule (Brussels). Monument to David in the church in which his funeral was held.

Fontainebleau Château (Fontainebleau, France). Displays Napoleon's official throne, which was designed by David.

Louvre Museum (Paris). Holds *Combat de Minerve contra Mars* (1771); *Andromache Mourning Hector* (1783); *Oath to Horatio* (1784); *Portrait of Charles-Pierre Pécoul* (1784); *Portrait of Mme Pécoul* (1784); *Paris and Helen* (1788); *The Lictors Bringing to Brutus the Bodies of His Sons* (1789); *Self Portrait* (1790); *The Otah of the Tennis Court* (1791); *Portrait of Mme Chalgrin* (1792); *View of the Luxembourg Gardens* (1794); *Self Portrait* (1794); *The Intervention of the*

Sabine Women (1794-1799); *Portrait of Mme Récamier* (1800); *Napoleon Crowning the Empress Josephine* (1805-1807); *Léonidas aux Thermopyles* (1814); *Three Women of Ghent* (1815).

Other Sources

Honour, Hugh. *Neo-Classicism.* Harmondsworth, England: Penguin, 1968. Provides a history of style and perceptive analysis of David's work.

Johnson, Dorothy. *Jacques-Louis David: Art in Metamorphosis.* Princeton, NJ: Princeton University Press, 1993. Places David in context of nineteenth-century art, culture and society.

Rosenblum, Robert. *Transformations in Late Eighteenth Century Art.* Princeton, NJ: Princeton University Press, 1967. David's work and doctrine are found not only in Neo-Classicism but also in the seeds of Romanticism, Realism and Academicism. Rosenblum provides a backdrop for tracing the development of style and ideas.

June K. Burton
University of Akron

Claude Debussy
1862-1918

Chronology

Born Achille-Claude Debussy on August 22, 1862, in St. Germain-en-Laye, France, son of Manuel-Achille Debussy and Sophie Manoury Debussy, both shop-owners; father subsequently becomes a traveling salesman, a printer's assistant, and later a clerk; mother works for a time as a seamstress; *1869* begins first piano lessons; *1870-1873* takes piano lessons from Madame Maute de Fleurville, a pupil of composer Frédéric Chopin and mother-in-law of the poet Paul Verlaine; *1871* father imprisoned for revolutionary activities during the Commune period in Paris; *1872* accepted into the piano class of Antoine Marmontel and the theory class of Albert Lavignac at the Paris Conservatory of Music; *1873-1879* studies at the Conservatory with teachers Émile Durand, Ernest Guiraud, and César Franck; *1874* performs Chopin's *Piano Concerto in F minor*, hoping for a career as a keyboard virtuoso; *1876* writes first known composition, *Nuit d'etoiles;* *1878* visits London; *1878-1879* does poorly on the Conservatory piano examinations and abandons hopes for a virtuoso career; *1879* composes *Trio for Piano, Violin and Cello;* *1880* wins first prize in a score-reading class; travels to Switzerland and Italy in the company of Madame Nadezhda Filaretovna von Meck, patroness of composer Peter Tchaikovsky; composes piano duet version of *Symphony in B minor;* *1881-1882* visits Russia as house pianist to Madame Nadezhda von Meck; *1883* wins Prix de Rome, second class, for his cantata *Le Gladiateur; 1884* awarded Grand Prix de Rome for his cantata *L'enfant prodigue; 1885-1887* spends an unhappy period at the Villa Medici in Rome; meets famous composers, including Franz Liszt, Giuseppe Verdi, Arrigo Boito, and Ruggiero Leoncavallo; *1887* meets Symbolist poet Stéphane Mallarmé and attends Tuesday meetings of a group of Symbolist poets; begins *La Damoiselle elue,* which is based on a text by poet and painter Dante Gabriel Rossetti; *1888* visits Bayreuth Opera House in Germany to hear the music dramas of composer Richard Wagner; *1889* visits Bayreuth again; introduced to Russian composer Modest Mussorgsky's opera *Boris Godunov;* enthralled by the exotic sounds of Javanese gamelan ensemble at the Paris World's

Exhibition; meets and cohabits with Gabrielle "Gaby" Dupont; *1890* severs connection with the Paris Conservatory after his symphonic poem *Printemps* is refused a place on the program with *La Damoiselle elue; 1891* meets pianist and composer Erik Satie; *1892* begins to make sketches for the opera *Pelléas et Mélisande; 1893 String Quartet* performed; *1894 Prelude to the Afternoon of a Faun* performed to either hostile or indifferent reception of the new style revealed in this composition; *1897* orchestrates two of Satie's *Gymnopédies; 1899* marries Rosalie (Lily) Texier; completes *Three Nocturnes for Orchestra; 1900* premiere of two of *Nocturnes for Orchestra* in Paris leads to public acceptance of his works; *1901* becomes music critic for *La Revue Blanche; Three Nocturnes for Orchestra* performed; *1902 Pelléas et Mélisande* premieres at Opera-Comique, Paris; *1903* writes music criticism for *Gil Blas*; meets Emma Bardac, the banker's wife and amateur singer; *1904* abandons Lily and moves in with Emma Bardac with whom he has one daughter; Lily attempts suicide but recovers; resulting public scandal causes some of Debussy's friends to sever contacts; begins his orchestral masterpiece, *La Mer*; seeks refuge from scandal at Eastbourne on south coast of England; records several songs with Scottish-born American soprano Mary Garden; *1905* divorces Lily; *La Mer* performs; *1906* begins to compose tone poem *Iberia; 1907* begins to tour widely as pianist and conductor, visiting England, Belgium, The Netherlands, Austria, Hungary, Italy, and Russia; *1908* marries Emma; *Pelléas et Mélisande* performed at the Manhattan Opera House in New York and at La Scala in Milan, where it is conducted by Arturo Toscanini; conducts *Prelude to the Afternoon of a Faun* at Queens Hall, London; begins an opera based on author Edgar Alan Poe's "Fall of the House of Usher"; completes *Iberia*; two British books about him and his music are published; *1909* becomes a member of the advisory board of the Paris Conservatory; *Pelleas et Melisande* premieres successfully in London; begins first book of preludes for piano; composes *Hommage a Haydn* for the piano; experiences first symptoms of cancer; *1910 Ibéria* and *Rondes de printemps* performed; conducts in Vienna and Budapest; *1911 The Martyrdom of St. Sebastian*, with text by Gabriele D'Annunzio, premieres; meets Richard Strauss and Sir Edward Elgar in Turin; *1912* composes two ballets, *Jeux* and *Khamma*, the latter of which is never finished; 100th performance in Paris of *Pelléas et Mélisande; 1913 Jeux* premieres in Paris, performed by the Diaghilev Ballet; composes *Syrinx* for solo flute; *1914* performs in London; composes *Berceuse heroique* as a contribution to war relief efforts, published in *King Al-*

bert's Book, a war charity publication with contributions from distinguished artists and public figures; *1915* composes song "Noel des enfants qui n'ont plus de maison" to his own poem; composes *En blanc et noir* for two pianos; composes sonatas for cello and piano and for flute, viola, and harp; undergoes serious operation for cancer; *1916* writes second version of a libretto for *The Fall of the House of Usher*; begins a sonata for violin and piano; begins *Ode a la France* for soloists, chorus, and orchestra but is unable to complete it because of declining health; *1917* completes a sonata for violin and piano and appears in public for the last time on May 5 to perform it with Gaston Poulet; undergoes second cancer operation, but grows steadily weaker; *1918* dies in Paris on March 25.

Activities of Historical Significance

Claude Debussy is one of the major revolutionary figures in the history of twentieth-century music. Usually credited as the founding father of musical Impressionism and for treating tonality in much the same way that Impressionist painters emphasized the changing nature of light, he remained loyal to many if not most aspects of the Western musical tradition dating back to the Middle Ages, all of his dramatic innovations notwithstanding. Although themes in his compositions may at times be amorphous and elusive, there is nevertheless form and structure underneath the veiled outlines. Debussy was not a Romantic in the tradition of Hector Berlioz or Robert Schumann, but he created works imbued with the deepest emotional sensibilities and the most exquisite subtleties. Debussy was most profoundly influenced in his early years by Russian classical music, particularly that of Modest Mussorgsky, and by the exotic Javanese gamelan sounds of gongs and percussion instruments that he heard at the World Exposition in Paris in 1889. Throughout his career Debussy was able to produce a number of seminal compositions that would profoundly influence twentieth century musical theory and practice.

Starting in the late 1880s, when he joined a circle of Symbolist poets and writers, Debussy became deeply influenced by the literary innovations of the closing years of the nineteenth century, particularly by the poetry of his favorite writers, Stéphane Mallarmé, Paul Verlaine and Charles Baudelaire. His musical adaptations of poetry resulted in some of the most exquisite songs in the entire literature of French music. His most celebrated orchestral work, the *Prelude to the Afternoon of a Faun*, was based on a poem by Mallarmé, and it used the tone of the poem to paint an extraordinary scene of pagan sensuality. In what is arguably his greatest creation, the opera *Pelléas et Mélisande*, Debussy used a Symbolist play by Maurice Maeterlinck to create a work in which the veiled allusions and images of the text are superbly matched by the restraint, subdued sonoroties, and exotic harmonies of the orchestra.

In his orchestral masterpiece, *La Mer*, Debussy created a portrait of the sea that was not a literal picture but rather an evocation of mood, as well as a personal reflection of the sense of awe that the unrestrained forces of nature can inspire. The sea always fascinated Debussy, and his recollections of childhood holidays spent by the Mediterranean and of later storm-swept crossings of the English Channel served as inspiration for this extraordinary orchestral composition. *La Mer* is one of the great works of twentieth century music, and it provides proof that the "impressionist" Debussy was also a master of orchestration and logical structure, using these talents to create in sound an unmatched tonal picture.

By the 1890s, Debussy was becoming increasingly confident in his own abilities to create a new and uniquely personal musical style. Even when he borrowed ideas from such contemporaries as the Norwegian composer Edvard Grieg, as he did in his *String Quartet* (1893), the final product became a masterpiece brimming with new and striking insights. From his earliest days as a student at the Paris Conservatory, Debussy exhibited traits of stubborn independence that would be essential elements in his struggle to achieve his artistic goals. He not only struggled to free himself from the bonds of the German Romantic tradition that culminated in Richard Wagner but as both a brilliant composer and a persuasive critic-journalist, he argued for the necessity of French music to be true to itself. In the last years of his life, suffering terribly from cancer, Debussy continued to explore new possibilities of expressing himself. His last compositions reveal this continuing open-mindedness, particularly the cello sonata of 1915, an experimental work that still can startle a casual modern listener. Deeply stirred by the destruction of World War I, the dying Debussy was somehow able to summon the energy to express his French patriotism in his final compositions, insisting that the title page of his last sonatas be inscribed with the words, "Claude Debussy, musicien français".

Overview of Biographical Sources

The earliest biographies of Debussy, published while the composer was still alive, were characterized by an emphasis on anecdotes and immediate first-hand descriptions rather than theoretical analyses of compositions that were still new and revolutionary to the great majority of the listening public. The decade following his death saw a number of monographs as well as collections of articles in special numbers of the journal *Revue Musicale*. The centennial of Debussy's birth in 1962 was marked by the publication of biographies, such as Jean Barraque's *Debussy* (1972) that invariably demonstrated a broad perspective, presenting the artist's life and achievements within the broadest possible context of a rich and complex European civilization struggling with many unresolved cultural issues on the eve of a devastating world war.

Edward Lockspeiser's biography, *Debussy* (1936), remains the best concise study of the great composer's life and works. The fifth edition, revised in the 1970s by Richard Langham Smith, emphasizes the life much more than the compositions. Lockspeiser's two-volume biographical work, *Debussy: His Life and Mind* (1962-1965), remains a monumental essay in intellectual history and provides immense amounts of detail on the cultural milieu that molded and nurtured the young, impressionable Debussy.

First published in French in Neuchatel, Switzerland, Marcel Dietschy's *A Portrait of Claude Debussy* (1962), is an excellent study of the composer's formative years but is not a complete biography. It does, however, provide important new details on Debussy's often difficult period at the Paris Conservatory. Of particular value are the details on the psychological development of the young man, including the profound impact made on him by his father's arrest for radical political activities after the collapse of the Paris Commune in 1871. Dietschy was extremely perceptive in structuring his book around the numerous women who appeared at each crossroad of Debussy's life.

Older volumes that are still readable and generally reliable factually, but nevertheless distinctly inferior to the one-volume Lockspeiser study, are Maurice Dumesnil's *Claude Debussy: Master of Dreams* (1979) and Leon Vallas's *The Theories of Claude Debussy, musicien francais* (1927). Although it is certainly readable, Victor Serof's *Debussy: Musician of France* (1956) contains a number of significant factual errors and is best avoided by those individuals who are beginning to study the life and achievements of Debussy.

Evaluation of Principal Biographical Sources

Barraque, Jean. *Debussy*. Paris: Seuil, 1962. (**A**) Published in Paris on the occasion of the centenary of Debussy's birth, this is an excellent study from a musical perspective, and includes a useful discography.

Chenneviere, Daniel. *Claude Debussy et son oeuvre*. Paris: A. Durand et fils, 1913. (**A**) Sums up most of the major critical impressions of the composer on the eve of World War I. Now of mainly historical value for Debussy scholars.

Cox, David. "Debussy, (Achille-) Claude 1862-1918." In Justin Wintle, ed., *Makers of Modern Culture*. New York: Facts on File, 1981: 124-126. (**G**) A brief but excellent sketch of Debussy's artistic achievement as seen in the context of twentieth-century culture.

Daly, William H. *Debussy: A Study in Modern Music*. Edinburgh: Methven Simpson, 1908. (**A**) One of the very first critical studies, this booklet remains of interest for a number of the author's astute judgements.

Dietschy, Marcel. *A Portrait of Claude Debussy*. Edited and translated by William Ashbrook and Margaret G. Cobb. Oxford: Clarendon, 1990. (**A, G**) Superbly researched and elegantly written, this study provides the best insights to date on the early, formative years of the composer's life, nicely balancing both his internal psychological development and the larger social and intellectual forces that formed his creative nature. A meticulously revised catalogue of works and a fine selective bibliography add many valuable details to the 1977 catalogue compiled by François Lesure.

Dumesnil, Maurice. *Claude Debussy, Master of Dreams*. 1940. Reprint. Westport, CT: Greenwood, 1979. (**G, Y**) Written in a style that now seems rather outmoded, this is nevertheless a study that contains a number of valuable observations. Although little is said about his music, the mood and atmosphere of Debussy's Paris is often captured in a novelistic fashion.

Harvey, Harry B. *Claude of France: The Story of Debussy.* New York: Allen Towne, 1948. (**Y**) Intended for young people, this volume is largely based on the first edition of Lockspeiser's biography.

Jardillier, Robert. *Claude Debussy.* Dijon, France: Editions de la Revue de Bourgogne, 1922. (**A**) One of the first books to appear after Debussy's death; marked by a strongly partisan and nationalistic tone. Now of mainly historical interest.

Koechlin, Charles. *Debussy.* Paris: H. Laurens, 1927. (**A**) Himself a composer of note, Koechlin here provided many fascinating opinions on the lasting importance of Debussy's work for French and Western music.

Laloy, Louis. *Claude Debussy.* 1909. Reprint. Paris: Aux Armes de france, 1944. (**A**) Written by a close friend and enthusiastic admirer of Debussy, this was the first French critical study. Laloy was an indefatigable journalist who wrote about, among other subjects, the civilization of China and "the future of music."

Lesure, François. *Debussy.* Geneva: Minkoff and Lattes, 1980. (**G**) This remains the best pictorial biography of the composer published to date; the text is in French and English.

Liebich, Louise. *Claude-Achille Debussy.* London: John Lane, 1908. (**A**) Along with the Daly volume, this is the first critical study of the composer, presenting him sympathetically as a "living master of music".

Lockspeiser, Edward. *Debussy.* 5th ed. Revised by Richard Langham Smith. London: Dent, 1980. (**A, G**) The best one-volume biography, based on Lockspeiser's definitive two-volume study.

————. *Debussy: His Life and Mind.* 2 vols. New York: Macmillan, 1962-1965. (**A, G**) Overall, the best detailed work on the composer's life and personality, arguing convincingly that the artistic achievements of Debussy can best be understood as part of a European revolution not only in music, but in literature and the visual arts as well.

Nichols, Roger. *Debussy*. Oxford: Oxford University Press, 1973. (**A, G**) An excellent brief introductory survey with many astute judgments and insights.

Nichols, Roger, and Robert Orledge. "Debussy, (Achille-) Claude." In *The New Grove Dictionary of Music*, edited by Stanley Sadie. Vol. 5: 292-314. London: Macmillan, 1980. (**A, G**) A succinct but excellent biography and analysis of the composer's output; provides a gratifyingly complete bibliography and listing of compositions.

Revue Belge de Musicologie 16 (1962): 43-149. (**A**) A special issue of the leading Belgian musicological journal, this volume emphasized the continuing impact of the composer in the French-speaking world.

Revue Musicale 1 (1920): 98-216. (**A**) This special issue of France's leading music periodical was "consecrated to Debussy" and contains a number of valuable articles on Debussy's legacy and style.

Revue de Musicologie 258 (1964). (**A**) This "golden book" honoring Debussy on the centenary of his birth contains a number of excellent technical articles that stimulated further research on a number of subjects.

Seroff, Victor. *Debussy: Musician of France*. New York: G. Putnam, 1956. (**G**) Written with energy and enthusiasm for its subject, but unfortunately this popular biography contains a number of serious factual errors. It lacks a bibliography and places too much emphasis on Debussy's early amorous adventures.

Slonimsky, Nicolas. "Debussy, (Achille-) Claude." In *Baker's Biographical Dictionary of Musicians*. 8th ed. New York: Schirmer Books, 1992: 402-405. (**A, G**) Brief but valuable article by the venerable and opinionated musicologist; includes a useful bibliography.

Suares, Andre. *Debussy*. 1922. Rev. ed. Paris: Emile-Paul freres, 1936. (**A**) A stimulating study published at a time when some readers still doubted Debussy's greatness.

Tienot, Yvonne, and Oswald d'Estrade-Guerra. *Debussy, l'homme, son oeuvre, son milieu.* Paris: H. Lemoine, 1962. (**A, G**) A sensitive popular biography written from a broad cultural perspective.

Vallas, Leon. *The Theories of Claude Debussy, musicien français.* Translated by Maire O'Brien. 1927. Reprint. Garden City, NY: Dover, 1967. (**A**) An important Debussy scholar argues that the composer was able, through the course of his career, to develop a consistent body of ideas on art and music.

—————. *Claude Debussy: His Life and Works.* Translated by Maire and Grace O'Brien. 1932. Rev. ed. Oxford: Oxford University Press, 1958. (**A**) An excellent translation of a study that tends to exaggerate Debussy's patriotism, depicting him a more politically-inspired artist than he essentially was.

Young, Percy M. *Debussy.* New York: D. White, 1968. (**A, G**) A brief introduction that contains some interesting and perceptive insights.

Overview and Evaluation of Primary Sources

Any serious investigation of Debussy's life and work must begin with three basic reference tools. The most recent work, James R. Briscoe, *Claude Debussy: A Guide to Research* (New York: Garland, 1990; **A**), provides an overview of research on the composer, followed by a chronology of his life and a listing of his compositions; an extremely rich critical bibliography completes the volume. All Debussy research must begin with this excellent book. Also valuable are François Lesure, *Catalogue de l'oeuvre de Claude Debussy* (Geneva: Minkoff, 1977; **A**), and Claude Abravanel, *Claude Debussy: A Bibliography* (Detroit: Information Coordinators, 1974; **A**).

Debussy's compositions are now in the process of being published as *Claude Debussy Oeuvres completes/Complete Works* (Paris: Durand-Costallat, 1986-; **A**). A journal specializing in all aspects of Debussy research is *Cahiers Debussy*, published since 1974 by the Centre de Documentation Claude Debussy in St. Germain-en-Laye, France. A fine compilation of Debussy letters, containing about one-fourth of all of his surviving correspondence, is François Lesure and Roger Nichols, eds., *Debussy Letters* (Cambridge, MA: Harvard University Press, 1987; **A, G**). The letters make clear how much effort Debussy put into his profound desire to be a leader in the transformation of music around 1900. Another collection of letters, edited lovingly by a non-scholar and Debussy enthusiast is Jacqueline M. Charette, ed., *Claude Debussy through His Letters* (New York: Vantage Press, 1990; **A, G**). A valuable selection of Debussy's musical journalism has been collected by François Lesure and Richard Langham Smith in *Debussy on Music: The Critical Writings of the Great French Composer* (New York: Alfred A. Knopf, 1977; **A, G**). Margaret G. Cobb's *The Poetic Debussy: A Collection of His Song Texts and Selected Letters* (Boston: Northeastern University Press, 1982; **A**) is an excellent compilation of the poetry that inspired Debussy to write over sixty songs and without doubt served to open new creative avenues for him to explore.

Fiction and Adaptations

Debussy's life inspired Pierre La Mure to write *Clair de lune, a Novel about Claude Debussy* (New York: Random House, 1962); a play by Curtis White, *Claude*; and a short story by Anthony Burgess, "1889 and the Devil's Mode." None of these works has been hailed as major artistic successes, but they nevertheless present nuances of the composer's complex personality, particularly his relationships with women. Of considerable interest is the 1991 video by Thomas Mowrey, *The Loves of Emma Bardac* (Sony Classical Laserdisc and VHS 46370), which features the piano-playing sisters Katia and Marielle Labeque. This video is a dramatic treatment of the life of Emma Bardac, Debussy's second wife, a gifted woman who had a romantic relationship with the composer Gabriel Fauré before she met Debussy.

Museums, Historical Landmarks, Societies

10 Rue Gustave-Doré (Paris). While living at this address from 1893 through

1899 with Gaby Dupont, Debussy composed much of *Pelléas et Melisande*.

11 Rue de Vintimille (Paris). Debussy lived here with his parents in 1867 and 1868.

24 Square de l'Avenue Foch (Paris). His last home, surrounded by a high iron fence, where he lived with his second wife Emma Bardac and daughter Claude-Emma ("Chou-Chou") from 1905 to 1918.

28 Rue de Constantinople (Paris). Debussy's early benefactress Mme. Blanche-Adélaïde Vasnier, with whom he had a love affair, provided Debussy with a room at her residence located here.

42 Rue de Londres (Paris). From 1888 to 1893, Debussy lived in an attic room at this address with Gaby Dupont.

58 Rue Cardinet (Paris). After abandoning Gaby Dupont, Debussy married dressmaker Rosalie "Lily" Texier and lived with her in a fifth floor apartment at this address from 1899 through 1903.

Chenonceaux (Indre-et-Loire, France). During the summer of 1879, Debussy was engaged as a pianist at the Château de Chenonceaux, where he came into contact with a more stimulating musical world than he had previously known, an experience that had a significant impact on his later intellectual development.

Eastbourne (East Sussex, England). Debussy completed *La Mer* while at the seaside Grand Hotel in 1905.

St. Germain-en-Laye (Yvelines, France). The room above Debussy's parents' china shop, where Debussy was born in 1862 and where he lived until 1864, is marked by a plaque. The Centre de Documentation Claude Debussy is also located here and publishes the scholarly journal *Cahiers Debussy.*

Tomb (Paris). Located in Passy cemetery.

University of Lowell (Lowell, MA). There is a statue of Debussy on campus.

Villa Medici (Rome). As a winner of the prestigious Prix de Rome, Debussy lived at the Villa Medici from 1885 through 1887, but the homesick young musician was miserable during his stay here, calling the Villa "abominable" and his room an "Etruscan tomb."

Other Sources

Boulez, Pierre. "Debussy and the Dawn of Modernism." In *Words on Music from Addison to Barzun*, edited by Jack Sullivan. Athens: Ohio University Press, 1990: 273-276. Suggests that Debussy remains one of the most isolated of all musicians, and that most music historians and critics have either misunderstood or oversimplified his creative legacy.

Brody, Elaine. *Paris: The Musical Kaleidoscope, 1870-1925.* New York: George Braziller, 1987. Superbly researched and beautifully written, this book places Debussy in the middle of an extraordinary collection of talented men and women. Of particular interest are the details relating to American musical influences on Debussy, such as the incorporation of jazz elements in his "Preludes" of 1910-1913.

Cortot, Alfred. *The Piano Music of Claude Debussy.* Translated by Violet Edgell. London: J. & W. Chester, 1922. Brief introduction to the subject, written by one of the great pianists of the century, this remains valuable for its insights, including the notion that Debussy's piano compositions subtly suggest emotions through a type of inference related to a spirit of "patrician reticence."

Cronin, Vincent. *Paris on the Eve, 1900-1914.* London: Collins, 1989. Presents a rich tapestry of Parisian cultural life in the years leading up to World War I, in which Debussy figured prominently.

Fleming, William. *Arts and Ideas.* 8th ed. New York: Holt, Rinehart, and Winston, 1991. An excellent introduction to a society's intellectual evolution and its art, this volume contains a cogently argued section on the central place of *Pelléas et Mélisande* in Impressionist art.

High Fidelity 12 (September 1962). The entire issue, which was dedicated to Debussy and his music, contains a number of valuable articles.

Howat, Roy. *Debussy in Proportion: A Musical Analysis.* Cambridge: Cambridge University Press, 1983. A technical study that provides evidence for the argument that Debussy was one of the great music theorists of the twentieth century.

Jarocinski, Stefan. *Debussy—Impressionism and Symbolism.* Translated by Rollo Myers. 1966. Reprint. London: Eulenberg Books, 1976. Argues that Debussy was much more profoundly influenced by symbolist concepts than by the ideas associated with the Impressionist school of painters. The author also emphasizes his artistic credo was essentially rebellious and revolutionary in spirit.

Long, Marguerite. *At the Piano with Debussy.* Translated by Olive Senior-Ellis. London: Dent, 1972. Written by the most renowned French female pianist of the first half of this century, an artist who personally knew and collaborated with Debussy, this is a book that is in many ways comparable to the writings of Alfred Cortot on the same subject. Besides providing many suggestions of a pianistic nature, Mme. Long notes that where music was concerned, Debussy "was totally involved from the moment he sat down at the piano."

Meister, Barbara. *Nineteenth-Century French Song: Faure, Chausson, Duparc, and Debussy.* Bloomington: Indiana University Press, 1980. An excellent survey of the work of the four most important French art song composers of modern times.

Mordden, Ethan. *A Guide to Orchestral Music: The Handbook for Non-Musicians.* New York: Oxford University Press, 1986. Contains a brief section on Debussy; analyses of Debussy's major compositions are rich in thought-provoking insights.

Myers, Rollo. "Debussy and French Music." *Musical Times* 108 (October 1967): 899-901. Suggests that while Debussy's impact on modern French music was a profound one, he actually had relatively little stylistic influence on specific French composers.

Nichols, Roger, ed. *Debussy Remembered*. Portland, OR: Amadeus Press, 1992. A significant source that contains reminiscences of Debussy by individuals who knew him intimately, including Marguerite Long, Colette, Maggie Teyte, and Sir Henry Wood.

Orledge, Robert. *Debussy and the Theatre*. Cambridge: Cambridge University Press, 1982. Presents a full picture of Debussy's often frustrating theatrical experiences, including abandoned opera projects both before and after the composition of *Pélleas et Mélisande*.

Palmer, Christopher. *Impressionism in Music*. London: Hutchinson, 1973. An important survey that places Debussy in the context of a series of cultural transformations that took place in the closing years of the nineteenth century in France and other European countries.

Parks, Richard S. *The Music of Claude Debussy*. New Haven, CT: Yale University Press, 1989. An impressive book that constitutes the first comprehensive theoretical-analytical study of Debussy's compositions.

Sadie, Stanley. *Stanley Sadie's Music Guide, An Introduction*. Englewood Cliffs, NJ: Prentice-Hall, 1986. An excellent introductory overview of Western music which is very successful in its mixture of musical description and background cultural information. Among the many valuable comments made about Debussy is the idea that his contact with Wagner's music convinced him of the urgent need to approach all aspects of modern music differently.

Schmitz, Elie Robert. *The Piano Works of Claude Debussy*. 1950. Reprint. New York: Duell, Sloan, and Pearce, 1966. This study by a noted French-born pianist who personally knew the composer has won praise from both pianists and composers.

Wenk, Arthur. *Claude Debussy and Twentieth-Century Music.* Boston: G. K. Hall, 1983. A perceptive study that examines Debussy's impact on the entire spectrum of musical development since the early years of the twentieth century.

—————. *Debussy and the Poets.* Berkeley: University of California Press, 1976. An excellent study of how Debussy's music was inspired by the poetry of Baudelaire, Verlaine, Mallarmé, and Louys.

John Haag
University of Georgia

Edgar Degas
1834-1917

Chronology

Born Hilaire Germain Edgar de Gas on July 19, 1834 in Paris into a privileged and wealthy banking family, the son of Pierre August-Hyacinthe de Gas, manager of the Paris branch of the family's Neapolitan bank, and Célestine Musson, daughter of a successful New Orleans French Creole businessman; *1845-1853* attends the Lycée Louis-le-Grand; *1853* earns his baccalaureate degree and enrolls in the Faculty of Law; *1854* enters the studio of Louis Lamonthe, a disciple of the Neoclassicist painter Jean-August-Dominique Ingres; *1855* enters the Ecole des Beaux-Arts; finds the formal academic program of the school confining and leaves to study classical composition in Italy; *1859* returns to Paris, establishing his own studio in an apartment on the Rue Madame, where he concentrates on painting portraits and historical subjects such as *The Bellelli Family* and *Young Spartan Girls Challenging Spartan Boys*; *1861* meets painter Edouard Manet, who influences his style, as evidenced in *Orchestra at the Opéra*; *1869* begins signing his works simply "Degas"; *1870-1871* serves in the artillery during the Franco-Prussian War, participating in the defense of Paris; *1872* leaves France for the United States; travels to New Orleans, where his uncle and two brothers are in the cotton business; stays six months and begins *Portraits in an Office: The Cotton Exchange at New Orleans*; *1873* returns to Paris; *1874* assumes a leading role in organizing the first exposition of artists of the Impressionist movement, under whose influence he has now begun to paint; *1874-1886* shows in seven of eight Impressionist Exhibitions; completes two of his best paintings, *Absinthe* and *The Dancing Lesson*; *1887* ceases to show in group exhibitions; becomes increasingly withdrawn from fellow artists, owing in part to his failing eyesight and misanthropic nature; continues experimentation in form and technique, becoming interested in engraving and sculpture; *1892* virtually gives up oil painting in favor of pastels, producing in this medium his most famous series of nude women: *Woman Drying Herself after the Bath* and *Woman at Her Toilet*; progressive blindness forces him to abandon artistic creativity altogether; *1912* forced to move from his long-time residence to new quarters on the boulevard de Clichy; distressed by the deaths of old friends, becomes even more withdrawn; *1914-1917* during World War I, is often seen wandering the streets alone, neglectful of his appearance; *1917* dies of a stroke on September 26.

Activities of Historical Significance

Painter, sculptor, and engraver, Edgar Degas mastered every medium he set himself to learn. Although associated with Impressionism, he never felt comfortable in that school, and with good reason. His solitary nature carried over into his art, which was individualistic and non-conformist. He never shared the enthusiasm of the Impressionists for working in the open. And even though he often chose out-of-doors subjects, he always preferred to finish his compositions in the controlled, safe atmosphere of the studio. He also remained true to the academic method in his taut, precise draftsmanship. However, his composition and use of color was truly innovative.

A student of photography, many of his pictures give the impression of fragmentary snap-shots taken at various angles, heightened by abstract, almost arbitrary, chromatics. Degas tried to maximize the drama of a scene rather than produce it realistically. He chose to illustrate the tension and grace of the ballet by ingenious artifice in an interplay of color and form. He was preoccupied with the depiction of motion, heightening this sensation through light reflected on clothes and gestures.

He found that pastels served his purpose better then oils because they made his figures seem a natural part of their environment. His pastels of nudes comprised about twenty percent of his total output and, except for his sculpture, dominated his output during the latter years of his life. The result was a further refinement of the free and easy spirit which already permeated the works of his earlier period, a more sophisticated reflection of the balance between technique, color, and environment. In these works Degas did not choose to depict the elegant beauties of the salon; he preferred lower-class women performing routine activities: bathing, drying their bodies, combing their hair, going to bed. Many of his models were prostitutes. This art, like that of Auguste Renoir, was distinguished by its appreciation of the richness and beauty of the human form, the display of grace even in mundane activity.

Despite the apparent naturalness of his creative process, Degas was a cerebral artist; his theatrical compositions the product of a long, painstaking, intellectual process. "No art is less spontaneous than mine," he wrote. "What I do is the result of reflection and the study of the great masters; of inspiration, spontaneity, temperament I know nothing. I must redo the same subject ten times, twenty times." The reality he portrayed was of his own creation. Degas owed little of this to others. Fellow artist Camille Pissaro believed him to be one of the greatest artists of his age, and he was certainly one of the most original. His place in the modern art movement is secure, although his stature as a major artist did not become apparent until after his death, and most of his works were not displayed during his lifetime. Degas even became one of the great collectors of his own work, buying back many of the paintings he had originally sold. The world knew even less of his sculpture. Only his *Little Dancer* had been displayed publicly. The sale of the contents of his studio in 1917 brought bidders from across Europe, including agents from the National Gallery in London, the Victoria and albert Museum, and the Louvre. For the first time, many people were able to appreciate his genius and were able to learn from it. In many respects, Degas defies classification, but his luminous use of color, his naturalness, spontaneity, and simplicity of design, his qualities of poetry and lyricism are major influences in the further development of artists who came after him.

Overview of Biographical Sources

The literature on Degas consists, on the one hand, of a series of memoirs, collections of letters, and biographies and, on the other, of various art books and exhibition catalogues. Biographers usually have a difficult time with their reclusive subject. Degas was determined to let few pierce his inner shell. As he told his friend Alexis Rouart, "I want to be famous and unknown." He got his wish. He chose a life of solitude, never marrying, indeed renouncing sexual gratification, and sacrificed his private life to his art. Art dealer Ambroise Vollard, who knew him as well as most, hardly goes beyond anecdotes about what Degas did and said in *Degas, an Intimate Portrait* (New York: Crown, 1937).

Degas's public life was, of course, his artistic output, which in his case was vast, as is the literature on it. In recent years, general works have given way to more narrow and monographic studies, which concentrate on particular aspects of his oeuvre like his sculpture, his pastels, and on various subjects: racing pictures, ballet, laundresses, and nude women bathing.

Evaluation of Principal Biographical Sources

McMullen, Roy. *Degas: His Life, Times and Work.* Boston: Houghton-Mifflin, 1984. (**A, G**) A scholarly presentation of the painter's life with a full-scale bibliography. The book is organized chronologically rather than by artistic period and relates Degas to his social class. Among the best and most readable biographies of the painter.

Sutton, Denis. *Degas: Life and Works.* New York: Artabras, 1991. (**A, G**) A comprehensive, scholarly synthesis of the artist's career that completely belies its coffee-table-book format. The discussion of Degas's art is divided according to subject matter: the nudes, the horseracing, the theater, the street scenes, etc. Sutton's enthusiasm for his subject shows in this interesting presentation.

Overview and Evaluation of Primary Sources

The basic catalogue of Degas's paintings and pastels is by P. A. Lemoisne: *Degas et son oeuvre* (4 vols. Paris: Arts et métiers qraphiques, 1946-1949; **A**). John Rewald prepared a catalogue of his sculpture entitled *The Complete Sculptures of Degas* (London: Lefevre Gallery, 1976; **A**).

A treatment of his nudes can be found in Richard Thompson's *Degas: The Nudes* (London: Thames and Hudson, 1988; **A, G**). This book was one of the first that specialized in such a study and presents the sculptures in an empirical framework, examining how they were made and what rules they followed or flouted. It traces Degas's interest in the human body from the early copies of Renaissance masters through the drawings from life and the later imaginings.

For another special subject see George T. M. Shackelford, *Degas: The Dancers* (Washington, D.C.: National Gallery of Art, 1984; **A, G**), which is a catalogue of the exposition celebrating the sesquicentennial of Degas's birth, presenting fifty-eight pastels, charcoals, oils, and chalks, and offering descriptions of their provenance and supporting literature.

Another important work is Jean Sutherland Boggs's *Drawings by Degas* (New York: Harry N. Abrams, 1966; **A, G**), an exhibition catalogue of the 156 drawings shown in St. Louis, Philadelphia, and Minneapolis. The illustrations are accompanied by incisive explanations of this most spontaneous aspect of the master's art. Also important is *Degas' Drawings* (New York: Dover, 1973; **A, G, Y**), which reproduces all the illustrations in the portfolio *Les dessins de Degas reproduits en fac-simile* (Paris: Demotte, 1922-1923), edited by Henri Rivière.

Special catalogues of Degas's works in museum collections can be found in Charles S. Moffet, *Degas Paintings in the Metropolitan Museum of Art* (Mount Vernon, NY: The Artist's Limited Edition, 1979; **A**), and Richard R. Brettell and Susan Folds McCullagh, *Degas in the Art Institute of Chicago* (New York: Harry N. Abrams, 1984; **A, G, Y**). Of more general interest is *Ministère de la Culture et de la Communication, Musée d'Orsay Guide* (Paris: Editions de la Rencontre, 1986; **A, G, Y**).

Degas wrote no memoirs, but he left behind many letters and various commentary. For these, see *The Notebooks of Edgar Degas* (2 vols. Edited by Theodore Reff. Oxford: Clarendon Press, 1976; **A**); and *Degas' Letters* (1945. Reprint. Oxford: Cassirer, 1947; **A**), translated by Marguerite Kay, which contains letters not found in the original French edition. Also of interest are Rachel Barnes, *Degas by Degas* (New York: Alfred A. Knopf, 1990; **G, Y**), and Richard Kendall, ed., *Degas by Himself: Drawings, Prints, Paintings, Writings* (Boston: Little, Brown, 1987; **A, G, Y**).

There is as yet no definitive edition of all his correspondence. Accounts of him appear in books published by friends and fellow artists, including Edmond Duranty, *La nouvelle peinture* (Paris: H. Floury, 1946); Daniel Halévy, *Pays parisiens* (Paris: Bernard Grasset, 1932); and *Degas parle* (Paris: La Palatine, 1960). Degas is mentioned in *Camille Pissaro, Letters to his son Lucien* (New York: Pantheon, 1943), translated by John Rewald; Berthe Morisot, *Correspondence* (Paris: Quatre Chemins-Editart, 1950); Odilon Redon, *A soi-même notes sur la vie, l'art et les artistes* (Paris: H. Fleury, 1922), and Maurice Denis, *Journals* (Paris: LaColombe, 1957-1959.

Principal Works

Paintings
Portrait of the Duchess of Morbilli (1855-1856)
Achille de Gas in the Uniform of a Cadet (1856-1857)
Young Spartans Exercising (1860)
Semiramis Founding Babylon (1861)
At the Races (1862)
Self Portrait (1862)
Portrait of a Young Woman (1867)
Mlle Fiocre in the Ballet 'La Source' (1867-1868)
Jacques-James Tissot (1868)
Les Musiciens à L'orchestre (1868-1869)
Madame Camus au Piano (1869)
The False Start (1869-1872)
Madame Camus (1869-1870)
The Dancing Class (1872)
Foyer de Danse (1873)
New Orleans Cotton Office (1873)
Sulking (Bouderie) (1873-1875)
Women Combing their Hair (1875-1876)
The Rehearsal (1877)
The Dancing Class (1880)
Two Laundresses (1884)
The Milinary Shop (1885)
Ballet Scene (1907)

Sculpture
A Dancer at the Age of Fourteen (1880)
Dancer Looking at the Sole of Her Foot (1900)

Museums, Historical Landmarks, and Societies

Most important museums in Europe and the U.S. hold at least one Degas. The most important works are in Musée d'Orsay and the Louvre (Paris); Courtauld Institute Galleries, National Gallery, and Tate Gallery (London); Pushkin Museum (Moscow); Kunsthalle (Hamburg); Ny Carlsberg Glypotek (Copenhagen); Nasjonalgalleriet (Oslo); Nationalmuseum (Stockholm), Foundation Calouste Gulbenkian (Lisbon); The Art Institute (Chicago); Museum of Art (Cleveland); Museum of Art (Philadelphia); Institute of Arts (Detroit); The Metropolitan Museum of Art and The Museum of Modern Art (New York); the Norton Simon Museum of Art (Pasadena); and National Gallery of Art (Washington, D.C.).

Places of Residence and Work (Paris). His birthplace is at 8 rue Saint-Georges; his boyhood homes at 21 rue de la Victoire, 24 rue de l'Ouest (now rue d'Assas), and 37 rue Madame. Apartments and studios in which he lived and worked are located at 13 rue de Laval (today rue Victor-Massé), 77 rue Blanche, 4 rue Frochot, 19 bis rue Fontaine Saint-Georges, 21 rue Pigalle, and 6 boulevard de Clichy. Most of the buildings, if they are still standing, bear a marker paying tribute to their association with the artist.

Portrait (Paris). Gustave Moreau's *Degas at the Uffizi* (1859) is in the Musée Gustave Moreau.

Self-Portraits. Degas in a Slouch Hat (1857-1858) is in the collections of the Clark Art Institute, Williamstown, Massachusetts, and *Degas Tipping His Hat* (1862) and *Artist in his Studio* (1873) are at the Foundation Calouste Gulbenkian in Lisbon. *Degas and Evariste de Valernes* (1864) is in the Musée d'Orsay.

Tomb (Paris). Degas is buried in the family vault in the cemetery of Montmartre.

Other Sources

Brown, Marilyn R. *Degas and the Business of Art: "A Cotton Office in New Orleans".* University Park, PA: Penn State Press, 1993. Degas's painting entitled "A Cotton Office in New Orleans" is one of the most significant images of nineteenth-century capitalism, in part because it was the first painting by an

Impressionist to be purchased by a museum. Drawing upon archival materials, Marilyn R. Brown explores the accumulated social meanings of the work in light of shifting audiences and changing market conditions and assesses the artist's complicated relationship to the business of art.

Fosca, François. *Degas*. Geneva: Editions d'Art Albert Skira, 1954. (**G, Y**) A short course on Degas's works, revealing his preoccupation with problems of form and composition.

Gordon, Robert, and Andrew Forge. *Degas*. New York: Harry N. Abrams, 1988. (**G**) A lavishly presented compendium of Degas's works. Coloristically superb, it reflects the high standards of the publisher. Along with the text are reviews of Degas's works by contemporaries.

Hüttinger, Edward. *Degas*. New York: Crown, 1967. (**G**) A book of illustrations held together by a text that explains the artist's personal development.

Lipton, Eunice. *Looking into Degas: Uneasy Images of Women and Modern Life*. (**A**) Berkeley: University of California Press, 1987. A militant feminist's attempt to evaluate the paintings and pastels of Degas as a reflection of the social struggles of the nineteenth century from the standpoint of women, class, and sexuality. The author is less concerned with objectivity than emotional responses, and the result is correspondingly more provocative than scholarly.

Millard, Charles W. *The Sculpture of Edgar Degas*. Princeton, NJ: Princeton University Press, 1976. (**A, G**) Originally a doctoral dissertation, the book provides a critical and historical framework in which to evaluate the artist's works. Millard takes issue with the commonly held belief that Degas conceived and used his sculpture as models for his paintings and pastels, stating categorically that they possessed their own unique integrity. Furthermore he argues that, although Degas was influenced by the small sculpture of classical Greece and Renaissance bronzes, he left no school of his own.

Reff, Theodor. *Degas: The Artist's Mind*. New York: Harper and Row, 1976. (**G**) Reff tries to discover what is unique about Degas's creativity by relating the man's artistic concepts to his academic precedents and current influences.

Rich, Daniel C. *Edgar-Hilaire-Germain Degas*. New York: Harry N. Abrams, 1951. (**G**) Consists mostly of color plates arranged in chronological progression, presenting his most famous paintings with an explanation about each one.

Terrasse, Antoine. *Degas*. Garden City, NY: Doubleday, 1972. (**G**) A conventional presentation, beginning with the obligatory biography, proceeding through the artist's life by categories of his works. There is a helpful year-by-year chronology of major works. Also of interest is a section on the art that Degas himself collected from Cezanne and Corot to Pissaro and Van Gogh.

William Laird Kleine-Ahlbrandt
Purdue University

Eugène Delacroix
1798-1863

Chronology

Born Ferdinand-Victor-Eugène Delacroix on April 26, 1798, in Charenton-Saint-Maurice (Seine), son of Charles Delacroix, a lawyer, and Victoire Oeben Delacroix; some scholars believe that his actual father was statesman and diplomat Charles-Maurice de Talleyrand, Prince of Benevento; *1800-1805* lives in Marseille and Bordeaux, where his father serves as Prefect; *1806-1815* attends the Lycée Impérial in Paris, where he receives a classical education; *1814* his mother dies; begins publishing etched and lithographed political cartoons in the popular press; *1815* enters the atelier of the academic painter Pierre-Narcisse Guérin; *1816* enrolls in the Ecole des Beaux-Arts as a pupil of Guérin; becomes friends with the future Romantic artists Théodore Géricault, Ary Scheffer, and Richard Parkes Bonington; *1816* publishes engravings and lithographs in the popular press; *1818* poses for Géricault's *Raft of the Medusa*; *1818 or 1819* copies Renaissance artists Raphael and Paolo Veronese, Flemish painter Peter Paul Rubens, and other masters in the Louvre, a practice he will never abandon; *1819* paints *The Virgin of the Harvest*, commissioned for the parish church at Orcemont (Seine-et-Oise); *1821* completes *The Virgin of the Sacred Heart*, a commission passed to him by Géricault, and four panels in the house of the actor François-Joseph Talma; *1822* exhibits at his first salon *The Barque of Dante*, a painting indebted to Géricault's *Medusa* and which the French government purchases; critical acclaim comes from the painter Baron Antoine-Jean Gros and the young journalist Adolphe Thiers, who heralds Delacroix as a genius and who later becomes a prominent politician and an influential patron; begins his *Journal*; *mid-1820s* admitted to the Restoration salons of Baron François Gérard and others, where writers, artists, and musicians mix with fashionable society; *1824* shows four paintings at the Salon, including *Scenes from the Massacres at Chios*, inspired by the Greek War for independence; although critical response is mixed, the government purchases the painting; begins to be acclaimed as the leader of French Romantic art, which opposes the neo-classical movement represented by Jean-Auguste-Dominique Ingres and the followers of

Jacques-Louis David; the *Journal* breaks off on October 5; *1825* visits England, viewing paintings by J. M. W. Turner and John Constable; renews his friendship with Bonington; sees performances of William Shakespeare and of German writer Johann Wolfgang von Goethe's *Faust*; returns to Paris, shares a studio with Bonington, and begins painting subjects from Shakespeare, English poet Lord Byron, Scottish author Sir Walter Scott, and historical novels of the Middle Ages; *1826* gains entry to the Romantic cénacle of authors Victor Hugo and Charles Augustin Sainte-Beuve but maintains his distance from this flamboyant side of French Romanticism; receives from the Conseil d'Etat his first important commission, *Justinian Drafting His Laws* (hung in the Palais d'Orsay and destroyed during the Paris Commune in 1871); paints *The Execution of the Doge Marino Faliero*, based on Byron's poem and which may allude to the recently crowned and unpopular Charles X; exhibits at the Galerie Lebrun works representing the Greek war, including the allegorical *Greece on the Ruins of Missolonghi*, a memorial for Byron, who died on his way to join the Greek forces, as well as for the Greek defeat; *1827* exhibits *The Combat of the Giaour and Hassan*, also based on the work of Byron and evidence of Delacroix's interest in oriental themes; shows thirteen paintings at the Salon of 1827-1828, including *The Agony in the Garden*, commissioned in 1824 by the Prefect of the Seine for the Church of Saint-Paul-Saint-Louis in Paris; *The Death of Sardanapalus* draws hostile comments from the press, temporarily costing him government commissions but its colorful violence and scandalous exuberance reinforces Delacroix's position as a leader of the Romantic school; *1828* publication of Albert Stapfer's translation of Goethe's *Faust*, with seventeen lithographs by Delacroix which won praise from Goethe himself; exhibits *Mephistopheles Appears Before Faust* at Hobday's Gallery in London; completes *Cardinal Richelieu Saying Mass in the Chapel of the Palais Royal* (destroyed during the February Revolution of 1848); *1828-1831* executes history paintings, *The Assassination of the Bishop of Liège* (1829), based on Sir Walter Scott's *Quentin Durward*, *The Battle of Poitiers* (1830), and *The Battle of Nancy* (1831), all of which combine historical accuracy with vibrant color and animated movement; *1829* publishes his first article, "Des Critiques en matière d'art," in the *Revue de Paris*; *1830* commences work on *28 July 1830. Liberty Leading the People*, an allegorical celebration of the Revolution of 1830 which brought the Orleanist Louis Philippe to power; *1831* exhibits the *Liberty* and seven other paintings at the Salon; although not well received by the critics, *Liberty* is purchased by the government, which later removes it (1832) from the public view as too revolutionary; made Chevalier (Knight) of the Légion d'Honneur; *1832* visits Morocco, Algiers, and Spain as a member of the Count de Mornay's diplomatic mission to the Sultan of Morocco; fills sketchbooks with notes and scenes of Arab life and customs, which he will later draw upon to paint such works as the *Jewish Wedding in Morocco* (1837-1841?) and the *Fanatics of Tangier* (1838); paints the *Portrait of Nicolò Paganini; 1833* receives, with the assistance of Adolphe Thiers, now Minister of Trade and Public Works, a commission to decorate the walls and ceiling of the Salon du Roi at the Chambre des Députés in the Palais Bourbon (completed 1837), the first of seven major government commissions for the decoration of public buildings; *1834* exhibits five paintings at the Salon, including the *A Street in Meknes* and *The Women of Algiers in their Apartment*; *1835* engages as his housekeeper Jenny Le Guillou, who will serve him faithfully until his death; suffers serious outbreak of the throat ailment that recurs periodically until his death; *1837* fails at first attempt to secure election to the Institut de France; exhibits at the Salon *The Battle of Taillebourg*, commissioned for Louis-Philippe's Galerie des Batailles at Versailles; paints a celebrated self-portrait; *1838* receives a commission to decorate the ceiling of the Deputies' Library of the Palais Bourbon (completed in 1847); *1839* travels to Belgium and Holland to study the work of Rubens; paints *Hamlet and Horatio in the Graveyard; 1840* receives commissions to paint a *Lamentation* for the Church of Saint-Denis du Saint-Sacrement (completed in 1844) and to decorate the the cupola of the Library of the Senate in the Luxembourg Palace (completed in 1846); shows *The Justice of Trajan* at the Salon; *1841* shows three paintings at the Salon, including *The Entry of the Crusaders into Constantinople* and *The Shipwreck of Don Juan; 1842* visits George Sand and Frédéric Chopin at Nohant; *1843* issues sets of lithographs, seven based on Goethe's *Goetz von Berlichingen* and thirteen illustrating Shakespeare's *Hamlet; 1846* shows three paintings at the Salon, including *The Abduction of Rebecca*; made an Officer of the Légion d'Honneur; *1847* resumes the *Journal; 1849* appointed to the Commission of Fine Arts and to the Jury of the Salon; receives a commission to decorate the Chapelle des Saints-Agnes in the Church of Saint Sulpice (completed in 1861); *1850* receives a commission to decorate the ceiling of the Galerie d'Apollon in the Louvre (completed in 1851); *1851* receives a commission to decorate the Salon de la Paix in the Hôtel de ville (completed in 1854; destroyed during the Paris Commune in May 1871);

named to the Paris City Council; *1855* shows thirty-six paintings in a retrospective at the Exposition universelle, which includes most of the famous canvases from the 1820s and the 1830s; wins Grand Medal of Honor; made Commander of the Légion d'Honneur; *1856* continues work on the Saint-Sulpice murals despite frequent illness; *1857* elected to the Institut de France, after failing seven times; moves to his last studio at 6, Place Fürstenberg; *1859* shows eight paintings at his final Salon; *1860* exhibits twenty-three paintings at the Galerie Martinet on the Boulevard des Italiens; *1861* completes the Saint-Sulpice murals; *1863* paints *Arabs Skirmishing in the Mountains,* his last major canvas; dies on August 13 in his house on the Place Fürstenberg, and is buried after a State funeral at the church of Saint-Germain-des-Prés in the cemetery of Père Lachaise.

Activities of Historical Significance

Eugène Delacroix in art, Victor Hugo in literature, and Hector Berlioz in music have, since the 1820s and early 1830s, symbolized the French Romantic revolution. Although a reluctant hero in the revolt against Neo-Classicism and the champions of monarchy, aristocracy, and church, Delacroix sought a radical renewal of painting. And his most controversial paintings, *The Chios Massacres* and *The Death of Sardanapalus*, aggressively juxtaposed at the Salons of 1824 and 1827 with *The Vow of Louis XIII* and *The Apotheosis of Homer* by his lifelong rival, neo-Classicist Jean-Auguste-Dominique Ingres, were proclaimed by supporters and critics alike as exemplars of the new movement. He must therefore be viewed first of all in this historical role. But to reduce Delacroix to this function is to minimize his achievement, for he was also the single greatest painter of this revolt. He not only continued to paint remarkable canvases after the battles over Romanticism had waned but also decorated with murals numerous public buildings in Paris, and he was a writer of considerable talent and insight.

Delacroix's paintings in the decade following 1822, when he exhibited *The Barque of Dante* at his first Salon, challenged and then helped transform French painting. Until that time, the conventions of the dominant neo-classical school of Jacques-Louis David and his followers, which had prescribed content as well as techniques of composition since the 1780s, required pure draftsmanship, carefully delineated forms, and the achievement of a smooth and impersonal painted surface.

During the first half of the nineteenth century, Ingres continued this tradition, epitomizing Neo-Classicism just as Delacroix symbolized Romanticism, and the conflict between these two schools persisted until the Universal Exhibition of 1855, at which each artist enjoyed separate shows.

Delacroix rejected Neo-Classicism, emphasizing instead the creative role of the imagination and the emotional and aesthetic qualities of color, which he considered independent of the subject. Energetic and visible brush strokes animated this color, and Delacroix left much undefined in his images, intimating that intangible qualities such as the inner spirit of genius or nobility of character can never be perfectly reproduced. Canvases such as the *Chios Massacres* or *The Death of Sardanapalus* were frequently tempestuous, and filled with drama, violence, movement, and contrast—indeed with the untidy passions and sufferings of life.

Critical reaction often divided along predictable lines, with the defenders of literary and political Romanticism praising Delacroix, and opponents such as Etienne Delécluze finding him wanting when measured by neo-classical standards. Delacroix's choice of subject matter during this period likewise evinces a repudiation of Neo-Classicism. Oriental scenes; horses, wild animals, and hunts; portraits; historical and literary subjects from medieval or renaissance history, such as the battle paintings of the late 1820s or *The Barque of Dante*; and literary subjects from contemporary writers, such as the illustrations for *Faust* or the paintings inspired by Byron were favored, as were religious paintings, landscapes, still lifes, and genre scenes. From these years also come *The Chios Massacres, Greece on the Ruins of Missolonghi*, and *Liberty Leading the People*, all of which deal with contemporary events.

After 1832 and while at work on the murals, Delacroix continued to paint easel pictures and to exhibit at the Salon, and he returned, with the exception of public events, to subjects and themes favored during the 1820s and early 1830s. During a working lifetime of less than 50 years, he would execute more than 900 oil paintings, several thousand drawings, some 1500 pastels and watercolors, 24 engravings, more than 100 lithographs and prints, and fill more than 60 sketchbooks, an immense body of work for a man often in fragile health. Late Romantic poet Charles Baudelaire surveyed Delacroix's achievement as an artist, concluding that he "was passionately in love with passion and coldly determined to seek the means of expressing it."

Between 1833 and his death in 1863, Delacroix executed seven commissions to decorate public buildings in Paris, evidence that despite the controversial nature of his art, he enjoyed considerable government patronage. Those found in the Church of Saint Sulpice and the Louvre aside, these wall paintings are little known, due partly to restricted access and partly to the difficulty of viewing them as a whole. Yet they are important, for their conception and execution required great intellectual effort, new techniques of composition, and the organization of a workshop of assistants. Complex allegories in the Renaissance and Baroque tradition, with their subject matter derived from classical sources, they often suggested concepts of government power and responsibility. The murals for the Palais Bourbon Library (1838-1847) and Saint Sulpice are of particular interest, for the former reveal much of Delacroix's philosophy of history and the latter his philosophy of life. For the Palais Bourbon, Delacroix devised an intellectually and artistically coherent program illustrating the birth and death of classical civilization. Indebted no doubt to contemporary philosophies of history, this program also reflects Delacroix's innate pessimism and his worries about the fragile nature of civilization. By implying a cyclical interpretation of history, it also critiqued then fashionable ideas of progress. The murals for the Chapel of the Holy Angels in the Church of Saint-Sulpice (1849-1861) were Delacroix's last major public commission. In the ceiling appears *Saint Michael Defeating the Devil*, while facing each other on the walls are *Heliodorus Driven From the Temple* and *Jacob Wrestling With the Angel*. Programmatic coherence for these works come from reiterated themes, such as the idea of human life as endless struggle, the triumph of good over evil, and the impossibility of resisting divine will or fate and hence the need for stoic resignation to the unchanging elements of the human condition.

Delacroix embodied Romanticism as much by his character and his writings as his art. His conception of himself can be elicited from his self-portraits, particularly that of 1837, and from his *Journal* and letters, and it can be confirmed by daguerreotypes taken late in his life, such as the portrait made by Félix Nadar in 1858, and by the perceptions of contemporaries such as poet and critic Charles Baudelaire. Delacroix was at once aristocratic and melancholy, elegant and fastidious, and somewhat of a dandy, and he viewed himself with detachment, insight, and candor. A solitary for whom the inner life ruled but who was welcomed in fashionable society for his witty and cultivated conversation, he was self-possessed and concealed much of himself behind a polished surface of exquisite manners and self-control. Absolutely dedicated to his work and capable of strenuous exertion despite his frail health, he never married but was rarely without female companionship, especially in his younger years. Delacroix held a romantic conception of the artist as one who was not only creative and exceptional but also destined to suffer because of these very gifts. And, although a stoic and a life-long pessimist, perhaps due partly to his temperament and partly to his reading of Roman philosophers, he shared the titanic aspirations of his Romantic brethren. "All my days lead to the same conclusion," he wrote in his *Journal* on April 26, 1824, "an infinite longing for something which I can never have, a void which I cannot fill, an intense desire to create by every means and to struggle as far as possible against the flight of time and the distractions that deaden my soul." Perhaps the best summation of Delacroix's complex character came from Baudelaire, who described him as a "volcanic crater artistically concealed by bouquets of flowers."

Delacroix exerted a powerful influence on the artists who came after him. But because the artistic tradition in which he worked—a tradition that took its subject matter from history and literature, that acknowledged its debts to past masters, and that accepted intellectually complex allegories—all but ended in the middle of the nineteenth century, it was not the content of Delacroix's paintings that proved influential but his artistic techniques and his use of color. As late-nineteenth-century painter Paul Cézanne noted, "we all paint through him," and artists from Impressionists such as Claude Monet, Auguste Renoir, and Edgar Degas to post-Impressionists like Georges Seurat, Paul Gauguin, and Vincent Van Gogh could copy and admire his work.

Overview of Biographical Sources

Comprehensive biographies of Eugène Delacroix are surprisingly few, considering not only his importance as an artist and his role in the French Romantic rebellion, but also the vast quantity of materials available, which range from his *Journal* and letters to the writings of his contemporaries. In contrast, there is no shortage of works dealing with his artistic output, as demonstrated by a perusal of the *Art Index* and the excellent bibliographies in the books by René Huyghe (1963) and Lucien Rudrauf (1942) and the 1963 exhibition catalogue by Maurice Sérullaz.

This discrepancy results from the considerable problems confronting prospective biographers of Delacroix, most notably the contradictions between Delacroix the man, whose ideas were as reactionary as his talent was romantic, and the style and subject matter of his paintings. Other writers, ranging from contemporary critics to modern scholars have emphasized the unresolved tension between the classic and the romantic tendencies in Delacroix's life and work and between the private man and the public persona. Not surprisingly, Frank Trapp, whose *Attainment of Delacroix* (1970) is the most complete biographical study in English, finds Delacroix's personality elusive. The enigmatic relationship between Delacroix and his art should seemingly make a psychological or psychoanalytical approach attractive, but few scholars have made this choice. Art historian Jack Spector is one exception, and in his *The Death of Sardanapalus* (1974), he advances a psychological explanation of the genesis of Delacroix's most controversial painting. If the complexity of Delacroix's character and personality confounds the biographer, so too does his artistic evolution. Trapp, for example, gives a chronological account of his early period and then adopts a topical format for the years 1832-1863, often blurring the lines of further development. The idea that Delacroix's career has two essential stages has also influenced Lee Johnson, whose catalogue raisonné of the paintings divides them into two groups, those executed 1816-1831 and 1832-1863, with a third part reserved for the public murals. The more or less chronological approach followed by René Huyghe in his *Delacroix* (1963) and by Tom Prideaux in his popular biography *The World of Delacroix* (1966) resolves some of the problems raised by the topical approach while bringing forth new ones.

To make matters yet more difficult, Delacroix appeared at a pivotal point in the history of France and of culture and painting, and he thwarts the desires of modern scholars to fit him into orderly categories, just as he frustrated contemporaries who sought to enlist him under the banner of Romanticism. Biographers aspiring to place Delacroix and his art within the context of his times must confront the problematic history of French Romanticism, helpful introductions to which are D. G. Charlton's *The French Romantics* and F. W. J. Hemmings's *Culture and Society in France, 1789-1848*. Romanticism was first and foremost a literary and artistic rebellion, but, unlike similar movements in Great Britain or Germany, the French variant also had a political and a generational dimension. So-called Romantics therefore often sympathized with one or more aspects of this rebellion but not with all of them, and this very diversity makes French Romanticism in general and individual Romantics difficult to characterize. For Delacroix, the question of the contradiction between his classicism and his romanticism naturally resurfaces here, with scholars generally stressing one tendency over the other; an exception is George Mras, who argues in *Eugène Delacroix's Theory of Art* (1966), that the artist achieved a synthesis of the two.

Other questions concern the nature of Delacroix's art itself, with scholars like Trapp arguing that it closes an era in French painting and Maurice Sérullaz, in his *Eugène Delacroix* (1971), contending that Delacroix heralded an era of pure painting. These two positions by no means exclude one another, for it can be argued that the subject matter of Delacroix's art belonged to his time or earlier periods, while his techniques were new and innovative. Delacroix painted during a period of radical transition in French art, and his work reflects the uncertainties of his time. A satisfactory biography of Eugène Delacroix must treat not only the man and the artist but also his place in the history of French Romanticism and French culture in the first half of the nineteenth century. Unfortunately, because Delacroix in particular and French Romanticism in general do not seem to stimulate the interest that the Impressionists, the post-Impressionists, and the Moderns do, such a biographical study remains to be written.

Evaluation of Principal Biographical Sources

Charlton, D. G., ed. *The French Romantics.* 2 vols. New York: Cambridge University Press, 1984. (**A, G**) Since Delacroix, like most of his contemporaries in the French Romantic movement, maintained a lifelong interest in literature and arts other than painting, it is necessary to set his biography within an intellectual and cultural context. Among the few works in English to do so is this valuable collection of essays by established scholars, which offers in addition to accounts of the Romantic movement as a whole studies of each of the arts, including painting. Particularly useful are Charlton's "The French Romantic Movement" and "Religious and Political Thought."

Escholier, Raymond. *Delacroix, peintre, graveur, écrivain.* 3 vols. Paris: Floury, 1926-1929. (**A**) A standard if dated biography in French, of which his *Eugène Delacroix* (Paris: Éditions Cercle d'Art, 1963) is a condensed version with color plates but no documentation issued for the centennial of Delacroix's death.

Faunce, Sarah. "Eugène Delacroix, 1798-1863." In *European Writers: The Romantic Century.* Vol. 5: 513-540. Edited by Jacques Barzun. New York: Charles Scribner's Sons, 1985. (**A, G**) Brief biographical sketch, together with a solid overview of Delacroix's letters, essays, and *Journal,* with a good introductory bibliography. Substantial quotations from Delacroix make this essay a useful starting point.

Hemmings, F. W. J. *Culture and Society in France, 1789-1848.* Leicester, England: Leicester University Press, 1987. (**A, G**) Comprehensive introductory survey of French culture between the Revolutions of 1789 and 1848, which, together with the Charlton collection cited above, establishes the context from which Delacroix emerged and in which he lived and worked.

Huyghe, René. *Delacroix.* New York: Harry N. Abrams, 1963. (**A, G**) Massive, learned, and reflective but often rambling biographical and artistic study which uses a wide range of published and unpublished materials. Filled with fascinating details and asides, it offers insightful readings of selected paintings, often with an emphasis on a picture's structure. Worth a careful reading are the excellent notes and an extensive critical bibliography, mostly of French language materials. Fine illustrations, both in color and black and white.

Johnson, Lee. *Delacroix.* New York: Norton, 1963. (**A, G**) An extended biographical essay on Delacroix as a colorist that argues for his influence on the Impressionists and the post-Impressionists. Citing Delacroix, "The foremost merit of a painting is to be a feast for the eye. That is not to say that reason should not find its place in it," Johnson argues that the *Sardanapalus* is such a "feast," that *The Women of Algiers* displays a reasoned use of color, and that a synthesis is achieved in the Saint Sulpice murals.

Moreau-Nélaton, Etienne. *Delacroix raconté par lui-même.* 2 vols. Paris: Henri Laurens, 1916. (**A**) A detailed and chronologically organized biography, based as the title indicates upon generous excerpts from Delacroix's *Journal* and letters. The black and white reproductions of paintings, drawings, and prints are poor by modern standards. The final chapter contains an analysis of materials relating to Delacroix appearing in the years between his death and the outbreak of the First

World War.

Mras, George P. *Eugène Delacroix's Theory of Art*. Princeton, NJ: Princeton University Press, 1966. **(A)** Mras identifies the sources of Delacroix's thought, seeks to disentangle Delacroix's original ideas from those he learned from past theoreticians, and considers the relation of the artist's theories to his artistic practice. Concluding that Delacroix was "tempered Romantic", Mras argues that he strove for "a reintegration of reason and passion in the creative act and in the human personality" and that his knowledge of classical theory restrained his Romantic temperament.

Pool, Phoebe. *Delacroix*. London and New York: Paul Hamlyn, 1969. **(G, Y)** Readable introductory biographical sketch, which offers in addition a biographical outline, excerpts from Delacroix's *Journal* and essays, and forty-nine color reproductions of his most famous works, with brief but pertinent comments on each.

Prideaux, Tom. *The World of Delacroix, 1798-1863*. New York: Time, 1966. **(G)** Informed but not scholarly, this clear and briskly written introductory biography is organized chronologically, with thematic essays on paintings and episodes in Delacroix's life occasionally interspersed. Although Prideaux notes in passing the paradoxes in Delacroix's personality and art as well as his appearance at a pivotal point in the history of art, the book is primarily a narrative enlivened with anecdotal detail and familiar passages from the *Journal*. Stories and legends about Delacroix's life and art are often repeated without comment. Color illustrations are abundant, and most of Delacroix's celebrated paintings are described and analyzed.

Rudrauf, Lucien. *Eugène Delacroix et le problème du romantisme artistique*. Paris: Henri Laurens, 1942. **(A)** A comprehensive historical and psychological study accompanied by an invaluable bibliography.

Sérullaz, Maurice. *Eugène Delacroix*. New York: Harry N. Abrams, 1971. **(G)** Overview of Delacroix's life and painting by a leading French Delacroix scholar, with notes on his drawings, a biographical outline, and a selected bibliography; drawings and forty-eight famous paintings or watercolors are reproduced in color, each accompanied by useful notes. Sérullaz emphasizes Delacroix's personality, his paintings, and the role of imagination and color in his art.

————. *Les Peintures murales de Delacroix*. Paris: Éditions du Temps, 1963. (**A**) A comprehensive and well-illustrated study in French of the wall paintings, from the early frescoes to those of Saint-Sulpice. While this study is valuable for its long quotations from Delacroix's *Correspondence*, documents in the Archives nationales, and contemporary reactions to the murals, there is little discussion or analysis of this material. For studies in English, see the catalogue raisonné by Lee Johnson and Spector's the study of the Saint-Sulpice murals.

Trapp, Frank. *The Attainment of Delacroix*. Baltimore, MD: Johns Hopkins University Press, 1970. (**A**) An authoritative, scholarly, and meticulously documented biography that makes extensive use of Delacroix's *Journal,* letters, and notebooks. Organization for the period before 1831 is chronological, while Delacroix's later years are treated topically, with chapters on his orientalism;, the illustrations for Goethe and Shakespeare; the paintings based on history, battles, and classical antiquity; the wild animal and religious paintings; the murals for the state; the Saint Sulpice murals; Delacroix's practice as a painter; and the critical reaction to Delacroix's work. Included also are richly detailed analyses of the genesis, content, and reception of famous paintings, particularly those of the 1820s. On the whole, coverage favors the artistic and literary aspects of Delacroix's work rather than the political, social, or intellectual context. Ever dispassionate and cautious, Trapp discounts many of the stories and legends associated with Delacroix. Color illustrations of the major paintings are adequate, and the inclusion of reproductions of works by contemporaries allows the unique qualities of Delacroix's art to stand out. No bibliography, but excellent notes serve as a guide for further research.

Overview and Evaluation of Primary Sources

Primary materials dealing with the life, thought, and work of Eugène Delacroix, with the contemporary reception of his art, and with his place in the cultural and intellectual life of France from the 1820s to the 1860s are voluminous. Most, however, are difficult to obtain outside major university collections and much remains untranslated from the French. Among the earliest is Achille Piron, *Eugène Delacroix. Sa vie et ses oeuvres* (Paris: Jules Claye, 1865; **A**). Published by a close friend just two years after Delacroix's death, it contains a portrait of Delacroix based on the recollections of his acquaintances, a biographical sketch, a catalogue of major works, lists of prices Delacroix received for his paintings, and reprints of fifteen essays and selected letters. Also useful is the early catalogue by Adolphe Moreau, *Eugène Delacroix et son oeuvre* (Paris: Libraire des Bibliophiles, 1873; **A**). Alfred Robaut's inclusive *L'Oeuvre complet d'Eugène Delacroix: Peintures, dessins, gravures, lithographies* (Paris: Charavay Frères, 1885; unrevised reprint, DaCapo Press, 1969; **A**), retains its value, although dated and rendered largely obsolete for the paintings by Johnson's catalogue. The *Paintings of Eugène Delacroix: A Critical Catalogue* (6 vols. Oxford: Clarendon Press, 1981-1989; **A**), edited by Lee Johnson, is the most recent and complete catalogue raisonné. Since drawings and prints are excluded by Johnson, Robaut's catalogue remains essential. For the prints, also consult the third volume of Loÿs Delteil, *Le Peintre-graveur illustré* (31 vols. Paris: Chez l'auteur, 1906-1930; **A**). The important *Faust* lithographs are clearly reproduced in *The Complete Illustrations from Delacroix's Faust and Manet's The Raven* (Bloomington: Lilly Library of Indiana University and Dover Publications, 1981; **G**). For drawings, see Kurt Badt, *Eugène Delacroix Drawings* (Oxford: B. Cassirer, 1946; **A**) and the *Dessins d'Eugène Delacroix* (2 vols. Paris: Ministère de la Culture, Editions de la Reunion des musées nationaux, 1984; **A**), which catalogues and reproduces the extensive holdings of the Louvre Museum.

Delacroix's *Journal*, his letters, and his critical essays on art and artists are all available in French editions; only excerpts have appeared in translation. André Joubin's *Journal de Eugène Delacroix* (3 vols. 3d ed. Paris: Plon, 1960; **A**) is standard. Dating from 1822-1824 and 1847-1863, the *Journal* reveals Delacroix as a thinker of considerable importance and an insightful and self-reflective painter. Available English translations by Lucy Norton, *The Journal of Eugène Delacroix* (1951. Reprint. Ithaca, NY: Cornell University Press, 1980; **A, G**), and Walter Pach, *The Journal of Eugène Delacroix* (London: J. Cape, 1938; **A, G**) offer comprehensive excerpts.

Five volumes of Delacroix's letters, which supplement his *Journal* as a principal biographical source, have been edited by André Joubin, *Correspondance générale d'Eugène Delacroix* (5 vols. Paris: Plon, 1936-1938; **A**); additional collections of letters have been published subsequently, including Lee Johnson's *Eugène Delacroix, Further Correspondence, 1817-1863* (Oxford: Clarendon Press, 1991; **A**). For an English version, see Jean Stewart's *Selected Letters, 1813-1863* (New York: St. Martin's, 1971; **A, G**). Delacroix's four major theoretical articles, his eight biographical studies of notable artists, and his miscellaneous writings have been reprinted by Elie Faure in *Oeuvres littéraires* (2 vols. Paris: Crès, 1923; **A**). Although no complete English edition has been undertaken, a translation of "Des critiques en matière d'art" by Walter Pach appears in *On Art Criticism,* (New York: Curt Valentin, 1946; **A**).

Accounts by Delacroix's contemporaries include Louis de Planet, *Souvenirs de Travaux de Peinture avec M. Eugène Delacroix* (Paris: Armand Colin, 1929; **A**), a journal of work on the murals for the Library of the Chamber of Deputies. Maurice Tourneux, *Eugène Delacroix devant ses contemporains, ses écrits, ses biographes, ses critiques* (Paris: Jules Rouam, 1886; **A**), provides an annotated bibliography of Delacroix's writings and contemporary comments about him, as well as excerpts from Salon and exhibition reviews. Of all the nineteenth writers on the life and work of Delacroix, the most important is Charles Baudelaire. His 1863 essay is available in English: *Eugène Delacroix. His Life and Work* (New York: Lear Publications, 1947; **A, G**). Additional selections are translated in the two volumes edited by Jonathan Mayne, *Art in Paris, 1845-1862: Salons and Other Exhibitions* (London: Phaidon, 1965; **A, G**) and *The Painter of Modern Life* (London: Phaidon, 1964; **A, G**). A one-volume collection also edited by Mayne is *The Mirror of Art, Critical Studies* (Garden City, NY: Doubleday, 1956; **A, G**).

Evaluation of Selected Critical Sources

Athanassoglou-Kallmyer, Nina Maria. *Eugène Delacroix: Prints, Politics, and Satire (1814-1822).* New Haven, CT: Yale University Press, 1991. (**A**) Original study of Delacroix's usually neglected sixteen political caricatures (five etchings and eleven lithographs). All of the cartoons are reproduced and set within a political and intellectual context that makes them comprehensible.

Johnson, Lee, ed. *The Paintings of Eugène Delacroix: A Critical Catalogue.* 6 vols. Oxford: Clarendon Press, 1981-1989. (**A**) With meticulous scholarship,

Johnson seeks to summarize all that is known about each picture, including the composition, content, and provenance. Volumes 1 and 2 cover 1816-1831, Volumes 3-4, 1832-1863, and Volumes 5-6, the mural paintings. Paintings are reproduced in black and white, and there are detailed bibliographies for each entry. Drawings and prints are not included. Johnson's focused approach on Delacroix's art often leads him to minimize the political, social, and intellectual milieux.

Sérullaz, Maurice. *Mémorial de l'Exposition Eugène Delacroix organisée au Musée du Louvre à l'occasion du Centenaire de la mort de l'artiste.* Paris: Editions des Musées Nationaux, 1963. (A) Catalogue of the centennial exhibition at the Louvre with detailed entries on each work shown, black and white reproductions, and an excellent bibliography. For important works like *Liberty Leading the People,* sketches and studies are included and discussed.

Spector, Jack J. *The Murals of Eugène Delacroix at Saint-Sulpice.* New York: College Art Association of America, 1967. (A, G) Spector confronts the paradox of the religious skeptic Delacroix painting great religious murals, situates them in a tradition that includes Old Masters like Raphael and Rubens, and traces the development of the murals using unpublished documents and sketches, many of which are clearly reproduced. Also treated is the actual painting of the murals, their content, the relation of color to their composition, and the contemporary reception.

—————. *Delacroix: The Death of Sardanapalus.* New York: Viking, 1974. (A, G) Detailed, learned, and well-illustrated study of the sources, genesis, and reception of Delacroix's most controversial painting. Spector's psychosexual interpretation of the relation between the *Sardanapalus* and Delacroix's personality occasioned a stimulating debate in the *Burlington Magazine* and the *Times Literary Supplement.*

Principal Works

The Barque of Dante (1822)
Scenes from the Chios Massacres (1824)

The Agony in the Garden (1824-1827)
Tasso in the Hospital of St. Anna (1824)
The Execution of the Doge Marino Faliero (1826)
The Combat of the Giaour and Hassan (1826)
Greece on the Ruins of Missolonghi (1826)
Justinian Drafting his Laws (1826-1827)
The Death of Sardanapalus (1827-1828)
Mephistopheles Appears Before Faust (1828)
The Battle of Nancy (1828-1831)
The Battle of Poitiers (1828-1830)
The Murder of the Bishop of Liège (1829-1830)
28 July 1830. Liberty Leading the People (1830)
Murals in the Salon du Roi, Palais Bourbon (1833-1837)
A Street In Meknes (1834)
The Women of Algiers in their Apartment (1834)
The Battle of Taillebourg (1837)
Medea (1838)
The Fanatics of Tangier (1838)
Murals in the Deputies' Library, Palais Bourbon (1838-1847)
Hamlet and Horatio in the Graveyard (1839)
Murals in the Library of the Senate, Palais du Luxembourg (1840-1846)
The Justice of Trajan (1840)
Entry of the Crusaders into Constantinople (1841)
The Abduction of Rebecca (1846)
Murals in the Chapelle des Saints-Anges, Church of Saint-Sulpice (1849-1861)
Murals in the Galerie d'Apollon, The Louvre Museum (1850-1851)
Murals in the Salon de la Paix, The Hôtel de Ville (1852-1854)
Arabs Skirmishing in the Mountains (1863)

Fictions and Adaptations

Delacroix does not seem to have appealed to novelists, playwrights, or film-makers. There is good reason to believe, however, that Honoré de Balzac intended the artistic ideas expressed by the painter Frenhofer in ''The Unknown Masterpiece'' to represent those of Delacroix. Be that as it may, it is generally agreed that Balzac consulted Delacroix when writing the story; see Anthony Rudolf's translation, *Gillette or The Unknown Masterpiece* (London: The Menard Press, 1988). Delacroix also appears as a character in the British film *Impromptu* (1991); starring Judy Davis as George Sand and Hugh Grant as Frédéric Chopin, it is available on video.

Museums, Historical Landmarks, Societies

Ackland Memorial Art Center (Chapel Hill, NC). Contains the painting, *Cleopatra and the Peasant.*

Albright-Knox Art Gallery (Buffalo, NY). Contains the painting, *A Street in Meknes.*

Art Institute of Chicago. Contains the paintings, *The Combat of the Giaour and Hassan, Arab Horsemen Attacked by a Lion,* and *Lion Hunt.*

Cathedral of Ajaccio (Corsica). Contains the painting, *The Virgin of the Sacred Heart.*

Church of Orcemont (Seine-et Oise, France). Contains the painting, *The Virgin of the Harvest.*

Kimbell Art Museum (Fort Worth, TX). Contains the painting, *The Bride of Abydos.*

Louvre Museum (Paris). With few exceptions, almost all of the renowned paintings of Delacroix's youth, including *The Barque of Dante, The Massacres at Chios, The Death of Sardanapalus,* and *Liberty Leading the People,* are owned by the Louvre, as are many of his mature canvases, such as *The Algerian Women, The Abduction of Rebecca,* and *The Entry of the Crusaders into Constantinople.* Also in The Louvre is a large collection of drawings. The Museé du Petit-Palais holds *The Combat of the Giaour and Hassan.* Delacroix's murals decorating public buildings and churches in Paris are not always easy to view; those in the Chapel of the Holy Angels in the Church of Saint-Sulpice and the Galerie d'Apollon in the Louvre are accessible, but those in the legislative buildings, the Palais Bourbon, and the Palais du Luxembourg are less so.

Luxembourg Gardens (Paris). Between the Orangerie and the Palais du Luxembourg is a monument to Delacroix by Dalou.

Metropolitan Museum of Art (New York). Contains the paintings, *The Abduction of Rebecca* and *Christ on the Sea of Galilee.*

Musée des Augustins (Toulouse, France). Contains the painting, *The Sultan of Morocco and his Entourage.*

Musée des Beaux-Arts (Bordeaux, France). Contains the painting, *Greece on the Ruins of Missolonghi,* and *Boissy d'Anglas at the National Convention.*

Musée des Beaux-Arts (Lille, France). Contains the painting, *Medea About to Kill her Children.*

Musée des Beaux-Arts (Nancy, France). Contains the painting, *The Battle of Nancy.*

Musée des Beaux-Arts (Rouen, France). Contains the painting, *The Justice of Trajan.*

Musée Fabre (Montpellier, France). Contains the painting, *Women of Algiers in their Apartment.*

Musée National Eugène Delacroix et Société de Amis d'Eugène Delacroix (Paris). Located in Delacroix's last studio at 6, Furstenberg Place, it houses memorabilia and is the site of occasional exhibits.

Musée national de Versailles (Versailles, France). Contains the painting, the *Battle of Taillebourg.*

Museum of Fine Arts (Boston, MA). Contains the paintings, *Lion Hunt* and *The Lamentation.*

National Gallery (London). Contains the painting, *Portrait of Louis Auguste Baron Schwiter.*

National Gallery (Washington, DC). Contains the paintings, *Arabs Skirmishing in the Mountains* and *Christopher Columbus at the Monastery of La Rabida.*

Père Lachaise Cemetery (Paris). Delacroix's neo-classical tomb, which he designed for himself, is located in Section 49.

Phillips Collection (Washington, DC). Contains the painting, *Portrait of Nicolò Paganini.*

Wallace Gallery (London). Contains the paintings, *The Execution of Marino Faliero* and *Mephistopheles Appears Before Faust.*

Walters Art Gallery (Baltimore, MD). Contains the paintings, *Christ on the Sea of Galilee* and *Christ on the Cross.*

Other Sources

The Art of the July Monarchy: France 1830-1848. Columbia: University of Missouri Press, 1990. (**A, G**) Published on the occasion of an exhibition held at the Museum of Art and Archeology, University of Missouri at Columbia in 1989, this book contains eight pioneering essays on the often neglected art of the July Monarchy and a catalogue of the pictures shown. Studies such as this provide a context for Delacroix's art of the 1830s and the 1840s. Reproductions in black and white and color are excellent.

French Painting 1774-1830: The Age of Revolution. Detroit, MI: Wayne State University Press, 1975. (**A, G**) Well-illustrated catalogue of exhibitions held in France and the United States in 1974 and 1975 that surveys the intellectual and artistic context in which Delacroix worked. See especially Robert Rosenblum's essay, "Painting During the Bourbon Restoration, 1814-1830" and the catalogue notes on the Delacroix paintings exhibited.

Friedlaender, Walter. *David to Delacroix.* Translated by Robert Goldwater. Cambridge, MA: Harvard University Press, 1952. (**A, G**) Originally published in 1930, this classic study sets Delacroix within the historical development of French painting, and it stresses the baroque elements in his work.

Mainardi, Patricia. *Art and Politics of the Second Empire: The Universal Expositions of 1855 and 1867.* New Haven, CT: Yale University Press, 1987. (**A**) Contains interesting material on the Delacroix and Ingres exhibits at the 1855 Exposition and argues for a radical transition in French painting during the Second Empire.

Marrinan, Michael. *Painting Politics for Louis-Philippe: Art and Ideology in Orléanist France, 1830-1848.* New Haven, CT: Yale University Press, 1988. (**A**) This study of history painting and political propaganda during the July Monarchy to promote its political agenda includes a discussion of images of the July Revolution, including Delacroix's *Liberty*.

Rubin, James H. "Delacroix's *Dante and Virgil* as a Romantic Manifesto." *Art Journal* 52 (Summer 1993): 48-58. (**A**) Rubin analyzes Delacroix's first Salon painting as a case study of a prudent young artist caught between the need to be successful and the desire to be original and address issues of contemporary concern, especially the on-going battles between conservativism and liberalism in politicism and between Neo-Classicism and Romanticism in literature and the arts.

Robert W. Brown
Pembroke State University

Hans Delbrück
1848-1929

Chronology

Born Hans Delbrück on November 11, 1848 on the Baltic Sea island of Ruegen, kingdom of Prussia, third son of Berthold Delbrück, a local court judge, and Laura von Henning, daughter of a Berlin University professor; *1867* graduates from classical secondary school in Berlin; *1867-1868* attends lectures in history, law, and philosophy at Heidelberg, Griefswald, and Bonn; *1868-1869* serves in the military, then returns briefly to the university in Bonn; *1870-1871* Franco-Prussian War breaks out; enters the war as a corporal and is later promoted to lieutenant in the 29th Rhenish Infantry Regiment; fights at St. Privat, and Saarbrücken; *1872-1873* returns to the university and under noted German historian Heinrich von Sybel's aegis, writes his doctoral dissertation, ''On the Credibility of Lambert von Hersfeld'', about an eleventh century historian; *1874-1879* serves as tutor in the household of Prussian Crown Prince and later German Kaiser Friedrich III; *1881* publishes the *Life of Field Marshall Count Gneisenau,* about the Prussian leader in the Napoleonic Wars; appointed lecturer at the University of Berlin, where he remains until 1921; *1885* marries Lina Thiersch, daughter of a professor at Dresden University and with whom he has seven children, the last of whom, Max Delbrück (b. *1908),* shares the Nobel prize for medicine in 1969; *1886* given German historian Heinrich von Treitschke's chair in World History at the University of Berlin; *1887-1890* begins publication of *Persian Wars and the Burgundian Wars* and *Strategy of Perikles Described through the Strategy of Frederick the Great,* the first two of his six groundbreaking books defining modern military history; *1882* elected to the Prussian Landtag; *1885* elected to the German Reichstag as a Free Conservative, leading to a career as one of the first political commentators of the new German state; *1885* begins a nearly forty-year association with the monthly journal *Prussian Annual,* which becomes, under his editorship (1889) the leading journal of political commentary in Imperial Germany; *1894-1898* nearly loses his job after a series of articles opposing policies of Germanization in the Prussian provinces of Schleswig and Posen; *1900-1920* publishes the

four-volume *History of the Art of War in the Framework of Political History*, one
of the first historical works to explicitly integrate military affairs with political,
economic, and social history; *1911* frightened by rising conservative nationalism,
cautions his readers against unrestrained military passions; *1913* publishes lectures
that he gave that year at the University of London as *Numbers in History*, one of
the earliest applications of quantitative methods in modern historical scholarship;
1914 World War I breaks out; works against the dual pressures of censorship and
propaganda; tries to combine contemporary military reporting and wartime political
criticism; *1917* his arguments are used to formulate the Reichstag peace resolution;
arguments against annexation of politically independent territories, especially
Belgium; is unable to influence government policy; *1918* with the passing of the
Second Reich, serves on the German Delegation to the Versailles Peace Conference; *1919* enters national politics and becomes a leading spokesman on the
reasons behind Germany's defeat in the war; *1920-1929* retires from the university;
maintains his position against increasingly malicious attacks by conservative war
leaders; testifies before the first legislative inquiry in German political history, the
Reichstag Committee to Investigate the Causes and Course of World War I; engages in celebrated legal battles against conservative and Nazi leaders; writes one
of the first histories of western civilization, the five-volume *World History*; *1928*
decorated by President von Hindenburg with the highest civilian award of the
German Republic; *1929* dies in Berlin on July 14 after suffering a stroke.

Activities of Historical Significance

Like his contemporary, German sociologist Max Weber, Hans Delbrück was a
pioneer of social thought. He was both the first modern military historian and one
of the first critical political commentators on the new German state. But throughout his life and despite his position as professor at the finest German university
and member of a distinguished family, Delbrück was continually perceived as
being on the wrong side of the German establishment because he was a liberal and
iconoclastic nationalist in a conservative and conformist empire.

Wars were considered by the professoriate as aberrations in the flow of human
affairs that were best left to those who fought them. Officers, who knew the
technical details, were unable to relate their knowledge of war to the larger spec-

trum of politics, society, and economy. Professors, who described this larger spectrum, did not know the technical details of armies and considered war of any kind to be an intrusion into human society. As a result, each group of specialists excluded or ignored the other in their historical writings. By pointing out this gap and criticizing both military and university historians, Delbrück tried to build a bridge between them but in doing so, he also incurred their wrath.

Delbrück's groundbreaking historical methods were based on three assumptions. First, he believed military affairs had to be included in general history because they were interrelated—each impacted upon the other. His concept of military affairs placed them well within broad cultural history: it included politics, economics, and society. This was evident in his earliest work, *The Life of Field Marshal Count Geneisenau*, in which he described the manner in which eighteenth-century military tactics were made obsolete by the French Revolution. In many of his works, Delbrück looked for the underpinnings of the military and found them in the political, social, economic, and technological aspects of culture. But to historians of his day, he was a generalist trampling on the traditional and institutionalized division of labor between the university and the army.

Second, Delbrück argued that historians had to master the technical and material details of armies in order to understand war. A memorable statement of this approach appears early in the first volume of the *History of the Art of War*, "a movement that is made easily by a detachment of one thousand men is an achievement for ten thousand men, a work of art for fifty thousand men, and an impossibility for one hundred thousand." His scholarship often debunked other historians' descriptions of wars, which he saw as misdirected because the authors had not applied critical historical methods to the material realities. His most famous critique concerned the corollaries between ancient and modern army size, and in fact he is recognized today as a pioneering quantitative historian: one who counted, measured, and compared, who always asked what was materially possible in ancient war and compared ancient events with what was feasible for modern armies. For example, the fifth-century B.C. Greek historian Herodotus had written that the army of the Persian king Xerxes numbered 4.2 million men. Delbrück demonstrated in *The Persian Wars and the Burgundian Wars* and in *The History of the Art of War* that this was highly unlikely. Based on the material relationships of the modern German army, an army corps of 30,000 men with its artillery took up approximately fourteen miles of road. A Persian army of 4.2 million would have taken up 1,960 miles of road space. If one accepted Herodotus, the first Persian ranks would have arrived on the battlefield of Thermopylae in Greece at the same time that the rear elements were leaving Susa, east of the Tigris River in Persia—an unbelievable stretch for any army. In another example, Delbrück questioned the statement that Greek soldiers at the battle of Marathon had run 4,800 feet: he noted that even modern Prussian infantry were forbidden to do this by regulations, it was simply too strenuous. By the time they engaged the enemy, formations would have been in disarray and the soldiers worn out. Such criticism of traditional sources and emphasis on material realities offended conventional practitioners.

The third assumption Delbrück made in his treatment of military history was his use of Hegelian methods which also brought criticism from traditional scholars. As such, he applied the comparative method and used ideal or paradigmatic forms as heuristic tools. Using the same process as sociologists Max Weber and Ferdinand Tönnies, Delbrück analyzed cross-cut slices of the military past and tried to make sense of them by comparing them with other events, both historical and contemporary. In one of his most controversial works, *The Strategy of Perikles Described through the Strategy of Frederick the Great* (1890), Delbrück suggested a bipolar continuum for all world military history—the strategy of annihilation at one end and the strategy of attrition at the other—and illuminated both strategies using the armies of fifth-century Greece (led by Pericles) and eighteenth-century Prussia (led by Frederick the Great) as examples. Both men, he argued, used the strategy of attrition in their warmaking, resulting from constraints placed on them by their respective social and political systems and by the material realities of the Athenian state and the Prussian kingdom. Thus Delbrück showed how two seemingly disparate armies separated by more than one thousand years, were limited by similar social and political frameworks.

Delbrück's paradigmatic thinking was grounded in economic and social analysis and based upon a reinterpretation of the legacy of military philosopher Carl von Clausewitz. In presenting a theory that stressed the fundamental duality of war, Delbrück aroused the ire of Prussian military leaders, who interpreted Clausewitz's theories to include only a single legitimate strategy—that of annihilation.

In an important sense, Delbrück was both one of the last of the nineteenth-century narrative historians, a group that included Leopold von Ranke, Sir Thomas Macaulay, and Edward Gibbon, and one of the first of the twentieth-century social science historians, which came to include such men as Weber, Marc Bloch, and Fernand Braudel. But because he did not entirely fit the former mold and because the latter had not yet been created, Delbrück was misunderstood. His professorship at the University of Berlin was in world history, not military history, because the faculty did not recognize that subject as part of a legitimate historical specialization. Sufficient military knowledge for historical scholarship could be learned by any generalist historian through part-time study.

Officers criticized him as a civilian outsider who, they argued, could not know the technical realities of armies because he was not a soldier. Professors also misunderstood his work, not knowing what to make of his integration of social, economic, and political history with military affairs. The socialist writer Franz Mehring and a few retired generals recognized Delbrück's accomplishment, but few of his peers were able to appreciate it. Indeed, a full understanding had to await the next generation.

Although sometimes considered a traditional Prussian monarchist, Delbrück was in reality a moderate liberal. His views are characterized by balanced humanitarianism and centrism. A modernist political commentator, he emphasized realism and materialism amidst an illiberal and idealistic society. And although he is considered to have been a supporter of Germany's hypernationalistic attitude toward world politics, Delbrück became increasingly uneasy about German naval and military policies after 1911. Warning in 1913 against the possible outcome of unchecked popular militarism, Delbrück came into conflict with the increasingly powerful conservative nationalist organizations that supported escalating defense budgets and an aggressive foreign policy. As this conservative tradition grew more reactionary under the pressures of World War I and Germany's subsequent defeat, Delbrück became more liberal in his opinions turning away from support for nationalism and toward a belief in world-wide cooperation.

Since Delbrück's paradigmatic interpretation of military history was well established long before the outbreak of World War I, he naturally applied it to the Great War. Early on, Delbrück understood that Germany had become involved in a new kind of war, a total war, and his speeches and essays in the *Prussian Annual* sought to explain it. After 1915, Delbrück began to suggest that his country had obtained its military goals and should seek peace. And when a thousand German professors signed the "petition of the intellectuals" supporting the government's position of victory at all costs, Delbrück was the moving spirit behind a counter petition, signed by several hundred leading intellectuals such as Albert Einstein and Max Weber, against forced annexation of independent countries. In 1916, he tried to warn his country against unlimited submarine warfare, the beginning of which in 1917 brought the United States into the war.

During the years 1914 to 1929, Delbrück changed his focus from academic scholarship to public history, concentrating his efforts on describing the greatest war in human history in terms that the German public could understand. His testimony before the Reichstag Committee from 1920 to 1926, his leadership of the famous "Stab in the Back" trial in Munich in 1924 and 1925, in which conservatives argued the view that Germany had not been defeated on the battlefield but had been stabbed in the back by the liberals and socialists, his membership on the Historical Commission of the Reich Archive (whose job it was to publish the official German history of the Great War), and his caustic book *Ludendorff's Self-Portrait* (1922), which indicted the German military leadership for pursuing its strategy of annihilation, all highlighted the public and final phase of his historical work.

Delbrück died without achieving wide recognition as a military historian in his own country, but his reputation began to spread abroad soon after his death. During the 1930s, *The History of the Art of War* was translated into Russian and published by the Soviet Defense Ministry, and when it was reprinted in a new German language edition during the 1960s, the book was hailed by European reviewers as a groundbreaking masterwork of historical scholarship. A decade later, it was translated into English, and today Delbrück is generally recognized as the first modern military historian.

Overview of Biographical Sources

During his lifetime, neither university historians nor military officers knew what to make of Delbrück's work. Contemporary reviewers found it difficult, if not impossible, to find a counterpart in the whole of historical literature written up to that time. Those who understood him best tended to be outsiders. General Sigismund von Schlichting, a German commander who was forced to retire for his unconventional views, wrote in 1900 in the official German government *Reichs-Anzeiger* a favorable response to the first volume of *The History of the Art of War*.

Franz Mehring, the socialist writer, wrote a full appreciation of Delbrück's histori-cal works in in his journal *Die Neve Zeit* (1908).

The first complete assessment of Delbrück's work was Gordon Craig's "Del-brück: The Military Historian," a balanced, objective essay based on Delbrück's published writings, which appeared in the classic Edward Mead Earle volume *Makers of Modern Strategy* (Princeton, NJ: Princeton University Press, 1943). It has been revised and included in Peter Paret's 1986 edition of the Earle work. Richard Bauer's essay, "Hans Delbrück" in Bernadotte Schmitt's *Some Historians of Modern Europe* (1942) is based on secondary accounts. In 1985 Arden Bucholz used the massive Delbrück papers in Berlin and Koblenz to describe his entire life, with emphasis on his contribution to military history. Noted French political and military theorist Raymond Aron addressed Delbrück's historical methodology and his controversy with officers and military theorists in extensive comments in his book *Clausewitz: Philosopher of War* (1976). German biographical accounts include Annelise Thimme's *Hans Delbrück als Kritiker der Wilhelminischen Epoche* (Düesseldorf: Droste, 1955) and Andreas Hillgruber, "Hans Delbrück" in Hans-Ulrich Wehler, ed., *Deutsche Historiker* (4 vols. Göettingen, 1972), IV: 40-52. Whereas his contemporaries were unable to understand Delbrück's empha-sis on economics and technology and his use of paradigmatic and comparative thinking as critical tools, today both officers and professors, specialists and mili-tary history buffs, can appreciate his pioneering methods as a narrative, analytical historian.

Evaluation of Principal Biographical Sources

Aron, Raymond. *Clausewitz, Philosopher of War.* 1976. Trans. Englewood Cliffs, NJ: Prentice Hall, 1985. (**A, G**) Originally presented as a series of lectures at the prestigious College de France, at its central core is Delbrück's redefinition of Clausewitzian ideas to include both wars of annihilation and wars of more limited scope and method. In the process of dealing with Clauswitz, Aron devotes forty pages to Delbrück's contributions as military historian and to his understand-ing of the world-renown Prussian philosopher of war.

Bauer, Richard H. "Hans Delbrück." In *Essays in Modern European Historiog-*

raphy. Chicago: University of Chicago Press, 1970. (**A, G**) Readable and popular biographical essay dealing with the whole of Delbrück's life based upon secondary sources. Its strength lies in its overall description of Delbrück's life in politics and in the university.

Bucholz, Arden. *Hans Delbrück and the German Military Establishment: War Images in Conflict*. Iowa City: University of Iowa Press, 1985. (**A, G**) Along with the publications of the German scholar Hans Schleier, the only book to use Delbrück's extensive personal papers in both the German State Library, Berlin, and the German Federal Library, Koblenz, as well as interviews with his surviving relatives. It describes Delbrück's work in military history as part of his complete biography. The bibliographical essay describes the sources for his life, both primary and secondary, and indicates what work is still to be done.

Craig, Gordon. "Delbrück the Military Historian." In Edward M. Earle, ed., *Makers of Modern Strategy from Machiavelli to the Nuclear Age*. 1943. Rev. ed. Princeton: Princeton University Press, 1986. (**A, G**) This classic and beautifully written brief essay on Delbrück, laying out the main structure of his life and work, was written and revised by a scholar considered to be a master interpreter of modern German history. There are notes and a full bibliography.

Gat, Azar. *The Development of Military Thought: The Nineteenth Century*. Oxford: Clarendon, 1992. (**A, G**) Gat has compiled a description and analysis of forty-three writers on military thought in nineteenth-century Europe and America. Delbrück figures prominently: his ideas and theories are described and he is compared with various other writers, for example, the American naval writer Alfred Thayer Mahan.

Marcu, V. *Men and Forces of Our Times*. New York: Knopf, 1931. (**G**) Written by a newspaper correspondent using popular sources and palace gossip, this book comments briefly on Delbrück's role and place in Berlin society and politics.

McClelland, Charles E. *The German Historians and England*. New York: Cambridge University Press, 1971. (**A, G**) Analysis of the role played by German historians in forming Germany's attitude toward England prior to World War I;

contains a thumbnail sketch of Delbrück's life and his changing attitude toward England.

Overview and Evaluation of Primary sources

Delbrück's major contribution to historical knowledge, considered the groundbreaking work in twentieth-century military history, is the four-volume *History of the Art of War in the Framework of Political History.* The paperback edition (Lincoln: University of Nebraska Press, 1990) contains numerous autobiographical asides and has been excellently translated by Walter Renfroe. Delbrück was a spirited and lively writer and those who read German will enjoy him in the original.

Delbrück's book *Numbers in History* (London: University of London, 1913) contains the edited versions of two lectures he presented at the University of London in 1913. They summarize the first three volumes of the *History of the Art of War.* Delbrück's pre-World War I lectures on the German government and constitution, published as *Government and the Will of the People,* were translated by one of his students at Berlin who went on to become a professor of government at Harvard, Roy S. MacElwee, (New York: Knopf, 1923).

Portions of Delbrück's testimony before the German Reichstag Committee investigating the causes and course of World War I and his analysis of the closing months of World War I are contained in R. H. Lutz, ed., *The Causes of the German Collapse in 1918* (Stanford, CA: Hoover Institution Library, 1934). Delbrück left an enormous collection of correspondence, personal documents, professional and political papers and publications. Most of these are in German, although he also knew English, French, Italian, Greek, and Latin. He was a spirited writer and his prose is livelier than that of most scholars of his generation. After his death in 1929, his wife spent the rest of her life (she died in 1943) cataloguing, organizing, collecting, and preserving these documents. This task was continued by his nephew, Cologne University professor Peter Rassow, through 1962. The Delbrück papers are available in two libraries, the German State Library, Berlin, and the German Federal Library, Koblenz. They include more than 26,000 letters sent and received, plus an unusually full variety of other sources. Also, Delbrück's introductions to his various works provide many autobiographical details.

Other Sources

Bucholz, Arden. *Moltke, Schlieffen and Prussian War Planning.* New York: St. Martin's, 1991. (**A, G**) For the context of writing military history in nineteenth century Germany and for details of Delbrück's main military critics—the officers of the military history section of the general staff—this book is useful. It describes the radical historical image produced within the German army, 1871-1895, which was used in support of the strategy of annihilation that undergirded the German war plans after 1897.

Craig, Gordon. *Germany, 1866-1945.* New York: Oxford University Press, 1978. (**A, G**) The standard interpretation of the era in which Delbrück lived by the greatest contemporary American historian of modern Germany. Beautifully written, penetrating and clear. The notes constitute a running bibliographical essay of the major historians, sources, and controversies.

Holger, Herwing. "Imperial Germany." In Ernest R. May, ed., *Knowing One's Enemies: Intelligence Assessment Before the Two World Wars.* Princeton, NJ: Princeton University Press, 1984. (**A, G**) A broad-based essay dealing with many aspects—political, economic, and military—of pre-1914 Germany, written by the leading scholarly expert on the German navy of this period. An excellent read with complete biographical notes.

Hull, Elizabeth. *The Entourage of Kaiser Wilhelm II, 1888-1918.* New York: Cambridge University Press, 1982. (**A, G**) The context of Delbrück's life, as viewed from the top of German politics, this is a witty, incisive and penetrating view of the intimate circle surrounding the last kaiser and the day-to-day life he lived. Based on broad and deep primary sources and using the most recent theory, particularly psychoanalytical, this book tries to make sense of the domestic power structures surrounding Kaiser Wilhelm II.

Ringer, Fritz. *The Decline of the German Mandarins: The German Academic Community, 1890-1933.* Cambridge, MA: Harvard University Press, 1969. (**A, G**) This pathbreaking analysis of the role of the German university system and its scholars in the great German crisis of culture and the demise of the Weimar

Republic, places Delbrück correctly as a modernist historian in contrast to the orthodox conservatives. Ringer's book is a complex philosophical analysis but well worth the study needed to understand it.

Arden Bucholz
State University of New York, Brockport

John Theophilus Desaguliers
1683-1744

Chronology

Born John Theophilus Desaguliers on March 13, 1683, in La Rochelle, France son of the Huguenot minister John Desaguliers and his wife, whose name has not been recorded; *1685-1699* his parents seek refuge in England as a result of the repeal of the Edict of Nantes by Louis XIV; educated by his father, who served as the minister of the French Congregation on Swallow Street in London; *1700-1705* privately tutored in the classics and sciences by a Mr. Sanders; *1706* enters Christ Church College at Oxford; *1710* receives his bachelor's degree, and is appointed to the Chair of Experimental Philosophy in Hart Hall College, Oxford; ordained as an Anglican minister; *1712* receives a master's degree from Oxford; marries Joanna Pudsey; *1713* serves as an experimental assistant to Sir Isaac Newton; *1714* elected to the Royal Society of London and named as the society's curator of experiments because of his knowledge of Newtonian physics; named chaplain for James Brydges, the first Duke of Chandos and a prominent aristocratic patron of the arts and sciences in London; *1717* lectures to King George I about Newtonian science; granted by the king a benefice in Norfolk, and named chaplain for Frederick, Prince of Wales; *1718-1725* reveals his commitment to Newtonian science and to Speculative Freemasonry in London; *1718* earns a Doctorate of Laws degree from Oxford; begins to lecture about experimental science in London taverns and coffeehouses; *1719* publishes *Lectures of Experimental Philosophy*; elected as third grand master of the Modern Grand Lodge of London; *1723* provides leadership to the grand lodge by helping Dr. James Anderson write the order's *Constitutions* and by developing its ritualistic system; *1725* active on the grand lodge's Charity Committee, believing that the new organization should be involved with the promotion of philanthropic projects; *1725-1732* assists in recruiting aristocratic and middle class gentlemen from England and Europe to the ranks of Modern Masonry; *1734* publishes *A Course of Experimental Philosophy*, a work embodying vivid explanations of gravity and motion, and describing his improvement's to Thomas Savery's steam engine; *1739* presents to the Royal Society his findings regarding the elasticity of bodies; delivers a major lecture to the Royal Society about his views regarding electricity; *1742* receives the annual award from the Bordeaux Academy for his studies concerning electricity; *1744* dies on February 29 and is buried in Savoy Chapel in London.

Activities of Historical Significance

John Theophilus Desaguliers taught monarchs, members of the nobility, and middle class intellectuals about the contributions of Newton to British Enlightenment science. His degrees from Oxford, his position as Chair of Experimental Philosophy in that university, and his involvement in the Royal Society of London enabled Desaguliers to become a leading apostle of the Newtonian creed. His experiments concerning Newtonian science, which were usually performed with his two assistants Richard Bridges and William Vreen, appear in *Lectures of Experimental Philosophy*, in *A Course of Experimental Philosophy*, and in the *Transactions of the Royal Society*. His lectures and observations contributed to the realistic marketing of Enlightenment science in British and European cities, and contain mechanistic and materialistic doctrines of Newtonianism. Desaguliers's lectures and experiments regarding mechanism stress principles of motion and gravity found in Newton's *Principia*; these lectures and experiments explain the movements of planets and moons around the sun through the Newtonian laws of motion and gravity. Desaguliers also explained, in non-mathematical terms, Newton's theories on the physical qualities and movements of objects in Nature. His experiments and lectures are of cardinal importance, for they illustrate the application of mechanistic principles to technology and demonstrate the operations of steam engines and his newly invented steam valve; of pumping mechanisms used in mines; of "Jack-in-the-box" machines utilized to eliminate impurities in water pipes; and of "rat's tail" cranes used for the raising and lowering of materials into carriages for shipment.

Desaguliers, too, distinguished himself as an advocate of materialism, explaining concepts from Newton's *Opticks* and emerging as one of the first Newtonians to do work with electricity. Desaguliers's demonstrations explained electrical properties and described the qualities of electrics, of non-electrics, and of the mystical "effluvial" charge. He even performed electrical experiments with metals and with human flesh to determine what kinds of bodies either conducted or rejected electricity.

Desaguliers became the most prominent Newtonian spokesman during the early British Enlightenment as he lectured and performed his experiments in such London coffeehouses and taverns as the Crown and Anchor, the Horn Tavern, and in other bars near Westminster and the Covent Garden. Thus, Desaguliers helped to link the Newtonian world with London tavern and coffeehouse life.

His promotion of Newtonian theories and Enlightenment ideas within the setting of London tavern and coffeehouse life seem to correspond to his efforts at providing leadership to Speculative Freemasonry. In 1719 he was elected grand master of the Modern London Grand Lodge and served as its deputy grand master in 1722 and 1723. As a Masonic administrator, he assisted Dr. James Anderson in 1723 in writing the *Constitutions* of the new order, thus helping to define the powers of the grand lodge and to transform it into a significant cultural institution. As a result of his efforts, the rites and ceremonies of modern Masonry were to embody Enlightenment ideas. Thus, Newtonian concepts of motion and light, the architectural ideas of Palladianism, the ethical concepts of deism, and the ideals of benevolence and religious toleration are vividly and visually explained in the degrees of modern Masonry. Desaguliers also proved to be a fine recruiter, attracting to the ranks of the Modern Grand Lodge individuals from the aristocratic, middle class, and intellectual elite. Under his leadership, local London lodges, for the most part located in taverns and coffeehouses, evolved into respectable fraternal institutions and assisted in the promotion of Enlightenment ideas.

Overview of Biographical Sources

Although there is no full-length biography, there are several short sketches tracing Desaguliers's career. The most analytical and comprehensive account of Desaguliers as an experimental scientist appears in I. Bernard Cohen, *Franklin and Newton* (1966). This splendid study portrays Desaguliers as an interpreter of Newtonian ideas and as a mechanist and a materialist. Three works of Margaret C. Jacob describe accomplishments of Desaguliers. In *The Cultural Meaning of the Scientific Revolution* (1988) Jacob presents terse but perceptive accounts about the role of Desaguliers in the Royal Society and about his work with various kinds of steam engines. In *The Radical Enlightenment* (1981) and in *Living the Enlightenment* (1991), Jacob explains and evaluates the place of Desaguliers as an administrator of modern Masonry. Three works of R. William Weisberger also assess the career of Desaguliers. In "The Cultural and Organizational Functions of Speculative Freemasonry during the Enlightenment" (Dissertation. University of Pittsburgh, 1980), in "The World of John T. Desaguliers" (*Proceedings of the Ohio Research Chapter,* 1980), and in "John Theophilus Desaguliers: Huguenot, Freemason, and Newtonian Scientist" (*Transactions of the Huguenot Society of South Carolina,* 1985), Weisberger evaluates the contributions of Desaguliers to Newtonianism and British Enlightenment culture, to Modern Speculative Freemasonry, and to London tavern and coffeehouse society.

Evaluation of Principal Biographical Sources

Cohen, I. Bernard. *Franklin and Newton.* Cambridge: Harvard University Press, 1966. (**A**) A persuasive study describing how the thinking and scientific methodology of Newton and his disciples produced an impact upon Benjamin Franklin. Cohen examines the career of Desaguliers, showing that his lectures about gravity and motion and his experiments relating to electricity were important to Franklin. The book contains a massive bibliography.

Coil, Henry W. *Freemasonry Through Six Centuries.* 2 vols. Fulton: Bell Press, 1966. (**A, G**) Contains a valuable chapter about the origins of modern Masonry in London and Desaguliers's contributions to it. Mentions little about the importance of science and culture to the new institution.

Findel, J. G. *History of Freemasonry.* Translated by Murray Lyon. London: Asher, 1869. (**A, G**) This is an old but fine study. Findel recognizes the importance of Desaguliers both as a Newtonian scientist and as a leader of Speculative Freemasonry.

Jacob, Margaret C. *The Cultural Meaning of the Scientific Revolution.* New York: Knopf, 1988. (**A, G**) Contains splendid accounts about Newtonian mechanistic and materialistic doctrines and about the place of the Royal Society in spreading doctrines of Enlightenment science. The study describes experiments and inventions of Desaguliers but mentions little about his role in Freemasonry. Contains a solid bibliography.

Purver, Margery. *The Royal Society: Concept and Creation.* Cambridge, MA: M.I.T. Press, 1967. (**A**) Explains the development of the Royal Society and the place of Newton, Desaguliers, and other Newtonians in giving it stature.

Robbins, Alfred. *English-speaking Freemasonry.* London: Benn, 1930. (**A, G**) An old but incisive account. Robbins explains the scientific and Masonic accomplishments of Desaguliers and the institutional development of the Modern London Grand Lodge.

Stewart, Larry. "The Selling of Newton: Science and Technology in Early Eighteenth Century England." *Journal of British Studies* 25 (1986): 178-192. (**A, G**) Shows how Desaguliers and other Newtonians marketed important scientific and industrial ideas to numerous groups in early eighteenth-century London.

Stokes, John. "Life of John Theophilus Desaguliers." *Ars Quatuor Coronatorum* 38 (1925): 285-306. (**A, G**) Describes major events concerning the career of Desaguliers but is not very insightful.

Weisberger, R. William. "John Theophilus Desaguliers: Huguenot, Freemason, and Newtonian Scientist." *Transactions of the Huguenot Society of South Carolina* 90 (November 1985): 63-67. (**A, G**) Discusses his schooling at Oxford, his involvement in the Royal Society, and his popularity as a Newtonian demonstrator. The article also focuses on an analysis of the *Constitutions* of modern Masonry and on an examination of its major doctrines and its rites.

―――――. "The Cultural and Organizational Functions of Speculative Freemasonry during the Enlightenment." Dissertation. University of Pittsburgh, 1980. (**A**) This dissertation contains lengthy accounts about the mechanistic and materialistic ideas of Desaguliers, about his leadership roles in modern Masonry, and about his abilities as a ritualist of the order. The author also assesses his impact on Enlightenment culture and on eighteenth-century Masonry.

————. "The World of John T. Desaguliers." *Proceedings of the Ohio Research Chapter* 15 (June 1980): 75-90. (**A, G**) Argues that Desaguliers introduced significant scientific and philosophical concepts into English Speculative Freemasonry and that he was an effective administrator of and recruiter for modern Masonry in London. The article also assesses the place of Desaguliers as a Newtonian scientist.

Overview and Evaluation of Primary Sources

In addition to those in British archives, primary materials about Desaguliers are also housed in American collections. A few of his works are found in the Library of Congress and in the libraries of Harvard and Yale Universities. The most extensive holdings are in Philadelphia in the American Philosophical Society and in the Library Company of Philadelphia—primarily because Benjamin Franklin purchased the writings of this prominent experimental scientist and Newtonian demonstrator.

Lectures of Experimental Philosophy (London: Mears, 1719; **A, G**) were delivered by Desaguliers in London taverns and coffeehouses and contain explanations about the importance of the scientific method, about the "First and Final Cause of the Universe," and about the movements of celestial bodies in light of the laws of motion and that of gravity. Desaguliers's other major work is *A Course of Experimental Philosophy* (2 vols. London: Senex, 1734-1744; **A, G**) and was financed in part by the Prince of Wales and by the Duke of Chandos. This work vividly describes the movements of bodies in nature in terms of gravity, mass, space, and time. It also discusses elastic and non-elastic bodies, the concepts of attraction and repulsion, and the operations of various steam engines and machines.

Some significant experiments performed by Desaguliers before the Royal Society have been recorded and include: "An Account on Some Experiments on Lights and Colors," in *The Abridged Transactions of the Royal Society of London* 29 (1716: 229-239; **A, G**); "An Account of A Machine for Changing the Air of Sick People," in *The Abridged Transactions of the Royal Society of London* 39 (1735: 12-13; **A, G**); and "Some Thoughts and Experiments concerning Electricity," in *The Abridged Transactions of the Royal Society of London* 41 (1739: 346-358; **A, G**).

Other Sources

Allen, Robert J. *The Clubs of Augustan England*. Cambridge: Harvard University Press, 1933. (**A, G**) A classic work describing Masonry and other clubs and organizations arising in early eighteenth-century London. Allen doesn't discuss the place of Desaguliers in the development of modern Masonry in London.

Baker, C. H., and Muriel I. Baker. *The Life and Circumstances of James Brydges: The First Duke of Chandos*. Oxford: Oxford University Press, 1949. (**A, G**) The Bakers offer a vivid depiction of Desaguliers within the cultural world of the Duke of Chandos. This study is well documented.

Clarke, J. R. "The Royal Society and Early Grand Lodge Freemasonry." *Ars Quatuor Coronatorum* 80 (1967): 110-119. (**A, G**) Provides a comprehensive list of members of the Royal Society who became Masons.

Ellis, Aytoun. *The Penny Universities*. London: Secker and Warburg, 1956. (**A, G**) Cogently demonstrates that taverns and coffeehouses functioned as inexpensive schools in early eighteenth-century London. Ellis describes how tavern and coffeehouse culture was important to aristocratic and middle class elites in the city.

Humphreys, A. R. *The Augustan World*. New York: Harper and Row, 1963. (**A, G**) Assess major scientific and cultural patterns in early eighteenth-century London.

Jacob, Margaret C. *Living the Enlightenment*. New York: Oxford University Press, 1991. (**A, G**) Contains solid chapters about the development of modern Masonry in London but says little about the involvement of Desaguliers in this new institution. Contains useful footnotes, but mentions little about the importance of Masonic learned societies.

————. *The Radical Enlightenment*. London: Allen and Unwin, 1981. (**A, G**) This detailed study stresses that Desaguliers and other leaders of modern Masonry in London were advocates of Newtonian and Whiggish ideologies, recruited to the new movement members from propertied elites and from learned societies, and were not associated with Masons who supported democratic movements in Europe. The book mentions little about the ritualism of Masonry.

Lennhoff, Eugen. *The Freemasons.* Translated by Einar Frame. London: Lewis, 1978. (**A, G**) This fine work explains the development of modern Masonry in London and the leadership role of Desaguliers in it.

Manuel, Frank. *A Portrait of Sir Isaac Newton.* Cambridge: Harvard University Press, 1968. (**A, G**) This work is a charming biography; Manuel chronicles the achievements of Newton, refers to the activities of Desaguliers, and illustrates the enormous impact of Newtonianism on the Enlightenment.

Roberts, J. M. *The Mythology of the Secret Societies.* London: Secker and Warburg, 1972. (**A, G**) Roberts alludes to the place of Desaguliers in the evolution of Freemasonry in London and explains how Masonry served as the paragon of European secret societies. The book contains detailed footnotes.

Timbs, John. *Clubs and Club Life in London.* Detroit: Gale, 1967. (**A, G**) This book is important for its description of coffeehouse and tavern culture in early Augustan England. Timbs also talks about the Crown and Anchor, the Goose and Gridiron, and other taverns and coffeehouses which were associated with early modern Masonry in London.

William Weisberger
Butler Community College

René Descartes
1596-1650

Chronology

Born René Descartes on March 31, 1596, in La Haye, France, the son of Joachim Descartes, a parliamentary counselor at Rennes, and Jeanne Brochard; *1597* mother dies; *1606-1614* studies the humanities, philosophy, physics, astronomy, and metaphysics at the Royal College at La Flèche, a Jesuit institution; exhibits a predilection for mathematics; *1614-1616* studies at the University of Poitiers, earning a law degree and license; *1618-1628* travels throughout Europe; *1618* in Holland, serves as an unpaid officer in the army of Maurice of Nassau, the Protestant prince of Orange; uses his mathematical ability in military engineering activities; in Breda, meets the Dutch philosopher, doctor, and physicist Issac Beeckman, who exposes him to recent developments in mathematics and becomes one of his close lifelong friends; writes the *Compendium Musicae* and dedicates it to Beeckman but does not publish it; *1619* leaves the army of the prince of Orange and joins the army of Maximilian, the Catholic duke of Bavaria; quits military life and travels through Denmark, Danzig, Poland, and Germany; envisions a new mathematical and scientific system of enquiry on November 10; *1620-1621* travels in Germany and Holland; *1622-1623* travels extensively in France, especially in Brittany, before ending up in Paris; visits his family in Poitou and sells property there that he had inherited from his mother; invests the profits from the sale in bonds and lives comfortably thereafter off the dividends; *1623-1625* travels extensively in Switzerland and Italy; makes meteorological observations, studies glaciers, and computes mountain heights; *1625-1628* returns to France and lives in Paris, spending time with members of the scientific community, especially the Franciscan friar Marin Mersenne, a close friend; *1628-1649* settles in Holland but changes residence almost yearly; produces his greatest works; *1629-1630* writes, but never publishes, a treatise on methodology called *Rules for the Direction of the Mind*, an incomplete work that reveals his preoccupation with a unified system of enquiry, possibly used as a reference for his later works; *1630-1634* undertakes independent study of optics, meteorology, the nature and structure of material bodies, air, water and earth, mathematics, especially geometry, and the physiological and anatomical sciences, with the belief that their unification by a new method will lead to a universal scheme of knowledge; *1633* learns of astronomer Galileo's condemnation by the Catholic church for advocating the heliocentric view of the solar system, and decides not to publish his nearly-complete draft of a comprehensive work called *The World*, which also supports this theory; *1635* his Dutch servant girl, Hélène, bears him a daughter, Francine; *1637* publishes in Leiden an anonymous volume containing three essays: "Optics," "Meteorology," and "Geometry," preceded by an introduction entitled *Discourse on the Method*, in which he sets forth his four principles for the pursuit of knowledge; *1640* daughter dies of a fever; *1641* continues to develop his method for the pursuit of a unified body of knowledge in *Meditations on First Philosophy*, which circulates in manuscript form prior to publication; provokes criticism with this work from religious thinkers whose formal objections, written up as the first six sets of *Objections and Replies*, are appended to the first published edition of the *Meditations; 1642* attaches a seventh set of *Objections and Replies* to the second edition of *Meditations*; accused of atheism by Professor Voetius of the University of Utrecht; *1642-1643* condemned by local Dutch authorities; French ambassador intervenes on his behalf; *1643* develops a friendship and lengthy correspondence with Princess Elizabeth of Bohemia on the relationship of the mind to the body and of reason to passions; his philosophy is condemned at the University of Utrecht; *1644* publishes *Principles of Philosophy* and dedicates it to Princess Elizabeth; attempts in his latest work to explain all natural phenomena in one single system of mechanical principles; *1645* reaches a compromise with the University of Utrecht after the school issues a decree forbidding publication of any work taking a position for or against the Cartesian doctrines; *1647* accused in Leiden of Pelagianism (the belief that the will is equally free to choose to do good or evil); attack produces yet another decree of neutral censorship; visits Paris and is awarded a pension by Louis XIV, the king of France; meets with philosopher Blaise Pascal to talk of their scientific experiments; begins a correspondence with Queen Christina of Sweden; publishes *Comments on a Certain Broadsheet*, in which he disavows the ideas of his former student and supporter Henricus Regius; begins work on *Description of the Human Body*; *1648* returns to Paris to meet with the physicist Pierre Gassendi, the English materialist Thomas Hobbes, and his friend and supporter Father Mersenne; *1649* outlines and publishes his ethical views in

Treatise on Passions and sends the manuscript as a gift to Queen Christina; leaves Amsterdam for Stockholm to serve as instructor to Queen Christina; *1650* catches a severe cold February 1; dies of pneumonia on February 11, and, as a Catholic in a Protestant country, is buried February 13 in a Swedish cemetery reserved for unbaptized children; *1793* the Convention Nationale decrees that his body should be transferred to the Panthéon, an honor never carried out, and Descartes is instead laid to rest in the garden of the Musée des Monuments Français; *1819* entombed in the Church of St. Germain-des-Près.

Activities of Historical Significance

As a philosopher and as a scientist, René Descartes was unparalleled in the seventeenth century. His influence on not only the French philosophers of the eighteenth century but on nineteenth- and twentieth-century thinkers as well is indicative of the extent to which his skeptical method of analysis has shaped western consciousness. Today, Descartes is considered to be the father of modern scientific and philosophic thought, the instigator of the Cartesian revolution in science and philosophy. This revolution, a testament to the originality of Descartes's mind, consists of two major advances pursued continuously throughout his life—the unification of all the sciences into one body of knowledge, and the creation of an analytic method of reasoning.

In philosophy, Descartes proposed a new way of thinking that threatened to subvert the traditional scholastic approach to knowledge. To Descartes, this method of using syllogistic logic to answer questions of a scientific or philosophic nature, that is, to use a three-part method of demonstration where the conclusion is already known on the basis of what is stated in the premises, was inadequate. He argued that scholasticism was useless for the discovery of truth and that it led instead only to elaborate rhetoric. For that reason, he devoted his life's work to creating a method that, when used correctly, would always lead to true knowledge.

In his unpublished work, *Rules for the Direction of the Mind*, written in the late 1620s, Descartes rejected outright scholasticism and the scholastic view that there are distinctions between various kinds of knowledge. Instead, he asserted that all knowledge was solely of one kind because its acquisition was entirely dependent on the use of the human mind. He also discarded the notion of preconceived ideas.

He instead proposed that inquiry must start from self-evident data that is known to be clearly and distinctly true and then continue to ensure that every step in the deductive progress from the data is self-evident.

Though *Rules for the Direction of the Mind* was not published during his lifetime [it was first printed in Amsterdam, 1701, in a posthumous collection of his works, *Opuscula Posthuma*], its ideas found expression in Descartes's later writings, including his first published work in 1637. This anonymously published volume contained three essays—"Optics," "Meteorology," and "Geometry"—and was preceded by a short semiautobiographical introduction, *Discourse on the Method*, which was later published separately.

Unlike most scientific works of the seventeenth century, Descartes's writings were produced in French instead of Latin, and were deliberately aimed at a wider audience than the narrow scientific community. The three essays presented many exciting scientific advances, including the creation of a new field in mathematics, the discovery of the law of refraction of light, the first attempt at a scientific explanation of weather including an explanation of a rainbow, a classification of curves, and the rejection of divine intervention as a useful explanation for natural phenomena. Yet it was the introduction to the volume of essays, *Discourse on the Method,* that received the most attention and is to this day Descartes's most widely-read work.

In the *Discourse*, Descartes elaborated on his new method of attaining certainty in knowledge. His four-step method for discovering truth began with a rejection of all accepted ideas and opinions and used skepticism as a way to build a new edifice of knowledge based only on certain truth. It was Descartes's search for that one clear and distinct truth upon which the rest of his method could be built that led to the famous dictum *cogito ergo sum* ("I think, therefore I am"). According to Descartes, doubting the existence of everything makes certain the existence of a doubting mind. From this one piece of knowledge, using the method of doubt, Descartes proposed that a body of knowledge could be constructed free from the superstitions and prejudices of the past.

Even though the *cogito*, as well as the mind-body distinction it created, has since been discredited, Descartes's method of total skepticism towards all preconceived ideas has become the basis of all modern scientific endeavors. The scholastic method of reliance on tradition and the interpretation of and debate over the classic texts to find scientific and philosophic answers had been effectively laid to rest. The advent of Descartes's philosophy dealt a death blow to the already crumbling medieval world view.

In 1641 Descartes came out with a Latin treatise, the *Meditations*, an elaborate development of the metaphysical doctrine of doubt described in the fourth part of the *Discourse*. It was the *Meditations*, circulated privately among scholars and scientists prior to its publication, which brought Descartes fame as one of the world's greatest living philosophers. Yet it was also the *Meditations* which involved him in bitter controversies concerning the idea of God. Even though Descartes's method derived the absolute certainty of God out of the knowledge of one's existence and of one's thoughts of God, and therefore claimed that the existence of God was a self-evident certainty, the circularity of his reasoning led his detractors to hurl charges of "atheism" at him, charges that were to harass the philosopher for the rest of his life.

In 1644 Descartes again restated his philosophical doctrines in the first part of another Latin work, the *Principles of Philosophy*. In the second through fourth parts, he attempts to give a logical account of all natural phenomena, as measured by physics, chemistry, and physiology, in one single system of mechanical principles. In these last three parts Descartes rejected all "spiritual" or qualitative notions in scientific explanations and refused to include teleological or purposive causes. It was his expressed determination in the *Principles of Philosophy* to explain all physical phenomena in mechanical terms and to relate these terms to geometrical ideas. Descartes's desire to rid science of spiritual explanations combined with his emphasis on the use of the hypothesis to aid generalizations led the way to the modern approach to scientific theory.

Overview of Biographical Sources

Biographies of Descartes are scarce, as most academics are primarily concerned with his groundbreaking philosophy rather than with his quiet private life. A few noteworthy biographies do exist, however. The earliest is Adrien Baillet's *La Vie de Monsieur Des-Cartes* (1691), a unique source of contemporary and slightly risqué information on Descartes. Although Baillet is occasionally apologetic, his work remains one of the most important biographies on the philosopher.

A few simplistic biographies, such as J. P. Mahaffy's *Descartes* (London: W.

Blackwood, 1901), were published in English during the early years of the twentieth century, but they have never earned, nor do they deserve any merit. Elizabeth Haldane's *Descartes, His Life and Times* (1905), is generally credited with being the first scholarly English-language life of Descartes. Haldane's academic work was completed just prior to the publication of the fundamental study of Descartes's works and life in Charles Adam's biography *Vie et Œuvres de Descartes. Étude historique* (1910. Vol. 12. *Œuvres de Descartes* Paris: Léopold Cerf, 1896-1913), edited by Charles Adam and Paul Tannery. In comparison to Adam's biography, Haldane's work lacks both an intense probing of Descarte's life and a close textual analysis. The significance of Haldane lies in the fact that her biography was the first scholarly attempt in English to analyze Descarte's life. Her work lacked an English-language rival until 1970. In that year Jack Vrooman published *René Descartes: A Biography* (1970). With the advantage of having Adam and Tannery's substantial work as a starting point, Vrooman offers much more insight into the life of Descartes than does Haldane. He adds little, however, by way of a deeper understanding of Descarte's philosophy.

There are few book-length biographies of Descartes in English, but most modern translations and analyses of Descartes's work devote a few pages to the life of the philosopher. The best of these sources is John Cottingham's *Descartes* (1986), which contains a detailed and interesting chapter on Descartes' life.

Evaluation of Principal Biographical Sources

Adam, Charles. *Vie et œuvres de Descartes. Étude historique.* 1910. Reprint. Vol. 12. *Oeuvres de Descartes,* edited by Charles Adam and Paul Tannery. Paris: Vrin/CNRS, 1958. (**A**) The first modern critical biography of Descartes, this work appeared as part of a 12-volume collection of Descartes's writings. As an editor of the collected works of Descartes, Adam had an incomparable knowledge of the texts and sources. Adam consciously chose not to include an analysis of Descartes's philosophy in the biography, however, focusing instead exclusively on the events of the philosopher's life. Adam makes up for this lacuna with numerous lengthy footnotes which further clarify the text and provide valuable references to the specific works of Descartes for those interested in pursuing his philosophy in more detail.

Baillet, Adrien. *La Vie de Monsieur Des-Cartes*. 2 vols. 1691. Reprint. New York: Georg Olms Verlag, 1972. (**A**) The virtue of Baillet's biography, published less than a half century after Descartes's death, is that it preserves numerous contemporary sources. Baillet inserts Descartes's letters and private family documents directly into the text of the biography. Some of these written sources have since disappeared in original form and would have been lost altogether were it not for Baillet's work. The main flaw of the book lies in Baillet's re-creation of specific conversations and events which he attributes to Descartes, but which cannot be verified by any other source. Baillet's desire to present a purified image of Descartes has rendered his biography suspect.

Haldane, Elizabeth. *Descartes, His Life and Times*. London: Murray, 1905. (**A, G**) For the purpose of analysis, Haldane breaks down Descartes's life into three distinct periods: his education, his travels, and what she calls his constructive period. In tracing Descartes's experiences, Haldane focuses much attention on his environment, both historical and personal. Haldane's analysis of his works is weak, and has been superseded by more recent studies. In spite of this flaw, Haldane's work is significant. Her biography of Descartes stood for over half a century as the most substantial account of his life in English since it was, until the publication of Vrooman's biography, the *only* account of Descartes's life in English which attempted to go beyond the anecdotal and attempt a scholarly rendering of his life.

Vrooman, Jack Rochford. *René Descartes: A Biography*. New York: Putnam's, 1970. (**A, G**) An easy-to-read yet thorough critical biography. Vrooman focuses on six distinctive periods in Descartes's life, relating the events of the first three to the development of Descartes's philosophy. Beginning with an analysis of how Descartes's world view was affected by growing up motherless, Vrooman explains Descartes's mercenary activities during the Thirty Years' War as part of his real-life search for truth; the development of his scientific method and his absolute conviction of its correctness are seen as a result of his night of dreams, November 10, 1619. The last three sections emphasize the different relationships he had with women, first with a servant, Hélène, who bore him his only child, and then with Princess Elizabeth of Bohemia and Queen Christina of Sweden. Extended passages from Descarte's personal correspondence are included in the text, some appearing for the first time in English. Vrooman's work is the definitive English-language biography of the philosopher.

Overview and Evaluation of Primary Sources

The classic edition of the collected works of Descartes is Charles Adam and Paul Tannery's edited collection, *Œuvres de Descartes* (13 vols. 1896-1913. Reprint. Paris: Vrin/CNRS, 1957-1968; **A**). This compilation is the definitive text of his work. Included are indispensable introductions, as well as textual and explanatory notes. The translations of the main works are those authorized by Descartes himself. Although the text of the correspondence can be considered authoritative, the dates and the identification of correspondents cannot.

This problem was corrected by Charles Adam and Gérard Milhaud in their indispensable eight-volume set, *Correspondance* (Paris: Presses Universitaires de France, 1936-1963; **A**), which includes many letters from the optical physicist Constantyn Huygens, that are lacking in Adam and Tannery's collection. The collection presents all known letters in chronological order, except for a few new finds, which appear in volume seven. The Latin and Dutch letters appear both in the original and in French translation. Because the dates and identification of the recipients are presumed definitive, and because the name index at the end of each volume gives a concise biography of all persons mentioned in the letters, this set makes an extremely useful reference tool.

The standard English edition of Descartes's work is *The Philosophical Works of Descartes* (1911. Reprint. New York: Cambridge University Press, 1978; **A**), translated by Elizabeth S. Haldane and G. R. T. Ross. However, this collection omits many works crucial for gaining an understanding of Descartes's philosophy, including *The Early Writings* (compiled from notebooks made during his travels in 1619-1622 and first published in 1859 as *Cogitationes Privatae*), *The World, Treatise on Man, Optics, Description of the Human Body*, and several sections from *Principles of Philosophy*. Most students, however, would do well to consult such relatively useful works as Elizabeth Anscombe and Peter T. Geach's *Descartes: Philosophical Writings* (1954. Reprint. Indianapolis: Bobbs-Merrill, 1971; **A**); Norman Kemp Smith's *Descartes' Philosophical Writings* (1952. Reprint. New York: Modern Library, 1958; **A**); and Margaret D. Wilson's *The Essential Descartes* (New York: New American Library, 1969; **A**). Wilson's anthology contains new translations of selections from the correspondence with Princess Elizabeth, and Smith's includes, along with the *Regulae, Discourse,* and *Meditations,* sections of the *Dioptric* and the *Passions.*

The most complete English-language collection of Descartes's work is *The Philosophical Writings of Descartes,* translated by John Cottingham, Robert Stoothoff, and Dugald Murdoch (2 vols. New York: Cambridge University Press, 1984-85; **A**). This comprehensive work contains *Early Writings*; *Rules for the Direction of the Mind*; *The World, or Treatise on Light and Treatise on Man*; *Discourse on Method*; *Principles of Philosophy*; *Comments on a Certain Broadsheet*; *Description of the Human Body*; *The Passions of the Soul*; *Meditations on First Philosophy*; *Objections and Replies*; and *The Search for Truth.* Descartes's *Compendium Musicae,* not often available in English anthologies, has been translated by Walter Robert under the title *Compendium of Music* (Rome: American Institute of Musicology, 1961; **A**).

The text of a dinner conversation between Descartes and Francis Burman, a twenty-year-old Dutch student, that took place in April 1648, is the basis for one of the most enlightening of Descartes's legacies. Over the course of the meal Burman raised more than eighty specific points covering some of the most vital issues in Cartesian philosophy. Based on Burman's detailed notes of that encounter, which were not discovered until 1895, the work, now entitled *Descartes' Conversation with Burman* (John Cottingham, trans., Oxford: Clarendon, 1976; **A**), offers the last recorded expression of Descartes's philosophical views.

Fiction and Adaptations

Three plays in which Descartes as a character was given a major role appeared during the late-eighteenth and early-nineteenth centuries. Only one of them, Jean-Nicolas Boully's *René Descartes: Trait historique en 2 actes et en prose par le citoyen Bouilly* (Paris, 1796) attempted to present a biography of Descartes. This play, a weird biographic fantasy, was performed at the first known Descartes celebration in La Haye-Descartes, and then later in 1796 at the Théâtre de la République after denial of Panthéon honors to the philosopher. The anonymously written *Le Club des Dames, ou le retour de Descartes: Comédie en une acte, en prose* (1784), and *Les Ombres de Descartes, Kant et Jouffroy à M. Cousin, par un professeur de philosophie*, possibly written by P. H. Mabire (1844), both feature the long-deceased philosopher returning to earth. In *Le Club des dames*, Descartes debates Newton, and in *Les Ombres de Descartes* he berates Victor Cousin. *Le Club des dames*, in particular, was used to heighten nationalist feeling against the English by portraying Descartes defeating Newton.

Museums, Historical Landmarks, Societies

Church Adolphe-Frédéric de Stockholm (Stockholm). Contains a commemorative monument to Descartes by J. T. Sergel.

Church of St. Germain-des-Près (Paris). Descartes's remains, with the exception of his skull, lie entombed here and are marked by a small medallion made by G. Guérin on the south wall.

Descartes's Birthplace (Descartes, France). Descartes's hometown of La Haye was renamed La Haye-Descartes in 1802 and is now known simply as "Descartes." His family home has been converted into a museum, which holds, among other rare items, the original parish register containing the entry for Descartes's baptism.

Louvre (Paris). Contains two portraits of Descartes, the first believed to be an old copy of a now-lost original by Frans Hals; the second attributed to Sébastien Bourdon.

Musée de l'homme (Paris). Descartes's skull is on permanent display here.

Palais de l'Institute (Paris). Houses a statue of Descartes commissioned by Louis XVI and sculpted by Augustin Pajou.

Other Sources

Cottingham, John. *Descartes*. New York: Basil Blackwell, 1986. An excellent introduction to Descartes's life and writings. Provides a useful short survey of Descartes's philosophy while emphasizing the main subjects of the *Meditations*. It also briefly touches on many of his other writings. Particularly useful are the long passages from Baillet's 1691 biography on Descartes's dreams, translated and reprinted in the appendix.

Grene, Marjorie Glicksman. *Descartes*. Minneapolis: University of Minnesota Press, 1985. Positions Descartes's philosophy in relation to the thought of his contemporaries. It provides good insights into the historical context of his work.

Hooker, Michael, ed. *Descartes: Critical and Interpretive Essays*. Baltimore, MD: Johns Hopkins University Press, 1978. An anthology of fifteen essays on Cartesian dualism. It also contains an English-language bibliography covering books and articles published about Descartes in the period 1966-1975.

Smith, Norman Kemp. *Studies in the Cartesian Philosophy*. 1902. Reprint. New York: Russell and Russell, 1962. The best general study of Cartesianism. Covers the failure of Rationalism from Descartes through Kent.

Barbara Whitehead
DePauw University

Denis Diderot
1713-1784

Chronology

Born Denis Diderot on October 5, 1713, in Langres, Champagne, France, son of Didier Diderot, a master cutler, and Angélique Vigneron; attends the Jesuit collège (secondary school) in Langres, where he studies Latin and Greek and wins a number of prizes; *1726* joins the clergy in order to inherit the ecclesiastical benefice of his uncle, the canon of Langres Cathedral; *c. 1728* goes to Paris to complete his studies at the Jansenist Collège d'Harcourt; may also have attended the Jesuit-run Louis-le-Grand; *1723* earns a master's degree from the University of Paris; enters the office of Clement de Ris, a solicitor, to study law; remains there about two years, but spends most of his time studying Latin, Greek, and mathematics; *1723-1733* supports himself by giving mathematics lessons, composing sermons, and doing odd literary jobs, including translations; receives money from his mother, but none from his father, who wants him to pursue a more settled profession; occasionally extracts money from friends and acquaintances, sometimes on false pretense; may have contemplated an ecclesiastical career as he studied theology during those years; frequently attends the theatre; *1741* meets Anne-Toinette Champion, a beautiful but penniless lingère (dealer in lace and linen) whom he courts under the pretense of needing shirts for his seminary trousseau; *1742* begins friendship with philosopher Jean-Jacques Rousseau; goes to Langres to obtain his father's permission to marry; *1743* forcibly "detained" in a Langres monastery on the orders of his irate father; escapes to Paris and goes into hiding; marries Marie Toinette at St. Pierre-aux-Boeufs, a Paris church agreeable to performing semiclandestine marriages; the marriage, which will last until the philosopher's death, will not be a success; supports himself and his wife mainly by translating English works; *1746* publishes the militantly deistic *Philosophical Thoughts*, which the Paris Parliament condemns to be burned as "scandalous and contrary to Religion and Morals"; *1747* publishes *Les Alleys, or the Sceptic's Walk*, a philosophical allegory probably written to procure money for an adventuress, Mme. de Puisieux, with whom he has begun a love affair; with his friend, mathematician Jean Le

Rond d'Alembert, signs a contract with publishers André-François Le Breton, Briasson, David, and Laurent Durand, as chief editors of a translation into French of Ephraïm Chambers' 1728 *Cyclopaedia*, the translation of which will grow into the great *Encyclopédie*; *1748* publishes an erotic novel, *The Indiscreet Jewels*, and *Memoirs on Various Mathematical Subjects*; *1749* publishes the *Letter on the Blind, for the Use of Those who See*, in which he presents daring materialistic views and for which he is arrested and imprisoned at Vincennes for several months; upon his release, resumes work on the *Encyclopédie*; *1750* writes the *Prospectus* that describes the purpose and outlines the content of the *Encyclopédie*; meets Melchior Grimm, who will become his closest friend; *1751* the first volume of the *Encyclopédie* appears, opened by a "Preliminary Discourse" authored by d'Alembert; *1752* a decree of the royal Council suspends the publication of volume II on the grounds that it threatens royal authority, religion, and morality; with Rousseau, Grimm, and d'Holbach, takes the Italian side in the "War of the Buffoons," a quarrel that divides Paris between the supporters of Italian opera and those of French music; *1753* because of pressure from Mme. de Pompadour, the king's mistress, and Lamoignon de Malesherbes, the state censor, volume III appears without explicit approval, but with tacit state tolerance; his wife gives birth to, Marie-Angélique, their only child who will survive into adulthood; publishes *Thoughts on the Interpretation of Nature*, a brief work that stresses the need to study external objects instead of reasoning in the abstract; *1754* with the fourth volume of the *Encyclopédie* behind him, visits his father in Langres while continuing work on the fourth and fifth volume; *ca. 1755* meets Sophie Volland, the learned and witty daughter of a well-to-do *bourgeois*, and falls in love; *1757* publishes *The 'Natural' Son*, a bourgeois drama that contains the line "only evil men live alone," which Rousseau takes as a personal attack, thus straining their friendship; publishes *Conversations on the 'Natural' Son*; oversees the publication of volume VII of the *Encyclopédie*, in which the article "Geneva" (written by d'Alembert) spurs J.-J. Rousseau to attack the Encyclopedists in *Letter to d'Alembert about Theatrical Performances*, published the next year; *1758* publishes another drama, *The Father of the Family*, accompanied by *Discourse on Dramatic Poetry*; assumes total responsibility for the *Encyclopédie* when d'Alembert, after a year of hesitation, withdraws from the overly controversial project; *1759* accused of impiety by the Attorney General, Omer Joly de Fleury, in a speech to the Paris Parliament; learns first that publication of volume VII has been suspended, then that the entirety of the *Encyclopédie* has been suspended by royal decree; finds out also that the *Encyclopédie* has been placed on the official Index of Prohibited Books; contributes critiques of Comédie-française performances and of the Salon (biennial painting exhibits) to Grimm's *Correspondance littéraire*, a periodical reporting Paris literary and cultural events that Grimm sends to a few, select subscribers, mostly German rulers; *1760* writes *The Nun*, which is circulated in the *Correspondance littéraire* in 1780 and published after his death in 1797; lampooned in Charles Palissot's highly successful comedy *Les Philosophes*; *1761* has *The Father of the Family* performed at the Comédie-française to a lukewarm reception; begins composing *Rameau's Nephew*, today considered his masterpiece but published only after his death; *1762* writes *Additions aux Pensées philosophiques*, circulated in the *Correspondance littéraire* but not published; *1763* makes the acquaintance of Edward Gibbon, John Wilkes, and David Hume; *1764* writes a treatise on freedom of the press, *Letter to a Magistrate Concerning the Book Trade*; to raise money for his daughter's dowry, seeks to sell his library; *1765* sells the library to Catherine II of Russia for fifteen thousand livres, and receives from the generous empress the appointment of curator of the library (to remain in his possession until his death) with a yearly stipend of a thousand livres; *1765-1766* brings out the last ten volumes the *Encyclopédie* and finds out, with great anger, that the publisher Le Breton has mutilated many articles to forestall action by the censors; *1766* secures for his friend Etienne-Maurice Falconnet a commission to erect a statue of Peter the Great in St. Petersburg; completes *Essays on Painting*, an attempt at integrating aesthetics and ethics; *1767* writes a particularly lengthy *Salon*; *1769* drafts one of his major works, *D'Alembert's Dream*, a daring flight of speculation about nature and the cosmos that is published after his death; *1770* begins negotiations for his daughter's marriage; writes *Conversation between a Father and His Children* (published 1772), and *The Two Friends of Bourbonne*, a moral tale; *1771* finally has his drama *The Natural Son* performed at the Comédie-française; *1772* writes the *Supplément au Voyage de Bougainville*, a description of a sexual utopia set in Tahiti (which is not published during his lifetime), and marries his beloved daughter to Abel-François-Nicolas Caroillon de Vandeul; *1773* sets off to visit Catherine II in Russia, stopping for several weeks in Holland, where he writes *Paradox of the Actor*; spends five months in St. Petersburg conversing frequently with Catherine, who is fascinated by his intellect and unmoved by his suggestions for reform; *1774* begins his journey home, stopping six months at The Hague, where he writes for Catherine II *Comments on the Instructions*, suggesting the need to liberalize her despotic government and emancipate the serfs; writes also a *Voyage de Hollande*, in which he praises Dutch liberty; publishes (anonymously) *Conversation between a Philosopher and Madame de ****, which gives a materialistic answer to the question of God's existence; *1775* at Catherine's request, drafts *Project for a University for the Russian Government;* 1776-1777 contributes extensively to Abbé Raynal's *Histoire des Deux-Indes*; writes a comedy, *Is he good? Is he mean?*, which will not be produced until 1955, perhaps because of its Pirandellesque approach to the nature of psychological reality; *1779* publishes *Essay on Seneca*; 1782 writes *Essays on the Reigns of Claudius and Nero*; *1784* suffers a stroke or a heart attack and moves to a large apartment in rue de Richelieu, rented for him by Catherine II; dies on July 31 and is buried in the chapelle de la Varge of Saint Rock Church in Paris.

Activities of Historical Significance

Denis Diderot did not make war, start revolution, or in any way make history. His participation was limited, if one can use such a word for one so influential, to changing the way people thought. For his contemporaries, Diderot was above all the general editor of the *Encyclopédie*. The very concept of an encyclopedia was new, so new that it had to be explained and its etymology given. The first edition of the *Encyclopedia Britannica* would appear twenty-one years after the prospectus which announced the publication of the *Encyclopédie*.

The *Encyclopédie,* as announced in its prospectus, would present the interrelationships of the sciences by a frequent use of cross references. It would also present the Enlightenment ideas and ideals, so much so that it would earn the ire of the French censorship and see its publication suspended several times. Articles such as "Government," "Political Liberty," "Absolute Monarchy," and "Limited Monarchy," advocated limiting royal power, a red flag to the partisans of divine-right monarchy. The article on "Salt" castigated the notorious "Gabelle," the salt tax, and condemned, as did the one on "Taxes," the injustice of the Ancien Régime tax system.

The early volumes avoided direct criticism of the established religion, Catholicism, but discussed chronology (in articles in "Chaldeans," "Chaos," and

"Chronology," for example) to impugn, indirectly, the historical validity of the Old Testament. In later volumes, articles such as "Priests," or "Theocracy" became virulent attacks on intolerance. Thus, the *Encyclopédie* was not an impartial compilation of knowledge, but a "war machine" designed to batter the walls of established religion and absolutist regimes in the name of free thought.

For twenty years the Diderot supervised this huge undertaking, writing thousands of articles himself. Diderot's voracious appetite for knowledge, his extraordinarily broad curiosity, and the deep respect for craftsmanship he had learned from his master cutler father stood him in good stead as he produced articles on topics as varied as "Steel," "Needles," "The Beautiful," "Political Authority," "Stockings," "Brewing," "Playing Cards," and "Philosophical Doubt." Under his leadership, the *Encyclopédie* was transformed from a mere reference work to a multi-volume Enlightenment manifesto directed against tyranny, inhumanity, and obscurantism. Yet, the *Encyclopédie* represents only a fraction of Diderot's manifold, multiform activities.

His dramatic theories, that plays should center around "social conditions," instead of characters, and should seek drama in the lives of ordinary people instead of crowned heads and mythical heroes have prevailed today, even if his plays were tedious and drowned in bathos. Most twentieth-century theatre, most television series, are derived from Diderot's bourgeois drama, not from classical tragedy or comedy.

He did not, as is sometimes stated, invent art criticism. Accounts of the biennial Salon exhibits had been written and circulated before he began contributing his *Salons* to the *Correspondance littéraire*. But he elevated the genre to a new importance and a new status, even if his praise of Greuze's sentimental village scene is a far cry from the reviews in *Art in America*. For Diderot, art was justified first and foremost by its moral content, not its formal perfection.

As a thinker, Diderot developed from a rather conventional early deism to a daring evolutionary materialism. Despite his old-fashioned talk of "fibers," the vision presented in *D'Alembert's Dream* of nature as a constantly evolving whole is both poetic and modern. This materialistic and evolutionary stand led him to question the basis for condemning moral monsters, as in *Rameau's Nephew*. He thus raised the problem of absolute ethical values in an amoral, materialistic universe. He did not solve the problem—the dialogue form he used in *Rameau's Nephew* suited his ambivalence about the topic—but he stated it with a rare intellectual honesty.

Diderot's thought and Diderot's art appeal directly to modern sensibilities. Robert Rimmer, the guru of the sexual revolution, has hailed Diderot as a precursor: the Tahiti of *The Supplement to Bougainville's Voyage* is a natural paradise where free love flourishes untrammelled by any restraint save the need to produce healthy children. *The Nun,* Diderot's bitter condemnation of clerical celibacy, especially when imposed upon girls forced into religious life (one of his sisters went insane in the convent) is still controversial today: the Jacques Rivette film version was forbidden by then French Minister of Culture André Malraux. And Diderot's brilliant novel, *Jacques le Fataliste* (1797), anticipates the most modern techniques of "le roman éclaté."

Overview of Biographical Sources

There are two major accounts of Diderot's life by his contemporaries and associates: Jacques André Naigeon's *Mémoires historiques et philosophiques sur la vie et les ouvrages de D. Diderot,* written by a friend and admirer; and Marie-Angélique de Vandeul's "Mémoires pour servir à l'histoire de la vie et des ouvrages de Diderot," most readily found in Denis Diderot, *Euvres complètes,* vol. 1, edited by Jules Assézat and Maurice Tourneux (20 vols. Paris: Garnier, 1875-1877). Both are indispensable though unreliable on details.

Two excellent biographies in English cover the philosopher's entire career: Lester C. Crocker's *The Embattled Philosopher: A Biography of Denis Diderot* (1954. Rev. ed. East Lansing: Michigan State University Press, 1966) is a lively entertaining account of Diderot's engaging personality by a premier scholar. Arthur M. Wilson's *Diderot* (1972) is as close to a definitive biography as one is likely to get with a personality as complex as Diderot's. Otis Fellows's *Diderot* is a convenient, brief synthesis (1977).

Various aspects of Diderot's manifold activities have been treated in monographs. The undertaking that absorbed twenty years of his life, the *Encyclopédie,* has been treated in English by John Lough in several monographs and articles, most importantly in *Essays on the 'Encyclopédie' of Diderot and d'Alembert* (London: Oxford University Press, 1968), and in French by Jacques Proust in *Diderot et l'Encyclopédie* (Paris: Armand Colin, 1962), which clarifies Diderot's role as editor and his overall contribution to the project, as does Lord John Morley's Diderot and the Encycloaedists (2 vols. 1878. Reprint 1923).

His importance as a thinker on scientific, political, aesthetic, and especially moral issues has been treated by Lester G. Crocker in *Diderot's Chaotic Order: Approach to a Synthesis* (Princeton, NJ: Princeton University Press, 1974). Charles Frankel's *The Faith of Reason: The Idea of Progress in the French Enlightenment* (New York: King's Crown, 1948) gives a good brief account of Diderot's thought, especially his transformism. John Henry Brumfitt treats Diderot's materialism in *The French Enlightenment* (London: Macmillan, 1972).

Emita B. Hill's "The role of 'le monstre' in Diderot's thought," in *Studies in Voltaire and the Eighteenth Century* (97[1972]: 147-261), is a brilliant study of Diderot's fascination with moral monsters and of his coping with the problem of evil within a materialistic framework. His concomitant preoccupation with "virtue" is analyzed by Carol Blum in a lively and original monograph, *Diderot, The Virtue of a Philosopher* (New York: Viking, 1974).

His contribution to art criticism is dealt with in Michael F. Cartwright, *Diderot critique d'art et le problème de l'expression* (Geneve: Droz, 1969); Lester G. Crocher, *Two Diderot Studies: Ethics and Aesthetics* (Baltimore: The Johns Hopkins Press, 1952); and especially in Yvon Belaval, *L'esthétique sans paradoxe de Diderot* (Paris: Gallinard, 1950), which shows his contributions to the theatre while covering his overall aesthetic thought.

His scientific thought has been studied by Jean Mayer in *Diderot, homme de science* (Rennes: Librairie "Les nourritures terrestres," 1960), and by Michèle Duchet in *Anthropologie et histoire au siècle des lumières: Buffon, Voltaire, Rousseau, Hebetiers, Diderot* (Paris: Maspero, 1971).

There are many studies of Diderot's individual novels, especially *Jacques le Fataliste*, but few overall surveys of Diderot the novelist. Among the most readily available are Roger Kempf's *Diderot et le roman ou le démon de la présence* (Paris: Seuil, 1964); as well as the relevant pages in Vivienne Mylne's *The Eighteenth-Century French Novel: Techniques of Illusion* (New York: Barnes and Noble, 1965); and English Showalter, Jr.'s *The Evolution of the French Novel, 1641-1782* (Princeton: Princeton University Press, 1972).

Evaluation of Principal Biographical Sources

Chouillet, Jacques. *Diderot.* Paris: Société d'Enseignement Supérieur, 1977. (**A**) Written by the eminent Diderot scholar, this biography is centered on Diderot's works, with careful analyses that provide new insight into Diderot's thought process, and into the social and political implications of his texts. Contains a bibliography. Untranslated.

Fellows, Otis. *Diderot.* Boston: Twayne, 1977. (**G**) Provides an excellent introduction to Diderot and his age for the general reader. Fellows draws on his extensive scholarship to present the life of the encyclopedist, tracing the crucial points in Diderot's development and situating these events in the larger historical context. Gives an excellent summary of the ideas and arguments of Diderot's major works and a sampling of critical opinion. Contains a helpful annotated bibliography.

Wilson, Arthur M. *Diderot.* New York: Oxford University Press, 1972. (**A, G**) The first part of this book was published in 1957 under the title *Diderot: The Testing Years, 1713-1759,* and is republished in this volume with Part II, *The Appeal to Posterity.* The work incorporates data from all available sources to present a detailed account of Diderot's life and a balanced view of the complexities of his personality and thought. Historical background is accurately provided, and the *milieux* in which Diderot moved is brought to life. Diderot's works are examined, sometimes at length, with particular attention given to the importance of the *Encyclopédie* and Diderot's role as editor. The book is richly annotated and there is a full bibliography. Indispensable for scholarly research, the work is immensely readable.

Overview and Evaluation of Primary Sources

There are Diderot letters, drafts, and manuscripts in numerous repositories. The most important collections are the papers deposited in the Saltykov-Shchedrin Library of Leningrad and the Fond Vandeul in the Department of Manuscripts of the Bibliothèque Nationale in Paris.

Diderot's extensive correspondence has been published in sixteen volumes by Georges Roth and Jean Varloot (Paris: Editions de Minuit, 1955-1970; **A**). The edition of the complete works prepared by Jules Assézat and Maurice Tourneux (20 vols.; Paris: Garnier, 1875-1877; **A**) has been superseded by the *Euvres complètes de Diderot* (Paris: Herman, 1875-1886; **A**), edited by Herbert Dieckman, Jean Favre, and Jacques Proust, with Jean Varloot as general secretary. Readable English translations of the main works are readily available, often in paperback.

There is an annual publication, the *Diderot Studies*, edited by Otis Fellows and Diana Gairagossian, and a semiannual published in Langres, *Recherches sur Diderot et l'Enciclopédie.*

Museums, Historical Landmarks, Societies

Boulevard St. Germain (Paris). There is a statue (1885) by Jean Gautherin.

Busts. The Hermitage in St. Petersburg contains a bust by Etienne-Maurice Falconet; the Musée du Louvre in Paris contains a bust (1777) by Jean-Baptiste Pigalle; and the Hôtel de Ville in Langres contains a bust by Jean-Baptiste Houdon.

Pierpont Morgan Library (New York City). Contains a drawing of Diderot (ca. 1767) by Jean-Baptiste Greuze.

Place Diderot (Langres, France). There is a statue by Frédéric-August Bartholdi (1884) outside his childhood home.

Portraits. The Musée du Louvre in Paris contains portaits by Jean-Honoré Fragonard and L. Michel Van Loo; the Musée d'Art et d'Histoire in Geneva, Switzerland, contains a portrait by Dmitri Levitskii; and the Musée Carnavalet in Paris contains a portrait by Jean-Simon Barthélemy,

Rue de Richelieu (Paris). The house in which he died is marked with a memorial plaque.

Other Sources

Archer, William. *Masks or Faces? A Study in the Psychology of Acting.* 1888. New York: Hill and Wang, 1957. An investigation of Diderot's *Paradoxe sur le Comédien,* based on actors' testimony of their own experience.

Creech, James. "Diderot's 'Ideal Model'." In *Diderot: Digressions and Dispersion.* Lexington, KY: French Forum, 1984: 85-97. In a collection of essays rejecting the attempt to integrate the diversity of Diderot's thought, this article examines the theory of the ideal model as a source of mimetic plurality.

Cru, R. Loyalty. *Diderot as a Disciple of English Thought.* New York: AMS, 1966. Discusses the English influence in all areas of Diderot's work, with a chapter devoted to its manisfestation in Diderot's theater and dramatic theories.

Undank, Jack. *Diderot: Inside, Outside & In-Between.* Madison, WI: Coda Press, 1979. Three chapters deal with the psychology of imitation in *Le Fils Naturel* and the *Entretiens.*

Mathé Allain
Southwestern Louisiana University

Fyodor Dostoevsky
1821-1881

Chronology

Born Fyodor Mikhailovich Dostoevsky on October 30, 1821, in Moscow, the son of Mikhail Andreevich, an ill-tempered surgeon, and Mariya Fyodorovna, a loving woman who played the guitar, liked to sing, and read poetry and fiction; *1837-1839* mother dies; studies at home, then at a boarding school, where he is mistreated by his peers; with his elder brother Mikhail, sent to the St. Petersburg Military School of Engineering, where he is a capable if somewhat impractical student who avidly reads classic Russian and European authors, especially Pushkin, Gogol, Balzac, E. T. A. Hoffman, Goethe, Schiller, Hugo, and George Sand; experiences periodic fits of epilepsy and is generally in poor health; father killed by his own serfs because he treated them inhumanely; *1843* graduates from the engineering cadet school and enters civil service in St. Petersburg; hates his job and gives it up to write; finishes translation of French author Honoré Balzac's *Eugenie Grandet*; *1844* begins writing *Poor Folk*; meets Dmitri V. Grigorovich, who introduces him to poet and publisher Nikolay Nekrasov; *1846 Poor Folk* published by Nekrasov, and Vissarion Belinsky, the leading critic of the time, receives it with high praise; publishes *The Double*, which is not as successful as his first novel; *1847* joins the "Petrashevsky Circle," a group of Utopian socialists named for its leader; *1849* with other members of the Petrashevsky Circle, arrested by the tsarist secret police and imprisoned at the Peter and Paul Fortress; after a two-week trial sentenced to death; tied to a stake at the Semenovsky Square in St. Petersburg for execution by firing squad, but sentence is commuted to four years of hard labor and four years in the army as a private in Siberia; the mock execution, probably ordered by Czar Nicholas I, results in one of the convicts going mad; *1850* incarcerated with hardened criminals under extreme conditions in Omsk; *1854* assigned to an army unit and eventually achieves the rank of second lieutenant; *1857* married Maria Dmitrievna Isaeva; *1858* released from the army; *1859* returns to St. Petersburg, where he is placed under secret observation for several years; as a result of his Siberian experience, becomes religiously and politically conservative and preoccupied with social and philosophical problems; with his brother Mikhail, the only one of his seven brothers and sisters with whom he had close contact, publishes the monthly journal *Time*; *1861* publishes "Memoirs from the Houses of the Dead," in which he describes prison life at Omsk; *1862* travels for the first time outside of Russia, visiting Germany, France, England, Switzerland, and Italy; meets Russian revolutionaries and philosophers Alexander Herzen and Mikhail Bakunin; *1863* in Paris, meets Apollinariya (Polina) Suslova, with whom he falls in love and who becomes the model for several female characters in his novels; in Baden-Baden, Germany, meets Russian author Ivan Turgenev; publishes a new journal, *Epoch*, with the first part of *Notes From the Underground* appearing in the premier issue; *1864* publishes *Notes from the Underground*, which describes his disturbing experiences at boarding school; wife, Maria, dies of tuberculosis; *1865* *Epoch* ceases publication due to financial mismanagement; leaves Russia to escape his creditors; moves to Baden-Baden, where he develops a gambling habit; *1866* his best-known novel, *Crime and Punishment*, appears in installments in the journal *The Russian Messenger*; publishes *The Gambler*, written in less than a month; *1867* marries his secretary, Anna Grigorevna Snitkina, an understanding, sympathetic and tolerant woman twenty-five years younger, with whom he has a daughter and a son, both of whom die in early childhood; *1868* publishes *The Idiot* in *The Russian Messenger*; daughter Sofia dies, which greatly affects him; *1871* returns to Russia after settling his debts; edits the journal *The Citizen*, in which he has a regular column, "The Diary of a Writer"; *1872* publishes *The Possessed*; *1875* publishes *The Adolescent*; publishes *A Raw Youth*, also a story based on his boarding-school experiences; *1877* elected Corresponding Member of the Academy of Sciences; *1878* son Aleksey dies; names the youngest of the Karamazova brothers in *The Brothers Karamazova* for Aleksey; *1879-1880* publishes probably his greatest work, *The Brothers Karamazov*; *1880* at the second meeting of the Russian Literary Society, delivers his famous "Pushkin Speech," in which he praises Pushkin as the greatest Russian genius and acknowledges Pushkin as his spiritual teacher; the address is received with great nationalistic enthusiasm; *1881* dies on January 28 in St. Petersburg and is buried at the Aleksandr-Nevsky monastery.

Activities of Historical Significance

Fyodor Dostoevsky is unquestionably one of the great novelists in the history of world literature. He is one of the most widely read Russian authors, and along with Nikolai Gogol, Ivan Turgenev, and Count Leo Tolstoy, he contributed to the nineteenth-century Golden Age of the Russian novel. As the creator of the modern psychological novel, his work also greatly influenced twentieth century writers.

Not only as a writer but also as a profound thinker, Dostoevsky touched upon some of the most essential problems of life common to all humankind. The depth of his spiritual thought can be compared to that of purely religious writers such as St. Augustine. Dostoevsky believed in the cathartic effect of voluntary suffering, which would teach humility and true love. His great novels are full of compassion, love for all living creatures, and willingness to forgive, all of which are projected against a background of a depressing world of cruelty, pain, suffering, crime, insanity, and absurdity.

Until 1885, when *Crime and Punishment* (1866) was first translated, Dostoevsky was unknown to the English-speaking world. Today he is admired as a brilliant psychologist in the field of literature. A complex personality himself, Dostoevsky probed the depths of the mind and the soul, and his work showed a remarkable anticipation of modern psychoanalytic theories. The contradiction in the personalities of Dostoevsky's characters are startling, and the author analyzes them at great length.

It is the spirituality, the profound thought, the emotional intensity, the balance between horror and humor, the suspense, and the psychological character analysis, rather than the frequently formless structure and the somewhat excessive style, that attract twentieth-century readers and writers to Dostoevsky. His influence on the novelists of the twentieth century is tremendous: Thomas Mann, Franz Kafka, André Gide, Friedrich Nietzsche, Maxim Gorky, Marcel Proust, Albert Camus, William Faulkner, and Robert Louis Stevenson are a few of the great names who found inspiration and models in Dostoevsky's writing.

The great period of Dostoevsky's writing began in 1864 with the publication of *Notes from the Underground*. Prior to this, his works were basically psychological character studies. In *Notes from the Underground*, Dostoevsky added philosophical and moral issues, and in *Crime and Punishment* and *The Brothers Karamazov* (1879-1880), he also dealt with fundamental religious questions. The mood of all

Dostoevsky's great novels can be characterized as emotionally intense.

Dostoevsky's characters reflected upon the author himself. He was a contradictory, complicated, often unpleasant dual personality, often expressing simultaneous feelings of sympathy and contempt, proud rejection of God and deep humility, belief and disbelief, love and hate. Even his philosophical and ethical views were at times inconsistent. Such also were Dostoevsky's heroes. They were constantly torn between opposite poles, and the author's own ability to empathize with them makes them frighteningly real and believable. The depth of Dostoevsky's psychological character analysis is considered by many critics to be unsurpassed in world literature.

Relationships in Dostoevsky's own life paralleled some of the psychological circumstances in his fiction. One in particular was his affair with Apollinariya (Polina) Suslova, whom he met in Paris in 1863. He fell passionately in love with this younger woman, who became his mistress. But, troubled by this illicit affair, he began to abuse her, and her love turned into hate. Dostoevsky did not stop loving her, though she continued to torment him even through his second marriage.

Dostoevsky considered himself primarily a novelist, and his non-fictional editorials are not as interesting as his novels and short stories. The critics see in him, in addition to the novelist, a remarkable psychologist, philosopher, and religious thinker. He was able to penetratingly explore and profoundly understand the human soul because he himself lived the life of his heroes.

Overview of Biographical Sources

There are numerous biographical sources on Dostoevsky of good or excellent quality. As is the case with many writers, much of this secondary literature combines the author's life with his work. Dostoevsky's work was known in Germany and France by 1890, but the 1885 English translation of *Crime and Punishment* initiated a gradual increase in the author's popularity in the English speaking world as well. Today, there are more books, articles, and dissertations on Dostoevsky in English than in any other language except Russian.

The earliest biographers tended to analyze Dostoevsky in one-dimensional terms. The great Russian religious philosopher, Nikolay Berdyaev, interprets Dostoevsky as essentially a religious writer in his *Dostoevsky: An Interpretation* (London:

Sheed & Ward, 1934). In this work, Berdeyaev's Dostoevsky defines a fallen mankind as constantly tormented by the freedom to choose between evil (violence and sin) and good (as epitomized in Christ). He finds that, in Dostoevsky, choosing Christ means choosing humanity over lack of humanity—the affirmation of the worth of every individual rather than the destruction of that ideal.

Some biographies have taken a popular, personal approach, such as Pierre Payne's *Dostoyevsky: A Human Portrait* (New York: Afred A. Knopf, 1961). Yet the specialized Dostoevsky biography is still being written—despite the numerous literary and socio-political biographies in intervening years—as evidenced by such works as Louis Breger's *Dostoevsky: The Author as Psychoanalyst* (New York: New York University Press, 1989), which views Dostoevsky as a literary precursor to Freud, writing psychoanalytic portraits that even now hold up against psychological theory.

Another major trend has been the literary biography, such as Leonard Grossman's *Dostoevsky: A Biography* (1975), which concentrates more on Dostoevsky as a stylist, a writer keenly aware of the meaning of every word, nuance, and characterization, for whom language and style were the tantamount concerns. Geir Kjetsaa's *Fyodor Dostoyevsky: A Writer's Life* (New York: Viking, 1987) is another example of this kind of literary biography, which places more emphasis on his development and style as a writer than on the often lurid details of his life.

Avraham Yarmolinsky's *Dostoevsky: Works and Days* (New York: Funk and Wagnalls, 1971) is an academic study that takes a critical approach to the literature while drawing a compelling biographical portrait of the creator. Likewise, Eugenii Soloviev's *Dostoevsky: His Life and Literary Activity* (New York: Macmillan, 1916) is a much earlier biographical sketch that focuses as much on the literature as on the life.

Some recent biographies have also cast him in a socio-political light, interpreting him as a product of his times and his work as product of his own, often melodramatic life as a gambler, revolutionary, exile, soldier, and finally, literary legend. Indeed, for the ultimate insight into Dostoevsky's life, one need look no further than his own fiction, the heart and soul of which was often based on the traumas of his life. Some of the most vivid incidents in his life—his near-execution by firing squad in December of 1849, from which he was saved by a last-minute reprieve; his experiences as an exile in Siberia; his four years working in a loghouse; his struggles with epilepsy; his years a soldier in Mongolia; and his painful gambling addiction—all appear in almost unadulterated form in such fictionalized accounts as *Memoirs from the House of the Dead* and *The Gambler.*

Evaluation of Principal Biographical Sources

Carr, Edward Halliett. *Dostoevsky (1821-1881): A New Biography.* 1931. 2d ed. New York: Houghton Mifflin, 1977. (**A, G**) A readable, well-researched, but somewhat out-dated biography with some original information. One of the early English-language biographies, with a preface by D. S. Mirsky.

Dostoevsky, Anna. *Dostoevsky: Reminiscences.* Translated and edited by Beatrice Stillman. New York: Liveright, 1975. (**A**) Published originally in 1925 by the distinguished Dostoevsky scholar Leonid Grossman, who selected the portions of Anna Dostoevsky's 798-page manuscript that described her fourteen-year marriage (1866-1881) to Dostoevsky. Introduction by Helen Muchnic.

Frank, Joseph. *Dostoevsky.* Princeton, NJ: Princeton University Press, 1976-. (**A**) A projected five-volume series on the life and work of Dostoevsky. The most comprehensive biographical work on Dostoevsky, written by a world renowned scholar; the most up-to-date biographical information. The three volumes in print are *Dostoevsky: The Seeds of Revolt. 1821-1849* (1976); *Dostoevsky: The Years of Ordeal. 1850-1859* (1983); and *Dostoevsky: The Stir of Liberation. 1860-1865* (1986).

Fueloep-Miller, René. *Fyodor Dostoevsky: Insight, Faith and Prophesy.* New York: Charles Scribner's, 1950. (**A, G**) A brief, analytical work about Dostoevsky and his work.

Grossman, Leonid. *Dostoevsky: A Biography.* Translated from the Russian by Mary Muckler. Indianapolis: Bobbs-Merrill, 1975. (**A**) Most important translation from Russian. Comprehensive biography by the great Russian Dostoevsky scholar.

Hingley, Ronald. *Dostoevsky: His Life and Work.* New York: Charles Scribner's Sons, 1978. (**A, G**) Good, basic commentary on the life and works of Dostoevsky with a useful index. Includes some interesting photographs.

Ivanor, Vyacreslav. *Freedom and Tragic Life: A Study in Dostoevsky.* Translated by Norman Cameson. Wolfeboro, NH: Longwood Academic, 1989. (**A, G**) A frequently reissued work by the great Russian symbolist poet who approaches Dostoevsky as the religious thinker and mythmaker. Ivanor argues that Dostoevsky created a new literary form, the novel-tragedy. Foreword by Maurice Bowra and newly introduced by Robert Louis Jackson.

Kjetsaa, Geir. *Fyodor Dostoevsky: A Writer's Life.* Translated from the Norwegian by Siri Hustvedt and David McDuff. New York: Elisabeth Sifton Books-Viking, 1987. (**A, G**) A good general biography with some pictures and an extensive 31-page bibliography.

Lavrin, Janko. *Dostoevsky: A Study.* 1947. New York: Russel and Russel, 1969. (**A, G**) Basic, compact, useful study of Dostoevsky's life and work.

Leatherbarrow, William J. *Fydor Dostoevsky.* Boston: Twayne, 1990. (**A, G**) A well-organized, useful work for readers just beginning a study of Dostoevsky.

Magarshack, David. *Dostoevsky.* New York: Harcourt, Brace & World, 1963. (**A, G**) An important biography, with all translations from the Russian made by the author himself; useful bibliography and index.

Mucholsky, Konstantin. *Dostoevsky: His Life and Work.* 1947. Princeton, NJ: Princeton University Press, 1967. Translated by Michael A. Minihan. (**A, G**) An important interpretation of the author's activities, recognized by many scholars as a classic in the field. According to literary critic George Gibian, it is "the best single work in any language about Dostoevsky's creative art and intellectual thought." Mucholsky (1892-1948) is long considered to be one of the most important critics of the twentieth century.

Payne, Robert. *Dostoevsky: A Human Portrait.* New York: Knopf, 1961. (**A, G**) Useful for academic and general readership.

Tarras, Victor. *The Young Dostoevsky (1846-1849): A Critical Study*. Paris: Mouton, 1969. (**A**) An excellent study of Dostoevsky's youth, focusing on the author's life and work prior to his arrest in 1849 and Siberian exile.

Troyat, Henri. *Firebrand: The Life of Dostoevsky*. Translated from the French by Norbert Guterman. London and Toronto: William Heinemann, 1946. (**A, G**) A classic biography by a great scholar; still useful for students today.

Yarmolinsky, Avraham. *Dostoevsky: His Life and Art*. New York: Grove, 1957. (**A**) A revised edition of *Dostoevsky: A Life* (1934). One of the most important biographical studies. Should be read by any serious student of Dostoevsky.

Overview and Evaluation of Primary Sources

Dostoevsky was more than a fiction writer—he was an obsessive keeper of diaries and journals, notebooks and ledgers, most of which served as his main resource materials for much of novels and short stories. Some of these journals and notebooks have been gathered and collected, either as works designed to show his literary development, or in annotated volumes relating to individual works. Ernest J. Simmons's *Dostoevsky: The Making of a Novelist* (1950. Reprint. Gloucester, MA: Peter Smith, 1962; **A, G**) provides a critical study of the development of Dostoevsky's art through extensive use of his notebooks.

The larger-scope journals and jottings have been published in English as *A Writer's Diary* in a new translation by Kenneth Lantz (Evanston, IL: Northwestern University Press, 1992; **A, G**); *Winter Notes on Summer Impressions*, translated by R. I. Renfield (New York: Criterion Books, 1955; **A, G**); and *Dostoevsky's Occasional Writings*, translated by David Magarshack (New York: Random House, 1963; **A, G**).

Specific editions of his notebooks relating to individual literary works were published in a special series by the University of Chicago Press, under the editorship of Edward Wasiolek. These are *The Notebooks for "Crime and Punishment"*, translated by Edward Wasiolek (1967); *The Notebooks for "The Idiot"*, translated by Katherine Strelsky (1967); *The Notebooks for "The Possessed"*, translated by Victor Terras (1968); *The Notebooks for "A Raw Youth"*, translated by Victor

Terras (1969); and *The Notebooks for "The Brothers Karamazov"*, translated by Victor Terras (1971).

Dostoevsky was also a devoted correspondent, leaving behind thousands of letters, many of which have been collected in English-language editions. The five-volume *Complete Letters of Fyodor Dostoevsky*, edited by David Lowe (Ann Arbor, MI: Ardis, 1989-1991; **A**) is the most comprehensive of these collections available. Another good, recent collection is *Selected Letters of Fyodor Dostoevsky*, edited by Joseph Frank and David I. Goldstein and translated by Andrew MacAndrew (New Brunswick, NJ: Rutgers University Press, 1987; **A**). Earlier collections include *Letters of Fyodor Mikhailovich Dostoevsky to His Family and Friends*, translated by Ethel G. Mayne (New York: Macmillan, 1914; **A**); *Dostoevsky: Letters and Reminiscences*, translated by S. S. Koteliansky (1923. Reprint. Salem, NH: Ayer, 1971; **A**); *The Letters of Dostoevsky to His Wife*, translated by Elizabeth Hill (New York: R. R. Smith, 1930; **A**).

A work which makes use primarily of the correspondence is Jessie Coulson's *Dostoevsky: A Self Portrait* (1962. 2d ed., New York: Oxford University Press, 1975; **A**). And correspondence as well as memory served as the basis for a work by Anna Dostoevsky (his second wife), entitled *Dostoevsky: Reminiscences*, translated by Beatrice Stillman (New York: Liveright, 1975; **A**). In this often painful remembrance, Anna tells of her courtship and marriage, as well as of Dostoevsky's love affair with Polina Suslova.

Fiction and Adaptations

There are numerous film adaptations of Dostoevsky's works. Most were produced in the former Soviet Union, but there are a few from other countries, including American versions of three of his most famous novels. *Crime and Punishment* was adapted in 1935 in a version directed by Joseph von Sternberg, and in a modernized 1959 version, directed by Denis Sanders. In the latter, *Crime and Punishment, USA*, George Hamilton (making his screen debut), portrays a modern-day American law student caught up in murder and imprisonment.

The Brothers Karamazov was adapted in a 1957 version directed by Richard Brooks, starring Yul Brenner, Claire Bloom, Lee J. Cobb, and Maria Schell. The films focuses on how the death of a domineering father effects his disparate sons.

The Gambler's American version was filmed in 1949 as *The Great Sinner*, and turned into a melodramatic gambling love story by director Robert Siodmak, with Gregory Peck and Ava Gardner in the lead roles. Other, less Hollywoodized versions were filmed in Germany in 1937 by Gerhard Lamprecht, in France in 1938 by Louis Daquin, and in the U.S.S.R. in 1972 by Aleksei Batalov.

The short story "White Nights" was adapted for the screen in 1957 in Italy by Luchino Visconti, with Maria Schell and Marcello Mastroianni in the leads; in 1959 in the U.S.S.R. by Ivan Pyriev; and in the U.S. in 1972 by Robert Bresson. The Soviet Mosfil Studios produced several adaptations: *The Idiot* (1959); *Nasty Story* (1965); *The Brothers Karamazov* (1968-1969); and *Crime and Punishment* (1970). N. M. Lary's *Dostoevsky and Soviet Film: Visions of Demonic Realism* (Ithaca, NY: Cornell University Press, 1986) is an excellent source on such films.

Dostoevsky has also inspired two major operatic works. Sergei Prokofiev's 4-act *The Gambler* was first performed in Brussels in 1929 (although it was originally intended for a 1917 debut, until the World War I canceled the production). It continues to be performed, including a recent, major staging at Chicago's Civic Center by the Lyric Opera of Chicago in late 1991. Leos Janacek's operatic version of Dostoevsky's *From the House of the Dead* first premiered in April of 1930, and also continues to be performed, including a notable staging by the New York City Opera in August of 1990.

Museums, Historical Landmarks, Societies

International Dostoevsky Society (Klagenfurt, Austria). Founded in 1971 at the University of Klagenfurt, it publishes *Dostoevsky Studies*, a journal of scholarly research on the author.

North American Dostoevsky Society (Salt Lake City, Utah). Currently based at the University of Utah, this is the American affiliate of the International Dostoevsky Society.

Aleksandr-Nevsky Monastery (St. Petersburg). Contains Dostoevsky's grave as well as those of a number of major figures in Russian history.

Other Sources

Chapple, Richard. *A Dostoevsky Dictionary*. Ann Arbor: Ardis, 1983. Identifies every character and the historical and literary allusions in Dostoevsky's fiction.

Fanger, Donald. *Dostoevsky and Romantic Realism. A Study of Dostoevsky in Relation to Balzac, Dickens and Gogol*. Chicago: University of Chicago Press, 1967. An interesting comparative study tracing various literary aspects through the works of these authors.

Murry, John Middleton. *Fyodor Dostoevsky: A Critical Study*. New York: Russel and Russel, 1966. A very basic study with a stress on literary analysis rather than on Dostoevsky's life. No index, no bibliography.

Pachmuss, Temira. *F. M. Dostoevsky: Dualism and Synthesis of the Human Soul*. Carbondale: Southern Illinois University Press, 1963. Primarily an analysis of Dostoevsky's works. Includes a chapter entitled "Biographical Factors."

Rowe, William Woodin. *Dostoevsky: Child and Man in His Works*. New York: New York University Press, and London: University of London Press, 1968. Although not a biography it has interesting references to Dostoevsky's life.

Simmons, Ernest J. *Dostoevsky: The Making of a Novelist*. New York: Oxford University Press, 1940. Uses biographical material to illuminate Dostoevsky's creative process.

————. *Feodor Dostoevsky*. New York: Columbia University Press, 1969. A short pamphlet appropriate for a first-time reader of Dostoevsky.

Wasiolek, Edward. *Dostoevsky: The Major Fiction*. Cambridge, MA: M.I.T. Press, 1964. A balanced presentation of Dostoevsky's content and craft.

Rado Pribic
Lafayette College

Émile Durkheim
1858-1917

Chronology

Born David-Émile Durkheim on April 15, 1858, in Épinal, Lorraine, France, son of Moïse Durkheim, rabbi of Épinal and Chief Rabbi of the Vosges and Haute-Marne, and Mélanie Isidor; *1858-1875* grows up in Épinal where he obtains his baccalauréats in Letters and in Sciences and observes the Prussian occupation of the city during the Franco-Prussian War; *1875* leaves Épinal for Paris to prepare for acceptance by the École Normale Supérieure; *1876* enters the Lycée Louis-le-Grand in order to continue his preparation; *1879* accepted into the École Normale Supérieure; *1882* passes his agrégation; *1882-1887* teaches in lycées in Sens, Saint-Quentin and Troyès; *1885-1886* studies in German universities in Marburg, Leipzig, and Berlin; *1885* his first publications appear in the *Revue philosophique*; *1886* appointed philosophy teacher at the Lycée de Troyes; *1887* appointed chargé de cours of social science and pedagogy at the Faculty of Letters at Bourdeaux; marries Louise Dreyfus, daughter of a Paris foundry owner; *1892* completes his Latin thesis, translated as *Montesquieu and Rousseau: Forerunners of Sociology*; *1893* completes and defends his doctoral thesis, *On the Division of Social Labor*; *1895* publishes *The Rules of Sociological Method*; *1896* forms the team that will publish the journal *l'Année sociologique*; *1897* publishes *Suicide*; *1898* first issue of *l'Année sociologique* appears; joins the League for the Defence of Human Rights and engages in Dreyfusard agitation in favor of a new trial; *1902* appointed *chargé d'un cours* in the Science of Education at the Sorbonne; *1902-1903* suffers nervous depression; *1904-1913* gives a course on philosophy of education at the École Normale Supérieure that will become obligatory for all students at the University of Paris seeking agrégations in sciences and in letters; *1906* given the title of professor at the Sorbonne; *1907* receives the Légion d'Honneur; *1912* publishes *The Elementary Form of the Religious Life in Australia*; *1913* his chair at the Sorbonne is renamed "Science of Education and Sociology"; *1915* writes propaganda pamphlets for French government in support of war against Germany: *Who Wanted War? The Origin of the War According to Diplomatic Documents*;

and *'Germany Above All': German Mentality and the War*; *1916* receives confirmation of the death of his son killed in action during the allied retreat from Serbia; suffers a stroke; *1917* dies November 15 in Paris.

Activities of Historical Significance

Émile Durkheim is the most prominent of the generation of "classical sociologists" that includes Ferdinand Tönnies, Max Weber, Georg Simmel, Vilfredo Pareto and Gabriel Tarde. He developed most of the basic concepts and methods that established sociology as a modern discipline. Durkheim propounded the idea that the scientific study of society involved a strict focus on what he called "social facts," as opposed to individual phenomena. The object of study must be upon the functional existence of collective institutions and mass behavior rather than upon historical development, political events or economic processes. Durkheim's work was a synthesis of his reading of Auguste Comte, of early German social thinkers like Tönnies, and of contemporaries like Tarde and Gustave LeBon, yet it was far more systematic than that of any earlier "sociologist." In addition, Durkheim worked single-mindedly to create an accepted academic discipline of sociology, taking pains to distinguish its subject matter from those of philosophy, political science, history, psychology or geography.

Durkheim's doctoral thesis and first major work, *On the Division of Social Labor* (1893) laid the foundation of his subsequent research. Its positing of the "mechanical-organic" typology of social organization (apparently inspired by Tönnies' concept of *Gemeinschaft-Gesellschaft*) resulted in a theoretical framework that could be used to explain the organization, behavior, and mentality of any civilization. Durkheim believed that societies and social "structures" in general were built according to the way in which essential tasks were allocated among the population and carried out. Societies were characterized by their division of labor and the way in which the different groups of people reinforced their interdependence through habits of thought and collective rituals. Durkheim considered the "morality" of a given society the index of its organizational sophistication. A scientifically "objective" concept in his schema, "moralité" constituted the affective bonds of a society manifest as laws, customs, rituals, and collective psychology. All of Durkheim's studies were based upon these two central ideas:

1) societies are essentially cohesive collectivities produced by the social allocation of necessarily interdependent economic tasks, and 2) collective and individual psychology must be explained in terms of the degree of social cohesion at a given time. Everything was a "normal" phenomenon in Durkheim's social universe, but some phenomena were "pathological" in that they did not contribute to social cohesion. This was a theory based upon the assumption that societies must be understood primarily in terms of their "integrative dynamic," and not in terms of their inherent divisions and conflicts.

His most famous application of this theory, and the methodology he elaborated in *Rules of Sociological Method* (1895), is found in *Suicide* (1897). Using government statistics, he demonstrated that the incidence of suicide could be considered a direct gauge of the extent of social disintegration, which he termed "anomie," a feeling of estrangement from society and other individuals resulting from the disruption caused by industrialization. Because anomie was a condition produced by actual social relationships, Durkheim disagreed with Gustave LeBon and Gabriel Tarde who maintained that the spread of certain kinds of ideas and behavior was due to the mechanisms of imitation and contagion. For Durkheim, changes in character and behavior were the surface signs of profound anxieties generated by the dissolution of social bonds.

These were the basic considerations that Durkheim carried to the study of social phenomena in Western societies and in "primitive" societies. His analyses ranged from the history of education in France in *L'Evolution pédagogique en France* (1938) to religious rituals and customs among Australian aborigines in *The Elementary Forms of the Religious Life* (1912). He attempted to institutionalize his ideas by forming a school of sociologists around his journal, *L'Année sociologique*. Its members, including Colistin Beagle, Maurice Halbwachs, Lucien Lévy-Bruhl, François Simiand and Marcel Mauss became the first generation of sociologists in the French university system. Their work led to the emergence of ethnological studies on a more wide-spread basis, influencing more recent figures such as Claude Lévy-Strauss and Michel Foucault. Durkheim's influence also has been strong outside France, especially in the development of the American functionalist school of sociology.

Durkheim's sociology must also be understood in relation to the social and political context in which he worked. His studies performed the dual political function of buttressing the class collaboration overtures of the Radical Party reformist politicians, by lending them scientific respectability and by denying validity to politics based upon the assumption that different economic interests necessarily lead to social conflict For example, Durkheim's lectures on socialism, delivered at the University of Bordeaux during the year 1895-1896, cannot be truly understood apart from the political issues current in the early 1890s and subsequent years. If Durkheim was unique in discussing the work of Karl Marx at a time when Auguste Comte was not considered intellectually respectable by much of the French university establishment, he did not do so because he admired either Marx or his work. In these lectures Durkheim attempted to invalidate the idea of a scientific socialism by denying any substantive originality or importance to Marx's ideas. It can even be said that Durkheim's sociology performed the ideological role of opposing Marxism at a time when it was rapidly gaining converts. However, it is also possible that the Marxist idea of class struggle was simply incomprehensible to Durkheim, who perceived modern societies so differently. As Jean-Claude Filloux states, "Durkheim did not understand that the extraction of surplus value and the existence of antagonistic social classes, defined in terms of their role in the productive process, form a structure of capitalist society." Rejecting Marxism and all forms of scientific socialism, Durkheim was more impressed by the writings of Henri de Saint-Simon, whose ideas permitted a collectivist, statist and non-revolutionary definition of socialism.

The most important political content of Durkheim's sociology was its tendency to discredit any view of society which held the antagonisms existing between social groups to be more important than their affective bonds. But, as for socialists, the problem of the cultural integration of the laboring population did present him with a theoretical challenge, and the source of political support he needed in order to promote and eventually institutionalize his ideas. No single person did as much as Durkheim to establish the idea that French culture was a homogeneous amalgam of customs and values which transcended all social, occupational and political differences. All of Durkheim's work figured into his attempt to establish the idea that the differences between groups in society are negligible in the face of what they all have in common. But whatever the normative content of his research, his efforts to establish a scientific method laid the foundations of contemporary academic sociology.

Overview of Biographical Sources

The works of Durkheim were not well-known outside of France during his life-time. With the exception of scattered book reviews, even specialists did not consider his work until the 1930s. The first full-scale analyses appeared in 1915 in the form of doctoral dissertations, notably those of Lucius Moody Bristol, *Social Adaptation* (Cambridge, MA: Harvard University Press, 1915) and Charles Elmer Gehlke, *Emile Durkheim's Contributions to Sociological Theory* (New York: Columbia University Press, 1915). Gehlke's work is a critique of Durkheim's basic premises, and it perhaps is indicative of the general American and British reactions to Durkheim's work. Gehlke claimed that far from resulting in the scientific objectivity he propounded, Durkheim remained highly normative in his consider-ations of social phenomena. Because of the abstractions of his formulations, Durkheim's work was generally inimicable to the empirical and philosophical traditions which dominated social science in the United States and Britain.

Interest in Durkheim increased in the 1930s. Major sociologists devoted articles to his work and introduced a new generation of American sociologists to it during a period of time when problems of social cohesion emerged. Important in this regard are P. A. Sorokin's *Contemporary Sociological Theories* (New York: Harper, 1928), George Simpson's "Emile Durkheim's Social Realism"(in *Sociology and Social Research* XVIII, 1933), Robert K. Merton's "Recent French Sociology" (in *Social Forces* XII, 1934) and his "Durkheim's Division of Labor in Society" (in *American Journal of Sociology* XL, 1934), and the chapter on Durkheim in Mabel A. Elliott and Francis E. Merrill's popular textbook, *Social Disorganization* (New York: Harper, 1934). This sudden interest can be at least partly explained by the fact that the era of the Great Depression saw the same kind of widespread socio-political discord, alienation and conflict-oriented ideologies that alarmed Durkheim at the end of the nineteenth century.

In this context, the first intellectual biographies of Durkheim were produced in the form of doctoral dissertations, notably Emile Benoît-Smullyan's "The Development of French Sociologism and Its Critics in France" (Harvard University, 1938), John Foskett's "Emile Durkheim and the Problem of Social Order" (University of California at Berkeley, 1939), and Harry Alpert's Columbia University dissertation which was published as *Emile Durkheim and His Sociology* in 1939. A major stimulus to these studies was Talcott Parsons' lengthy discussion of

Durkheim and his ideas in *The Structure of Social Action* (1937). Such introductory works, combined with the new social and political climate in the United States after World War II, infused American sociology with Durkheim's basic premises. The "mechanical-organic" dichotomy is reflected in David Reisman's *The Lonely Crowd* (New Haven, CT: Yale University Press, 1950); Robert K. Merton further developed the concept of "anomie" in *Social Theory and Social Structure* (Glencoe, IL: Free Press, 1959); and W. Lloyd Warner adapted Durkheim's approach to the consideration of social structure in his numerous studies of social status, most prominently in *Social Class in America: A Manual of Procedure for the Measurement of Social Status* (Chicago: Science Research Associates, 1949). The anti-Communist hysteria of the early post-war period, involving a rejection of conflict-oriented explanations of social phenomena such as Marxism, was expressed in various theories of "consensus" for which Durkheim's ideas were well adapted. At the same time, according to Robert Nisbet in *Émile Durkheim* (Englewood Cliffs, NJ: Prentice Hall, 1974), assimilation of Durkheim's ideas provided "a perspective that rescued social problems from the empirical atomism, the aimless individualism, that had so dominated the American sociological scene."

Since the 1950s, the volume of biographical research on Durkheim has increased considerably. The development of social theory in the 1960s resulted in a proliferation of studies centered specifically on both the man and his work, such as B. D. Johnson's thesis, "Emile Durkheim and the Theory of Social Integration" (University of California at Berkeley, 1964), and Steven Lukes' *Emile Durkheim His Life and Work: A Historical and Critical Study* (1973). If Lukes' book remains the most complete general biography, it is only one of many which have appeared over the last three decades. Detailed works of scholarship have elucidated unexplored aspects of Durkheim's life and the formulation of his ideas. Outstanding in this regard are Brian Turner's doctoral dissertation, "The Social Origins of Academic Sociology: Durkheim" (New York: Columbia University, 1977), which brought to light some instances of Durkheim's political partisanship; Bernard Lacroix's *Durkheim et le politique* (1981) which suggests how Durkheim's family history and personal psychology may have structured his sociological research; and, most importantly, W. S. F. Pickering's *Durkheim's Sociology of Religion* (1984), which has added new insights and brought together previous scholarship in a very clear way. More recently, a number of works have appeared indicating a heightened interest in Durkheim's thought: Frank Pierce, *The Radical Durkheim*

(London: Routledge, 1989); Michael Gane, *On Durkheim's Rule of the Sociological Method* (London: Kegan & Paul, 1988); José Pradès, *Durkheim* (Paris: Presses Universitaires de France, 1990); Frank Parkin, *Durkheim* (Oxford and New York: Oxford University Press, 1992).

Regardless of the existence of thorough biographical scholarship on Durkheim and the translation of the bulk of his work, it may be expected that such research will continue unabated. Durkheim's sociology, like Karl Marx's social analysis, is flexible enough to continue to inspire reinterpretation and rediscovery. Its scientific potential and its political applicability will ensure continued attention to a thinker whose ideas have laid the foundations of modern social science.

Evaluation of Principal Biographical Sources

Alpert, Harry. *Emile Durkheim and his Sociology*. New York: Russell and Russell, 1961. (**A**) The major introductory study written in the late 1930s which is now somewhat outdated because of the discovery of certain texts unavailable to Alpert, such as Durkheim's *Leçons de sociologie*. Nevertheless, this is an informed and clearly presented book that reflects the rapid and rich development of American sociology in the first decades of the twentieth century. Durkheim's ideas were quickly appropriated in the United States as his avoidance of the themes of class and conflict in favor of the dynamics of social and cultural cohesion bore a special appeal to researchers and educators in the (largely conservative) milieux of American universities.

Bierstedt, Robert. *Emile Durkheim*. New York: 1966. (**A, G**) A short biography and synthesis of Durkheim's ideas which contains a bibliography and a selection of texts. Excellent introduction for the general reader, although the reader should consult the more recently published introductory works that have benefitted from the important scholarship of the past thirty years.

Filloux, Jean-Claude. *Durkheim et le socialisme*. Geneva: Droz, 1977. (**A**) Lengthy academic study of an aspect of Durkheim's orientation which has raised considerable controversy: as to whether Durkheim was a socialist. The author, editor of some French republications of Durkheim's work, reveals the ambiguity of Durkheim's approach to socialist ideas. Further, he develops a strong argument that Durkheim never grasped the most essential insights in the work of Karl Marx. Unable to conceive of a qualitative transformation of social relationships, socialism for Durkheim was reduced to state intervention. Unfortunately, Filloux's book is not available in English translation.

Gane, Michael. *On Durkheim's Rule of the Sociological Method.* London: Kegan & Paul, 1988. (A) The central problem in the social sciences is that of "objectivity." Insisting that social phenomena were "facts" that may be analyzed according to well-defined criteria and a rigorous set of "rules," Durkheim helped a true "science" of society to emerge (in spite of his biases). By focusing on Durkheim's contribution to sociological method, Gane explains how his sociology laid the foundations for social thought and investigation in the twentieth century while failing to resolve certain philosophical issues.

Giddens, Andrew. *Durkheim.* London: Fontana, 1978. (A, G) A general introduction to Durkheim's ideas. Clearly presented and accessible to the non-specialist. Giddens summarizes and explains Durkheim's major works and the key ideas found there.

Greenberg, L. M. "Bergson and Durkheim as Sons and Assimilators: The Early Years." *French Historical Studies* 4 (1976): 619-634. (A) Psychoanalytic study which focuses upon Durkheim's relationship with his father. An extremely suggestive source which makes use of psychohistorical techniques of analysis in pursuing the thesis that Durkheim's social perceptions were structured by an ambivalent relationship with his authoritarian father and a family in which he was one of the only males.

LaCapra, Dominick. *Emile Durkheim, Sociologist and Philosopher.* Ithaca, NY: Cornell University Press, 1972. (A) LaCapra contends that Durkheim "attempted a reconciliation of liberal, conservative, and radical traditions" and that "above all," he "wanted the emergence of a society that reconciled legitimate order and progress, reason and sentiment, structure and creativity." Originally a doctoral dissertation, this is a disappointing intellectual biography. Its generalizations rely more upon a kind of urbane pretention than upon informed understanding and seasoned reflection. It is particularly deficient in its appreciation of Durkheim's social background and political orientation. This book was eclipsed by the publication of Steven Lukes's the following year.

Lacroix, Bernard. *Durkheim et le politique.* Paris: Presses de la Fondation Nationale des Sciences Politiques, 1981. (**A**) An erudite French-language work which combines a specialist's analysis of Durkheim's ideas and publications with fascinating new material on his family history and personal life based upon the discovery of documents hitherto unknown to scholars. The special merit of this book is that it combines a thorough analysis of the political thrust of Durkheim's sociology with a psychoanalytical examination of the man. Lacroix claims that "throughout his entire life, as his nervous breakdowns of 1902 and 1916 indicate, Durkheim was haunted by a poorly resolved oedipus complex; and it was poorly resolved because it could not be resolved." Although relatively unaccessible to the general reader, and unlikely to be translated into English, this is an important work.

Lukes, Steven. *Émile Durkheim: His Life and Work.* London, Allen Lane, 1972. (**A, G**) The major work in any language, this book is a clear and thorough account of Durkheim's life and a straight forward presentation of his ideas. At the same time, Lukes offers an extremely sensitive analysis of both Durkheim and his accomplishments. While not denying the latter, he nevertheless recognizes Durkheim's academic empire-building and his sometimes ignorance of evidence or arbitrary and unwarranted dismissal of arguments that conflicted with his theories. According to Lukes, "Durkheim was a bold and adventurous theory-builder, who, if he no longer claimed that 'the facts are wrong,' was, despite his aspirations toward objective, empirical science, often surprisingly insensitive to their role in falsifying, or verifying, his theories." This essential book is supplemented with a comprehensive bibliography, a list of courses and lectures given by Durkheim at Bourdeaux and Paris, transcripts of Durkheim's comments as a thesis examiner, and a list of the contributing editors of the *Année sociologique.* Available in an inexpensive Penguin edition.

Nisbet, Robert A. *Émile Durkheim.* Englewood Cliffs, NJ: Prentice Hall, 1974. (**A, G**) A long essay which presents Durkheim's ideas in terms of their contribution to modern sociology with a particular focus on his concept of milieu. Among the themes Nisbet discusses are analytical individualism, biologism, the critique of progress, the nature of authority, and the religio-sacred. Part two of the book comprises articles by five prominent sociologists: Robert K. Merton, "Durkheim's Division of Labor in Society"; Hanan C. Selvin, "Durkheim's Suicide: Further Thoughts on a Methological Classic"; Harry Alpert, "Durkheim's Functional Theory of Ritual"; Morris Ginsberg, "Durkheim's Ethical Theory"; and Robert N. Bellah, "Durkheim and History." A useful volume.

Parkin, Frank. *Durkheim.* Oxford and New York: Oxford University Press, 1992. (**A, G**) This concise yet comprehensive study (less than one hundred pages) manages to introduce Durkheim's thought and comment upon it critically. Parkin is particularly concerned to elucidate the critical content of Durkheim's work on the relations between juridical and social organization, between religion and social cohesion, and between state and civil society. He also touches upon Durkheim's considerations of women and sexual relations and his political engagements.

Parsons, Talcott. *The Structure of Social Action: A Study in Social Theory with Special Reference to a Group of Recent European Writers.* Vol. 1. New York: The Free Press, 1968. (**A**) The enormously influential work by a major authority who did much to introduce American scholars and thinkers to European social thought. Although written more than one-half century ago and criticized for its functionalist orientation, this book continues to have an impact on our understanding of Durkheim and, more generally, on the social sciences.

Pickering, W. S. F. *Durkheim's Sociology of Religion.* London: Routledge and Kegan Paul, 1984. (**A, G**) Lengthy, detailed study of Durkheim's work on religion and its general implications for the rest of his thought. Introduced by an analysis of Durkheim's life, psychology and career, and includes an excellent analytical review of other biographical treatments. Very readable presentation and analysis of Durkheim's ideas which pushes beyond Steven Lukes's study thanks to its clear synthesis of new material. An essential work.

Pierce, Frank. *The Radical Durkheim.* London: Routledge, 1989. (**A, G**) Pierce explores the socially critical and even "radical" dimension of Durkheim's thought.

Although conservative biases are evident in his life, politics and theories, Durkheim was nevertheless a member of a moderate left party, criticized the inheritance laws, and spoke out for separation of church and state legislated in France in 1905. His thought was, in fact, too complex to categorize easily in political terms.

Pradès, José. *Durkheim.* Paris: Presses Universitaire de France, 1990. (**A**) A recent French contribution to the effort to revitalize Durkheim's ideas by relating them to contemporary concerns. This is a logical and valid enterprise in that modern industrial societies and polities are necessarily preoccupied by questions of social representation and what Durkheim called "collective consciousness." Pradès's book shows clearly that Durkheim remains the most important theorist of "consensus."

Wallwork, E. *Émile Durkheim: Morality and Milieu.* Cambridge, MA: Harvard University Press, 1972. (**A**) A rather narrow consideration of Durkheim's attempt to build a science of morality that neglects the broader sweep and implications of his ideas.

Wolff, Kurt H., ed. *Essays on Sociology and Philosophy.* New York: Harper and Row, 1964. (**A**) An anthology of articles on Durkheim and his work by Henri Peyre, Joseph Neyer, Paul Bohannan, Hugh Dalziel Duncan, Talcott Parsons, Albert Pierce, Melvin Richter, Lewis A. Coser, Paul Honigsheim, Albert Salomon, Roscoe C. Hinkle Jr., and Kazuta Kurauchi. Includes a number of Durkheim's text and a bibliography.

Overview and Evaluation of Primary Sources

During his lifetime, Durkheim's major works were published by Félix Alcan in Paris. At present, French editions are published by the Presses Universitaires de France, including *Journal Sociologique* (1969), a selection of Durkheim's articles, notes and book reviews from his journal *L'Année sociologique.* Other articles were edited by the same publisher as *La Science sociale et l'action* (1970). It is to be noted that some of Durkheim's university lecture courses were compiled and published posthumously as *Le Socialisme* (1928), *L'Education morale* (1922), *L'Evo-*

lution pédagogique en France (1938), and *Leçons et sociologie* (1955). A large collection of texts has been edited by Victor Karady in three volumes as *Emile Durkheim Textes* (Paris: Les Editions de Minuit, 1975). Some letters can be found in the Bibliothèque Nationale and the Bibliothèque Victor Cousin in Paris. Most of the major works have been published by Free Press of Glencoe in English: *The Division of Labor in Society* (Glencoe, IL: Free Press, 1964), translated by George Simpson in 1933. According to Seven Lukes, this translation is "seriously defective." Indeed, Simpson translates the key expression-concept *conscience collective* as "common conscience," whereas it can be argued convincingly that "collective consciousness" is more accurate. This is Durkheim's seminal work. Within it are all the ideas developed in later texts. *The Rules of Sociological Method* (Glencoe, IL: Free Press of Glencoe, 1964), translated by George E. G. Catlin in 1938, this text explains the methods by which "social facts" may be observed, classified and explained. This is the book that established sociology as a science on a methodological basis. *Suicide: A Study in Sociology* (Glencoe, IL: Free Press of Glencoe, 1951), translated by George Simpson in 1950, is an application of Durkheim's methodological rules to a concrete social phenomenon.

Durkheim showed how a measure of scientific objectivity could be achieved through the use of quantitative analysis and rational classification. His famous concept of "anomie" is based on his determination that the rising level of suicides in industrial societies is due to increasing normlessness. *Sociology and Philosophy* (Glencoe, IL: Free Press of Glencoe, 1953) contains some collected courses and articles on key topics. *Moral Education: A Study in the Theory and Application of the Sociology of Education* (New York: Free Press of Glencoe, 1961), composed of the posthumously published lectures of Durkheim's course on education, is remarkable for how it illustrates the practical application of the sociologist's ideas to questions of public instruction, the formation of ethics, and the role of the state in social life. *Professional Ethics and Civic Morals* (London: Routledge and Kegan Paul, 1957), and *Socialisme and Saint-Simon* (Yellow Springs, OH: Antioch Press, 1958), with an introduction by Alvin Gouldner, are based on a course given at the University of Bordeaux in 1895, in which Durkheim offers different definitions of socialism before concluding that, essentially, socialism represents the rationalization of state intervention in social life. On this basis, Durkheim can be said to have been a proponent of a certain type of socialism. Durkheim's doctoral thesis, published as *Montesquieu and Rousseau: Forerunners of Sociology* (Ann Arbor:

University of Michigan Press, 1960), with an introduction by Henri Peyre, seeks to demonstrate how major social theorists of the eighteenth century prepared the way for Durkheim's own formulations. Various articles, lectures and letters have been compiled and published in *Emile Durkheim, 1958-1917: A Collection of Essays* (Columbus: Ohio State University Press, 1960), edited by Kurt H. Wolff; and *Selected Writings* (Cambridge: Cambridge University Press, 1972), edited by Anthony Giddens; R. N. Bellah edited *Emile Durkheim on Morality and Society* (Chicago: University of Chicago Press, 1973); W. S. F. Pickering edited *Durkheim on Religion* (London: Routledge and Kegan Paul, 1975); and *Durkheim Essays on Morals and Education* (London: Routledge and Kegan Paul, 1979); and M. Traugott edited *Emile Durkheim on Institutional Analysis* (Chicago: University of Chicago Press, 1978). Other translations include *Incest: The Nature and Origin of the Taboo* (New York: Lyle Stuart, 1963); *Primitive Classification* (Chicago: University of Chicago Press, 1963); "A Durkheim Fragment: The Conjugal Family" (*American Journal of Sociology* 70, 5, 1965); "Individualism and the Intellectuals" (*Political Studies* 27, 1969); and "Note on the Notion of Civilization" (*Social Research* 38, 1971).

Museums, Historical Landmarks, Societies

Societies (Paris). Groupe d'études durkheimienne, Maison des Sciences de l'Homme, Boulevard Raspail, 7th arrondissement. Coordinates research and publications concerning Durkheim and his work.

Other Sources

Bellah, Robert N. "Durkheim and History." In Robert A. Nisbet, *Émile Durkheim*. Englewood Cliffs, NJ: Prentice Hall, 1965. Important critique of the historical deficiencies of Durkheimian sociology.

Clark, Terry N. *Prophets and Patrons: The French University and the Emergence of the Social Sciences*. Cambridge, MA: Harvard University Press, 1973. An informed and detailed study of how Durkheim's sociology came to be "institutionalized'' in the French university system.

Coser, Lewis A. "Durkheim's Conservatism and Its Implications for His Sociological Theory." In *Essays on Sociology and Philosophy*, edited by Kurt H. Wolff. New York: Harper and Row, 1960. Excellent analysis of the normative content of Durkheim's concepts.

Portis, Larry. *Classes sociales en France. Un débat inachevé 1789-1989.* Paris: Les Editions Ouvrières, 1988. Places Durkheim's sociology within a context of social conflict and ideological evolution.

————. "Les fondements politico-idéologiques de la sociologie durkheimienne." *L'Homme et la société* 84 (1987). Uses archival material to demonstrate how Durkheim intervened directly in various political debates.

————. "Sexe, moralité et ordre social dans l'oeuvre d'Émile Durkheim." *L'Homme et la société* 99-100 (1991). Shows how Durkheim's less-than-progressive ideas about women, sexual relations and sex education were related to a pessimistic view of human nature in general.

Turner, Brian J. "The Social Origins of Academic Sociology: Durkheim." (Dissertation. Columbia University, 1977). Meticulous study of Durkheim's ideas and career in terms of university and national politics.

Larry Portis
American University of Paris

Arthur Stanley Eddington
1882-1944

Chronology

Born on December 28, 1882, in Kendal, in Westmoreland, England, son of Arthur Henry Eddington, headmaster of Stramongate School, and Sarah Ann Shout, a Quaker; *1884* father dies; moves with his mother to Weston-super-Mare; attends Brynmelyn School, where he distinguishes himself in mathematics and the physical sciences; *1898-1902* attends Owens College, Manchester, where he studies under the physicist Arthur Schuster and the mathematician Horace Lamb; *1902-1905* studies at Trinity College, Cambridge University, under R. A. Herman, one of the famous mathematical coaches of the era; influenced by the astronomer E. T. Whittaker; *1904* becomes youngest student to earn the highest score in Part I of the Mathematical Tripos examination; *1905* earns first class honors in Part II of Mathematical Tripos Examination and receives a bachelor's degree; lectures and tutors at Trinity; attempts abortive experiments on electron emission from hot metals at the Cavendish Laboratory; *1906-1913* becomes Chief Assistant at the Royal Observatory, Greenwich; gains experience making and analyzing routine astrometric observations; pursues his own research on the systematic motions of the stars; *1906* demonstrates that stars in the neighborhood of the sun are members of two intermingled groups drifting in different directions; elected a Fellow of the Royal Astronomical Society; *1907* wins the Smith's Prize from Cambridge University for his star-drift work; elected a Fellow of Trinity College; *1909* sent to determine the longitude of the geodetic station, Spencer's Monument, on Malta; *1912* travels to Passo Quatro, Brazil, to photograph a total solar eclipse but is thwarted by weather; *1913* returns to Cambridge to take over the prestigious Plumian Professorship; purchases and begins to edit *The Observatory*, a newsletter of the English-speaking astronomical community; *1914* publishes *Stellar Movements and the Structure of the Universe*, examining the motion and distribution of the individual stars making up our galaxy and endorsing the then-controversial idea that spiral nebulae are distant galaxies similar to our own; elected a Fellow of the Royal Society of London; appointed Director of the Cambridge Observatory;

settles permanently at the Observatory with his mother and older sister, Winifred; *1915* publishes "Gravitation," the first of his many writings on relativity theory, in the *Monthly Notices of the Royal Astronomical Society*; *1916-1926* rejects eclipsing binary models of Cepheid variable stars and attempts to explain the complicated variations in their light as radial pulsations of a single star; led by his interest in Cepheids to a decade-long study of stellar structure in general, publishing his results in a sequence of path-breaking articles appearing mainly in the *Monthly Notices of the Royal Astronomical Society*; engages James Jeans, a rival English astronomer and physicist, in a notorious series of public debates on stellar theory, mainly concerning the source of stars' energy, the physical state of stellar material, and the course of stellar evolution; *1918* publishes *Report on the Relativity Theory of Gravity*, the first full account of Einstein's general theory of relativity in English; becomes a major figure in the transmission of relativity theory from Germany to wartime England; *1919* photographs shifts in the positions of background stars during a total solar eclipse on the island of Principe, confirming the relativistic prediction that the path of light is deflected by a gravitational field; advocates the controversial point of view that stars' energy comes from subatomic processes; *1920* publishes the popular discussion of relativity, *Space, Time and Gravitation*; *1921-1923* elected President of the Royal Astronomical Society; *1922* begins to apply quantum physics to the problem of opacity in the stellar interior; *1923* extends his 1918 *Report* into a monograph, *The Mathematical Theory of Relativity*; *1924* publishes an observationally-confirmed relationship between the masses and luminosities of stars; *1926* publishes his greatest work, *The Internal Constitution of Stars*, a monumental analysis of the physical conditions inside stars; turns his attention increasingly to the popular exposition of science, to the philosophy of science, and to developing his "fundamental theory," an attempt to unify quantum physics and general relativity; *1927* popularizes the results of his stellar structure work in *Stars and Atoms*; *1928* publishes *The Nature of the Physical World*, in which he discusses the philosophical implications of recent advances in quantum theory, the general theory of relativity, and thermodynamics; *1929* publishes *Science and the Unseen World*, an exploration of the distinction between science and spiritual knowledge; *1930* is knighted; *1930-1932* serves as President of both the Physical Society of London and the Mathematical Association; *1933* publishes *The Expanding Universe*, a semipopular discussion of relativistic cosmology; *1935* publishes *New Pathways in Science*, a collection of his popular lectures; *1936* publishes the first of his monographs on fundamental theory, *Relativity Theory of Protons and Electrons*; *1938* receives the Order of Merit; becomes president of the International Astronomical Union; *1939* publishes *The Philosophy of Physical Science*, which enunciates his increasing interest in the epistemological bases of the laws of nature; *1944* dies on November 22 in Cambridge after a year's illness, leaving an unpublished manuscript, which is edited by E. T. Whittaker and published as *Fundamental Theory* in 1946.

Activities of Historical Significance

Arthur Stanley Eddington was among the great theoretical astrophysicists of the early twentieth century. Though his researches spanned quantum physics, subatomic physics, and general relativity—the three most active fields of physics in his day—his greatest and most enduring contributions were to astronomy. Eddington recognized that because stars are extremely hot inside, energy is carried from the interior to the surface of a star by radiation. This insight enabled him to calculate the temperature, pressure, and density inside the stars and to explain how internal parameters give rise to the conditions astronomers observe at stars' surfaces. Eddington's work culminated in his "standard model" of stellar constitution of 1926.

Eddington's achievement was a watershed dividing classical stellar models, based upon the simple, long-understood physics of convection and gravitational equilibrium, from a generation of modern models, successively incorporating the rapidly advancing results of twentieth-century physics. The new models of stellar interiors offered much more satisfactory representations of observation: first, a mass-luminosity relationship, and later, detailed explanations of stellar spectra. They solved long-standing problems, including identifying nuclear processes as the source of stellar energy. They provided a basis for decades of future stellar theory. Perhaps even more importantly, these models initiated a markedly closer relationship between astronomy and physics that continues to this day.

Eddington owed his widespread recognition outside the astrophysics community to his work on German physicist Albert Einstein's general theory of relativity. Despite the war-time climate of limited communication between England and Germany, and considerable hostility on the part of English scientists to the work of their German counterparts, Eddington welcomed papers on relativity sent by Einstein via the cosmologist Willem De Sitter in neutral Holland. Eddington relayed their contents to the Royal Astronomical Society, and in 1918 he presented his *Report on the Relativity Theory of Gravity* to the Physical Society of London. English reaction was immediate; Sir Frank Dyson, the Astronomer Royal, planned to help Eddington put the theory to one of its few possible observational tests. According to the theory of general relativity, gravity bends space and therefore bends the path of a light ray. Stars seem to change position when the sun is almost in front of them because their light is deflected as it passes through the sun's gravitational field. This effect can be observed only during a total solar eclipse, and the eclipse of May 29, 1919, provided an exceptional opportunity to measure it, because it occurred in front of the bright stars of the Hyades cluster. Eddington led an expedition to the island of Principe, located off the coast of West Africa, to photograph the eclipse at totality; a second expedition went to Sobral, in Brazil. Clouds obscured the Principe site for much of the eclipse, so the definitive photographs came from Sobral. Eddington, however, was responsible for the delicate task of measuring all the photographs, and he showed Einstein's prediction to be correct. As Eddington planned the expedition, measured the photographs, published both popular and scholarly accounts of relativity, and contributed to the mathematical development of the theory, history has allotted him chief credit for its observational confirmation.

By the middle of Eddington's career, his successes in astrophysics and relativity had elevated him to public fame. Originally an almost painfully quiet and private person, he learned to relish his stature as a statesman of science, and his hold on public attention tightened through ensuing decades with the publication of his superb popular expositions of up-to-the-minute physical and astronomical research. As a famous scientist and a devout Quaker, he was frequently called upon to lecture on science and religion, and he offered the reassuring message that because revelation and scientific knowledge deal with wholly separate realms of experience, religion and science can never conflict. The scientific community acknowledged him with honors too numerous to list, and his public recognition culminated in a knighthood in 1930 and England's Order of Merit in 1938.

In the midst of his apotheosis, however, Eddington embarked upon a project that eventually was to tarnish his image among scientists. Growing increasingly convinced of the subjectivity of observation, a point of view he elaborated on in his

Philosophy of the Physical Sciences, he set out to construct an account of the world that did not rely on the results of measurement. It is difficult to evaluate the "fundamental theory" to which Eddington devoted the last decade of his life. He hoped that by unifying the quantum mechanical and relativistic descriptions of the universe—descriptions that had previously stood as complementary but disparate accounts—he could uncover the underlying structure of the material world. The best-remembered feature of his fundamental theory is its emphasis on the discovery of mathematical relationships between constants of nature. (The velocity of light and the ratio of the masses of the proton and the electron are examples of natural constants.) Eddington believed that such relationships made it possible to calculate quantities that could not be found by measurement, including the number of protons and electrons in the universe.

Eddington died before his project was complete, and after his death, developments in quantum mechanics and relativity theory destroyed the foundation on which his fundamental theory was built. The physics community, which had already widely distrusted the theory as metaphysical, ill-founded and obscure, soon jettisoned it altogether. In spite of the theory's failure, Eddington deserves credit for developing new mathematical techniques in the course of his work, and for drawing physicists' attention to the significance of mathematical relationships between natural constants, a significance better appreciated now than in Eddington's day.

Eddington's Quaker belief inspired his pacifism and internationalism. During World War I, while many British scientists joined the war effort as soldiers or technical consultants, Eddington declared himself a conscientious objector. By doing so he risked internment, but at the insistence of the Astronomer Royal he was granted an exemption from national service on the condition that he prepare the expedition to photograph the eclipse of 1919. Eddington's student, Chandrasekhar, has reported that without this requirement, Eddington likely would not have undertaken the expedition, as he was already convinced of the truth of general relativity without observational confirmation. Because so much of the astronomical community was busy with war work, it is not clear who would have gone to photograph the eclipse had Eddington not been obliged to do it. And indeed, observational confirmation of relativity theory might have been delayed. Along with Eddington's pacifism came a deep concern for international cooperation. Writing in *The Observatory* at the end of the war he stood almost alone in arguing for the reintegration of German scientists into the international scientific community, while many of his colleagues fiercely objected, suggesting that Germany should be scientifically isolated. Eddington backed his conviction by publishing important papers in German scientific journals, and, in 1938, he served as president of the International Astronomical Union.

Eddington lived his adult life in Cambridge with his mother and his sister and seems to have found all the stimulation he required in the life of the mind. For recreation, he looked to books, chessboard, and bicycle. It is a memorable mark of his fastidiousness that at his death he bequeathed to C. J. A. Trimble, his sole intimate friend, a journal apparently listing every novel he had read and every mile he had pedaled.

Overview of Biographical Sources

Eddington's contributions to physics and astronomy are well known, but his life is less so because no full biography of him has yet been written. Most discussions of Eddington are obituaries, memorial lectures, or reviews by colleagues, competitors, and students, and are influenced by their authors' friendship or animosity towards him. Brief, sympathetic (and technical) accounts include W. H. McCrea and G. Temple's obituary in *The Journal of the London Mathematical Society* and H. C. Plummer's entry in *The Obituary Notices of Fellows of the Royal Society*. A. Vibert Douglas's *The Life of Arthur Stanley Eddington* (1956), discusses Eddington's life in much greater detail, but it is so adulatory and lacking in historical context that it is better described as a long memorial essay than as a true biography.

Arthur Stanley Eddington Memorial Lectures have been delivered annually since 1947 at Trinity College, Cambridge, and some half dozen of these have discussed aspects of Eddington's work. Chandrasekhar's "Eddington: The Most Distinguished Astrophysicist of His Time" (1983) was composed as one of these. Critical of Eddington's contributions to relativity, his fundamental theory, his refusal to accept Chandrasekhar's own work on the degeneracy of matter in dwarf stars, and his treatment of scientific adversaries in general, it is surprisingly unflattering for a memorial lecture. Chandrasekhar has, in turn, been censured by Eddington's defenders, among them McCrea. E. A. Milne's *Sir James Jeans*

(Cambridge: Cambridge University Press, 1952), a biography of Eddington's great rival, contains lengthy criticisms of Eddington's conduct of scientific controversies, drawing on both Milne's and Jeans's experience of disputes with Eddington.

Eddington scholarship has become more balanced with the work of recent historians of science, who have attempted to place Eddington's work within a historical context, but the technicality of his science and the dearth of primary sources concerning his personal life have so far limited their efforts to articles describing a few aspects of Eddington's story.

Evaluation of Principal Biographical Sources

Chandrasekhar, S. "Eddington: The Most Distinguished Astrophysicist of His Time." In *Truth and Beauty; Aesthetics and Motivation in Science*. 1983. Reprint. Chicago: University of Chicago Press, 1987. (**A, G**) Idiosyncratic sketch by Eddington's most illustrious student. Offers an appreciative summary of Eddington's astrophysics and a critical assessment of his contributions to relativity. Includes a modest amount of technical material, leavened with anecdotes.

Douglas, A. Vibert. *The Life of Arthur Stanley Eddington*. London: Thomas Nelson, 1956. (**A, G**) As close to a biography as Eddington scholarship has come. This is a charming account of his schooling and travels and an untechnical summary of his contributions to science. Assembled by a student of Eddington's who had access to the journal of his early career and some of his correspondence. Lacks historical context and critical analysis. Contains a bibliography of Eddington's publications, but is otherwise poorly referenced.

Graham, Loren R. *Between Science and Values*. New York: Columbia University Press, 1981. (**A**) Chapter two assesses Eddington's philosophy of science and its relationship to his religious beliefs.

Overview and Evaluation of Primary Sources

Eddington's most important books remain in print. *The Internal Constitution of the Stars* (Cambridge: Cambridge University Press, 1926; **A**), *The Expanding Universe* (Cambridge: Cambridge University Press, 1933; **A, G**), and *Space, Time and Gravitation* (Cambridge: Cambridge University Press, 1920; **A, G**) are still available in reprint editions. The first two contain useful new forewords by Chandrasekhar and McCrea, respectively. *The Mathematical Theory of Relativity* (Cambridge: Cambridge University Press, 1923; **A**) has been reprinted in unaltered form (New York: Chelsea, 1975).

Eddington's articles have, for the most part, not been collected and must be read as they were originally published, mainly in *The Monthly Notices of the Royal Astronomical Society*, *The Proceedings of the Royal Society of London*, and *The Observatory*. A good selection of extracts from the most important of them can be found in C. W. Kilmister's *Men of Science: Sir Arthur Stanley Eddington* (Oxford: Pergamon, 1966; **A**). The Kilmister, Plummer, and Douglas works give relatively complete lists of Eddington's publications.

Few of Eddington's manuscripts remain. Knowing of his impending, death, Eddington destroyed many of his papers. After he died, his sister Winifred and his friend Trimble destroyed most of the remaining personal material. Personal material coming into the hands of the Royal Society of London was also burned. There is a small Eddington archive at Trinity College, Cambridge, containing his journal for the years 1905-1914, a few letters, and some manuscripts of lectures and publications. Groups of letters can be found in the Einstein and Russell collections in Princeton, the Shapley collection at Harvard, the Weyl collection in Zurich, the library of the Royal Society of London, and scattered in the collections of other correspondents.

Other Sources

DeVorkin, David, and Ralph Kenat. "Quantum Physics and the Stars (II): Henry Norris Russell and the Abundances of the Elements in the Atmospheres of the Sun and Stars." *Journal for the History of Astronomy* 14 (October 1983): 180-222. Treats the justification for Eddington's misplaced belief that hydrogen is an insignificant component of the stars.

Hufbauer, Karl. "Astronomers Take up the Stellar Energy Problem, 1917-

1920." *Historical Studies in the Physical Sciences* 11 (1981): 277-303. Describes how Eddington placed the stellar energy problem on astronomers' research agenda.

Kenat, Ralph. *Physical Interpretation: Eddington, Idealization and the Origin of Stellar Structure Theory.* Ph.D. diss., University of Maryland, 1987. Considers Eddington's stellar model in light of semantic conceptions of theory and the problem of scientific realism.

Kilmister, C. W., and B. O. J. Tupper. *Eddington's Statistical Theory.* Oxford: Clarendon, 1962. An effort to show that theories of the nature of Eddington's fundamental theory can be fruitful.

Slater, N. B. *The Development and Meaning of Eddington's 'Fundamental Theory.'* Cambridge: Cambridge University Press, 1957. Compares various drafts of Eddington's manuscript.

Stachel, John. "Eddington and Einstein." In *The Prism of Science*, edited by E. Ullmann-Margalit. Boston: Reidel/Kluwer, 1986. Discusses Einstein's reaction to Eddington's work on relativity.

Yolton, J. W. *The Philosophy of Science of A. S. Eddington.* The Hague: Nijhoff, 1960. Criticism by a philosopher of science; takes Eddington's programatic statements too literally.

Joann Eisberg
Harvard University